Along the tracks of Cobb and Co.

Cobb's Coach Drivers

History speaking for itself ...

Research and compilation by Hazel Johnson

For my husband David, whose belief in me is unwavering.

Author's Note

"Into the mists of the past have gone the days of Cobb and Co.'s coaches, with their daring drivers who could 'spin' many a thrilling story of the days when 'the world was wide'." (Dick Craig's Fight, 28 Apr 1939, p.5)

*"These were the old days,
Days when the world was wide."*

I have always had a love for history, and I am a proud Australian. I believe the journey of exploring Cobb and Co., highlights such an important part of our history. The people of Cobb and Co., and other people who built this great modern Australia of today, have my admiration. Hard work, resilience and the ability to solve problems are reflected in the book's excerpts. In fact, my research has reminded me that the people who have come before us are very similar to the people of today—great business people, creative people, people with ingenious ideas, and of course people prepared to do the hard slog of 'day to day work', regardless of the weather (think of our vegetable farmers and those who work in the dairying industry). And of course they had a sense of humour e.g. "At an unnamed change station, the boss would flick off the covering of the food and say *What would you like lamb, mutton or ram!*"

You may ask *What makes my books different?* To share the positive history of how Cobb and Co., and the postal service, contributed to the great Australia of today, I have pieced together fragments written during the 1800s to the mid-1900s to tell the story, hence 'history is speaking for itself'. The original text may make you feel like you are the one sitting on the 'box seat' next to the driver, jolting along the many tracks of Cobb and Co.—at times, 'original words' have far greater meaning than when they are partially rewritten or in a different context. I have, I hope, selected excerpts that maintain the integrity of their context, the emotional response for the reader, and how they fitted into the big story of Cobb and Co.

'Along the tracks of Cobb and Co. - Cobb's Coach Drivers' explores some of the men, and the occasional woman, who handled the ribbons—at this stage over 800 drivers have been identified and my research continues. Each driver has referenced information that reflects that they have, in fact, driven for Cobb and Co. Wherever possible stories of bushrangers, floods, coach accidents, amusing anecdotes and the like are included. Further editions will follow, as I continue my research.

Special thanks to Mr John Osbourne OAM for his enthusiasm and support of my research, along with Mr John Elliot Writer/Photographer, Mr David Bolton and Mr Steve Cooper Manager, Operations at Cobb+Co Museum, Toowoomba.

Note, authenticity has been maintained as spelling, punctuation and grammar are as per historical sources. These features, in themselves, further enhance the story of change over time. In addition, the development in photography, including availability and quality of past photos, is evident. Author photo—Courtesy of John Elliott, writer/photographer.

I acknowledge that the accounts in this book series only fleetingly touches upon the rich, cultural history of Australia's First Peoples and their interactions with others during this period of colonisation.

Acknowledgement of Country

We acknowledge the Traditional Custodians of the land
on which the Cobb and Co. stage coaches travelled.
We pay our respect to Elders past, present and emerging,
and, extend our deep respect to all Aboriginal and Torres Strait Islander Peoples.

TITLES

Book 1
Along the tracks of Cobb and Co. —The Great Northern Road
(Tenterfield to Warwick)

Book 2
Along the tracks of Cobb and Co. —The Western Run
(Brisbane, Toowoomba, Roma & Charleville)

Book 3
Along the tracks of Cobb and Co. —The New South Wales Headquarters
(In & Around Bathurst)

Book 4
Along the tracks of Cobb and Co. —Back to the Beginning
(Victoria & the Goldfields)

Book 5
Along the tracks of Cobb and Co. —Cobb's Coach Drivers

Book 6
Along the tracks of Cobb and Co. —The Roaring Days !
(Amusing Anecdotes & Tales of Grit and Graft)

Book 7
Along the tracks of Cobb and Co. —Queensland
(Brisbane & Beyond) (Release date … late 2025)

Print | Audiobooks | eBooks
Copyright by Hazel T. Johnson

First Edition 2022, Second Edition 2023, Reprinted July 2025

Content mainly courtesy of Trove (The National Library of Australia) and their many partners including State Library of New South Wales, State Library of Queensland, State Library of Western Australia, and State Library of Victoria. Photographs taken before 1955 and maps created before 1955 are out of copyright (Australian Copyright Council). Special thanks to the other contributors of photos and/or information, to assist in the telling of part of the story of Cobb and Co. in Australia. Special thanks to Queensland Museum, Mr Ray Green, and The Sovereign Hill Museums, Ballarat. Spelling, punctuation and grammar as per historical sources. Every attempt has been made to ensure the correct use and acknowledgement of all sources. Corrections and/or contributions welcome for the next edition. Book cover image: Buster White—Courtesy The Sovereign Hill Museums Association Limited, Ballarat, Victoria.

Available from:
www.cobbandcotracks.au or local distributors

Further contact:
email   dvhtjohnson@gmail.com
phone   +61 4 1798 4455

ISBN 978-0-646-87010-6

This book was printed by: IngramSpark

Typeset in Garamond

Contents

4   Author's Note

8   Cobb and Co. in Australia
    Coaching
    Coaches
    Drivers
    Driving Methods
    Delivery of Mails
    Change Stations
    A move to the 'iron horse' ... and then to the 'motor buggies'

14 Chapter One: Drivers A-B
    'Long Jim of Cobb & Co.'

32 Chapter Two: Drivers C
    'Here's a song of Cobb and Co.'

46 Chapter Three: Drivers D
    'The Lights of Cobb & Co.'

56 Chapter Four: Drivers E-G
    Jehu and His Team

70 Chapter Five: Drivers H-I
    'So my mind goes harking backwards to the days of long ago'

86 Chapter Six: Drivers J-L
    'There was talk of flood or the fear that sprang'

98 Chapter Seven: Drivers M-N
    'The Roaring Days'

120 Chapter Eight: Drivers O-R
    'The Lights of Cobb and Co.'

142 Chapter Nine: Drivers S-V
    'The Roll Call of Cobb & Co.'

156 Chapter Ten: Drivers W-Z
    'The Olden Days of Cobb & Co.'

166 The Best Driver & Photographs

174 Remembering Cobb and Co.

178 Cobb and Co.
    Many spokes in the wheel ...

190 Reference List

Cobb and Co.
in
Australia

Supporting evidence:

Coaching

"The romance of road-coaching in Australia ... abounds with incident and accident by flood and fell, by field and forest. Over miles of drought-stricken plains, through leagues of raging bushfires, amid incessant rains and through the raging waters of swollen rivers, Cobb's coaches plunged along, beneath blazing sun-heat and in blinding storm, in heat and in cold, in midnight darkness and the crash of elemental war. The three great lamps have glowed in the blackest night as beacons of hope and messengers of civilisation, Cobb's mail-coach typifying a red link between the active world of affairs and the expatriated dwellers of the far Outback." (A Pioneer Of The Coaching Days: Late James Rutherford, 20 Sep 1922, p.26)

"In the boom days of the gold discoveries, when Bathurst, Ballarat, and Bendigo were so much in the eye of the get-rich-quick migrants from England and America, the means of travel to these goldfields was extremely slow, uncomfortable, and fraught with hazard, owing to the unmade tracks, the unbridged rivers and creeks, and the class of conveyance available. Metal-spring vehicles of a sort, and capacity, were soon catering for the hordes of travellers en route to these El Dorados of the early '[18] fifties." (The Lights of Cobb & Co., 17 Jul 1953, p.22) "About the middle of 1853 a change came over this mode of transit" (The Contributor, 25 Nov 1908, p.1405) with "Winslow Cobb and his brother (the founders of the coaching business of Cobb and Co)." (Personal, 14 Oct 1917, p.12)

Initially, "Freeman Cobb ... inherited some of the spirit of an adventurous sea-faring grandfather, Elijah Cobb ... became restless ... and it was agreed that he should go to Australia, but accompanied by an older member of the firm, Mr. George Mowton, while a number of the firm's drivers and express men would follow later in another ship ... He arrived with Mowton in Melbourne in April, 1853. The sailing ship Eagle had followed from New York with a number of Adams & Co.'s men and others also accustomed to Yankee methods of goods and passenger transport. They arrived later the same year ... three were John Murray Peck, James Swanton and John Lamber ... they had come to help with the establishment of Adams and Co.'s Express in Australia." (Gold, Men and Horses, 16 Jan 1954, p.14)

"Adams & Co.'s first announcement appeared in Melbourne newspapers on May 6, 1853." (Cobb & Co., 27 Mar 1933, p.4) "They commenced carrying from Liardet's (Port Melbourne) to the City of Melbourne for a start but 'no road' across the swamp between Emerald Hill, now South Melbourne, and the river was such a quagmire that their waggons sank to the hubs ... They advised their principals in the United States against the carrying business, but told them that there was a good opening for a real up-to-date line of coaches to the diggings ... the United States companies turned down the coaching proposition." (a [?] Drive, 31 July 1937, p.4)

However in 1854, Adams and Co. was still in business in Australia, and associated with Freeman Cobb. "NOTICE.—The undersigned, being about to leave in the Norma, for England and the United States for a short period, would respectfully inform the public that, during his absence, Messrs Samuel L. Cutter and Freeman Cobb will attend to the business of Adams and Co., in Australia ; the former will have the superintendence of the Banking and Exchange business, and the latter the General Business of the House, in the express department. GEORGE MOWTON, Resident Partner of ADAMS and CO., in Australia. Melbourne, Nov. 22nd, 1854" (Advertising, 24 Nov 1854, p.6) Meanwhile "George Francis Train, in his book 'My Life of Many States and Foreign Lands', 1902, says: *I told Freeman Cobb, who was then with Adams and Co., that I wanted him to start a line of coaches between Melbourne and the gold-mines, a distance of about sixty miles. I advanced the money for the enterprise, and a line was established, the first in Australia*" (My Life in Many States and in Foreign Lands, 1902, pp.133-134)

By "31 Jan 1854 Advertisement AMERICAN Telegraph Line of Coaches.—Daily Communication between Melbourne, Forest Creek and Bendigo—Cobb and Co. beg to announce to the public that they have determined to run a line of well-appointed Coaches between the above places" (Advertising, 31 Jan 1854, p.3) with the original proprietors of Cobb and Co. being Freeman Cobb, John B. Lambert, James Swanton, and John Murray Peck. Following this, in 1855, Adams and Co. was dissolved "NOTICE.—The Copartnership existing between the undersigned, under the name of Adams and Co., in Australia, was dissolved on the 1st day of March last. A. ADAMS, W. B. DINSMORE, E. G. SANFORD, S. M. SHOEMAKER, GEO. MOWTON, By their Attorney and Agent, Dyer Ames. NOTICE.—Removal.—After Monday, the 29th instant, the Agent of Adams and Co., Mr. Dyer Ames, may be found at the office of Messrs. E. W. Cobb and Co., No. 112, Collins-street west. All parties holding certificates of deposit will please present them before the 1st day of December next. ADAMS and CO., by their Agent and Attorney. Dyer Ames." (Advertising, 20 Nov 1855, p.3)

In the years that followed, until the 1920s, Cobb and Co. spread across many Australian states with a 'loose confederation of proprietors'. See 'Along the tracks of Cobb and Co.—The New South Wales Headquarters' (Book 3: In & Around Bathurst)

"Cobb and Co.'s Telegraph Line of Coaches.—The development of coaching enterprise in this colony is certainly as astonishing as any other of the wonderful things we have occasionally to chronicle ... but we venture to say that no one, not even Cobb himself, imagined that his enterprise would so rapidly approach the magnificent development lately, witnessed, when the humble half dozen passenger conveyance was represented by a gigantic car, holding fifty travellers and harnessed to fourteen greys, as fine specimens of horse flesh as one can hope to find in the southern hemisphere, 'tooled' by whips who are equalled by few, and excelled by none." (No Title, 14 Sep 1859, p.3)

Coaches

"A Cobb's coach is a 'Yankee notion' adapted for the rough roads of a new country—a thing of hickory wood, best steel, and much leather, exhibiting the greatest possible combination of lightness, springyness, and strength, with economy of space and carrying capacity. Ordinarily it carries six or nine passengers (jammed very tight) inside, and two on the box beside the driver. It is an animal (an animal being described as a thing of life and motion) with a large boot and an extensive tail, with a body between and a box in front, the boot and the tail being filled with mails and luggage. The body of the coach is swung on leather straps. Four horses are usually harnessed in front, under the guidance of coachy, who flourishes a long whip and keeps a firm foot on the break in descending inclines." (A Bush Trip, 3 Jan 1880, p.18)

Drivers

"The driver must be, and usually is, a man of firmness, activity and decision, with a most intimate knowledge of every road, rut, and stump on his line—his line being a distance of a day's drive, say about eighty miles, along which horses are changed as he travels backwards and forwards every twelve to fifteen miles, and the pace travelled at by the coaches is about 6 to 6 ½ miles an hour whilst going, or 5 miles an hour including stoppages to change horses, and for necessary meals to passengers" (A Bush Trip, 3 Jan 1880, p.18) "These old coach drivers were hardy men. Summed up in the words of an old driver of 82 years, their elixir of life was plenty of fresh air. *Except on a few occasions, we were early to bed*, he explained, a*nd at 5.30 a.m. we were up, breakfasted, and ready to face another day of anything up to 60 miles. Pay was small in those days, and the staple meal of mutton and damper was so scarce that we never suffered from indigestion. We smoked vile black tobacco sometimes, though people said it would kill us, and had a drink occasionally. There was nothing better, though, than the fresh bush air and the scent of the old gum trees!*" (One Secret of Old Age, 28 May 1937, p.12))

"A fine service it was, full of peculiar Australian characteristics, casual, happy-go-lucky in many ways, marked by good fellowship, good humor, courage, and an immense patience with the weather, the vicissitudes of the road, and the extraordinary development of out-of-the-way human traits. What has become of all those splendid drivers and horsemen of old Cobb and Co.? Gone where we all must go." (Cobb and Co. 6 Sep 1924, p.6))

Driving Methods

"Smart Yankee coachmen … introduced several driving methods that were new to us … were almost immediately seized upon and absorbed by the colonial youth in 'this land of the free, far away from the sound of the sea,' so that, in quite a few years, there sprang up a new set of drivers more suited to the back-country conditions of Australia … One cannot but applaud the great initiative, adaptability, and resourcefulness of the young Australian who so promptly picked up the ribbons … The imported American drivers introduced us to a quite new method of handling the ribbons … It consisted of four reins coming through between the same fingers as in the English fashion, but the near-side two crossed over the off-side pair in the palm of the hand, which was held horizontally, forming a roof over the lock, as a prevention against these parts of the reins becoming slippery in continuous wet weather." (The Lights of Cobb & Co., 17 Jul 1934, p.24) Yet another American innovation was the open 'Dolly Varden shield' to the winkers, permitting the horse to see everything that he should see, and nothing that he should not." (The Lights of [?]obb & Co., 17 Jul 1935, p.130)

Delivery of Mails

"The deliver of mails was carried out in the following manner:—On the righthand side of the coach, about level with the driver's seat, there was an extra strong iron hook. The mailbag prior to starting on the journey, were brought alongside in a cart and were hooked on in order of delivery. In the case of post offices of lesser importance the coach was not halted, the driver detached the bag, and threw it to a sturdy, rose-cheeked lassie who promptly caught it. Generally speaking the same little girl was on the spot, probably this was the great event in the daily life." (Memories of Myponga, 28 Oct 1927, p.13)

Change Stations

"Little time was lost at changing station. The outgoing team reins cleared, traces either hooked into the hames or thrown over the back, moved off to the stable. The incoming team were easily marshalled into their places. The drive 'All aboard,' the jar of the released break, and they were into their collars in one act" (Memories of Myponga, 28 Oct 1927, p.13)

1893 Edward Devine—Courtesy State Library Victoria

Driver of Coach.

A move to the 'iron horse' ... and then to the 'motor buggies'

1854 "a system of transit very much superior to anything I have yet seen in these colonies … and the vehicles are really the only attempt I have ever seen to adopt carriages to the rugged colonial roads … Thus the jolting incident to bad roads is very much diminished, and the chances of an upset almost extinguished." (Gleanings from the Victoria Gold Fields, 4 May 1854, p.5)

1924 "Slowly but surely of late years the horse coach has been disappearing from many parts of the State Queensland, until earlier in the week there appeared in our columns, that on August 14, the last horse-coach trip of the world-renowned firm of Cobb and Co. had been run front Surat to Yeulba. Cobb and Co. have played a leading part in the development of out-back Queensland and the announcement above referred to has been received with not a little sentimental regret by the many thousands who have during the long career of the Surat-Yeulba coach—or to be more precise the Yeulba-St. George coach as it was known for a considerable number of years—travelled by it. The motor coach has come in its place, but memory of the old conditions will long survive." (The Last Coach, 6 Sep 1924, p.4)

1920 "The name 'Cobb and, Co.,' is about all there ever was to associate Winslow and Freeman Cobb with the great system of passenger transport that served Australia so well in the pre-railway days of the country." (Stories of the Cobb & Co. Coaching Days, 19 Dec 1920, p.18)

"In its heyday, Cobb and Co. was the largest single transport system in the world" (The Days of Cobb and Co., 21 Jul 1951, p.12) In conclusion "very few persons, except those who actually lived in the past can have any idea what Cobb and Co. meant to the great outback. It carried to the families living in those lonely parts their letters and newspapers, to say nothing of numerous parcels, and now and then a stray friend" (Days of Cobb & Co. 1931, 16 Jan, p.8) "Around the name of Cobb and Co. will ever linger memories of the most romantic period in Australian history—the roaring days of the [18]'Fifties, the days of the bushrangers, the days of historic adventure by flood and field, the days of the sternest pioneering and the most daring exploration." (Sydney Mail, 20 Apr 1921, p.10)

1910 Heavy load of mail, Julia Creek, driver Fred Richards (J. Backwood N.Q.R photographer)—Courtesy Queensland Museum Collection

Corduroy roads, junction of Old Foster Road (Lydiards Track) and Nicols Road at Mirboo North—The Gippsland and Regional Regional Studies Collection (GRSC), reproduced courtesy of Federation University Australia

Chapter One
Drivers
A - B

Long Jim of Cobb & Co.

When he tells you of the leaders and the wheelers he has driven,

Of the colts that he has broken into harness raw and green,

You can bet upon the box seat he's past master with the ribbons ;

He's the *bean ideal* of drivers, perhaps the best that you have seen.

To the rattling of the traces

And the creaking of the braces

He keeps the conversation going with consummate easy flow.

He knows all about 'crook' wagers,

Handicaps, and weight-for-ages,

And he's just the very man to suit the firm of Cobb & Co.

Bullaman Aramac Hospital, July 9th, 1900.
(The Poet's Corner, 20 Nov 1900, p.10)

ca. 1920 Cobb & Co. coach No. 141, Surat to Yuleba Route, driver Fred Thompson—Courtesy Queensland Museum Collection

> "Fine covered in coaches, good horses and splendid drivers, built up a widespread and highly remunerative business for Cobb and Co. To handle the ribbons of this famous line, was a distinction amongst drivers, and in the long arduous and dangerous journeys through wild country, with bushrangers lurking in ambush." (Old Coaching Days, 11 Nov 1935, p.8)
>
> **BUSHRANGER TRICKED.** A good story is told of the late Mr. James Dennis, one of Australia's best known hoteliers. In the days of the decaying industry of bushranging, ruffian entered the bar, and, 'covering' Mr. Dennis with his revolver, cried 'hands up!' *Surely*, said Mr. Dennis calmly, *it does not require two men to bail me up?* The bushranger who was on his own, turned round to see who was following, Mr. Dennis whipped out his own gun, and the game was up." (Bushranger Tricked, 18 Mar 1911, p.4)

Supporting evidence:

Abbot, Bill ... 1921 See Griffen, Chas.

Adams, George (Tattersall)
1917 "Tattersall Adams was a frequent traveller on the North Coast, New South Wales. He was a beautiful driver, said Mr. Hampson [Bill]. He learned to drive with Cobb and Co … Whenever he got on the coach he would shift me off my seat and take the ribbons, and the way he would send those horses along was a treat to look at." (Coaching in Australia, 1917, p.27)

1923 See also Robinson, James (Robbie); 1925 Eddie, Nathan; 1932 Breen, Jim (Jimmy); 1935 Conroy, James (Jim)

Adams, J. G.
1889 "The new driver of Cobb & Co.'s coach to Charleville and Blackall is J. G. Adams." (Tambo Tit-Bits, 10 Dec 1889, p.2)

Adams, Peter ... 1921 See Griffen, Chas.

Aisbett Brothers ... 1937 See Atkinson, Frank

Aisbett, (Christian name unknown) Tom's Father
1953 "£5 by Cobb and Co. to Ballaarat COBB AND CO'S coaches have passed on but Ballarat remembers them with affection. For they played a tremendous part in the city's expansion goldrush days. It cost a digger £5 to get to the Ballarat gold fields. Then his luggage could follow later at a rate of £150 a ton. Memories were refreshed last month, when a 100 year-old coach drove from Melbourne to Ballarat as part of the Begonia Festival. It was driven by Fred Whiting and Tom Aisbett, both of Ballarat. Tom's father was one of the original drivers of Cobb and Co." (£5 by Cobb & Co. to Ballaarat, 16 April 1853, p. 30)

Aisbett, E. J.
1919 "The Cobb & Co.'s Old Coach Drivers' Association … old coach drivers employed by Messrs. Cobb & Co., kindred coaching firms in Australia and New Zealand, and others … Driver, district employed: Ballarat to Scarsdale and District" (Annual report / Cobb & Co.'s Old Coach Drivers' Association, 1919, pp.6-7)

1950 "One of the most disappointed men in Victoria on May 4 will be Mr. E. J. Aisbett, if he cannot get to the reunion. Mr. Aisbett, 83, of Mont Albert, is secretary of Cobb and Co. Old Drivers' Association. Writing to Mr. Harrison this week, he said he had been ill recently, doubted whether he would be along, but would be there if he possibly could." (Jehus of Yesteryear to be Guests, 26 Apr 1950, p.2)

Aisbett, James
1938 "Cobb & Co. Coach Again On Run To Ballarat. MELBOURNE. March 10. A Cobb & Co. coach drawn by four horses rolled through a maze of city traffic today on the first stage of a journey from Melbourne to Ballarat which is celebrating its centenary. The coach, which is in charge of Mr. James Aisbett, a former driver of the old Cobb vehicles, will take three days to cover the 75 miles of a journey which the ordinary steam train service now cuts out in less than three hours." (Cobb & Co. Coach again on run to Ballarat, 11 Mar 1938, p.10)

Aisbett, Jas. & Aisbett, J. M. T ... 1919 See Aisbett, E. J.

Aitken, James
1893 "Last Friday may be cited as the dawn of a new era in the advancement of communica between Geraldton and the goldfields inasmuch as on the afternoon of that day started from the office of Messrs. Marsh & McKenzie's (mail contractors) the first Cobb & Co. coach seen in the district. These conveyances are so well known and have now such a name for comfort and safety throughout Australia that it would be simply impossible to say anything that could place them in a higher position than they retain at present in the estimation of the travelling public. A large number of business men and others assembled to see the coach off. There were eight passengers, and a full cargo of luggage and mails. The masterly manner in which Mr. H. Ellis, a driver from Victoria, handled the seven splendid animals that made up the team was a display of driving that has never been equalled in Geraldton, except by Mr. James Aitken, who has hitherto been considered the master whip of the North, but we don't think Mr. Aitken has driven in this district the number of horses Mr. Ellis had under his control on Friday." (Our Members, 9 Jun 1893, p.2)

Alder, Amos
1930 "MEMORIES OF COBB & CO. The Old Coach Drivers. Reunion at Motor Show … Early in the afternoon the veterans began to assemble round the dilapidated stage coach that stands, a relic of the 'good old days,' at the main entrance to the show. On went the stream of reminiscences—yarns of the old coach routes, of adventurous drives through bush fires, of grand old horses, of cosy old 'pubs' along the roads, of the Kelly gang, and all sorts of things … The oldest driver of them all was Mr. R.H. Grover, better known as 'Bob,' who, in his 89th year, claims the honor of having been the first man to drive a six-horse coach across the Murray, from Beechworth to Wagga. He used to drive for Hiram Crawford, whose son, Walter Crawford, was amongst the veterans yesterday. One of Bob Grover's stories related to a different kind of stage from the type usually associated with coaches. Not so long ago—about 30 years or so,

he thought—he used to drive a coach and four across the stage in one of Bland Holt's plays at the Princess Theatre. But that was near the end of his coaching days. Before that he had driven in almost every part of Victoria. Another old driver who had many stories to tell was Harry Cornelius. Originally he drove coaches in New Zealand in the seventies, but when he came to Australia he drove carriages.

In 1880, he mentioned, when the present King and his brother, the Duke of Clarence, were visiting Melbourne, he used to drive the Marquis of Normanby between the city and Sandridge, where the Royal yacht was anchored. The Royal visitors always slept on board. Afterwards he was employed for private carriage work by the late Sir William Clarke. Stories of adventurous drives through the snow were told by Dave Carlisle, the pioneer driver on the road up a precipitous mountain. Amos Alder, another of the party, used to drive in the North-East in the days of the Kellys. *Not they* he said, when asked if the Kellys had ever bailed him up. *They were gentlemen.* Amongst the many others at the happy reunion were Ted Fowler (an old Gippsland driver), Charlie Matthews, Harry Payne (Bairnsdale to Omeo), Jim le Sueur (Cootamundra district), Jack Forbes (Bright to Omeo), Steve Holman (teamster and coach driver), George Page (blacksmith, who used to shoe the coach horses at Daylesford), Jim Laity (who drove the night coach from Daylesford to Malmsbury), Jim Bell (Balranald to Euston), Frank Edgecombe (Deniliquin and Echuca), and Alf Parker (Skipton district). Mr A. N. Vine, farmer, of Geelong district, who was the last manager and proprietor of coaches which ran under the name of Cobb and Co. in the Western district, was present also. Another guest was Mr. J. D. MacInnes, a member of the council of the Historical Society of Victoria. And yet another was Mrs. Letitia Barr, aged 88, who were a long black dress, shawl and toque, and discussed incidents associated with the coaching days before her husband died 38 years ago.

A MERRY DINNER. At the dinner in the evening Mr. Frank Smiley presided in his customary racy style. The chairman of the show committee (Mr. E.A. Bell) made a brief speech of welcome to the old coach drivers, who responded with 'cooees,' cheers and the singing of He's a Jolly Good Fellow. In response to cries for 'Horrie,' Mr. H. W. Harrison, secretary of the committee made a speech in which he predicted a time when old motor drivers would be attending a reunion at an annual aeroplane show. More cheers and singing followed. Then Mr. Smiley, after calling the crowd to order with a football umpire's whistle, made a speech himself. He went right back to his school days, when he won a prize for an essay on a horse. On behalf of the company Mr. Harrison presented Mr. Smiley with a set of jugs, with old coaching scenes, and the coachmen, through their chairman, presented Mr. Harrison with a blackwood walking stick. Someone struck up Silver Threads Amongst the Gold on a player piano, and the merry company joined in community singing in three or four different keys, and one of the old drivers, who had been a noted singer in his day (amongst his mates), sang Comin' Thru' the Rye, unaccompanied. In the midst of the second verse the company was called to order with the umpire's whistle, but the singer remained unperturbed, and finished his song amidst cheers and 'cooees.' At one stage the company stood in silence for a minute in memory of sixteen of their mates who had died since the last reunion. The toast of The Press was proposed by Mr. Boyce, the former chief of the Government Tourist Bureau, and the singing of the National Anthem ended a most enjoyable occasion." (Memories of Cobb & Co., 6 May 1930, p.11)

Alder, Jas. (Jimmy)
1938 "Cobb and Co. Coachman. As a veteran of the roads and as a 'digger' on the goldfields when the history of Victoria was in the making, the career of 'Jimmy' Alder was packed with incident. His death in Echuca in 1928 at an advanced age brought a venturesome life to a close. Alder was a platman at the Clunes mines at the time when the miners there declared a strike as a protest against a reduction in wages. One of the operating companies, in an attempt to break the strike, engaged a number of Chinese from Ballarat to work the Clunes mines. This aroused a feeling of bitter resentment, and a determination was formed to oust the foreign strike breakers from Clunes. About two miles from the town, a barricade of all sorts of heavy objects was erected, and when the Chinese arrived in the company of their police escort they were greeted with volleys of stones and bricks, bones and bottles and everything else lying handy which could be converted into missiles. This caused a hasty retreat of the Celestial invaders, whose one thought was to remove themselves as quickly as possible from the range of the infuriated mob. About 80 of the Chinese fled to Beechworth, and the route of their cross-country exodus included Shepparton. It must have been a strange scene when the picturesque proccesion presented itself before the astonished gaze of the puntsman at Shepparton. They had engaged William Bridges, an uncle of Mr. F. J. Cook, Baddaginnie, to transport their baggage for £1 apiece, while they themselves performed the long, arduous journey on foot. Weary and bedraggled, their garments rent from the hazards of the road and the impetuosity of their hasty retreat from distant Clunes, the visitation of this curious band of Oriental miners was a unique event in the annals of Shepparton.

As a result of the riots, Alder deemed it prudent to cultivate for a time a retiring disposition, until the episode had blown over. Accordingly, in 1873, and in company with the late James Campbell, of Loch Garry, and the late 'Bill' Campbell— whom Numurkah folk were later went to refer affectionately as 'King Billy'—Alder joined a party intent on making a new home in the virgin Goulburn Valley. Like the nomads of old, they travelled with their cattle, but when the wayfarers reached Shepparton they discovered that the old punt had sunk into the depths of the river, and the result was that they could not cross the Goulburn until after dark. While waiting for the new punt to be put in readiness, they camped with their 26 head of cattle in what later became High Street, in the vicinity of the 'News' office. Alder's recollection of Shepparton was that it then comprised the punt house, 'Jimmy' Hay's pub, Howe's store, the building formerly known as the Royal Hotel kept by a man named Evans., Day's Criterion Hotel, and a few scattered edifices all of an unpretentious class of architecture.

Later, Alder became a coachdriver for Cobb and Co., running from Shepparton to Violet Town. The rate at which the coaches ran was fixed at six miles an hour, including stoppages. He used to leave Shepparton at noon and complete his 32 odd miles journey at about 5 p.m.—a striking contrast with present day achievements of the motor car. Alder drove sometimes three horses, which were changed at what was called Caniambo creek. The roads were excrable, especially in winter, and Alder used often to recall in later years how, between Pine Lodge hotel and Kialla East school, the water had cut away the road so badly that there were deep hollows between, the roots of the trees. The coach horses—old and experienced campaigners—know just where to step and managed to get through safely but this was a feat beyond horses strange to the route. On one occasion, two horses in a doctor's buggy came to grief on this particular portion of the road, and their heads were being held up out of the water by men who had gone to their rescue, until they could be freed from their harness.

The opening of the Goulburn Valley railway line did away with the coach service from Shepparton to Violet Town, and then Alder drove the same firm's coach from Shepparton to Echuca for a considerable time. There were two stopping places on the 45-mile journey, one at Undera and the other at Vickers wayside hotel where a meal was available. Three sets of horses were thus needed for the trip, and there were at times, passengers enough to require four horses between each stage.

Alder had the honor of driving several of our State Governors to various functions in the district, among them being Sir Henry Brougham Loch, on the occasion of the Grand National Show at Shepparton, which extended for three days and, later, Lord Brassey. Alder was afterwards employed with his brother at Dolphin's soda water factory on the Goulburn river bank at Mooroopna where they were eye-witnesses of the sensational sinking of a horse and buggy into the flooded stream when cash and securities belonging to the Commercial Bank were lost. Despite the offer of a lavish reward by the bank, which attracted the leading diver in Victoria, the only article recovered was a revolver." (Veteran of the Road, 12 Oct 1938, p.18)

Alexander, Jack
1934 "T. J. Roberts … Matt Thornton drove the coach to Mount Pleasant for Cobb & Co. 60 years ago, he said. When he retired he prospected for gold at Mount Pleasant for many years. His successor was 'Sampson' Hall, who later drove the coach from Strathalbyn to Wellington. I believe his real Christian name was Stephen, but he was always known as 'Sampson,' because of herculean feats he performed with a tree outside the Belvidere Hotel, of which he became licensee.

In his day a guard, who had charge of the mails, sat at the rear of the coach, and blew a cornet when approaching a township. Sheridan, I believe, was the last of these guards. Jack Alexander, of boot polish fame, followed Sampson Hall, and he was succeeded by Jimmy Kelton. Jack Hynes of Gumeracha, supports me in the view that Jim Kelton was considered the crack whip on the mail road. Charlie Alford came after Kelton and, when he quitted the service, the last man to drive the Mount Pleasant coach was Goode, who now runs the mail car from Adelaide to Mannum. George Oakley used to drive the coach from the junction near Mount Pleasant to Mannum." (Out among the People, 25 Oct 1934, p.17)

1939 See also Chatfield, Harry

Alford, Charles John
1933 "ALFORD —On the 24th August, at Alfred Hospital, Charles John, beloved husband of the late Blanch Maud, loving father of Percival Alford, and brother of Annie (Narrogin, West Aus.), and Dorcas (Mrs. Lillaco, Albany West Aus.) (late driver Cobb and Co. coaches), aged 78 years." (Family Notices, 25 Aug 1933, p.1)

Alford, P ... 1919 See Aisbett, E. J.

Allan, (Christian name unknown)
1930-1940s "The photograph is of a coach and team outside a Cobb and Co. office. Note: On the reverse of the backing board are signatures of former coach drivers : Allan, ___ (coach driver); Freerer, ___ (coach driver); Danes, ___ (coach driver); Edwards, Bob (coach driver); Giles, Tom (coach driver); Hauman [or Harmon], A. (coach driver); Laity, ___ (coach driver); Mickle, D.J.; Millard, W.A. (coach driver); Milne, W. (coach driver); Mulholland, L. (coach driver); Partington; Kelly (coach driver); Rodgers, Mr. (coach driver); Smiley, Frank (coach driver); Sullivan, Mr (coach driver); Templeton [Templenton], ___ (later Mrs Burnside) (coach driver); Vines, T. (coach driver); Wallace, P. (coach driver)" (Cabbage Tree Ned : Cobb & Co's Coach Driver photograph, 1930-1940s – Newspaper Article, Royal Historical Society of Victoria)

Allan, John ... 1919 See Aisbett, E. J.

Amies, Tom
1917 "Of another driver Mr. Ruddle says: I was once going from Brisbane to Ipswich, Tom Amies was driving. At one of the stopping places a new chum groom brought out some water in a bucket to give the horses a drink, a mare in the pole on the near side, would not drink, so the fool took off the head stall. The mare, instead of drinking, put up her head and looked around. Tom kept repeating in a low stern voice, *Put on the winkers, put on the winkers*, which the new chum did; then Tom raised his voice, and what he said was unprintable. The groom seemed very much hurt at Tom's language and said, *An shure. I was only giving her a drink*. I was sitting on the box, Tom turned to me and said, *That's the quietest horse on the road, yet I thought we should have a smash*. So did I, but I sat very quiet, knowing what a splendid man Tom Amies was with horses." (Coaching in Australia, 1917, p.37)

1929 Cobb and Co.'s famous coaching days "With a merry rattle, trot, trot, clicketty clack … volumes could be written—tales of adventure, gold rushes, bushrangers, brave pioneers; drought and death and flood. Around them is woven a romance almost as old as Queensland itself, the romance of the famous coaching days of Australia … On one corner of the table lay some faded photographs and old prints—pictures of the coaches, and the hardy men who kept the roads open, and made habitable the uninhabited parts of Queensland; brave men and horses that made the bush ring with the rattle, trot, trot, clicketty clack of iron-shod wheel and hoof …

Last Tuesday in that same office gathered a group of people, men and women, young and old, the last shareholders of a company that has made history. They confirmed a resolution previously passed: That the company be wound-up voluntarily … But what a romantic page in our history has closed, a history that dates back to the early 1850's and the roaring days of the bushranger and the gold stampeder … Among the early Queensland drivers were H. Barnes, Jerry Murphy, Jim Hunter, Yankee Bill, Jimmy Murphy, Tom Elms, Nick Holden, Rob M'Rae, Tom Amies, and Tom Kidd … Here's to the old days. The ramping, roaring days of Cobb and Co … For much of the material in this article acknowledgement must be made to Mr. W. Long's History of Cobb and Co., published some years ago." (Cobb and Co's Coaching Days: colourful page of history closed, 30 Jun 1929, p.23)

Anderson, (Christian name unknown)
1870 "His Royal Highness was received on the arrival of the train by the mayor, Mr. T. N. Couves, and proceeded to breakfast at Bedford's Terminus Hotel, from whence the Royal party started shortly before nine o'clock in one of Cobb's carriages, driven by Mr. Anderson, a member of the firm, and escorted by Sergeant Toohey and a mounted constable." (Thursday October 27 1870, 27 Oct 1870, p.5)

Anderson, Jim
1917 "It is interesting also to recall the drivers on these lines of the [18]eighties, all good men and careful, if fearless. They brought in the coaches through flood or sunshine on time ... St. George and district to Thargomindah, via Bollon, Cunnamulla, Mitchell, and up the Balonne to Surat and Yeulba, lines of coaches ran with the following drivers:—Geo. Macgilcuddy, Jim Murphy, Bill Mitchell, Pat Toohey, Jim Davidson, now at Surat, Dave Teys, Ned Manning, Bill Woods, Fred Richards, now road inspector at St. George, Alf. Jensen, Harry Weaver, who lately died at Thargomindah, Tom Anderson and Jim Anderson, who a short while ago met his death in a bus accident at Toowoomba." (Coaching in Australia, 1917, p.41)

Written on the same page ... Bushranger in district of "St. George ... Vane, the bushranger, distinguished in the annals of New South Wales, has been sojourning on a neighboring station for some time past, but has lately left us to go farther north. He was engaged on a fencing contract, which he completed satisfactorily, and his mates found him very quiet and inoffensive. I have seen him in town, on one occasion, and he appeared an easy going customer, rather dull, if anything. I would have 'interviewed' him, only I heard he could cut the head clean off a duck with a revolver bullet at a hundred yards." (St. George, 14 Aug 1875, p.3)

Anderson, Thomas (Tom)
1901 "Georgetown Chips. (From the Mundic Miner, June 7.) Mr Samuel Cousens, the stalwart 6ft 4½ driver for Cobb and Co., has again severed his connection with that firm, and is now driving for Mr Harry Chatfield. His place has been filled by Mr Michael Enright, who arrived by Monday's coach ... Mr Edward Gallagher, who has been road manager for Cobb for many years, is leaving the firm, and Mr Thomas Anderson, who has been an old, experienced whip for Cobb out Cunnamulla way, has taken charge, having arrived on Monday night." (Georgetown Chips, 21 Jun 1901, p.3)

1938 "ON THE TRACK ... OLD WHIPS OF COBB AND CO. (The following lines were written in the days when Cobb and Co.'s coaches were still on the roads.) *I've been coaching down in New South Wales, riding in the Royal Mail, 'On the box' in Vic. and Tassie, in the boots in snow and hail; Riding in my sober senses, riding with my 'lamps' alight, Watching Jehu with the ribbons, seeing if he held them right ... So my mind goes harking backwards back to days of long ago, Back to old familiar faces in the ranks of Cobb and Co ...*

Wonderful books could be written about the bygone coach drivers of the West, and if the majority of Australians were patriotic enough to buy the literature of their own country, written by native-born author, several of us fellows who 'drive' a pen would make decent money putting such reminiscences between the covers of a printed volume. As matters stand, no Australian publisher can be found to accept this class of manuscript, knowing only too well, from past experience, that there would be little demand for such a book. It is a pity. The stories that could be told about these men should be handed down for the benefit of future generations, but I am afraid that even now it is too late, and they could not be collected ...

Not so long ago since I was in a one-pub settlement consisting of ten tin humpies and 83 goats, and while having one with the publican, a tall, wrinkled cove drifted into the bar and ordered a rum. *And how's the missus, Dan?* asked the publican. *I hear she's got another nipper.* The rum disappeared, and Dan accepted my invitation to have another. *Oh yaas, she's had another*, he said in a far-away voice. *What is it this time?* asked the man behind the counter. *Oh, It's a boy*, replied Dan, *and that's nine we've got now.* I reckon Billy Hughes ought to congratulate fellows like you, considering he reckons the country wants population, I said. *Well, I'm doing me best*, drawled Dan. *You'd better have another.* As the publican picked up the empty glasses he remarked, *When was the youngster born, Dan?* The man beside me scratched his head for a minute and seemed to be burned deep in thought *I'm blowed if I know*, he said, slowly. *Let me see now. Yes Strawberry had a calf on Wednesday—a fine calf—a heifer, and on Thursday old Dolly had a foal, and the missus give birth to her nipper on Friday.* The publican smiled. *Really*, he said, *and what kind of a foal did Dolly have Dan?*" (On the Track, 31 Aug 1938)

1917 See also Anderson, Jim; 1939 Warner, Jack

Andrews, Charles
1943 "Born in Bothwell ... in 1853 ... he was employed by Mr. M. Sheehan, as a driver for the famous Cobb and Co.'s coaches ... he drove the mail coach from Healesville to Melbourne." (Passing of pioneer coach man, 24 Apr 1943, p.3)

Athorn/Athorne, Edward
1920 "ALONE IN AGONY. COACH DRIVER'S ACCIDENT. MUNGINDI.—A serious coach smash occurred about 6 o'clock on Sunday evening three miles from St. George, when Cobb and Co.'s coach was travelling from Thallon and resulted in the driver, Edward Athorn, sustaining a broken thigh and severe internal injuries. It is reported that the lights of a car caused the horses to bolt and run up an embankment 5ft. high ... The driver, being alone, lay in agony, for hours before his cries attracted a man in the vicinity. Athorn was taken to St. George Hospital" (Alone in Agony, 14 May 1920, p.3)

1917 See also Wright, Bob

Athorn/Athorne, Ted ... 1948 See Herchberg/Hertsberg, Joseph (Joe)

Atkins, Andy ... 1917 See Wright, Bob

Atkins, W.
1925 "COBB AND CO.'S DRIVERS. TO THE EDITOR. Sir,—'Cobb s Coaches,' by T. J. Lonsdale is interesting reading but many 'good whips ' he left out. In my time Tom Gallagher (who subsequently became manager), Stan Wall, Ted Donohue, W. Atkins, Billy Richardson (now a car driver in Southport) and George Stevenson—all these men drove on the principal routes from Charleville; and a week before Christmas of 1904, I left Charleville for Adavale with the record heaviest loaded coach, so I was informed, and the ribbons were in the safe keeping of Stan Wall. He was only a little fellow but he could drive, and but for careful handling going over the Gray Range we must have toppled over. Yet those were the days and it did one good to see any of these men driving, and generally on time too. Lumley was the last of a good team of drivers to leave Cobb and Co. Mr Search who was secretary in Charleville for the firm for 20 years met every coach and saw every coach away each day—a fine record. It seems a pity that an old institution like Cobb and Co should die out, but of course now we are becoming too civilised, I am, sir, &c. OLD WESTERNER. Rathdowney, January 23." (Cobb and Co.'s Drivers, 29 Jan 1925, p.12)

Atkinson, F ... 1919 See Aisbett, E. J.

Atkinson, Frank
1937 "OLD COACHING DAYS. Veteran Driver's Grave.

BALLARAT, Sunday.—Memories of old coaching days were revived to-day at the unveiling of the headstone over the grave at the Ballarat new cemetery of Edward Devine, once known far and wide in 'the colony' as 'Cabbage Tree Ned,' most famous of Cobb and Co.'s coach drivers. The large assembly, presided over by the mayor (Cr. J. Pryor), included many old drivers. Among them were Mr. Frank Smiley (president of Cobb and Co.'s Old Coach Drivers' Association), who once drove in the Western district; Mr. Alf. Partington (secretary), who figured on the Ballarat-Streatham run; Mr. Frank Atkinson, the Aisbett brothers, Mr. Jim Edwards and Mr. Harry Glasson. Present also were representatives of the Historical Society of Victoria in Messrs. J. K. Moir (who was largely responsible for initiating the movement) and J. Alex. Allan.

It was Mr. Moir who two years ago found that Devine had been buried in a pauper's grave after his death at the Ballarat Benevolent Home in 1908, and took steps which, through the Cobb and Co.'s Old Drivers' Association, resulted in the old driver's grave being surmounted with an appropriate stone. Lending historical color to the ceremony at the graveside to-day was a typical Cabbage Tree coach driver's hat and brass-studded leather cash bag, traditional equipment of Cobb and Co. drivers in the early days. The mayor congratulated the sponsors of the movement for honoring one who was so closely associated with the early development of the State. Mr. G. R, Holland, chief president of the A.N.A., said that the name of Cobb and Co. would always be linked with early Victorian history, and 'Cabbage Tree Ned' represented all the best traits of the early drivers." (Old Coaching Days, 8 Feb 1937, p.14)

1937 See also Atkinson, Frank

Avery, Fred ... 1935 See Conroy, James (Jim)

Bain, Billy ... 1920 See Gales, A.

Balsall, Jack ... 1917 See Richardson, Alf

Bamberger, Louis
1878 "A culvert on the Gympie-road, which, with the accustomed thoughtlessness of our Road Department, had been left undistinguished by so much as a guide post amid the raging flood that covered it, has proved fatal to poor Louis Bamberger, the faithful and obliging driver of Cobb's coach, which, together with the horses, toppled over the side and was lost sight of for hours ... letters and papers were found ... had to be dried in an oven." (Maryborough, 28 Dec 1878, p.6)

Bannear, Harry ... 1921 See Griffen, Chas.

Barnes/Barns, Hiram
1864 "FORBES. Monday, 5 p.m. On Sunday morning, before daylight, Mr. Barnes, the driver of Cobb and Co.'s coach, was fired at by two men, one on each side of the road, about nine miles from Forbes, because he did not stop when ordered. The men were on foot, and could not follow the coach. Mr. Barnes distinctly heard the bullets whiz past him." (Forbes, 17 May 1864, p.4)

1875 "Accident to Cobb and Co.'s Coach. Yesterday, an accident occurred to Cobb and Co.'s Coach at Capsize Creek, between the Dawson and Rocky, by which Mr. Barns, the road manager, who happened to be driving, was seriously injured, and several of the passengers cut and bruised, and more or less shaken ... On Tuesday night we stopped at the Dawson township, where we met Mr. Barns, Cobb and Co.'s Road Manager, who was on his way to open a line of coaches to Springsure. Next morning we started on the coach for Rooky Creek, and had got as far as the Post Office, when it was proposed to take up three more passengers, viz., two policemen and a lunatic. Now, as the coach was full, and we had several lady passengers, I and others strongly objected to such a proceeding ; and in order to settle the matter the coachman drove back over the Dawson Bridge, to consult Mr. Barns.

The result was that a second coach was started, Mr. Barns holding the ribbons. The two coaches went on for about six miles ; Mr. Barns then exchanged seats, taking the reins of the first coach, in which were Mrs. Graham and niece, Miss O'Hara, Mr. C. J. Graham, Member for Clermont ; Mr. Blackiston, traveller for Messrs. Scott, Dawson, and Stewart ; Mr. Wallon, traveller for Mr. Alfred Shaw and Co., Brisbane and other passengers. As the coach was approaching the railway crossing near Capsize Creek, some men at work on the line held up their hands as a signal to stop, and Mr. Burns pulled up ; immediately afterwards, they waved for him to proceed, and he again put the coach in motion ; but at the same instant a ballast engine let off steam, and the horses, becoming frightened, slewed round and dashed forward, the result being that the coach was very nearly overturned, while the shaft, which seems to have come in violent contact with a stump, was broken to splinters.

Some of the male passengers leaped from the coach, which they fully expected would be capsized ; others seem to have been thrown out ; all were more or less injured. Mr. Graham was cut and bruised on the back, through two wheels passing over him. Mr. Wallen fell on his head, and sustained several contusions, besides losing consciousness for some time. Mr. Blackiston, who made a flying leap of about ten feet, escaped with a slight bruise ; but another passenger, whose name we did not ascertain, had one of his knee caps cut and a wrist dislocated. The ladies kept their seats, and were uninjured, as the coach was not overturned. This was owing, probably, to the horses getting free ; otherwise the result might have been most serious. Mr. Barns fared badly. He stuck to the reins, but was thrown from his seat, and dragged by the horses a distance of 40 or 50 yards, and was badly wounded on one side through falling on a stump. He walked for a minute or two after the accident, and then dropped down in an unconscious state.

The railway officials did all in their power for the travellers. A mattress was procured for Mr. Barns, and he and the rest of the passengers were taken down in a truck to Rocky Creek, and by ordinary train to Rockhampton. Mr. Burns was at once taken to the Leichhardt Hotel, and attended by Dr. Callaghan, who expresses the opinion that the case is not dangerous, as no serious internal injury has been sustained. The mishap seems to have been purely accidental." (Accident to Cobb and Co.'s Coach, 16 Sep 1875, p.2)

1917 "To the history of Cobb & Co. in Queensland. The first coaches ran in 1865, when Mr. H. Barnes, who died in April of this year, one of the oldest drivers and road managers of the firm, came to Brisbane to inspect, and shortly after brought the first turn-out, consisting of 16 coaches in all, made at the Bathurst factory of Cobb & Co. The first line was from Brisbane to Ipswich, Mr. Barnes opening the line with a team of twelve horses, he being strapped to the box. The writer of this notice well remembers travelling by coach to Ipswich in 1873. The vehicle was a 36-passenger coach, and was punted across the river at what was then known as Oxley Point (now Chermside). No luggage was carried, that being conveyed by the river steamers Settler, Shamrock, Glide, and other boats which used to ply between Brisbane and the confluence of the Brisbane and the Bremer." (The Genesis of Cobb & Co, 15 Sept 1917, p.11)

1865 "Queensland Organisation. Stables were built in Albert-street, on the site now occupied by Fleming and Sons, and on a certain day in the year 1865, the first coach set out on its dash with mails and passengers to Ipswich, with driver Barnes strapped to the box and a team of 12 horses straining at the reins. The opening of the Brisbane—Ipswich line was a great success. The journey occupied about three hours, there being three changes of horses, and each coach as a rule carried 30 to 35 passengers. The firm received its first setback the following year, when a disastrous fire occurred in the town, and Cobb and Co.'s premises were burnt to the ground. New premises were quickly erected further up Albert-street on the site now occupied by the Queensland Machinery Co. Ltd.

Still later the headquarters were built at the junction of Queen-street and Petrie's Bight, near Uhl's saddlery. By this time Cobb and Co.'s lines had been extended far and wide from the capital … Later the Gympie line was added and extended to Maryborough. Then came Brisbane to Sandgate, and one from Beenleigh and Southport, Nerang, Tallebudgera and Murwillumbah, while the Warwick line was extended via Stanthorpe and Maryland to Tenterfield, there joining on with the New South Wales systems, as also at Murwillumbah. Later other lines were extended north and west, and new routes established until Charters Towers, Aramac, Tambo, Emerald, and Roma were all linked up by Cobb and Co's coaches." (Cobb and Co's Coaching Days: Golourful Page of History Closed, 30 Jun 1929, p.23)

1923 See also Robinson, James (Robbie); 1925 Eddie, Nathan; 1929 Amies, Tom; 1932 Breen, Jim (Jimmy); 1935 Conroy, James (Jim)

Barnett, George
1913 "COBB'S AND A LEGAL PUZZLE. DRIVER WHO COUNTED HIS HOURS ONLY THIS SIDE OF THE BRIDGE. At the Geelong Police Court yesterday, Cobb and Co. were charged by Inspector Tipple that they did, in respect of the week ending 8th February, 1913, unlawfully employ one George Barnett, an adult, other than a casual hand, who during such week worked for 74 hours at a wage of 42/… The employe in question, in addition to other work, drove the coach to Barwon Heads." (Cobb's and a Legal Puzzle, 2 Apr 1913, p.4)

Barrie, Billie
1938 "QUEANBEYAN REMINISCENCES Sir,—As our 'Centenary' grows close, and I hear a Cobb and Co. coach is to be on parade … I would like to mention a few things of interest to my knowledge. My grandfather, John J. Barry, was one of the drivers from Goulburn to Cooma; and also to Harden. He died 12 years ago at Young, where he ran coach lines for many years … His driving mates were Tommie Moran, Battye Moran, Jack Moran (father of Jimmie Moran, of Queanbeyan), and Jimmie Moran, senr. nick-named 'The Fenian' because he always wore a green neck-tie. Tot Pooley and Malone were partners who also ran coaches, and Billie Barrie (my father) drove for them on the Tarago-Braidwood road afterwards. He was also a hurdle and steeplechase rider of note with his cousin, John Allsop, also of Monaro, who died in Sydney, a leading trainer for many years. My father, who has been a resident of Queanbeyan for 29 years, is it is safe to say, the only Cobb and Co. driver left around these districts. He drove on the Grenfell to Young line over the 'Weddin Mountains,' and Wyalong goldfields to Temora 44 years ago … Yours, etc., Queanbeyan, Sept. 13, 1938. MRS. MOLLIE BYRNE" (Queanbeyan Reminiscences, 20 Sep 1938, p.1)

Barrir, John … 1932 See Lowe, Bill

Barry, J … 1937 See Preston, R.

Barry, Jack … 1917 See Thompson, Joe; 1923 Robinson, James (Robbie); 1925 Eddie, Nathan; 1935 Conroy, James (Jim)

Barry, Jas … 1919 See Aisbett, E. J.

Barry, John J. (Father of Billie Barrie) … 1938 See Barrie, Billy

Barry, William
1932 "Mr. William Barry, who drove to Burrows for several years … later entered the employment of Cobb and Co." (Cobb and Co. Coachman, 21 Nov 1932, p.4)

Bates, Robert (Silent Bob)
1910 "A PIONEER JEHU GONE. The death of Mr. R. Bates (which sad event occurred on Sunday), has removed a personality whose history, were it able to be published, would form an interesting narrative. Deceased had attained the ripe age of 77, and was one of the pioneer coach- drivers of the State, having been contemporary with such expert knights of the whip as Gill, Wilkinson, and others, who have long since gone to their rest. Coming to Australia when quite a young man, the late Mr. Bates soon afterwards became associated with the mail service on the Great Northern Road, from Maitland to Armidale, about 66 years ago. He first drove on the line when Mr. John Gill had the contract, and subsequently entered the employment of Cobb and Co. Those were the days of bad roads and other difficulties, which rendered the coach driver's lot anything but a sinecure. The bushranging element was in evidence, too, and travellers found it no uncommon thing to hear the peremptory command to 'Bail Up!' The subject of this notice had experiences with the freebooting fraternity, and at least once, we believe, came into conflict with the notorious Thunderbolt.

In later years Mr. Bates drove regularly on the Glen Innes-Inverell line, until advancing years compelled him to relinquish the box seat for the less exacting demands of a quiet home life. A most skilful hand with the ribbons, deceased was also a singularly reticent man, and passengers found it difficult to engage him in conversation. This earned for him the sobriquet of 'Silent Bob.' Nevertheless, he was well liked by constant travellers between here and Inverell, the utmost confidence being placed In his driving abilities. Deceased was very strict in his attention to duty—no matter in what circumstances—and came to be regarded as the personification of punctuality. He had a grown-up family of seven, viz., Mrs. T. Goodwin (Gunnedah district), Mrs. Pitkin, Mrs. W. W. Nash, Miss A. Bates, and William, Charles, and John. The funeral took, place yesterday afternoon, the body being laid to rest in the Roman Catholic portion of the cemetery." Below was written "It is estimated that 250 tons of blackberries were gathered in Illawarra district during the season just closed. About 200 tons were sold to jam factories in Sydney at ld per lb." (A Pioneer Jehu Gone, 17 May 1910, p.2)

1933 "Old Link Broken. Cobb and Coy.'s Stables Demolished. Sacrificed to Progress. How old is Cobb and Co.'s stable? Well, I'm here 75 years and it was there when I got here. In those days Tattersall's Hotel was a very small weatherboard pub. It was kept by a Mrs. Molloy, and she was a wild woman. I remember one day there was an election fight on and she was soon in the thick of it. Her wig got knocked off in the scuffle, I remember. Yes, she was a pretty wild sort of a woman was Mrs. Molloy.

The speaker was Mr. Larry Andrews who, in spite of his great age, has all his faculties. He well recalls the days when the delivery of the mails depended upon the pluck, determination and skill of Cobb and Co.'s drivers. They were wonderful men, continued the veteran, and the way they got through on some of those roads was marvellous. They followed the same routes as the mails travel today but the roads were terribly rough and boggy. I can't remember them all, but some of them were Bob Bates, Dick Palmer, Larry Madden, Jack Johnson (who died not long ago), Bill O'Dell, and Jimmy Nairn. They were great fellows ... I never drove for Cobb and Co., but 1 drove the Hillgrove coach for a long time: I knew Cobb's stables well enough though.

The historic old stable—a nerve centre of New England in the days of the pioneers—has run its course. It is now being demolished in the yard of Tattersall's Hotel, a sacrifice on the altar of progress ... The old building was 64 feet long, 21ft. deep and 25ft. in height, and was built of hand made bricks, and was in a wonderful state of preservation ... all the woodwork was held together with wooden pegs, and the timbers were in such an excellent state of preservation that much of it would be embodied in the new building. The bricks were being broken up and would be used to make the concrete for the garage. Mr Robinson has had his sample rooms completely renovated and is providing enlarged accommodation for cars. These changes are inevitable, but one cannot but feel a pang of regret that such an historic old spot as Cobb and Co.'s stables should have to be sacrificed to meet the demands of a more modern age." (Old Link Broken, 9 Jan 1933, p.4)

1923 See also Robinson, James (Robbie); 1925 Eddie, Nathan; 1932 Breen, Jim (Jimmy); 1935 Conroy, James (Jim)

Bell, Jim ... 1930 See Alder, Amos

Bell, Samuel F.
1929 "PENSIONER FOUND DEAD. Old Cobb's Coach Driver. KALGOORLIE, Dec. 5.—About 4.30 o'clock this afternoon ... dead in his camp near the Mt. Charlotte reservoir ... Bell has no relatives in this State. He came to the goldfields about 30 years ago from New South Wales. In Menzies, in the early days, he drove one of Cobb and Co's coaches for several years." (Pensioner found dead, 12 Dec 1929, p.27)

Bennett, Jim
1936 "I knew Mr. and Mrs. Benussi and all the children. Not long ago I stayed with the late Frank Benussi at Sale, where he conducted the Star Hotel. Before the railway was extended to Daylesford, Cobb and Co.'s coaches used to run in all directions. We boys would frequently 'whip behind', and I shall never forget on one memorable occasion I was whipping behind the Creswick coach in Vincent-street, outside the school, when the driver, Jim Bennett, swished round his whip, and the lash twined round my neck, dragging me off the boot and for some distance along the road before it unwound itself and set me free. It might have been serious for me, but it cured me of the habit of whipping behind." (Daylesford, 4 Apr 1936, p.7)

Bernie, Joe
1927 "News has been received of the death in Sydney of Mr. Joe Bernie an old time and well known resident of Young and an uncle of Mrs W. Jasprizza. Mr Bernie was 78 years of age. His wife predeceased him a few years ago. Before the Railway went through from Young to Cowra, he used to drive Cobb

ca. 1920 Bainbilla horse change on Yuleba Surat route, Fred (Tommy) Thomson driver, Charlie Horrobin nursing niece Marguerite, Edith Horrobin (cousin), Bob Horrobin and Louie Horrobin standing; The Horrobin family ran the Bainbilla station and mail change—Courtesy Queensland Museum Collection

and Co's coach, and was well known throughout the district. Twelve months ago he had an accident, from which he did not completely recover." (Obituary, 29 Aug 1930, p.4)

1927 See also Payne, Jack

Bernie, William ... 1927 See Payne, Jack

(Surname unknown), Big Bingy
1867 Big Bingy's heroism "Surat ... the river Ballone still heads in the same direction. I was pained to witness a most distressing scene in the bed of this well-known stream ... A respected Suratter managed to get stuck, dray, bag and baggage, in the treacherous depths of the river. Horse flesh could do no more ... an act of manly heroism on the part of our old friend Big Bingy, which really deserves recording ... a plunge in the water, and ere the miserable quadruped in the shafts had time to cock his ears, and give a snort, he was wrenched out of his harness, and his place filled by the *Big 'un*. An appalling yell, apparently from under his tail, startled the leader into activity, and up the bank they went, as if the ponderous dray had been only a wheelbarrow ... An unfortunate horse was left in a deplorable state, and all from catching a glimps of his driver.

The said Jehu had mounted a terrific hat a la Cobb and Co. And I may remark here that these hats have a charmed reputation. The moment a Roman mounts one, his character as a 'whip' is established. In an evil moment the man in the hat left his perch, and dismounted for the purpose of blowing his nose. (His own, not the horse's). The poor animal evidently took him for something supernatural, and was seized with gripes of so enduring a character, that he was abandoned to the crows and dingoes. A fabulous price has since been offered for the hat, under the impression that no jibber could stand it." (Roma, 5 Oct 1867, p.3)

(Surname unknown), (Billy the Whip) ... 1925 See Paine, William

Birrell, Charles
1873 "BATHURST. [From our Correspondent.] September 30. Cobb's coach for Orange met with an accident, which threatened dire consequences to the driver and passengers, on Friday. One of the pole traces broke as the coach was descending the long ridge near Dunkeld ; the horses bolted, and one fell and was dragged by the rest some 30 yards. Ultimately, the leaders broke the pole and severed the harness, and got away. The coach was on the point of overturning several times. The driver, Charles Birrell, showed great courage and presence of mind, and was assisted at the break by Mr Lewis Lloyd, of Goldrich, who was a passenger." (Bathurst, 30 Sep 1873, p.2)

Bissel, Frank ... See Appendix 1.6

Bissell/Bissel, Charles (Charlie)
1896 "Death of a Mudgee Whip. Charles Bissell, one of the oldest and best known coach owners of the western district, died at Mudgee on Tuesday, aged 66. Bissell for many years drove Cobb and Co.'s coach over the Blue Mountains. He also drove the mail coach between Wallerawang and Mudgee until the railway was constructed to Mudgee, since which time he has driven the Mudgee-Gulgong mail. He has made many friends on the various routes over which he has travelled." (Death of a Mudgee Whip, 17 Sep 1896, p.2)

1925 See also Whitney, Frank; 1925 Eddie, Nathan; Appendix 1.6

Bissu, C ... 1932 See Lowe, Bill

Blackwell, R. & Blackwell, T ... 1919 See Aisbett, E. J.

Blake, Andy
1941 "Rural Reminiscences ... Crunching of iron-clad wheels over a rocky creek bed; the *Up Paddy—Get along there, Joe!* Of the driver; crack of whips, and welcoming 'hoorays' of a small band of settlers at Journey's End. No better stimulus, in these days of high-powered motor transport, can be obtained for the conjuring up of a mental picture of the pioneer days, when Cobb and Co. flourished, than a talk with Andy Atkins, of Noraville, between Adavale and Windorah. For our mutual friend, now in his 75th hale and hearty year, is the only ex-Cobb and Co. driver in Queensland. With pride he says: *We knew how to handle a horse those days*, and, with a chuckle, he watches the coming generation trying to hold the reins of a single nag properly ... *You've read 'The Cattle King'?* he asked me yesterday. *To me that book reads really like life, because one of the men mentioned in it, Andy Blake, a Cobb and Co. driver, taught me how to drive a four-in-hand.* The light of battle comes back into his eyes... *We had no roads to travel over .... we made our own tracks, lost horses, broke axles, and often finished up with broken harness and traces .... but we always got through all right."* (Rural Reminiscences, 6 Feb 1941, p.4)

1925 See also Snell, Charlie

Blake, Arthur ... 1888 See Swanton/Swanston, James

Bloomfield, Alf
1886 "From Brisbane to Adavale ... about 2 o'clock in the morning, the word 'Dulbydilla' ... About an hour after arrival a cold collation was served up, and as if infected by the gloom that overhung everything, we sat down and silently and solemnly ate the corned and roast beef before us. The coach office is attached to the hotel, and the clerk is a quiet and methodical little man of business. His office was rendered cheerful and comfortable by a fire brightly burning in a little stove, and he kindly invited us in, and presented us with a late number of the Saturday Review, which proved most acceptable. About 4 o'clock, the cheery voice of Alf Bloomfield, the coachman, was heard lustily shouting 'all aboard', and mounting the box seat with a friend we dashed out of Dulbydilla at a fine pace behind six beautiful dapple-grays (Cobb's best) and over two tons weight on the coach.

The air at this time was not very cold, but crisp and delightful and the moon, like a globe of silver hung straight before us, simmering gently on the tree tops, and lighting up the avenues through which we dashed. Wrapped in our overcoats and mufflers, and bound round with rugs, a gentle glow suffused our bodies, and the drive proved most enjoyable. Bloomfield, as a driver, is one not easily surpassed. The manner in which he tooled the six splendid animals round trees and stumps, over logs ruts, and stones, went far to confirm us in the generally expressed opinion that he is one of the best drivers King Cobb has in his employ. On the road we passed numerous teams, some laden with wool, others with produce, and the flames from the camp fires flickered and fell, casting grotesque shadows that danced among the trees weirdly. But the moon soon disappeared, and the ghostly dawn with its grim light came in succession, bringing with it a keen cold that made the flesh on one's face tingle. And when the great golden sun arose a pleasant warmth was quickly diffused among the chattering and shivering travellers, and later on beads of perspiration stood on the foreheads of those on the box." (From Brisbane to Adavale, 8 May 1886, p.733)

1876 See also Murphy, Jeremiah (Jerry)

Blue, Dr ... 1921 See Griffen, Chas.

(Surname unknown), Bob (Little Bob) ... 1917 See McPherson, Jim

Bolton, Bill ... 1917 See Corbett, Sandy

Bourke, Harry ... 1917 See Richardson, W.

Bourne, Henry Arthur (Harry)
1940 "Former horse attendant for Cobb & Co. and later coach driver, funeral director, hotel licensee, and road ganger, Mr. Henry Arthur (Harry) Bourne, is one of Menindee's most colorful personalities ... his first link with the coach business when he joined the services of Cobb and Co. in 1884. He was then engaged in attending to the horses at Forbes. Later he was promoted to coach driver, and had charge of the coaches being driven between Condobolin and Euabalong, Condobolin and Wyalong, Bourke and Wilcannia, and White Cliffs and Wilcannia ... In 1915 Mr. Bourne said he drove the first motor lorry mail between Broken Hill and Tibooburra." (Link With Cobb and Co, 2 Mar 1940, p.3.)

Bowes, Bill ... 1875 See Turner, Bob (Big Bob)

Bowes, Will
1860 "An accident has at length arisen out of the unnecessary display of flash driving, in turning the corner of the Market Square, opposite Messrs Dalgety, Ibbotson, and Co ... it is said that a horse dray was nearer the leaders' head than the whip (Will Bowes) anticipated—and the vehicle got locked, and over it went ... It was also fortunate that the ring bolt sprang out, the horses (which were vigorous and fresh) being thus left free of the capsized vehicle. Off they dashed down Malop street west, and were brought up by a cart, without doing damage to themselves or anything else ... Will Bowes, who is considered one of the safest whips on the line, had mounted the box of another coach ... and was on his way to Ballarat." (Current Topics, 11 Jun 1860, p.2)

Bradley, (Christian name unknown) (Hoppy Brad) ... 1937 See Peck, John Murray

Bradley, Jack (Hell-fire Jack) ... 1929 See Mesbitt, Bill; 1936 Richardson, Bill

(Surname unknown), Bradley (Lame Bradley/Brad)
1875 By Robert P. Whitworth ... republished in 1889 "I remember being amused by the following:—*Well, 'taint much of a story to speak of, but such as it is, you're welcome,* said Hiram Crawford, as we; rattled over the hard Beechworth road at a steady ten-mile-an-hour trot, on the long stretch between Donnybrook and Wallan-Wallan. It was a bright summer's day, not a cloud in the blue vault overhead. The cattle stood dreamily under the fictitious shade of the bare gums, lolling out their tongues, and whisking their tails to keep away the flies ; the cicadas kept up a ceaseless chirruping in the cherry-trees, the jackasses screeched out their discordant laugh, and lazily flew from one limb of a tall iron bark to another as we bowled past. There was a quivering haze in the atmosphere, as if it were simmering in the sunshine, for it was December, and hot, broiling, burning, baking hot. The dust flew up beneath the batter of the horses hoofs, and the white road stretched mile after weary mile before us. But, borne on the wings of the balmy afternoon breeze, came floating over our senses the aroma of new-mown hay, that aroma so softly sweet, so sweetly pungent, that reminds us of green hedgerows, of waving oaks, of shady woods, of lowing kine, of the wild hedge strawberry, of the ferns and burdocks by the brook, in the long-past days of our childhood. Something of this, as the grateful perfume mingled with the also grateful perfume from

the pipes that garnished our lips— for, let me tell you, there is nothing in the world a greater relief on a hot day than what an Irishman would call 'a blasht o' the poipe.'

Taint onlikely, said Hiram, you've heard tell of Lame Bradley; maybe be'n on the box with him ; he was a quare fellow, was old Brad, and there's many a comical yarn told about him. I don't know of one, however, better than that I'm going to tell you. Lame Brad., you see, was one of the old stock, real grit, and no mistake, no funk, no holding off. Rain or shine, drought or flood, bad road or good road, road or no road, 'twas all one to him. He'd got to go, and he went ; and his cattle 'd got to go, and they went. He wa'nt what you call a very particular driver, nor if he was late or in a hurry, and as he was generally in a hurry, why, travelling with him wa'nt altogether like lying in bed reading the newspaper. Oh no, not much. The Ballarat and Geelong road, when he was driving, was pretty bad here and there, stiff pinches, deep ruts, heavy clay, occasional swamps, and now and then a, nice stretch of corduroy, broken, every few yards, and mended, maybe, by throwing in a post or a rail from the next fence. Oh, it was lovely, lovely enough to jar every tooth out of your head.

Well, one miserable, drizzly, cold day, there was a crowd of passengers waiting about the door of the office in Ballarat waiting for Brad. A cold, wet, miserable crew they were, sure, and you may bet your bottom dollar their tempers wer'nt improved by being kept waiting. The horses were hitched up, the mail bags aboard, the luggage strapped under cover on the rack, everything ready for a start, except the driver. There was the coach sure enough, but where was the coachman ? Ah, where ? He wa'nt there, that was clear enough, and without him, you know, there was no go. A quarter of an hour passed—no Brad. The minute-hand crept slowly, oh, so slowly, round to the half hour—no Brad. The swearing round that coach was getting awful, but for all that there wasn't any Brad. There was a row, but that wa'nt Brad. And why wa'nt Brad. there ? Because Brad. was in the hotel playing euchre. Very wrong of Brad., no doubt, but it was so. At last, when they'd given him up, and were going to send somebody else on with the coach, along comes Brad. up the street. Well, he climbed on the box without a word of reply to the complaints of the passengers, but with a wicked twinkle in his eyes that meant mischief.

Three-quarters of an hour late, am I ? he muttered to himself. All right, we'll see. The coach, was full inside, and with a fair sprinkling outside too ; full when he started, but—well, I'll tell you. Brad. got his team of six well in a line, shook up his reins, sent his whip curling round like a snake, and brought it whack across the flanks of his leaders, that sent them off with a jump that threatened to snap the swingle-bars, and away he went at a steady trot down the street. All right, so far : all right, too, until he got well outside the town, and then, muttering Late, eh ; am I ? he began to put the horses to their mettle. Go was the word, and he went—first at a gentle canter, and then as the cattle began to get warm to their work, at a gallop that sent the wet sand and mud flying in all directions. Still, beyond an occasional lurch, there was nothing much to grumble as yet, for the road, except a few ruts, was in fair order all the first stage. Very late this morning, ain't you, Bradley ? said Joe, the ostler, as the coach pulled up for a change of horses at Buninyong. Am I ? replied Brad., surlily. Never you mind ; give me a nobbier of gin, and put a fresh point on that whipthong ; and look sharp, d'ye hear ? Not another word did he vouchsafe, but, as soon as the horses were put to, started off with a plunge and a jerk that sent the insides tumbling into one another's laps, as if they had been in a railway train at the time of a collision. A mile further and the trouble began. The made road came to an end there, and the heavy rain had transformed what there was of the track into a mass of stiff clay, varied with pools of liquid mud. Creaking, straining, tugging, on went the coach faster, now labouring heavily through the tenacious clay, now plunging over the wheel-hubs into deep holes filled with sludge like pea soup. It was holding on by your eyelids then, you bet, for Brad, went at it totally regardless of the black eyes and contused heads of his passengers, who were jolted and pitched about like parched peas on a drumhead, and who yelled at, and objurgated him in vain.

This yer coach has got to be in Geelong at three o'clock, that's what's the matter with me, was all that could be got from him, and another whirl of the whip sent the half-maddened horses on floundering through the flying mud. It was in vain that at the next change the passengers prayed him to moderate his transports and go along a little more gently. Gents, he said, I've got to get in Geelong up to time, and by the living, jumping Jehosaphat, I'm going to get there. The next stage was still worse, for the road before getting to Meredith was terribly cut up, and pretty long streaks of corduroy had been laid down in the worst parts. At them Brad, went, as if he were determined to shiver every plank in the machine. All one to him, whether the logs were sound or broken, he never stopped to look, swaying, toppling nearly over, quivering in every bolt from the jar against some big stone or tree-root, on he went helter skelter. One of the outsides was sent flying through the air in a somersault, and landed neatly in a ditch, while two of the insides, thinking it better to risk their necks by a jump than to be killed cooped up in a narrow coach with a madman (for they thought he had taken clean leave of his senses), opened the door and leapt boldly into the puddle through which they were plunging at so furious a rate. No matter to Brad. He never stopped to pick them up, not he ; never even looked round to see whether they were lamed or not, but kept right on in his wild race against time. This made matters worse for those left in the coach, for while they were packed they were jammed together, and partly prevented one another being knocked about much. But now they were hurled from one side to the other, shot backwards and forwards like shuttlecocks, jolted, battered, banged, now against the roof, then with a flop and a thud against the back, only to be sent bodily forward against the stanchions, or cannoned against a neighbor.

In sad plight they reached Meredith, bleeding, bruised, sore from head to foot. In vain they stormed and raved. Brad, only smiled grimly, and asked for another point to his whip. But flesh and blood could not stand it, and, in a body, they refused to go another yard with him. They would, they said, stay where they were, and make the company pay for it ... He pulled up at the office door just as the clock struck, the hour, threw down the reins to the ostlers, and quietly handed his waybill to the manager. Just saved your time, Brad., old man, said the latter, and the roads must have been mortal heavy ; but—looking over the waybill—'where the -deuce are the passengers ? ... I guess old Brad, got hauled over the coals some, about that affair, but folks wa'nt so particular in those days, and it was looked on as only a good joke after all." (Velvet and Rags, 26 Oct 1889, p.2)

1875 See also Turner, Bob (Big Bob)

Bradley, T ... 1937 See Preston, R.

Brady, Mick
1917 "Two other lines ran in this district also, but for only a short while. One was from the Boonmoo Junction on the Chillagoe line to Mount Garnett, and the other, a branch of the Herberton line, from Mount Albion silver mines to Mungana, via Oakey Creek, in the early days of Chillagoe. Cooktown and the Palmer goldfields: Mick Brady drove this line for 17 years." (Coaching in Australia, 1917, pp.45-47)

1925 See also Eddie, Nathan

Brady, Thomas (Possible Cobb and Co. coach driver)
1874 "Thomas Brady, coach-driver and mail contractor, was charged at the Police-office, to-day, with stealing a horse, the property of Messrs. Cobb and Co. Constable Francis arrested the prisoner, and locked up the horse in a stable at Cannonbar. The staple of the stable door was drawn at night, and the horse taken away. It was found on Friday dead in the creek. The animal had apparently been shot, its throat was cut, and the brands cut out. A mass of evidence was taken to-day, and the prisoner was committed for trial." (Dubbo, 3 Jun 1874, p.2)

Brayshaw, Charlie ... 1951 See Leary, Jack

Breen, James
1917 "DEATH OF OLD ORANGE COACH DRIVER. Following close on the death of the late James Breen, one of Cobb and Co's coach drivers in the early days of western settlement, comes word of the death on Saturday, at Stuart Town, of a contemporary of his in the person of Mr. Thomas Willcock. Born near Molong, nearly 9 years ago, the son of Mr. and Mrs Michael Willcock, he worked in his father's flour mill as a youth, and subsequently carried on a bakery business, and also engaged in mail contracting. He ran the Murrumbidgerie Hotel before Murrumbidgerie changed its name to Wongarbon, and later on took charge of the Commercial Hotel, Wellington, about the time the old flour mill was erected. He prospered, and built the old Carriers' Arms Hotel at the corner of Percy and Maxwell streets. He went back to the road as a driver with Cobb and Co., and was with that firm for 20 years. He ran between Orange and Wellington before the railway to the latter place was completed; then between Wellington and Dubbo. On the 'iron horse' reaching Dubbo he drove from Dubbo to Cobbora, and through to Coonabarabran, and did a little more coaching till the line was constructed to Nyngan and Coban. A spell at carrying followed, and he next landed back at Farnham, where he worked at the Prince Billy mine. In fact he did mining for the rest of the time he was able to work. He was twice married. The children, of the first union were Messrs William Genge, Jack, Harry (Wellington), Thomas (Sydney), and Mrs. J. Sibraa, of the Hawkesbury Experiment Farm. The children of the second marriage are Mr. A. and Miss Willcock. The funeral on Saturday was largely attended." (Death of Old Orange Coach Driver, 5 Sep 1917, p.1)

Breen, Jim (Jimmy)
1929 "I don't think Jimmy was ever held up, but he had a coach that had been driven by Hiram Barnes, which had two bullet holes in the side. Those holes illustrated many a tall yarn he told to new chums, and always they were *fired there on my last trip down*." (Whips of Cobb & Co., 20 Feb 1929, p.5)

1932 "Whips of Cobb and Co. ANY of the skilled drivers of the great coaching firm of Cobb and Co. were famous in their day—especially the days of the bushrangers and gold rushes, when the roads of adventure threw them so much into public notice. No name was better known in Australia than that of George Adams, long of Tattersall's Hotel, Sydney, and well known by his other activities. He was one of the whips of Cobb and Co. in the adventurous days when names were made on the roads. He was a pupil of Bill Hampson, one of the best of the old time drivers, and the most respected by the outlaws that sometimes infested the tracks on account of his skill as a revolver and rifle shot. George advanced from driver to road manager, but later on he left the coaches to work the mid-eastern rivers as a commercial traveller.

BILL HAMPSON was tutored by Silent Bob Bates, a very careful driver, who seldom said anything but 'Gid up.' As a rule the coach-driver was a genial sort, and dispensed a lot of information about the country, interspersed with tall yarns about the local inhabitants. He entertained the box-seat passenger, who in return was expected to open the gates.

NICHED among the immortals is Jack Fagan, the most exciting of whose many thrilling experiences was the hold-up at Eugowra Creek. The coach, under escort, was carrying a big 'swag' of gold, and at Eugowra Rocks encountered a volley of shots, fired from the bush. In the sudden excitement the horses bolted and capsized the coach. Fagan escaped with a bullet hole in his hat and another in his coat. On another occasion he was driving down a steep hill with a load of passengers when the brake dropped off. He kept the horses at a gallop, whizzing round bends and roaring down the slope—to keep the coach from running over the horses, he explained to the terrified passengers when the thriller was over.

Other old-timers of the same district were Dan Mayne, afterwards proprietor of the 'Bathurst Sentinel,' Peter Torbury, who had the reins when Frank Gardiner stuck the coach up on the road to Lambing Flat; and Ned Nathan, a little chap of nine stone, but strong and full of fire, who advanced to a managership, and later became Mayor of Orange. Three notable whips were Jimmy Breen, Hiram Barnes, and Jim Conroy. The first-named was a skilful handler of young horses, and revelled in rough and twisty roads with newchum passengers on board. Jimmy Breen was a great admirer and caustic critic of his boss, Jim Rutherford, who founded Cobb and Co. and was manager till about 1905. When Jimmy's hands had lost their deftness he was given a pension and a well-stocked farm by Rutherford, but died out west.

Hiram Barnes, after driving on Victorian and New South Wales roads, pioneered many of the Queensland routes. He was not sorry to go north, for on the Orange-Forbes line, where he was best known, he was a special mark for the Hall and Gilbert gang, whom he had several times outwitted, and who had several times fired at him. Jim Conroy, who passed out in 1906, and who was twice stuck-up by bushrangers, missed 'big things' more than once. For a while Jim's driving activities centred about Goulburn, and he told that often on dark nights he had a [First Nation's person] walking in front with firesticks. On one occasion, while Jim was driving through Bargo Brush, a long way from everywhere, the coach was crippled by the bursting of one of the rear tyres. Lashing a pole across the coach behind the box-seat, he fastened another along the side so that it rested on the projecting end of the cross-pole, and passed under the hind axle and trailed some yards back on the ground. In that way it did duty for the crippled wheel, but the prop had to be renewed three times before the journey ended.

OF the hundreds of Cobb and Co.'s drivers, none caught the popular fancy or stamped himself on the tracks of time like Cabbage-tree Ned. As a whip he was famous in the boom days of Ballarat, and to the end of the coaching days his star remained undimmed by any driver on any road. Yet Ned never did anything very wonderful that scores of others did not do, except that he drove a huge coach that carried 70 passengers, besides mails, luggage, and parcels. But Cabbage-tree Ned (officially Edward Devine) was a picturesque figure, who got his classic title from the fact that he always wore a good Australian cabbage-tree hat. Ned was a Tasmanian, a dare-devil with the reins, who rattled down hills and swung round bends at a pace that made nervous passengers grip their seats and hold their breaths. It was said that when he was in a hurry, or had to make up time, some of the passengers shut their eyes in panicky anticipation of the crash of doom. E. S. .Sorenson." (Whips of Cobb and Co., 24 Feb 1932, p.15)

1923 See also Robinson, James (Robbie); 1925 Eddie, Nathan

Brenyer, Donald ... 1951 See Leary, Jack

Bristow/Bristowe, George
1873 "FATAL COACH ACCIDENT ON THE WESTERN ROAD (From the Bathurst Times, June 11.) An accident of a very terrible nature, by which one man lost his life and three other persons were severely injured, occurred on the Sofala

road, within a mile or so of the village of Peel, late on Monday afternoon last. It appears that the mail coach on that day left Sofala, at the usual time, driven by a man named George Bristowe, and when the deplorable affair happened there were in the vehicle three passengers—namely, a man named George Du Crano (a Frenchman) and two women named respectively Mrs. Baker and Mrs. Dickson. The road was in an exceedingly boggy state, but all went on well until a hill had been reached leading down to a place known as Folley's Gully—a locality, which appears, is dangerous to travel in any weather, especially so after rain—and upon arriving here the horses set off at a gallop, the driver apparently losing all command over them ... the horses descended the incline at a furious pace, and all of a sudden the coach, which had been swaying fearfully from side to side, capsized. Bristowe was pitched on to the road, and killed almost instantaneously, his neck being broken ... Du Crano ... He then left the spot, and by dint of great perseverance, for he had to rest on the road more than once, he reached a farmer's house, and there communicated intelligence of the disaster. The owner of the farm (Mr. Betts) at once proceeded to the scene of the catastrophe, and upon assistance being procured the dead body of Bristowe was conveyed to Peel, and the two women were also attended to. It was then found that the fore part of the coach had been carried away by the horses, which were found in a scrub close at hand, and that the vehicle had separated the front, by the king bolt being twisted out of it place." (Fatal Coach Accident On The Western Road, 14 Jun 1873, p.2)

1908 See also Byrne, F. A.; 1917 Ward, Joe

Britten, Thomas
1954 "OBITUARY. MRS. M. E. BLANCH. Mrs. Mabel Evelyn Blanch who died at her home in Phillip Street, Gloucester, last Thursday was a member of one of the oldest families in the town. She was a daughter, of the late Mr. and Mrs. Thomas Britten and was born at Gloucester 69 years ago. Her father was one of the earliest Cobb and Co coach drivers in this district, driving the mails from Raymond Terrace and also to the Copeland goldfields and over the new road to Taree. He was one of the first residents to settle in the new township of Gloucester, when it consisted of only a hotel, a store and a few houses, and was one of the most colourful personalities of the coaching days. Mrs. Blanch's mother; who died in Gloucester not so many years ago in her nineties, was known as Granny Britten, and was a great source of information on the early days. She claimed to have known the famous bushranger, Thunderbolt, when he operated in this district.

Mrs. Blanch spent all her life in the Gloucester district. After her marriage to Mr. Charles Blanch at Dungog, the family lived in Gloucester and shortly after Mr. Blanch returned from the first world war they moved to the Buckett's Road where they engaged in dairy farming for nearly 20 years. Mrs. Blanch was predeceased by her husband in 1942. After his death she continued to live in Gloucester, having resided at Phillip Street ever since ... Mrs. Blanch is survived by a family of 10 children: Mrs. Murray (Florence), New Lambton, George Charles, Gloucester, Claude, Wallsend, Mrs. Gillfillan (Doris), Taree, Leslie, Mograni, Cecil, Mt. George, Mrs. Newton (Joyce), Gloucester, Mrs. Foster (Beryl), Gunnedah, Dudley, Gloucester and Robert, Taree. She is also survived by seven sisters: Mesdames R. Oldfield senior, W. Morris and L. Britten, Gloucester, Creagh, Bowman, F. Smith and Gorton, Taree, and Mrs. Wratten, Quirindi. The funeral took place at Gloucester on Friday, leaving for the Church of England section of the Gloucester cemetery after a service in St. Paul's Church of England. In the absence of the Rector, Rev. D. R. May. the services were conducted by the Rector of Stroud, Rev. S. C. Blakemore." (Obituary, 21 Sep 1954, p.2)

Britton, W. & Bromley, Geo ... 1919 See Aisbett, E. J.

Browden, Abraham (Possible Cobb and Co. coach driver)
1904 "Thunderbolt ... On four different occasions he stopped and robbed the Warialda mail ... In February, 1867, the mail was being driven to Tamworth by Abraham Bowden, who had with him a passenger named Derrington. They had just passed Manilla when the command to 'bail up' was heard, and having obeyed the mandate the two men were ordered to pass into the bush ... Here Bowden was commanded to hand out the mailbags and take up his position with Derrington about thirty yards distant while the bushranger rifled the bags, taking from the letters all the notes, cheques and orders which they contained ... Having resumed his journey towards Tamworth he met Constables Norris, Shaw, and Doherty ... To these he told his story, and then pushed on to Tamworth to acquaint the police there ... Shortly after this 'Thunderbolt' made his appearance on the road with a boy as his robber companion, and the queerly-assorted pair committed many depredations on the road, her Majesty's mails still forming the chief attraction. The boy's name was Mason, and it was not long before he established a reputation for reckless daring equal to that of his chief. In many instance they abstained from robbing the passengers or the driver, and contented themselves with rifling the bags and 'sorting' the letters." (Thunderbolt [Fred Ward], 27 Aug 1904, p.8)

Brown, Jesse ... 1953 See Rutherford, James (Jas./Jimmy)

Brown, Jim ... 1917 See Wright, Bob

Brown, W.
1873 "Mr. W. Brown was recently presented by several gentlemen at Glen Innes with a purse of something like twenty sovereigns, in recognition of his services as mail coach driver, while in the employ of Mr. W. W. Frazer, and Cobb and Co., and for his kindness and attention to passengers, and his proficiency as a 'whip'." (Country News from Country Papers, 13 Dec 1873, p.765)

Bruce, Harry
1917 "Among the drivers on the Western run were Jack Hill, Charley Wild, Bill Reade, and Harry Bruce, and their return passengers often included a police escort for some poor looney shepherd, whose mind the loneliness of the bush had deranged." (Coaching in Australia, 1917, p.37)

1938 "ON THE TRACK ... OLD WHIPS OF COBB AND CO ... Watching Jehu with the ribbons ... *So my mind goes harking backwards back to days of long ago, back to old familiar faces, in the ranks of Cobb and Co ... Harry Bruce and big Jack Warner—both were demons in the dark, They could drive their bloomin' 'carriage' where a dingo couldn't bark ... And they'd break her into gullies like a hearse that bore the dead*" (On the Track, 31 Aug 1938, p.11)

1917 See also Richardson, W.

Brumfield, A.
1885 "A first-class driver this, as good a man as I would wish to sit beside on a box-seat, but he cannot make this early fasting ride agreeable ... The rain begins to fall, quietly, slowly, and assiduously, and before I know it I am wet through ; Mark Tapley might have enjoyed this, but I do not. The soil here is

of a quality that soon makes and clogs the coach wheels after a little rain. Now driver Brumfield has a hard task and shows his mettle and what he can do with the whip and ribbons, and by his voice in encouraging his horses. On through the scrub, past dead cattle and prowling dingoes, we stop at Mr. M'Kenzie's station to deliver some letters. This is a poineer homestead, slab with bark roof; its owner works hard and deserves success. The rain continues, there is a vague chance that the coach may stick up, and we shall have to walk into Charleville." (A Winter Tour in Queensland, 15 Aug 1885, p.4)

1917 See also Corbett, Sandy

Brummy, Jimmy ... 1925 See Paine, William

Buchanan, Johnny
1874 "Johnny Buchanan, one of Cobb and Co.'s drivers, was fined £5 at Yea this week for carrying more than the authorised number of passengers. We do not approve of over-crowding passenger coaches, but at the same time we have much sympathy with those who come to a coach-office specially to get a passage, and no matter how important their journey, they must wait for twenty-four hour. We think that much consideration should be made for the good nature of the driver, who has no pecuniary gain by the number of passengers, yet runs the risk of losing his situation by accommodating an occasional passenger. The fine of £5, which the driver has to pay out of his own pocket, is too severe, and considering it was Christmas time, some allowance might have been made." (Alexandra Times, 17 Jan 1874, p.2)

Buckland, James (Jim/Jimmy)
1934 "A PIONEER COACH DRIVER ... brings to mind the memory of one of the old-time residents of Kilmore in the person of the late Mr James Buckland, who resided in Sutherland street. Mr Buckland was one of the old-time coach drivers for Cobb & Co. about fifty years ago, he being on the Kilmore Heathcote route. The terminus at this end was Kelly's hotel, long since demolished. The hotel, which contained 50 rooms, occupied the corner of Sydney and Foote streets, where the soldiers' monument now stands. The coach stables then were the bluestone buildings, now owned by Mr C. Dillon, at the rear of the post-office. Mr Buckland, who was familiarly and favorably known to public and passengers as Jimmy Buckland, held the complete confidence of travellers during the long term of about 30 years he occupied the box seat of the coach." (A Pioneer Coach Drover, 13 Sep 1934, p.2)

1939 "Back beyond Jack McDougall's period of service, a Cobb and Co. coach, driven by Jim Buckland, supplied the necessary means of transport and delivery. One would need to engage in some tiresome research work before publishing definite particulars concerning that far gone period. This much however, we do know, Jim Buckland was driving a coach for Robertson, Wagner and Co. (Cobb and Co.) along that track in the late sixties of the past century." (Reminiscences, 2 Mar 1939, p.1)

Buller, Jimmy
1939 "The Old Time Bush Patrol. TALES OF A LONELY LIFE. By Garth Owen. A TRIP WITH COBB & CO. From time to time I have mentioned the regular coach, which came from Wilcannia twice a week, on the way to Mount Browne, and, of course, made the return trip just as regularly. It was rather astonishing that in those days of poor roads and frequent inconveniences, that the timetable should be so closely adhered to. The coach was seldom more than a quarter-hour late, and the drivers lost little time in picking up and delivering of mails. Of course, there were times when floods or bush fires upset the schedule, but these were rare incidents, and were looked upon as 'acts of God.'

The down coach to Wilcannia usually arrived fairly late in the afternoon, and on one occasion I can remember, it was running very late, and we had all gone to bed, when we heard the rattling vehicle lumber up. Ned and I slipped across the verandah and heard the driver explaining that a tyre had come off about five miles from Cobham, and that it was about eight hours before the station blacksmith had been able to fix things up. *It might have been a lot worse*, said Jimmy Buller, the driver, *but, as it happened, I only have a couple of passengers, and they know how to look after themselves*. There are many minor accidents to vehicles, which are easily overcome, if there is a coil of fencing wire near at hand. Wire and greenhide and a copper rivet or two will just about overcome any trouble when coupled with the resourcefulness and initiative of the average bushman. But runaway tyres are another proposition, and on this occasion the wheel had to be taken to the blacksmith, and had to have the tyre cut and shut, a rather slow job at any time. When the boss explained the reason for the coach's delay at the breakfast table next morning he chuckled and said it brought to his mind an incident in which he was personally concerned, about 25 years earlier.

Aunt Fanny at once scented a story, and, though the boss demurred at first, he finally promised to try and remember the circumstances of what he admitted was a rather remarkable experience. *I hope you won't be disappointed*, said the boss ... *I'll do my best, though, goodness knows, I'm not much of a hand at spinning yarns*. You can bet we were all there when the storytelling began. *First of all*, said the boss, *it is necessary to keep in mind that road conditions were vastly different 25 years ago, from what they are today ... settlements were pretty far apart. In these times you are seldom more than 20 or 30 miles from help if anything goes wrong, but, except for the mail changes, which were much farther apart than they are to day, there was mighty little to break the tedium of a long journey. On the occasion of the trip, which forms the basis of this yarn, I was travelling from down near Sydney to a station beyond the mountain country ... I picked up Cobb and Co., at a railway terminus about 20 miles out. There were only two other passengers from the same town, but we picked up others as we went along. There had been a gold find a couple of hundred miles out and the coach went through the main diggers' settlement. Most of the time we were at some sort of a town at night, until we passed the goldfields, when we used to stop for a few hours at a convenient mail change. I was the only through passenger and was privileged on that account to the box seat next the driver. His name was Con Sawyer, an Irishman who had come to Australia as a youth and had gone straight into the bush, where his aptitude for horse management, soon attracted attention, and he was one of Cobb & Co.'s most trusted drivers. He was a burly sort of chap and never went out of his way to avoid a quarrel. He was credited with being handy with his fists, and this reputation helped to maintain peace between Con and his associates. Con's left hand fascinated me. There was no middle joint in his thumb. His first finger had been chopped off about midway between, the first and second knuckles, and the stump without a nail was the same length as his smooth, jointless thumb. I learnt later that the top of the finger had been chopped off by Con himself when he had been bitten by a snake. To add to the queer appearance of the hand, the little finger had been broken at some time and had not been reset properly, so that it was a permanent hook. Despite these disabilities, Con handled the ribbons of his four in-hand team like a magician. By the slightest turn of the wrist he could control a prancing team and was never flurried or upset, even though the leaders backed out of their traces and turned to have a look at him. He didn't talk much as a rule, but when the fancy seized him, or a drop of potent liquor loosened his tongue, he had many interesting tales to tell ... At every stop Con went round the old bus, tapping the wheels and inspecting bolts and bearings. There was a powerful foot brake, the leverage of which was surely remarkable, for the hind wheels would often skid, when Con put his weight on. The brake blocks were reinforced with a pair of discarded bushman's boots, thick in sole and studded with hobnails. Looking at one of these boots one day, while we were waiting at a mail change, I could not help wondering what history might lie behind it."* (The Old Time Bush Patrol Tales of a Lonely Life, 20 Jul 1939, p.62)

Bullock, S ... 1891 See Miller, George Trenchard

Burgess, (Christian name unknown)
1896 "St. George. February 22. Cobb and Co.'s Mungindi coach met with an accident yesterday, when near Nindy Gully Hotel, the horses bolted, and the driver, Burgess, was thrown out and had his skull fractured. A son of Mr. M'Mahon, a publican here, was also thrown out, but he was not hurt. M'Mahon ran back to Nindy Gully and informed Mr. Noud, who immediately proceeded to the scene of the accident, and brought Burgess into the hospital, where he now lies in a critical state." (St. George, 25 Feb 1896, p.2)

Burgess, Jack ... 1947 See Richards, J. Frederick (Fred)

Burgess, John Edward
1937 "Mr. John Edward Burgess, aged 84 years, died at his home at Humevale, near Whittlesea, last week. Mr. Burgess was the oldest member of the A.I.F. having joined up with the 1st Remount Unit as a corporal in October, 1915. He was then aged 62 years. His service was of 883 days, 767 of which were served abroad. Mr. Burgess in the early days was employed as a driver on Cobb and Co's coaches in the Broken Hill district." (Obituary, 14 Sep 1937, p.2)

Burke, John Conway
1943 "Those old-timers drove through frost and cold, over unmade roads, and swam their horses over creeks. Taxi drivers of to-day may find these details of interest: their daily mileage averaged 60; their weekly pay was 15/-, and their keep ... Conway Burke was the first man to take the mail from Melbourne to Sydney, and his memory (with that of other Cobb pioneers) is kept green by the Cobb & Co. Old Coach Drivers' Association ... This year, on May 2, a pilgrimage is planned to the graves of John Conway Burke and Hugh Mitchell at the Melbourne General Cemetery" (Memories and Musings, 29 Apr 1943, p.10)

Burke, Tom ... 1917 See Manning, Ned

Burnside, Mrs ... 1930-1940s See Allan, (Christian name unknown)

Burrowes, H.
1909 "Serious Coach Accident. Cobb and Co's. coach leaving Lawlers on Wednesday morning for the train terminus met with an unfortunate occurrence ... As soon as the leaders moved, the driver, Mr. H. Burrowes, found that he had no command over them owing to the rein of the near side leader becoming in some way caught in the harness ... the coach collided with the Road Board lamp and capsized over the kerbing ... the driver escaped unhurt ... The public lamp which had only recently been erected, was literally torn to pieces, and portions of the lamp proper were separated, while the pillar itself was twisted and practically ripped open, besides being uprooted. The unfortunate occurrence very much affected the driver, Mr. Burrowes, one of the best known whips in the firm's employ—a sober, careful, and reliable servant, and one who is held in high esteem by all classes of the travelling public." (Serious Coach Accident, 30 Jul 1909, p.2)

Burrows, Henry William (Harry)
1953 "COBB AND CO. DRIVER DIES. LEONORA, Sat: One of the last Of the old Cobb and Co. coach drivers has died here ... Henry William Burrows (75) ... Mr. Burrows used to recall that while driving for Cobb and Co. one year, Wiluna had 28in. of rain. Its mean annual rainfall is eight inches. One of his biggest droving jobs was in 1913 when he took with another drover 1000 cattle from the Kimberleys to Wangawal Station, 120 miles north-west of Wiluna." (Cobb and Co. Driver Dies, 2 May 1953, p.2)

Burrows, John
1903 "The sad news reached Malcolm yesterday of the death of Mr. John Burrows, who was seriously injured in the coach accident which occurred between Doyle's Well and Lawlers on the 8th inst. Deceased had been at Poison Creek Hotel since the accident, and was being attended by a trained nurse and Dr Myles, of Lawlers. He had been making such satisfactory progress that it was expected that he would soon be well enough to be brought down to his home at Malcolm. Consequently the news of his death come as a great shook to his many friends in this district. On Tuesday he took a turn for the worse, hemmorahage of the injured lung having set in. Mrs Burrows was sent for but deceased only lasted till 3 p.m. on Wednesday. Deceased leaves a wife and three children, the youngest of whom is only eighteen months of age. Heartfelt sympathy is expressed throughout the district for the widow and children in their bereavement. Deceased was a native of New South Wales, and has been for a number of years with Messrs Cobb and Co. He was well known on all the coaching tracks on the fields, and highly respected by all with whom he had come in contact." (Obituary, 27 Nov 1903, p.2)

Burstall, Jim ... 1917 See Corbett, Sandy

Butler, (Christian name unknown) ... 1912 See Miller, Ted

Byrne/Byrnes, E. A.
1917 "It is stated in Mr. E. A. Byrne's memos (he was an old Cobb and Co.'s driver) that the partners of the original firm of Cobb and Co ... Cobb, Peck, Swanson and Blake sold out to a Melbourne man named Thomas Davies, who was obliged to dispose of it very soon after, and the business fell into the hands of a company comprised chiefly of coach agents, drivers, etc. calling themselves *The Victorian Stage Company*." (Coaching in Australia, 1917, p.15)

1935 See also Conroy, James (Jim)

Byrne, F. A.
1908 "THE CONTRIBUTOR. A GREAT COACHING FIRM. THE RISE AND DECLINE OF COBB AND CO. BY F. A. BYRNE, ex M.L.A. To the present generation of Australians the name of Cobb and Co is only a memory. They have heard, of Cobb's being connected with the early back country passenger traffic before the advent of railways, and have no idea of the important part this great and enterprising firm took as pioneers in developing the Australian continent. When gold was discovered in Victoria, in 1851, and up to the middle of 1853, the only means of conveyance to the then existing gold fields, Mount Alexander, Bendigo, and Ballarat, was by paying a carrier so much for head for the carrying of the passengers' swags and tools, the men walking, and, of course, camping out at night ... About the middle of 1853 a change came over this mode of transit. In that year four Americans, Freeman Cobb, John Peck, James Swanson, and Anthony Blake, went into partnership as coach proprietors, and imported from Abbott Downing and Company, Connecticut, several coaches, suspended on leather springs (or thorough braces) adapted to bush and rough roads ... to and from Melbourne and Liardet's Beach, now Port Melbourne, or Sandridge ... to Forest Creek and Bendigo ...

The mail ... a contract for their conveyance was now entered into between the Government and Cobb and Co., with a very large subsidy. The firm rapidly extended their operations ...The drivers at this time were all Americans ... Those drivers were young, strong men, to whom the handling of large teams of six and seven horses was a science new at that time in Australia ... The firm extended their business in every direction, quickly sweeping aside the opposition which every now and again appeared ... whole western division fell to the invincible Cobb and Co. Very soon they attacked the northern road from Singleton to Tenterfield ... In connection with the coaching business, the firm established five coach-building factories—at Goulburn, Bathurst, Castlemaine, Hay, Bourke, and Charleville ... It can truthfully be said, too, that never had a firm a more capable, loyal, and faithful body of servants. Several of them filled important positions in the public life of the Australian States; amongst whom may be mentioned Mr. John Taverner, the present Agent-General for Victoria in London, who was a stage coach driver on the Bendigo to Swan Hill Road in Victoria. Mr. A. R. Outtrim, the present M.L.A. for Maryborough, and ex-Minister for Mines in that State, and F. A. Byrne, driver, agent, and manager, and ex-M.L.A. for Hay, in New South Wales. In this connection it may be mentioned that the father of Mr. Alfred Deakin, an old coaching man, and member of the old-time firm of Bill and Deakin, was accountant to Robertson, Wagner, and Co. for several years.

A remarkable fact in connection with that great business was the wonderful immunity from fatal and serious accidents which it enjoyed, notwithstanding the dreadful bush roads which had to be negotiated by day and night in the early days ... After a service of 35 years with Cobb and Co. in Victoria and New South Wales the writer can only recall four fatal accidents to drivers. These were:—Hal Hamilton, killed at Frying Pan Hill, on the Bathurst road (I think in 1866), through the failure of the brake; George Bristow, killed coming down Mount Victoria, brought about by a bridle coming off one of the horses, causing the bolting of the team and capsize of the coach; Tommy Hoyle, killed at Badaginnie on the Beechworth-road, caused by the team shying and capsizing the coach over a pile of broken road metal; and Joe Ward, killed on Pyke's Hill between Melbourne and Ballarat through the failure of the brake in 1872. And whilst the roads at that time were infested by gangs of Bushrangers, and coaches were frequently bailed up and robbed, there were no fatalities among the drivers from that cause." (The Contributor, 25 Nov 1908, p.1405)

Byrne, Patrick Joseph
1930 "MR. P. J. BYRNE ... death occurred in the Moree District Hospital early on Thursday afternoon of Mr. Patrick Joseph Byrne, aged 69 years. The deceased, who followed the occupation of a carrier, was one of the most familiar figures in the North-West. Born at Winniford Swamp, near Maitland, in 1861, his death probably removes the last connecting link with the old coaching days. Shortly after his arrival here in 1883 he took up driving the coach for Messrs. Cobb and Co ... working at different periods on the whole line from Maitland to Mungindi, but principally between Moree and Narrabri. When the railway was opened to Moree in 1893 he entered into a contract to convey the mails from the railway station to the post office, and still held that contract at the time of his death. Besides a wife, one son and four daughters survive him, the former being Mr. W. Byrne (Moree), and the latter Mrs. J. Melville (Gunnedah), Mrs. L. Brown (Sydney), Mrs. J. Valentine (Sydney), and Mrs. E. Hulbert (Perth). He is also survived by three brothers and three sisters, the brothers being Mr. Thomas Byrne (Moree), Mr. John Byrne (Sydney), and Mr. Keiran Byrne (Inspector of Police, Orange), and the sisters Mrs. Dunn (Sydney), Mrs. Ryan (Moore Creek, Manilla), and Mrs. Smith (Tamworth)." (Mr. P. J. Byrne, 4 Aug 1930, p.3)

1921 Bainbulla Mail Change as it was in the time of the Cobb and Co. Coaches, standing is my dad holding my brother Bob, my mother and Abraham Horrobin sitting. The two children are myself & brother Alice—Courtesy State Library of Queensland

Byrnes, David
1951 "Mr. David Byrnes who died at the South Coast District Hospital, was born at Currency Creek 85 years ago. In his young days he drove coaches in the North for Cobb & Co., and on returning South in 1905 he married Miss Nell Johnston, of Goolwa, a daughter of the late Capt. Johnson, well-known river skipper who piloted the 'Queen of the South' through the Murray Mouth, with only one minor mishap, perhaps more than any other boat. The late Mr. Byrnes is survived by one son, Max, of Goolwa." (Obituary, 10 Aug 1951, p.3)

Byrnes, Patrick (Paddy)
1912 "MR PATRICK BYRNES. The death of the familiarly known 'Paddy,' Byrnes, under sad circumstances, brought a thrill of sorrow to his many friends and relatives. Last Wednesday whilst drafting some stock at Booberoi station, where he was employed, his horse fell over a beast, coming down heavily upon the rider, breaking his leg and, causing internal injuries. He was brought at once to Condobolin Hospital, where notwithstanding the best attention and treatment and the medical skill of Drs. Kearney and Boazman (who held a consultation) he succumbed on Saturday afternoon. He was buried next day in the Catholic portion of the local cemetery, the Rev. Father Howard officiating, and there was a large gathering of people to pay their last tribute of respect. Deceased, who was close on 60 years of age, was born at Brotherony and grew to fine proportions, stalwart and fearless in character, which led to his being renowned in feats of horsemanship. In the old days of Cobb and Co, for whom he used to drive a mail coach from Forbes to Condobolin and other parts, and subsequently his own coaches, he was one of the best known whips of the west, and the older commercial travellers to this day will reel off some of their daring trips, through floods and other obstacles, under the strong hands and care of 'Paddy' Byrnes, who never failed to land them safely. He fairly revelled in the handling of young and refractory horses and it adds but a touch of keener pathos that his ending should have been brought about so simply when in his sturdier days he had successfully braved so many hazardous feets of horsemanship. He leaves a widow and family of 5, all grown up, to whom we offer our sincere sympathy." (Mr. Patrick Byrnes, 31 Jan 1912, p.5)

Hotel Loafers.
"There was usually, a chap, hanging about a pub who as a coach drew-up would offer, to tie up your bootlace, or perform some small service that he considered would entitle him to a tip or drink on the cheap. Jack. He was a man of a good county family but, alas, he was a remittance man, and became much of a loafer. One day, in company with a man likewise minded, he was sitting in the bar of the Finniss Vale Hotel. One of them had just made 'a rise.' They were celebrating the event with a feed of bread and cheese, and beer ... One day, after holding a horse for quite a spell, the rider came out and rode off without bestowing the usual tip. Jack let him get about 100 yards away, then hailed him. The rider came back. *What's the matter ? If any one axes me what may be the colour of your money, what am I to tell,'em ?* An extra tip was forthcoming. Jack could quote scripture freely and correctly when he was 'three, sheets in the wind' ..."
(Memories of Myponga, 2 Nov 1927, p.2)

Charleville Post Office—Courtesy Ray Green, Bathurst

Chapter Two

Drivers

C

Here's a song of Cobb and Co.

Here's a song of Cobb and Co.,

And coaches 'rhythmic rattle.

Crack o' whip and lusty voice,

On the uphill battle.

Distant views and rounding turns—

Ever still ascending—

Lilt of birds and hillside streams.

With men's singing blended.

Marion Miller Knowles, 6 June 1942
(Annual report / Cobb & Co.'s Old Coach Drivers' Association, 1919, pp.6&7)

1910 Coach leaving Surat, driver may be Jack Mathieson—Courtesy Queensland Museum Collection

Supporting evidence:

Cairns, (Christian name unknown)
1899 "Coach Accident. An accident occurred to the mail coach which runs from Tenterfield to Casino via Drake on the 10th inst., about 19 miles from Tenterfield in going down a place called 'the black pinch.' The brake gave way and the driver, Cairns, exercised great care, but near the bottom of the incline the wheels collapsed and the passengers were thrown out, the coach being entirely smashed. Cairns was cut and bruised." (Coach Accident, 19 Aug 1899, p.10)

Cameron, W. & Cann, H ... 1919 See Aisbett, E. J.

Cann, Harry
1949 "Those were the days of the last bushrangers, who raided gold escorts and coaches on the roads from Blackwood and Bendigo to Melbourne. Mr Cann was born in Blackwood's oldest hotel, which, at that time, was Cobb and Co.'s coach office. His elder brother Harry, now 80, was a coach driver." (Found his Happiness in Hills, 8 Nov 1949, p.7)

Cann, James
1951 "OBITUARY ... Another of the few remaining Cobb and Co. coach drivers passed away in the Townsville Hospital on Tuesday afternoon in the person of Mr. James Cann. Deceased, who was 83 years of age, drove the coaches for many years on the Muttaburra—Tangorin—Hughenden run and later came to Kuridala, where he was engaged in a carrying business for several years before joining the railway department as a fettler. The Cann family moved to Cloncurry about 17 years ago and took up residence in the town. The late James Cann was a man whose pleasant disposition and charitable nature had earned for him many friends, and although small in statue, he had always been a hard worker, which he always said, contributed much to his long livety. The evening of his life was spent in retirement and he lived in Townsville with his daughter, Mrs. H. Walduck and in Toowoomba district with his son Jim since leaving here with his sick wife some three years ago. His wife predeceased him six months ago and he leaves 4 sons and 6 daughters." (Obituary, 19 Oct 1951, p.1)

Carbis, J ... 1871 See Hall, S.

Carbis, Jack ... 1921 See Griffen, Chas.

Carlisle, D ... 1919 See Aisbett, E. J.

Carlisle, Dave ... 1930 See Alder, Amos

Carr, James Michael
1955 "The late Mr. Carr was born and educated at St. George, and as a very young man was employed by Cobb & Co. as a driver in the St. George area. Later he was transferred to Richmond, where for many years he drove a Cobb & Co. coach between that town and Cloncurry. After this period of service he was transferred once more, and this time to North Queensland, where he operated a coach from Alma Den to Georgetown, and later from Georgetown to Croydon." (Obituary, 10 Nov 1955, p.2)

Carr, Jim
1938 "Watching Jehu with the ribbons ... *The Andersens and Davey Teys and Jim and Mick Carr, could steer a team through forest box or stunted Coolabah*" (On the Track, 31 Aug 1938, p.11)

Carr, Mick ... 1938 See Carr, Jim

Carr, Terence ... 1917 See Richardson, Alf

Carter, (Christian name unknown) (Long) ... 1937 See Peck, John Murray

Carter, Dick ... 1921 See Griffen, Chas.

Carter, George ... 1935 See Conroy, James (Jim)

Carter, John (Jack)
1934 "Mr. John Carter—who drove Cobb and Co. coaches in the early days ... in his reminiscences, Mr. Carter says ... *Cobb and Co. had the mail Binalong to Boorowa, Marengo and Young. My mate, James Toy, had driven from Binalong one morning, and I came through from Young the same day, and then had to go on to Binalong. Before I started, Toy informed me that a gentlemen came with him to Boorowa, and intended to start a newspaper there ... Toy told me to be very careful what I said to him*" (The Days of Cobb & Co., 19 Oct 1934, p.14)

1935 See also Conroy, James (Jim)

Carter, R.
1897 "In another column is published a list of subscriptions in aid of Mrs R. Carter and family. Mr Carter was formerly well-known in Ballan as a driver of Cobb and Co's. coaches. He recently met with an accident that resulted in a very badly broken leg, necessitating his removal to the Melbourne Hospital. As he had been out of work for some time the timely help rendered to his family by Ballan friends will prove very acceptable." (Local and General News, 30 Sep 1897, p.2)

Carter, Robert
1889 "COUNTRY NEWS ... Robert Carter, the driver of Cobb and Co's coach between Ballan and Bacchus Marsh, met with a severe accident this afternoon. He was proceeding to his own house with an express wagon belonging to Mr. Gusser, cordial manufacturer, when he was unfortunately jerked off on to the street. He received a number of severe injuries." (Country News, 25 May 1889, p.11)

Carter, Thomas William (Thos)
1940 "LITHGOW PIONEER ... former Cobb & Co. driver Mr. Thomas William Carter ... He was a driver of a Cobb and Co. coach running between Mudgee and Sydney ... born in Lithgow, and, living here all his life, saw the town grow to its present proportions. As a miner, he worked in the old Vale of Clwydd and Hermitage pits. When coaches were the fashion, Mr. Carter was a coachman for the late Andrew Brown, of Cooerwull, who erected the CooerWull Academy and donated it to St. Andrew's Presbyterian Church.

BUSHRANGING DAYS The possessor of a jovial disposition, Mr. Carter told a host of interesting stories concerning his experiences during the days of bushrangers. He was a good citizen, and a hard working man in all his activities. His wife predeceased him nine years ago ... Sympathy will be extended to his four daughters, Mrs. E. Bennett (Hurstville), Mrs. W. Smith (Workmen's Club, Lithgow), Mrs. J. Price (Gordon), Mrs. W. Kirkland (Pottery Enclosure), his son, Mr. L. Carter (Mort's Estate), four brothers, Messrs. Alfred, (Lithgow), John (Sutherland), James (Penrith) and a sister, Mrs. Stanford (Leichardt)." (Lithgow Pioneer, 26 Apr 1940, p.2)

1940 "EX-COBB AND CO. DRIVER DIES ... A former Cobb and Co. driver between Mudgee and Sydney died in Lithgow Hospital today ... He often related thrilling stories of the bushranging days." (Ex-Cobb And Co. Driver Dies, 27 Apr 1940, p.5)

Cartrini, Jack
1899 "ACCIDENT TO COBB'S COACH. An accident, which fortunately was not serious, happened to Cobb's coach seven

miles from Mt Malcolm, on the Mt Margaret track, last evening. The driver, Jack Cartrini, was taking a pull on the horses, when the reins broke, causing the horses to bolt, and throwing him out, a wheel passing over his ankle. Mrs Robertson, a lady passenger, jumped off behind and received a severe shock. The horses travelled on for two miles with seven passengers and then collided with a stump, which brought them to a standstill." (Accident to Cobb's Coach, 15 Mar 1899, p.5)

Cawker, Tom (Tommy)
1918 "Tom Cawker was driving the mail in 1852 and '53, when I was going to school. Many a time I jumped on the rack of his coach and had a ride when I lived at Russell's Creek. Some years after he gave up mail driving and went into the livery stable business in Portland. Jack O'Brien and Jack Kemp were the next drivers, and they drove a few years. O'Brien took an hotel at Panmure and then in Warrnambool, and Kemp went into one in Port Fairy. Then the next drivers were Jack Lovett and Jim Bambrick, Frank Smiley and Scott, and they stuck to it until the railway opened. I have given you the names of all the drivers from the first mail coach to the opening of the railway." (The Early Days of Warrnambool, 5 Aug 1918, p.4)

1926 "PASSING OF THE COACH ... Yesterday (June 30) saw the passing of the old-time coach route between Mount Gambier and Casterton (Vic.). Mr. T. Cawker, of Casterton, who drove the first coach (and with it the mail) some 56 years or more ago, finished as a last farewell, by driving an old Cobb & Co. coach with a four-in hand into this town. He said that he had driven the first and driven the last. The motor car service started to-day (July 1). The veteran whip, in his eighty-eighth year, looked impressive with his long white flowing beard. ... Old Tom is known throughout the length and breadth of Victoria and the south-east. He is one of the few Cobb & Co. old-time drivers left.

He drove His Majesty the King from Penola to Casterton when His Majesty overlanded from Adelaide as a youth, with the Duke of Clarence, to Melbourne. When King George was out here as the Duke of York he had Tom called, and renewed acquaintanceship with him. Also when the present Prince of Wales was in Melbourne he had old Tom called up, and had a long yarn with him about the old coaching days and the driving of his father, and presented Tom with a souvenir gift to mark the event. Mr. Cawker is a remarkably cheery old chap, and nothing delights him more than to yarn and spin tales of the old days. He says that his good health is the result of an abstemious dieting and having been 'on the water wagon' for the last 50 years. He used to come over the 47 miles drive sometimes without having had breakfast. He says that so much as he loves a good horse, and the joy of holding the ribbons behind the prancing steed, he has to realize that the horse must pass for jobs like this, and the motor comes into its own. He never misses a Grand National meeting at Flemington, and has owned many a good jumper himself. He lives in Casterton." (Passing of the Coach, 10 Jul 1926, p.60)

1941 "Extracts taken from his book, *Pioneering Days of Western Victoria*, published in 1923, by James L. Hamilton, who took a trip during the late 'fifties to Tasmania ... I found a small express wagon, which carried the mails to Hamilton ... The driver was the well known and capable Jehu, named Tom Cawker ... It was pitch dark, and no bridge, with the river running pretty fast, but Cawker sent his team straight at it, and got through to the other side. Here, though, there was a slippery bank, and the horses wouldn't tackle it, so I jumped into the water and, taking the leaders by the head, steadied them while they scrambled up the bank. I did not much relish that plunge ... but a blazing fire and a good supper made us soon forget our troubles." (Annual report and balance sheet / Cobb & Co.'s Old Coach Drivers' Association, 1941, p.10)

1923 See also Lyall, Jimmy

Chamberlain, (Christian name unknown)
1917 "Chamberlain was another old Cobb's driver on this Northern track. He came from the Central district. Special horses and harness were kept for crossing the steep Newcastle range. Once the horses bolted down the range and the coach hitting a granite boulder was smashed to matchwood, and the leaders killed. The driver came off without very serious injury." (Coaching in Australia, 1917, p.48)

Chamberlain, George
1876 "A Big Snake.—This morning ; Mr. George Chamberlain, the driver of one of Cobb's Gympie coaches, brought us for inspection ... a dropsical bottle of vast dimensions, which just furnished coiling accommodation for a huge black snake—as evil a looking beast as one would wish to see ... six feet long ... Chamberlain saw him in the road this side of the Caboolture, and, jumping off the coach, 'nobbled' him, and consigned him to one of the coach lamps." (Adelaide, 22 Apr 1876, p.2)

1878 "A few local residents gladly availed themselves of an invitation from Mr. Barnes, the representative of Cobb & Co., to go as far as Newsa on the occasion of the first trip via the new route ... Barnes, Ike, and Chamberlain worked like Trojans, and it struck me that they were quite prepared to do the driving, grooming or anything else to make the trip a success ... Little time was lost in changing horses, and Chamberlain was entrusted with the coach, Barnes taking George's place on horseback." (To Newsa by Cobb & Co's Coach, 12 Jan 1878, p.3)

Chatfield, Harry
1939 "Mr. Harry Chatfield passed away after a long illness at his home in Herberton on Saturday last, January 7, at the age of 82 years ... At the age of 16 years he was driving for Cobb and Co. in the Riverina" (Obituary, 14 Jan 1939, p.14)

1941 "The Day Before Yesterday ... DEAR 'John,—Cobb and Co. and what memories the name revives! Memories of the old travel methods after the passing of the bullock dray and pack and saddle horse. As one who practically all my life has been interested in transport, I have taken a keen interest in modes of transport in this and other parts of the world, but I do think the coaching days in Australia were thrills and pleasure combined. In the Eastern States where Cobb and Co. originated (the firm established itself in this State when the gold rush started) coach travelling was the favourite and only method of reaching the interior. On every road the familiar old coach was met; its prancing horses and skilful drivers were a lasting sight to residents of the Australian bush. Of the old drivers, skilled knights of the ribbons and whip, many are now over the last trail; probably very few remain to recount their varied experiences in times of drought, flood and bush fires. In North Queensland coaching days were rough and of those old drivers probably there are some readers who remember and probably travelled under the guidance of Tom and Ned Gallagher, Joe Hertzberg, Martin Warnemindi, Joe Mosch, Harry Chatfield, Rod Macrae, Jack Warner and others who for many years piloted the coaches over mountains and rivers. Their only slogan was 'Get there,' and they always got there, no matter what obstacle came in their way. With as many as eight powerful horses in the team, and a riding light attached to a standard on top of the coach, side lights on each side of the body of the vehicle, they travelled from sunrise and in many instances to midnight, as stages had to be made.

CHANGE HORSES. At frequent intervals were the stage horses or changing stables. Here a groom in charge was always in readiness to yoke up a fresh team, in many cases partly-broken in horses, and away to the next change. Many were the tales, humorous and tragic, recounted of these old stage horses and their keepers. Most of the old stories were true, others, due to the imagination of the old jovial drivers, intent on keeping his passengers amused, were doubtful. Of these latter, the gem of the road from Hughenden to Cloncurry was that of the courteous stage keeper, renowned for his gallant treatment of the fair sex. On one of the day stages where night accommodation was not provided, he never failed to respond to strange requests. In the case referred to a woman passenger demanded a bath, an unknown luxury at that particular time of the year. There certainly did exist, an old bag-enclosed space with a pull rope shower (out of order). To this the woman was escorted. Previously the gallant had filled a bucket with water, and standing on a box, waited until the lady pulled the rope, then he decanted the contents of the bucket over her fair form. Unfortunately she had retreated to a corner, and the water did not reach her. She was startled by a voice overhead, *Say, miss, stand in the middle, I'm blowed if I can reach you over there.* The woman collapsed, as also did the gallant water dispenser. After persuading the lady to resume, he conducted operations with his eyes closed, with the remark, *We will still continue to make your stay very comfortable.* So when she was about to retire she was handed a couple of squares of calico, dubbed sheets, but which were the only tablecloths in the establishment. As morning dawned the woman was disturbed from a peaceful slumber with the request: *Say, miss, please hand out the sheets, as I want to lay the table for breakfast.* On another stage the story was told of the bloke and the pickles. He was a young commercial traveller, not yet used to bush tucker. When his portion of goat was handed to him, he asked the waitress for pickles. The fair damsel walked to the kitchen door and in a loud voice passed on the request as follows: *Missus, there's a bloke in here must think it's Christmas; he wants PICKLES ...*

The ranges had to be crossed time after time and the 'Blackguard Pinch' was the most dangerous. To ascend double horse power was required, and passengers walked; to descend trees were felled, and attached to the back of the coach to act as a drag ... Thousands of fire-flies flitted to and fro ... Carpet snakes also abound in this particular district and at times became mixed up with the horses, providing much excitement to passengers, more so when they were picked up on the wheels and eventually deposited on the box seat ... But these old knights of the road always 'Got there' day or night. Then in the dry season, especially on the western runs, they had the 'wiily willy' or rotary dust storm to contend with, which would sweep across the downs in full blast. These caused not only discomfort to passengers and horses, but held up the journey many hours. Then when the rains came the whole country would be turned into a quagmire, wheels being rammed with black mud till they looked like balloon motor tyres." (The Day Before Yesterday, 18 Dec 1841, p.41)

While written in the same paper Fighting Disease *Wars are only stepping stones in the path of medical and surgical research*, the doctor said. *We doctors are always at war, but our fight is against disease. It is a fight that will never end. But from the mud and horror and bloodshed and death of every war we are able to pluck a few more scraps of knowledge that will help all humanity ...* In the middle of the dense tropical scrub of Northern Australia a convalescent depot has been established. It is a lonely station of incessant dust storms. An invitation out to dinner is as rare and as welcome as a first prize in Tatt's. One of the doctors had received such an invitation. He was excitedly making preparations when he was told that an urgent case was waiting outside. A young digger was standing by the tent with a neat hole in his lower lip. *What the devil has happened?* asked the M.O. *You know my pet frilled lizard, doc? Well, I had 'im in me hand. Just in fun, you know, I bent my head down to give him the raspberry. The lizard got in first !* The man was patched up. The doctor hastily continued his preparations for dining out. Just as he was ready to leave an excited and almost incoherent orderly raced into the tent, vaguely gasping that someone had been bitten by a snake. The doctor followed him, pounding through the dust to the tent lines. Very much the worse for drink, a husky soldier was lying down beside a dead snake ... Anxiously the M.O. examined him. There was no sign of the deadly little punctures that would indicate snakebite. Desperately the M.O. asked questions, searched for a clue. Another soldier walked up to the tent. *You don't want to. worry about him, doc,* he advised. *He's drunk ! I know he's drunk,* angrily snapped the doctor, whose dinner invitation had by now vanished like a pleasant dream. *But he's been bitten by this snake. No, he ain't,* was the casual reply. *That snake was killed yesterday. And if anybody's been bitten it's the snake. Last time I saw Bill he was staggering back to his tent. He saw that snake on the ground and decided to try out the new set of false teeth the dentist had made him this morning. When I left him he was lying on the ground with his new teeth sunk into the snake, worrying it like a kitten. You needn't waste your time on him, doc. Why not have a look at the snake?"* (Australia, 18 Dec 1941, p.71)

1939 See also Patterson, Jim

Chick, Charley (Charlie)
1898 "Forty Years Ago December 19, 1898—An accident to Cobb and Co.'s five horse coach, plying from Menzies to Malcolm, was reported in the 'Kalgoorlie Miner' 40 years ago today. The coach left Menzies at 6 a.m. and was due at Malcolm at 8 p.m. At Tampa, 19 miles from Malcolm, a change of horses was made. Only 200 yards from Tampa the team shied and ran the coach into a stump, upsetting it and throwing out two men seated on the driver's seat and three women in the back seat. The horses bolted and the driver, Charley Chick, was dragged some 300 yards, with his hands tangled in the ribbons. A cyclist had to ride to Niagara to get medical assistance for Chick, who was in a precarious condition." (Forty Years Ago, 19 Dec 1898, p.4)

1912 See also Miller, Ted

Chisholm, Geo ... 1919 See Aisbett, E. J.

Clapp, F. B ... 1929 See Mesbitt, Bill

Clapp, (Christian name unknown) ... 1875 See Turner, Bob (Big Bob)

Clark, Billy
1932 "AUSTRALIANITIES. No. 178. COBS & CO. DRIVERS. By Will Carter, Hurstville. Roll up, you old Cobb and Co. drivers or should I say, rattle up ... Looking back over the years as an outsider ... They were no ordinary types the men of Cobb and Co., not mere steerers of horses, but highly interesting fellows, who, from long and intimate observation along their stages through ear as well as eye in daily contact with all sorts and conditions of men and women, could entertain their passengers right through their journeys. What tales they could tell of the old days when life was vastly more exciting than it is today, the digging days. the bushranging days, the rough-and-ready days, the days of lively romance ...

SOME OLD DRIVERS. My memory carries me back to two drivers along the Great Southern Road ... My father then kept the 'Coach and Horses Hotel' at the Adelong Crossing, now Tumblong. He had a store adjoining, and was also the postmaster. The mails arrived from Gundagai, 8 miles distant, and after sorting, the fine of Cobb and Co.'s thoroughbrace coaches sped on their way. One was driven by Billy Yabsley, and the other by Joe Pittman. One of them kept straight on along, the Great Southern Road to Tarcutta and the other went to Adelong, then a lively goldfield. One morning Joe Pittman was sitting at his meal—I forget whether it was breakfast, lunch or tea—and seeing me loafing around, he handed me a teacup and mildly requested me to shy it at a large rugged mass of blue granite outside the door. That was a time when green juvenility respected the judgment of age; it was a time when the commands of seniority met with prompt obedience at the hands of youth. Theirs not to reason why, theirs but to do and—take the consequences. I took the nice, clean, shiny cup which was of the old leaden-white hue and not too superb in quality ; I took the cup joyfully and shot it with precision, smashing it to bits. Joe Pittman was guping a slug of sausage at the time the crash came, and the old sinner started to splutter and hiccough and laugh and half-choke in his delight. In came my mother, who presided at an immediate inquiry, and, but for the intervention of Jo, I fear me I should have suffered a severe reverse. I never forgot Joe Pittman, who must have gone off the earthly roads long years ago.

A TRIP TO CALCUTTA. One lovely bright sunny day my father mounted the box seat with Billy Yabsley—I shall be mortified to learn that he was Jimmy Yabsley... —and presently I was handed up and deposited in my father's lap. Away went the jolly old bays and browns down that long level white strip of road and round the sharp elbow-turn to the left and on past Billy Manns' smithy arid wheelwright shop. Down we clattered till we reached Mundarlo. and finally came to our destination, Tarcutta. I cannot say whether we returned that night or next day, but I got it firmly fixed in my mind that I had been to Calcutta instead of Tarcutta, and it was not till I had aged sufficiently to tackle "jography" that I discovered my error. Just 40 years later I met a kinsman of Yabsley at Moss Vale.

FREEMAN COBB. Freeman Cobb, the founder of the old coaching firm, came over from the United States with a view to engaging in carrying goods to the interior. Good money awaited such an enterprise then, as the goldfields were all aglow with gold-fever. Population had rushed into unthinkable excess, resulting in food shortage. Scores of teamsters were on the road with their slow dawdling bullock drays, but their load capacity was light and their despatch incapable of meeting the demand. Cobb was going to hop in and win a fortune. For some reason or other, doubtless a practical one, he decided upon establishing a line of coaches to carry passengers and limited merchandise. How it flourished is history ... I wonder why he dropped the reins just as he had got the wheels of enterprise well greased.

FAMILIAR NAMES. Take any old country town you like. Poke along down the main street and drop in at the local hairdresser's, and, while the artist of the clippers is at work, start a yarn going like this : 'I remember arriving at this town of your about thirty years ago on one beastly wet night on Cobb and Co.'s coach.' You won't get much further than that. The barber will, in all probability, stop clipping, switch back in thought for a space of six and a half seconds, and then remark: 'Thirty years ago, thirty years ago, that would be Johnnie Jones you were with? Johnnie would be driving then. I didn't know him, but I've heard the dad tell many a yarn about him. Left-handed with the whip, wasn't he?' He would then run off the names of about half a dozen other drivers of the line with many associated incidents. For my own part I can remember certain names, such as Billy Clark, Dick Corbett, George Fox, and so on, men who drove in my own district. Now, what an array of them could be found in each State if a systematic search were made. Only recently Dick Palmer died at Cronulla at the age of 94. The majority are gone over the border, alas, but there are many veterans using the knife and fork still and what a fine thing it would be to bring them all together for an annual corroboree." (Australianites— Cobb and Co. Drivers, 6 May 1932, p.9)

Clark, Joe
1917 "COBB AND CO.'S COACH TRIP FROM SELWYN TO BOULIA. From Selwyn it is 123 miles to Boulia. Leaving Selwyn at 5 a.m. with Driver Joe Clarke, one of the best with the ribbons and universally popular, the first mail change is Mistake Creek, 18 miles ... The Western country towns acknowledge the great debt of gratitude they are under to Cobb and Co. for their efficient coach services. The writer recalls the time during the 1901 drought when Cobb and Co, carried per parcel post practically all the supplies for Boulia and district, and many other Western towns have to thank Cobb and Co. for their food supplies during the same drought." (Coaching in Australia, 1917, p.100)

1949 "FATAL ACCIDENT. Whilst mustering cattle on Coolullah Station on Wednesday last, Mr. Joe Clark, a stockman employed on the station, was killed when his horse stumbled, fell and rolled on him. Before going to Coolullah, Mr. Clark was an employee of the Cloncurry Shire Council, working at both Mount Isa and Cloncurry. For many years he was a Cobb and Co. Coach driver, and drove the mail coach on the Selwyn—Boulia, and McKinlay—Winton routes. The deceased's capabilities as a stockman were well known throughout the North West, where he had been employed on various stations. His ready wit and cheery personality won for him a wide circle of friends." (Fatal Accident, 22 Jul 1949, p.6)

1917 See also Wright, Bob

Clifford, J. (Possible Cobb and Co. driver)
1887 "Yesterday morning the team of football players from Adelaide with a number of their friends who accompanied them from South Australia, were taken for a tour of inspection of the town and suburbs ... started from the Victoria Hotel in three large conveyances supplied by Cobb and Co., of Malop-street ... coach drawn by four horses, under the control of Mr J. Clifford, formerly a mail-coach driver in South Australia; and a dray drawn by three horses, the whip being taken by Mr T. Moss" (The Adelaide Football Players And Visitors, 9 Jun 1887, p.3)

Clint, J. (Possible Cobb and Co. driver)
1928 "Back-to-Orange Celebrations. Wonderful Historic Procession. Also basking under the sunshine of the protection of this noble coterie was Cobb and Co's coach, lent by Mr. O'Neil and driven by Mr. J. Clint. Stores to the diggings, just as in those days long gone, came the heavy waggon drawn by a team of horses, the next exhibit lumbered into sight, on its mission from the old firm of Wright, Heaton and Co. it was followed, however, by a scene of the present day, a number of racing riders mounted on Superb cycles, while in their rear came an ancient high wheeled bicycle lent by Mr. J. Hamilton." (A Triumph in Organisation, 28 Dec 1928, p.6)

Clowry, Frank
1882 "Coach Accident. As the outgoing Sydney mail was leaving Cooma for Goulburn on Monday night, it met with a serious mishap that was happily unaccompanied with loss of life. After crossing Cooma Creek, the coach reached within a short distance of Alderman Harris's residence, when the hind wheel of the near side of the coach came off, the vehicle tilting on one side. Intently, the driver turned the horses round, and in another moment he was thrown heavily to the ground. Mr. John Reedy was an inside passenger, booked to Micalago. He looked out, and saw the driver (Mr. Frank Clowry) lying on the ground. The driver told Mr. Reedy to jump out, which he did, landing on some timber, and cutting his hand. This was no sooner done than the horses galloped furiously over Cooma Creek ... At the corner, the coach was stopped by a post, the horses dashing into the verandah of Mr. Fisher's store. The lamps of the coach were

smashed, and the vehicle almost wrecked … the mails were transferred and a new coach sent on with but little delay." (Coach Accident, 8 Nov 1882, p.3)

Cobb, (Christian name unknown)
1855 "FRIGHTFUL ACCIDENT.—One of the most alarming accidents we have heard of in the history of coaching, and one that but for the skill and prudence of the driver might have terminated fatally, occurred on Friday last, near Keilor. Most of our readers know the tortuous way in which the new road runs round the large hill over the Deep Creek, having on one side the high embankment from which the road is cut and on the left a frightful precipice … As one of the daily line of coaches to Bendigo was … descending the hill … the head-stall of the off-wheeler gave way, and in an instant the team became unmanageable … Fortunately, Mr Cobb (a most accomplished whip) was himself driving … with the utmost presence of mind coolly approached the yawning precipice, at the same time taxing every nerve to keep his horses towards the embankment on the right. On the second turn of the road it appeared utterly hopeless that the coach, containing sixteen passengers, could be saved, when luckily a loaded dray, proceeding the same way as the coach, intervened between it and the abyss … Wonderful to say, neither the horse under the dray nor his driver were in the least injured by their perilous descent. After a short delay the conveyance proceeded safely to its destination—Mr Cobb having been entertained handsomely by the passengers in acknowledgment of his presence of mind.—Courier of the Mines. (Beechworth, 22 Dec 1855, p.6)

1856 "Night travelling on the Bendigo Road … it would be extremely unfair in us not to do justice to the eminent skill and courage of the drivers of both lines of coaches who traverse this dangerous route by night. Nothing less than thorough knowledge of the road, combined with skilful handling of their horses, could avert some serious accident from the numerous stumps and ruts which abound on it. The slightest negligence, or indulgence in liquor on their part would almost certainly be attended with some serious if not fatal accident, and it is in the highest degree creditable to them that this has not been the case … drivers courageous and skilful" (Night-Travelling On The Bendigo Road, 30 May 1856, p.2)

Cobb, Hiram … 1953 See Rutherford, James (Jas./Jimmy)

Cole, (Christian name unknown)
1856 "Accident.—We regret to state that Mr. Swanton, manager of Cobb's line of coaches, met with a severe accident on Friday last. While standing in the yard at the Taradale Hotel, one of the coach horses struck out and kicked him on the lower jaw which it fractured. Mr. Swanton is at present lying at the Castlemaine Hotel, recovering rapidly …

Coach Accident.—News reached Ballarat on Thursday morning that the Melbourne coach had broken down, but that all the passengers had escaped uninjured, with the exception of the driver whose shoulder had been dislocated. Subsequently rumour had magnified the damage to four men killed and nine seriously wounded. The afternoon coach from Melbourne arrived about seven in the evening, and confirmed the first version of the story, which had grown from transmission like the three black crows. We subjoin the following letter from Dr. Crane relative to this accident :—*Coach accident at Bacchus Marsh.—On reaching Bacchus Marsh the particulars of the accident were soon gathered. It appears that the passengers had taken their seats at the station for Melbourne, during the time the leaders were left unguarded, and*

1897 A Cobb and Co. coach on the road to Bulong (Mrs. F. L. Watkins, 6 Hope Road, Applecross)
—Courtesy State Library of Western Australia

when about to start, and before the driver had taken his seat, they became frightened. Mr. Cole, the driver, made an effort to secure the leaders, but failing to reach them, he caught the wheel horses, and was carried a distance of twenty yards or more, in letting go he was hurled against a log, causing dislocation of the shoulder. On his being disengaged, they rushed on for a distance of one hundred yards or more, when they came in contact with a tree, which separated the horses from the coach, without much damage to the coach or the slightest injury to the passengers. Mr. Cole is doing well. S. E. Crane, M.D.— Ballarat Times." (Castlemaine Town Council, 12 Nov 1856, p.3)

Coleman, Sydney (Sid)
1947 "Cobb Coach-Driver to Commercial Pilot. ROMANTIC CAREER OF NEW SUPERINTENDENT OF FAR WEST CHILDREN'S HEALTH SCHEME. To most of us, the famous Cobb and Company coaches seem to belong to another century—to early Australian history, and the days of the gold-rushes and bushrangers. An announcement that a man who was once a Cobb's coachdriver has just been appointed superintendent of the Far West Children's Health Scheme is likely, therefore, to cause raised eyebrows and the doubting comment, *Surely something wrong there somewhere?* Certainly, it is almost a century since the grand ; old coaches came into being … their services were famous not only for their, regularity and speed but also for the skill and popularity of their drivers. As new railways were gradually built through the Eastern States, the coach services were rushed out to serve the back-blocks …

But these sturdy old coaches were still running over red Australian roads when Sir Charles Kingsford Smith, then just plain 'Smithy,' was beginning to soar above them, starting a new transport era. Thus it was possible for … Mr. Sidney Coleman, for many years mayor of Bourke and for 16 years on its municipal council, to begin life as a Cobb's coach-driver but graduate to flying through the clouds over his old coaching routes. And, in that fascinating period of transition from old to new, Sid Coleman not only learned to fly but gained his commercial pilot's certificate and eventually flew his own plane and passengers over his old coaching trails. *The Cobb and Co. coaches certainly seem to link me with early Australian history*, he says, with a laugh, *but I would like to point out that as late as the twenties these coaches were still running between Thallon and St. George, up Mungindi way … I began the coach-driving, on the route between Winton and Boulia ; and I think those were, the happiest years of my life."* (Cobb Coach-Driver to Commercial Pilot, 16 May 1947, p.4)

1948 "Mr Sid Coleman, revisited for the first time in 27 years the place where he drove Cobb and Co. coaches as a lad up Mungindi way. He was a senior driver for Cobb and Co. on the Thallon to St. George route" (Drove Over His Old Cobb and Co. Coach Route, 26 Jul 1948, p.4)

1953 "The death occurred in Sydney on December 28th, of Mr. Sidney Charles Coleman, a well-known personality of the West, at the age of 53 years … deceased leaves a family of three children : Myrtle, Cecil and Bonnie. Myrtle is married (her name now being Mrs. W. Bailey-Pikes and she has two children, a boy and a girl, the only grand-children. Bonnie's married name is Mrs. David Warburton … story of his life … born 1st March 1899 at Winton, Queensland … *At the age of 12 I began work with Cobb & co. as a groom at Dunbar mail change. My job was to care for the coach horses, have them groomed and ready in the yard when the coach arrived and to change them with those in the coach. My wages were £5/10/0 per month and I had to find my own keep. I remained at this job for 6 months.*

1925 Cobb & Co. coach from Yuleba to Surat at Beranga Station, driver Fred Thomson (Alice Coleman [nee Wilson] photographer)—Courtesy Queensland Museum Collection

This 6 months was the loneliest period of my life. I was alone at the 'change', living in a tent, and at night I could hear the howling of the dingos and curlews. After leaving this job I tried my hand at droving ... working on sheep and cattle stations ... well boring ... horsebreaking ... tank sinking ... I then rejoined Cobb & Co. as a driver on the Winton-Boulia run, a distance of 240 miles. This was in the year 1913 and I was 14 years of age. The two coaches on this road ran once every week, passing each other at Maskunda. The trip took 3 days.

In 1915 I became leading driver in charge of all lines running out of Winton and in 1916 I became overseer in the Winton and Longreach districts. During this period I had many, happy times and many exciting (but some not so happy) experiences. My path was often blocked by fierce bushfires and I sometimes came face to face with their tragic consequences. I remember clearly one occasion when being completely encircled by fire. I decided to drive my coach into the Hamilton River. I let my horses go and walked two miles to the Hamilton Hotel with my three passengers. When the fires died down a little I returned to the coach and took it to Hamilton. The next morning it was impossible to go on, so we decided to ride out and see how 4 men, who we knew were fighting a fire some 10 miles from the hotel, were faring. The sight that met my eyes turned my stomach. Lying side by side, with their hands covering their faces were the charred remains of three of the party ... Australia, being the land of contrast that it is, gave me also my share of its floods. There were many rivers on the run, the largest of which was the Diamantina which we crossed 52 miles from Winton ... when in full flood is 3 ½ miles wide. It was during one such flood that I had my marathon swim ... On this particular ocassion the river was at its peak and the boat was on the other side. There was no way of communication with Elderslie—telephone and wireless were unknown in that region. On reaching the river I saw the impossibility of crossing and settled down to wait—living for the first week on food supplied by boundary riders ...

At the end of three weeks 40 people were gathered by that wide expanse of water. Food was short. Our diet consisted of mutton (without salt) and tea. Smokers had to satisfy themselves with a mixture of tea and gum leaves. The situation became serious and something had to be done. I volunteered to swim the river. I knew the country well, I knew the position or the channels and I knew where the shallow water would be. At six in the morning I stripped off my clothes and waded into the river. I made for what I thought to be shallow clay pans but to my exasperation found that they had been moved and that the constant attempts to find the bottom was taking too much out of me. I decided to swim from tree to tree, but found that the snakes had beaten me to most of these sanctuaries. All day I swam then night came upon us. Dusk made my surrounding eerie and unnatural, and I was struck by the fear that I might lose my way. Then I spotted the evening star in the east and guided by it finally reached the other side at 9 p.m.—exhausted, my face raw from sand fly bite but with a great feeling of relief that I had succeeded in my arduous task and defeated the elements. I staggered eleven miles to Elderslie where I arrived at 3 a.m. I was given hot coffee and put to bed, where I remained for three days. The next morning provisions were ferried over to those on the other side ...

At the end of 1919 the old Cobb & Co. 'folded up' in North Queensland, but I believe that they were still running until 1922 in the South West of that State. In 1921 I was married in Townsville. My wife and I drove overland to Sydney in a Buick ... first became interested in the Far West Children's Health Scheme ... In 1930 I got the urge to fly. I came down to Sydney and joined the Royal Aero Club ... I used the plane commercially and for pleasure and carried out many 'mercy' flights such as transporting doctors for urgent operations, bringing patients from out-of-the-way places to hospitals and the far." (Death of Mr. S.C. Coleman, 16 Jan 1953, p.6)

Colke, J. C ... 1919 See Aisbett, E. J.

Colman, Charlie & Colman, William ... 1921 See Griffen, Chas.

Comerford, R ... 1919 See Aisbett, E. J.

Conroy, James (Jim)
1917 "Jim Conroy, who died in June, 1906, aged 82, was another old driver. Born in Manchester, he came with his parents to Melbourne in 1842. His father erected a humpy on a block of land (where Buckley and Nunn's premises are now) but, attracted to Sydney, he sold the paddock for £12 ... *Coach driving wasn't all beer and skittles in those days ... have often had (First Nations Peoples) with fire sticks in front of me on dark nights. Bushrangers? Well I was stuck up twice ... the only time I ever travelled on the road without a match ... one of the lamps inside the coach he laid it flat down instead of standing it up. The result was, of course, that it went out, and after the bushrangers had gone, we were compelled to continue the journey in the dark."* (Coaching in Australia, 1917, p.26)

1935 "FIFTEEN years ago last March, after sixty-eight years of continent-wide activities, the great old firm of Cobb and Co. passed-in its final cheque, and entered into the mists of our memories, taking along with it many pleasant recollections of its coaches, their equipment, and their drivers ... COBB AND CO. were on the road in an amazingly short time, and became popular from the jump. The firm very soon erected their own coach-construction and repair shops, and in these they built additional coaches on the Abbott design, but of various transport capacities to suit the varying conditions of the roads radiating to the several diggings. From the first, and throughout the firm's subsequent existence, a uniform colour scheme for the coaches was adhered to. The superstructure was a deep rich coach-red, with the whole of the undercarriage and wheels a striking variety of stone tints, varying from a rich chrome-yellow, down to a light stone, and most of these were picked out with black lining, giving the vehicles a very striking and attractive appearance that is now historic. At odd places around about Australia there still remain decaying specimens of these coaches, wherein the standard Cobb and Co. painting, stout canvas blinds, and heavy-weight brown leather cushions are identifiable ... Cobb and his partners, soon secured the mail contracts, with large subsidies, and they added very prominently, in rich yellow paint, the letters V. R. on a side panel under the driving seat of each vehicle, as a public intimation that the coach carried Her Majesty's postal matter and was entitled to certain free-way passage on the road. The profits of the company swelled and swelled ...

Cobb's next expansion was in 1862, when they exploited the coaching lines of New South Wales. It was a memorable event in coaching history when, as travelling manager, H. Barnes, one of Rutherford's experienced Victorian drivers, set out from Bendigo for this colony, after the uncorking of considerable champagne, having in his care 10 coaches and two feed-waggons, and some 103 horses, of which about 80 were in use on a stage ... in quite a few years, there sprang up a new set of drivers more suited to the back-country conditions of Australia. Without detracting in any way from the capabilities of those Yankee coachmen, who taught us much that was new and left their mark on many of the driving methods of to-day, one cannot but applaud the great initiative, adaptability, and resourcefulness of the young Australian who so promptly picked up the ribbons when the Yank let them drop.

The doyen of this new school of Australian drivers was Edward Devine—or Cabbage-Tree Ned, as he was affectionately termed, though I never learned why. Ned was Tasmanian-born, and he was the very first to adopt the methods of the American driver, and excel him. During the middle fifties, and early sixties, while Cobb & Co.'s other drivers were drawing the extraordinary wage of £10, £12, and £14 a week, with all meals free on the journey and free lodgings at night ... At the time Devine was driving eight and twelve greys in his 'Leviathan,' the firm of Cobb & Co. was running, on its various lines, teams matched in color, including six matched blacks driven by the Yankee, Emanuel

Levi, six greys driven by W. P. Jackson, six roans by Harry Netterfield, and six bays by George Carter ... Coach driving in the [18]fifties and sixties was a princely occupation, with a corresponding princely pay, and, as a consequence, it attracted a class of intelligent and well-educated men, to whom the love of adventure, the love of a horse, and the love of a constantly varying body of travelling companions appealed, as a call to the fascinations of handling the ribbons and whip from the throne of a box seat. In due course many of these men succeeded to important positions with the firm as inspectors, road managers, and agents; but by reason of advancing years, and a natural desire to settle in one place, many finally entered upon a variety of other pursuits. Some turned to grazing and farming, some to running smaller mail-contract lines, purchased from the big firm, quite a number took to butchering and stock dealing, while no small number entered upon the lucrative business of hotel-keeping.

THERE are many traditional, and differently related, tales of these old coach-drivers, some of which are more or less fabulous. Mostly, however, these tales arose from actual happenings, and these, in the fading mists of our memory, appear gilded with romance, and loom pleasantly through the softening haze of time, as we resurrect them after so many years. Drivers possessed a variety of qualities. Some were loquacious, some were reticent and spoke but little, some were recognised leg pullers, when they had box-seat travellers from the city, but it is reasonably fair to say that all were entertaining, and excellent company, helping materially to while away many an otherwise weary hour of a long journey. IN the following biographical sketches a few only of the Jehus of the past are dealt with, and these are listed somewhat alphabetically, irrespective of any order of precedence or the years in which they were in evidence. GEORGE ADAMS.—Learnt the art with Cobb and Co., and rapidly became famous on their North Coast mail lines. It was said of him by W. H. Hampson, an excellent Cobb driver himself, that Adams had no peer in the art. George later succeeded to the position of a road manager for the firm, then became a commercial traveller and finally settled down in Tattersall's Hotel in Sydney, where he inaugurated the racing sweeps still bearing his name, and accumulated considerable funds. FRED AVERY—Drove for Cobb, and for G. Nowland, in the late eighties between Dubbo and Coonamble. Fred was a prince of drivers, under many difficult situations, and it was a treat to sit beside him at night and note the cleverness with which he would negotiate a strip of gilgai country over blacksoil, cutting out curves and figures of eights on the hard pans between the pools where a foot or two off the crust meant a bogged wheel, his leaders having often to be manoeuvred on a left curve, while the wheelers and coach were completing a right-hand one. H. BARNES.—One of Freeman Cobb's original drivers in Victoria. He remained in the service of Cobb & Co. when Jim Rutherford came into the picture, and was placed in charge of the notable cavalcade of plant brought from Victoria in 1862 to open a Cobb service on the N.S.W. roads. For some years he was the most popular driver between Orange and Forbes, on which road he hit up against Gardner's satellites on several occasions. In 1866 he went to Queensland, and drove on the Brisbane-Gympie road, and then became roads manager for the firm. W. H. Barnes, M.L.A., of Queensland, was a son. JACK BARRY.—A Cobb driver, operating chiefly in the Mudgee and adjoining districts. He was a noted joker and leg-puller, and renowned as one of the best of drivers. E. A. BYRNES.—One of Freeman Cobb's drivers in Victoria, and an excellent whip. BOB BATES.—'Silent Bob.' Said nothing when he had nothing to say. A fine cheery old soul, when you understood him well and talked little. He was an excellent driver, employed on Cobb lines in the northern parts of New South Wales, and was a contemporary of George Adams and H. W. Hampson there. GEORGE CARTER.—a Cobb driver in Victoria, later settling in Albury, and running a bus service from that town to the Victorian railway terminus at Wodonga. JACK CARTER.—A live-wire Cobb driver on coach lines from Binalong to Burrowa and Young. A great whip, and full of interesting tales of the road. EDWIN J. COOMBES—A Cobb driver on various roads diverging from Orange. Later ran a bus service at Parkes where, at 80 years of age, he died only recently. JIM CONROY.—Perhaps the most outstanding driver on the main Southern road between Campbell town and Goulburn. First drove for Manning, then for Crane and Roberts, and later for Cobb & Co., when this mail line fell to the big firm. Jim then joined the railway service, and was for 30 years mail-guard on the Sydney to Bathurst track. A noted teamster of interesting, coach road stories. He died in 1906, at the age of 82. NED DEVINE.—'Cabbage-Tree Ned.' Justly regarded as the champion of champions in the clever handling of multiple teams and, mammoth coaches. He was a Tasmanian by birth, and the first of Freeman Cobb's colonial trainees on a box-seat. He was regarded as having no peer in the safe handling of big teams in the jumbo coach, the 'Leviathan,' constructed to carry 75 passengers. He was a most entertaining man, and immensely popular with his passengers. In 1802 he was deputed to drive Stephenson's team of English cricketers to various places from Melbourne, and at the end of the tour was presented with a purse of £300. Opposition coach lines to Cobb were always fishing to catch Ned, but the water was too deep, an his salary of £17 a week was augmented by sideline 'perks,' and his total income must have approached £1000 a year. JIMMY DONOHOE.—A fine old driver for Cobb. & Co. and for himself on mail lines about Hay, Deniliquin, Booligal and Echuca. He died in Hay last year at the age of 82. TOM ELMS.—A heavy-weight driver on Queensland lines, but an excellent whip, and sociable with passengers. Tom made a feature of his bugle-calls, and their variety, as he entered a town on his Cobb coach. JACK FAGAN.—An excellent all round driver on the road from Forbes to Bathurst for Ford and Co., one of this company being the late Phil Mylecharane, so long connected with Shute, Bell & Co. Jack became particularly famous as the driver of the escort coach bailed up in June, '62, by Gardner's gang at Eugowra Rooks. Old Jack throughout his life retained and treasured his big Californian hat and coat showing bullet holes in them as a reminder of Gardner's intentions. Fagan later drove for Cobb & Co., finally settling down as a grazier on Mulyan and another holding in the Cowra district. JACK FOREMAN.—A heavy, burly man who drove McCullough mail coaches between Nevertire and Coonamble. A good driver if he liked, but was prone to find new glue pots, and perhaps did not nurse his teams to advantage. Still, he was popular, and could tell numerous fabulous tales of the road, when he got a box-seat passenger who would listen to his romances and leg-pulling. JACK GIRDHAM.—An acknowledged good and careful driver through the sixties, on various coach lines radiating from Forbes, where he later settled down as proprietor of livery stables before the advent of motors. Old Jack was a recognised authority on the habits of the [First Nations Peoples], and was always their friend. W. H. HAMPSON.—'The Invincible.' Steered many Cobb coaches on the North Coast, and was credited with saying that George Adams was the prettiest driver he ever saw. Later he drove on Upper Murray coach routes. NICK HOLDEN.—Sometimes erroneously called Oldham. A highly regarded Cobb driver on Queensland tracks. It is related of Nick that once, on descending a long steep hill with a culvert and curve at the bottom, he galloped his team to keep them free of the coach, and none knew but himself that his brake had broken, until he explained the reason for his haste. DICK HOUSTON.—A very trusted and careful driver for Cobb's on various parts of the northern road between Newcastle and Glen Innes. W. E. JACKSON.—An old-day Cobb driver in northern parts of Victoria, and became a roads manager with headquarters at Albury. TED

KEIGHTLY.—A very good and reliable driver for Cobb's between Tamworth and Armidale. He knew the bushranger Thunderbolt (Fred Ward) well, and had several meetings with him. LEVI.—One of the Yankee drivers imported, in 1852 by Freeman Cobb, and was contemporary with 'Cabbage-Tree Ned.' OWEN MALONE.—A Cobb's driver on Bathurst via Blayney to Orange road. In the early sixties he was bailed up by three men—not of Gardner's gang—about eight miles from Bathurst. Arundell Everett, a passenger, was relieved of £6 and Malone of the mail bags containing nearly £1000 in notes, belonging chiefly to the Bank of New South Wales. Two of the trio were caught by Capt. Battye and sentenced to 15 years' hard. BILL MALONEY, Sr.—Drove his own line of coaches between Hill End and Bathurst, and later was succeeded by his sons, Pat and the ever green Bill Maloney Jr., who was the subject of an article in 'The Land' a few months ago. DAN MAYNE.—What a name to conjure with in the West, when we think of his later activities in journalism in Bathurst. He previously drove Cobb coaches, and was quite a good one. GEORGE TRENCHARD MILLER.—'Handsome George.' An excellent driver on the southern roads, during the early sixties and onward, for Crane and Roberts, but transferred to Cobb & Co. when this firm bought out the latter. George was a well-educated man, of good physique, and extremely popular with travellers. His period of driving was renowned for freedom from accident, and if any man had conquered the art of nursing teams on bad stretches it was Miller. He then became a roads manager and inspector for Cobb's. E. Trenchard Miller, of Sydney, is a son, with much commercial activities, and prominent in yachting and Boy Scout circles. HERB McCULLOUGH.—Owned and drove his own mail coaches on the roads from Coonamble to Dubbo, Nevertire and Walgett, in the late eighties, and later ran mail lines up the coast above Newcastle. Now, I think, he is grazing not far from Coonamble. Never saw George Adams drive, but I cannot easily imagine a cleaner, cooler, or more finished driver of multiple teams than the same Herb. He was a great nurser of horse-power on difficult stretches through glue-pots, gilgais, and tricky sand-monkies, and he was never known to turn a hair. MONTGOMERY.—'Old Monty.' Last known to me as driving for Herbie McCullough on the Coonamble Walgett mail track. His plant was somewhat culled from his boss's more important lines, and how he got anything at all out of some of his crock horses was a mystery. Monty dozed a good deal on those long lonesome black-soil plains, but was easily awakened by the sight of a passenger's hip-pocket contents, and, when invited to refresh, his invariable expression was *It's as good as grease on the wheels, it makes the 'orses go*. Once, discussing the depth of a flooded warrumbool near Bugil, Monty told me *It's pretty full at time, but I 'as to go through, an' was thinkin' of askin' McCullough to give me 'orses with longer ears*. Poor old Monty—how we loved the old chap. JIMMY NAIRN.—Another of Cobb's drivers in the Bathurst district, before he drove for so long between Armidale and Glen Innes. On retirement from the bugle road, he kept a little inn in Armidale and ran a bus service to and from the railway station. TED NATHAN.—A great feature of the Cobb & Co. lines in the West, where he drove between Bathurst and Forbes. Serving a long apprenticeship on the box-seat, he became roads manager for the firm and settled in Orange where, on his retirement in 1890, he entered into town activities and became Mayor. Since his death in 1915, the Orange townspeople erected a handsome fountain in Robertson Park to his memory. Ted Nathan was a short, stocky man, but weighed tons when measured by his energies. JIM NICHOLAS.—A well-known Cobb driver in Riverina. JACOB RUSSART.—'The Hard Doer.' A well known Cobb driver in Queensland and the western parts of N.S.W. On retirement from the road, and after some mining ventures, he settled down as boniface at the Royal in Parkes, and has many descendants of note about that district. BILL ROCHESTER.—A very fine driver between Dubbo and Coonamble, excellent travelling company, and informative. JIMMY SMALL.—An expert and pretty driver of multiple teams about Bathurst, Orange, Forbes and Molong. Retired from coaching and kept a hotel in Orange back in the late eighties. PETER TOOHEY.—A very fine old driver between Bathurst and Lambing Flat, in the diggings and bushranging days. Made a bold and clever escape with coach and passengers, when a bail-up was staged out Crowther way in 1862. He left sons to pick up the ribbons and whip when he laid them down. JIM TOY.—A driver of Cobb's outfits between Binalong and Burrowa. Was contemporary with Jack Carter there.

So that any remaining members of that line old body of Cobb & Co. change stable grooms, chancing on these lines, might not feel angered if passed over, I have a few words in conclusion to say of them, seeing that they played a very big part in the upkeep of these pioneer lines of transport throughout the colonies. Yes! Ben, Dick, Crazy Tom, Old Jack, and the rest of you were fine fellows, and when a passenger by coach, with my love for a good horse and everything to do with him, I never failed at your stables to look you over, to look at your stalls, and at your well-groomed four-footers, with clean soft ribbons hanging loosely to the hame-rings while they nibbled at a last handful of oats and bran, awaiting the call to come out and fall into place, to be reined and hooked up for their stage often to fifteen miles in the great scheme of transport. Yes, old chaps! You were a fine lot; and one of the chief spokes in Cobb & Co.'s wheel of the road." (The Lights of [?]obb & Co., 17 Jul 1935, p.24)

1916 "Mr. James Conroy … 1859, entered the employ of Crane and Roberts as a driver of one of their coaches. His track lay between Campbelltown and the Bargo Brush, and he continued his calling as a mail coach driver when Cobb and Co. took over the business. When the railways ousted the coaches from the road he followed the times, and became a mail guard on the Southern Line." (Death of Mr. James Conroy, 17 Jun 1916, p.2)

1923 See also Robinson, James (Robbie); 1932 Breen, Jim (Jimmy)

Cook, W … 1919 See Aisbett, E. J.

Cooke, Archie … 1921 See Griffen, Chas.

Coomber, Edwin John
1935 "Death of Cobb and Co's Driver. One of the few remaining links with the old days of Cobb and Co.'s coaches, which plied between Orange, Parkes and Forbes … passed away during the week at Parkes, in the person of Mr. Edwin John Coomber, aged 80 years. Born at Ophir in 1854, when that locality was a hive of industry, and miners of all nationalities were tearing up the country in their search for the precious nuggets, he grew to manhood on his parents' farm there, in company with his five brothers. Later, he became a driver for Cobb and Co., and tooled his team on the length from Orange to Molong for many years. When Parkes was in the heyday of its mining boom, the deceased forsook the road, and engaged in mining work at that centre, where he remained for 15 years. Mr. Coomber was married at Molong 55 years ago to Miss Sarah Frances Archer, who survives him, as do two daughters and one son. His only living brother is Mr. A. T. Coomber, of Sydney." (Death of Cobb and Co's Driver, 22 Feb 1935, p.2)

1935 See also Conroy, James (Jim)

Coomber, Jim & Coomber, Ted … 1929 See Corbett, Alec.

Coombes, Edwin J … 1935 See Conroy, James (Jim)

Cooper, Bill … 1917 See Wright, Bob

Corbett, Alec.
1929 "DEATH OF MR. CORBETT. Coaching Days Recalled.

News came to hand on Saturday night, of the death in Queensland of Mr. Alec. Corbett ... Mr. Corbett was about 65 years of age, and left Orange in 1893. When Cobb and Co.'s coaches were the passenger carriers between the railways and large western towns, Alec Corbett was known on the line from Orange to Forbes as the greatest of all the great drivers who handled the coaching teams of 40 years ago, in the days when men knew how to drive. Those were the days of five horse, corn fed teams, doing long stretches over unmade roads in 15 and 20 mile stages. It was a pride of Cobb's coaches to always get through on time, and never refuse the rawest colt that the winkers could be placed on. Unbroken colts were brought in, mostly from the Cowra and Canowindra districts—JG half circle and other brands—and after a few runs in the 'brake,' graduated into the crack teams. Alec. Corbett's driving brought to his lot the roughest and wildest of these, and he handled them like an artist.

The coach drivers were then men of public importance along the bush highways. They passed the news along their routes, delivered all the medicine, watches and other things, too fragile for the parcels section of the weigh-bills. They were known to all by their Christian names, and along Cobb and Co.'s 'telegraph line of Royal Mail coaches' there was none so popular and obliging as Alec. Corbett. The old roads were long stretches of ruts, linked up with patches of metal, the driving hours were long, the winters very wet and boggy, and the summers hot and dusty ...

Yet coaching had its romance, and there are now many grey heads in back country towns who still longingly recall the days on the box seat and Alec. Corbett. His death recalls many names of the old school of coach drivers who have nearly all passed out, as their occupation, too, passed out, first by the railways, and then by the motor—Jim Little, Ted Yeomans, Pat Donovan, Bob McGroder, Jack Piesley, Alec. Ross, 'Old Clem,' the Coombers, Tom and Mick Willocks, Bob Field, Joe Strickland, the Frosts— 'Old Jim' and his sons, Tom and Jim, Pat Gilligan, and a lot of others, whose names the fading memory of the past does not at the moment yield. Of these, the Coombers (Ted and Jim) are still living, and the veteran who was 'Old Jim Frost' forty years ago, is still enjoying good health, somewhere in Sydney." (Death of Mr. Corbett, 4 Mar 1929, p.5)

Corbett, Dick ... See Clark, Billy

Corbett, Sandy
1917 "It is interesting also to recall the drivers on these lines of the eighties, all good men and careful, if fearless ... Roma to Charleville, via Mitchell and Morven, had as drivers, Tom Merritt, Jim Burstall, Luke O'Malley, Jim O'Leary (now at Cunnamulla), Bill Bolton, R. Nicholson, Sandy Corbett, and A. Brumfield" (Coaching in Australia, 1917, p.41)

Cork, (Christian name unknown)
1875 Crammed into Cobb and Co. coach "ORIGINAL CORRESPONDENCE. PASSENGER CONVEYANCE FROM DALBY TO ROMA. To the Editor of the Queensland Times. Sir,—For some time back the public have borne patiently with the style of conveyance provided by Cobb and Co. between the above named localities. In the coaches—a perfect nickname—three passengers are stowed away where there is room only for two, and so crammed is the space allotted for the feet with occasional bags of corn, as well as packages for which a high carriage in paid, that, setting aside danger, the journey has become a terror to travellers. From the Condamine horses and coach become worse, and, unfortunately ... a new driver has been put on in place of Mr. Cork, who resigned ... Yesterday a lady and her little baby had a most narrow escape. It appears the driver was 'indisposed,' and while the lady's husband and another gentleman were walking the driver brought the so-called coach foul of a stump or tree, pitching her clean out, and sending the little innocent out of the mother's arms right amongst the horse's legs. Luckily the gentlemen were on foot, and they immediately rescued it from its dangerous position, when, to the surprise and delight of both parents, the little thing was found to be uninjured ...

The whole line seems to be managed without regard to people's comfort or safety ... It was only this morning a gentleman told me of his being pitched three times from the coach during one journey. As there are to be some changes, I hope this letter will catch the manager's attention ... Seeing that we have a country 700 miles at the back of us, all of which has been eagerly taken up and, further, that large portions of it are superior to the Darling Downs—I think the Postmaster General might pay us a visit ... I will guarantee that we will give him a feed of beef and mutton such as cannot be produced on the Downs." (Original Correspondence, 2 Jan 1875, p.5)

Cornelius, Harry ... 1930 See Alder, Amos

Cousens, Samuel ... 1901 See Anderson, Thomas (Tom)

Cousins, Sam ... 1948 See Herchberg/Hertsberg, Joseph (Joe)

Cox, Bill ... 1917 See Richardson, W.

Coyle, (Christian name unknown)
5 Jun 1925 "THE DAYS OF COBB AND CO. Through the death in Sydney recently of one of Cobb and Co.'s old coach drivers, Mr. Coyle, father of the well-known barrister of that name, memories are revived of the days when Cobb and Co.'s line of mail and passenger coaches plied between Orange and the far west, to Cobar and Bourke, and between Orange and Forbes, at the time when the gold fever was at its height. In those faraway days there were 15 or 16 hotels between Orange and Forbes, and the coaches were loaded on every trip, while the event of the week was the arrival of the gold escort. At different times opposition to Cobb and Co. was tried, but the big firm always won in the end. On one occasion the late Fred. Richardson, of Forbes, sent in a tender for the conveyance of mails between Orange and Forbes, and his tender was so low— £1000—that it was accepted, but he was soon to learn that he could not fight Cobb and Co. He was obliged to sell out to them." (The Days of Cobb and Co., 5 Jun 1925, p.5)

Coyle, Thomas (Tom)
1905 "Old Sofala ... James Rutherford (Cobb & Co.) made thousands with his coaches up that way. Tom Coyle, one of the pioneer drivers over the Wyagdon and Monkey Hills, afterwards drove on the Towers (Q.), and is, I believe, now a wealthy man." (The Lands Scandals, 12 Aug 1905, p.10)

1925 "PASSING OF COBB & CO. PIONEER COACHING DAYS. Surviving Partner's Reminiscences. The announcement that the last coach owned by Cobb and Co., now being used between Yeulba and Surat, Queensland, is to be supplanted by a modern motor service has awakened a host of reminiscences in the mind of Mr. Thomas Coyle, an alderman of Annandale for 16 years, and one of its most respected citizens, for the best part of a quarter of a century. *I think I am the only one of the old timers left*, said Mr. Coyle *and although I have been out of the firm a good many years now, it is pleasing to think of the old stirring days. Men were men then, and fought their battles man to man. The first coach services I remember, went on the veteran were from Sydney to Penrith, run by rival proprietors, Bob Elliott and Crane and Co. Then there was a service to Bathurst, linking up with the Penrith route, run by a man named Minahan (whose nickname was 'Scrawny Jack'), and another by Dinny Gaynor. Mr. James Rutherford, a man of great enterprise, bought out the lot. To give you some idea of his operations even in those early days, it may be only necessary for me to state that at one time in his earlier career his liability to the bank financing him was said to be £400,000. When I entered the service of the firm, late in the [18]60's, the firm consisted of Frank Whitney; Walter Hall, James Rutherford arid, a wealthy Melbourne racing man named Power. When I got my first start at Bathurst, at a salary of £3 per week, I felt that my fortune was made. There were no wages boards in those days; no basic wage, or any of that latter-day foolery and a man was paid what he earned and was glad to get it. In less than five years I was sent to take charge of the whole of Northern Queensland, but not before the firm's operations had extended from Orange to Bourke, and some of my most stirring adventures occurred in New South Wales.*

BUSHRANGING DAYS *Yes, they were days when bushrangers flourished,* said Mr. Coyle, *in reply to a question: and, although I often held the reins on coaches carrying many thousands of pounds worth of gold —my record consignment was 1 [?]ton 1 cwt. from Hill End — I was only stuck up once. That was at Piper's Flat; and, fortunately, it was at a time when there were neither gold nor mails aboard. There was a schoolmaster named O'Connor on the box seat with me, and, as a double-barrelled gun was pushed right in front of his face, he called out, 'Take that thing out of my mouth; I won't resist.' Afterwards he said to me 'The beggar's hand was shaking so I thought the blamed thing might go off by accident.' One of the hold-up gang said to me, 'I suppose you know who I am ?' and I replied 'I don't but I suppose you are Gardiner.' I knew jolly well he was not Gardiner, but I had to pass that way two or three times a week late at night, and it was good policy for me to pretend that I did not know who they were. As a matter of fact, they were only a bunch of local amateurs, and their luck was out, for they only obtained a small amount of cash and, jewellery, of little value, from the passengers. There was a more serious hold-up a week or two later near the same spot, however when a relief constable named Carmody was shot, dead, and it was afterwards estimated that the real bushrangers this time were busy disposing of the body while my coach, carrying half a ton of sold, passed by safety. When I was appointed to the charge of the North Queensland branch,* continued Mr. Coyle *it was not all beer and skittles. One of the stages out Hughenden way meant a span of 80 miles without water, and that was no joke in such a climate ; but I never lost a horse, much less a driver. There was soon a net-work of Cobb and Co's. coaches serving the sparsely settled districts of Cloncurry, Winton, Hughendon Croydon, Normanton, Port Douglas, Herberton and a score or two other outposts, the names of which I cannot now remember, but I know I had charge of 300 men and 2,000 horses. After about ten years of management I was taken in as a partner, with a fifth share in the whole concern. Then the railways came along, and, as I saw the coaching days were doomed I managed to get out at the right time.*

A HAWKESBURY NATIVE Born of Irish parents, Mr. Coyle is a native of the Hawkesbury, the nursery of our sturdiest pioneer stock. He was born at Llandilo, on the South Creek, about nine miles from Windsor, in 1847, and if his present rugged bearing may be taken as a criterion, he should be in a condition to enjoy his 78th birthday on the last day of 1924. A distinguished nephew is Mr. W. T. Coyle, K.C., Chief Crown Prosecutor." (Passing Of Cobb & Co, 16 Jan 1925, p.3)

Coyne, J.
1917 See Wright, Bob

Cozens, Bob
1928 See Grover, Robert H. (Wharparilla Bob)

Crewes, Fred
1921 See Griffen, Chas.

Crimmins, John
1912 "Constable John Crimmins, a native of Mudgee, and who has been in the police force for 32 years, has resigned owing to ill-health. For years John was on duty at the Redfern railway station, in the early days he was a great man with horses … and for a considerable time drove one of Messrs. Cobb and Co.'s coaches on the stage from Mudgee to Coonamble." (Local Brevities, 28 Mar 1912, p.21)

Crogan, James
1884 "Coach Accident in Victoria. MELBOURNE, Thursday.

ca. 1925 Main street in Surat, Fred Thompson driver, Tom Leonard sits next to Fred; Cobb & Co's last coach run Surat to Yuleba 14/8/1924 (Photo and information from Jim Crack; Photo used in 'Telegraph' newspaper 29 August 1924)—Courtesy Queensland Museum Collection

A shocking accident occurred last evening to Cobb and Co.'s coach, coming from Mornington to Frankston. The horses shied near Frankston and the conveyance was upset. Miss Coates, daughter of the late Dr. Coates, who was on the box seat, was killed, and the driver, Crogan, severely injured. The latter was removed to the Melbourne Hospital, where he is now a little better. The inside passengers, who included Mr. Call, P.M., were much shaken." (Coach Accident in Victoria., 19 Apr 1884, p.760) " James Crogan, aged thirty-five years, a single man, residing at Ascot Vale … The coach was somewhat damaged and one of the horses injured." (Dreadful Coach Accident, 22 Apr 1884, p.4)

Crossen, H. J. (Possible Cobb and Co. driver)
1937 "OLD COACHING DAYS. Memories of former years— of times they drove the mail and passenger coaches owned by Cobb and Co. and associated Arms ... Fifty members of Cobb and Co. Old Drivers' association attended the meeting, Mr. H. J. Crossen (Ballarat), who is 83 years of age, was the oldest driver present." (Old Coaching Days, 25 May 1937, p.19)

Crow, (Christian name unknown)
1874 "Two accidents have occurred to Messrs. Cobb and Co.'s mail coaches during the past week, either of which might have been attended by serious and even fatal consequences. In the first instance, the afternoon coach proceeding to Warwick on Friday last (fortunately without any passengers), on arriving at the Gap Hotel, a horse belonging to Mr. W. Gillum was substituted for one taken away by the up-coach. The driver, Mr. Crow, then started to cross the Gap, accompanied by Mr. Gillam, and on arriving at the top of the Range Mr. Gillam returned, the horse appearing perfectly quiet, but on descending the other side, however, the fresh animal became obstinate, and after short struggle caused the buckle of one of the reins to go through the hames-ring, the driver thus losing all power over the horses. He then tried to capsize the coach to prevent the horses from getting away, but could not succeed, and the horses bolted away down the precipitous ridge, running the coach over a log, which threw the driver out, and after that against a tree with great force. We are sorry to say the driver was very seriously hurt. The second accident occurred on Wednesday last. When the mid-day coach ... driven by Mr. J. Highfields, was nearing Fagg's selection, one of the reins broke, and the horses immediately started off, running the coach against a tree. We believe the passengers were not injured, and succeeded in getting as far as the Gap Hotel." ('Latest News from the North, 28 Feb 1874, p.10)

Cummings, Pat
1951 See Leary, Jack

Cunningham, Johnny
1873 Newly painted coach "Condamine. Mr. Welch, Inspector of Telegraphs, passed through this on Friday, on his return from Cunnamulla, St. George, Roma, &c. Cobb and Co. have got a new coach radiant with fresh red paint and gold letters running on this line. If the coaches and horses are up to the mark, there will be no fear that the driver—Johnny Cunningham—will be up to time. He is a first-rate whip and a general favourite." (Condamine, 19 Apr 1873, p.10)

Currie, (Christian name unknown)
1870 "DEATH of A Jehu. The Ballarat Courier reports that an old driver for Cobb and Co. died suddenly on Tuesday. A few hours before, while driving the Malmsbury coach, he was seized with a cramp, from which he did not recover. His name is Currie, and he was held in considerable respect by those who were acquainted with him." (Licenses Under The Land Act, 16 Dec 1870, p.3)

Cuthbertson, Jas.
1919 "Driver, district employed: Bendigo District" (Annual report / Cobb & Co.'s Old Coach Drivers' Association, 1919, pp.6&7)

1902 Finish of the Melbourne Cup, the race was one by 'The Victory'—Courtesy of Ballarat Heritage Services Picture Collection

Chapter Three
Drivers
D

The Lights of Cobb & Co.

The bullock-driver scarcely feels

His way on new-cut track

Ere Cobb and Co., with lighter wheels

Have run the marks out-back ;

And while the seasons come and go

And through the changing years

All flags are dipped to Cobb and Co

The western pioneers ;

What reck if all the creeks are dry

And hot winds blight and blow

We'll meet and fill our glasses high -

"Good luck to Cobb and Co.!"

Will H. Ogilvie, Glenrowan 1895
(Cobb and Co., Verse 4, 30 Mar 1895, p.4; The Daily Telegraph, 6 Sep 1924, p.13)

1915 Coach in Procession, Ned Gallagher driver—Courtesy Queensland Museum Collection

Supporting evidence:

Dailey, Johnny ... 1932 See Horton, John

Dallas, George D.
1933 "Mr. George Dallas rode on the box many a time in New Zealand with one of the finest drivers in the world, Cabbage Tree Ned ... Mr. Dallas first drove in New South Wales forty years ago. His horse bus used to cover the distance between Sydney and Parramatta in three hours. After sixteen years in Sydney he drove a bus for the tramway companies in Dandenong road, High-street and Malvern road. He is now, in charge of the boat sheds at Xavier College." (Cobb and Co. Coach Drivers, 21 Jun 1933, p.11)

1937 See also Preston, R.; 1919 Aisbett, E. J.

Dallis, Jack
1936 "ECHOES OF THE PAST COBB AND CO.'s COACHES (By 'Gooragooby,' Dalveen.) In the days of Cobb and Co. the coaches completed the 40 miles that stretched between Warwick and Stanthorpe in about six hours! Today one hour, or a little more, suffices for a motor run between the two centres. An important factor associated with early coaching days was the establishment of commercial branches of the firm of Cobb and Co. throughout the various colonies ... To maintain order at Quart Pot Creek, 16 constables, under the charge of Sub-inspector Harris, left Warwick by special coaches for the tin mines on April 11, 1872. This was in answer to a request by a gentleman on the field who feared serious trouble from the populace, owing to his having dismissed a number of Britishers, in receipt of 7/per day for 10 hours work, to allow of the introduction on the field of Chinese cheap labour. However on arrival at Quart Pot Creek, it was found that the distressful condition of affairs on the field had been considerably exaggerated, and the police took their departure for Brisbane a few hours later. Eighteen years previous to this episode (1854) there were only 14 police all told, in the whole of what is now Queensland territory, Brisbane having six, and Ipswich, Warwick, Drayton and Gayndah two apiece. In June, 1872, Pickworth, of Percy-street, Warwick, started a line of opposition coaches between Warwick and Stanthorpe, but they did not prove a success, for on December 7, of the same year, they were purchased by Cobb and Co. for the sum of £350, and the fares between Warwick and Stanthorpe went up immediately to 10/, in place of the ruinous, competitive fares of 2/6 each way previously. Eventually Cobb and Co. put the price up to 25/ each way.

On May 18, 1875, Cobb and Co's coach, running from Gympie to Maryborough, met with an accident. When approaching the ferry at a rapid pace the brakes became useless, and the horses careered down the steep incline on to the punt and over into the river. None of the passengers lost their lives, but the driver had a narrow escape. The coach and mails were subsequently recovered, but the four horses were drowned. In April, 1876, Cobb and Co's stables at Oakey Creek, on the old Warwick Stanthorpe road were destroyed by fire and five valuable coach horses perished in the flames. When first proclaimed a penal settlement in 1867, the first white prisoner to be sent to St. Helena was a man whom Judge Lutwyche, at Warwick, sentenced to 14 years penal servitude, for having committed a mail robbery ...

The years 1864-65 saw a long series of robberies on the roads west and south of Goulburn, the Gilbert-Hall gang alone being responsible for 10 robberies in 14 months. Thos. Clarke robbed six of Cobb and Co's coaches in 1865, and between 1864 and 1870 'Thunderbolt' became the terror of coach drivers in the New England district. About the early seventies valuables and money were taken from the mails in large amounts by the bushrangers Cummins, Williams, and Dunn. Mention of 'Thunderbolt' reminds me of a speech made at a public gathering some 14 years ago by my old friend, Mr. Donald Gunn. Inter alia, he stated that he came on the Downs with his father in 1865. His wife (since deceased) was a daughter of John Deuchar, who came over here shortly after the Leslies, and they all helped to develop the Darling Downs. Deuchar had employed 'Thunderbolt' as a stockman.

This stockman first of all stole a horse somewhere in the south and escaped from the police, and, if it had not been for that incident, possibly there would have been no 'Thunderbolt.' So far as he knew Fred Ward ('Thunderbolt') had never committed any outrageous crime. He remembered an occasion when his father whilst riding home from Tenterfield met with 'Thunderbolt' and they rode along together. His father was wearing a gold watch and chain, but the bushranger did not interfere with it. After travelling along the road for some miles 'Thunderbolt' said he would have to push on. He did so, and the next thing he heard was that the bushranger had stuck up Nick Hart and relieved him of £110 won by him at Tenterfield races, when his horse (Minstrel) appropriated the 'double' threat. Sergeant Waldron, from Bonshaw, with other members of the police force, came over in search of the highwayman, and he distinctly recollected 'Thunderbolt' calling at Pikedale, sometime previously. However, while the police were absent 'Thunderbolt' visited Bonshaw and stuck up that place. In some districts, both in Victoria and New South Wales, the conveyance of mails by Cobb and Co.'s coaches became so hazardous through almost continuous trouble with bushrangers, that the firm found it difficult to retain its drivers, and quite a number sought and obtained transfers to Queensland. Respected descendants of these men are living in this State at the present day. The adventures of coach travel, however, were not only to be experienced in running the gauntlet with bushrangers.

The old coach driver was a character, about whose oddities a whole book of anecdotes could be written. It was a matter of honour with him to run to time, and emergencies were the test of his prowess. For a number of years prior to the last of Cobb and Co's coaches in Queensland—that plying between Yeulba and Surat—being taken off the road, steel springs were dispensed with owing to frequent breakages, and a leather contraption was used to perform their function. With a few rough tools the coach driver would improvise and repair breakages; a piece of wire filched from a selector's fence would bind a broken part; and a sapling would keep the body of the coach off the ground should a trailing wheel collapse, as 'Jack' Dallis, in charge of the Goondiwindi-Warwick coach, experienced on an occasion back in the eighties or nineties when nearing Warwick ...

The firm of Cobb and Co. went out of the coaching business when the last coach was taken off the Yuelba-Surat road in 1924; and the Blackall coach, which did its last run in 1922, was travelled to Sydney to be placed in the Museum. There are only three of these vehicles now in existence, so far as I can gather.

One is, or was until recently, in the Brisbane Museum, and the other two are in Sydney—one in Vaucluse House and the other in the Museum." (Echoes of the Past, 29 Feb 1936, p.8)

Daly, Dick
1913 "A noteworthy event (writes 'Vagrant') was the appearance in the papers of an ad. announcing the disposal by auction of Cobb and Co's interests at Leonora, including the right to run their coaches along the track to Lawlers, and elsewhere. This means that the firm, as represented by Jimmy Nicholas, Charlie Kidman and Ted Miller, has made up its mind to go off the road for good. Probably some of the old drivers, Dick Daly and other noted whips, will take over the concern, that is if the price required is not too much for their joint finances. Of late years, but particularly since mining at Lawlers declined, as a consequence of the Northern Mines closing down, coaching in the north has been a rather tame investment, but the outlook is good in view of the Consolidated at Wiluna having overcome treatment difficulties which prevented that large proposition from getting on a paying basis. When in full swing the Wiluna mine will provide a lot of work for the coaches and the carrying industry." (The Countryman's Column, 12 Jan 1913, p.7)

1925 "Coaching in the Commonwealth. Experiences of Half a Century. 'Jimmy' Nicholas Handles the Ribbons ... Cobb and Co.'s drivers were very often, like myself, boys grown up in their employ and taught to drive; but many of their very best men, with big teams and heavy loading, had been horse and bullock teamsters. And yet I think if I had to decide as to who was the very best driver I had ever known I would pick an ex-Jockey named Jimmy Foy, weight about eight stone. He was one of Crawford and Connolly's men, and drove the big 45-passenger seven-horse coach on the Wagga-Albury line for years. I once heard Mr. Hall say that in all his experience of coach drivers he had not seen Foy's equal. We (Kidman and Nicholas) had many first-class drivers in our employ during our coaching partnership, and if I were asked to pick the best of them I should select Dick Daley, a big strong man with wonderful hands and patience. He came to me in New South Wales, I think, in 1892. He drove there for us, and when I came over here. I brought Dick with me. He went through the West Australian coaching with us, and when horses had to be discarded for motors he took on the latter and made a very solid driver. Dick is still with me at Shark Bay, and, like myself, is trying to forget coaching and learn something about the best way to make money out of sheep." (Coaching in the Commonwealth, 24 May 1925, p.11)

1925 "Last week, through a typographical error, the name of a famous coach-driver was given as Jimmy Foy. It should have been Jimmy Loy.— Ed. S.T."(Coaching in the Commonwealth, 31 May 1925, p.9)

1912 See also Miller, Ted; 1953 Kidman/Kiddman, Charles (Charlie)

Danes, (Christian name unknown) ... 1930-1940s See Allan, (Christian name unknown)

Davidson, James (Young Jimmy)
1927 "Mr. James Davidson, who had resided in the Surat-St. George district for the past 45 years, died at Surat on September 8, at the age of 72 years. He had been in failing health for some time. The late Mr. Davidson in his younger years was head stockman on Dareel Station, then managed by Mr. Hill for the A.P. Company. Later, in the employ of Messrs. Cobb & Co., he was a well-known figure as the driver of the coach between Yeulba and St. George for over 30 years. Forty years ago he married Miss Clarke, a daughter of a well-known Surat family. He retired in 1912 from his position as driver, and engaged in farming in the Surat district. His wife and a daughter predeceased him seven years ago. Four sons served in the Great War, the youngest of whom died abroad, and was buried in Sierra Leone. The deceased is survived by three daughters and seven sons." (Obituary, 14 Sep 1927, p.17)

1917 See also Anderson, Jim; 1925 Eddie, Nathan; 1925 Mitchell, Bill (Billy); 1939 Warner, Jack

Davidson, Jimmy (Old/Father of Young Jimmy Davidson)
1925 "REMINISCENCES OF FORMER DRIVERS ... The Jimmy D—, of the Yeulba track, referred to old Jimmy Davidson, who, after leaving the box seat, looked after the mail change at Rosehill outside of Surat, on the St. George road, and the coach travellers could always rely on a good meal there." (Cobb's Coaches, 17 Jan 1925, p.17)

Davis, Geo ... 1919 See Aisbett, E. J.

De Graves, (Christian name unknown) ... 1937 See Preston, R.

De Graves, J ... 1919 See Aisbett, E. J.

Devine, Edward (Cabbage-tree Ned)
1933 "A man who could delicately flick the ash off your cigarette with his whip, a man whose popularity later was Victoria-wide" (Cobb and Co. Coach Drivers, 21 Jun 1933, p.11)

1903 "A tall man, of military appearance ... recently returned from a far off field, after an absence of 36 years, is Mr. Edward Devine, who, from 1853 to 1862, was known as 'Cabbage Tree Ned,' the famous coach driver for H. Dewing and Cobb and Company between Geelong and Ballarat in the stirring days of the golf diggings. In 1853 'Ned,' who is still hale and hearty, was only seventeen years of age, but, having received a thorough training as an ostler from Mr. James Dewing, an early settler in the Geelong district, he soon became 'king of the highway' as a coach driver. His team always consisted of a six-in-hand ... On several occasions he narrowly escaped falling into the hands of 'Captain' Melville and 'Black Douglas' on the road to Geelong ... Mr. Devine received the name of 'Cabbage Tree Ned' from the early Ballarat diggers, because he usually wore a cabbage tree hat, a kind of head dress which became very popular with some of the gold seekers of the early fifties." (Cabbage Tree Ned, 12 Dec 1903, p.6)

1932 "Cabbage-tree Ned, Cobb and Co's. famous whip, never wore anything else but the cabbage tree. Its manufacture began in the bush, and subsequently one or two Brisbane and Sydney firms used to turn out the high-priced article. In some places the hats were made by selectors' wives for the men and children. Some made them for sale. I knew one woman, who, with the help of her children made £600 in five years out at these hats. The leaves for plaiting were usually got for them by (First Nations Peoples) along mountain gullies and creeks, where the cabbage palms wen plentiful." (Tales of the Bush, 20 May 1932, p.6)

1875 See also Turner, Bob (Big Bob); 1923 Robinson, James (Robbie); 1925 Eddie, Nathan; 1932 Breen, Jim (Jimmy); 1935 Conroy, James (Jim); 1933 Grover, Robert H. (Wharparilla Bob); 1937 Atkinson, Frank

Dickson, W.
1891 "Activity was displayed yesterday in regard to carrying out all arrangements decided upon for the speedy removal of the cargo from the steamship Bancoora, which was wrecked on Monday morning on the beach in the vicinity of Bream Creek ... The handling of the whip and reins for the occasion was entrusted to Mr. W. Dickson, one of Cobb and Co.'s skilful and trusty drivers, and the work was effectually accomplished without the breakage of a strap, bar or spring." (The Wreck at Bream Creek, 16 Jul 1891, p.2)

Dilworth, J.
1875 Coach breakdown "The Great Northern line of road, between Tenterfield and Glen Innes is getting as almost as bad as the streets in this Municipality ... On the Monday after the mail had crossed the Bluff ... here the coach capsized, but fortunately without accident to the passengers. Some few miles further on, the thorough-brace broke ... no person was injured, owing to the exertions of J. Dilworth, the coachman, and R. Bowers, of the coaching staff, who was present. Again ... on the return trip ... breaking of the axle, some of the passengers being much shaken and slightly bruised. Those who travelled by the coach that day, speak, in terms of praise of the coachman and his assistant, and justly attribute the accident to the right cause—the dangerous state of the road. Trial Railway surveys are progressing in the district" (Tenterfield, 25 Aug 1875, pp.2-3)

Dilworth, John
1877 "Armidale—51 years ago. Memories of the Past. In the early part of the week Mr. Walsh, of the Ben Lomond Hotel (on behalf of himself, Mr. Shannon, and the men in the latter gentleman's employ), presented Mr. John Dilworth, Cobb and Co.'s driver between Glen Innes and Armidale, with a handsome watch and guard, for Mr. Dilworth's carefulness and civility, in looking after and delivering letters to the residents of Ben Lomond (who have not as yet, succeeded in having conferred upon them the benefits of a local post office). They have, by this souvenir, testified their appreciation of the services rendered them by this courteous and obliging mail driver." (Armidale—51 years ago, 31 Aug 1928, p.9)

Discom, Tom ... 1921 See Griffen, Chas.

Discombe, Thomas
1897 "A Golden Wedding. On Monday last Mr. and Mrs. Thomas Discombe, of North Woodside, celebrated their golden wedding ... He then left to engage in the driving of a mail coach, and for 20 years he served in that capacity in the employment of Messrs. Rounsevell, Cobb, & Co. and Hill & Co., and for about four years he kept the hotel at Mount Torrens. On relinquishing driving he purchased the brickyards at North Woodside, where he has resided since, and by a comprehensive system of irrigation he utilised the water that accumulates in the pughole for a portion of his ground. The family consisted of eight children, six of whom survive, there being in addition 13 grandchildren, and seven great grandchildren." (Miscellaneous News, 10 Mar 1897, p.6)

Doherty, James
1907 "In our last issue we referred briefly to a serious accident which befel Mr James Doherty, of Benalla West, who was severely injured through a dray loaded with wool passing over

Coach at Langlo Hotel, Ernie Parr Smith driver, Andy Atkins on wheel (Cobb and Co. driver)—Courtesy Queensland Museum Collection

his shoulder and chest. Hopes were entertained that the sufferer would pull through, but later on serious complications set in, causing his medical adviser to entertain no hope of recovery, and the unfortunate gentleman quietly passed away on Monday last. The late Mr Doherty, who was a native of the North of Ireland, was one of our oldest pioneers, having arrived in Benalla as far back as 1857, and with the exception of a few years absence on a visit to America, had remained in the district ever since. Mr Doherty was well-known in the old coaching days, having wielded the ribbons for Cobb and Co." (Obituary, 19 Apr 1907, p.3)

Doherty, Jim
1888 "On the morning on which this story opened, there was more than usual interest attached to the departure of the coach from the Shearers' Rest Hotel. Christmas week had arrived, and there were people on the move ... Then the drought was becoming serious. People speak of the severity of the droughts in the old times, but the fact is there never has been a drought in Australia like that which prevailed in Queensland in 1885. Residents know that it began in 1883 ... Suffice it to say that the residents of Camptown, and the people who had driven into it by stress of weather outside on the western downs were eager after any event that might turn their thoughts from the humdrum of daily life, and from brooding nervously over the probabilities of the future ... the mail was a heavy one ... the coach must go, and so Jim Doherty had to get his horses fed and ready for the road ... he had determined to do the first stage with two horses ... he would save feed and water at the halting place ...

He gave a shake of the reins and a 'Get up' to the pair, but 'Dandy'—a staunch old grey horse ... made a pull that drew the coach round a bit ... in the meantime 'Bally' had jibbed. Then the fun begun, and Camptown turned out to enjoy it ... Beerie, the hotelkeeper, tried to lead them off at a walk. Not a bit of it would 'Bally' move ... Just then Beerie's dog, a nondescript sort of mongrel, seemed to take it into its towsy-shock head that it could assist its master, and went for Bally's heels, barking and biting ... a swift kick ... he slunk off ... Allan Fairlie, the Scotch blacksmith, brought from the carpenter's shop a flat thin board ... but did not start him ... Ultimately another horse had to be procured, and yoked in 'Bally's' place. Happily it went off all right" (Cobb's Coach, 22 Dec 1888, p.1)

Doherty, Mick
1935 "Mick Doherty was one of the greatest wags and yarn-spinners who ever ruled the reins aboard a Cobb and Co. coach in Victoria. His fund of funny stories seemed inexhaustible, although it must be remembered that his audience changed from day to day which gave him free fling to ring the old chime with original embellishments, time after time ... On one occasion he was staying a night at a big and fashionable hotel ... Late that night a civil engineer was stricken ill ... *We have a doctor on the premises* ... M. Doherty, M.D. was located in No. 36 ... *You're a doctor Who said so? You said so yourself in the visitor's book tonight. You're mad as a snake ... M.D. stands for mule-driver; I'm a Cobb and Co.'s man, as all the country knows*" (Out in the Bush, 17 Sep 1935, p.12)

Doil, Deny ... See Appendix 1.6

Donnelly, (Christian name unknown)
1892 "Young Blood. As Mr. Donnelly was driving one of Messrs. Cobb and Co.'s brakes down William-street, on Saturday, with one young unbroken horse and one steady old stager, the former, after one or two frantic plunges managed to get his hind

Charleville Rail Station—Courtesy Ray Green, Bathurst

legs straddlewise over the pole, which of course led, to more frantic plunges than before. In a very short time however one of the occupants of the break was at the head of the unruly colt, and managed after a minute or two to quiet him down, when it was found necessary to unharness him and detach him from the break before his legs could be righted. Immediately the animal felt himself free he gave a springing plunge and in no time was twenty yards from the vehicle, but he was evidently in the charge of a practiced horseman, and his head was not free for a moment. No damage was done with the exception of a slight scratch on the off hind leg. The animal was a really shapely bit of horseflesh and looks well worth the trouble of breaking in." (Young Blood, 28 Mar 1892, p.2)

Donohue, E ... 1917 See Wright, Bob

Donohue/Donohoe, Jimmy ... 1935 See Conroy, James (Jim)

Donohue, Ted ... 1925 See Atkins, W.

Donovan, Pat
1932 "Mr. Hood says that the Duke came through from Queensland by coach to Warren and Dubbo, the driver being the late Bill Walden of Gilgandra, to whom the Duke made a present of a silver-mounted pipe. Mr. Hood drove his grace from Dubbo to Wellington, and received a tiepin as a gift, and Pat Donovan took him on the stage to Orange. The latter also got a pipe from the visitor." (Cobb and Co, Driver Disappointed, 18 Mar 1932, p.2)

1929 See also Corbett, Alec.; Appendix 1.6

Donovan, Sergeant
1925 "THE ADVENT OF THE MOTOR COACH. A CURIOUS COINCIDENCE. W. Carmody (94 Silas-street, East Fremantle) writes:- Reading the most interesting articles in your valuable paper, giving as they do the history of the good old coach days now past, through interviews with Mr. Jas. Nicholas, the then king or the outback coach track, I am enclosing an old photo, taken in Leonora, on the corner of Tower-street (main street) and in front of the old office of Cobb and Co. This photo was taken about the beginning of or in the early part of 1911, 14 years ago. I was struck with one portion of the story where Jimmy (Mr. Nicholas) describes how, a couple of years before, it struck him real hard when he saw in Laverton the first motor-driven vehicle, and its passenger was the then general manager for Bewick-Moreing ... for it spelt the end of the good old horse coach and all his activities for half a life-time. I remembered after reading the articles that I had this old photo, somewhere stowed away, and I thought it would be of interest to you and your readers ...

This photo portrays the first real motor coach of the road, and its run was from Leonora to Lawlers (95 miles, I think). It was a great day, I well remember, in the old town when she (the coach) was duly assembled and turned up. A trial run, or joy run, was made around the town and district to the wonderment and curiosity of young and old. This photo was taken by old Roy Millar, the pioneer photographer of Kalgoorlie and other centres in the early days. Mr. Jas. Field, Cobb and Co.'s first motor mechanic and driver, also acted as tutor to a lot of the old horse drivers, Dick Daly, C. Chick and others. At the crank is Mr. J. Farley (now gone west), host of the Exchange Hotel, on the extreme left is Andy Anderson, cordial manufacturer and good fellow, on the seat behind the driver (right hand side) is Geo. Gamel, of Gamel and Trim, builders and contractors, now I believe living in Perth, and next to him your humble servant. I was then in the carrying business, but well remember being called up for duty, to take part in the trial run. I might add that the only 'dry' advocate that was on the coach that day was the driver, Field. On the back seat, with pipe in mouth, is Davie Bernes, host of the Leonora Hotel, one of Menzies and Leonora's earliest pioneers ... He has also gone to his forebears.

You may make what use you can of the scrappy reminiscences I have scribbled down. I can well remember setting out on the trial run, but have a very poor recollection of coming back. All I know was that the coach and driver fulfilled our fullest expectations. There was a strange coincidence in connection with the picture you published of the gold escort taken leaving Malcolm, as I was a passenger on that coach. That photo was taken at about a quarter to 5 in the morning (it was summer time), and true enough old Sergeant Donovan was in charge on the box seat. On that run I was initiated into the game of horse loo, 1s. in.; and the winner had to shout at the first stop or pub. It was a favourite method of beguiling the journey on those old coach runs." (The Advent Of The Motor Coach, 7 June 1925, p.11)

1925 See also Eddie, Nathan; 1935 Conroy, James (Jim)

Doran, Jimmie ... See Appendix 1.6

Dougharty, Mick
1909 "The little Alpine town of Bright presented an animated appearance on the occasion of my visit by reason of the large number of visitors intent on visiting Mount Buffalo, or 'The Garden of the Gods,' by which name it is perhaps best known lately. Our little preliminaries having been arranged, we stepped into one of the coaches ready to set out to the summit. It was our good fortune to have as whip that crack driver of Cobb & Co. fame, Mr. Mick Dougharty. For over 30 years this veteran of the roads has done service in these and other parts, having driven in his time almost every Governor of the state, and many are the stories—books could be filled—of his skill and daring in these wild mountain regions." (A Glimpse of the Buffalo, 30 Apr 1909, p.4)

Douglas, George ... 1939 See Warner, Jack

Douglas, W.
1930 "*Motor bus driving in London is easy. I'd startle them with a bush six-in-hand*, Mr. W. Douglas, a former Cobb and Co. driver now on a business trip to England ... Mr. Douglas sighs for the old Cobb and Co. days, when he was reprimanded for fording rivers at a hand gallop and drenching the passengers." (Old Coach Drivers Scorn, 6 Aug 1930, p.5)

1938 "ON THE TRACK ... OLD WHIPS OF COBB AND CO ... Watching Jehu with the ribbons ... *And Douglas with his ready wit, and ever cheerful smile, could drive a team of five abreast or in single file.*" (On the Track, 31 Aug 1938, p.11)

Douglass, Joe
1879 "Reward of Merit.—Travellers on the Orange coach will

be sorry to hear that Joe Douglass, the well-known, whip, who has been driving for Cobb and Co. during the past four years and eight months on that route, has received notice that his services are no longer required. He informs us that during the time he has been driving the Orange mail he has never before received a reprimand from the company. Such being the case it is very strange that Cobb and Co. should dismiss, without any inquiry, a driver who is known by all travellers between here and Orange to be a steady and careful man, one who looked after all the interests of his employers and the comfort of his passengers. We hear that some of our principal towns people are making a move towards presenting Mr. Douglass with a testimonial in recognition of his attention and civility to passengers during the long period he has been driving into Forbes. We hope it will receive a hearty response from the travelling public.—Forbes Times." (Late Telegrams, 14 Jun 1879, p.4)

Dowdle, Samuel
1933 "Mr. Samuel Dowdle, aged 70, another well-known Hillston district identity has died. In his early days Mr. Dowdle was well-known throughout the Riverina as a coach-driver employed by Cobb and Co." (Personal News, 23 Jun 1933, p.46)

Dowling, Nicholas
1938 "Reputed to be the oldest driver yet living of the famous coaching firm of Cobb and Co. Mr. Nicholas Dowling, of Beechworth, celebrated his 87th birthday on Tuesday. He left that firm's employ in 1862, going to Beechworth where he was employed by Crawford and Co. When that firm gave up business, Mr. Dowling became a cab proprietor, retiring only a few years ago. Mr. Dowling's health is good and he has many interesting reminisences of the old coaching days." (Personal Items, 27 May 1938, p.5)

Doyle, (Christian name unknown)
1878 "Serious Coach Accident. On Friday, May 2, as Cobb and Co.'s mail coach was proceeding from Gundagai to Albury, an accident of a most serious nature happened to Mrs. M'Evoy, who was passenger on the coach. The Yass Courier gives the following particulars :—*There were two drivers, Doyle and Egan, on the box, and when they were about a quarter of a mile from Tarcutta crossing, the box of the wheel burst, and caused the driver, Egan, to be jerked from his seat to the ground. The other driver got off quickly, and left Mrs. M'Evoy in the coach; and she, not wishing to be in the couch, jumped clean away from the wheels, but fell heavily on her left side insensible, and severely injured her left arm.*" (Serious Coach Accident, 11 May 1878, p.5)

Doyle, Billy
1878 "Billy Doyle, a driver of Cobb›s coach, was fined £3 for assaulting Mr Holroyd, Master in Equity, between Gundagai and Bowning. The cause of this *fracas* originated by the driver placing a horse-collar and a bag of potatoes amongst the inside passengers." (Telegraphic Intelligence, 18 Jan 1878, p.2)

Doyle, D ... 1932 See Lowe, Bill

Drew, Billy ... 1921 See Griffen, Chas.

Drew, Jim ... See Appendix 1.6

Drood, Sammy ... 1951 See Leary, Jack

Dryer, Billy ... 1921 See Griffen, Chas.

Duffell, Jack
1947 "Cobb & Co Veteran. Dailies were in error when they put forward 82-year old Charleville man as the oldest surviving driver of Cobb and Co. coaches. Living in Herston-road, Kelvin Grove, is Mr. Jack Duffell, aged 84. In good old days he was known in every corner of central, southern and south-western Queensland, as a driver of famous old vehicles ... Jack Duffell held the first car-driving licence, Charleville district, with early Model T." (Cobb & Co Veteran, 9 Nov 1947, p.39)

1948 See also Herchberg/Hertsberg, Joseph (Joe)

Duncan, (Christian name unknown) ... 1919 See Aisbett, E. J.

Dunleavy, F. J.
1925 "A Wagga District Native. AN ADVENTUROUS CAREER. FROM COBB'S COACH DRIVER TO MINING ENGINEER. In his youthful days in Australia, Mr Dunleavy drove a Cobb's coach out on the Lachlan, but he was ever a wanderer. He was known on the Yukon as a journalist ... its venturious career was brief. It lasted only a short northern summer season ... became famous in many parts of the world as a mining engineer" (A Wagga District Native, 21 Apr 1925, p.3)

Dunn, James
1874 "ACCIDENT TO A MAIL DRIVER.—An accident, which nearly proved fatal (says the Bathurst Times), happened to Mr. James Dunn, mail-driver in the employ of Messrs. Cobb and Co., on Thursday afternoon last, at Trunkey. Dunn had driven out to Trunkey with the coach as usual, and, after having delivered the mails and seen his team attended to, he mounted a young horse for the purpose of quieting it. He was riding up the street when the animal shied and bucked, and threw the rider heavily to the ground. The unfortunate man fell on top of his head, and landed on the edge of a newly-made road, inflicting a terrible gash, triangular in shape, a little above his temple. He was rendered completely insensible, and as he remained in that state it was thought advisable to remove him to Bathurst. He was placed in a waggonette and brought into town, where, under the care of Dr. Machattie he recovered consciousness, and is now progressing favourably." (The Sydney Morning Herald, 10 Nov 1874, p.5)

Dunstall, G.
1878 "On Wednesday evening, September 4, a number of gentlemen assembled at the Crown Inn, Truro, to present the maildriver, Mr. G. Dunstall, with a sum of money and to entertain him at dinner, which was provided in excellent style by Host White. The Angaston Brass Band was in attendance, and played appropriate music during the evening ... Mr. Price proposed *The health of the guest*, remarking that Mr. Dunstall had been in the employ of Cobb & Co. as maildriver for 11 years ... It gave him great pleasure to bear testimony to the sterling qualities of the guest, whom he had always known as an honest, diligent, careful, and indefatigable servant, both of his employers and the public ... The Chairman handed over to Mr. Dunstall a purse containing £20 2s. 6d. as a token of the esteem in which he was held by the public, and also a whip presented by one of his fellow drivers. Mr. Dunstall returned thanks for the testimonial and the great kindness manifested towards him." (Presentations, 14 Sep 1878, p.9)

Durack, M. P.
IN THE DAYS OF COBB AND CO. Personalities Of The

Track By MARY DURACK Mention was made in a recent edition of 'The Sunday Times' the passing of another of the old Cobb coachdrivers. Reading this my father, M. P. Durack, recalled that he too could claim to have driven for Cobb and Co., albiet in a strictly unofficial capacity, and to jog his memory of the episode he turned back the yellowed pages of his 1898 diary. His reminiscences of the journey be made in July of that year from Cammoweal to Hughenden cast some interesting sidelights upon conditions of travelling and outback ...

There was a great deal of drinking and merry-making going on, and the attractive young girl serving behind the bar drew my attention to one of the heaviest drinkers. *He's your coachman for the final 80 miles to Hughenden*, she said ... It was bitterly cold when we set off at 7 in the morning with a team of five horses, three in the lead and two in the pole. I had the box seat next the driver, which was probably as well, because we had not gone far when I realised that he was sound asleep. I woke him, and suggested that I took the reins. *Can you drive?* he asked. I said I thought I could manage, so he handed over to me and watched for a few minutes. Oh, you're all right, he said, and crawled gratefully into a large box that was used for carrying parcels. I saw no more of him then till 4 in the afternoon.

It was an interesing experience, and one I recall very clearly. At distances of 15 or 16 miles a fresh team of horses was in readiness and attended by grooms whose duty it was to release the incoming teams and harness-up a fresh relay. Cobb and Co.'s 'new man' was questioned at various stages regarding the former driver. *You're new to the game. What's happened to Bill?* I explained that Bill was temporarily indisposed owing to a slight colic attack, and they seemed to understand ... Next morning I caught the train for Townsville, and saw no more of Bill, though I heard some months later that he had been sacked, poor devil. I was sorry, for he was a good chap, Bill, what I saw of him, and if it hadn't been for his little weakness I could never have claimed to have driven for Cobb and Co." (In the Days of Cobb & Co., 22 Oct 1944, p.4)

Durieu/DuRieu, William (Billy)
1867 "The Commissioner of Public Works availed himself of the opportunity offered by his visit to the Finniss to inspect the various public works in the neighbouring townships. After the proceedings connected with the laying of the foundation-stone of the Finniss Bridge had terminated Cobb and Co.'s fine coach, with the six greys driven by the well-known whip, Mr. Durieu, started for the Goolwa with the Commissioner and his friends, who put up at the Corio Hotel. The party arrived soon after 7 o'clock on a beautiful moonlight night

Next morning a visit was paid to the wharf, which has been very considerably enlarged, and is now more adequate to the requirements of the trade. When the alterations are fully carried out the accommodation will be greatly increased. Goolwa is certainly improving, but a great deal still remains to be done before the wishes of the inhabitants and the wants of the township are met. On the Wednesday morning a special carriage left Goolwa for Port Elliot and Victor Harbour, under the direction of Mr. Jones, the manager of the line. We observed several new buildings in both places. Port Elliot is a beautiful spot, and when the railway is opened to Strathalbyn it must become the watering-place of South Australia. It possesses unrivalled advantages. The fine granite rocks which project far into the ocean must become a favourite resort of the dusty and baked Adelaide people ... As a place of business Port Elliot has gone down, being fairly eclipsed by the new port of Victor Harbour. But while it has lost its business importance it will be all the more desirable as a marine township ... In the evening the [First Nations Peoples] got up a special corroboree in honour of the visitors, and with a view to their own special interests. The native entertainment was on a large scale, and did great credit to the performers." (The Commissioner of Public Works in the South, 23 Mar 1867, p.3)

1913 "A VETERAN WHIP. THE PASSING OF THE COACH. [By a Special Reporter.] The day is fast approaching when the old-fashioned stage coach will vanish for ever from the streets of Adelaide. The times have changed. The population in the country surrounding the city has multiplied largely and production has increased in proportion. This has necessitated the construction of railways, and where these have not been supplied the coaches have given place to faster-moving petrol-driven vehicles. These methods of transport certainly have their advantages, but the picturesque atmosphere is absent.

I can remember the drive to Mount Barker before the days of the iron road, and can recall the keen invigorating air of the hills as I looked out over the canvas apron on the box seat, and marvelled at the dexterous manner in which the driver tolled his five horse team over hills and gullies. These men required nerve in addition to skill ... they were men who could think and act quickly in case of emergency. Just such a Jehu was William DuRieu ... Any one to see his kindly face and note the gentle bearing of the fine old man would find it difficult to imagine his handling a six-horse team over the Willunga road for years ... He told me he was born in England, and arrived in South Australia by the ship Planter in May, 1839. He was then nine years old. Shortly after this, owing to his father marrying a second time, he left home and was engaged for a while by Capt. Walker, of Walkerville. His first job was that of picking up potatoes as the men dug them out, but after about three weeks of this he found that he was not strong enough for the task. Capt. Walker told him he was no good for the work. Mr. DuRieu chuckled quietly at the recollection, and then resumed:—*I asked him then for my money*, and he replied, *'I'll give you your money,' and he pretended to kick me*." (A Veteran Whip, 15 Sep 1913, p.14)

Exciting Incidents
"No, *my driving career was not free from exciting incidents* ... There were no brakes on the coaches in those days, and when those heavy vehicles, sometimes carrying 25 passengers, gathered impetus it was not easy to pull them up." (A Veteran Whip, 20 Sep 1913, p.40)

1870-1875 Williamson's Corio Hotel, Hood's coachbuilding and clocktower in the market square, Geelong (American & Australasian Photographic Company)—Courtesy State Library of New South Wales

ca. 1920 Cobb and Co.'s Royal Mail (W. Roy Millar & Sons, photographer)—Courtesy State Library Victoria

Chapter Four

Drivers

E - G

Jehu and his team

"I wonder whether any persons have noticed the seemingly perfect understanding that exists between an experienced driver, who is also a lover of horses, and his team. Well, I have, and gained much pleasure, and have acquired a better knowledge of human nature—yes, and horse nature, too. This driver knows the temperament and ability of each horse. The off-wheeler may be disposed to be doing more than his fair share. A slight pressure on the rein, and *Easy does it, old man,* from a canter to a steady trot immediately follows. A slacking in the traces of the near-side leader, a reminder is at hand, just a flick of the whip over his hindquarters, with the admonition, Bob, get a move on, and the chap is into, his collar, again, and so on. Meanwhile the man at the wheel is engaged in some story of the road; yet his eyes are ever on his charges. As a rule each horse, has his assigned position in the team—it may be a 'poler' off-side or a 'leader' near-side. Circumstances may make it necessary to change positions. I have noticed a 'poler' moved to a leader's position look round to see how the chap that has taken his place is getting on." (Memories of Myponga, 28 Oct 1927, p.13)

1912 Cobb & Co. Coach No. 118, between Yuleba to Surat, driver Fred Richards
—Courtesy Queensland Museum Collection

Supporting evidence:

Eales, Dan
1883 "A SMART DRIVER.—A correspondent who is an eye-witness of the occurence described, writes as follows:—Dan Eales, the driver of Cobb's coach which left Germanton for Little Billabong on the morning of Friday, the 31st August last, was guilty of conduct worth recording. Dan had two passengers, both of whom on account of the cold and rain preferred the inside of the coach. When about two miles from the Little Billabong post office the off-rein of the off-side horse got adrift from the bit. Dan tried to steer his team (only two) square up against the fence, but in vain. Seeing nothing for it but a smash as things were, Dan jumped off on the near-side with the reins in his hands, and despite the fact that he was encumbered with the usual coachee's three overcoats and muffler, he managed to keep his legs and get to the near-side horse's head. By this time the horses had a full head of steam, and it was only by sticking most pluckily to the near-side nag—who, by the way, is the hero of half-a-dozen smashes—that Dan managed to steer clear of the trees and at last to steady the team. At this time the insides, feeling the trap swirl round in an unaccountable way, looked out, and to their surprise and no slight alarm beheld Dan being lifted off his legs and occasionally shaken like a rat by the gentle quadruped he was trying to stop. Altogether it was a display of presence of mind, pluck, and activity, such as is but seldom witnessed, and Dan Eales well earned the thanks of his passengers. But for his admirable conduct, too, Cobb and Co. would no doubt have had to pay a swinging bill of damages for dead or damaged passengers." (No Title, 14 Sep 1883, p.13)

Eastley, William
1939 "Pioneer Driver ... one of Cobb and Co's drivers. He drove from Coonamble to Dubbo for many years, and from Carcoar to Blayney and Cowra. He had lived at Lithgow for the past 30 years." (Pioneer Driver, 10 Feb 1939, p.2)

Eddie, Nathan
1925 "COBB AND COMPANY'S COACHES. From the far-off torrid Gulf of Carpentaria to the wind-swept littoral of Bass' Straits, spread the tentacles of a mighty organization, which, in the zenith of its fame, appeared monopolistic, yet presaging nought but good; the acme of efficiency in its extensive ramifications, with not a, scintilla of nefariousness to mar its onward course; moulded on the highest conception of idealistic foresight; of lofty aims, and imbued with an intensity of patriotism, that, in comparison with that ruling in these days of dubious standards of ethics, stand revealed as a model of amazing incongruity.

No form of mental analysis; no meticulous course of deductions;, no regular channel of erudition exists that could assess, with any reasonable modicum of accuracy, the immensity of its services in the progress and development of the three, and perhaps four, of the present States of the Commonwealth of Australia. Victoria, New South Wales, Queensland and in a minor degree, Western Australia, owe much to the existence of that famous and outstanding firm of Cobb and Co. founded at Melbourne in 1853 by four young Americans. Freeman Cobb (then 23 years of age), James Swanson, John Murray Peck and John Lamber — the latter retired and was succeded by a compatriot, Anthony Blake. This opportunity-seizing quartette secured the necessary coaches from Abbott Downing of Co., of Connecticut, at a cost of 3000 dollars each.

The first coach, under the aegis of Cobb and Co., left the Criterion Hotel, Melbourne, at 6 a.m. on Monday, January 30th, 1854, en route to Bendigo (110 miles). Gold had been discovered at Ballarat in August, 1851, and at Bendigo in December, 1852. The gold fever had smitten hard the early and meagre population of Melbourne, and few begrudged the payment of the £5 fare and the tedious journey out over the Dividing Range, traversing the tortuous track through the notorious and heavily timbered Black Forest, Forest Creek, Mt. Alexander (now Castlemaine) into Bendigo, the land of hope for the thousands attracted to this shrine of Croesus. Thus was the genesis of this epoch-making and momentous organization launched, an organization that owed its stupendous success to the administrative genius, the amazing intuition, the resolute courage, the indomitable energy and dogged determination of James Rutherford, the governing director of Messrs. Cobb and Co., Ltd., for over 50 years, who died in harness at Mackay (Q.) on 13th September, 1911, aged 84 years. An American by birth, he was undoubtedly one of Australia's greatest patriots, and his was an organizing genius of exceptional merit. Nor did he confine his activities for good to those directly associated with transport services—his unparalleled mental vigour and versatility of purpose were almost uncanny. In the words of Milton, it may be truly said of him —*Thou in our wonder and astonishment, Hast built thyself a live-long monument.* Fifty-five years ago this rampageous firm of pioneer transport contractors, in Victoria, New South Wales and Queensland, harnessed up daily, for their coaching services, 6000 horses; the teams covered 28,000 miles weekly; the firm received £95,000 a year for mail subsidies, while the aggregate pay roll worked out at £100,000 a year! Thus is it possible to portray the immensity of operation of this wonder fully enterprising organization.

THE BIRTH OF THE GOLD INDUSTRY. In the van of every big gold rush in the three eastern States since the early sixties, Cobb and Co. made it possible to complete the development of the newly-found fields by ensuring access; by providing transit under escort for the precious gold; by making provision for the conveyance of officials and carriage of mails and parcels. By blazing the track into almost inaccessible outback tracts, the service provided by Cobb and Co. invariably proved the forerunner of permanent railway communication, and formed roads ... The history of Victoria, in this respect, had its counterpart in New South Wales, Queensland, and, in a more circumscribed sphere, in Western Australia, where, in 1895, Cobb and Co., directed by Charlie Kidman (a brother of Sir Sidney Kidman) and Jimmy Nicholls (an old Riverina driver of Cobb's) operated between Geraldton and Mullewa and Southern Cross and Coolgardie and Hannan's Find (Kalgoorlie) ...

NEW SOUTH WALES INVADED ... 1862 ... Bathurst ... On the driving box of the first four coaches to enter Bathurst were James Rutherford (destined to become one of the greatest benefactors and residents of that 'city' of the plains'), Frank Whitney, Hal. Hamilton and Charlie Bissell ... Jack Fagan, the driver of Cobb's coach on 15th June, 1862, at the time of the hold-up by Frank Gardiner's gang of bushrangers at Eugowra

... became the owner of Sunny Ridge Station, in the Carcoar district ... W. H. Hampson, Robt. Bates, Eddie Nathan (afterwards Mayor of Orange), Jake Russert, H. Barnes, Jim Breen, Dan Mayne ... Jim Nairn, Jack Barry and Joe Thompson were prominent drivers in the service of Cobb and Co ...

Cobb and Co. obtained their first footing in Queensland in 1865 ... Heat waves and dust and droughts; rain, mud and floods made little difference. Some of the heaviest floods on record did not deter the intrepid coach drivers from the performance of their duty to the Government and the isolated pioneers of outback—they were prepared to, and did, face the gravest dangers that assailed them at times, often at the peril of their lives. Decimating droughts, with their long dry stages, found Cobb and Co. playing the game with all their proverbial pluck and determination—not once did they throw up the sponge and jeopardize or disorganize the coach service and mails. The roaring, all-devouring bush fires that periodically followed in the wake of a flush season, with under-stocked holdings, at times mercilessly swept all before them on the broad open western plains. There were men on the driver's seat of Cobb and Co.'s coaches who feared nothing, and who grimly saw their mission through, regardless of the consequences. Many cases of sticking up of the Queensland mail coaches by armed desperadoes during '67, '68 and '69 are recorded—yet the service was maintained with a clock-like regularity. West, nor'west, and south, found Cobb and Co. extending out their fine and deeply appreciated conveniences—unquestionably, they aided settlement and development in that country of distances, as no other factor in its history has done has done or was capable of doing.

KNIGHTS OF THE WHIP. What fine men, those who wielded the whip for Cobb and Co., were! They left records, not humanly possible to equal or excel. Jim McCormack, on the Cunnamulla to Barringun route, cracked his whip for an unbroken period of 30 years; anyone who has seen the Warrego in flood will appreciate his record of endurance. J. Thompson ran the Thomson down for 16 years, on the Hughenden to Muttaburra run. Old Bill White headed his 'leaders' from Croydon out to Georgetown during a big stretch of the 30 years spent with the firm. From humid Cooktown, out over the rough barren country to the Palmer, Mick Brady faced the spears of the notoriously hostile myalls, and the intense heat and flies of the Peninsula for 17 long years. One of the most noted of characters as a whip in 'the sixties' was Ned Devine ... he was deputed to carry as his distinguished passengers the Duke of Edinburgh and suite. One could go on indefinitely recounting many such similar records. A number of these old drivers did well for themselves—Hiral Barnes became very wealthy, George Adams, of Tattersall's fame, was driver, and subsequently road inspector; Fred Richards became a road inspector, so did Ted Palmer and Tom Gallagher; Jno. Robertson and Frank Whitney became men of affluence ... Their old 'C.O.B.' brand, known throughout the length and breadth of the continent, is now the registered brand of Thomas Purcell, owner of Galway Downs Station, and other holdings on the Cooper.

Many old Queenslanders will remember that 47 mile trip south from Yeulba (on the main Southern and Western railway, 281 miles from Brisbane) to Surat, an old-fashioned, straggling hamlet on the Balonne River, passing en route Duffs and Tinawon. Ten hours to do the trip, and one pound for the fare, unless fortunate enough to secure a box seat, when one willingly paid the extra half-crown for it, if available. It was not a pleasure trip, as the first part of the journey was through prickly pear country, of a low sandy, ridgy character, and was by no means appealing! Nearing Surah, belar scrub, sheoak and coolibah grew intermittently, while the black soil flats provided the food for language, in wet seasons. The usual team consisted of seven (four polers and three leaders), two changing stages, one at Mainbilla and one at Waldegrave, were provided. Incidentally the numerous letter-boxes en route spelt slight delays for the delivery of mails and parcels. The extra trip down the river to St. George entailed an 80 mile additional run, a thirteen hours' possesion of a coach seat, and a 30/- disbursement for an ordinary fare. Jimmy Davidson, Bill Mitchell, Bill Lumley and the Palmer Bros, made their whip-cracks re-echo, for many years, on the old Yeuba coach run with Cobb and Co. The firm still retain their stores and motor mail connection at Yeulba, Surat, St. George, Thallon and Dirranbandi, a mere skeleton of their past glory. Mr. W. Ross Munro, of Boombah Station, near St. George, is one of its directorate.

During this week, the last of Cobb and Co's coaches, the old Yeulba mail coach referred to, was handed over by the Queensland Government to the Commonwealth, for permanent sanctuary in the Federal capital of Canberra. An official, though comparatively insignificant, recognition of the glorious and unparalleled national service of one of the finest pioneering institutions ever founded under the Southern Cross. Its great accomplishments are unassessable, and its incomparable records should be engraven in gold, for the enlightenment of the future generations. In the years to come, at Canberra, many will gaze abstractedly at that romance-saturated old 'battler,' the last glorious relic of a once mighty organization, so indissolubly intertwined with Australia's early progress and prosperity. To them another out-of-plumb head stone of a neglected, weed-strewn graveyard, covering the forgotten records of its dead— the dead they knew not! Not understanding—they will pass on!! To those its significance will be lost—to those it will be just .... just a ludicrous-looking old coach!!! — W.D.E. (The Stirring Days of Cobb and Co., 10 Apr 1925, pp.28)

Edgcombe, F. & Edgecombe, Frank ... 1930 See Alder, Amos

Edwards, Bob ... 1930-1940s See Allan, (Christian name unknown)

Edwards, James
1883 "ACCIDENT TO COBB AND CO.'S COACH ... GORDON, Tuesday ... An accident befell Cobb's coach, which runs between Gordon and Egerton daily, at two o'clock this afternoon. Tho horse bolted, and turning a sharp corner broke a shaft, and overturned the vehicle. The driver, James Edwards, was thrown out, but uninjured. Fortunately no passengers were in the coach." (Accident to Cobb and Co.'s Coach, 18 Apr 1883, p.3)

Edwards, James H.
1949 "Veterans Recall Pioneering Days. When the first dinner of Cobb & Co.'s old coach drivers was given at the Exhibition in Lord Stradbroke's Motor show year of 1925 there were

110 drivers present. Some brought along their old clay pipes to smoke. Yesterday, 35 drivers were in the gathering of over 40 in the Aquarium dining room at a 2 p.m. dinner and, although two of them were 88 years old, not one clay pipe appeared. James Laity, who made a speech about old Castlemaine days, and William Cooper were the oldest drivers present. Mr. Percy Rogers, president of the Chamber of Automotive Industries, was host. Oldest guest was A. J. Sullivan, 93 years 7 months, born in Melbourne in 1855, and still an expert mathematician. Bill Kinnear, saddler, who is 88, was another guest. Motor Man, too. The veteran James H. Edwards, who is 81, produced documentary evidence of a unique career. He drove for Cobb and Co., Ballarat, up to 1889, took out his locomotive driver's certificate in 1909, and, for 14 years, from 1919, drove electric trains. His motorman's certificate, issued by the Victorian Railways, is a pioneering link with modern transport. Tom Vines recalled steeple chases in which he rode at Warrnambool and Hamilton over 50 years ago. I went down that way the other day, he told the gathering. But the roads were a sad sight. Too many motor cars." (Veterans Recall Pioneering Days, 20 May 1949, p.2)

Edwards, James Henry
1952 "Cobb Driver Dies. An old coach driver, whose associations with Cobb and Co dated back to the seventies, died at Middle Park recently. He was Mr. James Henry Edwards, who joined the Victorian Railway after the steam train ousted Cobb's coaches from the State highways. Then, in turn, he saw the introduction of the electric and diesel powered trains. Edward's father was manager of Vines and McPhee, the firm which controlled Cobb and Co in the Western District." (Cobb Driver Dies, 18 Oct 1952, p.2)

Edwards, J. H ... 1919 See Aisbett, E. J.

Edwards, Jim ... 1937 See Atkinson, Frank

Egan, (Christian name unknown) ... 1878 See Doyle, (Christian name unknown)

Egan, Charlie
"The old drivers to at last lay down their reins were: Charlie Egan who drove Cobb's last coach on the Mitchell-Bollon run 1920." (Communications Across the Generations, Read 1971, p.188)

Egan H.
1919 "Driver, district employed: Western District" (Annual report / Cobb & Co.'s Old Coach Drivers' Association, 1919, p.7)

Egan, Mick
1928 "In these days of magnificent six cylinder Hudsons, Buicks, etc., it is interesting to read of the hardships endured by bishops and priests in the outback districts a quarter of a century ago ... some particulars appearing in the 'Freeman' in April ... the thermometer racing above 120 degrees ... *Early next morning Mick Egan, Cobb and Co's renowned driver, drove his team of five horses up to the presbytery and the Bishop and Father Carroll took their seats. Mick cracked his whip and the prancing horses plunged forward and the party were on the Muttaburra-road long before the rising sun had tinged the sky with its bars of gold. It was one of the hottest days on record, and going over the plains the breeze seemed to come from a furnace.*" (Looking Backwards, 11 Oct 1928, p.16)

1950 See also Hickson, Harry

Egan, Nick ... 1917 See Wright, Bob

Ellis, H ... 1893 See Aitken, James

Elms/Elmes, Thomas (Tom)

1870 "The state of the weather interferes most inconveniently with the transmission of the inland mails, and human life is not unfrequently jeopardised, and even sacrificed, in performing the arduous service which mailmen are called to undergo. Cobb's coach from Brisbane to Gympie started on Monday morning, and the driver, Thomas Elms, when he reached the Glass-house Mountains stage, found the creeks so swollen that he had to abandon the coach, and swim across the creeks with the leading horses. He then went on with the mail-bags in the saddle as far as Coochin Creek, and tried to cross, but could not do so. He made several attempts, even at the risk of his life, and at last succeeded, though not without considerable venture. Our telegram informs us, too, that the Gympie and Brisbane coach was prevented by the flood from crossing Deep Creek. The drivers of the coaches are certainly worthy of commendation for the plucky manner in which they endeavour to carry out their instructions. Often, at the risk of life, have they done so, and this is especially the case on the Gympie-road, which is undoubtedly the worst in the colony for coach traffic." (Current Topics, 5 Feb 1870, p.2)

1929 See also Amies, Tom; 1936 Richardson, Bill; 1935 Conroy, James (Jim)

Empson, Mrs. (Took the reins)
1887 "A Croydon (Queensland) paper reports that on the 27th September Cobb's coach, on the way up to Croydon, stopped near Rocky Creek and the driver and some of the passengers got down, leaving only a young man on the box seat in charge of the reins, and Mrs. Empson and a young lady inside. The horses took fright, and suddenly bolted down the road at full gallop. The young man on the box got frightened, and was quite powerless to check them. Mrs. Empson seeing this, with great pluck and at no small risk, managed to climb outside the coach on to the box, and when there seized the reins, and succeeded in pulling up the runaway team. While doing so they turned short round, and breaking off the swingle bars, three leaders dashed off into the bush, and two of them were not recovered ; the third one was caught, and the remainder of the stage had to be accomplished with only three horses. Had it not been for Mrs. Empson's pluck and presence of mind there is no doubt that a very serious accident would have occurred." (Ball's Head, 26 October 1887, p.7)

Enright, Michael ... 1901 Anderson, Thomas (Tom)

Evans, E.
1935 "The death occurred at Cootamundra on Friday, of Mr. E. Evans, 73, a former alderman of the Municipality. Before joining the railway service he was a driver for Cobb and Co., on the Monaro routes." (Obituary, 8 Jun 1935, p.2)

Everett, J ... 1919 See Aisbett, E. J.

Eyre, Ben
1938 "ON THE TRACK … OLD WHIPS OF COBB AND CO …Watching Jehu with the ribbons … Now, there was Ben Eyre—he might still be alive—but it's a long time since I last saw him in Longreach. Away back—I think it was in '94—Ben Eyre was driving the mail coach on the Birdsville-Windorah track … He was a good all-round bushmen, knew something about droving, and could break in any horse that was brought to him." (On the Track, 31 Aug 1938, p.11)

Fagan/Fegan, John (Jack/Old Jack)
1903 "FEGAN AND FAGAN. TO THE EDITOR OF THE SHOALHAVEN NEWS. Sir, — Re your par in last Saturday's News about the Hon. J. L. Fegan. He was not the driver of Cobb & Co's. coach when Ben Hall and party stuck it up at Eugowra. The driver was John Fagan. Fagan kept the Royal Hotel at Carcoar after, leaving Cobb and Co., and was also the proprietor of the mail coaches from Blayney to Cowra. He also owned a email sheep run at Mandurama. At the time I knew, him he owned the Royal Hotel, but had let it. When the railway was opened from Blayney to Harden he gave up the coaches and then went to live on his sheep run at Mandurama, and still lives there, I believe. I have often heard his cronies 'chaff' him about that hat and whip.— Yours, etc., SHOALHAVEN RESIDENT." (Correspondence, 11 Apr 1903, p.3)

"Jack became particularly famous as the driver of the escort coach bailed up in June, [18] '62, by Gardner's gang at Eugowra Rocks." (The Lights of [?]obb & Co., 17 Jul 1935, p.131) "Jack Fagan, the driver of Cobb's coach on 15th June, 1862, at the time of the hold-up by Frank Gardner's gang of bushrangers at Eugowra, and which resulted in two of the gold escort being shot (Sergeant Jim Condell and Senior-Constable Henry Moran) Turner alias Manns was subsequently executed for the affair" (The Stirring Days of Cobb and Co., 10 Apr 1925, p.28) "all the others had narrow escapes, the driver having a bullet through his tall Yankee hat. The horses bolted, and overturned the coach, and the bushrangers had an easy task in securing the booty." (Coaching in Australia, 1917, p.25) "Old Jack throughout his life retained and treasured his big Californian hat and coat showing bullet holes in them as a reminder of Gardner's intentions." (The Lights of [?]obb & Co., 17 Jul 1935, p.131)

1923 Robinson, James (Robbie); 1925 Eddie, Nathan; 1932 See also Breen, Jim (Jimmy); 1935 Whitney, William Franklin (Frank); 1935 Conroy, James (Jim); Eugowra Escort Robbery

Farrar, J … 1919 See Aisbett, E. J.

Farrell, Pat … See Appendix 1.6

Fawcett/Forcett, Sir Alexander (Bob/Alec)
1935 "Mr Smiley has in his possession a whip on which is inscribed the letters 'F. W. Haines.' Mr Smiley said that it belonged to a coach driver named Bob Fawcett who one day presented it to Mr Fred Haines, the son of a squatter at Deniliquin. When asked why he was giving the whip away Fawcett explained that he would not drive the coach any more as he had received word from England that his brother had died. He was the next of kin and had become Sir Alexander Fawcett. He returned to England, and for many years had kept up correspondence with Mr Haines." (Veteran Coach and Coachman, 8 Jun 1935, p.24)

1884 See also Hole, (Christian name unknown); 1929 Mesbitt, Bill

Ferguson, Jack … 1947 See Richards, J. Frederick (Fred)

Fergusson, J … 1919 See Aisbett, E. J.

Field, Bob … 1929 See Corbett, Alec.

Fillery, E.
1893 "A COACH ACCIDENT. Cobb and Co.'s coach from Wilcannia arrived at Louth on Monday morning 19 hours late. The driver (E. Fillery) and three passengers had a most miraculous escape on Saturday night. It appears that since the river has risen the coach has been compelled to travel along the top of an embankment which is erected across the mouth of the Nelyambo dam. When going over this dangerous pass a bolt came out of the pole disconnecting the two leading horses from the pole. They made a dash forward, pulling the driver off the coach and the fore-wheel passing over his chest. The remaining horses bolted, the passengers (three men) being thrown out. The horses swerving off the track, rushed down the embankment about 40ft., smashing the coach to atoms. One horse was turned over, and lay jammed in between pieces of the broken coach. Driver Fillery was much hurt through the wheel passing over him, but was able the next day to drive his passengers on to Tilpa. Most miraculously the passengers all escaped with only a severe shaking. Had they not been thrown out before the coach went over the embankment, they must have been seriously injured, or probably all killed. They were compelled to camp alongside the dam all night, and next morning obtained a springcart from Nilyambo by which the passengers and mails were brought on. On Thursday last week some excitement was occasioned in Louth by the horses bolting down the street with this same coach, one of the bars having broken. Had there not been a skilful driver on the box an accident would most probably have happened." (A Coach Accident, 1 Apr 1893, p.4)

Finemore, John
1926 "Finemore, one of the old Cobb and Co. coach-drivers on the Monaro. Born at Parramatta in the [18] fifties, he arrived in Cooma while a stripling fifty years ago, and was employed in the mail-coach stables, and subsequently being elevated to the position of coach-driver from Goulburn to Braidwood, Queanbeyan, Bungendore, Cooma and Bombala. Deceased was regarded as one of the most reliable jehus in the State, and was popular amongst all his associates. The advance of the railways dispensed with most of the mail coaches, and Mr. Finemore made for Shepardstown, where he earned a livelihood with his horse and dray until he became ill with dropsy. Kind friends did all that possible in the way of nursing and attention to make his last days pleasant." (Obituary, 6 May 1926, p.2)

Fitzpatrick, Jimmy … See Appendix 1.6

Flannery, James
1925 "OBITUARY. ADELONG.—The death occurred on Sunday of Mr. James Flannery, aged 80. He was connected with Cobb and Co. for many years, when the Adelong gold field was booming, and drove coaches also between Temora and Cootamundra until the advent of the railway. In later years Mr. Flannery drove coaches between Cootamundra, Gundagai, and Adelong. His wife predeceased him five months ago." (Obituary, 1 Sep 1925, p.2)

Fogarty, F ... 1937 See Preston, R.

Fogarty, F. E.
1933 "Mr. F. E. Fogarty, of Garden Vale, has a remarkable record. His driving career lasted 35 years, during which he pioneered the Broken Hill trails when the rush to that town began, and in all that time he never met with a serious accident of any kind. He afterwards became a mail contractor and drove a motor car. *Give me, a horse anytime*, he said. *Start with a team of horses and you know you will get there.*" (Former Cobb and Co. Drivers, 21 Jun 1933, p.11)

Forbes, Jack ... 1930 See Alder, Amos

Foreman, Jack ... 1935 See Conroy, James (Jim); Appendix 1.6

Forsyth, A.
1884 "A very serious accident occurred to Cobb and Co.'s Deniliquin and Moulamein coach … The driver of the coach, which also had a very heavy cargo of luggage, was A. Forsyth. After the coach had proceeded about 10 miles from Deniliquin it ran against a stump, which smashed the pole, and threw the driver out onto his head … After an hour's delay and the recovery of the horses, a fresh start was made with the same driver … the coach came into collision with a tree, completely, smashing the vehicle, and throwing the passengers with great force out on to the ground … The whole town is reported to have turned out and gone to the scene of the accident … Forsyth is a fresh driver on this line, this being his second trip, and he had not quite recovered from a broken jaw, the result of an accident." (Serious Coach Accident, 15 Apr 1884, p.2)

Fossett, Alick ... 1925 See Jones, Bill

Foster, Jim
1911 "COACH ACCIDENT. THE DRIVER SEVERELY SHAKEN. WINTON, November 22. Cobb and Co.'s coach left for Longreach this morning with seven passengers, and when a few miles out the leading reins broke at the coupling, and the leading horses became beyond control. The driver, Jim Foster, was thrown from the box and severely shaken, the pole of the coach was broken, and the harness damaged. The passengers escaped without injury." (Coach Accident, 23 Nov 1911, p.5)

1917 See also Richardson, W.

Fowler, E. J ... 1937 See Preston, R.

Fowler, Ted ... 1930 See Alder, Amos

Fox, George
1931 "TAMWORTH TO GUNNEDAH. In the days, of Cobb and Co. we used to pay 7s 6d for a twelve-miles' lift from Adelong to Tumut in the old red and yellow coach with its leather-leaved springs, with good old George Fox steering his old prads up over the sweetbriar-embroidered gap road to his destination in about two hours. George is still aboard the planet, I learn with much pleasure, and is driving his team at eighty-odd years with the same old dash at Gundagai." (Australianities, 27 Oct 1931, p.10)

1936 "Cobb & Co. Driver. The death occurred at Gundagai on Wednesday of Mr. George Fox, 90, one of the oldest district identities, and a link with Cobb & Co. Born in Somersetshire, he came to Australia at the age of 12. He commenced his driving career at 18 and joined Cobb and Co. in 1877. He was one of the first drivers between Gundagai and Cootamundra, Bowning and Adelong. Fox was never molested by bushrangers, but met

1887 Cobb & Co.'s mail coach on the Port Douglas-Herberton Road, Queensland—Courtesy State Library of Queensland

Morgan on one trip near Wagga, and Moonlight and his gang near Gundagai." (Cobb & Co. Driver, 18 Jul 1936, p.4)

1925 See also Paine, William; 1932 Clark, Billy

Fraser, George
1932 "GEORGE FRASER. George Fraser, 79, a native of Dungog, died at the home of his daughter, Mrs. E. Fox, Tamworth (says an exchange). He drove Cobb and Co. coaches from Armidale to Bendemeer, Glen Innes to Inverell and Tenterfield, and was the only driver of a team of five piebalds. He was for 25 years a councillor of the Severn Shire." (Obituary, 16 Dec, 1932, p.5)

Frayer, A. H ... 1919 See Aisbett, E. J.

Free, A ... 1937 See Preston, R.

Freerer, (Christian name unknown)
1930-1940s See Allan, (Christian name unknown)

French, Christie ... 1917 See Wright, Bob

Frisco, Ming
1922 "Once on the long road from Cobar a German and a Dane sitting on the back seat of the coach were saying nasty things to one another for 25 miles, or more. Then Ming Frisco, the driver, took a hand, pulled up the coach, and ordered them to get down and fight it out. They got down and sat on opposite sides of the road, and nothing would induce either to leave his 'corner.' Sarcasm and exhortation alike were unavailing. *I'd drive on and leave them there*, said Ming, *if I didn't have to collect their fares at Nyngan*. And for the rest of the journey they were quite courteous and friendly." (When Cobb & Co was King, 16 Apr 1922, p.15)

Frost, James (Old Jim Frost)
1926 "Old Cobb & Co. Driver. LAST LIVING LINK WITH COACHES. Mr. James Frost, who is 91 years of age, and resides with his daughter at Thirroul, is hailed as the oldest living driver of Cobb and Co's. coaches ... old Jim Frost drove on various routes, including Bathurst, to Sydney, and Forbes to Orange. He knew Ben Hall and his gang well." (Old Cobb & Co. Driver, 9 Aug 1926, p.4)

1926 "Mr. Jim Frost, Last of the original Cobb & Co. Coach Drivers. *And when the camps were dreaming. And fires began to pale, Through rugged ranges gleaming, Would come the Royal Mail.* Mr. Jim Frost, father of the well known representative ... for Singer Sewing Machines, has seen 91 summers and still going strong. He is now the last of the old original Cobb & Co. drivers, and was called Old Jim Frost when on the roads 30 year ago, and he is still 'Old Jim'—not much older, save for the marks on the calendar ... Jim was born in Penrith and went to school between the years 8 and 10 ... learned to read when full grown. His primer was the Bible, the only publication no one wanted until he had read it. Learned to write with charred stick until he was able to buy the orthodox tools ... a sister, Mrs. Barlow ... Oldest son is a stalwart youth of 70, youngest lad 40 ... He was the first N.S.W. man to earn a shilling of the late James Rutherford's money after Cobb and Co. came to the colony ... George (Tallersall) Adams was one of his fellow whips ... Dan Mayne ... was another of the men he drove with. Jim Conroy was also one of them ... He drove from Bathurst to Penrith and over other routes ... bushranger ... Ben Hall ... used to bring them what they required in supplies and papers to be left at

ca. 1915 Joe Hirschberg's coach, Croydon to Forsayth—Courtesy Queensland Museum Collection

prearranged places, with news of the movements of the police ... not so considerate of some drivers ... held up Tom Hunter ... Jack Fagan was ambushed at Eugowra Rocks in June, 1862 ... One of the events of the gold days of Gulgong was Cobb and Co's race ... Old Jim drove for the company and won ... But all this is behind the old chap. His driving days are done. For him now only the whip of the ribbons of dreams." (Mr. Jim Frost, 6 Jul 1926, p.2)

1928 "OLD WESTERN PIONEER. EARLY COACH DAYS. The following interview with one of Cobb and Co's. old western coach drivers is supplied by Mr. Jas. O'Donnell: As I passed through Thirroul a few days ago I dropped in to have a word with Mr. J. Frost, who resides with his son at that town. The name Frost to the old Western men must set them thinking back 50 or 60 years ago, when James Frost, one of the smartest coachdrivers in New South Wales ... During the course of an interesting chat he said: *For 30 years I was driving for Cobb and Co. My stages were from Bathurst to Orange. I remember well the day that Muggerage was murdered on the road between Guyong, and Bathurst. I drove to Forbes in the roaring 60's when Frank Gardiner and Ben Hall held the road.* He added that in those far-off days one had to hold his tongue—and heard nothing and saw less as to the movements of the bushrangers. He mentioned many of the old drivers—Jack Fagen, Jimmy Little, the Keagans (2), Joe Strickland, and the Coombers, also Pat Gilligan. Fifty years ago he drove the coach from Orange to Parkes, via Molong ...

In those days they used to change horses at the Freemason's Hotel. He asked after, and mentioned the names of old hotelkeepers from Molong to Parkes—Denny Toohey, Cottingham, Mrs. Packham (Bumberry), Geo. Peck, and Billy Williams ... At big sporting events in olden days James Frost's services were always requested to drive the big buses—seven and eight in hand ... When asked of the great progress made to-day with regard to motor cars, flying machines, wireless, etc., he replied: *Wonderful! Wonderful! In my day I was the wireless. I often had 40 or 50 people waiting along my stage to hear news as to who won the boat race or what won the Melbourne Cup.*

But, do not forget those days had their compensation. There was not the hurry or bustle, but the people were kind and hospitable, and helped one another. When the railway opened to Forbes in 1893 and Cobb and Co. began to disband ... He was a very reliable driver and the travelling public had great confidence in him. He was always kind-hearted and obliging, and thousands of little acts of courtesy by getting small articles for 'this and that one' are to his credit. To many a footsore traveller he gave a lift, when not overloaded." (Old Western Pioneer, 11 Aug 1928, p.16)

1929 See also Corbett, Alec.

Frost, Jim (Jimmy) ... 1929 See Corbett, Alec.; Appendix 1.6

Frost, Tom ... 1929 See Corbett, Alec.

Gales, A.

1920 "ON THE ROADS WITH COBB & CO Apart from being stuck up by robbers, which now rarely happens, coach drivers have had many sensatioual experiences in traversing the thousand rugged roads of the country. I was waiting for the mail at Tibooburra, N.S.W., one evening when word was brought that the coach had been swept away in a creek down the road— an exciting event in that dry corner. Four horses were drowned, the coach partly wrecked, but the mail bags were recovered later along the channel. There had been little rain on the road, but a storm had dropped a deluge on the hills at the head of the creek. In that quarter the duststorm often enlivens the way. Once the Hungerford-Bourke coach was blown over and dragged on top of the driver (Scott). The one passenger escaped unhurt, and had to repair a broken pole and other damage before the journey could be resumed. Another flood disaster happened about the same time on the Braidwood-Jerriga-road. When crossing the Colang [?] the horses took fright, and team and coach were swept down stream. A man, who happened to be on the opposite bank, saved the horses, but some of the mail was lost.

The bush fire has to be reckoned with, too. Many a wild race the coach-driver has had with the rushing flames, and narrow escapes from falling trees and branches in burnt bush. When flames are rapidly closing on a narrow road, and there is no escape but straight ahead, passengers get some thrills in the dash through smoke and cinders. On the Glen-Wills line, in February, 1905, the coach and load were destroyed, and three horses and an unlucky swagman named Tom McBride, who had been picked up a couple of miles back, were burnt to death. The team had been jogging along a cutting on the side of a hill when broad sheets of flame suddenly leaped over the road and enveloped it. The driver, Arthur Kilpatrick, who was severely injured, escaped by crawling into Lightning Creek.

Once on Walhalla-Traralgon road (Vic.), while Driver Billy Bain and two male passengers were in the Copper [?] Hotel at Cooper's Creek, leaving woman and three children in the coach, the horses bolted, and for half mile galloped along the edge of a precipice. The woman was jolted out while trying to get hold of the reins, one of the children jumped out, and finally the coach with the other two youngsters went over the cutting and smashed against a tree 20ft. below, which saved it from a drop of hundreds feet. Neither passengers nor horses were injured, and the coach very little damaged.

A more serious results attended a bolt on a road running north from Murwillumbah (N.S.W.) in March, 1902. The brake broke on the steep descent ... to Currunbin Creek, and the coach, driven by Dave Jarvis, was overturned. Of seven passengers aboard one was killed and several injured. The same month the Moruya-Bega (N.S.W.) coach, piloted by A. Gales, and carrying five passengers, had a smash-up in Bega while mail bags were taken into the post office. One passenger, Roger Heffernan, of Moruya, was killed, and Nurse Allen, of Begu Hospital, who was returning from a holiday, had both legs broken. Not long after this happening T. Latewood, driving for Cobb and Co., between Narrabri and Wee Wan (N.S.W.), was left in midstream at Mollee Crossing with a coach-load of passengers through, the pole-hook breaking. The three leading horses dashed up the bank and collided with a tree, one breaking its nose, and another being so badly injured that it had to be shot.

A couple of months later the Port Augusta-Tarcoola (S.A.)

coach was found overturned near Wilgena, Driver Hugh Williams being helpless with fractured collar bone, fractured ribs, and other injuries, and his only passenger, a woman, having both legs broken. Many other coaching sensations occurred that same year 1902, in different parts of the country, including two robberies between Broken Hill and White Cliffs (N.S.W.), £3000 worth of opal in one instance being lifted from the White Cliffs mail while under armed escort, and the escape of three prisoners and a lunatic one night from the Cliffs-Cobar coach. The escapees were shortly recaptured, except one, named Wm. Hall, who exchanged his prison garb for the lunatic's suit before bolting. He was rearrested on a racecourse nine years afterwards.

Even the common gohanna had a finger in the thrills. While the coach was travelling from Albury to Howlong (N.S.W.) a startled lizard ran up the legs of one of the horses, causing a bolt and a smash-up against a tree. About the only thing, that escaped unhurt was the gohanna.—Edinbury Swan." (On the Roads with Cobb & Co., 4 Sep 1920, p.9)

Gallagher, A. D. (Ned) ... 1941 See Chatfield, Harry

Gallagher, James
1895 "QUEENSLAND. (FROM OUR OWN CORRESPONDANT) CHARLEVILLE. June 2. His Excellency the Governor, who was driven by Mr. Gallagher, of Cobb and Co., arrived this afternoon from Bourke, via Cunnamulla." (Queensland, 3 Jun 1895, p.5)

1926 "PERSONOGRAPHS *Let Her Go, Gallagher!* ONE of the hale and hearty old men of Brisbane is Mr. James Gallagher, formerly general manager in North Queensland for the great coaching firm, Cobb and Co ... He and his brother, the late Thomas Gallagher, came to Queensland while they were young men, and both became managers for Cobb and Co., Mr. Tom Gallagher being located in the south-western district, with St. George as one of his chief office centres. Mr. James Gallagher, the 'boss' of many drivers, was himself a splendid whip, and even as manager it was sometimes his pleasure to handle the reins when the District Court judge or any other 'distinguished visitor' was a passenger." (Personographs, 13 Jun 1926, p.10)

Gallagher, John
1917 "Mention here may well be made to the brothers Gallagher, Tom, John and Edward, who from the early 80's were intimately connected with Cobb and Co ... Tom and John, in 1879, took up the mail contract between St. George, the Bollon, Cunnamulla, and Thargomindah. This was a 340 miles run, then the longest in Queensland. In 1881 an arrangement was made to amalgamate this line with the firm of Cobb and Co., which then was in the form of a syndicate. It was then decided to form the whole concern into a limited liability company." (Coaching in Australia, 1917, p.37)

1930 "OBITUARY. The death occurred at St. George on Thursday, of Mr. John Gallagher, at the age of 83 years. The late Mr. Gallagher was an old resident of St. George, and in his youthful days was one of Cobb and Co.'s 'whips,' in the coaching days in Western Queensland. Later he became district manager for the firm and was employed in that capacity till he retired three years ago." (Obituary, 2 Jun 1930, p.18)

Gallagher, Thomas (Tom)
1912 "Mr. Thomas Gallagher, the well-known general manager of the coaching firm of Cobb and Co ... He started with the company as a coach-driver, and there are many people in Australia, and especially in Queensland, who can still remember the 'capable whip' of 'Tom' Gallagher ... in his day he was recognised as one of the most capable drivers in the coaching line." (Messrs. Cobb and Co., 29 Ap 1912)

1917 See also Gallagher, John; 1925 Eddie, Nathan; 1941 Chatfield, Harry

Gardener, Tom ... 1917 See Richardson, W.

Gardiner, (Christian name unknown) (Dad) ... 1898 See Hampton, Al.

Geaghan, Bill ... 1925 See Paine, William

Getson, George
1913 "CROSSING SMASH AT MARSHALLTOWN. COBB'S COACH WRECKED : TWO HORSES KILLED. DRIVER'S MIRACULOUS ESCAPE. A sensational accident occurred at 11.45 last night at the open railway crossing at Marshalltown, where a special goods train from Warrnambool, travelling at the rate of 38 miles an hour, crashed into a covered conveyance and pair of horses belonging to Cobb and Co. Both horses were killed, the vehicle was shattered to pieces, but the driver, George Getson, who resides at 117 Swanston-street, had a miraculous escape from serious injury. He was carried along the line on the cow catcher for about 50 yards, and came out of the smash with only a nasty gash over the head and forehead ... He was proceeding along easily at about six miles an hour, and knew nothing of the approach of a train. When he got on to the crossing the train apparently caught the vehicle full on ... With such destruction all round him, it was a wonderful escape for the driver that he did not meet instant death ... The unfortunate man soon afterwards left in the ambulance for his home. He stated that he was feeling pretty right. Mr. A. N. Vines, proprietor of Cobb and Co., came from his home at Newtown and personally saw to the comfort of his employe ... Getson who is an experienced and careful driver, said he was always on the look-out for trains, and knew their times of arrival at the different crossings. This train, however, was a special. Getson is a married man." (Crossing Smash At Marshalltown, 11 Jan 1913, p.3)

Gilbert, George
1932 "MR. GEORGE GILBERT. On Friday Mr. George Gilbert, an old resident of the district, who had been engaged as a general carrier, passed away after a period of ill-health. Mr. Gilbert was well known throughout the district and also around Bundaberg. He was an old coach driver for Cobb and Co. in the days when Winton was a tent town." (Mr. George Gilbert, 10 Nov 1932, p.23)

Giles, Tom ... 1930 1940s See Allan, (Christian name unknown)

Gill, (Christian name unknown) ... 1910 See Bates, Robert (Silent Bob)

Gillespie, John (Senr.)
1925 "LINK WITH THE PAST. EARLY COBB & CO

DRIVER The death has occurred of Mr. John Gillespie, Senr., one of the oldest residents of the Orange district, at the age of 81 years. The deceased was born at Donegal, Ireland, and came to Australia in 1864. In 1876 he removed to Orange, where he remained for practically the rest of his life. He was one of the early drivers for Cobb and Co., and by his death is removed the last link in the district of the old coaching days. His first engagement was to drive from Orange to Bathurst, the route being reversed at a later period, whilst his final trips included Carcoar. Attracted by the promise of the older mining centre of Carcoar, he relinquished his connection with Cobb and Co., and conducted the White Horse Hotel at that centre for twelve months. He then returned to Orange to take over the old Daniel O'Connell Hotel, in Byng street, and after holding the licenses of various other hotels in the town, gave up the calling some years ago to spend the evening of his days in retirement with his life's partner in the cottage in which he lived. In the earlier days Mr. Gillespie took an active interest in politics, and he was also a prominent member of the Hibernian Society. He leaves a widow and one son." (Link with the Past, 30 Jan 1925, p.2)

Gillespie, W.
1903 "ILFRACOMBE. (From Our Own Correspondent.) Mr. W. Gillespie, who was driving Messrs. Cobb and Co.'s coach from here to Isisford for a considerable time some years since, has returned to his old billet and Mr. E. Jones, whom Mr. Gillespie succeeds on this line, has gone over to Charleville to drive for the same company. Mr. Gillespie was always a popular driver and many old friends are glad to see him back." (Ilfracombe, 10 Jan 1903, p.31)

Gilliam, Fred
1932 John Horton "was offered a job by Mr. Colin Robertson, manager of Cobb and Co.'s Goulburn branch, and gladly accepted, taking over the Goulburn-Yass run in succession to Fred Gilliam, a brother of George Giliam of Ashton's circus fame, who was compelled to resign from Cobb and Co. owing to ill health." (Cobb and Co. Coachman, 21 Nov 1932, p.4)

Gilligan, Pat ... 1929 See Corbett, Alec.

Girdham, Jack ... 1935 See Conroy, James (Jim)

Girdlestone, Walter ... 1921 See Griffen, Chas.

Glasson, H.
1937 "Memories of old coaching days were revived to-day at the unveiling of the headstone over the grave at the Ballarat new cemetery of Edward Devine, once known far and wide in the 'the colony' as 'Cabbage Tree Ned,' most famous of Cobb and Co.'s coach drivers ... assembly ... included many old drivers. Among them were Mr. Frank Smiley (president of Cobb and Co.'s Old Coach Drivers' Association), who once drove in the Western district; Mr. Alf. Partington (secretary), who figured on the Ballarat-Streatham run; Mr. Frank Atkinson, the Aisbett brothers, Mr. Jim Edwards and Mr. Harry Glasson." (Old Coaching Days, 8 Feb, 1937, p.14)

1937 See also Preston, R.

Glasson, Harry ... 1937 See Atkinson, Frank

Glasson, H. C ... 1919 See Aisbett, E. J.

Goode, (Christian name unknown) ... 1934 See Alexander, Jack

Goodfellow, C. A ... 1919 See Aisbett, E. J.

Gordon, Alexander (Alick)
1877 "On Sunday last, says the Southern Argus of March 1, about noon an accident occurred to the mail coach (Cobb and Co 's) from Bowning to Gundagai. As the coach was going down a steep hill about a mile from the latter town the horses suddenly took fright at two women on horseback carrying parasols over their heads. The horses bolted, breaking the king-bolt and taking away the fore-coach with them, and the portion of the coach with the passengers in it went over the side of the road into a paddock a few feet underneath, taking a summersault and landing topsy turvey. The passengers, of which there were three, escaped uninjured, excepting Mr. Solomon, of Albury. Dr. McKillop, of Gundagai, was speedily summoned, and arriving at the scene with as little delay as possible, he discovered that Mr. Solomon had his collarbone broken and his right side severely bruised. The sufferer was conveyed to Mr. Fry's hotel, were the doctor set the broken bone and otherwise afforded relief to his patient. When the agent (Mr. Fry) heard of the mishap he forwarded another coach to bring on the passengers and mails. The driver, Alexander Gordon, was thrown from his seat, and escaped with sundry bruises." (Undaunted v. Midlorn, 6 Mar 1877, p.7)

1925 "It was in the year 1850, when the first sod of the first Australian railway was turned, that Mr. William Paine made his first journey to Gundagai ... Other drivers of those days were 'Billy the Whip.' and 'Paddy the Boy,' and, later, the late Bill Geaghan, George Fox, Alick Gordon and Jimmy Brummy." (Dead At 93, 10 Dec1925, p.5)

Graham, F. S.
1929 "COBB AND CO. KING PASSES On the eve of his 80th milestone, Mr. F. S. Graham died at his home at Oberon. In his hey-day, he was the crack whip between Blarney and Grenfell, and later ran coaches between Oberon and Tarana. A fine old character ... Cobb and Co's, drivers were a type by themselves. They had to be he-men to hold down their jobs." (Cobb and Co. King Passes, 4 Sep 1929, p.1)

Graham, Sam
1930 "It is averred that the first willow tree planted in Bathurst grew from a straight branch which was planted by a police magistrate who had been on circuit at the Oberon court. This gentleman used the willow branch for a switch as he rode on horseback from Oberon to Bathurst ... In the bad old days the Great Western mail was carried by pack-horse from Hartley to Bathurst, twice a week. It went through Oberon, and carried all the mail matter from Sydney to Bathurst and nearly every town of importance in the west. Mr. John Bourke ... was one of the contractors. Two other well-known contractors were Mr. Sam Graham, father of the late Sam Graham, and Mr. J. B. Keen, father of Mr. Ned Kern, of Oberon. Both were residents of Oberon. Mr. Sam Graham was afterwards one of the well-known drivers on Cobb and Co.'s coaches, and is well remembered by many of the old residents of Oberon and Bathurst districts." (Oberon News, 26 Sep 1930, p.6)

Grant, David
1899 "Coach Accident. Driver Killed. Sydney, June 2. A terrible accident occurred on Wednesday night, about 7 o'clock, to the Deniliquin coach. On approaching the Hay bridge the leading horse shied at a lamp on a passing sulky, and the team bolted down an incline towards the river. The coach capsized, and the driver, David Grant, was thrown heavily, and suffered a fractured skull, dying about an hour afterwards. The other occupants of the coach, Bud Dugan (a groom), and Mr. Norton (a passsenger) had a miraculous escape. The latter received slight injuries to one of his legs. The coach was badly damaged, and the mails scattered about. Grant was an old and trusted employee of Cobb and Co., and leaves a widow and four young children, for whom sympathy is felt." (Coach Accident, 2 Jun 1899, p.5)

Green, Jos ... 1917 See Richardson, W.

Greer, (Christian name unknown)
1911 "COACH OVERTURNED. An accident happened on December 30 to Cobb's coach, running between Charleville and Adavale, near Ambathalla Lake (Q.). A man named Campbell, Cobb's groom, at the Range Tank, who was a passenger in the coach, had his leg broken, and Greer, the driver, sustained injuries to his ankle. The accident was caused by the reins breaking. One horse fell, and the others, falling over him, overturned the coach. The coach proceeded to Adavale, conveying Campbell to the hospital there. The services of another driver were obtained." (Coach Overturned, 2 Jan 1911, p.2)

Greer, Jimmy
1955 "The Roll Call of Cobb & Co (By H. J. Bennett, Rocky Creek, Yarraman, Qld.)
The frosty morning clear,
Those hands that held the ribbons,
Belonged to Jimmy Greer.
Hold on Jim ; though they bolt through hell,
Emerge with their hooves aglow,
Steer them straight through the Boombah Gate,
For Good Old Cobb & Co,
Ah; those were the days, I remember,
Trotting along on the plain." (The Roll Call of Cobb & Co, 30 Jun 1955, p.5)

Griffen, Chas.
1921 "JOTTINGS. By J.W.E ... Mr. Chas. Griffen ... *These remarks*, he says, *of the old days may interest a number of your readers as they date back to the year 1864, when my father was the manager of the stables (Cobb & Co.'s) at Nairne, then known as 'Bythorn'. There were no railways this way in those days, and the big coaches were very different to the vehicles one sees nowadays, many of them being hung on leather springs. Passengers for the inside had to board them from side doors, most of them carrying eight persons in fair comfort, three also being accommodated on the 'box' seat, the luggage, which was always limited as much as possible, being strapped on the top and back of the coach. Mr. Ben Rounsevell, who was a son of the pioneer John Rounsevell, in those days had command of all the traffic for the south, and I think he is still living in the city area. He used to periodically come along and inspect the horses, stables, and employees and see that everything was going right.*

Horses, and good ones they were too, were very cheap in the sixties, and nothing was thought of knocking one on the head if it showed signs of failing, some splendid foals being treated thus also, so that the mothers of them could be put to work in the coach without much delay. The animals did not get as much grooming as they do nowadays, and I remember once when my father asked for some brushes and curry combs he was told to use a brush of straw if he wanted to doll his horses up so. It would cost more than a new horse to get a good set of brushes and combs and so there was little of grooming done. Long hay was the chief feed, not much chaff being used, although plenty of bran and oats were supplied, and as often as possible the horses were turned into paddocks at night.

The first of the fine old drivers that I knew was Billy Moyse, and it was he who was selected to act as whip for the Duke of Edinburg [Edinburgh] on his trip through the hills to Strathalbyn. When the coach got here it was pulled up under a big arch of welcome that had been erected across High Street just where Mr. Williams and Mr. Clarke have their shops now, a second one being put up near St Andrew's bridge. While he was here the Prince was interviewed by several of our people, and after a fairly long stay the party went back to the city via Mount Barker. At this time the coaches right through the colony were nearly all run by the great firm of Cobb & Co., who also had the chief contracts for the mails in other colonies, but soon afterwards the South Australian branch was taken over by John Hill & Co., and a new order of things came with the change of the firm, John Hill being a great judge of and as great a lover of horses, and under his rule our coach horses were the finest to be seen in the class of work in Australia.

The principle drivers in my Nairne time were Ike Prater, Ned Rook, Tom Discom, Oliver Lawrence and Billy Dryer. About 1870 my father was transferred to Strathalbyn. The stables then stood near where Mr. Tom Fallon's house now has been erected, though originally they had been situated about a mile out of the town on the Adelaide road. Billy Moyse was one of the drivers on this line then, but he only remained a little while after we came here, going to the Mallala district where he also went in for farming, remaining there till he died a little while ago about the age of 86. He farmed for about twenty years and then for a while went back to Hill & Co., for the spell of the road never deserted him. Ned Rook was also transferred from Nairne, and the two Thompsons, Alf and Bill followed us here. Jark Carbis, Sampson Hall, Fred Crewes, Mat Thornton, Peter Adams, and Billy Drew were other drivers on this line the latter being a sort of travelling inspector for the firm as well. On the Wellington route the chief toolers were Dick Carter, Tom Treloar, Harry Bannear, Jack Simmons, and Billy Morris, and on the Milang route Jim Keough, James Whisson, Bob Northway, Bill Abbott and myself, the overland mail coach, which was a special one three times a week being driven by Walter Girdlestone, whose long late drive was one of the most wearisome in the whole state much as he tried to make it enjoy able for his passengers. They were generally a fine lot these drivers I have mentioned, and of them all I think Mat Thornton was the one who could get most out of his horses, seeming to have a thorough understanding of them in all their moods. Give him a team of colts and nothing would delight him better, and in a few minutes he would have complete control of them though another man would soon have come to grief.

Mr. Griffen alludes to several other drivers who were temporarily on the line, including Jack Alexander, and he closes a very interesting letter by mentioning the fact that connected with the old booking-office (which was first in the building of which Mr. T. Moore's shop forms a part, and after wards in that which is now Elder, Smith & Co.'s office) the late John Downing, Sam Austin, and Jonathan Sanders were the most prominent of the holders of position here as the agents for the firm which for very many years controlled all of the coach traffic of the south. *There were several amateur whips who used to do a good bit of driving in an informal, or perhaps I ought to say in an irresponsible way, the list of them with perhaps the one exception of Charlie Colman being alas now one of men passed on to another existence! Let me see— There was William Colman, who had driven in the Coach Club in his native England, Charles, his son, alluded to above, Dr. Blue, Will Rogers, Alan McFarlane, John McFarland, J. L. Stirling, Archie*

Cooke, oh yes, and another survivor I had overlooked for the moment—Judge Gordon. All of these good old pioneer residents used to get hold of the reins when they did the journey by coach to the city or back, it being an understood thing—arranged do doubt by a little judicious preliminary negotiation that the place of honor on the box seat in their case carry the privilege of relieving the driver for a portion of the trip.

There were very good whips too, the passengers incurring no special risks at their hands. Once—I am only whispering this to a few of my readers whose absolute secrecy I can rely on—once, a lady was allowed to hold the ribbons—once only, for she let go of the reins while taking them over, and for a mile or two the team did some fast work with a leader running free on one side, while a flicking loose rein flapped the heels of the other horses. I was not there at the time, but other passengers said that the language Jack Carbis used with regard to lady drivers for some weeks later was scarcely fit for publication in a Sunday school magazine. I do know this, that never after that incident would the fine old Jehu let any aspirant handle the reins of a team he had in his care. Like the Scotchman of the whiskey story, he 'took nae mair risks'." (Jottings, 15 Sep 1921, p.3)

Grover, Robert H. (Wharparilla Bob)
1933 "OLD COBB AND CO. DRIVER. Born in 1844, when Melbourne was still a village, Mr. Robert Grover, one of the first of the many, famous coach drivers for Cobb and Co., died at his house, Hawthorn Park, Preston, last week. Mr. Grover was a member of Cobb and Co's. Old Drivers' Association. How swiftly time is thinning the ranks of these men, who form a living-link with days when we had no railways, is shown in Mr. Grover's death, it being the 35th. among the members of the association since its last reunion in May, 1930. The average age of its members is 76 years. Mr. Grover was a horse lover from his boyhood, and took a deep interest in the coaches with which he later became associated. He witnessed the landing in Melbourne of the first four American coaches that were used in Victoria, and was on friendly terms with the famous American drivers of the day. Among those were Levi Rich, 'Ike' Haigh, 'Big' Sampson, and also the well-known 'Cabbage-tree' Ned Devine, of Tasmania. Mr. Grover was associated with Dick Harris in driving the first six-horse coaches from Albury to Wagga—the first stage of the Sydney mail." (Old Cobb and Co. Driver, 23 Feb 1933, p.3)

1928 *"Those were the Days!* Seventy Cobb & Co.'s Coach Drivers. *Him ? Pooh ! He's only a metal-road driver; don't take any notice of him !* A mere youngster of sixty years or no, with hardly a grey streak in his black thatch, had presumed to boast a little of the teams he had handled as a coach-driver, and the white-haired old gentleman sitting beside me was properly contemptuous. It was at the Exhibition last night, at the annual dinner given by the Motor Show executive to the surviving coach-drivers of the Cobb and Co. days. There were 70 ripe and happy old boys who sat at the decorated tables in tho Olde Englishe Inn ... Each guest was brimful of yarns and reminiscence, and each was bubbling with excitement, and keen to begin his, 'I remember—'They revelled in 'the days when my beard was black', these white-whiskered, ruddy-faced old chaps. *Yes,* said the old driver beside me, *there were no metalled roads in our day. We had to drive, all day and all night, moon or no moon, over rough bullock tracks, carrying passengers and Her Majesty's mails, and we were always on time. Ah,* said William Keast, one of the original Cobb and Co. drivers, *we did that! Really we were your true pioneers. And it didn't need special legislation to put us off the roads, either. The railways did that! a sly slap at current happenings this.*

A good coach-horse cost anything from £21 to £67 in those days, said another old man regretfully; *you won't see such prices again for working horses.* Just then the chairman made an odd request to the gathering. *All those who were actually stuck up by bushrangers, please stand up.* But tho old chaps were as full of fun as so many schoolboys, and every man Jack of them stood up. It turned out, however, that a couple of them had actually been 'stuck up.' *I was stuck up by Jack Morgan,* said Harry Watson; *that was in 1869, when I was driving the mail between Albury and Wagga. At Munga Park, it was, and*—But his voice was lost in a babel of 'I remembers.'

"*Were you ever stuck up?* I asked of Bob Grover, of Wagga, aged 87. *Me? No,* said Bob, *but I've had some encounters with real bushrangers. In the Kelly days passengers and drivers alike were all keyed up and expecting the worst. I drove in the Kelly country, but I was never stuck up, because I always carried a bottle of brandy in the boot. More than once or twice I've swung round a bend to see Ned Kelly himself with his hand up to stop me. All he wanted was a stiff nip, and he always got it from me, and we'd swap a word or two. He was always alone. I fancy he was inclined to keep Dan, and Steve Hart and Joe Byrne in the background a bit. They were a bit too flash for Ned, I was in Jerilderie, New South Wales, when the Kellys stuck up the town and held it for three days. That would be early in 1879. There was a Government reward of £8000 offered for the gang after that, but no man, woman or child in the North-East squealed. They didn't dare. Only Aaron Sherritt, but the Kellys shot him dead at his own door. I remember ... I remember,* said S. C. Holman. of Maryborough, *driving 40 Chinese diggers on a 'Jack' coach between Castlemaine and Maryborough. They were making for Fiddler's Creek, and I remember all their umbrella hats hanging behind the luggage at the back of the coach like a lot of big mushrooms ...*

And I drove the reporters and divers down to the wreck of the Loch Ard at Curdie's Inlet, 27 miles from Cape Otway, in June, 1878, says Bob Cozens, *Only Tom Pearce and Eva Carmichael were saved out of 52 souls.* ... Fifty-one years ago that day, Frank [Smiley] drove his first coach for Cobb and Co. from Wickliffe to Warrnambool. Down through Caramut and Hamilton the route lay, over the best roads in the colony in those days ... Then they had a silent toast for those old comrades of the roads who had driven to the Elysian Fields since last year's reunion. Pioneers, oh, pioneers! — N.C." (Those were the days!, 8 May 1928, p.6)

1930 See also Alder, Amos

Ostlers, Important Personages.

"Ostlers. occupied responsible positions , in the coaching business. They. had the care cf the horses, carefully, examining them for possible defects, paying special, attention, to the-: hoofs and condition of shoes, attended to the feeding and grooming; also they had to look after the harness, seeing that the collars were in perfect condition, and so prevent the possibility of galling, and keep up the supply of horse rations. They needed to be sober, reliable men ; otherwise they would soon lose their job. There was an ostler at the Noarlunga Hotel, which was kept by Tom Dungey, who was. an artist. He used to carve curious articles on the bones of cuttlefish, such as bouquets of flowers, Prince of Wales feathers, and such like. Some of these he sold to passengers, thereby considerably adding to his :pay.: He told me he used to go to the beach on Sundays and, collect the objects he worked upon." (Memories of Myponga, 2 Nov 1927, p.2)

1893-1895 Post Office Hotel and Post Office, Forbes (Ryan & Thompson)—Courtesy National Library Australia

Cobb and Co. at Bathurst—Courtesy Orange & District Historical Society Collection

Chapter Five

Drivers

H - I

"I remembered a piece of poetry that was written over 30 years ago and was found amongst the effects of the late 'Billy' Mitchell, one of Cobb's oldest drivers, its title was 'The Whips of Cobb and Co.' It read as follows"

So my mind goes harking backwards to the days of long ago,

Back to old familiar faces in the ranks of Cobb and Co.

And I see a whiskered chivvy—you can guess the 'chiv,' I mean—

It was known as Billy Mitchell ; is he still above the green?

Many miles I've ridden with him ; many yarns to me he's told ;

Many drinks we've had together—'ginger beer'—in days of old ;

Many times I've blown his bugle when we reached the sandy lane ;

Many times I've held the ribbons when we crossed the Myall Plain.

Author unknown
(Cobb's Coaches, Verse 3, 17 Jan 1925, p.17)

Cobb & Co. coach departing—Collections of the State Library of Western Australia and reproduced with the permission of the Library Board of Western Australia

Supporting evidence:

Haig, Ike
1929 See Mesbitt, Bill; 1933 Grover, Robert H. (Wharparilla Bob); 1951 Winkler, Eddie

Haines, F ... 1919 See Aisbett, E. J.; 1937 Preston, R.

Halcroft, Richard
1929 "Richard Halcroft ... was 84 years of age ... In his earlier days, Mr. Halcroft was a driver of the line of Cobb and Co's. coaches between Forbes and Toogong, and also between Wellington and Dubbo. On several occasions he had valuable cargoes of gold on board, but had never been interferred with by bushrangers. Afterwards he was in charge of Cobb and Co's. depot at Toogong." (Mr. Richard Halcroft, 3 Aug 1929, p.8)

Hall, S. (Possible Cobb and Co. driver)
1871 "Omnibus Accident.—On the 21st inst. As Cobb & Co.'s omnibus was proceeding to Adelaide, when near the Mountain Hut, the leaders shied at some water on the road, and swerved suddenly to the near side of the road. By skilful management, and timely application of the whip, the driver, J. Carbis, drew them to the other side, and the front off wheel ran against the bank. He was immediately deposited on the bank, but retained his hold of the reins, and, the horses moving on, was dragged between it and the vehicle, sustaining sundry abrasions of face, hands, &c. There were eight passengers on the top, seven of whom were thrown off, and one of them, Mr T. P. Jones, of Glenelg, feeling that he had sustained considerable injury, was driven to the Hon. J. H. Barrow's, where he was attended by Dr. McIntyre, who found that one or two of his ribs were broken. The others did not sustain any serious injury.

There were four horses in the conveyance at the time, one of them a young one, and the others old mail horses of five or six years standing, and they were proceeding at about the rate of five miles per hour. The spot where the accident occurred seems to be a very dangerous portion of the road, as it is only a short time since the bus driven by Mr. S. Hall capsized at the same place, and on this occasion had not the driver succeeded in pulling the horses to the right hand side of the road nothing could have prevented a most serious accident; which must inevitably have been attended with loss of life ...

The Fresh Mail Contracts.—Considerable interest is excited in this District as to who are the successful mail contractors, but up to the time of our going to press no definite information had been received. We believe there have been 461 tenders sent in, so that it is probable that sometime will elapse before the results are made known." while recorded in the same article "Punt Accident.—On Saturday last a mob of 526 cattle belonging to S. Davenport were being crossed at Wellington, when one batch rushed on too suddenly, and the ropes gave way. The punt immediately floated away with the stream, and the cattle jumped overboard and swam ashore ...

Fire near Wellington.—We have heard that a day, or two since a stack of barley belonging to A. McFarlane, Esq., Wellington was destroyed by fire. The full particulars have not yet reached as." (General News, 25 Feb 1871, p.2)

Hall, Stephen (Sampson/Big Samson)
1921 See Griffen, Chas.; 1929 Mesbitt, Bill; 1933 Grover, Robert H. (Wharparilla Bob); 1934 Alexander, Jack

Hall, Walter Russell ... 1935 See Whitney, William Franklin (Frank)

Halliday, (Christian name unknown)
1878 "LOUTIT BAY. (COMMUNICATED.) For a thorough change of air commend me to Lorne, Loutit Bay. Snugly ensconced on the shores of one of the numerous little bays on the southern coast of Australia, sheltered from the north winds by the dense forest and the high hills which skirt the seaboard south of Winchelsea and Birregurra, and open to the cool sea breeze wafted in from the Southern Ocean, the little watering place of Lorne, unpretentious, unpretentious, natural, and beautiful, stands destined some day to be one of the most delightful sea-side resorts in Victoria. The place is easily reached from Geelong, Ballarat, or Melbourne.

The rail takes you to Winchelsea, and from thence on Mondays, Wednesdays, and Fridays, Cobb and Co.'s coach, piloted by one of the best of whips (the obliging and careful Halliday), takes you amid scenery of the wildest kind to this secluded little place. The way is uninteresting until you reach Dean's Marsh, where the coach stops to enable its passengers to obtain dinner; but beyond that place the road begins to ascend, winding its way through dense scrub and lofty gum trees, here and there affording beautiful little peeps of forest scenery. From the summit of some of the high spurs along which the road winds, you peer down far beneath into almost impenetrable valleys, at the bottom of which graceful branches of fern trees spread out their beautiful fronds amid a dense undergrowth of bush shrubs, here and there the sun glinting down upon them through the foliage of the lofty gum trees high above. On nearing the coast the sea bursts all at once on the view, and after calling at the Post-office and allowing passengers for Mountjoy's boarding house to alight, you drive on to the Lorne Hotel, kept by Host Gosney, where you can enjoy the comforts of a well-conducted hostelry, and have a splendid view of the sea.

A walk next morning to Tommy's Look-out, a high promontory at the entrance of St. George's Creek, is very enjoyable, and is amply repaid by the extensive view sea ward and landward. Then, after refreshing the inner man at the hotel on your return, a walk up that delightful ravine, the bed of the Erskine, is one of the most beautiful strolls to be had in this romantic neighborhood. The rippling of the water over the rocks and amid the moss-covered boulders, through ferns and fallen trees, is most refreshing and pleasing to the eye, whilst the sweet scent of the undergrowth, consisting of musk and other shrubs, together with the woody aroma from the forest, is most exhilarating to those who have left the close atmosphere of town and the daily routine of office life. The rapids on the Erskine are well worth a visit, and so are the falls farther up, but considerable physical exertion is required to reach the latter ; however, it amply repays one for the labor and fatigue. Excellent fishing may occasionally be obtained at the month of the Erskine, where bream are at certain times plentiful; crayfishing may also be enjoyed about three miles along the coast at low water, and those who are fond of boating and sea fishing may indulge in both, as an excellent boat is kept for hire by an experienced boatman." (Loutit Bay, 31 Jan 1878, p.3)

Hamilton, Albert ... See Appendix 1.6

Hamilton, Allan
1868 "THE MAIL COACH ACCIDENT. From the Bathurst Times THE INQUEST. ON Saturday morning last, at 10 o'clock, the district coroner, Dr. Busby, commenced an inquiry at Duny's, Golden Grain Inn. Bentinck-street, touching the death of the late Allan Hamilton, who was killed on the previous morning by the upsetting of the Sydney mail coach on Frying Pan Hill ... *I was a passenger by the mail from Sydney on Friday last ; I came to One Tree Hill by the railway, and from thence by coach. At Bowenfels we changed coaches. We started from Bowenfels with, I believe, six men, four women and a child, and myself. I took my place inside, where I remained until the coach arrived at Meadow Flat (Durack's). I then got outside, and sat on the near side of the box, with Mr. James, solicitor, and the driver, the deceased Allan Hamilton, whose body has been viewed by the jury ...*

We came on quite well until we reached the top of Frying Pan Hill, when suddenly the driver exclaimed something to the effect of 'Good God ! the break is gone !' He asked Mr. James to put his foot and help him on his side, and at two or three different times asked me, in God's name, to press on the break all I could on my side. Immediately after Hamilton said the break had gone, the horses broke into a gallop and became uncontrollable ; but the deceased managed to keep them clear of any impediments in the road until the near fore wheel struck against a guard log ; the coach got clear of it, and swayed to and fro, and after running about a hundred yards further, the off fore wheel struck another large guard log on the righthand side of the road, and the coach immediately fell over on the right-hand side, and the horses bolted away with the pole and fore carriage ... On recovering myself, I immediately proceeded to see what was the matter with Hamilton and Mr. James, who were also thrown from the box and I found them both powerless. Hamilton appeared to be dreadfully injured, and was lying across Mr. James's head ... Hamilton was dead ... Mr. Lambert, Mr. Moore, and myself, after having examined the coach, deemed it best to walk into Bathurst to give information of the accident ...

MONDAY, 1ST JUNE, The jury re-assembled at 10 o'clock, and again proceeded to examine the coach after which the following evidence was taken : Francis Jeffs, being duly sworn, deposed : *I am a blacksmith, and reside at Bowenfells. I am in business for myself. I sometimes do work for Cobb and Co. I remember the coach that left Bowenfells on Friday morning. I have seen the coach since. I saw it yesterday morning in Cobb and Co.'s yard. The groom at Bowenfells in the employ of Cobb and Co. instructed me to do some work to the coach on the Thursday before the accident. He told me to put a new handle (foot-rest) to the break, and a new block to the break. I did not see anything else the matter with the coach.*" ('Monday 1st June' 5 Jun 1868, p.3)

Hamilton, Hal ... 1908 See Byrne, F. A.; 1925 Whitney, Frank; 1925 Eddie, Nathan

Hampson, (Christian name unknown)
1935 "OLD COACHING DAYS. RISE OF COBB AND CO. ROMANTIC 71 YEARS. GOLD ESCORT WORK. (BY WALTER E. BETHEL).
*The roaring camps of Gulgong and many a Diggers' Rest:
The diggers of the Lachlan; the huts of farthest west:
Some twenty thousand exiles who sailed for weal and woe;
The bravest hearts of twenty lands will wait for Cobb and Co.*

From September, 1851, to September, 1854 gold to the value of £43,161,418, was found in Victoria. The banks, loaded up with specia, suffered from an embarrassment of riches. There were not stores enough to hold the immense quantity of goods poured into Melbourne from all parts of the world. Men flocked to the gold rushes on foot. Two-wheel drays drawn by bullocks, were the main means of transit to the diggings, but the supply was inadequate to the demand. The drays carried the swags and tools, while the miners walked ... The first coach was introduced by James Watt, landlord of the Border Inn, at Bacchus Marsh; a fare of 25/ was charged ... The great demand for better transport led in 1853, to a coaching business under the name of Cobb and Co ...

In 1861 he [Rutherford] advocated the extension of Cobb and Co.'s business into N.S.W ... It marked a new era in transit for Bathurst, and the residents cheered at the prospects of the reliable and speedy service inaugurated in the old town. With a full realisation, of what lay before Cobb and Co., Rutherford made Bathurst not only his business centre, but his home. In the yard of the Black Bull Inn, he erected blacksmith's and wheelwright's shops. This forge developed in 1862, into the company's great central depot for all the coach-work required for Victoria, N.S.W and Queensland, and up to 50 men were constantly employed ... Fine covered in coaches, good horses and splendid drivers, built up a widespread and highly remunerative business for Cobb and Co.

To handle the ribbons of this famous line, was a distinction amongst drivers, and in the long arduous and dangerous journeys through wild country, with bushrangers lurking in ambush, the personalities of the drivers became established in the public mind, and each one became celebrated in turn for some outstanding point of character ... Jack Fagan ... Edward ... Robert Bates ... George Adams, better known as 'Tattersall' ... and was, it is said, a beautiful driver ... *he used to send those horses along* remarked Driver Hampson ... I have a memory of taking one of these journeys—56 years ago—leaving, the train at Murrumburrah and driving, through Wombat, Muriumburrah to Burrangong Creek on the road to Grenfell. I was trying to hold a kangaroo pup and myself as well on the back seat of the coach, and it took some doing. On this journey I met a Mrs. Sarah Musgrave at her home at Burrangong. She was then a woman of 50 years: she is now a somewhat famous centenarian, having reach 105 years of age." (Old Coaching Days, 11 Nov 1935, p.8)

Hampson, Wright Harrison (Bill/The Invincible)
1917 "W. H. Hampson ... learned to drive under Robert Bates—'Silent Bob'—the most taciturn of Cobb and Co.'s drivers. It is recorded that a traveller asked 'Bob' one day what was growing in a field they were passing. A week after when the traveller was returning Bob suddenly ejaculated, *Loosum, I tell yer*, and relapse into silence." (Coaching in Australia, 1917, pp.26 & 27)

1917 "W. H. Hampson, 'the invincible', an old-time driver, was a dead shot with the revolver. He was a splendid driver, and always to time. Hampson drove the coaches from Kempsey to Port Macquarie, Taree to Gloucester, Glen Innes to Inverell, Tenterfield to Drake, Lismore to Murwillumbah, Warialda to Goondiwindi and under Cobb and Co., from Dora Dora to Tooma in the Murray River district." (Coaching in Australia, 1917, p.26)

1918 "DAYS OF COBB & CO. MAIL DRIVER FOR 54 YEARS … For fifty-four years and four months, with the exception of a period spent fighting with the First Imperial Bushmen's Contingent in the South African War, Mr Hampson handled the ribbons. He has seen much adventure, but he has never lost a mailbag—even under the Webster regime." (Days of Cobb & Co., 4 Oct 1918, p.7) "Recently there retired from the honorable occupation of driving his Majesty's mail a veteran of three score years and ten—Mr. Wright Hampson, of Crown-street, Surry Hills … The veteran has since his early days rejoiced in the name of 'The Invincible,' for his skill in handling four and five horse teams, his unbreakable record of being always on time, and his known skill with the revolver … drove coaches … for Cobb and Co., from Dora Dora to Toomba in the Murray district." (Mail Driver 54 Years, 26 Sept 1918, p.2)

1924 "A COBB & Co. VETERAN. MR. WRIGHT HAMPSON. In town last week we noted Mr. Wright Harrison Hampson, still hale and hearty and despite his seventy-odd years. He was well-known in Kempsey years ago as a mail coach driver of wide repute … The veteran has since his early days rejoiced in the name of 'The Invincible', for his skill in handling four and five horse teams, his unbreakable record of being always on time, and his known skill with the revolver. Perhaps it is the last attribute that is responsible for the fact that he was never molested by bushrangers, although he was often at close quarters with them. Mostly, Mr. Hampson drove coaches from Kempsey to Port Macquarie, Taree to Gloucester, Glen Innes, to Inverell, Tenterfield to Drake, Lismore to Murwillumbah, Warialda to Goondiwindi, and, for Cobb and Co., from Dora Dora to Toomba in the Murray district. He knew the Dora Dora [First Nations Peoples] …

His last eight years as a mail carrier were spent on the Waverley round. The old whip talks glibly of tragedies of nearly fifty years ago. There was, instance, the shooting of Cranley in 1873. Cranky put up at the hotel at Bendemeer, on the Northern Rivers, kept by William Avery manager for Cobb and Co. He stayed for a fortnight, and then asked for his account. Mrs. Avery gave him the bill, and he handed her a cheque, which she went into the bedroom with to get change. Cranley immediately followed and covered her with a revolver. However, a groom in the yard saw the incident through a window and ran off to the police station. A Constable Bowen was there, and, having his horse saddled, he immediately mounted and galloped along to the hotel, to be met at the door by Cranley, with the revolver in his hand. *What the hell are you doing here?* asked Cranley, as Bowen dismounted. *Put up your hands,* called Bowen ; but his command was answered by a shot, which missed. Bowen whipped his hand to his holster, and Cranley fired again and again missed. Bowen then fired in return and Cranley went down on his knees, shot through the abdomen, but he fired again and missed once more. Bowen again pulled the trigger, and this time he made no mistake, for Cranley got it fair between the eyes and fell dead. Bowen, a fine officer was himself shot dead a little time later in an affray with bushrangers.

In the same year Mr. Hampson was at Moonbi, 15 miles out of Tamworth, when the mysterious Mulla murder was perpetrated. A fine young girl, Bridget Coleman, was minding a flock of her father's sheep at the 10-mile Mulla. Her brother, who had charge of another flock, not meeting her as usual, made search, and found her lying on the grass with her skirt around her throat. *He did! He did! He did!* gasped the girl. The youngster ran home ; but when he returned with his mother and father his sister was dead. A large money reward was offered for the apprehension of the murderer ; but the affair remains one of the many unsolved mysteries of New South Wales. It was only recently that the mother of Bridget Coleman died at Moonbi at the age of 90 years …

During the career of the notorious Thunderbolt, Mr. Hampson drove through the terrorised countryside ; but although the bushranger frequently saw him, he never offered interference … For a long time Thunderbolt outdistanced all pursuers with this speedy animal; but he was shot at last at Kentucky Waters by Sergeant Walker who was acting as outrider of a gold escort. That was the end of Thunderbolt. We may add that Mr. Hampson's father was Const. Edward Hampson in charge of the then lock-up at East Kempsey, way back in the sixties. Const. Hampson was killed in an accident while riding near Yarrabandinni gates on Christmas Eve 1862. Mr. Wright Hampson was 14½ years of age at the time." (A Cobb & Co. Veteran, 7 May 1924, p.3

1934 "[Hampson] was tutored by Silent Bab Bates, a very careful driver, who seldom said anything but *Gid up*" (The Whips of Cobb & Co., Pioneers Of Outback Trails, 26 Jan 1934, p.8)

1923 See also Robinson, James (Robbie); 1925 Eddie, Nathan; 1932 Breen, Jim (Jimmy); 1935 Conroy, James (Jim)

Hampton, Al.
1898 "THE OLD COACHING DAYS … Famous Whips of the Pioneer Times. Red-Coated Mail Guard. Who that has passed beyond the youthful stage in Australasia has not heard of Cobb and Co., that magic title so closely associated with the gold-fever days, which had so much to do with moulding the history of the country, and which all who were identified therewith look back upon with fond recollection? Cobb and Co. are practically extinct, but their good deeds live after them … stirring times when Cobb and Co. were kings, and the dashing, daring, warm-hearted drivers their prophets … a writer in the 'Australasian' supplies interesting particulars of the history of Cobb and Co. They are from Mr. J. M. Peck, stock and station agent, one of the original partners … Freeman Cobb … with Jas. Swanton, John Lambert, and J. M. Peck, he formed the original Cobb and Co., though other companies soon adopted the name, which spread all over Australia …

In the early days the coaches carried the red coated mail guards, but these were afterwards dropped. In all the excitement of the early digging days Cobb and Co. were never stuck up on the road to Bendigo, though the gold escort were once or twice under fire. Amongst the most celebrated of the old drivers were Harry Nettlefold, still living in New Zealand, and 'Long Carter,' who was in New Zealand a few years back. Other identities of the road were Levi Rich—well known as Levi, but never rich—'Dad' Gardiner, 'Dirty-faced Ned,' Al. Hampton, well known on the Bacchus Marsh line, Ned Divine or 'Cabbage Tree Ned,' celebrated on the Geelong side, Geo. Woodworth—now living at Gisborne, 'Lame Bradley,' and a few others. Bradley had a bent leg, yet was a very awkward man to meet in a row, and he was reckoned the finest driver of a five-horse team in forest country. 'Dad' Gardiner, who was very powerful, had no peer in holding up a team of eight, a task that takes some muscle. Teams of eight were frequently driven over the heavy Castlemaine grades. All were drivers typical of a class. Bradley would have none but the best horses, and generally palmed a duller off on some other driver; his teams were the clippers of the road. Once, after ripping through from Keilor to Digger's Rest in 17 minutes, he took out his watch, and remarked: *That's a bit too quick—I should have taken 20 minutes.* He ran some meteoric trips later in the opposition days, when coaches leaving Bendigo at 6 o'clock were in front of the Albion at 2, and he is said to have been identified with a story often told.

He started from Ballarat to go through in fast time, and shook off all his passengers but a sailor, who said: *I'll stick to you while she has a rag on her.* Mr. Peck considers Lame Bradley the quickest and pluckiest driver who ever sat behind a team, and a wonder in forest, country. When night coaches were started he drove through the Black Forest, a task that on bad nights demanded wonderful eye and nerve, yet one broken leg was the only accident Cobb and Co. had reported to them in those early days. 'Levi' could and would drive anything, and after handling the worst kind of brute, he would drawl, in his slow Yankee way: 'Purty fair hawse.'

'Sampson' was a thorough Western 'Hoosler' and a rough diamond, but with a capacity for effective, long-drawn rejoinder that won him fame on the road. Handing a badly-written telegram out on the line, the postmaster objected to the spelling: *Heow du you expec' a man to spell when he's had no sleep for two nights?* said the driver. There were short stops for breakfast at Keilor, and passengers were hardly seated at Jackson's before the driver's 'All aboard' was heard. One morning Mr. Stubbs, the famous auctioneer, asked for a few minutes extra. *I'm Mr. Stubbs — a friend of Mr. Cobb ... Wal! I wouldn't wait for ye if you were Stubbs and Sons*, said Sampson. After Cobb and Co. disbanded, Watson and Hewitt were for a long time the leading coach proprietors, then Robertson and Wagner, with Walter Hall (now of Sydney, and well known in mining and sporting circles), Rutherford, and others—known as 'the Canadian Crowd'—became Cobb and Co., and in their time saw the glory of the coaching days pass away." (The Old Coaching Days, 25 Sep 1898, p.12)

Hampton, Jimmy ... 1935 See Rochester, William George (Bill)

Hanning, Robert
1895 "*Robert Hanning, who has been well-known locally as a driver of the mail coach, sailed for Western Australia last Saturday, where we hope he will make his pile. Hanning was a most obliging driver, and a flush of customers did not prevent his going out of his way to oblige one or more passengers who desired to be put down elsewhere than in Grant Street.* Speaking from personal knowledge, it is safe to say that Hanning had some of the roughest country in that colony to drive over, consisting of mountains, gullies, rivers, and creeks, and is not only an experienced, but a careful and most expert whip. Cobb & Co have secured an acquisition, and those who have the good fortune to secure a box seat alongside Hanning, will find him a most genial Jehu." (News of the Week, 5 Jun 1895, p.14)

1895 "Mr. R. Hanning, who has just started to drive the mail coaches on the Southern Cross to Coolgardie line." (Colonial Governors, 1 Jun 1895, p.2)

Harding, John S.
1947 "DROVE COBB AND CO's. COACH! TOOWOOMBA, Nov. 10.—Mr. John S. Harding, who celebrated his 91st birthday this year, claims to be the oldest surviving driver for Cobb and Co.'s coaches. He was driving before his 21st birthday ... Mr. Harding drove for Cobb and Co. for about 10 years in the western districts of New South Wales." (Drove Cobb and Co.'s Coach !, 11 Nov 1947, p.1)

Harman, A ... 1919 See Aisbett, E. J.

Harman, Arthur ... 1947 See Wallace, Peter

Harris, Dick ... 1933 See Grover, Robert H. (Wharparilla Bob)

Hart, Nicholas
"Nicholas Hart was born in Glebe, Sydney to parents Nicholas and Elizabeth (Nerney) Hart ... The first record of Nicholas Hart junior (after his birth) is when he was before the courts on a charge of stone-throwing in 1858, aged thirteen and fined 30 shillings ... The young Nicholas Hart found work at Maryland Station close to the Queensland border. Family oral history relates that he was an excellent horseman with a passionate love of animals ... It is unknown at this stage where Nicholas met his future wife, Emma Susannah Judge but the record of their marriage shows they were married in Warwick Queensland on 24 July 1865 ... As the children of Nicholas and Emma were born the addresses of the parents are revealed as Maryland at first with occupations given variously as groom, ration carrier and Cobb and Co. groom ... The bushranger Thunderbolt held him up (*A Ghost Called Thunderbolt* by Stephan Williams.) ... The family oral history fits well with this version with the addition that the most important thing passed down orally by my mother was the great relief on Nicholas' part, that Thunderbolt had not caught the horse. If he had managed to catch Mistral its fate would have been to have been run to death—Thunderbolt, though an expert horseman asked so much of his mounts that they did not last long.

At some stage Nicholas must have become a Cobb and Co. coach driver as he is listed as one of only three drivers on the Warwick—Maryland—Tenterfield run in the Queensland Museum Publication *Cobb & Co. – Coaching in Queensland*. The coaches ran between 1870 and 1881 and from 1876 to 1879 ran every day. A search of the Deeds of Grant in the Queensland State Archives reveal that in February 1876 Nicholas Hart was granted 320acres of first quality grazing land at Canning Downs South (near Warwick) at a cost of nineteen pounds ... The story passed down within the family is that he was gored by his 'favourite pet jersey bull' and was unable to continue running the property. Presumably this was behind the move to Roma, perhaps for work there, although once again the railway had arrived no doubt lessening the demand for carrier work although short distance work would have still been required ...

The widow, Emma Hart and her eight surviving children ranging from ages of two to seventeen continued to live in

Roma for nearly 20 years ... The eldest son, also Nicholas, was with the Postal Department from 1889 when he was 17, becoming Assistant Postmaster in 1896 ... The last mention of any of the Harts in Roma is on the 28 March 1900 when there is a newspaper report of a 'sale of a valuable and choice selection of furniture' being offered up for sale on account of Nicholas Hart. He was resident at Greenmount, southwest of Toowoomba during the First World War as his son, Cyril Vivian Hart is mentioned on the honour roll of the War Memorial in this town. Greenmount is also given on the wedding certificate as the address of both Maud Hart (my grandmother who grew up in Roma, sister of this Nicholas Hart) and her future husband Claude Lister (born 1889 at Muckadilla where his father was station master)." (Information provided by Lynn Roberts [nee Clunn] great- granddaughter of Nicholas and Emma Hart, 1 Oct 2013)

Hart, Nick ... 1936 See Richardson, Bill

Hauman/Harmon, A ... 1930-1940s See Allan, (Christian name unknown)

Hayden, George
1930 "Cobb's Coaches Recalled. The death occurred recently at Casino of Mr. George Hayden, brother of Mr. H. Hayden, of Warren. The deceased was one of the pioneer coach drivers, in these arts, and before the advent of the railway to Warren, he 'handled the ribbons' of coach teams for years between Coonamble via Warren and Nevertire, and on other western coach routes for Cobb and Co. He was 62 years of age." While the same article stated "Another Snake Victim. Mrs. Ina Murray, aged 38 years, of Albury, was bitten by a large, tiger snake on Sunday and died several hours later ... Snakes arc very prevalent this year, and country residents are warned to be careful." (Cobb's Coaches Recalled, 27 Nov 1930, p.7)

Heap, Francis Albert (Frank)
1953 "The death has occurred of Francis Albert (Frank) Heap, of Kedron. He was born in 1867 at St. George and in his young days was a driver for Cobb and Co. coaches in western towns." (Death of a Cobb Driver, 5 Feb 1953, p.5)

Heathwood, James
1873 "Serious Accident to Mail Driver ... Mr. James Heathwood one of the drivers in the employ of Messrs. Cobb and Co ... was driving, a coach (luckily an empty one) down the steep hill which slopes to Jugiong Flat. Two teams were on the road before him. He passed one safely ; but whilst attempting to pass the other ... his leaders were frightened by the rumbling of the teamster's break. They shied and then bolted ... Heathwood was thrown from his seat ... the wheel of the coach passed over his temple ... He jumped up, and endeavoured to run after the horses ... On passing Mr. Flynn's public-house, where the mail coaches change horses, the coach was observed to be driverless ... Mr. Flynn mounted a horse ... succeeded in securing the horses" (Serious Accident to a Mail Driver, 19 Nov 1873, p.4)

Heelan, (Christian name unknown)
1887 "Cobb's large coach ... met with an accident ... Fortunately the driver, Heelan, one of the oldest and most experienced in the firm's employ, although thrown down kept hold of the reins, and thus prevented his team of four horses from bolting ... The party proceeded on foot to Frankston." (Accident To One Of Cobb's Coaches, 23 Dec 1887, p.2)

Hemers, John
1927 "Mr. Hemers has had a widely varied career. Born at Portland, Victoria, in 1858, he assisted his father in the transportation of mails in the good old days when the horse was not the despised animal it is today. When a youth he secured a job driving one of the famous Cobb & Co. coaches in his home district, and he can still relate many humorous and exciting experiences met with on the roads." (Off the footplate, 22 Sep 1927, p.1)

Herchberg/Hertsberg/ Hertzberg, Joseph (Joe)
1948 "50-60 years ago OLD COBB and CO., DRIVERS Writing in the 'Charleville Times', 'Plain Bill' Wynnum states: The passing of Joseph Herchberg aged 88, at Armidale recently bring memories of these old drivers of years ago, when Cobb and Co. was King. He was one of the old brigade of knights of the road who kept the wheels moving on the old coach routes of west Queensland: Charleville to Cunnamulla, Thargomindah, Barringun, Adavale, Tambo. I can recall the names of many of these old veterans—young men in those days—Joe Hersehberg, Sam Cousins, Ted Palmer, Fred Richards, Jim McCormack, Jack Duffell, Alex Teys, Ted Athorn and many others ... What strength of arm and nerve had these old drivers, when handling teams of six or eight corn-fed horses, swinging away in the early hours of the morning, with their thorough-brace coaches loaded with, passengers and mails on their day's stage of about 80 miles. The day's stage usually taking from 10 to 12 hours depending of course on the state of the roads. No bitumen or built up roads in those days—black soil plains and raw sand hills. But, rain or shine the mails got through and mostly on time." (50-60 years ago, 3 Jun 1948, p.3)

1941 See also Chatfield, Harry; 1947 Richards, J. Frederick (Fred)

Hewson, Charley ... 1917 See Wright, Bob

Hickson, Harry
1950 "REMINISCENCES OF COACHING DAYS In 1880 Cobb and Co. bought a number of mail services throughout Western Queensland, and the general regularity and convenience of their coaches served to open up the country. Their coaches are now of the past, but the time was when Cobb and Co.'s name was a synonym for efficiency and, when humanly possible, for punctuality. Time marched on and the motor vehicle displaced the coach. The coach drivers left the West for fresh fields. As years passed the ranks of the drivers dwindled. Today there are few left. However, here and there one meets either an old coach driver or a passenger who had experienced the thrills of coach travelling.

Two old drivers for Cobb and Co. reside in Rockhampton—Harry Hickson and Lou Sheraton. They were mates for some years. They shared a room at a Winton hotel. Both of them well remembered one of their passengers who also lives in Rockhampton—Sid May. Harry Hickson drove the coach from Longreach to Winton in 1911 and the following year took over the Winton to Kynuna run. A year later he went to Boulia and after 12 months there went to Jundah, where he stayed 18 months. In the middle of the big drought of 1915 Mr Hickson, to use his own words, 'got sick of the job.' Securing a couple of horse teams he entered into partnership with his brother, and they engaged in carrying in the West. Produce was carried to the stations and wool was carried on the return trip. After three years in this business Mr Hickson left it to go droving, purchasing a plant of his own. In 1926 he returned to Alpha, *Back to where I was born*, he said. He put in four years working round the Alpha district, and then came to Rockhampton where he engaged in general work till 1941 when he secured employment with CQME Co. at Lakes Creek, and at present is train driver for the company.

Mr Hickson said that when Tom Golligher retired as travelling manager, the business of Cobb and Co. was declining on account of the advent of motor vehicles. When the coaches went off the road T. Uhl and Sons, of Brisbane, were the biggest shareholders. The last coach run was from Thallon to Dirranbandi. Speaking of the days of the coach, Mr Hickson said that drivers had many thrilling experiences. They were a good team of men. One of the drivers that Harry Hickson remembered well was Steve Wall, father of Bill Wall, who owns the racehorse Auction. Bill now conducts an hotel at Winton. It was unusual to hear of a driver who was not familiar with all the embellishments of the English language. Mr Hickson said there was one driver—Alex McMullen—who was never known to swear at his horses, but on special occasions he could perform brilliantly on any human objective which seemed to need it.

RAN OUT OF RATIONS On one occasion in 1913 during a flood Mr Hickson and his eight passengers were stranded at the Girlie mail change. They were stuck for eight days and ran out of rations. Hickson and two shearers named Whitbread and Currie swam the Diamantina to get relief. It was a nightmare swim. By swimming from tree to tree they eventually reached the other side, where the boat was moored. After a short rest on the eastern bank the trio set out to walk to Elderslie station, managed by Mr C. J. Brabazon. Mr Brabazon sent a buckboard loaded with rations to the stranded passengers. Mr Hickson secured a horse from the station and rode into Winton where he secured a coach and brought out another load of mail and passengers.

The passengers were boated across the river. *There was one horse worth its weight in gold*, said Mr Hickson. When a boat was loaded with goods, passengers or mail the horse would swim with the boat tied to its tail. *And it could pull a good weight*, added Mr Hickson. Some coach trips were risky on account of the roads—or the absence of roads. On one trip from Winton to Muckunda, Mr Hickson warned the passengers that the was a possibility of the coach turning over on account of the washouts. He advised them that in their own interests it would be better for them to get out of the coach. However, one woman refused to budge. The coach did turn over. The openings of the coach were narrow. Investigations showed the woman to be uninjured. In attempting to get the woman out of the overturned coach it was found that she could not be pulled through the opening on account of her size. So she was left there. The horses were unyoked and the coach unloaded of mail and goods. With the aid of ropes the coach was pulled back on to the road. The woman squeezed herself out, and in reply to the other passengers *It was a wonder you were not killed*, she replied *It would take more than that to kill Mother Muckunda* (which was the nickname of the licensee of the hotel at Muckunda). But all trips were not over flooded, country. Times out of number the roads were dry and dusty. On the road from Winton to Boulia there were a number of hotels, including the 20-Mile, 40-Mile, Britcher's Creek, Middleton's, Muckunda, Min Min, and Hamilton's. They all did a good trade. From Winton to Boulia was 260 miles, and on a dusty summer day the halt at each hotel was a welcome break. It was a four day journey and it was a prosperous run for Cobb and Co., who received £1500 a year for the contract.

A GOOD FRIEND Mr Hickson said there was one person in the West whose name he would never forget that was C. J. Brabazon, manager of Elderslie station … Mr Brabazon was always on the spot to help coaches in difficulties. Drivers were always sure of the loan of a horse to ride for help when they were near Mr Brabazon's property, Mr Hickson said that one who did quite a lot of travelling by coach was Sid May. *Sid was in his prime in those days*, said Mr Hickson, On one occasion the mail was being brought from Muttaburra to Longreach by packhorse. Sid May was mounted on a black horse which was tired at Weewondilla. When he leaned from the horse to pick up a mailbag from one of the letter boxes the horse put on an excellent exhibition of bucking. Sid, not being skilled in the art, soon parted company with his mount and was sprawled in the mud. *Sid was no Skuthorpe*, added Mr Hickson …

GOOD OLD DAYS *Those were the good old days*, said Mr L. Sheraton yesterday when referring to his employment as a coach driver with Cobb and Co. Lou Sheraton took up coach driving at 16 years of age and was the youngest driver ever to be employed by the company. His first run was from Winton to Longreach, a three-day journey. There were five passengers on the coach and the travelling manager of Cobb and Co. (Mr Tom Golligher) The first trip was Mr Sheraton's first encounter with wet weather as a driver. Later he became accustomed to it. *Wet or fine the mails had to get through*, he added. Western roads in the old days were not the best, said Mr Sheraton; in fact, *they are not much better today*. On his first trip it rained and as the coach chugged along the wheels collected heaps of black soil. At various stops the driver would have to 'debus'—to scrape the mud from the wheels. After four or five months on the Longreach-Winton run, Mr Sheraton took over the Boulia to Muckunda trip. A coach ran from Winton to Muckunda, and Mr Sheraton's coach picked up passengers and mail and transported them to Boulia.

All western trips were similar during the wet weather, said Mr Sheraton. Black soil roads had to be traversed and swollen rivers crossed. He recalled a man named Spencer who was groom for Cobb and Co. and camped at the Girley mail change. Spencer had plenty of pluck and he had no fear of flooded creeks. When the Diamantina was in flood Spencer used to swim the river with a rope in his mouth attached to which was a tub. First taking the mails across he would return for the passengers … *And we were always on time*, he added. *They were strict in those days. If the mail was late there were 'please explain' forms to be filled in*. …

SMALL PAY The pay was poor, for a coach driver, said Mr

Sheraton. Starting at £10 a calender month, the salary rose to £12, then £14, and when he finally left the pay was £16. The groom's salary was much smaller, and he had to be content with £6 per calendar month … When Mr Sid May was asked, if he remembered travelling with Harry Hickson and Lou Sheraton on Cobb and Co.'s coaches, he said he had made many journeys with them. He remembered Harry Hickson particularly well because he was an excellent billiards player—one well above the average. Other drivers Mr May remembered were Bill White, Mick Egan, Alf Lewis and the Richardson brothers. White was on the run from Longreach to Winton. Mick Egan was on the 'down the river' run (down the Thomson River from Longreach to Jundah). Alf Lewis drove from Blackall to Tambo. Alf Lewis used to harness up a team of seven greys. *Believe me*, said Mr May, *it was a great sight to see this team stepping out from Northampton Downs to the Northampton Hotel. This hotel was kept by the Russells, but it has now vanished* …

GOOD COMPANY Mr May said travellers were great company on the coaches. The coaches had flaps which could be dropped. These were supposed to keep out the dust, but in dry weather one could always bet on arriving at his destination weighed down with a thick layer of dust. In wet weather there were many rough experiences. The coaches had leather braces instead of steel springs. With mails, parcels and passengers aboard, the coach swayed like a ship on a choppy sea. There was always competition for the box seat, for which an extra 5/- had to be paid … Other knights of the road Mr May remembered were Joe Edgley (who travelled for Walter Reid), Bill Minnie (for Headricks), Arthur Dearman (for Denhams), Billy Badger (for Robert Reid and Co.), Harry May (for David Storey and Co., Sydney). *They were a happy crowd,* said Mr May … *When the destination was reached everyone would be tired, sunburnt and as red as a lobster. But in those good old days we had no rationing, there was plenty of beer, plenty of butter and there was no need to worry about petrol*, he added." (Reminiscences of Coaching Days, 23 Mar 1950, p.9)

Highfields, J ... 1874 See Crow, (Christian Name Unknown)

Hildebrand, Conrad
1869 Traralgon "The Early Days. The following account of the early days was written by the late Mrs Mapleson:—Leaving Melbourne in Cobb & Co's. mail coach on its way to Sale on the 22nd July, 1869, my passage was booked through to Traralgon. The passengers' list was not a large one, the roads being almost impassable at that time of the year. All on board, besides the driver (Conrad Hildebrand) were one gentleman, a well known Rosedale citizen, the late Mr Paul Kensie, tanner by trade, and one young lady on her way to Hazelwood Station as governess to the late Mr McMillan's family, and so left our company at Morwell Bridge, where the mails for that place were put off and other bags taken aboard. After leaving the great city all went well till the evening shades were closing in, and after a few

changes of horses, the driver told us to stick tight to our seats for we were now approaching the far famed Glue Pots, a delightful and well known piece of the old Melbourne road to Gippsland. The next thing we heard was all hands must get down and walk as the mud was very deep. So with the aid of a lantern provided by the coach driver, Mr Kensie led the way through scrub and mud by the side of the road till we got past some of the worst parts. Then all mounted the coach again right glad of a seat. By the way, we passed two of Cobb & Co's. coaches stuck hard and fast in the mud, and very much the worse for wear. After our halt for supper, and another much needed change of horses, it was a rough spin through the long night, nothing to see but the high wall of trees and a scrub at either side and the starry blue sky above us. Travelling on without anything startling taking place, we arrived at Moe early in the morning at the well known hostel, kept by Mr and Mrs Miller, where breakfast was ready and waiting, and very acceptable after such a rough stage. Well a short rest, a fresh change of horses, then on again over the old corduroy road to Morwell, where our companion—the Governess, left us. Then on again to my own destination (Traralgon), where my brother was waiting to meet me at the Old Traralgon Hotel, leaving our jolly companion, Mr Kensie, to travel on to Rosedale alone—his stopping place.

At the time of writing, July, 1923, there is only three persons left in Traralgon, who were living here at the time of my arrival, namely, Miss M. Campbell, her sister (Mrs Wallace) and their cousin, now Mrs A. Cole. The Old Traralgon Hotel, and the only one, and just changed hands from Mr Duncan Campbell to Mr Martin. The Police quarters were standing on the corner where the Post Office now stands. The town was composed mostly of large strong cattle yards to accommodate the large mobs of Queensland fat bullocks on their way to the Melbourne fat cattle markets. The little cemetery nestled on the bank of the creek, where the Railway Station Master's residence low stands. There is still one of its land marks left—the willow tree and poplar, which were planted at one of the little graves.

The surrounding locality was dense scrub and timber—one could scarcely walk through it. Bridges and culverts were not heard of, and roads, other than the main Melbourne to Sale road, were not in existence—only little bridle tracks, as they were called then. The low-lying ground between the Hotel and Traralgon Creek was a sea of water, and the coach groom used it as a swimming bath for the horses, when they arrived covered in mud. He would ride one and lead the others all about in the water to clean the dirt off them. What was known as Loy Yang station was held by the Bros. Henderson as a cattle station—they had not long taken it over from a Mr Turnbull. Many families were on the lookout for land at the time, and gradually found their way to Gippsland to select land. It was then that the old station was divided into many selections. Amongst the first

Coaches and horses in front of the Cobb & Co. offices in Bayley Street, Coolgardie—Collections of the State Library of Western Australia and reproduced with the permission of the Library Board of Western Australia

were A. McDonald, on the Creek; Mr G. Sligh, Mr R. Mills, Mrs L. Liddiard, Mr R. W. Liddiard, Mr T. Burton, Miss Robinson, and several others. Then the uphill fight began for the pioneer." (The Early Days, 17 Aug 1928, p.4)

Hill, H. J.
1867 "THE BROMPTON\WESLEYAN PICNIC. The third annual picnic of the Brompton Wesleyan Young Men's Association took place on Monday, December 30, and was most successful, the weather and the site (St. Bernard's, at Magill,) combining to secure this result. The picnicers started from the Wesleyan Chapel at Brompton, at half-past 9 o'clock in the morning, the procession, which consisted of a number of omnibuses and private vehicles, being headed by Cobb & Co.'s Leviathan, driven by Mr. H. J. Hill, six-in-hand. A most enjoyable ride of seven miles brought the pleasure seekers to the grounds selected for the day's amusement ... all kinds of games were indulged in and a very agreeable day spent" (Foundations of the Colony, 31 Dec 1867, p.2)

Hill, Jack ... 1917 See Bruce, Harry

Hill, Thomas
1953 "WAS A COBB AND CO. COACH DRIVER The death occurred in the Hillston Hospital recently of Mr. Thomas Hill at the age of 75 years ... Mr. Hill, who was born at Hay; spent the major portion of his life in the Hillston district, where he was well-known and highly respected. In his early years he drove coaches and worked for Cobb and Co., his father at that time being road manager for that firm." (Was a Cobb and Co. Coach Driver, 28 Sep 1953, p.2)

Hiller, Jack ... 1951 See Leary, Jack

Hillman, (Christian name unknown)
1905 "WINTON ... A very important civil case ... John W. Lancashire summoned Cobb and Co., for the recovery of two horses or their value £30, also £10 damages caused by illegal detention ... For Cobb and Co. Mr. Kruck (secretary of the firm in Brisbane), Henry White (hotelkeeper at Longreach), and Mr. Hillman, (coach-driver) were examined." (Interesting Court Case, 8 Dec 1905, p.3)

Hirschberg, Joe
1948 "Mr. Joseph Hirschberg, 77, who died in Armidale, N.S.W., last week, was one of the few remaining links with Cobb and Co., and one who afterwards owned his own coach lines in North Queensland. In the early days he drove from Warwick to Goondiwindi, Stanthorpe, to Texas. Later he took over the coach route from Almaden to Croydon. Retiring from coaching, he took up land for cattle raising at Cockatoo Downs, but after a few years returned to horses. He entered the remount trade from Townsville to India and retired in 1939." (Obituary, 14 May 1948, p.2)

Hitzman, Bill ... 1917 See Wright, Bob

Hobbs, H ... 1937 See Preston, R.

Hodgson, C. E.
1937 "Mr. C. E. Hodgson, who was for many years a driver of Cobb and Co.'s coaches on the Hay-Deniliquin route, has died at Deniliquin, aged 82. A native of Yorkshire (England), the late Mr. Hodgson was for 20 years with the Orient Line, most of the time as chief purser of the line. He took a position as station book-keeper at Yanco station before joining Cobb and Co. His body was taken to Numurkah for burial alongside his wife." (Obituary, 26 May 1937, p.6)

Hogan, T ... 1937 See Preston, R.

Hogan, Thomas
1940 "DROVE FOR COBB AND CO. Mr. Thomas Hogan. Another link with the famous coaching firm of Cobb and Co. was broken when Mr. Thomas Hogan, a former driver, died during the week-end. Mr. Hogan was well known in Fitzroy, for he had lived there for more than 70 years. As a young man he was head driver for Cobb and Co., and he drove their coaches on the Frankston, Hastings, and Whittlesea routes for many years. At the age of 9 Mr. Hogan became an apprentice to a racing stable, and he afterwards rode for Mr. Samuel Hardy. He earned a reputation as a steeplechase rider, and he often gave exhibitions with visiting travelling circuses. During one of these exhibitions his riding partner was killed, whereupon Mr. Hogan gave up horse-riding as a profession. It was then that he joined Cobb and Co. Mr. Hogan was also a great friend of Constable Fitzpatrick, who was shot by Ned Kelly as he was trying to arrest Dan Kelly. Many years ago Mr. Hogan was a driver for 'The Argus'." (Obituary, 20 Aug 1940, p.2)

Holbery, Robert
1914 "DEATH OF AN OLD-TIME' COACH DRIVER. An old colonist, Mr. Robert Holbery, died at his residence, Bolmont, Spring Vale, aged 78, last week. Arriving in Melbourne from Capetown in 1853, he became associated with Cobb and Co., and Crawford and Co., and soon became almost as well known on the roads as the famous 'Cabbage Tree Ned,' who was also in the employ of Cobb and Co. Mr. Holbery was a driver for this latter firm for over 40 years. He had charge of a coach for 35 passengers between Adelaide and Glenelg, and between Kapunda and Burra. For many years he was in Southern Riverina, driving between Adelong and Albury, via Tumut, Wagga and Junee." (Death of an Old Time Coach Driver, 21 Jul 1914, p.4)

1914 "Mr. Robert Holbery ... The deceased, who was twice married, left an adult. family. Twelve months ago he was injured in a railway accident at Tunstall railway crossing, and never recovered from its effects." (Obituary, 25 Jul 1914, p.45)

Holden, Nicholas (Nick)
1917 "Mr. W. Ruddle writes: Nicholas Holden, a coach driver on one of the early Gympie coaches, was a witty fellow, and up to all sorts of larks. On one trip from Gympie, and coming down a steep, ridge where at the bottom was a creek spanned by a culvert, about half way down Nick started the horses into a trot, then a canter, and then towards the bottom at full gallop. Over the culvert they dashed to the terror of a load of passengers. After passing the creek he slowed down, and pulled up; the passengers thought it was a bit of his devilment, as he was whistling or yelling the whole time, and they began to berate him thoroughly. Nick jumped down and said *Got a bit of a fright? Well you would have had a bigger fright had you known that the brake was gone, and I was keeping the horses going so that the coach should not run into them.*" (Coaching in Australia, 1917, p.37)

1929 See also Amies, Tom; 1935 Conroy, James (Jim)

Hole, (Christian name unknown)
1884 "Serious coach accident ... The driver was Alexander Fawcett. When within two minutes drive of the Pretty Pine Hotel ... a collusion with a stump ... the driver being thrown violently upon his head ... Mr. Hole, of the Pretty Pine Hotel , who was an old driver for Cobb and Co., seeing that Fawcett had been severely shaken ... offered to take his place ... Fawcett declined the assistance ... Fawcett began to experience the ill effects of his fall ... it was arranged Mr. Murray should temporarily take his place ... on going down the decline ... rocking so violently that Mr. Murray, fearing it was about to capsize leaped from the driver's seat to the ground ... Information at once was telegraphed to Cobb and Co's office at Deniliquin" (Serious Coach Accident, 30 Apr 1884, p.4)

Hole, Mat.
1934 "On arrival at Deniliquin, the coach pulled up at The Sportsman's Arms Hotel, on the outskirts or the municipality, where it was met by a number a cabmen touting for the job of conveying passengers from the Royal Hotel—where the coach office was situated—to the railway station. When a start was made from the Sportsman's Arms Hotel for the town, the cabs escorted the coach, and one cab man, who was a good bugler, was in the habit of sounding a horn as the coach proceeded into the town. The arrival of the coach at Deniliquin was thus made an event. It was a mail contract regulation that the coach driver should sound his horn when approaching a post-office, but, excepting at Deniliquin, I never knew this to be done. I never knew a driver who could have sounded a horn.

The drivers of the coaches were a very fine body of men. The best and most resourceful were employed on the Deniliquin road. Of these, some of the most notable were Charley Lee, Mat. Hole, Mat. Thornton, and Bill Keast. Of these, Charley Lee was the most experienced. He had been driving between Hobart and Launceston before he came to Riverina. He drove the coach right through from Hay to Deniliquin, before the railway was opened to the latter place, during the flood years of 1867-1870, and his skill and courage was so greatly appreciated that in1868 he was presented by the pastoralists of Deniliquin and Hay with a gold watch and chain, which he wore to the day of his death, not long ago, and which, I believe, his son, Mr. Charles Lee, of Park Estate, Booroorban, still wears. This was the most signal act of recognition I ever knew of a coach driver receiving at the hands of the public. Charley Lee was one of the most successful drivers that Cobb and Co. ever had: he never cost the firm a shilling through an accident resulting in in-jury to a passenger.

The drivers I have referred to were engaged on the Deniliquin road. There were many other notable and successful drivers on the Booligal and other roads. Some excellent drivers did not come to Hay. Charley Lee, who selected land near Booroorban, whilst he was still driving, worked it and added to it and died a comparatively wealthy man. But, as a rule, the coach-drivers did not save or make money. Some of them, after retiring from driving, took to hotelkeeping. In one of his books relating to 'Life on the Mississippi' in the river steamboat days, Mark Twain relates how it was the ambition of every boy in every river hamlet, to be engaged on a boat, so that he could be seen scraping a dirty bolt on the boat's deck when it drew into the local wharf. It might be said of many boys in Hay, that it was their ambition to become coachdrivers. The drivers were very much sought after. They were news-carriers and message-carriers. They were never asked to pay for accommodation at any hotel, and if they had partaken of a drink whenever they were asked to do so they would not have been much good for their work.

One of the Australian poets has referred to 'the singing coaches,' which is an allusion to the way the passengers, especially at Cup time and holiday times, indulged in singing on the coaches. Another, who wrote a set of verses, called 'The Ghosts of Cobb and Co.' wrote in one of them: I hear the shouts of coaches 'out,' Whip cracks and straining traces; The clanging bars, the driver's shout, The creak of the thoroughbraces. At Running Stream and Cudgegong, I see the headlights show; And list to the travellers' happy song, Who ride with Cobb and Co. This singing was most common on the night coaches, and usually started about dusk. Some drivers were very fond of getting the box-seat passengers to sing, and on the 14 and 17 passenger coaches, on which there were five passengers on the box, they generally made a good showing of community singing—although the term community singing was not then coined. The songs were usually of a sentimental nature, and with long lines to suit the rythm of the horses' action. Some favourites were: Spanish Cavalier, Blue Alsatian Mountains, All that Glitters is not Gold, Won't you buy my Pretty Flowers, His Galloping Horse, Abyssinian Gold ... But all previous melodies took a back seat when 'The Sweet Bye and Bye' came out. It was a favourite everywhere—not only on coaches—for quite a long while.

The recognised fare on a coach was 6d. per mile. Thus the fare to Deniliquin was 40s.; to Booligal, 25s.; and to Wagga, 90s. There was not much traffic on the Wagga road, and a five-passenger coach sufficed. That was a road of long stages—20 miles—and plenty of grass-fed horses. When 'opposition' was keen, the fares were reduced considerably, and passengers at 10s. were sought for to go to Deniliquin. It was a rule that the coach should never be sent out without a passenger as company for the driver and to assist in the event of accident. In the very rare instances in which no passenger was booked, a man had to be engaged to go. Such man was usually termed 'a gate-opener' and for going to Deniliquin he was usually paid £1. It was not unusual for a man without money to wait on-the coach-agent and ask if there were any chance of a gate-opener's job ...

It is difficult for young people to visualize , the coaching days — days when there were no such things as motors,: wireless, moving pictures, talkies, or telephones—and in the coaching districts, no such things as trains. In the late seventies, Mother Shipton's prophecy, written about 1510 was, frequently quoted. It began, *Carriages without horses shall go; accidents fill the world with woe. Round the world thought will fly, with the twinkling of an eye.* And ended, *And the world to an end will come in eighteen hundred and eighty one.* Many of the predictions had come true before 1880, such as the telegraph, and not a few people were superstitious enough to believe the world would end in 1881 ...

There were many Chinese engaged in the district, mainly as

gardeners and cooks, but sometimes as station hands and burr cutters. Another feature was the hotels. There are now eight hotels in the municipal area. In 1880, all the existing eight were here, except the Terminus, and also eleven others, in addition to three which were on the outskirts, of the town. All the hotels were required to have stabling accommodation, and to keep a stock of horse feed. There were also two breweries. Attached to one of the hotels, the Niagara, was a theatre, the Theatre Royal, nearly opposite the waterworks tank in Leonard St., where nightly performances were given. The Niagara and the Wharf Hotel were burned down in the late eighties and the old theatre was for a time used as a cordial factory. Even more marked is the disappearance of the road-side hotels, due to the motor car supplanting the horse drawn vehicle. No one in the coaching days would think of driving past a road-side hotel. It was the thing to pull up and have a drink at least, and usually a meal and a feed, for the horses. Now it is not unusual for cars to drive through from Hay to Melbourne with but one stop—for lunch and petrol. This lack of trade has put the road-side hotel, with few exceptions, out of business.

A feature of coaching which I might mention was the liberal way the pastoralists treated the mail contractors. At practically every stage a paddock was provided for them. At Hay, Cobb and Co. had use of a beautiful frontage paddock, on Illilawa, which is still referred to as Cobb and Co.'s paddock, and the only consideration the then owners, Messrs McCulloch, Sellars and Co. asked for it was that their manager and his family should have free passes between Hay and Deniliquin. A bad season was a very serious matter for Cobb and Co., as the horses had to be corn-fed, and feed was dear. Moreover it cost a great deal for transport from Hay to the cout-back stages. In the drought of 1884, it cost the firm a small fortune to send chaff and oats out to Ivanhoe and the other changing places on the Booligal—Wilcannia line.

As an example of the difference in the times, I might mention that in 1877, when Mr. Colin Simson, of Mungadal, was elected to Parliament, a bullock was roasted whole on the reserve, now the tennis courts, and barrels of beer provided as liquid refreshment. Could such a happening occur now? When the railway was opened to Hay on 4th July, 1882, the train which brought Governor Lord Loftus here to perform the official ceremony was the first many of the residents had ever seen, and quite a third of Hay's then population had not seen the sea. Whether we are the better for all this change in circumstances and ideas might profitably form the subject for a debate. We were more contended then, so far as my observation goes, and I remember writing in my copy-book at school, 'Contentment is great gain.' The subject I have talked about is an engrossing one, and it's not easy to know when to stop. I hope I have not wearied you with this retrospect of a by-gone age—an age which provided plenty of scope for ambitious men and noble women who did great work for their country and their generation, but an age that can never return." (Coaching and the coaching days, 13 Feb 1934, p.4)

Holland, Harry ... See Appendix 1.6

Holliday, W ... 1919 See Aisbett, E. J.

Holliday, William
1946 "VETERAN COACH DRIVER DIES. GEELONG ... Mr. William Holliday, 86 years, who was a pioneer driver with Cobb and Co ... spent most of his life in the Geelong district. For 32 years he was a driver for, Cobb and Co., and later ran a hackney cab at Geelong. In more recent years he operated motor vehicles." (Veteran Coach Driver Dies, 27 Jun 1946, p.3)

Hollister, D. & Hollister, F ... 1919 See Aisbett, E. J.

Holloway, Noah
1932 "In connection with Cobb and Co.'s coaches which used to run from Geelong through to Warrnambool, of the drivers, Mr. Castles remembers best was Noah Holloway, and he had sound reason for so doing. George is a thorough humorist and tells this tale against himself with much gusto. Walking along the road in the Birregurra district one day the coach passed him and he hopped on to the step on the opposite side to the driver, Holloway. All went well for three or four hundred yards, when the long lash of the driver came round and caught him across the nether garment, but Castles hung on and received more cuts ... eventually jumped off the step and fell on his knees on the hard macadamised road, sadly damaging his trousers and sustaining grievous wounds to his knees." (Early Camperdown History, 9 Jun 1932, p.5)

Holman, S. C.
1938 "COBB & CO. VETERAN DEAD MELBOURNE. Friday. After a long illness, Mr. S. C. Holman, who was said to have been the oldest survivor of the drivers of Cobb and Co. coaching days in Victoria, died in a private hospital last night, aged 91. He will be buried at the Melbourne general cemetery tomorrow. Mr. Holman was a driver of the coach which used to carry mails between Melbourne and the Bendigo district." (Cobb & Co. Veteran Dead, 19 Mar 1938, p.6)

Holman, Steve ... 1930 See Alder, Amos; 1937 Preston, R.

Holman, Stephen Charles
1934 "Mr Stephen Charles Holman, veteran ... 87 ... started driving for Cobb and Co. at the age of 17, and is a well-known figure at Sandringham, where he plies his trade. He is hale and hearty but is concerned over the action of Sandringham Council in having removed the cabmen's shelter—a building which had stood for 30 years." (Cobb Coach Veteran, 26 May 1934, p.1)

1928 See also Grover, Robert H. (Wharparilla Bob)

Hood, A. R ... 1932 See Lowe, Bill

Hood, Massey
"The old drivers to at last lay down their reins were: Massey Hood and Ollie York on the Cunnamulla-Thargomindah run 1922." (Communications Across the Generations, Read 1971, p.188)

Hood, Ross
1916 Wellington "COACHING IN FLOOD TIME. MR. ROSS HOOD'S REMINISCENCES ... In Cobb and Co.'s old coaching days, Wellington did not have any formed streets and parks, such as there are at the present time. The principal street was along from the Macquarie bridge, what is now Lee-

street and Nanima-crescent, on to the Royal Hotel in Percy-street (then kept by Harry Hughes), then on to the post office Mr. Alexander, postmaster, and afterwards Mr. Alex. Chrystal, now retired and living at Comobella). The principal business places started from the bridge, and the old public house is still going strong, in those days kept by Jim Malloh. On the opposite corner was a butcher's shop kept by the Cornwell family, now vacant land. On the east side of the street Tom Cunnington had his watchmaker's business in a small shop, now a private residence. The public school (afterwards the public. library) was further along on the opposite side (Mr. Turner, master), and opposite was Lake's Hotel, kept by a man named McKay.

Across the road in a small paddock, were Cobb and Co 's stables, looked after by Tom Robinson. The gate into the yard stood about where Payne's plumber's shop now is, and Habgood's fruiterer's shop is about where the stable stood. Bob Porter's barber's shop and the Masonic Hall stand on the other corner of the stables paddock. Then came the shop of the late Mr. Forwood, who used to do all the harness and general repairing. Round the corner in Warne-street was Bernasconi's general store (where Kimbell's bakery now stands), and next to him was Jim Thompson and Wilson's blacksmith's shop, where W. Gardiner did the horse-shoeing and general coach repairs for Cobb and Co.

The coaches travelled the road up to the Royal Hotel, and pulled up in front of the hall door, when the passengers would step out of the coach on to the verandah, and if they so wished they could step on to the balcony of the hotel from the top of the coach. There were no footpaths in those days. After letting down the passengers we would drive on to the post office. Tom Robinson always met the coaches as they passed the stables, and came on and got the mails and delivered them. Then we would go to the hotel and deliver the passengers' luggage, and pick up the next driver who had to go on to Orange. Some of the old travellers will remember the gentlemanly waiter (Harry Thomson) who used to be at the Royal Hotel, and was always up at that early hour to give them a bit of breakfast for a modest two and six per meal, and the passengers never grumbled at that. Harry always had my tot of rum and milk ready for me ; and so I would then go to bed. The coachman's room was off the public dining room (portion of the bar now takes in the dining room).

It was not all beer and skittles with the mailmen from Wellington to Orange in those days, any more than it was to Dubbo. The only difference was that they had the greater portion of the journey in daylight. If Harry Nolan and I had been willing to have knocked off, the Orange mailmen would have done so too. That was how it was put to me at one time by them, but I said I would keep going as long as I could keep the horses above ground with the coach ... The first lot of passengers I carried came through from Bourke way with Billy Waldron, the driver from Warren. They told me the flood waters were 60 miles wide below Warren, and that the coaches had to travel through the flood waters for miles below Canonbar, with Phil Ryan and Bob Watmore as mail-drivers. We came along all right, until we were coming down Stephenson's-lane at a walk, when we bogged up to the axle in places, and I got my front axle caught on one of the short stumps, which were so thick that we could not straddle the tracks, so had to come along carefully in that part of the road.

I said to the two passengers alongside of me, *I am stumped or snagged*. I got my axe, and got down, and was chopping the stump, when Rev. Canon Smith, of Bathurst, who was an inside passenger asked, *What are you doing, Ross? I am chopping a stump that has got me fast*, I answered. *Oh, is that all. Can't we back the coach and get clear?* I said, *It is boggy, and I would have to back the coach up hill.* To which he replied, *Well, we will have a try. You get into your seat and pull the horses back with the reins.* I said, *Yes, but you will get all over mud. Oh, mud, that's nothing, it will wash off*. With that the Canon took off his coat and invited the rest of the passengers to do the same, and with a good strong shove at the wheels, as well as pulling the horses back, we got clear enough so that I could chop the stump well down level with the ground. I may mention that Canon Smith was the father of Mrs. Franks, wife of the Government Inspector of selections ...

The road was terrible for the Orange coaches to travel over. Up along past Donohue's and Harris' it was up to the axle, and also at other places up Baker's Swamp way ... On one of my trips to Dubbo I got along as far as across Deep Creek, and was going along the side of the ridge on a hard-looking track opposite Lynch 's farm, when all of a sudden the hard top broke on the near side and let me bog down to the hub of the wheel on the low side of the ridge. The coach was held fast, and as it was a straight pull I could not slew to the right or left, for I would break the pole of my coach or capsize. The eight passengers got out (men and women) and I went and roused up some of the Lynchs and got the loan of a spade and pick and broke the crust of the track away from in front of the wheel, and got out after a couple of tugs, and then loaded up again and continued through to Dubbo." (Coaching in flood time, 21 Sep 1916, p.3)

1935 "With Montefiores is linked the name of Mr. Ross Hood, whose death took place at the District Hospital last Saturday. It was not altogether unexpected, as he had passed his 83rd milestone, and had been in declining health for some months. It is over sixty years since he first traversed these roads as a coachman engaged by the well known firm of Cobb and Co., and many thrilling stories he could tell of his adventures in the days when highwaymen and bushrangers were often met on the roads. It was at one of the hotels in Montefiores that he met the young lady who was to be his life partner, and as such she shared his joys and sorrows until God called her to His heavenly home just two years ago.

The late Mr. Hood was a man of stern, conscientious but kindly disposition, and made many friends during his long residence here. During the greater part of his life, he took a keen interest in politics, and an active part in all matters that concerned the general welfare and advancement of the town he had watched grow from its infancy to its present state. He leaves behind him a grown up family of two sons and two daughters, the latter being Mrs. Hoffman (Parramatta) and Mrs. Hodge (Campsie). The sons are Albert (Wellington), Robin (Bega). One son was killed at the great war, and another son was accidentally killed while driving the Gulgong mail some years ago. After a service at St. John's Church of England, the body of our departed friend and pioneer was laid to rest in the Church of England portion of the Wellington cemetery, both services being conducted by Rev. K. D. Norman, and Mr. Brindley read the services of the Loyal Orange Lodge, of which he was a member for many years."

(Wellington District News, 29 Aug 1935, p.4)
See also Appendix 1.6

Hopkins, E. L ... 1919 See Aisbett, E. J.

Horton, John
1932 "DRIVERS OF THE PLAINS. COBB & CO. MEN REMEMBER. WHITE HEADS Do you remember ... Bill, and Wagga Bob, the Wizard of the West, the Black Bull Hotel, and Brady of the Barwon? Of course you don't. You never drove a coach for Cobb and Co. But half a dozen old men who did remember these fantastic figures of Australia in the making met last night in the basement of the C.T.A. to talk over old times and look at lantern slides of coaches they had driven, drivers they had drunk with, and roads down which they had rocked with passenger and mail. The father of the gathering was John Horton, 83 years old, who drove his first Cobb coach to Yass from Goulburn in 1870, and his last—when the last coach ran on the track.

REMINISCENCE The youngest was a lad of 60 something, from Bourke. After the first few moments the white heads were nodding to a chorus of 'Do you remember?' and 'Did you know?' and something of the glamorous discomfort of early travel was revived. They talked with equal affection of horses and men, [First Nations Peoples] and squatters, landlords and their inns, mule teams, pack-mails. They recalled the Tom Thumb coach with its white horse and its black one, and the Leviathan coach which seated 75 passengers and needed a team of 16 matched horses. And for an evening at least they heard again the creaking of the Cobb and Co. and the hoof-thunder of the six-in-hand team." (Drivers of the Plains, 1 Apr 1932, p.9)

1932 "Mr. John Horton, of Goulburn, who claims to be the oldest surviving driver of Cobb and Co's coaches, gives some of his recolections ... Mr. Horton recalling an instance where a loaded team took a week to travel a mile. As the condition of the roads prevented him from running to schedule, Mr. Horton soon tired of his position and returned to Goulburn. Within a fortnight of his return he was offered a job by Mr. Colin Robertson, manager of Cobb and Co.'s Goulburn branch, and gladly accepted, taking over the Goulburn-Yass run in succession to Fred Gilliam, a brother of George Giliam of Ashton's circus fame, who was compelled to resign from Cobb and Co. owing to ill health. Mr. Horton commenced driving with Johnny Dailey, at that time one of the State's veteran coach drivers. That was in 1870, the winter proving to be one of the wettest seasons experienced for years. Lake George was almost overflowing and the coaches did not have a dry trip for almost five months ... Mr. Horton remained in the service of Cobb and Co. for some time ... He subsequently brought a hotel on the Yass Road four miles from Goulburn." (Cobb and Co. Coachman, 21 Nov 1932, p.4)

Houligan, Pat ... See Appendix 1.6

Houston, Dick
"Still, even now, thirty minutes by rail will enable us to leave the crowded streets behind, bringing us to cultivation paddocks and long, red roadways that lose themselves in the silent bush beyond ; and as we continue our journey, and feel the fresh country air in our faces, we think of the stern austerity of the pioneering days retreating slowly before the onward march of civilisation, and we remember once again the ramping, roaring days *When the Royal Mail was run by Cobb and Co*. What a wealth of romance and adventure the very name suggests. Well do I remember, although it is thirty years ago, my first boyish experience with Cobb and Co., between Newcastle and Glen Innes. What a hero wild Dick Houston, the driver, appeared in my juvenile mind. I shall always remember that journey ; and what a flood of recollections swept across my mind as one day, ten years after, my attention was directed by the sight of Cobb and Co. sweeping down Great Bourke-street, Melbourne, from the Albion Hotel to Wood's Point and Mansfield!

Since then, I have met Cobb and Co. in many places, Sometimes I enjoyed a box seat, sometimes I had no seat. Cobb and Co. just loomed large on the edge of the black soil plains and passed me by in a cloud of dust. Sometimes Cobb and Co. was a big affair, six steaming horses, fresh from the last change, and three big lamps, one on each side of the box seat and one overtowering the middle. As such I knew them 'along the dusty road to Hay'. But the finest turn-out was the mail that climbed up the Australian Alps, from Bairnsdale to Omeo, in Gippsland. Then again, Cobb and Co. was represented by the little red bone-shakers, familiar around Geelong and Lilydale in Victoria, and along several tracks in this State—around Bathurst and the Turon. But oh ! they were good days ; rough days, quart pot days, damper days, perhaps ; but still they were big, brave generous days—days 'when the world was wide,' to quote Henry Lawson. What lies some of those old hands could let out without blinking—lies with the gloves off ; and what feats of driving some of these knights of the road could accomplish !

I remember hearing of one of Cobb and Co's drivers who was never known to be late reaching his destination. One day he was delayed on the road by a flood or a fallen tree. Determined to reach home in time, he 'let her go' for all she was worth and came down the mountains at the rate of 100 mile or so an hour. The only box passenger was bumped up into a passing gum tree, where he remained, awaiting orders. Then the boot and its contents parted company. Still the driver piled on the pace. Then that coach started to distribute itself over the surface of sundry parishes. Nothing daunted by these circumstances, the driver hung the mail bags around his neck and drove into the depot on the axle, fourteen seconds in front of schedule time. I did not see this with my own eyes ; but I have no reason to doubt it, because I met that driver and he told me all about it. The front of his head was quite bald, where the wind had blown his hair off. His name was Buck, and out back, when the boys were going it pretty strong, they used the expression 'Let her go for Buck's the rider.'

Some of us, doubtless, remember the bush publican who bossed a certain mail change. When the company were seated at dinner he would whisk off the covers with a flourish and exclaim *Now then, gents, what'll yer 'ave ? There's lamb, ram and mutton*. They were the days when there was work and enough for all hands to do, A snack and a shake-down for a traveller too.— W.F."
(The Day of Cobb and Co., 19 Dec 1908, p.12)

1935 See also Conroy, James (Jim)

Hoyle, Tommy ... 1908 See Byrne, F. A.

Hoyt, (Christian name unknown) ... 1875 See Turner, Bob (Big Bob)

Hunter, James
1906 "The Cobb and Co. drivers are dying out one by one, and must soon be more rare than Crimean veterans. The latest to throw down the reins for good is James Hunter, of Emu Plains. He started driving for the Company in Melbourne, went on the Southern line, and finished in the West. His daughter is married to W. Howell, the well known Australian cricketer." (From Day to Day, 4 Sept 1906, p.4)

Hunter, Jim ... 1929 See Amies, Tom; Appendix 1.6

Hunter, Nick ... 1955 See Yankee Bill; 1955 Yeomans, Edward (Ted)

Hunter, Robert
1936 "The death has occurred in Sydney of Mrs. E. J. Cronin, a Mudgee native, at the age of 65. Mrs. Cronin was the daughter of the late Mr. Robert Hunter, a driver of the Cobb and Co. coach which plied between Mudgee and Coonamble many years ago." (Mainly About People, 12 Nov 1936, p.12)

Hunter, Tom ... 1923 See Robinson, James (Robbie)

Hussey, Charles
1925 "Another of the old residents of Healesville in the person of Mr. Charles Hussey, passed away on Saturday, June 13, at the age of 67 years. Deceased, who was born at Brushy Creek, was a well-known coach driver between Warburton, Lilydale and Woods' Point 45 years ago, and was also amongst the first drivers when the lime kilns at Cave Hill, Lilydale, were opened. Mr. Hussey was prominent in the recent re-union held in Melbourne of Cobb and Co.'s old coach drivers. For the past 20 years he had been employed at the Terminus Hotel, Healesville, and was highly respected by all who knew him. He leaves a widow, four daughters and one son to mourn their loss." (Obituary, 20 Jun 1925, p.2)

Hussey, W ... 1937 See Preston, R.

Hutchinson, (Christian name unknown)
1879 "An accident occurred at midnight, last night, to Cobb's coach, which left Merriwa for Casilis, Hutchinson driving … The agent hero states that, at about 6 o'clock this morning, two of the coach horses, with a portion of their harness on, walked into the yard. This was the first intimation of the accident. He at once left to ascertain the cause, and found the coach completely shattered, the harness scattered along the road, the lamps smashed, and, strange to say, the driver, who says that his arm is broken and that he is otherwise injured, was found coiled up in the boot of the coach asleep. He says that no assistance being anywhere near at hand, he remained to protect the mailbags" (Colonial and Intercolonial Messages, 12 Jul 1879, p.9)

Hutchinson, H ... 1919 See Aisbett, E. J.

Hutchinson, Henry
1948 "HUTCHINSON … late member of Cobb and Co. Coach Drivers' Association." (Family Notices, 3 Aug 1948, p.2)

Hutchinson, Jim
1944 "Early-day Hughenden … a few corrections … My father was storekeeping at Prairie in 1884 which was the railway terminus before the line was continued to Hughenden in 1887. I think that was the year, but these notes are from memory. Cobb and Co. were running coaches from Prairie and that old timer, Jim Hutchison, was the man in charge on the box seat. After Cobb's left Prairie they changed horses at Jardine Valley, on Deep Creek, a mile away, and which runs into the Flinders" (On the Track, 13 Nov 1944, p.3)

1917 See also Richardson, W.

Hutchinson, W ... 1937 See Preston, R.

Ike, (Christian name unknown) (Bendigo Ike)
1927 See Redfern, Jim; 1878 Chamberlain, George

Circa 1920 Joe Hirschberg on Duchess to Camooweal route—Courtesy Queensland Museum Collection

Chapter Six

Drivers

J – L

There was talk of flood, or the fear that sprang

Like a frightened bird when the 'Hold-up' rang—

The 'halt' at forty paces

When, 'hell for leather' or lose the lot,

The whip cracks echoed the pistol shot.

And the horses leapt to the traces.

E. R. Murray, Queensland (Verse 4)

ca. 1925 Main street in Surat, Fred Thompson driver, Tom Leonard sits next to Fred; Cobb & Co's last coach run Surat to Yuleba 14/8/1924 (Photo and information from Jim Crack; Photo used in 'Telegraph' newspaper 29 August 1924)—Courtesy Queensland Museum Collection

Supporting evidence:

Jackson, (Christian name unknown) ... 1875 See Turner, Bob (Big Bob)

Jackson, Pegleg/Peleg Whitford
1858 "CASTLEMAINE. (From the Mail and Miners Right.) COBB'S NEW COACHES.—The second of the new coaches, which are exciting so much attention just now among the traveling portion of the public, arrived in Castlemaine on Tuesday, with twenty-eight passengers, driven by Jackson, one of Cobb's crack whips. The coach which arrived yesterday carried thirty passengers. The coaches are made at Concord, in New Hampshire."

While also written on the same page in the paper "HOG CHOLERA.—The hog cholera has found its way to Castlemaine. The animal appears to be attacked in the first instance in the head, something after the manner of a cranky sheep. A portion of the tail may then be cut, and a small slit made in the ear, for the purpose of bleeding, and a little opening medicine given. About a couple of nobblers of brandy should then be poured in the trough, with a little oatmeal, which the pig will take with avidity and relief. If remedial measures are not speedily adopted, the disease proves fatal in about twenty-four hours." (Castlemaine, 13 Jan 1858, p.2)

27 Jul 1860 "We, the undersigned, do hereby give notice. that the PARTNERSHIP hitherto existing; between us, under the style of the VICTORIAN STAGE COMPANY, EXPIRED by effluxion of time on the 25th of June ult. All claims against the said company up to that date must be sent in to A L. Blake, the manager, in Melbourne, or to one of the agents mentioned below on or before the 21st of August, or they will not be recognised. The names of the agents are as follows :—J. F. Britton, Sandhurst ; P. W. Jackson, Castlemaine ; J. M. Connoll, Digger's Rest ; C. D. Pollock, Maryborough ; H. T. Millie. Shamrock Hotel, Ararat ; A Montegani, Creswick's Creek ; E. T. Foley, Ballarat ; James Hay, M'Ivor ; Wm. Jones, Echuca. (Signed) ARTHUR LINCOLN BLAKE. PELEG WHITFORD JACKSON. JOHN FRANCIS BRITTON. OLIVER BLAKE CLAPP. CHRISTOPHER IVES. JOHN MURRAY PECK. CHARLES CULWELL GARDINER." (Advertising 27 Jul 1860, p3)

1858 See also Levi, Emanuel (Manny); 1929 See Mesbitt, Bill

Jackson, W. P ... 1917 See Levi, Emanuel (Manny); 1935 Conroy, James (Jim)

Jarvis, Dave ... 1920 See Gales, A.

Jenkins, Isaac ... 1860 See Mack, James

Jenkins, Jose ... See Appendix 1.6

Jennings, H ... 1919 See Aisbett, E. J.

Jensen, Alfred
"One of the great men who lost his life whilst serving the people of the bush" (Memorial plaque, Surat Cemetery, Qld) "Alfred was born in Denmark in 1879. His family emigrated from Denmark in 1885. They came aboard the RMS Merkara, via London. The family disembarked in Rockhampton. At that time his father August was 34, his mother Karen was 33, his brother Anders was 4, and his sister Agnes was 1. They all remained living and working in Queensland, in Rockhampton and Brisbane. After Alfred's death on the 7th March 1911, aged 39 years, Cecil's son (born 1939) remembers the old pioneers acknowledging Alf when they spoke to his Dad, Cecil, (Alfred's son), lamenting his loss. After his death, the family all moved back to Barcaldine where Alf's wife Harriet was from. Harriet ran a lolly shop in Barcaldine for years, and in addition did many other odd jobs like washing, ironing etc to keep the family fed. Alf and Harriet also lost two children in infancy–Alfred Jnr (died in Barcaldine in 1900) and Annie (died 1908 in Yuleba and is buried in the same cemetery as Alf). Harriet never remarried and is remembered by her grandson, (Cecil's son, who grew up in Barcaldine), *as a resilient, strong and austere woman, greatly respected by the community. The hardships she must have endured are almost unimaginable, and we are very proud of her.*

Direct descendants of Alf include senior officers in the Australian Army, Navy and Air Force (including operational service), a doctor, a magistrate, an Order of Australia recipient, an Olympic swimmer, the Chief Pilot of Qantas, Shire leaders and in the mining industry. Many descendants also worked in the outback as stockmen, shearers, carriers and publicans, important jobs in these remote communities.

Community service and a strong work ethic remain strong values in our family, and have been hallmarks of each generation of Alf's descendants. The notification of Alf's death in the Balonne Beacon, shows he was a well-known and well-respected Cobb and Co driver. Incredibly, over 100 years since his passing, he is still publicly acknowledged through his employment with Cobb and Co, one of the most iconic and respected Australian institutions of all. *We are very proud of Alf, and our family's unique connection to Cobb and Co.*" (Contribution by Alfred's Great Grandson, Mac Jensen, 2023)

1917 See also Richardson, Alf; 1917 Anderson, Jim; 1947 Richards, J. Frederick (Fred)

Jinkins, J ... 1932 See Lowe, Bill

Jinks, Mrs. Mary C.
1951 "COBB AND CO. DAYS Former Cobb and Co. coach driver Mrs. Mary C. Jinks, 78, of Garden City, Victoria, says *the girls of to-day lack pioneer spirit. So you can't expect the young men to have that spirit. Girls of to-day are ruining themselves with smoking and gay life*, she said. Her remedy: *Bring back the Cobb and Co. coaches and give the young Australians a year on the run*, she says. *I used to drive a coach from Broken Hill to White Cliffs opal fields (150 miles). I made the trip with a gun in one hand, the reins in the other. We had to watch the sundowners those days.*" (Cobb and Co. Days, 26 Jul 1951, p.10)

1951 "She drove for Cobb and Co. The Cobb and Co. coach that rolled into Ballarat last Monday carried as a passenger the only woman driver registered with the Victorian association of Cobb and Co.'s Old Drivers. She ... still retains the love of adventure that caused her to follow her pioneering husband to the opal fields in western New South Wales half a century ago.

For three years she ran the 'Mail Change' at Kapala, along the route from Broken Hill to the Bunker Creek opal fields, and many a time she drove a change of horses out to replace a tired team and bring the coach in to the house. The drivers would blow their horns as soon as they were within hearing, distance and, according to the tune, Mrs Jinks would know whether all was well or not. If the tune was 'Hot Potatoes' she could leave the change horses in the stable and devote herself to preparing a meal of goat meat, potatoes and dried vegetables for the passengers. If it was not she would leave the meal and set out with a fresh team to bring the coach in while the driver followed with the tired horses. At that time the opal fields were served by coach twice a week and, four days out of seven, Mrs Jinks had to provide a meal for passengers and driver. If her husband was away, she had also to see that fresh horses were available for the next stage of the journey. For part of this time she lived, in a tent. Her kitchen was a bark and tin humpy ... Now that she has settled down in Melbourne, where she lives with one of her 14 children, Mrs Jinks finds an outlet for her boundless energy by collecting for charity." (She drove for Cobb and Co, 22 Aug 1951, p.32)

(Surname unknown), Joe
1902 "ALONG THE LINE March 5th. Storm clouds, and a Westerly wind coming up off rain. Some showers fell last night, in odd Western plains. It's just the recent kind of showers, two drops to the acre. Some places are moderately well off, but no one speaks confidently of the season. I daresay, however, you'd find a few Gulf places well enough off to be past anxiety, and from the talk, I should reckon Coalbrook and Woolgar places fairly independent. I was speaking to Joe, I mean Cobb and Co. Joe, about the Richmond road, and he tells me there's fair feed for sheep all the way along from Hughenden." (Along the line, 7 Mar 1902, p.6)

Johnson, Billy
1926 "COLLINS'S HOTEL. A REMINISCENCE BY 'CESTUS.' Fire has robbed Charters Towers of one of its old landmarks for the well known Exchange Hotel was burnt down on Tuesday morning. When Hugh Mossman, George Clarke and Fraser developed the North Australian and Mossman reefs, the population first settled at Milichester began to trend from that 'Sea-port' to Charters Towers ... Jimmy Anderson, good looking Harry Speakman, a prince amongst football players. Jack Benham, 'Dad' a forward of force, a crack walker and noted oarsman, venerable George Summers, white haired, and patriarchal, the Highlander Simon Fraser with the song of the Celt in his voice, Paddy Guinane, the last three cordial manufacturers, whose carts were never out of Collins's yard, Freddie Johnson, a keen worker in anything political, municipal or national, Billy Johnson, the old Cobb and Co. driver and cabman, Meeson, Jack Lewis, Dobbs, Charley Sutton, Arthur and Joe Clark, Mick Anderson, and Harry Reddel, all 'cabbies,' and speculators, and amongst the last but by no means least, 'Faugha-Ballagh' a giant who could and did eat as much on three ordinary miners." (Collins's Hotel, 19 Jun 1926, p.6)

Johnson, Jack ... 1933 See Bates, Bob

Jones, Bill
1925 "Experiences of Half a Century ... Jimmy Nicholas Handles the Ribbons ... Victorian Cobb and Co (Robertson and Wagner) ran these coaches on the night mail between Hay and Deniliquin, while the big passenger traffic was on there, for many years. They seated about 30 passengers, and with very deep lazybacks, ditto cushions, they were most comfortable, being conveyances of luxury in the coaching days. I think this line might easily be classed as one of the best equipped coaching lines, if not the very best, that Australia has had.

It was 80 miles across the Old Man Plains, lovely to travel over on a summer night, but a quagmire of mud and slush in the winter time. This line passed the notorious Trotting Cob Swamp, near Wanganella. A legend used to say that a headless grey cob, with a rider who was also headless, sometimes was to be seen trotting at a great pace and disappearing most mysteriously, just as it had appeared to be coming close to you. I don't think a coach ever passed that place day or night but that all the passengers were anxious to be shown the Trotting Club Swamp. However, the bubble burst some years later when it came to light that the cob and rider were both very human and did the ghost stunt to cover up a method of stock duffing, from any travelling mob that might be along that way ...

Some of the drivers I remember on it were Bill Keast (a champion driver, careful and capable), Tom Ploughs, big Bill Jones, Jack Keast, Alick Fossett, Saltbush M'Kenzie and others whom I cannot just recall, as the time I speak of is some forty years ago one forgets things. These men were all masters of their profession in the days when Australia was carried mostly by Cobb and Co. ahead of the railways." (Coaching in the Commonwealth, 17 May 1925)

Jones, Johnnie (Left handed with the whip) ... See Clark, Billy

Jonson, Andes
1897 "COBB'S COACH TO ORBOST. Mr Andes Jonson, who drives the mail coach from Cunninghame to Orbost, is a young man whom it is well to know." (Cobb's Coach to Orbost, 20 Nov 1897, p.20)

Jordan, W. E.
1906 "MR. W. E. JORDAN, a well-known resident of Goulburn for many years, died in Prince Alfred Hospital, Sydney, on Monday, at the age of 61 years. Mr. Jordan was at one time a mail coach driver in the employ of the historic firm of Cobb and Co. Later he drove the coach between Braidwood and Tarago for Mr. Malone, and relinquishing that employment came to Goulburn, where he went into business as a cab proprietor, following that occupation for many years ... Mr. Jordan was highly respected, and the news of his death will be received with regret. He leaves a widow and family." (Obituary, 22 Aug 1906, p.2)

Kavenagh, John
1926 "On Tuesday night there passed away at the District Hospital practically the oldest identity of the Hillston district in the person of John Kavenagh, at the ripe old age of 80 years. Deceased in the early days was employed driving one of the renowned Cobb and Co. coaches—the only method of transport from one place to another in the [18]50's. The deceased had lived the greater part of his life in the Hillston district ... A few days

previous to his demise he sustained serious injury owing to his clothes becoming ignited when trying to do something at a fire. Had it not been for the presence of his adopted daughter in the house at the time something more serious may have occurred. Regardless of injury to herself she promptly wrapped something around the old man to extinguish the fire, and subsequently obtaining assistance had him conveyed to the hospital, where he succumbed as stated." (Obituary, 14 Jan 1926, p.6)

Keast, (Christian name unknown)
1924 "Drivers were paid up to £14 a week, and grooms £4 10s a week. Cobb and Co. were just and liberal with their vast army of employees … there was never any difficulty between the management and the men, and no firm ever had a more reliable, loyal and faithful body of servants. The old coach drivers were original and forceful characters, and most delightful travelling companions. I have ridden thousands of miles with them in the olden days, they always gave me the box seat and I would take the reins sometimes, while the worn out Jehu slumbered in the 'boot,' on top of the mail bags. It was a common occurrence for a man to go for days and nights without a real rest …

I travelled once with a man named Keast, from Wilcannia to Hay, some three or four hundred miles, and we recited poetry all the way, turn and turn about. Such journeys would kill the modern young man who feels tired if he goes for a 10 mile ride, and talks about fatigue if he travels for a few hours in a buggy, or railway carriage, but in the olden days men were made in a stronger mould and thought nothing of going for a week without a stop." (Cobb & Co., 13 Dec 1924, p.2)

Keast, Bill … 1925 See Jones, Bill; 1934 Hole, Mat.

Keast, Jack … 1925 See Jones, Bill

Keast, John William
1907 "DOUBLE BEREAVEMENT. HAY, Wednesday.—John William Keast, a very old and well-known coach-driver for Messrs. Cobb and Co., died at Melbourne today, after undergoing an operation. The young man, Albert Keast, who was found in the river yesterday, was the second son of deceased. Young Keast was buried at Hay this afternoon, the funeral being largely attended. The town band played the 'Dead March' to the cemetery as a mark of respect to their late member. Deep sympathy is everywhere expressed with the family in their double bereavement." (Double Bereavement, 19 Dec 1907, p.8)

Keast, William … 1928 See Grover, Robert H. (Wharparilla Bob)

Keightly, Ted … 1935 See Conroy, James (Jim)

Kellier (?), Edward (Barney)
1951 "Mr Edward (Barney) Kellier—one of the best known of Townsville's old residents … A resident of T C Avenue, Railway Estate, he was aged 94 years. Seventy-four years of his life he had spent in Queensland. His varied career had made him one of the most romantic figures in the city, having landed at Townsville on St Patrick's Day 74 years ago. He was early in Charters Towers and was also associated with Cobb and Co. coaches. His first run being from Blackall to Whi?town (now Isisford). Later he drove from Bogantungan to Blackall, and then to Pine Hill, Beta and Jericho, and finally between Blackall and Tambo." (Obituary, 11 Aug 1951, p.3)

Kelly, (Christian name unknown)
1892 "Coach Accident. An accident happened to Cobb and Co.'s coach, running between Broken Hill and Milparinka, on its last trip down, which, though fortunately unaccompanied by injury to anyone, placed the driver in considerable jeopardy. Constable Breen, who was on his way to attend the Circuit Court sittings here, was the only passenger, and when near Fowler's Gap descended from the box seat to open a gate. The horses became restless, and the driver, in order to facilitate Constable Breen's ascent, held his team very firmly. Just as the constable mounted to the box the leading rein broke and the horses bolted. Breen jumped to the ground before the team had top speed on, so as to secure the heads of the animals, but the pace was too fast, and he could do nothing. The driver, Kelly, however, displayed much coolness and courage in his difficulty. The country was open, and he managed to keep the team going in a circle until finally the coach capsized. Kelly was, of course, thrown from his seat, but sustained no material injury beyond a bruise on the knee. The pole was broken, but the safety-strap which keeps the fore carriage attached to the coach held the horses, and with Constable Breen's assistance they were secured. After the vehicle had been patched up in some fashion, Euriowie was reached, 20 miles distant, only a little after the contract time. The accident is attributed to faulty reins." (Coach Accident, 19 Apr 1892, p.2)

1930-1940s See also Allan, (Christian name unknown)

Kelly, Charles
1921 "ECHO OF COBB AND CO. Train passengers to Cowra will miss a familiar face from the local railway station (writes Cowra Guardian), for all who knew the genial busman Mr. Charles Kelly. His patriarchal figure and happy voice made him a notable on the station, where he was a general favorite. Death claimed him on Saturday afternoon last at the fine old age of 73 … Deceased was a native of Monaro, and in his early days was a driver for Cobb and Co. between Young and Grenfell. Afterwards he was in the employ of Wright Heaton and Co. Some 35 years ago he settled down in Cowra and remained here for that long spell, nearly all the time driving his own vehicles for hire. Mr. Kelly was twice married. Sons by the first marriage are Eugene, William and George and daughters Mrs. Martin, Mrs. Patterson and Mrs. Waterbury, nearly all of whom are resident in Sydney. His son Joseph issue of the second marriage, follows in his father's footsteps as busman in Cowra." (Echo of Cobb and Co., 10 Sep 1921, p.4)

Kelton, Jimmy … 1934 See Alexander, Jack

Kennedy, (Christian name unknown) … 1937 See Preston, R.

Kennedy, Tom … 1932 See Lowe, Bill; Appendix 1.6

Keough, Jim … 1921 See Griffen, Chas.

Kidd, Tom … 1929 See Amies, Tom; 1923 Robinson, James (Robbie); 1955 Yankee Bill

Kidman/Kiddman, Charles (Charlie)
1953 "Coach Runs in Early Days ALL NAMED COBB AND

CO. To the Editor. Sir,—I have been interested in the many letters concerning early-day life on the goldfields which have appeared in the 'Kalgoorlie Miner,' as during the past 57 years my home has been at various places between Coolgardie and Meekatharra. I first saw Coolgardie in August on 1896. These anecdotes have brought to mind the manner in which the women of those days had to 'rough it.'

For instance, I remember being at the teamsters' camp at Menzies on a Saturday night in October, 1896, when a team arrived from Coolgardie at 9 p.m. With that team were a miner's wife and some school-age children. That journey, meant four, if not five, nights' camp in the bush. You had to be in the money to pay Cobb and Co. fares, which on some of the back-country trips, were as high as 1/ per mile. Incidentally there were some who thought that Cobb and Co. were the one great firm operating all over Australia, which was not the case. In the Geelong district of Victoria, which was my family's first Australian home after leaving Ireland 64 years ago, there was a man named Vines, who ran district coaches under the name of Cobb and Co. I believe that on these goldfields Kiddman and Nicholas were trading under the name. The partner was Mr. Charles Kiddman and not his more famed brother, Sir Sidney Kiddman, as I have sometimes seen in the press. I have also been told that a man named McKenzie and a partner, whose name I have forgotten, ran the first coaches from Cue to Peak Hill, trading as Cobb and Co. The first coaches to Lawlers were run by Crews and Co. from Mt. Magnet and they continued until Sandstone became a settled community, when Kiddman and Nicholas bought Crews and Co. out.

Cobb's last horse mail, somewhere about 1913 or early 1914, was up the back track from Sandstone to Wiluna and the late Dick Daly was the last driver on that line. Both Dick Daly and Jimmy Matthews took over motor coach driving when the horses were gone. Places I have been employed at on the ‹fields are Darlot, Lawlers, Leonora, Sandstone, Meekatharra, Youanmi, Errols (near Barrambie) and finally Kalgoorlie. When I first saw Canon Collick he was holding services in a dining room in Menzies. That was about November, 1896. There were no churches or halls then. — Yours etc., LEN LAMBERT, 41 Colins street, Kalgoorlie." (Coach Runs in Early Days 17 Jun 1953, p.8)

1925 See also Eddie, Nathan

Kidman, Sir Sydney (Syd) ... 1925 See Nicholas/Nicholls, James (Jim/Jimmy)

Kilpatrick, Arthur ... 1920 See Gales, A.

King, Charlie
1925 "Coaching in the Commonwealth. Experiences of Half a Century. 'Jimmy' Nicholas Handles the Ribbons ... There used to be a rather notorious place of its kind on the road between Urana and Jerilderie called the Cockeydejong Swamps. This place, had some fearsome phantom lights floating about it during the winter months, when the swamps used to be filled with water after the winter rains. There was quite a good deal of interest taken in these mysterious lights, and one of the Sydney papers—the 'Bulletin,' I think—sent its agent up to have the matter investigated. I do not know what opinion he formed of the apparitions, but there was considerable comment in the papers about what it was and what caused it.

However, all Cobb and Co.'s drivers called this part of the road The Dog's Road, and none of them cared to take it on. The driver there at the time I mention, named Charlie King, used to swear they were ghosts, and towards the end got very nervous of them. He had to cross this swamp ten times a week at night—he left Urana at 8 p.m. five nights a week and ran down towards Jerilderie (25 miles) where he met an up coach and then returned to Urana at 4 a.m. I was on the Urana to Wagga road at the time, and had to turn out as soon as King came in and take my coach on to Wagga. I remember be used to come in some mornings very scared of these lights, and say he knew they were some kind of ghosts, as they rose out of a little creek on the edge of the swamp each night as he got there. If he was running late, they would be well over the swamp and die out on the other side, and if he were early they sprang up from the same creek and followed him across the swamp. He reckoned the starting place of this creek from which these lights sprang up nightly was to be the place where he was going to meet his end, in a coach accident.

Strange to say on Christmas night 1877, I landed with my coach at Urana to find that King had that morning been thrown off his coach at the very place he had always been afraid of, and been, fearfully smashed up. He had both arms broken and one leg and his head fearfully cut about, and altogether he was pretty nearly finished, but he recovered after being in hospital eight or nine months, though he was never able to drive again." (Coaching in the Commonwealth, 31 May 1925, p.9)

King, Harry ... 1932 See Lowe, Bill; Appendix 1.6

Kingsland, Daniel (Dan)
1933 "Sydney Morning Herald of March 10, 1908 ... The R.M.S. Asturias, which arrived on Saturday, counted among her passengers Mr. Daniel Kingsland, one time, horse breaker and driver of Cobb and Co.'s coaches in this and other parts of Australia and now the owner of five estates in Hampshire. There are many with whom Mr. Kingsland was associated in the seventies and eighties, particularly in this State, Queensland, and Victoria, who will remember 'Dan' Kingsland only as an individual into whom fear could not be struck by the wildest horse that was ever bred, and who will be interested in the story of how their quondam friend succeeded in rising to the position he occupies to-day.

Briefly the story may be summed up in the few words—he has spent the last 20 years of his life in the Argentine Republic. This in itself conveys a good deal to those who are acquainted with the rich republic. Mr. Kingsland went to Buenos Ayres in 1880, became interested in the horse and cattle trade, ten years later was responsible for more than half the cattle, exported from the republic, and twelve months ago retired altogether from the control of freezing works that cost £500,000 and are amongst the largest of their kind in the world ... three testimonials from the manager of Cobb and Co., the manager of Kirk's Bazaar, Melbourne, and Hill and Co., proprietors of a horse bazaar in

Adelaide, all declaring that Mr. Dan Kingsland was a competent horsedriver and horsebreaker. Mr. Kingsland is very proud of those and does not hesitate to declare that he found them of considerable value when in 1880, after a residence of 22 year, he left Australia to seek his fortune in other parts ... The climax came when Mrs. Kingsland died in Brisbane. He resolved to seek new fields" (Fame and Fortune, 23 Mar 1933, p.55)

Kirk, K. (Volunteered to take the reins)
1888 "QUEENSLAND. Coach Accident, BRISBANE, This Day.—Cobb's coach met with an accident yesterday at Saint George. While going out with the mails, the driver took ill, and a traveller named Kirk volunteered to take the reins. The horses soon afterwards shied and over turned the coach. Kirk, in falling was pulled off the box and the horses bolted. One of the horses was killed and the passengers were slightly injured." (Queensland, 13 Mar 1888, p.6)

Lairy, Jack
1937 "Cobb & Co's Coaches ... Three times a week Cobb & Co's coaches plied between Gunnedah and Walgett. Passengers booked their seats in advance at various offices along the route. The drivers had to be picked men who drove as many as six in hand, all spirited corn-fed horses which were changed at short distances along the road. From the instant they were harnessed up they danced and plunged, eager to be off on the journey.

There was very little whip required unless it was to let some too free a horse know that there was a master over him. These dexterous men of the reins, however, were just as capable of using the whip as they were of 'holding the ribbons.' They could whip four or five horses at once, an art only acquired after long practise and experience. Jack Lairy and Ted and Bill Lunley were amongst the drivers.

Horses were changed at Narrabri and at two or three places between there and Wee Waa. At Wee Waa the old Commercial Hotel (now burnt down) was a changing place. It was opposite the Oddfellows' Hall and was conducted by Mr. Ben Harris. Another changing place was in the vicinity of Molee. Here crossed the coaches, coming and going. They changed again about 10 miles lower down on the Pilliga road, again about 12 miles nearer Pilliga at a place called Boolawa Creek, at Talumba Creek, and so on to Pilliga and Walgett." (Wee Waa and District News, 2 Sep 1937, p.2)

Laity, (Christian name unknown) ... 1930-1940s See Allan, (Christian name unknown)

Laity, James/Jim
1950 "Coaching Reunion. Cobb Drivers. On Old Run ... The veterans will travel up the old Melbourne-Sydney road by coach again—this time by motor-coach ... Oldest driver present is likely to be Mr James Laity, of Black Rock, 89, who began coaching at 16 and drove the night coach to Daylesford. In its heyday Cobb and Co. harnessed 6000 horses a day in the eastern States of Australia and the coaches covered 26,000 miles a week." (Coaching Reunion, 28 Oct 1950)

1919 See also Aisbett, E. J.; 1930 Alder, Amos

Lakewood, Thomas (Tom)
1933 "MR. T. LAKEWOOD. OLD COBB & CO. DRIVER PASSES. The death occurred in the local hospital on Thursday last of Mr. Thomas Lakewood, at the age of 70 years. Deceased, who was a son of the late Mr. and Mrs. T. Lakewood, had been ailing for some time. In the old coaching days deceased's father was a driver in the employ of Cobb and Co., and deceased was later also employed by the same firm as a driver. At one time the family resided in a cottage situated on the allotment next to the Royal Hall. Two sisters (Mesdames F. Beake and J. Kerr) still reside in Grenfell." (Obituary, 19 Jun 1933, p.2)

1951 See also Leary, Jack

Lambell, E ... 1919 See Aisbett, E. J.

Lambell, W. E.
1932 "An old resident of the Birregurra district, Mr. W. E. Lambell, has died. He was one of Cobb and Co.'s coach drivers." (Colac, 31 Oct 1932, p.11)

Lambert, J. R ... 1888 See Swanton/Swanston, James

Land, Ted
1926 "THE SILENT MEMBER. Picturesque figure in Queensland Parliament is Ted Land, grey-moustached member for the great western plains of Balonne electorate. Land's voice has not been heard in debate since 1917, when he spoke on the land laws and the rabbit menace. His silence is due to an illness in 1918, when doctors advised him to refrain from speaking in public, because of the danger of excitement over interjections. In the last three elections Land has been returned without taking the public platform. His kindly advice to passengers, as a driver of Cobb and Co.'s coach to Cunnamulla, earned him Parliamentary representation 22 years ago. He likes the atmosphere of the House, and perhaps spends more time in the Chamber than any other member. Land's distinguishing marks in the House are a soft shirt, without a collar, and a red rose in his coat. He has never been known to dress any other way.— Galleryite." (Gossip, 20 Nov 1926, p.15)

Langdon, Bill ... 1917 See Wright, Bob

Langley, George Wey
1894 "There are many people still in Victoria whose memories carry them back to the time when King Cobb established his lines of coaches to the gold fields. Amongst the number of coach drivers whom Cobb and Company brought to Victoria was one George Wey Langley, a native of Newport, Rhode Island." (A Romance Of Early Colonial Life, 29 Jan 1894, p.4)

Latewood, T.
1920 "Incidents on Lonely Roads. By Bill Bowyang ... Very few persons, except those who actually lived in the past can have any idea what Cobb and Co. meant to the great outback. It carried to the families living in those lonely parts their letters and newspapers, to say nothing of numerous parcels, and now and then a stray friend ... T. Latewood, driving for Cobb and Co., between Narrabri and Wee Waa (N.S.W.), was left in midstream at Mollee Crossing with a coach-load of passengers through, the pole-hook breaking. The three leading horses dashed up

the bank and collided with a tree, one breaking its nose, and another being so badly injured that it had to be shot … It is with something akin to regret that I state that the glamor of the old coach days has departed for ever, and no more the gleaming lights of Cobb and Co., and the loud whipcracks and cheery shout of the driver will be heard through the still night air to herald the coming of the 'Royal Mail,' and the arrival of the hungry wayfarers, for whom the well kept table of the landlady at the half way hotel gleamed as a veritable oasis in the dessert." (Days of Cobb & Co., 16 Jan 1931, p.8)

Latewood, Thos.
1919 "The death occurred at Grenfell last, week, of Mrs. Ann Latewood, aged 89 years. She came from Ireland to Australia in 1830, and at the early age of 11 was left to fight life's battles alone, a sister who came out with her having died. She was fortunate to find a home with the late Mr. Jas. Roberts, uncle of Sub-inspector Roberts, who brought her up. Later she married Mr .Thos. Latewood, a coach driver for the old firm of Cobb and Co. Deceased was at Braidwood in the early gold digging days, and, often spoke of the times when the diggers lit their pipes with Bank notes. She also resided at Gundagai at the time of the big flood, in 1852. She could converse freely about the doings of the bushrangers. On more than one occasion she came in contact with Ben Hall and his gang." (News and Notes, 25 April 1919, p.1)

Lawrence, Oliver ... 1921 See Griffen, Chas.

Leary, Jack
1951 "I have received a letter … asking me to refresh their memories of the Cobb and Co. days of long ago … here goes … I took on mail running from Brewarrina to Walgett in 1891 and followed the game right up till 1910. In 1892 (if my memory serves me correctly, that was the year Glenloth won the Melbourne Cup) I became a full-blown mailman. In 1902 (I think Victory won the Melbourne Cup) I started with Cobb and Co and came to know such fine men and drivers as Jack Hiller, Sammy Drood, Jack Leary, Pat Cummings, Tom Lakewood, Donald Brenyer, Charlie Brayshaw, Bill Lumley and others—all great men with the ribbons … Jack Leary, was the man who drove the first Cobb and Co coach to Walgett and drove the last Cobb and Co coach out of Walgett, after the train had taken up the running. Our wages were £14 a month … a bugle—better known as a mailhorn … every mailman was compelled to carry one of the mailhorns strapped on the driving side of his coach.

BROKEN COACH POLES … drivers carried hemp clothes lines … driver got to a mail change or a roadside pub and he would be knocked up and lie down and perhaps doze off to sleep. … he would probably be an hour late arriving …what kept you? … Prior to this the driver … bound up the coach pole with a clothes line and his excuse would be that the horses played up and broke the pole.

GREATEST DRIVER … Tom McDonald was a marvel with the reins" (In the Days of Cobb & Co., 19 Jan 1951, p.2)

Lee, Charles (Charley/Charlie) ... 1923 See Robinson, James (Robbie); 1934 Hole, Mat.

Leftwitch, Thos ... 1919 See Aisbett, E. J.

Lennon, Jack
1917 "The first coach was driven through from Port Douglas to Normanton by Harry Bruce, an old driver. During the Etheridge and Croydon booms no route was busier in the whole of Queensland. The coaches ran three times a week from sea to sea, once a week to Georgetown, once a week from Normanton to Cloncurry, and twice a week from Port Douglas to Herberton … C. E. Search, now inspector at Charleville, took charge at Normanton, Kruck taking the Croydon management, and among the drivers on this perilous road were Jack Lennon, Jack Warner (the old St. George-Surat driver, who, in crossing the flooded Balonne River, was swept away, losing coach and horses and almost his life)" (Coaching in Australia, 1917, p.48)

Leonard, Jack ... 1917 See Richardson, W.

Le Sueur, Jim ... 1930 See Alder, Amos

Levi, Emanuel (Manny)
1858 "A Colonial Pic-Nic.—We guess we can beat the old country in pic-nics. At least this was the opinion of forty gentlemen who took their seats on Cobb's coach yesterday morning, for a pleasure trip to the Loddon. There were Jackson and Levi at the helm, driving ten horses ; there were 'creature comforts' ad infinitum; there was a magnificent country, and William Henry Fancourt Mitchell and Frederick Taylor appeared upon the scene, and Her Majesty was drunk, and the President of the United States was toasted, the Victorian Stage Company was drunk, and 'The Ladies' were duly honored, and all the elements of enjoyment were imported into the occasion. The resources of the Victorian Stage Company must be enormous, and fully equal to all the requirements of our present internal communication. A pic-nic under these auspices is a thing worth enjoying, and when they next give one, may we be there to see." (Uncertainty of Mining Law, 29 Oct 1858, p.3)

1917 "In the sets of teams used by the firm were the six matched blacks driven by Emanuel Levi, an American, six greys driven by W. P. Jackson, six roans driven by Harry Netterfield, six bays driven by Carter. All were well bred, handsome, well groomed horses, and intelligent as one could wish. A fine sight was the coach and its 12 white horses as they moved through the crowd in front of the Bull and Mouth, Bourke street, Melbourne, on their way to Ballarat." (Coaching in Australia, 1917, p.20)

1935 See also Conroy, James (Jim)

Leviston, W.
1919 "The Cobb & Co.'s Old Coach Drivers' Association … old coach drivers employed by Messrs. Cobb & Co., kindred coaching firms in Australia and New Zealand, and others … Driver, district employed: Rokewood and Ballarat" (Annual report / Cobb & Co.'s Old Coach Drivers' Association, 1919, pp.6-8)

1933 "The oldest man present was Mr. J. Stephen, of St. Kilda, who used to drive between Sale and Port Albert, and the youngest was Mr. W. Leviston, of Ballarat, a youth of 58, who carried the whip for 38 years." (Former Cobb and Co. Drivers, 21 Jun 1933, p.11)

Lewis, Alf ... 1917 See Wright, Bob; 1947 See Richards, J. Frederick (Fred); 1950 See Hickson, Harry

Lewis, Peter ... 1932 See Lowe, Bill; Appendix 1.6

Little, Jim (Jimmy) ... 1928 See Frost, James (Old Jim Frost); 1929 Corbett, Alec.; Appendix 1.6

Lloyd, Charles
1909 "COUNTRY NEWS. QUEENSCLIFF. DEATH OF A PIONEER COACH DRIVER. Mr Charles Lloyd, livery stable proprieor, of Queenscliff, died at his residence on Friday. In the early days he was employed as a coachman by Cobb and Cos., and one of his duties was to convey the English mails, which were then landed at the Heads, from Queensland to Geelong." While on the same page "PORT FAIRY. THE SEALING SYNDICATE.The Melbourne syndicate which had a charter from the Government to kill 500 seals on Julia Percy Island, has been keenly disappointed with the undertaking. The men employed to carry out the work, all of whom are experienced, have returned, and stated that there were not nearly as many seals on the island as reported, and hose there were very wild. Somepersons had evidently been there recently, and been indiscriminately shooting a number of seals. This had had the effect of driving the seals away. An inspector of fisheries accompanied the men on their expedition, and it is his intention of making full enquiries into the matter." (Country News, 30 Aug 1909, p.6)

Lloyd, H.
1912 "With the fall of the leaf (writes our Castlemaine correspondent) the death roll of local pioneers has been considerably lengthened during the past week. The latest addition is Mrs. Lloyd, widow of Mr. H. Lloyd, one of Cobb and Co.'s coach drivers in the early days. She was 39 years old" (Obituary, 27 May 1912, p.6)

Lloyd, Jack ... See Appendix 1.6

Long, Jack ... 1917 See Wright, Bob

Loveday, (Christian name unknown)
1927 "COACH ACCIDENT. The Glen Innes correspondent of the Armidale 'Express' 50 years ago recorded ; Cobb and Co's coach, on the trip from Tenterfield to Glen Innes, again met with an accident on Tuesday last. On a very rough portion of the road, between Halliday's mail station and the Deepwater River, the axle gave way in the centre, necessitating the leaving of the coach on the road. Mr. Loveday, the driver, was obliged to convey the mail on horseback to Dundee, where Mr. Utz kindly lent him a vehicle with which to proceed on his journey The mail, was, however, delivered in Glen Innes in due time." (Coach Accident, 5 Nov 1927, p.4)

Lovelock, Johnny
1914 "Mr. 'Johnny' Lovelock, born in 1839, native of Berkshire, came to Melbourne from New York on 12th August, 1853. Nine ships left at same time. Spent his 16th birthday at Border Inn, Bacchus Marsh. Went to Blackwood rush. Was employed at Golden Point store of Oxenham, Cohen & Hagard. Had driven coaches for Cobb & Co. on several routes in Victoria. Died at Carlton, 26th. April, 1912. An affable unpretentious man.

(Bacchus Marsh, 19 Sep 1914, p.3)

1870 "ATTEMPTED STICKING-UP OF THE DUNOLLY MAIL ... The Dunolly mail coach, a light two-horse vehicle, left Cobb's office at twelve o'clock on Friday night, driven by Johnnie Lovelock well known to travellers on that road ... a man rushed out of the bush and seizing the bridle of the near side horse cried out to the driver to 'stand' and stop the horses. The sudden appearance of the man from the scrub on the side of the road startled the horses, and caused them to swerve to one side so violently that the vehicle nearly ran on to the embankment, but the driver with great presence of mind kept his horses well in hand and steered clear of the bank, and drove on so fast that the man had to let go the bridle. He then ran up close to the box and again ordered the driver to stand ... the pistol exploded, but neither passengers, driver, horses, nor coach were hit with the ball ... Lovelock then applied the whip to the horses, with vigor, and galloped into Creswick to Anthony's American hotel, where the coaches always stop. As may be imagined, both driver and passengers were in a great state of excitement ... the man who endeavoured to stop the coach ... had what appeared to be a dirty handkerchief over his face." (Attempted Sticking Up Of The Dunolly Mail, 22 Feb 1870, p.3)

Lowe, Bill (Son of James Lowe)
1932 "COBB & CO. DAYS (To the Editor) Sir,—Mr. A. R. Hood, of Wellington, is quite correct when he states that there were very few Cobb & Co. coaches on the road 30 years ago. In the west there was one running between Nevertire and Warren, and a few others connecting outlying districts with the railway. Your correspondent stated that the Duke of Manchester travelled from Bourke to Wellington, and that Bill Walden drove him from Warren to Dubbo. I knew Bill well, and a good driver he was, too. With H. Nowel Bill Walden drove on the Dubbo end of the Bourke-road. Mr. Hood declares that he himself drove the Duke to Orange. I was not aware that His Grace was out here more than once. Anyhow, none of these drivers seem to have received much of a tip. The Duke gave me a 'fiver,' and the gentleman who accompanied him 'shelled out' very well.

Cobb & Co. did not use many six-horse coaches. Five horses was usually the largest team, and a very good team to handle. For Mr. Hood's information, I drove six horses when Mr. Rutherford (one of the proprietors) gave the children of Bathurst a picnic at Hereford. Five coaches conveyed the children—four 30-passenger with five horses, and one 45-passenger with six horses. The drivers were Bob Rogers, Harry King, Peter Lewis, Tom Kennedy and myself. An argument arose as to who would drive the six-horse team, but Mr. Rutherford settled it by taking the box seat and calling me up to take the reins. I was only 17 at the time. After this I drove a six-horse thorough-brace van between Dubbo and Buckinguy and a similar team in a coach on the Sunny Corner-road. I would like to know when Peter Lewis drove six horses from Bathurst to Albury, I never knew that there was a line of coaches between these towns, and if there was it must have been a very long time ago. I worked with Peter and I never once heard him refer to this run. At the time I was driving from Dubbo to Buckinguy Mr. J. Weldon was the branch manager and Mr. Hamilton was in the office at Bill Orble's Royal Hotel. The railway bridge over the rise was just being completed at the time, and Dubbo was a very lively place then. I knew John

Barrir, J. Jinkins, D. Doyle, B. McGroda, and C. Bissu, all drivers, and I think I remember Mr. Hood, too. Probably he remembers me. Yours, etc., BILL LOWE. Portland." (Cobb & Co. Days, 22 Mar 1932, p.2)

1932 "Bill Lowe, who resides at Portland, is one of the old drivers of Cobb and Co's, coaches still to the land of the living, and one whose hands are still as capable of handling the ribbons as when he drove the Duke of Manchester from Bathurst to Hill End, to 1881. Bill was the youngest driver ever employed by the famous overlanding firm, being only 18 when he was given charge of a coach, and for 33 years he tooled his team over all kinds of roads and in all kinds of weather, until the railways forced the company to wind up." (Cobb & Co., 19 Feb 1932, p.5)

1932 "COBB & CO. DRIVER DISAPPOINTED After all, Mr. Bill Lowe, of Portland, the old Cobb and Co. coach driver, did not drive the historic mail coach ... in the Bridge procession on Saturday." (Cobb & Co. Driver Disappointed, 23 Mar 1932, p.3)

1919 See also Aisbett, E. J.; Appendix 1.6

Lowe, James (Jim)
1937 "Gold Digging Days. Stories of the Old Coach Drivers. Safe Deposit for a woman's gold By Will Carter (Copyright) *Tah—tutta-tah—tutta-tah—tutta-tah-tutta-tah—tutta-tah—tah!* Hark, there's the coach man's bugle! Now the coach enters Bathurst town with a rattle of wheels and a clatter of hooves, and Jim Lowe, always to time, now hauls up his steeds to deliver, the royal mail at the old-time post office. All the way from Hill End, where thousands are talking of Beyers and Holtermann's great bonanza, hauled up at Hawkins' Hill, where the rich mica-veins are yielding fabulous returns, the team stands with trembling forelegs, and streaming with sweat, for Jim has had to send them over the last 10 miles to make up for some lost time on Wyagdon. Now they are off to their quarters for a rub-down and stable comforts for the night.

On the morrow the coach will start again for the gold fields about 4 a.m., be the weather what it will, and there will be corridor-calls in the hotels half an hour before that time to rouse intending passengers from their slumbers. A flourish and crack of the whip, and they are away for Peel, Wyagdon, Wattle Flat, Sofala, and Hill End. One day the coach was nearing Hill End when two bushrangers suddenly appeared and bailed it up. The passengers were compelled to hand out their valuables. Among the company was a woman seated by the driver, nursing a six-months' babe. When the thieves had disappeared, and the coach was jogging on its way, the woman flourished a calico bag containing a hundred sovereigns. *How on earth did they miss them?* inquired the fleeced travellers in amazement. *The moment I saw the men rush from the bush*, said the woman, I *slipped the bag into the folds of the baby's napkin; they didn't think to search the child.*

HIDE AND SEEK Jim Lowe told a story of a certain Bathurst jeweller's wife who used to make fortnightly trips to the diggings to collect watches for repair, as well as to buy gold, and take orders for rings, brooches, earrings and other jewellery. She would be loaded with valuables each way, and always carried her stock inside a carcase of mutton. Some placed their money in a dripping tin well down on the 'bed- rock,' under the rendered fat. Others sewed it in the lining of their clothing, or concealed it in the box of one of the wheels, or in the harness.

One day Lowe had reached Jack White's Flat, between Peel and Wyagdon when he was balled up by a masked, armed man, who ordered him to drive off into the bush a bit. The bushranger was about to rip open the mailbags when up rolled Billy Moloney with a big load of Irishmen, straight out from the old sod, and making for Sofala. A few minutes later a cavalcade of their compatriots galloped up to give them a hearty welcome, and accompany them to Sofala. The bushranger was not observed in the excitement of the meeting, and he made good his escape, and was never apprehended. [Billy Maloney] recalls the names of many noted drivers, among whom are Jim Hunter, Martin Murphy, Peter Lewis, and Bob Pelsley."(Gold-Mining Days, 21 Jun 1937, p.1)

1937 "Cobb and Co's first driver on the Sofaia-Bathurst run ... Well, here we are, all aboard, and . . . away we go. Who is the sturdy driver who handles the ribbons so confidently, and flourishes that long-tailed whip of his for a slacking leader, or to warn off the youngsters who love to hang on behind the coach? His face is full of determination, and an urging word or two from that deep baritone voice sends the team off at a brave pace. The neddies know his grip, and they know their old master's will, and away they go, giving their last ounce and dash of speed. The driver is Jim Lowe, who drove the first Cobb and Co. team from Bathurst to Sofala, and who drove long before that for Foreman ... one of the earliest line-proprietors, who sold out to Coyle, who kept the old Barley Mow at Sofala for a time, and later went to Hill End after selling to Mendle ...

Lowe was born at Wilberforce and was out on his own among horses at 13, with McDonnell, of Penrith, who supplied coachmen and teamsters with produce. Later, he drove an express van for Woods, from Parramatta to Bathurst with passengers and luggage, and thereafter he mounted the box for Foreman. A great driver was Jim all through winning the admiration and confidence of all who entrusted their lives and luggage to him in those risky days, when outlaws were about, when the driver had to carry an axe and other tools for repair, or clearance, of the roadless roads in the daylight or the darkness, in the sunshine, or the rain, or snow ... On one occasion, when the coach was loaded heavily, a passenger said to the driver, *How comes it that you have three classes of passengers and three prices? We all seem to be crammed to suffocation. You'll pretty soon get to know all about it*, said the driver ... *First-class passengers will keep their seats; second-class will get out and walk to the top of the hill; third-class will walk and push the coach.*" (Gold Digging Days, 2 Aug 1937)

See also Appendix 1.6

Lumley, (Christian name unknown) ... 1925 See Atkins, W.

Lumley, Bill ... 1925 See Eddie, Nathan; 1925 Mitchell, Bill (Billy)

Lumley, Harry ... 1936 See Richardson, Bill

Lunley, Bill & Lunley, Ted ... 1937 See Lairy, Jack

Luscott, (Christian name unknown)
1880 "Luscott, the driver of Cobb's coach, was thrown off near Emerald, and died from injuries received." (Pugh's Queensland almanac, directory and law calendar, 1880, p.84)

Lyall, Jimmy
1923 "THE BALLARAT TURF CLUB RACES, 1st JANUARY 1876 … One can fancy that again one hears the rattle of the squatters' handsome teams and the crack of 'Jimmy' Lyall's whip as he dashes up with Cobb and Co's big four horse coach as he did half a century and more ago … The Railway has encroached upon his domain, till only the short 10 mile stage between Balmoral and Harrow is left to him. One cannot resist having the pleasure of a ride beside the wonderful old 'Jehu'. He assures us with a twinkle in his eye that he knows the road quite well. He has been driving over it since 1870, he explains. Jimmy Lyall, of Harrow, and Tommy Cawker, of Casterton are the two remaining divers of the old coaching days of Western Victoria. Jimmy remarks that he is 11 years younger than Tommy" (Far Western[?] Victoria, 10 Nov 1923, p.8)

Lyall, William
1931 "OCTOGENARIAN'S SAD END. Killed by Tram in City. After a strenuous life of 80 years in the days of Cobb and Co's mail service, fate played an unkind trick when Mr. William Lyall, an octogenarian of Casterton, was knocked down by a tram in Bridge Road, Richmond. He died in the Melbourne Hospital at 11 o'clock the same night from his injuries. These constituted a fractured skull and two broken legs. The elderly gentleman (who was 80 years of age) for the past ten years has been employed by Mr. Jack Cawker, on whose property on the Mt. Gambier road, about five miles from Casterton, he had a very comfortable home.

Recently Mr. Lyall journeyed to the city for a holiday, stating he would be back again for the Casterton races. He was completely deaf, and it can be assumed that this affliction may have accounted in some way for the accident, news of which was telegraphed to Mr. Cawker by Mr. Lyall's daughter (Mrs. Tomison). Born near Warrnambool, Mr. Lyall, on the death of his parents, worked as a lad for the late Mr. Thomas Cawker, with whom he was associated at different periods during his life. Deceased was a great horseman, and in his young days was a well-known rider.

For many years he was a driver for Cobb and Co. in the old mail coach days, driving between Portland and Hamilton and Portland and Casterton. He also rode and drove with the mail between Casterton and Mt. Gambier when that line was first opened, travelling between Argyle and Lindsay, then known as 'Mickey Springs.' In later years deceased was groom at the Ardno mail stables and also at the Nine-Mile Creek stables when they were controlled by the late Mr. Thos. Cawker. An uncle of deceased, Mr. William Lyall, of Harewood Park Estate, Cranbourne, was the first man to bring hares to Australia, and was also a noted importer of Shorthorn cattle and Shetland ponies. Deceased is survived by a widow (formerly Miss Kate King, of Portland) who is at present living in Sydney with her son. Other known members of the family are two daughters —Mrs. Tomison, of Richmond, and Mrs. Geo. Barker of Hamilton. A son of deceased was Mr. Jack Lyall, a well-known jockey, who died in Adelaide some years ago." (Octogenarian's Sad End, 18 May 1931, p.4)

1911 Bogged coach, Mary Ann Creek, Fred Richards driver—Courtesy Queensland Museum Collection

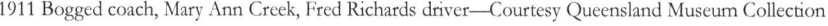

Flooded Balonne River, St George, Queensland (John Thanasis Tsonakas photograph album)—Courtesy State Library of Queensland

Chapter Seven

Drivers

M – N

The Roaring Days

Oft when the camps were dreaming,

And fires began to pale,

Through rugged ranges gleaming

Would come the Royal Mail.

Behind six foaming horses,

And lit by flashing lamps;

Old 'Cobb and Co.'s' in royal state

Went dashing past the camps

Henry Lawson, 1889
(In the days when the world was wide, Verse 6, 1900, p.33)

1894 Cobb & Co. coach at Coolgardie—Collections of the State Library of Western Australia
and reproduced with the permission of the Library Board of Western Australia

Supporting evidence:

MacDonald, John
1942 "Death of Cobb & Co. Coachman. The death is announced from Camperdown, Victoria of Mr. John MacDonald, who in his young days, was one of Cobb and Co.'s coachmen. At the time, the Kelly gang was on the 'rampage' he was in charge of the telegraph line. He was 90 years of age." (Death of Cobb & Co. Coachman, 18 Jun 1942, p.1)

Macgilcuddy, Geo ... 1917 See Anderson, Jim

Mack, James
1860 "Police Court ... practising imposition on the public, by assuring intending passengers by the coach that the fare was 5s, and after securing them and their luggage exacting 7s from the same ... The Mayor said he was somewhat surprised to find that characters of the description of the defendants, Jenkins and Mack, were employed by respectable firms such as Messrs Cobb and Co." (Central Police Court, 23 Aug 1860, p.3)

Mackenzie, Jack
1925 "HIGHWAY ROBBERY. A STORY OF 1867. COBB & CO.'S COACH. (By 'Red Gum.') The recent holding up of a motor bus on the North Ipswich side, by a masked man, brought to memory the consternation caused by the report of the 'sticking up' of the Ipswich Brisbane mail coach between this city and Oxley on January 7, 1867, by an armed bushranger ... Cobb and Co.'s coach, with Driver 'Jack' Mackenzie handling the ribbons.

The scene of the robbery was at a point about two miles from Oxley, known as 'The Blunder' ... he called on the driver 'to pull up.' Driver Mackenzie, thinking that all was not right, whipped up his horses, and a hard race ensued between the highwayman (who wore a dark covering over his face, with eye-holes cut in it), and the coachman, the former still ordering the driver to stop. As the driver continued to refuse to obey, the bushranger drew a pistol from his belt (in which was also attached a large sheath-knife), and deliberately fired at one of the leading horses, but did not inflict any injury. Driver Mackenzie kept up endeavouring to drive over the highwayman, as well as also vigorously using his whip on the robber's pony, with a view of making it throw the rider. It was only when the horses had become thoroughly exhausted that Mackenzie was compelled to pull up.

The highwayman, covering the passenger with his firearm, then ordered them to alight and throw down on the road all the money they possessed, remarking in a gruff tone of voice that *less coffins would be wanted* ... The highwayman then dismounted and gathered up the money deposited (£10 in all). The ruffian did not trouble to search the passengers, otherwise, he would have made a large haul ... After taking up the money deposited, the bushranger approached the driver and demanded the Goodna mail. Mackenzie refused, and pointed the revolver previously given to him at the robber, who had covered the coachman with his firearm. Things at this stage evidently assumed an aggressive form, but, in spite of most strenuous efforts on the part of the coachman to fire, the trigger refused to budge. His determined action had aggravated the highwayman, who, it is said, exclaimed, *You-Wretch!* and then threatened to *put a pellet through him*. The driver still refused to pass out the Goodna mail bag ...

He then commanded Mackenzie to take the coach into the bush, but the driver stubbornly refused to carry out the highwayman's orders. The bushranger angrily rode off with the contents of the Ipswich mail bag, which was later on, discovered by the mounted police in the bush, hanging on a branch of a tree." (Highway Robbery, 21 Mar 1925, p.14)

Macnamara, (Christian name unknown) (Mac.)
1873 "Disastrous flood at Inverell. December 28. We have been visited with a flood, unknown for its severity and destructive consequences, even to that old authority ... Never has the water risen so high, run with such violence ... It is idle to conjecture the loss sustained ... till we hear all accounts. The loss strictly confined to the town must be calculated by thousands, nothing less ! Tons of goods, merchandise of every description ... has been ruthlessly sacrificed by the unrelenting element ... whilst articles of every description were being washed in every direction—horses, cows, calves, pigs, fowls, cats, dogs, turkeys, casks, cases, bags of flour, boxes of soap, candles, dogs, sheep, furniture, bedding, machinery, saddlery ... with women screaming , children crying, men shouting ... Too much praise cannot be given to those gentleman who so kindly placed themselves and houses at the disposal of the distressed people. Cobb and Co's coach, under the management of its expert driver, Mr. Macnamara, did great work. Mac. turned out at first alarm, had his team harnessed, and went round the town, removing the living freight to security. He is an expert whip, and sticks at nothing ; for instance, in driving along in one place, his leader's hocks were covered with water. *Nevermind*, said Mac., *if the pole holds they are bound to go through it*—and through it they went, amidst the screams of women and applause of men." (Disastrous flood at Inverell, 7 Jan 1873, p.3)

Macnamara, John
1884 "TALLAROOK (From our own Correspondent.) THURSDAY Mr John Macnamara, who was known as a coach driver for Cobb & Co., on Yea line, died at Alfred Hospital, Melbourne, on Tuesday. Deceased was a most obliging man. He was greatly respected in the district." (Tallarook, 18 Jan 1884, p.2)

Macrae, Rod ... 1941 See Chatfield, Harry

Madden, Edward (Teddy)
1929 "Another Veteran 'Whip' DEATH AT YOUNG. Following the death of Mr. Larry Madden, probably the last of the old Cobb and Co. coach drivers in the north, comes news of the death of Mr. 'Teddy' Morgan, of Wambanumba, Young, who drove the mail coaches for 65 years. A resident of the Young district for 69 years and probably, the districts oldest resident Edward (Teddy) Morgan, died in the Sacred Heart ... He was 91 years of age and has had a romantic career. For sixty-five years he drove the mail coaches, and was driver for Cobb and Coy., being one of His Majesty's oldest mail drivers, and a man who was known throughout the whole country side. Deceased leaves a wife and four daughters, Mrs. J. Grime (Sydney), Mrs. E. E. Grounds (Bendick Murrell), Mrs, W. McCabe (Wambanumba), and Mrs. H. Perrin (Young), Billy Grime, the famous boxer, is a grandson." ('Teddy' Morgan, 6 Aug 1929, p.4)

Madden, Lawrence (Larry)
1881 "Glen Innes.—Mr. Blythe held a Land Inquiry Court at Glen Innes, and investigated some 29 cases. On Tuesday evening, at the Commercial Hotel, Mr. L. Madden (Messrs. Cobb and Co.'s driver between Armidale and Glen Innes), was presented with a handsome and valuable watch and Albert. The watch, which was purchased from Messrs. K. Marcus, jeweller, Grey-street, is appropriately engraved. The presentation was made by Mr. Mayor Jones, who referred to Mr. Madden's unvarying kindness to the public at large, and to his desire to carry out faithfully the work entrusted to him by his employers. The mayor also mentioned, as an evidence of Mr. Madden's general popularity, that Mr. John Moore, of Armidale, had voluntarily contributed £1 1s towards the cost of the present. Mr. Jones concluded by proposing Mr. Madden's health. The toast was enthusiastically received, and the company—some 40 gentlemen—declared him to be a 'jolly good fellow.' Building has taken another start in Glen Innes, and now we have several new structures in course of erection.—GUARDIAN" (Northern Districts, 23 Jul 1881, p.39)

1913 "Fifty Years on a Mail Coach. One of the oldest drivers of mail coaches in the State is Mr. Lawrence Madden, or 'Larry,' as he is known in New England and along the Grafton road. With the passing of the mail coach service to Grafton, Larry retired from driving, after half-a-century as 'whip' ... A more popular driver than Larry it would be hard to find. No man in New England is more respected than this old Cobb and Co. man ... *it was like parting with my oldest friend when I had to step down from the box seat and throw in the reins. Drivin' and horses came natural like to me, as I was born on a station and had to do with horses most before I could walk. I've been driving now for fifty years ... I c'n handle 'em ... better at night than in daylight. The horses seem to go better at night, and the road doesn't seem so long ... Cars might be all right ... but when they stop they stop* ... He began driving 50 years ago on the first coach service between Armidale and Glen Innes ... from Glen Innes to Tenterfield, and also to Stanthorpe in Queensland. The veteran Cobb and Co. driver is extremely modest in to his abilities as a whip." (Fifty Years on a Mail Coach, 13 May 1913, p.3)

1929 "The worst one I ever had was about nine years ago, about three miles out on the Grafton road. I was by myself on the coach that night, and a bitter cold night it was. We were crossing Beardy Plains. The coach lurched into a rut, and I was thrown under the wheel as I tried to bring the team to a standstill. My arm was held down by a wheel. The horses stopped dead, and it was snowing hard at the time they would not move an inch, and I lay there with the wheel pressing on my arm for nine hours. Early in the morning they moved a bit, and my arm was released ; but the experience, was nearly too much for me." (Fifty Years on a Mail Coach, 23 Apr 1913, p.19)

1929 "There were few more widely-known men in Northern New South Wales than Mr. Larry Madden, whose death occurred on Monday night. Mr. Madden was born at Gara station, near Armidale ... He began driving 66 years ago, on the first coach service between Armidale and Glen Innes. Mr. Gabriel Wardrobe had the mail contract, and he used to run a two-horse coach. The late Mr. Madden spent six years with Mr. Wardrobe, and then drove a four-horse coach from Glen Innes to Armidale for Mr. E. Potter. He afterwards spent three years driving on the same route for Mr. W. W. Fraser, and when Cobb and Co. bought Mr. Fraser out Mr. Madden continued to drive in that service. When the train was coming North, in the 'seventies, he drove from Glen Innes to Tenterfield, and also to Stanthorpe. He afterwards bought out part of Cobb and Co.'s outfit, and continued to drive between Tenterfield and Wallangarra until the ballast train ran him out. On one occasion a bushranger, named 'The Hairy Man,' conversed with him on the Inverell-Bundarra road but later rode off through the bush. That was a particularly narrow escape, for on that occasion Mr. Madden had nearly £20,000 on the coach." (Obituary, 3 Aug 1929, p.14)

1933 See also Bates, Bob

Maddicks, John
1886 "Mr. H. B. Taylor, the contractor for the Tambo and Alpha mail service, has secured Mr. John Maddicks as driver again. He was well known on the road some years ago, while in Cobb and Co.'s employ." (Tambo, 2 Oct 1886, p.25)

Madrill, Ambrose
1953 "Ambrose Madrill, now living at Nukarni, is believed to be the last of the Cobb & Co. coach drivers in the West." (Drove for Cobb & Co, 17 May 1953, p.27)

Maher, Michael
1933 "OLD-TIME COACH DRIVER ... Mr. M. Maher ... SWAN HILL ... age of 87 ... Born in Ireland, he came to Australia at an early age, and drove for Cobb and Co. in the Deniliquin district for many years. From 1886 to 1901 he drove the Moulamein-Swan Hill coach" (Old-time Coach Driver, 7 Mar 1933, p.5)

Mallon, William Garret (Garry)
1896 "... from Thursday's issue of the Kilmore Free Press :—Deceased gentleman, who had attained a good age, will be remembered by many in the district, where in the old coaching days he was employed by Cobb and Co., when 'Garry,' as he was familiarly termed, was as prominent a figure as any other who then frequented the old Kilmore-Hotel ... always bearing the highest reputation for straightfowardness, manliness, and loyalty to his employers ... We believe we are right in saying that deceased, who was a man of iron nerves, yet genial and good-natured, was the first man who took Her Majesty's mail overland from Sydney to Albury, and during his long career he was deservedly esteemed and respected." (A Veteran Coach Driver, 9 May 1896, p.2)

Malone, Owen ... 1935 See Conroy, James (Jim)

Maloney, John
1927 "A PIONEER MAILMAN. A man who was familiar with the bush roads of this State in the early days when the name of Cobb and Co. was a household word, died at Wagga Wagga last week. This was Mr. John Maloney, aged 91 years. He was for many years a driver of Cobb and Co's mail coaches and could tell stories of stirring adventures of the 'roaring days' of the goldfields and the bushrangers." Another article on the same page says "AIRMAN'S THRILL. Captain Giles, theAustralian

airman who set out from California to fly to Honolulu and Australia, had a rough experience. He had travelled 500 miles when his plane went, spinning into an 'air pocket' and turned upside down. His charts, food, and instruments fell into the sea. He was obliged to return, and landed in Southern California. He is to make another attempt when the moon is full. (A Pioneer Mailman, 25 Nov 1927, p.6)

Maloney, William (Bill/Billy Snr) ... 1935 See Conroy, James (Jim); 1937 Lowe, James (Jim)

Mannin/Manning, Ted ... 1938 See Anderson, Thomas (Tom); 1939 Warner, Jack

Manning, (Christian name unknown)
1884 "SURAT. [FROM OUR OWN CORRESPONDENT.] July 27. Mr. Weber has kindly furnished me with the following particulars of the Yeulbah mail robbery. The coach started from Yeulbah on the night of the 19th July at 10 p m , Mrs. Cole of St George, and two children being inside passengers, and Mr. Walker, of Dalby, and Mr. T. O'Brien, of Tinowan, being on the box with the driver. On arriving at Appletree, the first stage, twenty miles from Yeulbah, at 1:30 a.m., Mr. Weber went to the back of the coach to see if the rack was secure. The rack appeared to be lower than it should be, and he then discovered that two straps were cut and two unbuckled, and that the St. George mail bag, a very large one which had been fastened on the rack at Yeulbah had vanished.

Mr. Weber at once got two horses, and he and Mr. O'Brien started back to Yeulbah, noticing on the road a fire in a scrub, about a mile from Yeulbah on the side of a hill, not used for camping thus drawing their attention to it. On arriving at Yeulbah, just before daylight, they went instantly and reported the loss to tho police. The police sent for their horses, and Senior-constable Burke, Constable Quilter, and two [First Nations] trackers went back with Messrs. Weber and O'Brien, who also got fresh mounts. On arriving at the fire they found pieces of torn up letters strewn about, and the remains of the mail bag smouldering in the fire. The trackers then picked up the tracks to where the robbers (two in number) had cut the bag from the coach, about 500 yards distant. They then returned to the fire, and tracked the footprints of two men in the direction of Yeulbah, and then to the cattle yard on the line about a quarter of a mile from Yeulbah, and then lost all traces on the rails.

The case, of course, is in the hands of the police, but as this is the third robbery of the mail at Yeulbah and the thieves have hitherto escaped, it is thought that the same result will follow this. Amongst the plunder were two watches and a huge amount of postage stamps and notes. The general impression appears to be that as robbing the mail appears to be a vested interest at Yeulbah the mail should travel by day instead of by night ... I forgot to state in connection with the robbery, that Mrs. Coe heard a noise as of someone pulling at the rack and heard a box which had been placed on the mail bag striking on the rack, but did not give an alarm to the driver.

The travelling public will regret that Mr. Manning who has driven for Cobb and Co. for the last two years, has resigned his situation. A more courteous and able coachman never handled the ribbons, and the St. George people are getting up a testimonial to be presented to him. Mr. T. Naylor has a fine field of wheat growing in Surat, and Messrs. Simpson and Wood have gone in for wheat cultivation , both fields are in splendid condition. Heavy rain last night; the roads in a fearful state; the coach did not arrive until 12 o'clock to-day (Sunday). Weather fine to-day." (Surat, 1 Aug 1884, p.6)

Manning, Ned ... 1917 See Anderson, Jim; 1917 Richardson, W.

Markus, H ... 1919 See Aisbett, E. J.

Markwell, Billy ... 1940 See McMillan, Alexander

Markwell, W. S.
1953 "LONGREACH-WINTON FOR COBB & CO. The old days when the only transport between Longreach and Winton was that provided by Cobb and Co.'s coaches, and the average speed was seven miles an hour, were recalled when Mr. W. S. Markwell, of Glenagra, Kynuna, visited Longreach recently. Mr. Markwell was a Cobb and Co. driver at the age of 18. That was in 1911, when two drivers and two coaches operated the service. The other driver was Billy White. The coaches used to pass half way between the two towns and there were six changes of horses in the 128 miles.

Leaving Longreach at daylight, the coach would reach Winton at 4 pm the following day. Drivers were paid £12 a month and grooms £6, which did not include keep. In 1912 Mr. Markwell found more lucrative employment in Winton, where he remained until 1915, when he enlisted in World War I. While still in France, he drew a selection at Richmond, and after working it for 10 years purchased his present holding, Glenagra, of 40,000 acres, which is now stocked with cattle. Mr. Markwell still has an eye for a good horse and had a particular reason for his interest in Mr. Bullfinch's success as champion hack of the Longreach and Blackall shows. Mr. Bullfinch is owned by his daughter, Mrs. Betty Cooper!" (Longreach-Winton for Cobb and Co., 11 Jun 1953, p.14)

1917 See also Richardson, W.

Martin, Bob
1870 "THE ROBBERY OF SILVER FROM ONE OF COBB'S COACHES:—The Queensland Express relates that a few weeks ago the Bank of New South Wales sustained a loss of £100 through a bag of silver having been carelessly left in one of Cobb and Co.'s coaches by the driver (Martin), to whom the money had been entrusted for conveyance to the branch bank at Roma. The bag disappeared most mysteriously ; and up to a few days since, no tidings of the missing treasure could be obtained, notwithstanding the efforts of the police ... About a week ago Sergeant Francis, of the Ipswich constabulary, received some information which led him to suspect that the cash had found its way into the hands of a man named McDermott, a groom employed at Tattersall's Hotel, Ipswich ... it was found ... but nothing like the amount lost by the bank." (The Robbery of Silver from one of Cobb's Coaches, 9 Feb 1870, p.4)

1917 "Bob Martin, a brother of a well-known Brisbane auctioneer, driver between Dalby and Roma, coming to Brisbane to be married, was entrusted with £100 worth of 5s. pieces for the Bank of N.S.Wales, Roma. These were stolen from the buggy at Ipswich, but traced later through a game of general pool, whereat a number of new 5/ pieces turned up. A search at the house of a groom of Cobb and Co. revealed £70 more, and the groom received a sentence of nine months." (Coaching in Australia, 1917)

Martin, Charley ... 1917 See Wright, Bob

Martin, Thomas
1936 "COBB AND CO. DRIVER. Mr. Thomas Martin, of Annandale, who is spending some months with his daughter, Mrs. T. Keelan, of Bald Nob, celebrated his eightieth birthday last week. Mr. Martin, who was a Cobb and Co. coach driver in his day, is still hale and hearty, writes the Bald Nob correspondent of the Glen Innes 'Examiner'." (Cobb and Co. Driver, 3 Jul 1936, p.10)

1942 "Cobb and Co. Coach Driver's Death. The death ... of Mr. Thomas Martin, at the age of 86 years and four months. Mr. Martin, who was born at Moruya, was one of Cobb and Co's coach drivers along with the late Mr. Bob Bates ... He was always happy with his horses, and was well known and liked for his kindness and consideration to passengers. He was a cheery soul, and never failed to give a lift to pedestrians and also school children on their long walks to school." (Cobb and Co. Coach Driver's Death, 12 Nov 1942, p.7)

Martin, W ... 1919 See Aisbett, E. J.

Mason, Jim ... 1923 See Robinson, James (Robbie)

Matheson/Mathieson, Jack ... 1947 See Richards, J. Frederick (Fred)

Matthews, Charlie ... 1930 See Alder, Amos

Matthews, Jack
1931 "Jack Matthews, who was 77 years of age, came to the Hay district from Melbourne, off which place he was a native, half a century ago, and was one of the staff of drivers on Cobb and Co.'s coaches for years." (Administration of Justice Bill, 9 Jun 1931, p.2)

Matthews, Jimmy ... 1953 See Kidman/Kiddman, Charles (Charlie)

May, Frank
1908 "Death of an Old Time Coach Driver. Mr Frank May, at one time one of Cobb a Co's most popular coach-drivers ... He was a kindly man ... Amongst some of Mr Frank May's most thrilling experiences was the sticking-up of his coach by bushrangers 49 years ago ... The following is the account of the mail robbery, which took place on 24th May, 1859 ... from 'The Examiner':—Old times appear, to be again returning. When everyone seemed to be under the impression that the time when desperadoes would attempt to stop and rob a mail coach was gone by, and when such an occurrence, was least expected, the evil day came, and the coach, was stopped and robbed of all the valuables that could be found ... When the coach from Beechworth had reached within about four miles of Broadford, on its way to Kilmore and Melbourne, three men made their appearance with blackened faces, and with revolvers and a gun, and ordered the driver, Frank May, to stop." (Death of an Old Time Coach Driver, 23 Jul 1908, p.2)

Mayne, Dan
1917 See Thompson, Joe; 1923 Robinson, James (Robbie); 1925 Eddie, Nathan; 1932 Breen, Jim (Jimmy); 1935 Conroy, James (Jim)

McAnally, (Christian name unknown)
1869 "A distressing accident occurred at Bowenfels to Messrs Cobb and Co.'s day coach from Bathurst, on the 24th December. The coach started from Bathurst at 4 a.m., and proceeded on its journey as far Bowenfels. When it was passing Mr Lee's public house the leading horse all at once swerved off the road down an embankment, and overturned the coach. At the time of the accident there were twelve passengers on it, who were all more or less injured ... The driver McAnally had his shoulder put out and his wrist broken. The coach was smashed to pieces ... The driver is said to have been in no way to blame." (The News of the Day, 1 Jan 1869, p.2)

McCleary, William ... 1919 "LANDSBOROUGH. OBITUARY. Mr William McCleary passed away at Landsborough, at the age of 66 years. In the early days he was engaged with the firm of Cobb and Co., and for 20 years between Ballarat and Landsborough." (Landsborough, 22 Jan 1919, p.6)

McCormack, Jim ... 1948 See Herchberg/Hertsberg, Joseph (Joe); 1925 Eddie, Nathan

McCormack, Martin
1927 "Back in the days of the backblocks, Martin McCormack was one of the crack whips of Cobb and Co. Last week, the old chap, now past this four score years and ten, went through from Peak Hill to ... Randwick, where he will rest till the time comes for the sunset trail. Martin was right through the bushranging days, and knew most of the 'outlaws'." (Press Error, 1 Jul 1927, p.6)

McCrae, Roderick ... 1917 See Richardson, W.

McCullough, Herb ... 1935 See Conroy, James (Jim)

McDonald, (Christian name unknown)
1947 "Last year Mr. Wallace Mitchell, well-known Melbourne bookmaker, whose father was a Cobb and Co. driver, unveiled a bronze tablet in Bourke-street, Melbourne ... to identify the starting place of a coach run begun in 1854 ... About the same time Mr. McDonald, himself a former Cobb and Co. driver, presented a short wooden ladder to the Historical Society of Ballarat. It had been used by Cobb and Co. passengers to reach the seats of coaches travelling to Melbourne." (Cobb & Co. Coaches for Aust. Picture, 6 Jun 1947, p.5)

McDonald, Geo ... 1919 See Aisbett, E. J.

McDonald, Tom ... 1951 See Leary, Jack

McDonald, Wm. (Bill/Billy)
"The old drivers to at last lay down their reins were: Bill McDonald who drove Cobb's last coach on the St. George-Thallon run." (Communications Across the Generations, Read 1971, p.188)

McFarlane, Alan & McFarland, John ... 1921 See Griffen, Chas.

McGlinchy, Arthur
1903 "Arthur M'Glinchy, 76, Tamworth, a familiar figure of Cobb and Co.'s coaching days. He died on his birthday." (Obituary, 20 May 1903, p.1228)

McGroder/McGroda, Bob ... 1929 See Corbett, Alec.; 1932 Lowe, Bill

McIntyre, John
1888 "A MAIL COACH ON FIRE. By Electric Telegraph ... Windorah, August 6. Cobb and Co's coach conveying the Barcaldine, Rockhampton and Southern mails caught fire about fourteen miles from here on Saturday. The driver, John McIntyre, managed to save the Isisford and Jundah mails for this place, but all the correspondence from other places was destroyed and the coach itself was almost entirely consumed. There was a strong breeze blowing at the time the driver's hands were severely burnt. An exhaustive inquiry into the matter was held here to-day before Messrs. F. Smith and J. Lonergan, JJP., but there was no evidence to show how the fire originate. It is generally thought there must have been some combustible substance in transit in the mail bag made up in Rockhampton." (A Mail Coach on Fire, 7 Aug 1888, p.5)

McKenzie, (Christian name unknown)
1867 Coach breakdown "rain here which has done a good deal of good ... Mr. S. Bassett came to the Condamine with 7,000 sheep from Euthulla on the road to Tenterfield, but receiving a telegram from Roma, he has retraced his steps and gone back to Euthulla ... Messrs. Cobb and Co.'s coach broke down about five miles this side of the Kogan, and the driver (Mr. McKenzie) had to go back there to get chains, &c., and managed to fasten the coach so as to proceed here. He reached here about ten o'clock; two hours late. The mail generally keeps capital time, and the letters are always given out at any time by Mr. King; certainly the most obliging postmaster I was ever brought into contact with in the colony." (Condamine, 5 Oct 1867, p.3)

McKenzie, (Christian name unknown) (Saltbush) ... 1925 See Jones, Bill

McKenzie, Jack
1867 "Report of the 'sticking up' of the Ipswich Brisbane mail coach between this city and Oxley on January 7, 1867, by an armed bushranger. Considerable excitement prevailed when, at a later period of the day, the receipt of a telegram confirming the news was announced, especially as some 10 local residents, including a lady, had left as passengers at 6 o'clock on that morning by Cobb and Co.'s coach, with Driver 'Jack' Mackenzie handling the ribbons. The scene of the robbery was at a point about two miles from Oxley, known as 'The Blunder.' While toiling up a rough hill at that stage, a horseman was noticed to be riding alongside the road, swaying about in the saddle as if intoxicated, and, when the coach came opposite to him, he called on the driver 'to pull up.' Driver Mackenzie, thinking that all was not right, whipped up his horses, and a hard race ensued between the highwayman (who wore a dark covering over his face, with eye-holes cut in it), and the coachman, the former still ordering the driver to stop. As the driver continued to refuse to obey, the bushranger drew a pistol from his belt (in which was also attached a large sheath-knife), and deliberately fired at one of the leading horses, but did not inflict any injury. Driver Mackenzie kept up endeavouring to drive over the highwayman, as well as also vigorously using his whip on the robber's pony, with a view of making it throw the rider. It was only when the horses had become thoroughly exhausted that Mackenzie was compelled to pull up. The highwayman, covering the passenger with his firearm, then ordered them to alight and throw down on the road all the money they possessed, remarking in a gruff tone of voice that 'less coffins would be wanted.' He further commanded the driver to turn the horses towards Ipswich, which was accordingly done, but not too cheerfully, as one of the passengers, who had a revolver in his possession, had handed the weapon to Mackenzie just previous to the order to alight being given.

GATHERING THE SPOILS. The highwayman then dismounted and gathered up the money deposited (£10 in all). The ruffian did not trouble to search the passengers, otherwise, he would have made a large haul, as the late Mr. Harry Hooper (father of Mr. H. T. Hooper, of this city, and Mr. C. W. Hooper, of Laidley), who was one of the passengers, anticipating the turn of affairs, had in the meanwhile 'stowed away' on his person a considerable amount of money, which he was taking to Brisbane for business purposes; he also 'planted' from view a valuable gold watch. Subsequently, Mr. Harry Hooper received by post a note, cut in halves, supposed to be the one he had deposited on the ground in compliance with the bushranger's request. Mr. W. D. Tamlyn, a well known clerk in the employ of Messrs. Clarke, Hodgson, and Co, was also a passenger, and some little while previous to the robbery, had sold a brace of pistols, identical with those found subsequently in the possession of the highwayman, when arrested in June of 1868.

After taking up the money deposited, the bushranger approached the driver and demanded the Goodna mail. Mackenzie refused, and pointed the revolver previously given to him at the robber, who had covered the coachman with his firearm. Things at this stage evidently assumed an aggressive form, but, in spite of most strenuous efforts on the part of the coachman to fire, the trigger refused to budge. His determined action had aggravated the highway man, who, it is said, exclaimed, *You Wretch!* and then threatened to 'put a pellet through him.' The driver still refused to pass out the Goodna mail bag (which was supposed to contain a lot of money), and handed him instead the Ipswich mail bag, which the robber ripped open there and then, with his sheath-knife, emptying the contents on the ground, and afterwards gathered it up again. He then commanded Mackenzie to take the coach into the bush, but the driver stubbornly refused to carry out the highwayman's orders.

The bushranger angrily rode off with the contents of the Ipswich mail bag, which was later on, discovered by the mounted police in the bush, hanging on a branch of a tree. Mr. Harry Hooper recognised the pony ridden by the daylight robber as being the property of the late Mr. J. J. Johnston, a general storekeeper of Little Ipswich at that time. Mr. Hooper also noticed that there was a patch of mud on the animal hiding the brand. This pony, it had been discovered, had been 'removed' a couple of days (proir) to the date of the robbery ... Bill Jenkins's ...

From the Ipswich Police Court, the highwayman was remanded

to Brisbane, where he stood his trial for highway robbery under arms. Sub-Inspector Lloyd prosecuted, and to the surprise of everyone in this district, Jack Johnston's pony, which Jenkins rode when he stuck up Cobb and Co.'s coach, on January 7, 1867, was 'resurrected.' That completed the chain of evidence. Jenkins was found 'guilty,' and sentenced to 18 years' hard labour. Jenkins was only an assumed name." (Highway Robbery, 21 Mar 1925, p.14)

McLean, John
1872 "COACH ACCIDENT. A serious accident occurred on Thursday to the coach leaving Ballarat at 1 p.m. for Talbot. There was an unusual crush of passengers, and when the vehicle—one of Cobb and Co.'s largest coaches, drawn by live horses—was nearing Clunes, there were no less than thirty-seven men, women, and children crowded upon it. At this point a brewer's lorry on the road frightened the horses, and made them shy, the result being that before John M'Lean, the driver, could recover command of them they had drawn the near wheels over the side of an embankment several feet high. The coach was of course capsized, and its numerous living freight thrown violently out." (Coach Accident, 6 Apr 1872, p.7)

McMahon, Tom ... 1932 See Smiley, W.

McMillan, Alexander
1940 "The death of Mr. Alexander McMillan, which occurred this week, at the age of 68 years, has removed one of Queensland's early coach drivers. The late Mr. McMillan was employed by Cobb and Co. for 22 years, leaving their service in 1907. At 15 years of age he drove the first conveyance over the New England range from Casino to Tabulam in New South Wales ... Later, when he was driving between Lismore and Murwillumbah. Mr. Shaw, the then manager of Cobb and Co., engaged him to drive their coaches on the Tambo-Alpha line. The late Mr. McMillian was wellknown to old-time drivers for Cobb and Co., such as 'Billy' Markwell, Frank Ward, Steve Wall, Fred Richards, and many other western drivers ... Mr. McMillan spent most of his life in the Boulia-Winton district. In the severe drought of 1905, with Frank Ward, he carried water in a 30-gallon tank on the rack of the coach to water his team of six horses." (Late Mr. A. McMillan was Cobb & Co. Driver, 12 Oct 1940, p.2)

1940 "COBB AND CO DRIVER PASSES ... The late Mr. McMillan ... For many years he lived in Cloncurry. Later he spent some time in Lismore but eventually returned to the west. His death occured after a severe illness. He is survived by his widow, three daughters—Patricia, Mary, and Anne all of Brisbane; and a son—Walter of Southport." (Cobb and Co Driver Passes, 18 Oct 1940, p.4)

McMullen, Alex ... 1917 See Richardson, W.; 1950 See Hickson, Harry

McNickle, George
1864 "The Coach Accident.—George M'Nickle, driver of Cobb's Raywood coach, was brought up on the remanded charge of furious and negligent driving, and was again remanded for a week, bail being allowed." (Municipal Police Court, 7 Jul 1864, p.2)

McPhee, A ... 1919 See Aisbett, E. J.

McPherson, Jim ... 1917 See Richardson, W.

McRae, Bob ... 1955 See Yankee Bill

McTiernan, Barney
1930 "Barney McTiernan. Fifty Years of Coaching ... Barney McTiernan, tall and unbent 50 years of coaching, stands up six good feet and his voice rings out a voice of brass. His hands are rough and strong, yet gentle, for many a horse they have coaxed over broken, unmade roads—for 50 years ... He has a thousand views of life and love ... he rolls out whole verses from Paterson, Kendall, or Gordon. A talker, Barney, but's not one to cause apprehensive yawns ... Barney's basso profundo was first raised in an infantile wail at Michelago in 1861. Life was not all peace at Michelago in those days, for the Clarke gang was active, and when Barney was very young Levi's store was robbed. His brother was in the habit of arming himself heavily against lurking bushrangers before setting out to court the lady of his heart.

ROUGH ROADS AND LONG. Barney first started coaching with Cobb and Co. on the run between Murra Murra and Young ... After Federation he acted as the coachman to Sir George Reid, Sir Richard Baker, Sir Austin Chapman, Colonel J. C. Neild, and others from Cooma down to Eden, via Bombala and Dalgety. They were in search of a federal capital site, and Sir John Forrest favored Dalgety. But we now have Canberra ... Varied have been his adventures, and the perils of the road have been many. Swollen creeks seem to have been the main danger. Once, with a lady of dignity and avoirdupois on his back, he was obliged to swim across one. The lady was half drowned, and Barney was on his third descent before he landed her ... he must have been very powerful. All the world has been his friend, and he has a name for open handed generosity and great good fellowship. He is as honest as the day and as straight as a Roman road." (Barney McTiernan, 14 Nov 1930, p.5)

1931 "An Old Coach Driver... Here is a well-known story of Barney. Two gentlemen, whose business interests took them upon the broad highway, had a wager between them of £10. One of them wagered that if a letter was posted at Adelaide and addressed 'Barney, Coachdriver, Australia,' that same letter would be successful in finding him ... Within 48 hours of his having despatched it Barney received it in his letter box at Nowra. Ten pounds changed hands ... A great lover of horses, he fought his horses against the motor until machinery triumphed over flesh and blood. Today, outside his old stables hangs the sign *If you can't afford a Ford, remember ye good old horse is still here, also Barney.*" (An Old Coach Driver, 27 Feb 1931, p.4)

Meagher, Pat ... See Appendix 1.6

Merritt, Tom ... 1917 See Corbett, Sandy

Mesbltt, Bill
1929 "Crack-o'-the-Whip. The Romance of Early Coaching. (By L. T. Luxton) Bright red were the embers in the fire, warm the room, mellow sounding the voices. In that atmosphere of suburban ease and security it was difficult to envisage the hardships, the perilous adventures, and the rugged romance of the days of Cobb and Co. I watched the glowing embers and

listened, and gradually my mind caught something of the fervour of my informant and color by color pictures of the past rose up before me. I saw the horses and the stout-sprung vehicles, rolling and jolting over roads of all degrees of roughness, sunk to the axles in mud and lashed by rain, tearing through the burning forest, rumbling down the streets of country towns with a grandeur that drew children from their play. I saw the burly drivers with their long curling whips. 'Cabbage' Ned Devine, who drove Stevenson's English Eleven around Geelong in 1862 with 12 big greys in the traces ; 'Hellfire' Jack Bradley, who feared nothing on earth ; 'Alec' Forcett, of the Hay-Deniliquin run, who inherited a baronetcy and died Sir Alexander Forcett ; Bill Mesbitt, who used to flick lizards off the road into the air with his whip and hit them as they come down again ; 'Big' Samson, Peg-leg Jackson, Ike Haigh, and many others. That the past was brought so vividly before me was entirely due to the fine enthusiasm and rare skill in anecdote of Mr. Frank Smiley, of Prahan, who was a well-known coach-driver on the Colac to Warrnambool run in the days before motor cars. Looking into the fire and drawing slowly at his pipe, Mr. Smiley passed from incident to incident. *Cobb and Co. was a famous old name*, he remarked. *But it was not one big company as many people think. Nearly every coaching firm called itself Cobb and Co* ...

All Picked Men. The early coach-drivers were all picked men—most of them Americans from the Rocky Mountains and the prairies. Later some of the 'big' drivers were getting £10, ,£12, and £14 a week, and the wages of a few touched £1000 a year. The reason was that some of the drivers were so popular that the proprietors were glad to pay them their own price to keep them from opening in competition ... My father was an American from Maine, and it was when he was in charge of the horses at Blow's Flat—now called Myrniong—in the [18] 'sixties that I had my first taste of coaching. I was too young to remember much, but my mother told me all about it in after years. Wood was practically unprocurable, so everybody had to live in tents, men and horses together. My mother cooked for everybody. One cold, wet day she was cooking in the tent when Mr. F. B. Clapp, the father of the present chairman of Railway Commissioners, came in. Mr. Clapp was a well-known figure in the coaching business, and be had the reputation of being as straight as the proverbial die. Everybody swore by him. Watching the water flowing through the tent past my mother's feet, he shook his head and said in his American accent, *Little woman this won't do. I must send you down enough lumber to floor this tent, and an American cooker* ... Sure enough, a couple of days later up swept 'Hell fire' Jack Bradley with his fiery Van Dieman's Land team of four blacks, and dropped a load of flooring planks and a first quality American stove.

Bare-knuckle fighting was very popular at that time. The battles were tremendously long. At Skipton, where I was schooled, I remember there was a lad who was handy with his fists. After several successful scraps he was backed to fight a prize-fighter in Melbourne. His father anxiously awaited the result at Skipton. At last the long expected telegram arrived. 'Won easily ; only 76 rounds' ... Later I was on the Colac to Warrnambool run at the time of the Kelly gang, when people along the road used to wait up half the night to get the latest news of the bush rangers. The teams I drove were nearly all six horse, but I remember that there was a driver at Castlemaine who drove 22 greys with 51 passengers on board for a wager. The famous old Leviathan coach, which ended its days as a water carrier, was licensed to carry 75 passengers, and it had 14 horses in the traces ... Smashes were part of the business. You expected them. But all the same there were suprisingly few serious accidents. One night in the Stony Rises one of my horses shied at a load of dead rabbits and swung round until be smashed the wheels of the coach and killed a fine leading horse, named 'Hell-fire' Jack. Another time the brake broke going down the Fyansford Hhll, near Geelong. We went down so fast that we got most of the way up the next hill before the horses had to pull again. The only time I can remember a team beating me was when five greys bolted from Pirron Yalloak to Stonyford, a distance of about three and a half miles. I was pretty strong in the arms, but I had to give them their heads.

In the back country, fording flooded creeks and being dug out of 'glue pots' in winter and galloping down forest roads during bush fires with trees crashing all round in summer were part and parcel of the work in almost every season. It was a hard game, with the great popularity which nearly every coach driver enjoyed as its only compensation. The reunion of Cobb and Co. drivers ... is a splendid idea. Old comrades separated for perhaps 50 years meet, and with the old coach as a back ground get the 'tang of the leather' again ... *We're passing out* ... The fiery, glossy-coated horses steaming in the frosty stillness of early morning, the travel stained coaches, with their dignity, spanking over the plain with whips cracking, the genial, burly drivers with their twinkling eyes and weather-tanned faces, the blare of the bugle in the forest and the twinkling of lanterns as the mail bags were hauld on in the darkness at some remote posting station—all would be gone from human rememberance. Once again the machine age will have fliched from life something that was picturesque and dear to the hearts of men." (Crack-o'-the-Whip, 5 Jul 1929, p.2)

Mickle, D.J ... 1930-1940s See Allan, (Christian name unknown)

Miles, J.
1873 "STANTHORPE. During the past week the weather has entirely put a stop to all mining operations in this district. The rain set in early on Monday morning and continued without intermission, we may say, till Wednesday at noon. When the clouds began to break and the sun showed its face again one and all were delighted and hopeful, but we fear that the downpour ceased too suddenly, as now, as we are going to press, the sky is overcast and a nasty drizzling rain falling. Cobb and Co.'s coaches have been working under great difficulties, and their drivers cannot be too highly commended for their pluck and perseverance in bringing in their coaches intact and without any grumbling on their part. On Tuesday last the early coach was stopped at the Eight-Mile Creek owing to the flood; we believe, however that the mails were sent on to Warwick that day. There was no early coach on Wednesday, but Mr. J. Miles, the driver ... managed to cross the creek with his four horse team, the leaders having to swim, and the water being about six inches above the body of the coach. He tells us that at Deuchar's Creek, going into Warwick, the bridge was almost impassable, and that the road from the Four-Mile Creek to the Seven-Mile was entirely under water; nevertheless the driver was not in much after the usual time. We hear from Warwick that the whole of the lower

part of the town was inundated and that the approaches to the new bridge were washed away. The rainfall there must have been considerably more than in Stanthorpe.—Border Post." (Stanthorpe, 23 Jun 1873, p.3)

Miles, Jimmy
"There were the great days of coaching in this country. Cobb and Co. started a large coach from Geelong, via Batesford, Shelford, Skipton, and Streathan, to meet at Streathan another coach, which left Portland the same hour in the morning, and passed through Heywood, Branxholme, Hamilton, etc. Passengers and mails were exchanged at Streatham, after which each coach started on its return journey ... They had splendid teams of 4 and 6 horses, groomed like racehorses, and full of life. Miles, the driver from Portland end, had on his last stage into Streatham (or the Hopkins, as it was then called) a team of six light coloured chestnuts as nearly alike as it was possible to get them ... He often disturbed the minds of nervous passengers, but I do not think he ever made a mistake ... As he pulled up his team, he sat on the box with a satisfied smile on his face like a man who has had a good dinner and subsided into an armchair" (Pioneering days in western Victoria : a narrative of early station life, 1927, p.87)

Miles, Johnny ... 1936 See Richardson, Bill

Millard, O. A ... 1919 See Aisbett, E. J.

Millard, W. A. ... 1930-1940s See Allan, (Christian name unknown)

Miller, George Trenchard
1891 "Fatal Coach Accident Near Grenfell. [By Telegraph.] (From our correspondent.) Grenfell, Tuesday. A lamentable occurrence took place near here this afternoon. The coach for Young left with a number of passengers, and about three miles out met the in-coming coach, where the drivers change. George Miller, Cobb and Co 's manager at Young, and driver of the up-coach, had dismounted with the intention of changing seats, the reins being in the hands of Samuel Robinson, police-magistrate of Young. Mr. Robinson dropped one of the reins, which fell upon the horses, causing them to start. The driver, with one rein and his foot on the brake, circled the horses in the hope of stopping them, but failed, and the coach upset. Mr. A. E Hopkins, of Roma, Darling Downs, Queensland, who was returning home his wife and family after disposing of a lot of cattle at Wodonga, was so terribly injured that he died in a cart on the way to Grenfell. Mr. Robinson has his collarbone and a number of ribs broken, and is in a serious state. Miss Dent suffered severe injuries, the others escaping comparatively unhurt. The coach was wrecked. No blame attaches to the driver, who is one of the most careful and experienced men in Cobb's service. A friend endeavoured to persuade Mr. Hopkins before starting to remain till to-morrow, when he would drive him down the other road to Cowra, but the deceased said as he had booked he would go on. Besides, it was understood he wished to visit his sister at Goulburn, this was the last trip, as he intended to make with stock." (Fatal Coach Accident Near Grenfell, 21 Oct 1891, p.6)

While on the 11 Nov 1891 "for the information of others ... On Tuesday, 20th October last, the coach from Young brought in news of a terrible accident through the capsizing of the coach from Grenfell at a spot about four miles out, where the coaches met and the usual exchange of drivers took place. The accident was attributed to the dropping of one rein by Mr. Robinson, one of the passengers, while in the act of handing them to Mr. G. Miller, the driver who had just exchanged seats with Mr. S. Bullock. The rein dropping on the near side horse causing him to start ... On Thursday the inquiry ... resumed ... —Samuel Robinson, being examined by Mr. Crommelin, deposed: I am a police magistrate residing at Young; was in Grenfell on 20th October last ; started on the coach shortly before 1 o'clock, taking a near side box seat ; a young lady named Miss O'Brien, and S. Bullock were also on the box, the latter being the driver; about four or five miles out, the coach met the incoming one from Young driven by George Miller ; Bullock handed me the reins and got down ; Miller also got down from his coach ; he then took his seat in the coach I was in, and I handed him the reins complete ... I am ... quite capable of holding the reins ; have driven myself for 50 years and had only one accident." (Grenfell Coach Accident, 11 Nov 1891, p.2)

1910 "Mr. George Miller, well known to the travelling public as mail coach driver in the service of Cobb and Co., died at Young on Saturday afternoon. Forty-five years ago he drove the mail coach from Yass to Gundagai, and later on from Murrumburrah to Young. When the railway line was opened to Young he continued in the same service, driving between Young and Grenfell." Advertising on the same page included "IN THE BUSH. Wolfe's Schnapps. Is the safe Stimulant. It has recognised Medical Properties" while "Mr, Frank Allan, chief inspector under the Vermin Destruction Act, is a strong believer in the efficacy of poisoned apples as a means of killing rabbits! He has, he says, discovered a simple, machine, for slicing apples, which should greatly increase the use of this bait in the country." (Personal & Social, 10 Jun 1910, p.2)

1927 See also Payne, Jack; 1935 Conroy, James (Jim)

Miller, John
1897 "Grenfell Police Court : TUESDAY. Before Messrs. T. Bembrick and Beck. Inspector of Nuisances v John Miller (late driver of Cobb and Co.'s coach)—Plying for hire within the municipality without a license. Mr. Crommelin, for defendant, pleaded : first, that his client did not ply for hire ; secondly, not guilty. William Henry Sadleir, Council Clerk, Grenfell, deposed that defendant had not applied for any coach license. By Mr. Crommelin : He had been Council Clerk for three years, and during that time had never heard of the driver of a stage coach being licensed as a driver under the municipal regulations ; thought present proceedings the outcome of an inspiration of the inspector who, he understood, initiated the case ; the driver of the other coach was not licensed, nor, so far as witness was aware, were proceedings taken against him." (Grenfell Police Court, 10 Jul 1897, p. 2)

Miller, Ted
1912 "The motor, has knocked the charm out of coaching despite the fact that the long tracks are encompassed, more swiftly. There was something congenial in sitting behind a jogging team, notwithstanding the roasting of the gleaming sun, and the cloud of dust that rose about the coach as it slowly trundled on. Cobb and Co.'s office at Leonora is not what it

used to be, the motor is too suddenly off the mark, there is no lingering in the early gloom getting the horses under weigh, no 'let 'em go,' as the driver cracked his whip and gallantly tooled his prads away … The famous whips, Charley Chick, Dick Daley, Butler, and others, have vanished from sight but not to die for we know that … coach-drivers are immortal, yet their absence is to be deplored. One link with the glorious past remains … Percy Toy … Ted Miller, another remnant of other days, periodically comes to light from somewhere in the remoteness, of the outer-back, and Jimmy Nicholas." (Mulgaland Mems, 29 Sep 1912, p.7)

Milne, E … 1919 See Aisbett, E. J.

Milne, W … 1930-1940s See Allan, (Christian name unknown)

Mitchell, Bill (Billy) … 1917 See Anderson, Jim; 1925 Eddie, Nathan

1925 "REMINISCENCES OF FORMER DRIVERS. A number of the drivers mentioned were known to men I have met in the city. I know some of them, including 'Billy' Mitchell, who reared a family in Charleville. One of his sons is now a school teacher in Brisbane, and a married daughter also resides in the metropolis. The Jimmy D—, of the Yeulba track, referred to old Jimmy Davidson, who, after leaving the box seat, looked after the mail change at Rosehill outside of Surat, on the St. George road, and the coach travellers could always rely on a good meal there. Young Jimmy Davidson also was a driver for Cobb and Co. along the Yeulba and St. George tracks until he went to the war, and I think that he was in charge of Cobb and Co.'s stables and office at Augathella when that firm ceased operations as mail contractors on the Charleville-Tambo line. Old 'Bill' Lumley was the last of Cobb and Co's drivers on that line, although it may be claimed that Ted Palmer and his brother were the last of the drivers out there, but they were independent contractors when they took the line over from Cobb and Co, and continued the coaches until they were replaced by motor cars and lorries.

Cobb and Co's last line was on the Yeulba track, and it seems that it was this track that gave Cobb and Co. a big lift in the days before the railway went to Thallon and Dirranbandi. Before that line was built all of the mails and merchandise for St. George and lower down the Balonne, as far south as the New South Wales border, went via Yeulba. When the railway was constructed beyond Goondiwindi, there was a noticeable falling off of packages, &c, for St. George and lower down that used to go via Yeulba, and it was then that the coaching business in that part of the country commenced to wane. A trip from Yeulba to St George was all right when the seasons were good. The coach left Yeulba at 8 am on Wednesdays and Saturdays. The first days stage was 17 miles to Surat, where the coach arrived about 4.30 p.m. Surat was left at 4 o'clock next morning and St. George reached about 6 o'clock the same day. A change of horses was provided about every 12 miles, about 60 horses being used for each trip, and there were some tough ones amongst them. The last stage into St George, about 14 miles, was done behind 8 grey ponies, which perhaps, comprised the best team I have ever seen. These little fellows never needed the whip—the brakes were more necessary than the whip. A couple of miles out of St George the driver would blow a bugle that he carried, and by the time the coach arrived at the post office half of the population of St. George would be there to meet it. Those were great old days, and many an old man treasures them in his memory. It is meet that the last of Cobb and Co's coaches should be preserved for future generations to see." (Cobb's Coaches, 17 Jan 1925, p.17)

1939 See also Warner, Jack

Mitchell, Hugh (Hughie)
1876 "A Coach-Driver in Trouble. ALLEGED EMBEZZLEMENT BY THE DRIVER OF THE LILLYDALE COACH. Hugh Mitchell, a man who has been for many years past employed as a driver by Messrs, Robertson and Wagner, the well-known proprietors of Cobb's coaches, was charged … The prisoner formerly drove the coach between Kilmore and Melbourne, but for some years past has been engaged on the Lillydale and Melbourne line, and it is on this line that the alleged embezzlements are said to have been committed." (A Coach-Driver in Trouble, 21 Jan 1876, p.3)

Mitchell, John … 1936 See Rochester, William George (Bill)

Montgomery, (Christian name unknown) (Marvellous Monty/Old Monty)
1880 "Cobb and Co.'s mail coach met with a very dangerous accident this week, between Walgett and Coonamble, through the shameful and culpable conduct of certain Crown lessees, who wilfully obstruct the mail coach road by unlawfully placing closed gates across these highways, contrary to the Act specially prohibiting these obstructions. The driver (Montgomery) states that while attempting to get through one of the gates, the horses became restive and unmanageable ; the leaders reared over, and the whole team, affrighted, kicked and plunged violently, breaking through the harness and materially injuring the coach, which arrived in a shattered state and bound together with the reins." (Walgett, 8 Jan 1880, p.5)

1887 "One notable change with the new year is the exit of Cobb and Co. from our town. It is ten years since this well-known coaching firm made its debut in this quarter by inaugurating the western mail service from Dubbo and Mudgee to Walgett, and right splendidly has that service been maintained. Careful drivers, safe coaches, good staunch horses, and moderate fares has been the rule of the road throughout, while punctuality and civility has been the motto of the whole system. Without being invidious, it requires to be said that this excellent management is the result of Mr. John Barry's experience and sound judgment in coaching business … It may be added that 'Monty,' the original whip who 'tooled' the first team across the *terra incognita*— the country, was on the maiden trip of this Western service. 'Marvellous Monty'—which his ten years graduation declares him to be—has transferred his allegiance to the new contractor. This is a guarantee of the due fulfilment of all engagements at this end of the line, as Montgomery, with the old Cardinal, believes 'there is no such word as fail'." (Walgett, 29 Jan 1887, p.13)

1935 See also Conroy, James (Jim)

Moore, Thomas B.
1951 "PASSING OF T. B. MOORE. With the demise last

evening of Thomas Bailey Moore at the age of 81 years, Innisfail lost an old and respected resident. Deceased spent his early life as a driver for Cobb and Co., and on various stations in the west. In the latter part of his working life he was employed by the Railway Department in Townsville and Ingham districts where he was very well known. After his retirement he lived many years in the north, mostly with his daughter, Mrs. G. Curro, of Innisfail." (Obituary, 5 Sep 1951, p.6)

Moorhouse, J ... 1932 See Smiley, W.

Moran, Battye & Moran, Jack (father of Jimmie Moran) ... 1938 See Barrie, Billy

Moran, James
1932 "Drove for Cobb's. ... No one, perhaps is more anxious to participate in Sydney Harbour Bridge celebrations than James Moran, a veteran Goulburn coach-driver, who spent several years in the service of Cobb and Co ... engaged in taking ... coaches ... to as far south at Eden until the railway was opened at Albury." (Drove for Cobb's, 15 Feb 1932, p.2)

Moran, Jim ... See Appendix 1.6

Moran, Jimmie, senr. (The Fenian) & Moran, Tommie ... 1938 See Barrie, Billy

Morecroft, John Telford
1879 "It appears that Cobb and Co.'s buggy picked up the mails at the usual hour ... and went on its journey, carrying two passengers ... Mr. Levoi, traveller for Messrs. Hoffnung and Co., merchants, Brisbane and Sydney, having in his possession a large amount of valuable jewellery, amongst which was a tin box containing about £1000 worth. After travelling about a mile ... the occupants of the coach observed a temporary fence of saplings stretching across the road. The driver, John Morecroft remarking that some boys were playing him a practical joke, pulled up at the obstruction, and then observed a powerfully built man on the whip-hand side of the coach, resting himself on one knee and presenting a gun at him, with a peremptory order *to bail up and get off that coach*. The intruder had some white calico wrapped about him, which concealed the lower part of his face and body, and he presented rather a spectral appearance ... *I want that box of jewellery* ... Following up the tracks, Jones came on the box, hid under a bush. It had been much battered in, but was found unopened." (Sticking up the Gympie Coach, 8 Sep 1879, p.4)

"Knew Thunderbolt. Guildford Ex-Coachdriver. WORKED FOR COBB & CO. Talked to 'Thunderbolt.' Bailed-up by a bushranger. Driven a mail coach 110 miles without a spell. Nearly 85, but still hale and hearty, John Telford Morecroft, ex-driver of Cobb and Co.'s coaches, has a wealth of interesting reminiscences ... It's a long way from 1932 Guildford to the rollicking [18]'seventies on the Gympie and Charters Towers goldfields, but John can take you there in a jiff. Born in Balmain a few months short of 85 years ago, the lure of coaching gripped him early; and at the age of fourteen he joined up with Cobb and Co., who had the mail coach monopoly in Victoria, Queensland and New South Wales. He was one of the youngest drivers in the service. From the western and New England districts of New South Wales to the Gympie and Charters Towers goldfields in Queensland his profession took him, as he worked up from the modest two horse coach to the spanking five horse mail with its 25 passengers. He has vivid memories of the days when Frank Gardiner and Frederick Ward—Captain Thunderbolt' to most people—held the roads. *I've spoken to Thunderbolt hundreds of times*, he said *A real good fellow. The whole district was sorry when he was shot by the police.*

John's acquaintance with the bushranging fraternity wasn't always so happy. It was at dawn one morning, a mile outside Gympie. As the mail coach, with its golden load, approached a clump of trees, a masked figure leapt out. *Bail up!* he ordered sharply. A loaded revolver is a strong argument; and John bailed up. But later John's identification led to the robber's capture and sentence to fifteen year's imprisonment. John still chuckles when he thinks of that. It was all in the day's work; and there was £10 at the end of each month, with everything found except the whip.

His longest trip, with several changes of coach, was in the western districts of New South Wales. With the return journey it made a total of 110 miles. Those were the happy-go-lucky times. Someone offered John a couple of gold-reefs at Charters Towers. He turned them down—couldn't be bothered. *I was sorry later,* he added. *But I was young in those days.* Fire, flood, loneliness—the coachman's life had its ups and downs. But some times there was a little romance. A young English girl came out to spend a holiday in Brisbane. John met her. Took her out. Took her out again. The third time it was to the church, and the couple, married fifty-three years now, have never regretted it. As John explains, a coachman had to be quick about it. He was here one day and fifty miles away the next.

Mrs. Morecroft is almost as expert with the whip as her husband. He taught her, and tells with pride how quickly she learned to handle the five powerful steeds that could keep up a pace of nearly fifteen miles an hour. Incidentally, John's been motoring with someone else at the wheel. He likes it. *But I'd sooner be on the seat of a coach—if I had the reins,* he added. *Aeroplanes! No!* John's emphatic. *I haven't been up; and I don't want to. This is high enough for me.* It's forty years now, since John gave up his whip. The glamor of the gold fields, the romance of the days when the flashing wheels of Cobb and Co's coaches maintained the lines of communications with the outposts of the young colony, before the razor slasher and gangster supplanted the hard riding, hard shooting bushranger—all have gone. But John, gardening in his Clement street home, remembers." (Knew Thunderbolt, 15 Dec 1932, p.7)

Morgan, Edward (Ted/Teddy)
1929 "Another Veteran 'Whip.' Death at Young ... comes news of the death of Mr. 'Teddy' Morgan, of Wambanumba, Young, who drove the mail coaches for 65 years. A resident of the Young district for 89 years and probably the district's oldest resident, Edward ('Teddy') Morgan, died in the Sacred Heart Hospital last week ... and has had a romantic career. For sixty-five years he drove the mail coaches, and was driver for Cobb and Co., being one of His Majesty's oldest mail drivers, and a man who was known throughout the whole countryside. Deceased leaves a wife and four daughters, namely, Mrs. J. Grime (Sydney), Mrs. E. E. Grounds (Bendick Murrell), Mrs.

ca. 1880 G.P.O. corner of Bourke and Elizabeth Streets
(Caire, N. J., 1837-1918, photographer)
—Courtesy State Library Victoria

Wellington Inn, Orange, NSW, on the northwestern corner of Summer Street and Lords Place, built in 1859, the first two-storey hotel in Orange, Booking Office for Cobb & Co., (later renamed the Royal Hotel), licencee's name James Torpy, licencee from 1872 to 1876—Courtesy of Central West Libraries

1910 Cobb & Co. coach arriving in St George, Queensland—Courtesy Brisbane John Oxley Library, State Library of Queensland

Wm. McCabe (Wambanumba), and Mrs. H. Perrin (Young), Billy Grime, the famous boxer, is a grandson." ('Teddy' Morgan, 9 Aug 1929, p.4)

1929 "Edward (Teddy) Morgan … For sixty five years he drove the mail coaches, and was driver for Cobb and Co., being one of His Majesty's oldest mail drivers a man who was known throughout the whole country side." with the following article appearing on the same page "CIGARETTES Hints for Smokers. Cigarette smokers, beware! Those who inhale smoke from the humble fag absorb three times as much nicotine as those who do not. Roll your cigarette, tightly and make them long and slender. Short thick bumpers produce twice as much nicotine as the amaciated looking thing many men roll when time is short or tobacco is running out … These and many other facts of great interest to smokers and the medical profession are given in the June issue of the London 'Lancet,' as a result of the research work of Drs. Winterstein and Arenson, of the Tecliincal High School of Zurich, Switzerland." (Mail Driver's Death, 6 Aug 1929, p.3)

1929 "Ted Morgan spent most of his life in the employ of Messrs. Cobb and Co, as a driver of mail coaches. He was born … 91 years ago. At the age of two years he came to New South Wales … For 65 years Ted Morgan drove the mail coach … including between Goulburn and Taralga, Goulburn and Wheeo, Burrowa and Young, Burrowa and Cowra via Breakfast Creek, Burrowa and Cowra via Murringo, Young and Grenfall, Young and Bimbi, Young and Temora … Ted Morgan used to speak of when he drove the mail through a 7-mile flood in the Bland. Picking the road by means of a stump here and a post there was no easy task. Yet another adventure in the Bland was when he was crossing a flooded creek in a sulky. The horse slipped and floundered in deep water, throwing Ted off his seat. Ted succeeded in cutting loose the breeching straps and traces, caught hold of the horses tail, and was taken to safety by the animal, which swam to the nearest dry ground." (Obituary, 9 Aug 1929, p.6)

Morris, Billy … 1921 See Griffen, Chas.

Morris, D.
1893 "Coach Horses. CASES AGAINST WESTERN DRIVER. The case, Police v. D. Morris, cruelly beating one gray gelding, was disposed of at the Blackall Police Court, before Messrs. W. J. Hartley, P. M., and V. Desgrand and H. J. Hewer, JJ.P., on Thursday, the 6th instant, the case being dismissed without costs. The decision of the beach (as supplied to the Western Champion), reads as follows: The bench are of opinion that the defendant was endeavoring to carry out his duties as a driver for Cobb and Co. to the best of his ability, and that there is insufficient evidence to warrant them in convicting him of cruelly beating the horse in question, while it is apparent from the evidence elicited that the manner in which Cobb and Co. ran their mail coaches on this road during the late drought must be repugnant to the feelings of every humane person, unfed horses being compelled to drag heavy coaches for long stages. Some of the magistrates forming the bench have often travelled by coach under similar circumstances, and realise the difficulties under which a driver labors when he has to take a coach loaded with passengers and mails to its destination in a given time, drawn by horses unfitted for their work by semi-starvation. In the case of a mail contract by coach between a railway station and a town distant 78 miles, the bench think there is not the slightest excuse for neglecting to properly feed during a drought the horses required for the service; and, as they understand, Cobb and Co. declare large dividends annually, the company cannot possibly have the excuse of being unable to do so. The bench hope that the present prosecution will have the effect of drawing the company's attention to late existing state of affairs, and that they will take the necessary steps to prevent its recurrence. Two other cases were dismissed on similar grounds." (Coach Horses, 26 Jul 1893, p.3)

Morris, Frank … See Appendix 1.6

Morris, G. M … 1919 See Aisbett, E. J.

Morris, Tom … See Appendix 1.6

Morris, Wally … 1936 See Rochester, William George (Bill)

Mosch, Joe … 1941 See Chatfield, Harry

Moyse, Billy … 1921 See Griffen, Chas.

Mugridge, Bob … See Appendix 1.6

Mulholland, L. … 1930-1940s See Allan, (Christian name unknown)

Murphy, James (Jemmy)
1879 "Accident to Cobb and Co.'s Coach, at St. George. The Standard of the 8th instant supplies the following particulars of the accident which happened to Cobb and Co. 's coach (of which only Telegraphic information was previously to hand):— An accident of a serious nature occurred to the down coach, which left St. George on Tuesday morning last for Yulebah. Mr. James Murphy, better known as 'Jemmy Murphy,' was the driver, and we need scarcely add to that statement the fact that it was an accident pure and simple.

Mrs. Dickens and three children were unfortunately for them, passengers at the time, one of the little boys being seated on the box beside the driver. On reaching the eight-mile gate from St. George it became necessary for Jemmy to get down and open it, and after taking the team through, and while closing the gates, the horses started. Jemmy at once rushed to stop them, and with great presence of mind lifted off one of the youngsters who was standing with one foot on the step, out in safety as he passed. Seizing the reins, in the endeavor to pull up, he received a tremendous kick from the near-side leader which broke his thigh and knocked him down. Still sticking to the reins he used his best endeavours to head them round for the fence, but was eventually compelled to let go. The team then headed for the river, only about two chains distant; but again swerved along the bank and headed for their stable at Burgorah at a smart trot. Before going far they ran the coach against a tree, cleared themselves from the wreck and made home. The violence of the shock threw Mrs. Dickins and her daughter from the coach, severely bruising and disfiguring her, and at the same time the boy on the box seat was thrown off and also considerably hurt.

Miss Dickins then walked to Burgorah station, a distance of

about two miles, and in & short time every available help and kindness was placed at the disposal of the sufferers by Mr. and Mrs. Healy. A message was sent to town and a number of gentlemen at once went out to render all the assistance possible. Jemmy was laid on a mattrass and driven in, in company with the passengers. He was at once taken to the hospital, and the broken limb set right by Dr. Marks, and we are pleased to be able to state that he is progressing favorably. It is also satisfactory to record that Mrs. Dickins and the children are recovering from the rough treatment they experienced. That the results were not of a much more serious nature is a source of astonishment as well as congratulation, and is no doubt to be attributed to the pluck, and nerve displayed by Jemmy in sticking to the reins as long as he did.

We understand it to be the intention of some of the residents to initiate a movement for a testimonial to be presented to him on his recovery as a mark of their appreciation of his conduct, and we have no doubt it will be well received and supported in the district where Jemmy is so wellknown and so deservedly popular. A very general opinion prevails, however, that some precution should be taken by coach proprietors to prevent the possibility of such a disaster again. When there are no passengers in the coach, or when as in this instance, they consist of ladies and children, the coachman is compelled to leave the box to open the gates or take down the numerous slip rails along the line of road and in so doing has to trust to chance and the disposition of his horses, for the opportunity of regaining his place on the coach. The risk of such, accidents as the one now recorded would be materially lessened, if not altogether prevented by sending a boy from, either end, to accompany the coach, and assist the driver where there are no passengers, or at least none who can be expected to take down and replace the sliprails, such as those which ornament the St. George line, some of which are as large as the royal yard of a 120 gun-ship, and not nearly so easy to handle." (Accident to Cobb and Co.'s Coach, at St. George, 15 Nov 1879)

1880 "Action for Damages. DICKENS AND WIFE V. COBB & CO. We reprint from the Courier the report of the above case heard at the District Court, Brisbane, on Wednesday,, before Mr. Judge Paul and a jury. This was an action brought by Mr. Dickens, post and telegraph master at St. George, and his wife, to recover £200 damages for injuries sustained by the latter and caused by an accident to a coach owned by the defendants, which accident occurred through the negligence of defendants' servant. Defendants admitted the negligence, and lodged £50 in court in satisfaction of damages. Mr. V. Power, instructed by Messrs. Edwards and Marsland, appeared for the plaintiffs ; and Mr. Griffith, Q.C. with Mr. Rutledge, instructed by Messrs. Wilson and Wilson, for the defendants. The case was postponed from last sittings of the court, a commission then having been appointed to take the evidence of the plaintiffs and their witnesses. The evidence de bene esse was read by the registrar of the court.

The plaintiffs' evidence was in effect that, on the 4th of November last year, Mrs. Dickens, her two sons and daughter, left St. George about 7 in the morning by one the defendants' coaches for the Western Railway terminus. She was proceeding to Brisbane for her approaching confinement, in order to be within reach of better medical attendance, and with a view to diminish the attendant expenses. After starting, the horses which were fresh, were driven eight miles without accident, until a gate near the residence of Mr. Healy was reached. The driver, James Murphy, gave the reins to Charles Dickens, a boy of six years, descended from the box, opened the gate, mounted again, and drove the coach through. Having done so he again gave the boy the reins, and having closed the gate, spoke to Mrs. Dickius' second son, who was inside the coach, and who wished to be taken on the box. Murphy said he would take him, and Mrs. Dickens objected, saying he (Murphy) had enough to do to take care of the one outside. Murphy, however, lifted the child out, and while in the act of doing so the horses started. Murphy clutched at the reins, and did his utmost to stop them ; but one of the leaders kicked him, breaking his thigh. The horses then ran down the bank of the Balonne River, passed under a leaning tree, which knocked the top off the coach, and ran the vehicle against a stump, the shock throwing Mrs. Dickens out of the vehicle, and disengaging the horses from it. Her daughter ran to Mr. Healy's for assistance, and Mrs. Dickens was picked up insensible. Both her eyes were blackened ; she had a contusion on the forehead, and another on the side, which caused her great pain. She also suffered great pain of mind, fearing the shock would bring on premature confinement. Dr. Marks attended her from the 4th until the 14th November. He afterwards attended her on her confinement, which was not premature, but one of malposition, which was unusually severe and necessitating the use of instruments, and from which she recovered but very slowly. He attributed her increased sufferings and slow recovery to the injuries she had received by being thrown from the coach.

The plaintiffs' claims was made a follows :—For medical attendance, £40 ; for medicine and medical assistance, £40; for medicine and medical comforts, £25; nursing, £12; extra domestic assistance, £10 ; and £113 for general pain of body and mind. For the defence, James Murphy, the driver of the coach at the time of the accident,' deposed that, on coming to the gate, before descending from the box to open and to shut the gate he twisted the reins round the guard iron, and handed the ends to the boy Charles Dickens; he did not know why he gave the child the reins, except to keep him quiet, after shutting the gate he saw the little boy who was inside with Mrs. Dickens standing with one leg outside on the step ; he came round to him and just then the horses started ; he lifted the child out and placed him on the ground, and caught at the reins of the near wheeler, but the horse reared, and he then snatched at the reins of the near leader; when he gripped the rein the horse jumped away, kicked him, and broke his thigh ; from where he was he saw the coach coach until it was brought up to a stop by a stump ; the horses at first cantered a few yards but had slowed to a trot when the coach struck the stump ; he saw Mrs. Dickens at the time ; saw her sitting in a stooping position with her hat off, after the coach stopped and the horses had broken away from it ; about ten minutes after the accident Mrs. Dickens walked up to where he was and abused him for being such a fool as to permit the accident to happen; she spoke in her ordinary voice ; she remained near him for a few minutes, and then removed away some distance. Mr. G. M. Kerr saw Mrs. Dickens at the scene of the accident about 10 O'clock ; she knew him and spoke to him. Dr. Sharpnell gave evidence to the effect that a shock from being thrown out of a coach to a woman in Mrs.

Dickins' condition would be almost certain to be followed by premature confinement. He gave other evidence of a scientific nature, and as the to fees charged by him in similar cases, which were very much less than those charged by Dr. Marks. Some further evidence de bene esse having been read for the defence, and for the plaintiffs in rebuttal, Mr. Griffith addressed the jury, and was followed by Mr. Power. His Honor having summed up, the jury retired, and returned into court in ten minutes with a verdict for the defendants." (Action for Damages, 26 Jun 1880, p.3)

Murphy, Jeremiah (Jerry)
1870 "Wednesday, July 13. (Before the Police Magistrate.) Breach of Municipal By-Laws. Jeremiah Murphy, driver of Cobb & Co.'s coach, appeared to answer a charge of driving that vehicle across the foot-path in East-street. Mr. Hellicar for plaintiff and Mr. Batho for the defence. W. A. Smith deposed that about half-past 12 o'clock on the 12th instant he saw the defendant drive a coach from the yard across the foot-path in East street; a water-table had been formed opposite the gate, which was injured. The Bench found the offence proved, and fined the defendant 10s. and 3s. 6d. costs. The Police Magistrate added that he thought a notice should have been issued by the Corporation warning parties to erect bridges across the water-tables. Mr. Hellicar said the public were well aware that it was necessary to do so; the by-laws had been published, and this was not the first case of a similar nature that had been brought before the Bench." ('Wednesday, July 13', 14 Jul 1870, p.3)

1876 "Charleville to Dalby per Cobb and Co's Coach. On a bright January morning, 1876—well, to be precise, it was on a Sunday morning, the 2nd January, 1876, that the celebrated Cobb and Co. started their first coach from the fair city of Charleville to that equally as fair city Roma. At 7.20 the well-known cry of 'All aboard' sounded on the sweet morning air, when your humble servant having taken his seat, together with A. Broomfield (the driver that is to be) and Jerry Murphy of happy memory, who handled the ribbons on this auspicious occasion, started away with a spanking team of four horses, which Jerry tooled along at 'knots' an hour, the country looking black, dry, and parched, and no grass.

Made Bradley's farm at 9.20, and got to the dam mail-station at 10.12, where we had the first change of horses. This time Broomfield took them in hand, and away again over parched, and grassless country. The fine clear morning air having sharpened our appetites, we had recourse to a goodly-sized package of sandwiches and a small 'wee drap' out of the flask, and we all felt considerably better. (I may here state that it is necessary for passengers to take a little refreshment with them, as at present there is no accommodation on the road until you reach Maryvale.) Pulled up, and watered the horses at the 'tank,' where Murphy intends having a mail-station; away again, the horses much refreshed after imbibing. It was now we began to feel the heat : it was like a furnace. I may say that I felt as hot as two furnaces : about 140° in the sun. It was now that our water-bags came into action. I can tell you that a drink of cold water in a waterless bush, under a blazing January sun, is a luxury not to be thought too lightly of ; and the man that invented water bags ought to have a front seat in heaven." (Charleville to Dalby per Cobb and Co's Coach, 22 Jan 1876, p.3)

1879 "A familiar favorite and pioneer of our old coaching days, Mr. Jeremiah Murphy, who, in connection with Cobb and Co.'s coaches, was widely known and respected throughout the colony, has passed away, after a painful illness. Mr. Murphy was in the employment of Messrs. Cobb and Co. for the past eighteen years, having entered their service in New South Wales in 1861, whence he accompanied the first coaching plant of the company to Queensland, in January, 1866, when the company extended their operations to this colony. For some four years after his arrival he was driving on different lines of road—between Brisbane and Ipswich, Dalby and Roma, and Bigge's Camp, Helidon, and Toowoomba—and old travellers over the Main Range will long remember their favorite whip.

About nine years ago he was made road manager between Dalby and Roma, and subsequently he organised the extensions to Charleville and St George. About six years ago he was appointed to be road manager between Brisbane, Roma, Warwick, and Tenterfield, and he was subsequently promoted to be general line inspector for their coaches throughout the colony. During his long career in connection with Queensland coaching the deceased, in every department of his work, gave the greatest satisfaction to his employers and to the public, and he was esteemed as a faithful servant and a popular favorite to the last. Mr. Murphy returned to Brisbane from a tour of inspection on the northern roads about six weeks ago, since which time he suffered acutely from the illness that terminated fatally on Tuesday last. The deceased, at the time of his death, was only thirty-six years of age. His funeral, which took place last Wednesday, was numerously and respectably attended. Through all the breadth of Queensland are men who will sincerely regret the early death of 'Jerry Murphy,' for he was a man whose life, while largely identified with all the toil of outside settlement, was invariably equal to all emergencies. Courteous he was, and considerate to all with whom be came in contact but, above all, loyal to Cobb and Co." (Current News, 19 Jul 1879, p.69)

1929 See also Amies, Tom

Murphy, Jim (Jimmy) ... 1917 See Anderson, Jim; 1929 Amies, Tom

Murphy, Martin ... See Appendix 1.6

Murray, Patrick
1926 "OLD COACH DRIVER. DEATH OF PATRICK MURRAY ... Mr. Patrick Murray, at the age of about 81 years ... He terminated his connection with Cobb and Co. some 30 years ago, after driving the Dubbo to Coonamble mail for several years." (Old Coach Driver, 2 Jul 1926, p.3)

Murray, Tom ... 1932 See Smiley, W.

Nairn, Jim (Jimmy) ... 1917 See Thompson, Joe; 1925 Eddie, Nathan; 1933 Bates, Bob; 1935 Conroy, James (Jim)

Nankervis, J ... 1919 See Aisbett, E. J.

Nash, Les.
1919 "The Cobb & Co.'s Old Coach Drivers' Association ... old coach drivers employed by Messrs. Cobb & Co., kindred

coaching firms in Australia and New Zealand, and others ... Driver, district employed: Mt Buffalo " (Annual report / Cobb & Co.'s Old Coach Drivers' Association, 1919, pp.6-8)

Nathan, Edward (Ned/Eddie)
1917 "Edward Nathan, another of Cobb and Co.'s men, died in March, 1915, in Sydney. He was a little man, and weighed but 9st. 2lb., but it is stated that on the occasion of the visit of the Australian Eleven to Bathurst he carried two massive players of whom one was Bonor, across the road together. For several years he was road manager, and, when he retired in 1893, he was presented with a public testimonial and purse of sovereigns ... He was a good sportsman, and president of half a dozen country jockey clubs" (Coaching in Australia, 1917, p.27)

1932 See also Breen, Jim (Jimmy)

Nathan, Ted ... 1935 See Conroy, James (Jim)

Naylor, Joe
1912 "I hear Joe Naylor has disposed of his coach, and mail service to a local buyer. This coachman will be remembered starting driving for Cobb and Co. on the Jericho-Blackall line about 18 years ago. About eight years ago he left Cobb and Coy., and started driving on the Blackall-Isisford line for Messrs William Atkinson and Coy. Later he acquired the coach service from Listowel to Blackall, and held proprietorship of this service up till now. Joe is going in for another profitable business, having had sufficient coach driving." (Blackall Notes, 5 Aug 1912, p.6)

1930 "THE GOOD OLD DAYS. Living in Blackall (Cent. Q.) is Joe Naylor, one of Cobb's old-time drivers, and, one of the best with the ribbons. No gate was too small for him to drive a team of seven horses through, and young horses were put straight into the coach without being broken. Men suffering from nerves had no right on the box-seat when Joe's call, *Let 'em go!* rang out.—Barcoo" (Gossip from Everywhere, 16 Aug 1930, p.13)

Naylor, Tom ... 1947 See Richards, J. Frederick (Fred)

Nesbitt, W ... 1937 See Preston, R.

Netterfield, Harry ... 1917 See Levi, Emanuel (Manny); 1935 Conroy, James (Jim)

Newman, William (Bill/Billy)
1884 "TRIP TO MARYSVILLE ... a descriptive article which appeared in The Australasian under the head of 'Easy Trips from Melbourne:'—We started from Lilydale under luxurious conditions, having chartered for the use of our party, six in all, the comfortable 'Tom Thumb' coach of Cobb and Co., which, with its well-padded sides and back, is to the ordinary coach what a first-class railway carriage is to a second-class. The day was bright and warm, and the rich level of the Yarra Flats, after the showery weather which had preceded, looked its best ... we turned back to our coach, to which our careful and civil Driver Newman had, by this time, attached the horses, we all felt that we had reached the turning point of a very pleasant outing." (A Trip to Marysvale, 9 Apr 1884, p.7)

1893 "We hear that the popular 'whip,' Mr William Newman, who was for a number of years in the employ of Cobb and Co., has leased the well-known livery and letting stables belonging to Mr. M. Sheehan, of Healesville."Advertised on the same page "THE CAVE HILL BUTTER FACTORY will be opened on and after 1st of September, 1893, For the Reception of Milk ... D. Mitchell ... PUBLIC NOTICE Cave Hill Bacon Factory. Best quality pickled pork, heads, feet, gams, &c. can be obtained at the factory." (Local and District News, 13 Oct 1893, p.2)

1899 "Death of a Victorian Identity.—A well known identity in the coaching days of Victoria, in the person of William Newman, died rather suddenly in the Fremantle hospital on Monday. For many years 'Billy' Newman was Cobb and Co.'s favourite whip on the bush roads of Victoria, and he was also in the service of Robertson, Wagner and Co for a long time. He was best known, perhaps, in the Lilydale and Wood's Point districts. About two years ago the deceased came to Western Australia, and latterly he was, in the employ of Mr. K. McKenzie, bus proprietor, of Fremantle. Newman was about 56 years of age." (News and Notes, 29 Jun 1899, p.5)

1932 "OLD COACHING DAYS MELBOURNE TO MARYSVILLE. How many people are there in our metropolis to-day who ever left the old Albion Hotel, Bourke-street, in Robertson and Wagner's (Cobb and Co.) Royal mail coach, on a trip to Marysville? Bill Newman, was the popular whip on that run, and for many years his quips and jests created great merriment on the journey ... put the clock back to the early eighties, and once again travel over the old road (says 'The Age') ... Punctually at 6.30 Bill's call, 'All aboard for Marysville' ... a stop was made at the White Horse Hotel for a refresher, then on to Ringwood to change horses at the Coach and Horses Hotel. Off again. Rounding a bend in the road to Lillydale an old man kangaroo came hopping along. Bill shook his whip at him, exclaiming, *No mails to-day, Jacky*, and with that the old man bounded into the scrub to tell the bush people who were waiting for him. An American lady traveller sitting alongside Bill exclaimed, *Wa-a-a-l, if that don't beat creation. Do you mean to tell me, driver, that that animal, with that long tail and sawn-off arms carries the mail round these parts? Yes, madam*, Bill replied. *He is very intelligent. Have you got anything in America to beat it? Sure, you win*, the lady replied, to the great delight of the listeners ... On reaching Rosemount Hill further diversion was created by a swarm of bees flying over the coach." (Old Coaching Days, 18 Oct 1932, p.4)

Nicholas/Nicholls, James (Jim/Jimmy)
1908 "In Western Australia, there was no large service in coaching, until the finding of Coolgardie, followed by other great discoveries, where a highly efficient mail and coach service was established ... by Sydney Kidman (the Cattle King) and James Nicholas, the latter an old-time driver for Cobb and Co. in Riverina. The service then established assumed very large proportions, and was a well-equipped and well-managed business." (The Contributor, 25 Nov 1908, p.1405)

1925 Part I "Coaching in the Commonwealth. Experiences of Half a Century. 'Jimmy Nicholas' Handles the Ribbons ... I have only heard of the original Mr. Cobb, who did some coaching in the early days of Victoria, also of different other early day coaching owners, but the most of these early day men, if not all, did not stick at the business anything like the time that the six men I am going to mention did, and neither did they do one-fiftieth part of the coaching these men have done. Their names were—Alick and John Robertson, John Wagner, Walter Hall and James Rutherford. A sixth man, Mr. Whitney, was connected with the firm, but I never saw him, and think he must have gone out of the business before my time. They were, I think, all Americans, and no doubt Rutherford Wagner and Hall were super men, who would have been great at any calling they took up. The two Robertson brothers were more of the office-type—good financiers, but not nearly the ginger in them the other three men had. I think they all came across from America to get to the Victorian goldfields. They had had coaching experience already in America with Wells, Fargo and Company, and I take it that when they saw the possibilities coaching offered in Victoria they at once grasped it, and were soon the King Cobbs of Australian coaching, a position they retained for many years ...

Somewhere in the [18]'sixties they dissolved the partnership in Victoria. Jim Rutherford and Walter Hall took New South Wales as their base of operations, and traded as 'Cobb and Co., Rutherford and Hall, Proprietors, Sydney.' The two Robertson brothers and Jack Wagner retained the Victorian portion and traded as 'Cobb and Co., Robertson and Wagner, Proprietors, Melbourne.' The two firms were known as Victorian Cobb and New South Wales Cobb. Victorian Cobb did nearly all Victorian coaching. They crossed the Murray at Echuca and ran all that western portion of New South Wales out as far as Tibooburra, some 700 miles from Echuca. Sydney Cobb did the balance of New South Wales, and were largely interested in the Queensland Cobb and Co., which was I think, another registered company ...

I drove for the two firms for about ten years, and was driving out of Wagga when I was fifteen, and afterwards on the several roads to Narandera, Urana, Jerilderie, Deniliquin, Wilcannia, Milparinka, and for a while on a network of roads Sydney Cobb and in New England running from Tamworth, Armidale, Glen Innes, Inverell, Walcha, Bundara, Tenterfield, and on into Stanthorpe in Queensland. I could not stand the cold of New England after the years I had spent on the hot Riverina plains, so soon cleared back to the Darling, and drove from Wilcannia to Mr. Brown, the last town out west in New South Wales. There was a very bad drought on there, sheep and other stock dying in thousands, as also did the coach horses. As to keep them working would have meant carting chaff some 500 miles, an impossible proposition. Cobb and Co. had for the first time to relinquish horses and get camels to carry the mails, and they did it well. I think that was the first time in Australia that camels had carried mails. Kidman and Nicholas ran Esperance to Norseman with camels for a month in 1896 ... I left the Cobbs in 1884 ... in 1887, Sid Kidman bought O'Neil out, and he and I carried, on mail contracting for a good many years, running into big contracts at times. We traded as Kidman and Nicholas, and our operations ran into all the States except Victoria, but much the biggest in New South Wales and W.A. Sid and Sac Kidman held a half interest in the firm and I the other half. They very rarely came amongst the coaching, as their business of stock dealers, station holders, etc., kept them busy in another direction. We mostly had about 1000 horses at work coaching,

in the different States, and at times up to 1200 ...

Sydney Cobb amalgamated with some brothers named Morrisson in all that, network of mail contracts going west from Dubbo and out on to the Darling at Bourke, and as far down as Wilcannia, Milparinka and back Cobar way. Kidman and Nicholas were this firm's principal opposition. We got practically, all their contracts on one or two occasions, but they finally got our lot back in 1897, and we sold them all our coaching plant, including horses, in one line. At this time we had been established in W.A. for over a year and were not sorry to have a good cleaning up over East." (Coaching in the Commonwealth, 17 May 1925, p.9)

1925 Part II "Coaching in the Commonwealth. Experiences of Half a Century 'Jimmy Nicholas Handles the Ribbons ... We will allow Mr. Nicholas to tell the story in his own words ... I came West in 1894, after tendering for all our New South Wales mails, and at Southern Cross attended a meeting of the Coolgardie Coaching Company and got them to give me a month's option over their coaching plant from Southern Cross to the goldfields. I had intended buying them out, but when I got back to the hotel after the meeting there was a wire for me from Kidman saying our tender had been accepted for all the western portion of the New South Wales mail contracts. So it was a case of abandoning, my option over the Coolgardie Coaching Company's lines and hurrying back to get several hundred horses, coaches, plant, etc., ready to start our new contracts by New Year's Day. I told the Southern Cross people I would be back and make a deal with them as soon as I could sell some of our less suitable routes, which I did, but it took me longer than I thought. Meantime the railway had been opened to Coolgardie, and the Coaching Company had registered their company and named it Cobb and Co., Ltd. There were six members in the company, namely, our old and genial friend Charlie Saw, that wonderful old man William Marwick, Billie Milne, Wilkinson, Jack Day and another. They were the originals of Cobb and Co., Ltd., here. I think some of these members had sold out to the others, however, in June, 1896, when Kidman and Nicholas made them an offer of £10,000 for the 24 shares in the company on a walk-in-walk-out basis. This they accepted, all but Jack Day, so we let him retain his shares and bought him out somewhere about a year later. The deal was a good one.

We got our money back in seven months, thanks to the fact that Wilkie Brothers were about that time cutting those two cement hills out close to Coolgardie and could not get their engine through to carry the traffic on to Kalgoorlie. And so the company rolled along. Sometimes not making much profit, and at others—when any fresh rushes were about and plenty of people were travelling—showing good profits. I kept buying members out until after a year or so I had 20 out of the 24 shares, the balance being held by my old bookkeeper, Ted Miller and my family. This position continued until about three or four years ago, when I finally wound Cobb and Company, Ltd. (W.A.) up. I remember some years ago thinking coaching, with its monopoly, would go on for ever, and it did not seem likely there would ever be any way of carrying mails and traffic successfully other than that by horsed coaches. The first little set-back that forced itself upon us was the advent of the bike. Many of the younger travellers went by bike instead of coach, and the next had set-back we got was when New South Wales adopted the parcels post. This meant our carrying free in mail bags for the Postal Department tons of parcels for which we had previously been paid coach rates. One line running at the time, suffered more than any other. It was from Cobar to Wilcannia, and the direct route from Sydney to the Middle Darling districts. We had to put on additional coaches there occasionally to carry the parcels post ; However New South Wales had to pay a higher rate for their mail contracts in the succeeding years, so we in a way got some compensation, but of course the advent of motors soon extinguished the old horse coaches.

The first time I saw a motor car outback was at Laverton. It was taking one of Bewick, Moreing's managers (W. Hoover, I think) around the different mines inspecting, and the car got along, so well I could see the quick demise of all other methods of carrying traffic. So I at once began cutting big coaches down and making them into vans, and sold them at about half their original value. I also disposed of horses and other coaching equipment as soon as possible, and began carrying on the business of Cobb and Co. per motor cars instead of the old methods. I could see the days of holding monopolies, as had been done by the different Cobb and Co, were finished, and the sooner I drifted into some other line of business the better. This I did as soon as I could, realising that all my life's studies and education in coaching were gone in one swoop. My plant with a good many thousands of pounds as a coaching concern, was nearly useless against motor traffic. So thus ended W.A. Cobb and Co., as well as all other coaching companies' business, for anyone with a tin Lizzie can run opposition more or less successfully with any other car on long bush roads such as Cobb and Co. used to cater for." (Coaching in the Commonwealth, 24 May 1925, p.11)

1925 Part III "Coaching in the Commonwealth. Experiences of Half a Century. 'Jimmy' Nicholas Handles the Ribbons. [Coaching, now fast dying out throughout the Commonwealth, in inextricably bound up with the history of Australia, and the story of its evolution is one of the most interesting it is possible to imagine. No one is a greater authority on the subject than Mr. James Nicholas, of Peron Peninsula Station, Sharks Bay, and in an interview granted to a representative of 'The Sunday Times,' Mr. Nicholas has given us a narrative of coaching in Australia as he has seen it during the last 50 years ... We will allow Mr. Nicholas to tell the story in his own words ... I was one of Cobb's old drivers, grooms, agents, managers and owners, and also one of the good old firm's biggest opposition as regards their main contracts in after years. My whole life had been spent coaching a business which I liked and thoroughly, studied in all its branches, and if I did not know enough to run a coaching firm after seeing both the best and worst coaching in Australia I must be a booby indeed. Now, as regards Sid Kidman, I don't think Australia has seen many men as smart as he was. I have not seen anything of him for the last 20 years or so, but as a young fellow we were great pals. He in those days was one of the nicest men you could meet—a great horseman, could ride or drive anything and was probably Australia's best judge of a bullock. He could hop off the top rail of a yard on to any bullock, ride him around and slip off him on to the top rail well before the bullock knew just what had happened. He would buy or sell anything from a pocket knife to the biggest station, and one deal did not disturb him a bit more than another. In fact, I think Sid., now Sir Sidney Kidman, is one of Australia's super men. He never drank, swore, or lost his temper in his life, could box if necessary as well as the best of them, and was not a bad poker player, but five 'bob' rises were his limit. So I think—he with those few different characteristics in his favor and I with a lifetime of knowledge—we should have been able to run Cobb and Co., Ltd., of W.A. Anyhow, we did, and successfully, too.

Our coaches, horses, men, etc., were always the best we could procure. Most of our drivers were as good as Australia has had at any time. I question if any other road had its big daily traffic carried better than the Menzies to Malcolm and out back traffic was carried. I have seen our coach arrive at Menzies at night with twenty to thirty passengers regularly; and twice a month, in addition to this load, we had from half a ton to a ton and a half of gold on her. The only other road I know of that has carried such a traffic was the one I have before, referred to—Hay to Deniliquin—that is, for a number of years, and even that road was just a passenger, letter and paper mail traffic. They had not in those days the tons of parcels post mail we had to carry over here. Coaching was a much more expensive business to run here in the early days of Coolgardie, Kalgoorlie, and other goldfields rushes owing to the water supply being mostly obtained from condensers. Our water bill alone was not less than £5000 a year. It's a pity, in a way, that coaching has passed out, because it was a man's job. Each individual, driver, groom, etc., had the personal responsibility of his coach or charge—he was out on his own, and had no boss to be continually referring to but had to solve all his own problems, etc. without assistance.

The following may give some idea of what used to occur on the Old Man Plains in the winter, at a place called Holy Box change, near Mossgiel. About the middle of winter, when all lakes, swamps and such like places were well filled and creeks all flooded, the following little conversation between groom and driver at 10 o'clock on a dirty night might be heard; *Any news of the Willandra Crossing to-day?* from the driver. The groom: *Oh, yes; the water is still rising. It is now half a mile wide, and ten or a dozen teams are stock there. They have had to doublebank each waggon across with 40 or more horses on them. The road is ripped to pieces there, so look out, but the teamsters sent word to say they will have a team of horses ready to pull you through if you get anchored there to-night* This Willandra was no doubt a rotten place ... And so it generally was the horses, used to the mud and slush and bog of the plains, if not bustled, would scramble through somehow. Coaches were built for that special kind of work—low and strong and very hard to turn over, so that while they kept on their wheels the horses would tug them out of their own volition ... Old time Victorian drivers used to say the glue pot on one of the Victorian roads was, in winter, the worst bit of road in Australia, but in that stretch of plain from Echuca to Ivanhoe, about 300 miles, I think there were numerous places of the glue-pot calibre. I remember another scene taken at Ben Lomond mail change on the top of the New England mountains, on the road between Armidale and Glen Innes, time midnight, in midwinter. The two mail coaches used to meet here about midnight every night. Very often there was 6ft or 7ft of snow piled up against the side of the stables, with a laneway cut in it to get to the door. This was supposed to be a metal road, but at the time I speak of they were building the railway along there, and what was metal had been pushed down into the mud in many places. The roads were fearful, and the grades very steep in places. Cobb and Co. only allowed two passengers to be carried on the night mail coaches, but accommodated all passenger traffic on the day coaches that ran over that road. The next change towards Armidale from Ben Lomond was at a lake called The Mother of Ducks. A couple of miles after leaving this change you had to go down what was called The Devil's Pinch, a fall of, I think, 1600 feet in one and a quarter miles. It was a ribbon road cut into the side of the mountain, with a fall of several hundred feet on one side and the steep side of the mountain on the other. A good stiff post and rail fence on the precipice side of the road at places helped to make one feel a bit more secure, and saved many lives, I am sure. In cases of brakes giving way, by preventing vehicles from toppling over the cliff. The down coach used to pass over this portion of road about 4 a.m., and on a clear night, when you could almost see the frost falling and everything was frozen and the surface of the road like glass, the passage down the pinch was a most unpleasant one. Patches of the road, sometimes yards wide, would be frozen hard and slippery as glass. The leaders, as soon as they got on to it, would slip about, and finally be on their haunches by the time they got across it. Then the wheelers would slither along over it in the same way, and when the coach came on to it brakes were of no use, and you had the hair-raising feeling of slipping along without having the slightest control over either coach or horses until you struck the gravelly surface again. It was a most unpleasant and very dangerous predicament to have to face, one way or the other, each night, and I don't know any coach drivers in Australia who earned their money better than the men who drove the night mail from Armidale to Glen Innes." (Coaching in the Commonwealth, 31 May 1925, p.9)

1925 Part IV "Coaching in the Commonwealth. Experiences of Half a Century 'Jimmy' Nicholas Handles the Ribbons No. IV. (Conclusion.) ... Cobb's manager ... Mr. Powell ... said that if I saw any of those alarming lights I would not stop on it. I remember the old man replied: *You won't, see any there, Jimmy. You don't drink whisky and Charlie has been taking more than was good for him for some time.* Anyway, on I went, and saw nothing ... I had several times seen similar lights but took them for swaggies' camp fires, etc., or some night birds' eyes, such as the big owls you sometimes see on those plains—their eyes would take the reflection of the coach lights at such a long way off. Anyway, I decided the next time I saw such a light I would get down and examine it to satisfy myself. So one night, a month or so later, when nearing the creek I saw the light about a hundred yards off the road up along a fence. I had a passenger with me who could drive, so I got him to hold the reins, while I investigated the light. I took the four-horse whip well coiled up, ready for action in one hand, and a coach lamp in the other, and stalked along until I got within twenty yards of the light, when it promptly disappeared. I examined the spot-where it had been most carefully but could find no trace of any animal or bird tracks in the soft mud. But I remembered that just when the light disappeared I heard something like a bird's wings flutter, and felt in my own mind that the lights were a reflection from some big bird's eyes. I frequently saw the lights afterwards but took no notice of them ... but lots of the people who had seen them and knew how King had been smashed up at the place where they were generally visible first, still clung to the idea that they were something in the ghost line ...

Some idea of the difference of running the old style of horse coaches as against the present day motors may be gleaned by what follows. Kidman and Nicholas ran a line with horses from Morgans in South Australia to Cobar in New South Wales. This line connected up with the South Australian and New South Wales railways, and was about 620 miles long. It passed through Renmark, Wentworth, Pooncarie, Menindie, Wilcannia and Cobar. We ran along the Murray and Darling Rivers for the first 500 miles, roughly and then cut across to the Sydney rail head at Cobar, some 150 miles from the Darling. Another road we ran was from Booligal on the Old Man Plains through to Tibooburra, passing through Mossgiel, Ivanhoe, Wilcannia, White Cliff and Milparinka, with a branch running down to Tarrawongee, a distance of 510 miles. A third was from Broken Hill to Wentworth, 200 miles, and a fourth from Broken Hill to Menindie, 75 miles. Another of our lines was from Farina, S.A., to Cadilio Downs, in Queensland, a distance of 400 miles, and still another from Hergott, S.A, to Birdsville, Queensland. The Bourke to Wilcannia contract we had once or twice, but sold it to the original contractors, Morrison Bros. These different lines ran into something over 2000 miles of coaches. Some services were run three times a week others twice, and some once a week. It took some 1400 horses, 40 coaches and 150 men to run these services properly. These, of course, did not include our West Australian contracts. To-day these same services can be run with 16 motor cars and in half the time we used to take with the horse coaches. Imagine the difference when you come to consider the cost of purchasing 1400 horses, harnesses, and other equipment, to say nothing of the outlay on some 40 coaches, the wages of 150 men and feed for, say, 600 horses in bad seasons! What a tremendous advantage the comparison is in favor of motor transport! But of course as against that, as each of our 150 men would represent the wage earner for a family of four on an average, this meant that the old coaches, provided keep. etc., for about 600 people, big and small; whereas the motors, on the same basis of families, would only provide a living for 64 people ...

Victoria Cobb & Sydney Cobb Factories "Further, as regards coaches, Victorian Cobb had two coach-building factories, one at, I think. Castlemaine, Victoria, and the other at Hay, N.S.W. Sydney Cobb had two factories, one at Bathurst, and the other at Bourke, N.S.W. We got all our coaches we used in the Eastern States from one or other of these factories, and brought a lot of them over when we bought Cobb and Co., Ltd., out here. Furthermore, a large number of our best coach horses were brought over here from our Eastern roads. The head of Victorian Cobb (New South Wales representative) was a Mr. Maurice Parker, who had under him Mr. G. A. McGowan, an American, and a very smart coaching man in his day, also Mr. Frank Byrne.

Their headquarters were in Hay, N.S.W. Sydney Cobb's principal manager was Mr. W. Lee, a very smart man at his business. Mr. McGowan might be remembered over here years ago, as when Victorian Cobb's business was about finished he came over here and found Charlie Kidman and myself. We bought out the Perth

Omnibus Company, and McGowan managed it for a while ... Charlie Kidman joined 'Kidman and Nicholas' here when we bought Cobb and Co., Ltd., but, and was an active member for a couple of years, when I bought him out." (Coaching in the Commonwealth, 7 June 1925, p.11)

1925 See also Jones, Bill

Nicholson, Bob ... 1917 See Wright, Bob

Nicholson, Geo ... 1938 See Templeton, Herb.

Nicholson, Ryby
1938 "COBB AND CO. A VETERAN DRIVER QUEENSLAND 50 YEARS AGO—Mr. Ryby Nicholson, of Turramurra drove Cobb and Co.'s coaches in western and southern Queensland more than 50 years ago. He was with the company for nearly 20 years, and, though now about to celebrate his 83rd birthday, he remembers vividly the days and nights spent on the six-horse coaches which served this vast district before the days of trains, motor cars and aeroplanes. Mr. Nicholson first drove a coach from Roma to Charleville, a distance of 180 miles, which was a three days journey. This line extended also to Cunnamulla, Thargomindah, and Hungerford, on the New South Wales border, where it linked up with the coach running to Bourke. The trip from Roma, then the railhead, to Thargomindah, took nine days. Later, he was on the run from Barcaldine, north west to Cloncurry. The company also ran coaches to Croydon, in the Gulf country.

Those were the days, Mr. Nicholson understood, when Cobb and Co. paid its shareholders as much as 25 per cent. Mr. Nicholson was manager at Hughenden when he resigned. He was the last of the road managers in Western Queensland. On the Charleville line, where he was for six months, he never carried fewer than eight passengers on a 14 passenger bus. He had had as many as 20. On these occasions two would travel on the boot and others on the roof of the coach. There were no metal roads outside the towns, and seven or eight miles an hour was reasonable travelling, for some tracks were very rough. On the black soil plains in wet weather it was necessary to stop every half-mile to clean the wheels. He had driven three days and two nights, stopping only to change horses and eat. In the whole of the 20 years with Cobb and Co., Mr. Nicholson never had a serious accident. When he was in Barcaldine, he was deputed to drive Governor Norman round the town and district, in his coach with six greys in thee harness. It was nothing unusual to have a couple of tons of mails on board. Mr. Nicholson took up land to engage in horse and cattle breeding. In 1915 he came to New South Wales. His father arrived in Melbourne from England in 1848, acting as salesman in Kirk's bazaar for many years." (Cobb & Co., 27 Jan 1938, p.10)

1917 See also Corbett, Sandy

Nolan, Adam ... See Appendix 1.6

Nolan, Harry
1916 "Coaching in flood time. Ross Hood's Reminiscences ... There was one place at the foot of a limestone ridge on the track along by M'Kenzie Bros.' Geurie station, that was very treacherous country. It was towards Murrumbidgerie station (Furlong's). That is the reason why each coachman had to carry an assistant with him. It was necessary to have him to get through these boggy places, and to keep a look out for stumps, for fear that we got stumped on the low ground towards Cobb and Co.'s change stables at Murrumbidgerie side of Deep Creek. When the coaches met the drivers always told each other where to look out for bad spots on the tracks. After leaving Deep Creek we kept along through a pine scrub, just beyond Lynch's farm. Towards the stables there was a long flat with a cowl that went behind the stables. That we had to cross, and it was dangerous on account of the stumps and falled timber. As the flood was coming out so strong Harry Nolan and I had arranged that if the down coach got to the stables he was to wait until the up coach came up, so that we could give directions one to the other. The cowl, which went behind the stable's and the hotel (Joseph Jackson, proprietor), crossed the road a quarter of a mile below the stables towards Dubbo, and as Harry was coming out one night his horses had to swim across between a big stump and a tree that used to be our guide." (Coaching in flood time, 24 Aug, p.5)

See also Appendix 1.6

Nolan, Jim ... 1917 See Manning, Ned

Nolan, Tom ... 1917 See Wright, Bob

Norris, George ... See Appendix 1.6

Northway, Bob ... 1921 See Griffen, Chas.

Nowel, H ... 1932 See Lowe, Bill

Pipe-Lighting Feat.
"I wonder whether many, have seen a driver achieve this almost impossible performance of that of cutting up tobacco, filling, and light his pipe, while driving a team of five horses ? I have seen this performed time and again. I took lessons, and with practice accomplished the job, that is, so far as just lighting my pipe when going full tilt ahead. My mentor insisted on two things. Face the wind, and let the match get well alight before applying to cupped hands. I remember seeing a man use up nearly, a box of matches, and then failed. A fellow-passenger turned to him. *I say, mate what brand of lucifer do you smoke?*" (Memories of Myponga, 12 Nov 1927, p.22)

Chapter Eight
Drivers
O – R

The Lights of Cobb & Co.

Not all the ships that sail away since Roaring Days are done—

Not all the boats that steam from port, nor all the trains that run,

Shall take such hopes and loyal hearts—for men shall never know

Such days as when the Royal Mail was run by Cobb and Co.

The 'greyhounds' race across the sea, the 'special' cleaves the haze,

But these seem dull and slow to me compared with bygone Roaring Days!

The eyes that watched are dim with age, and souls are weak and slow,

The hearts are dust or hardened now that broke for Cobb and Co.

Henry Lawson, M.L., Sept., 1897
(The Lights of Cobb and Co., Verse 8, 1897, p.9)

1920 Ballon River Ferry, crossing the Balonne River in flood near Surat, Fred 'Tommy' Thompson in front of boat/Cobb and Co. driver (Photo from Henry Senyard, son of Harry Senyard who was Cobb and Co. manager in Surat)—Courtesy Queensland Museum Collection

Supporting evidence:

Oakley, George ... 1934 See Alexander, Jack

O'Brien, Andy
1927 "Her Majesty's Mails were carried under contract ... For some time there was daily communication by mail coach from Adelaide to the Talisker Silver-lead Mine, near Cape Jarvis ... The first change of horse was made at Reynella, the next Noarlunga ; then Norman's Victory Hotel, at the foot of Sellick's Hill. The change before reaching Normanville took place at Myponga ... Cobb & Co.'s contract really ended near Normanville ... Andy O'Brien, Humorist ... used to drive between Adelaide and Willunga ... He was a bright, merry Irishman, guileless perchance, except in the matter of horses ... about 60 years ago ... on one occasion just as the ostler released the new team, the offside leader started rearing, and finally bolted ... 'hell for leather' down the hill ... temporary easing of the pace enabled Andy to regain control of the team." (Memories of Myponga, 28 Oct 1927, p.13)

O'Brien, Maurice ... 1917 See Wright, Bob

Obrien, P ... 1919 See Aisbett, E. J.

O'Connor, John
1937 "Cobb And Co. Driver Dies. Mr John O'Connor, who drove Cobb and Co.'s coach between Bendigo and Swan Hill, died today at his home in Kerang at the age of 79." While written on the same page was "CLOSE SEASON ALWAYS FOR KOOKABURRAS. Kookaburras enjoyed a permanent 'close' season, on official of the Fisheries and Game Department said today, referring to the imposition by a suburban court yesterday of fines for keeping kookaburras in captivity." (Cobb And Co. Driver Dies, 24 Jun 1937, p.10)

O'Dea, James
1914 "Mr Michael James O'Dea died yesterday afternoon at 3 o'clock at his residence, Nolan Street, Kerang. The deceased was 60 years old at the time of his death. He was a native of Bendigo and was for many years engaged coach driving for Cobb and Co. from Bendigo to Heathcote and Kilmore. He also acted as driver for Bruce and Sons, Bendigo. About 4 years ago he came to this district and settled with his wife and family in Kerang ... Deceased leaves a wife and family of four sons and four daughters." (Obituary, 1 Dec 1914, p.3)

O'Dell, Bill
1933 "WHEN BILL O'DELL HELD THE REINS. Recently reference was made to the demolition of the old stables at Armidale which were the New England headquarters of Cobb and Co., 75 to 80 years ago. The report mentioned some of the coach drivers of those days, including Bill O'Dell, who was the father of Mr. W. O'Dell, of Manilla. The 'Manilla Express,' which reprinted the article, says: Mr. W. O'Dell brought a photo of the famous old Cobb and Co. driver into this office. It was taken many years ago, the occasion being when a grateful travelling public presented the popular coach driver with a four in-hand whip as a memento of their appreciation for his faithful services. The late Mr. Bill O'Dell, when a youth, travelled from Maitland to Tamworth in the early coaching days. Maitland was then the railway terminus. Arriving in Tamworth he requested the coach driver to allow him to sleep in the coach during the night, as he only possessed 1/6, which he required for tucker. The coach driver took compassion on the youth and arranged for a hotel-keeper to give him a bed for the night. Next morning young Bill O'Dell was given a job as a general useful at the hotel, which he held until he went to work for Cobb and Co. in the stables. Gradually he worked himself up until he became a driver on the coach between West Tamworth and Murrurundi ... Tamworth and Armidale ... On several occasions was O'Dell stuck up by Thunderbolt, a tree on the Murrurundi Range, which still stands, marking the first occasion ... the late Mr. O'Dell reared a family of 11 children, and when he died in 1894, was able to leave them all something to face life's troubles with. There were no eight-hour shifts, the driver being on duty until his job was done. Such was the spirit of the men who paved the way in the old coaching days of Cobb and Co." (The Days of Cobb's Coaches, 3 Feb 1933, p.3)

1933 See also Bates, Bob

O'Donnell, Dick ... 1947 See Richards, J. Frederick (Fred); 1917 Richardson, W.

(Surname unknown), (Old Clem) ... 1929 See Corbett, Alec.

Oldfield, Richard ... 1936 See Rochester, William George (Bill)

O'Leary, Jim
1917 "Another, J. O'Leary, I met at Cunnamulla. He joined Cobb and Co. in the 60's at Ipswich, when the firm, changing from the old North Star stables, put up at Lennon's. From there he went to Warwick, and then along the Western Line to Cunnamulla and Barringun ... Later, O'Leary went on the Warwick line, when the Stanthorpe rush broke out, and the coaches ran the 40 miles out and back in a day, loaded with 16 to 18 passengers. A rough and expensive road on coaches and horses ... O'Leary then, in the early 80's, went out to the Western line, when the run was from Charlie Moore's pub at Roma to Bindango change, then to Muckadilla, Amby Downs, Mitchell (Quinn's), Womalilla, Moore's Creek, Woodhatch, Black's Water Hole, Morven, Mrs. Corbett's (then Saddler's Water Hole), the Dam ... (Dirty Dam), Bradley's Dam, and to Ted Bradley's at Charleville. From Charleville a coach went down the Warrego to Cunnamulla via Wallal (old Bubbligig), Green's pub, Jenning's Mangalore station, Murweh, Mack's Creek, Garner's Claverton, McCormack's pub, Coongoola (Armstrong manager), Tickleman out station, to Tattersall's Hotel, Cunnamulla, where the office of Cobb and Co. remains to this day." (Coaching in Australia, 1917, p.37)

1917 See also Corbett, Sandy

O'Malley, Arthur Michael
1934 "87 years ... Mr. O'Malley was a pioneer of the Lachlan district, and was in the early days a driver for Cobb and Co. He was a native of the Goulburn district." (Mr. Arthur Michael O'Malley, 22 Aug 1934, p.2)

O'Malley, Luke ... 1917 See Corbett, Sandy

Orbel, Billy ... See Appendix 1.6

Orbell, William George (King)
1937 "Two Sterling Citizens … The late Albert Orbell, who was 59 years of age, was a son of William George Orbell, who, in the early days, kept the old Royal Hotel, and was a driver for of Cobb & Co.'s coaches." (Dubbo Mourns, 30 Mar 1937, p.1)

1935 See also Whitney, William Franklin (Frank)

O'Sullivan, J ... 1919 See Aisbett, E. J.

Ottey, T ... 1937 See Preston, R.

(Surname unknown), Paddy the Boy ... 1925 See Paine, William

Pack, J ... 1888 See Swanton/Swanston, James

Page, Harry .... See Appendix 1.6

Paine, John
1925 "Mr. John Paine … A native of Sydney, Mr. Paine drove the mail coaches for Cobb and Co. for many years, first on the Juglong-Wagga run, then between Cootamundra and Temora, and finally between Young and Grenfell. He gave up with the coming of the railways, and settled at Young … He married, when 22, Miss Forde, of Wagga, who survives him; and of his family of 16, eight sons survive: Messrs. John T. (Young), William James (Q.), Reginald (Young), Cecil A. (Q.), Louis. M. (Young), Arthur E. (Q.), Joseph Patrick and Robert E. (Young)." while in another article "Wirth's circus arrived at Kerang on Tuesday morning. A horse valued at £50, belonging to the local butter factory, completing a trip to the station, dropped dead on seeing the elephants approaching along the road. A similar incident occurred in Wagga some years ago when the passing of a circus caused a horse to drop dead in the shafts of a cart owned by the late Mr. Patrick Moran in front of his shop, on the site of the present Commonwealth Bank building … HORSE FALLS INTO WELL A horse owned by a man named Ward, fell down a well on a vacant allotment fronting Burrowa street, Young. The animal, which was harrnessed to a cart, was being driven home, when it suddenly slipped down an old well, hind feet first. The shafts of the cart and the harness prevented the animal from falling to the bottom of the well. It remained suspended in the well mouth for several hours, meanwhile making desperate efforts to free itself. Willing hands worked for hours and finally succeeding in rescuing the animal." (Local and General, 26 Jan 1925, p.2)

Paine, William
1925 "DEAD, AT 93. Australia's Oldest Jehu. DROVE A COACH IN PRERAILWAY DAYS. It was in the year 1850, when the first sod of the first Australian railway was turned, that Mr. William Paine made his first journey to Gundagai, and, from thence on, he has been associated with this district, until his death took the reins on Monday evening last, at 'Surrey,' Gundagai, where the old jehu had lived in retirement for many years. Born in London in 1830, Mr. Paine came to New South Wales with his parents at a very early age, and when he left school, his first job was driving the mail coach from Penrith to Hartley. Then he secured service, as a driver, with Messrs Garry and Sheahan, who ran the mail from Sydney to Albury. The journey used to occupy three days and two nights, and horses were changed every 10 or 12 miles. The fare was £21, being at the rate of 1/- per mile. Other drivers of those days were 'Billy the Whip.' and 'Paddy the Boy,' and, later, the late Bill Geaghan, George Fox, Alick Gordon and Jimmy Brummy. Going to Bendigo goldfields, deceased was amongst the first to open the White Hills. Returning to N.S.W., he went back mail driving, chiefly between Campbelltown and Yass. Next he was engaged as manager of Kimo station, near Gundagai, when it was owned by Mr. Collins, and when there was no river road, the track to Kimo and Nangus being through Reno. Afterwards he opened a butchery in Gundagai, and next he secured the Bridge Hotel, South Gundagai. He sold out there in 1880, and purchased the Royal Hotel, Gundagai (now owned by Mr. A. Hogan). For eight years he was boniface of the Royal, when he retired into private life, and for over a quarter of a century he lived quietly. Over 40 years ago, when driving for Cobb and Co., from Gundagai to Cootamundra, deceased was thrown from the coach, whilst going down a hill, near Cootamundra, and had a leg broken. Deceased was twice married, his second wife being a daughter of the late Mr. John Benton, of Gundagai. His widow and one son by the first wife survive." (Dead at 93, 10 Dec 1925, p.5)

Palmer Brothers ... 1925 See Eddie, Nathan

Palmer, Dick ... 1932 See Clark, Billy; 1933 Bates, Bob

Palmer, George Guild
1948 "Mr George Guild Palmer Passes WAS FORMER COBB COACH DRIVER. The death occurred on Sunday evening of Mr George Guild Palmer, of 29 Anderson street, Bendigo, at the age of 81. The deceased … was one of Cobb and Co.'s mail drivers for many years commencing employment with them at the age of 15 … He was also regarded as a very outstanding judge of horses and his opinion was often sought in this regard." (Mr George Guild Palmer Passes, 12 Nov 1948, p.2)

Palmer, Keppel
1908 "Keppel Palmer, late driver Cobb & Co. Tambo" (Civil Sittings, 26 Sep 1908, p.9)

Palmer, Ned ... 1917 See Wright, Bob

Palmer, Richard (Dick)
1931 "WITH COBB & CO. Old Driver's Story … Mr. Richard Palmer, a native of the Hawkesbury River district who is 94 years of age, tells interesting stories of the early coaching days. For 14 years he was a driver for Cobb and Co., and he helped to blaze the track over a considerable area of the western and other districts. Once he was bailed up by bushrangers, and on another occasion he was present when a bushranger was shot dead by a constable. He lives with his married daughter Mrs. Stan Latta, of Cronulla … with Cobb and Co. he ran from Mt. Victoria to Bathurst. *The roads were so frightfully rough*, says Mr. Palmer, *especially the descent of the mountains, that it took all my skill to get through punctually, and with safety to myself and passengers.*

ROUGH WORK. At a later stage he was on the box of the coaches running from Orange to Wellington; it was a cold and dreary job, and there was plenty of night driving over terrible roads. He had twelve months on the run, and then took on a new line from Bathurst to Trunkey, a Mr. Phillips having acquired the contract. One of the most exciting experiences on this run occurred at Mail Road Creek, just out of Bathurst, when in fording a flooded stream the coach and horses narrowly escaped being swept away. Every horse had to swim for its life, but skilfully piloted by Mr. Palmer, they got through. There was only one passenger—a woman. Mr. Palmer later left Phillips and rejoined Cobb and Co., and took on the run from Wallerawang to Cunningham Creek.

It was in this service that his coach was stuck up by bushrangers. Mr. Palmer had pulled up to water the horses; he had twelve women and two men aboard that day, and the usual mails. Captain Riley, who owned a station at Rylstone, was one of the male passengers, and the other was Mr. Bennett, Cobb and Co's manager at Wallerawang. The coach was being driven along quietly when two rough-looking fellows, named Stapleton and Rose, jumped out of the bush and called out *Bail up!* at the same time covering the driver and those on the box seat with revolvers. A third member of the gang, McGrath, was holding his mates' horses in the bush. Mr. Bennett was driving the coach at the time and he was ordered to drive on and follow the leader—Stapleton—and the other bushranger into the bush; Mr. Bennett hesitated, but Mr. Palmer, seeing the awkwardness of the position, took the reins and followed the bushrangers; he did not want to be shot, he explained. The coach followed the highway men about half a mile into the bush, and the passengers were then searched, the leader at the same time threatening that he would blow out the brains of anyone who attempted to move. The women were searched first—some of them had tried to hide their money in the curtains of the coach, but it fell out, and the bushrangers seized it. *Whilst one robbed the passengers the others had us covered with his revolver*, says Mr. Palmer. *As for me I never carried a pistol the whole time I was driving; it was no good trying that on, for if I had done so, and the bushrangers got wind of it, they would have shot me. For that reason few drivers carried arms.*

SAVED HIS WALLET. Captain Riley, who had just sold some property, had a wallet containing some hundreds of pounds. This he managed to slip, under cover of his overcoat, into Mr. Palmer's hand, and it was saved. The mail bags were rifled, and the driver told to move off. *Later, however,* says Mr. Palmer, *I drove the coach back to the spot and recovered what was left of the mails. The bushrangers had hoped to obtain gold, but as it happened, they just missed a big haul by being a day late.* Stapleton was subsequently arrested, and identified by Mr. Palmer, and after being duly tried, was found guilty and sentenced to 10 years. Rose was arrested and sentenced to seven years. McGrath, the third member of the gang, was in the court room listening to the evidence when his two mates were tried. The police got wind of it, and he was arrested, tried and sentenced to 10 years. Mr. Palmer knew the mother of Rose, a young man, and subsequently put in a good word for him with Judge Josephson, who tried the case, with the result that his sentence was reduced to two years. Leaving the Wallerawang service, Mr. Palmer next had a change to the northern tablelands across the Liverpool Range, where he found the conditions even rougher than before. He had to drive from Tamworth to Bendemeer. Mr. Palmer tells how he came to Sydney from the Hawkesbury River, when in his 'teens, and remembers the Tank Stream extending to Hunter-street, with a half-penny bridge for passengers at the foot of Pitt-street. He claims to have seen the last man hanged over the old gaol gate at Darlinghurst by hangman Green. He was one of the first at the wreck of the Dunbar at the Gap in 1857, and helped to pull the sole survivor (Johnston) up from the cliffs from a ledge of rock upon which he had been thrown after the vessel struck. Mr. Palmer made £7 per day in bus fares carrying sightseers from the city to the scene of the wreck. After retiring from Cobb and Co's service, Mr. Palmer went into the hotel business. His wife, who lived to be more than 100, died some years ago, Mr. Palmer has two sisters living at Carringbah, near Cronulla ; both are more than 80 years of age. Mr. Palmer still has a ruddy, healthy look, although he admits that his 'wind is not as good as it was'. He attributes his longevity to the fact that he was always in the open air, and even at this late stage of his life he still makes little of the daily walk of about three miles to see his sister." (Early Days, 24 Jul 1931, p.7)

1932 "Good Old Dick Palmer ... One day, with one passenger aboard, and a lady at that, he found himself, during a stormy period of weather, confronting a raging flooded creek, just a little way out from Bathurst. He pulled up at the over flowing bank, and stared pretty solidly at the roaring current, sweeping through a narrow channel. His passenger looked up anxiously at him and ventured : *What are you going to do, driver? Dashed if I know,* answered Dick, *it's ten to one we'll go down if we tackle that flood. Well, I simply must get over. I have a sick mother a few miles on who is without a single person near to help her in her trouble. If you are game to cross I shall not be afraid, and, perhaps I may be able to help you,* said the plucky bushwoman. *Well, you're a game one,* said Palmer, *I'll have a go for it, come what may. I'll go back a piece and put the horses at a gallop, and maybe we'll get over before they've time to funk.* Sure enough, they did get over, too, but it was a touch and go" (Australianities, 3 Sep 1932, p.2)

Palmer, Ted
"The old drivers to at last lay down their reins were: Ted Palmer and Billy White on the Charleville-Augathella-Tambo run 1921." (Communications Across the Generations, Read 1971, p.188)

1925 See also Eddie, Nathan; 1947 Richards, J. Frederick (Fred); 1948 Herchberg/Hertsberg, Joseph (Joe)

Parker, Alf ... 1930 See Alder, Amos

Parrington, J.
1934 "Cobb and Co. Driver Now a Squatter. Mr. J. Parrington, of Bulla Park, Cobar, who, with Mrs. Parrington, has been holidaying in Dubbo, was a 'gun' driver of the old coaching days out back, from Broken Hill to Tibbooburra, to White Cliffs and Wilcannia. He was the driver of the White Cliffe coach, which was stuck up and robbed of a valuable consignment of opal, under an armed guard, in connection with which Jack Burgess stood his trial. Like so many of the old coach drivers, Mr. Parrington has made good, and is now the owner of 100,000 acres of land situated in the fertile area between Wilcannia and Cobar. All who visit his homestead vote him a wonderful host." (Cobb and Co. Driver Now a Squatter, 16 Mar 1934, p.4)

Partington, Alf ... 1919 See Aisbett, E. J.; 1937 Atkinson, Frank

Partington, Kelly ... 1930-1940s See Allan, (Christian name unknown)

Patrick, Johnny ... 1875 See Turner, Bob (Big Bob)

Patterson, (Christian name unknown)
1917 "Port Douglas-Georgetown ... Georgetown-Normanton ... The latter was a run of two days, the Half-way House being kept by Patterson, an old-time driver and road manager for Cobb and Co. It was at times an awful track, flooded creeks, boggy country, and heavy loads making of it a rough coach ride. Then in summer the dust and flies were fearsome." (Coaching in Australia, 1917, p.48)

Patterson, Jim
1939 "I am not here buying into an argument, but my friend has his own opinion about alligators and crocodiles. Thus: *Naturalists say that there is no distinction between our alligators and crocodiles, but if they had lived as long in the Gulf as I have, they would get rid of that idea. The 'alligator' is a saurian that frequents tidal water and large permanent water holes adjacent to tide water. He is very timid but a low down cunning cadger. On hearing the least sound he disappears. If he is basking on a mudbank he will glide into the water with just a ripple—no splash. When investigating something that has caught his attention he will come up within a short distance of the bank and only its eyes will be visible. If cattle or horses are within his view, or indeed anything else he fancies, he will make a dash for his prey travelling at a terrific speed. If a grip is obtained there is no letting go, as his teeth are interlocked. The female 'gator grows to a greater size than the male and is twice as nasty. She lays from 45 to 60 eggs on a sheltered bank near the water. In calling to his mate the male gives forth a sound not unlike the sound made by a bull. The alligator grows to an enormous size. Several have been shot up to 25 feet in length. He is a thick set stodgy brute with a shortish head and snub nose. The dingo fears the alligator, and has his special method of circumventing him. When a pack of dingoes wish to cross an infested river the pack congregates, on the bank and howl mournfully and fully tuned in. Then when the unneighbourly alligators in hearing distance come to investigate the cause of the serenading the dingoes scamper a good distance ahead and swim over.* Reminds one of the 'false alarms' raised in the game of hide and seek.

The crocodile never interferes with human beings ... He lives in fresh waterholes, and if the hole goes dry he migrates to other water. His principal food is fish and game. If you shoot a few wild ducks you will probably lose some before you gather them in. If any animal gets bogged and dies in the water he will never eat any of it. The crocodile is not timid. You will see dozens floating in the water or basking on the banks any day. If he is on a bank or a leaning limb he flops into the water like an amateur swimmer. They lay their eggs on a sand bank and cover them over. When hatched the young crocodile are a prey to everything. The [First Nations people] consider young crocodiles a delicacy. The crocodile grows up to nine or 10 feet in length, but never has much weight in him. If you fire a gun near him he will sink to the bottom of the water hole and make a grunting noise not unlike the grunt of a pig. In the Broadwater Lagoon on Glenore Station holding it is common to hear as many as 20 or 30 grunting at the one time. Crocodiles do not like to mix with the alligator. The crocodile has a long thin head with protruding nostrils, and he is a gentleman compared to the alligator. Their different water habits and different food give my friend his own ideas on alligators and crocodiles. He states that never has he seen a cross between the two and further that as long as there is a bushman left there will always be a recognised difference between the alligator and the crocodile.

Fifty-three years' residence in the Gulf entitles my informant to speak with authority on Gulf subjects, hence the above ... The old days of Carpentaria are done. Newer ones are beginning. Cairns maintains its air line with Normanton. That rail connection between Forsayth and Croydon must eventually be made, thus linking up Trinity Bay with the Norman River township that is six years older than Cairns. Names of others prominent in the life of the town are recalled. R. G. Shanklin (auctioneer). Dr. Dyson, and much later Dr. Taylor. Mr. Alf. Chargois, photographer, whose family are now in Cairns. Joe Grittner, saddler; Alf. Grittner, his son, is in Atherton. Messrs. C. Mullins and A. Menzies were undertakers. Cordials were manufactured by W. Lawrence; Bakers were J. Kiely, W. Hudson and —Wachter. Cabs, no cars then, were owned by Joe Bailey, P. Madigan and A. McNab. Carpenters included A. Menzies, P. Cook, J. Scott and M. Whyte. Carters were J. A. Cornwall, Ned Schreck and Bill Harris. Soap works were conducted by Herman Bechtel, who then went to Mareeba and built a similar works. Morgan, Richards, gunsmith and engineer. A bank not previously mentioned was the London Chartered Bank. More carriers are remembered, Charlie Brown, J. Molloy, D. Mitchell, J. Gregory, T. Topdell, J. Radford, H. Hannaford. An Athertonite of to-day, Mr. Allender, may remember these tin-smiths, Mann and Fooks and J. L. Peake. River captains included Captain Gunderson and Geordie Palmer. Then there was Captain Vipan and the Kanahooka's Captain Campbell, who was in charge of the vessel when she was wrecked in the Gulf. The captain and another man managed to get to the mainland near where Inkerman station now is ...

The old bush tracks have become indistinct. If slightly bushed we find ourselves just blame it on the dust haze into which the years have disappeared. Under Mareeba's tree of knowledge opposite the post office another of the Gulf pioneers talks of the past. Frank Stubley, of Charters Towers and Evelyn, died at Foote's Lagoon, on the Normanton-Croydon road—in the 'eighties. A busy road that Croydon highway. There was an hotel at the Eight Mile. The mail coach stage was about 20 miles from Normanton. Alf. Fleurty had charge of it for a time. Cairns knew Alf. later as one of its cab drivers. At Collar Camp there was another hotel, Harry Nielsen's. No Grand Centrals along the way; hospitable sheltering roofs albeit. Mrs. Ovens had an hotel at the Carron Crossing. Jim Patterson was at the 50 mile. He was one of Cobb and Company's drivers. Harry Chatfield was familiar with the sandy stretches and the grades that lay between Normanton and Croydon.

Floods! It doesn't rain those floods any more. In the '90 deluge you could, 16 miles from Croydon, launch a boat and float right down to Normanton; the water went up to the second storey of Patterson's Hotel at the 50-mile. Ward brothers, Harry Hopdell and Jack Towle were camped with their teams at the 'Tin Grave,' four miles from Creean Creek. The flood went over the waggons, spoiled their loading and drowned bullocks and horses. Early Normanton—that is of the mid 'eighties— knew Charlie Furber. He came overland from Barcaldine and steered his bullock team between Normanton and the goldfield. Brother Tom had Normanton's Carriers Arms Hotel at one period. Time, like memories, possess elasticity, so let us leave the Gulf country and its strangeness." While "PERSONAL

Miss Gunderson (Melbourne) has left for the south after five weeks' holiday at Lake Berrine Guest House."(Pathways of Yesterday, 9 Sep 1939, p.39)

1917 See also Wright, Bob

Payne, Albert Edward (Jack)
1925 "LINK WITH COBB & CO. OLD-TIMER MAKES HIS LAST HALT. PASSING OF MR. JACK PAYNE. Another link with the roaring days of the diggings, and with the strenuous pioneering of the [18]seventies, has been snapped with the passing, in his 75th year, of Albert Edward (familiarly known as Jack) Payne, of Young. An Australian by birth and with the average Australian's love of horses, and outstanding ability in handling them, he took to the bush early in life, and by the association with Cobb and Co.'s coaches in the heyday of their existence, helped to blaze many a bush track and to carry on the arduous work of transporting passengers and his Majesty's mails over long distances. He was a well known figure throughout the south and south-west. Before the coming of the railroad, he dexterously handled the ribbons on Cobb's coach between Temora and Cootamundra, Juglong, Junee and Wagga, Young and Grenfell, and 'along the road to Gundagai.' Amid all the vicissitudes of those trying times, and in all weathers, he maintained the reputation of Cobb and Co. for reliability ...

He lived for a while at Gundagai, where two brothers and a sister now reside, and later on at Wagga, where he married a Miss Forde. Later on they went to, live at Young, and here the family has been settled for over 30 years. It was at Young that Jack Payne severed his connection with the famous firm. The railways were gradually pushing Cobb's coaches off the map. For some time the deceased was employed on Quamby Station, and later he was engaged as a driver by Wright Heaton and Co., a position he held for many years. Reticence was always a characteristic of the old driver, and he could not be encouraged to talk much of his early experiences. He was the father of a large family-fourteen sons and two daughters. Six sons and two daughters predeceased him, some of them in their infancy. His widow and eight sons survive, three of the boys having gone to Queensland. They are John Thomas, Reginald, Louis Mark, Joseph and Robert, of Young, and William, Cecil and Arthur, of Queensland. Heart trouble was the cause of death." (Link with Cobb & Co., 27 Jan 1925, p.6)

1927 "COBB AND CO. SIGN ON HOTEL. Old Booking Office... That sign painted in white, was revealed when workmen removed an Qld liquor trade. advertisement from the walls of the Albion Hotel, Young. According to reliable statements, the sign is 60 years old. The Albion Hotel, which was the booking office of Cobb and Coy., was built in the early seventies by the late Abraham Cohen. His son succeeded him, and later the old hostelry was taken over by the late W. T. Bolton. The coaches were taken off the Murrumbarrah run 42 years ago, when the railway line was built through to Young, but the Grenfel run was continued until the branch line was constructed from Koorawatha about 25 years ago. On the Murrumburrah run, horses were changed at Wombat ; and, on the Grenfell run, at Buller Creek.

NOTED DRIVERS. Mention of Cobb and Coy. brought back names of old drivers, now dead and gone, such as William and Joe Bernie, George Miller, and Jack Payne. There were two other notices under the old sign. One read 'M'Ewan's ale, October brew. Just landed by mail steamer,' and the other was a cardboard sign, which had evidently slipped down behind the older one, inviting people to see the 'greatest film ever made.' Old hands say this was written by the town's first picture showman, Mr. W. Martin, who later established a tailoring business in the town." (Cobb and Co., 9 Jun 1927, p.10)

Payne, Harry ... 1930 See Alder, Amos

Pearse, Harry ... 1938 See Pearse, Thomas

Pearse, Thomas
1938 "A diary of the day describes the over land journey from Geelong thus:—*On September 17 I made my first trip to Louttit Bay to lay out a garden and orchard for Thomas Mountjoy. We were able to get as far as Big Hill by coach, thence by packhorse to the bay. The journey took 11 hours. The first coach to cross the ranges ran from Geelong, and started from Brady's grocery shop, in Moorabool street. The regular drivers were two brothers, Tom and Harry Pearce. The road was certainly rough, but the old coach bumped along : sometimes it missed and sometimes it deepened the numerous ruts along the track. As we came to each stream I wondered just how deep it would be, but the fords just slipped behind, and Big Hill was reached. Here we changed over to packhorses for the remainder of the journey.*" (Romance and Tragedy of the Otway, 5 Nov 1938, p.4)

Peck, John Murray
1937 By S. H. Earp "WHEN SLEEP DROVE COBB & CO. In the winter of 1853, four young Americans who were in the employ of one or the other of the two leading U.S.A. Express (or Carrying) Companies Wells, Fargo and Co., and the Adams Express Co. came out to Victoria with the intention of starting carrying to the gold diggings for their firms. They were Freeman Cobb, of Brewster, Massachusetts; John Murray Peck, of Lebanon, New Hampshire; James Swanton, of Omar, in New York State; and John B. Lamber, of Leavenworth, out in the far west of those days, Kansas. They commenced carrying from Liardet's (now Port Melbourne) to the City of Melbourne for a start, but the 'no road' across the swamp between Emerald Hill, now South Melbourne, and the river was such a quagmire that their waggons sank to the hubs and had to be dragged through on their floors. On this experience they, advised their principals in the United States against a carrying business, but told them that there was a good opening for a real up-to-date line of coaches to the diggings, and a certainty, if established, of getting the mail contracts, as those then in existence were only an apology for coaches, and the mails often days behind ... the four 'Boys,' as they called themselves, raised all the capital they could, and on January 30, 1854, started, as Cobb and Co., their first coach from the Criterion Hotel, Collins street, Melbourne, for the Forest Creek diggings, now Castlemaine, under the title of, as advertised in 'The Argus' of the day ...

The new firm, with their splendid organisation and equipment, cut the usual time between Melbourne and Forest Creek down by half, and were an immediate success, and becoming very popular for their promptness and regularity soon obtained the mail contracts and ran their predecessors off the road. They quickly extended the lines to Bendigo, and opened branches to Maryborough and other centres, and later to Swan Hill. Soon other Americans and Canadians ('Yankees' and 'Canuks') followed, some joining Cobb and Co. as drivers … In 1857 the original partners sold out to Tom Davies, another American, whose son, 'One-armed Tom,' years after became famous at Newmarket (V.) for his working sheepdogs, and there are now four grandsons in the employ of different Newmarket firms … On the dissolution of the original firm in 1857 all but Swanton returned to the United States comparatively speaking well-off men. But Peck subsequently returned to Australia with a cargo of the famous American 'Jack' coaches and the harness to equip them … The new great 'Jack' coaches brought out by Peck were the first of their class in Australia, and created great interest in the coaching world, as they carried 40 passengers, and put all others completely in the shade …

George Woodworth was fond of telling of his first experience driving one of the 40-passenger 'Jacks' with a six horse team. He had the Castlemaine to Bendigo stage at the time. Another driver brought her up from Melbourne, and George, being a very short-backed man, on getting on the box, the level of the roof was so high above his head that he said he thought that when she made the first pitch the big coach, being very lightly loaded, was going to somersault right over on top of him. To those who have never experienced the comfort of riding in a Cobb Yankee leather-braced coach, the motion may be described as similar to that of a well balanced schooner sailing down wind over gentle swells, as there are no jars from inequalities of the road usually given by steel springs …

Barnes, who was a great raconteur of the bush ranging days in New South Wales, and who had driven in the 1850's for Cobb and Co. in Victoria, pioneered Cobb and Co. through Queensland till they reached right out to the Gulf of Carpentaria, and literally Cobb's coaches were then covering Australia from sea to sea, from Burketown on the Gulf to Hastings on Westernport. The Sleeping Driver John Murray Peck was the only one of the four original partners who stayed on in Australia … he took over the management of the Bendigo road, and my father, Harry Huntington, was born in that year at Gisborne … 1862 big Dal Campbell offered him the position of cattle sales man to Dal Campbell and Co, he readily accepted. Though coaching in the gold-rush years of Cobb and Co. was doubtless more profitable, Peck never barked back, remaining in the stock agency business till his death in 1903.

Of Peck's tales of the early coaching days the one that stands out was of driving the Bendigo night mail a six-horse team over six miles of corduroy in the Black Forest while fast asleep. Peck and the road overseer had both driven a night coach on the first night and on the second night danced till daylight at a big ball at Castlemaine. Both were kept busy during the third day at that centre. When mighty tired, just about ready to turn in early that evening, with thoughts of a well-earned rest, the coach from Bendigo to Melbourne arrived with the driver hors de combat and unable to go on, with a sudden attack of colic. The coach carried the mail, and a late arrival in town meant breaking a wonderful record Cobb's drivers held for being on time despite all obstacles, and a heavy penalty for the firm.

TOSSED—BUT SLEPT Only Peck and the overseer could drive a six-horse team, so it was one or the other 'for it,' in spite of both not having had a wink for 60 hours. Peck could have ordered the overseer to take on the job, but instead he tossed him for it and lost. It was a bitter winter night, and so all the passengers preferred to ride 'inside.' All went well till the Black Forest, between Woodend and Gisborne, where six miles of the track in one stretch was corduroyed, and Peck afterwards just had a hazy recollection of driving on to it, but nothing more, till the bumping of the wheels and the consequent rocking of the big coach on its leather braces over the corduroy ceased when the coach ran off at the end of the six miles on to the soft earth track. He had been rocked off, and had driven the six horses the whole six miles, sound asleep. He awoke with a start, but with 'the bunch of ribbons' still intact in his hands. Realising what would have happened if he had met anything or his leaders had shied, he pulled up and called out to his passengers. *If you folks wish to reach Melbourne alive you will have to come out on to the box in turns and keep me awake, for this is my third night without sleep, and I have driven the last six miles sound asleep.*

The passengers, only too readily, acquiesced, and kept Peck awake for the rest of the journey, about 40 miles, by sticking pins into his thigh or arm. He said that 40 miles, in the effort to keep awake, was the most miserable drive of all his experience. After daylight he dropped his whip three times across the Keilor Plains, but delivered the mails at the G.P.O. on time, and driving round to Cobb's stables threw himself into a groom's bunk and slept the clock round … Such experiences of long hours without proper rest and exposure to all weathers, as Peck went through that night in the Black Forest, in the long run told on the strongest constitutions, for none of the drivers of the first ten years of Cobb and Co., with the exception of 'Long' Carter, lived to be really old men." (a [?] Drive, 31 July 1937, p.4)

1953 See also Rutherford, James (Jas./Jimmy)

Peckman, Harry
1929 "Mr. Henry Peckman, of Albion-St, Katoomba, who celebrated his 88th birthday on Thursday, has resided at Katoomba for 40 years, and remembers the district when there was not a house on the site occupied by the present town … born on Kurrajong Heights, and in his younger days acted as a driver for Cobb and Co., carrying a regular service between Lithgow and Penrith. Although he was never molested by bushrangers, he saw the outlaws, Moran and Smith, captured at the Blue Mountains Hotel, where Lawson now stands." (Veteran Coachman, 21 Aug 1929, p.3)

1934 "HARRY PECKMAN. EIGHTY-EIGHT NOT OUT Last Wednesday, Mr. Harry Peckman was tendered a complimentary concert in Katoomba Town Hall. Many a column of copy the veteran poet has provided for the writer over the last 20 years … Harry was one of Cobb and Co.'s early drivers. He drove the present King and Queen over the Blue Hills in their young days

… the writer's only hope at this distance is that the house was a bumper one, making for a decent glad-hand to the old whip, who is one of the landmarks of the Blue Mountains capital." (Harry Peckman, 11 Jan 1934, p.2)

Pedrara, Andy
1947 "Following In Father's Dust. Sydney, December 6.—Where 60 years ago Cobb and Co. driver, the late Andy Pedrana, was raising the dust on the Hay-Deniliquin Road, his son now drives the mail. As driver of one of the famous Cobb and Co. mail coaches, Andy's timing was considered brilliant. It took seven changes of a six-horse team to get the coach over 80 miles in 12 hours. Today, his son. Bill Pedrana, is carrying on the good work as mail coach driver—but six times faster." (Following in Father's Dust, 11 Dec 1947, p.9)

Peters, Billy ... See Appendix 1.6

Peterson/Paterson, Fred. F.
1885 "Fred. F. Petersen, Cobb & Co.'s driver, got drowned whist swimming the second channel of the Thompson River." (Colonial and Intercolonial, 12 Mar 1885, p.2)

1885 "QUEENSLAND.—BRISBANE, THURSDAY. The Blackall police telegraphed to-day, stating that Paterson, the driver of Cobb's coach to Windorah, and a lad named Eagan had been drowned in the Thompson River. No particulars have been received. Patrick Green, a lad of 18, who was employed in Messrs. Dath. Henderson and Co.'s saw mills at Brisbane, had his leg drawn into a planing machine to-day, and the limb was badly mangled. He was removed to the hospital, where amputation was found to be necessary." (Queensland, 13 Mar 1885, p.6)

Petrasson, T.
1912 "COACH IN BUSH FIRE. BETWEEN TWO BELTS OF FLAME. On Friday last a fierce bush fire swept through the Anglesea forest, near Jan Juc. Cobb and Co.'s coach, with a five-horse team, driven by T. Petrasson, was headed off by the fire near Addiscott, and before the coach could turn, the flames were within a few yards of it — in fact, one of the horses was slightly singed. Petrasson skillfully avoided the main body of the fire and went back towards Jan Juc. There he found another belt of flame in the way. Between the two sections the coach remained in safety, but the roar of the flames made the six passengers uneasy, and the smoke-charged atmosphere was very trying. The coach was two hours late in reaching Geelong. A change of wind to the south soon arrest the progress of the fire towards the settlements." (Coach in Bush Fire., 21 Feb 1912, p.4)

Phillips, Charles
1864 "Bursting a blood vessel.—Yesterday morning Charles Phillips, a driver in the employ of Cobb and Co., while in the charge of the Murray coach, suddenly burst a blood-vessel. Luckily at the time the coach was nearing Seward's, on the Campaspe, to which place he was quickly conveyed. We have since heard that he is in a dying state. —*Bendigo Advertiser*" (No title, 7 Jul 1864, p.4)

Pickering, (Christian name unknown)
1883 "SPRINGSURE, March 7. On last Saturday afternoon, soon after the arrival of the Comet mail, our usually quiet little town presented a scene of excitement not frequently witnessed. All the commotion was caused by the running away of Cobb's coach and three horses. It appears that Pickering, the driver, has, in addition to his other duties, to act as groom at this end. After delivering the mail at the post office, he drove as usual to the stables, at the Commercial Hotel, and proceeded to unharness the horses. After detaching the leader, and while unloosing the others, one of them managed to dispose of his winkers, and bolted. The leader, although quite free from the coach, caught the spirit of the other horses, and away they went at a speed beyond control. As the horses started Pickering seized the reins, and at great personal risk did his utmost to pull up the animals; but he might as well have tried to stop the late comet in its course. After nearly running over several children, the coach was brought to a standstill by coming in contact with the corner post of the divisional board's paddock. I regret to say that Pickering, in attempting to stop the horses, was severely bruised and much shaken. The coach was considerably damaged, having the hind wheels smashed and other parts broken."

Other stories of the day included "Current News. TYPHOID fever is now very prevalent at Ballarat. BENHAMO'S circus is in Brisbane, playing to good houses. MARY BENSON has been committed for trial in Sydney for attempting to commit suicide by throwing herself across the tram rails in front of an approaching tram.DURING the week ending 10th instant, 129 saloon and 130 steerage passengers arrived in Brisbane per steamers from the Southern colonies; and 70 saloon and 136 steerage passengers left this port for the South. THE barque Scottish Lassie, 9GB tons, commanded by Captain Kerr, and having Dr.Ledingham as surgeon-superintendent and Miss Ware as matron, left the port of Glasgow for Townsville on the 1st of December last, with a total of 320 immigrants. THE list of Brisbane entries for the Southport regatta closed on Tuesday evening at the Imperial Hotel. THE Rev. T. O'Conuell, P.P. of Toowoomba, invites designs for the new church which tho Roman Catholic residents of that town propose to erect. The building is to be of stone, 60ft. wide inside the walls, and a present length of 100 ft., exclusive of a temporary sanctuary and chancel, and the cost is not to exceed £5000. £25 will be given for the design and specifications eventually adopted by the building committee." (Country News, 17 Mar 1883, p.407)

Piesley, Jack ... 1929 See Corbett, Alec.

Pillett, Charles
1898 "Mr. Charles Pillett.—We are sure that all those who know 'Charlie,' the affable and obliging driver of the Esperance—Norsema mail coach, will be sorry to hear that he is leaving the district to-day, Messrs. Cobb and Co. have no more faithful servant or careful driver than the genial Frenchman who has been in their employ for so many years, and we hope he will continue in their service, even if not on our road, for many years to come. We shall miss his excellent rendering of the 'Marseillaise' at our little 'sing songs,' but somehow or other we fancy he will be back this way before long." (Local and General, 16 March 1898, p.2)

Pittman, Joe ... 1932 See Clark, Billy

Ploughs, Tom ... 1925 See Jones, Bill

Plows, Tom ... 1886 See Simmons, Frederick Langton (Fred)

Plush, Fredrick
1944 "Mr. Frederick Plush, of Renmark, whose death occurred recently, was born at Angas Park (now Nuriootpa), in 1862. Mr. Plush had spent the whole of his life on the river except for a few years when he was in Western Australia driving for Cobb & Co. As a mail contractor Mr. Plush was on the Wentworth run for 21 years. He was also associated with the Chaffey brothers, and spent some years at Mildura. Mr. Plush was recognised as an outstanding horseman, and had ridden many winners in both showring and race track. He was an able bushman, who had often helped in bringing in brumbies from the back country. Even after his 80th birthday Mr. Plush was to be seen in Renmark both riding and driving horses, including youngsters he was breaking in. He leaves a widow, formerly Miss Ada Johnston, and two sons and two daughters." (Obituary, 1 Jun 1944, p.2)

Pollard, G ... 1919 See Aisbett, E. J.

Potter, Warren
1861 "King Cobb. Sir,—My attention has been attracted more than once to certain sarcastic remarks referring to the grasping monopoly of King Cobb. I am an old traveller in all sorts of conveyances, but more particularly on that line, must with your kind permission remark that I have watched the progress and admired the systematical and mechanical method by which the affair has been worked; the almost insurmountable difficulties overcome at the commencement of their career, when roads were literally made by the coach track; the cool courage of the drivers, whose self-possession when danger stared them in the face have saved the lives of the affrighted passengers; their success in getting the mail contracts; their punctuality in making time. Unappalled by floods and rapid streams, means are speedily and successfully devised to get the mail across: instanced only a few weeks since, when M'Callum's Creek was impassable, and Mr Warren Potter caused a rough construction to be made, by which the mail was sent across. How at head-quarters they have been appreciated by again and again having the contract, though higher than some competitors—the importance of punctuality in that branch of the service being a public benefit. No wonder the company has created an honorable monopoly, as pioneers of a line the model of management. No one can be astonished, and few envy, the Bianconi of Victoria." (King Cobb, 15 Feb 1861, p.4)

Powell, (Christian name unknown)
1873 "On Saturday last an accident occurred to Cobb and Co.'s mail coach while on its passage up from Murrurundi. From what we can gather on the subject it appears that the driver had occasion to remove some horses from one stable to another further up the line, and, in accordance with the usual custom, had attached one to the leaders this trip. Some water lying on the road caused the horse to shy, which startled the leaders, and turned them off the road, up a sideling, of course taking the coach with them. Powell, the driver, received some slight injury to his ankle, but otherwise there was no serious damage done.

On Tuesday night, a more serious affair occurred, which resulted in the driver (Whiteman) getting two of his ribs broken. The first mischief was caused by one of the horses getting his legs over the pole in some way, and in endeavouring to set himself free, broke a trace and his own leg ; the result of which was the necessity of shooting the horse. The coach then proceeded without interruption until a little this side of Goonoo Goonoo, when the horses, from some cause not defined, bolted. In endeavouring to stop them one of the leading reins broke, which had the effect of turning the horses' heads suddenly round, the king-bolt broke, and the horses went away with the fore part of the coach. The driver was thrown forcibly against a stump, which broke two of his ribs and severely bruised him otherwise. Some of the passengers received slight injuries, but we have not heard of any serious accident happening to either of them. The mails were brought into Tamworth in Mr. Lumley's coach. No blame can be laid to the drivers, who are very careful men." (Epitome of News, 5 Apr 1873, p.2)

Power, Patrick Edward
1909 "Mr. Patrick Edward Power ... the age of 67 years ... The deceased was probably the oldest native of the Orange district, he being born at Broken-shaft Creek. He was poundkeeper in Orange for about 20 years. He occupied a similar position at Condobolin for about the same period. Mr. Power was an expert horseman, and drove for Cobb and Co from Orange to Forbes. About two years ago he came to reside with his son-in-law, Mr. John Clarke, at the Gladstone Hotel. He was absent from Orange for a brief period, but returned and lived with his daughter till his death. Mrs. Power predeceased her husband some 16 years ago. There are 3 daughters and one son, 12 grandchildren ... Mrs. J. Clarke (Orange), Mrs. Jones (Sydney), Mrs. J. Wright (Orange), and Mr. P. Power (Orange), are the children of the deceased ... Possessing a tall commanding form, Mr. Power was a most interesting personality. Even in his advanced years he was considered one of the best whips on the Lachlan. He was brimful of reminiscent anecdotes, and could tell many an interesting story of the past. Mr. Power was particularly keen upon a road race which occurred as far back as 1870; and which should prove of interest to many of the old residents. The contest was between Mr. Robert Frost's chestnut horse *The Colonel* and Mr. Edward Tarrant's bay mare *The Barmaid* ... The race was from Dubbo to Orange; from post office to post office, a distance of 104 miles. Roger Davis had the mount on *The Colonel* and Walter Higinbotham, of Melbourne, who trained Carbine, the famous cup winner, rode *Barmaid*. Mr. 'Paddy' Power, the subject of our obituary, was an active participant in the race, in it he had a considerable cash interest, which added zest to the enthusiasm and ardor which he felt in the issue. The race was for £100, and each horse had to carry nine stone. *The Colonel* led and made the pace throughout, and won easily." (Obituary, 8 May 1909, p.2)

Prater, Ike ... 1921 See Griffen, Chas.

Preston, R.
1937 Victoria "Cobb and Co.'s Coachmen Live To Grand Old Age. Coach driving in the 'roarin' days' must have been a healthy occupation, for 21 of the old drivers of Cobb and Co.'s coaches in Victoria who will hold their annual reunion on Sunday and Monday are more than 70 years of age—and, of these, seven

are more than 80. Galloping four-in-hands over country roads, day and night, in burning sun or drenching rain; washing down damper and salt meat with pannikins of strong tea; and the bumps and fatigues attendant upon the strenuous lives they led, seem to have toughened their sturdy constitutions. Steve Holman, who was the oldest of them, was 90 when he died just before Christmas. Their president, Frank Smiley, is 80, and is in a real estate business at Prahran. The good fellowship of the coach routes has lived on in him. A merry laugh and the optimism of perennial youth add a vigor to his fund of stories. He inherited a coachdriving tradition. His father, S. P. Smiley, drove the open coach from William's Town to Melbourne Town before the construction of the first railway between these centres in 1857. And 75 years ago, Smiley senior drove the first stage of the Royal Mail line of coaches on the Gippsland run.

WAS A YANKEE Smiley senior was one of the famous Yankee drivers who came from America with the early coaches, before vehicles were made here. The old timers will meet at the Police Depot, St. Kilda Road, on Sunday afternoon, and, at 2 p.m., will drive in one of the famous old coaches on the annual pilgrimage to the grave of John Conway Bourke in the Melbourne general cemetery. Bourke was Victoria's first mail man, taking the mails round the Port Phillip district in '39 and onward by packhorse. Among those expected to attend are: T. Hogan (83). H. Glassen (83), T. Bradley (83), W. H. Watson (82), H. Hobbs (81), W. Hussey (80), R. Preston (19), W. Nesbitt (78), F. Haines (78), E. J. Fowler (78), W. Hutchison (78), T. Ottey (77), A. Free (76), J. De Graves (75), G. Dallas (73), J. Barry (73). C. H. Watt (73). F. Fogarty (72), T. Vines (68), A. Vines (65), and a great many of the 'young fellows. Only 17 can be accommodated in the coach, with another at the ribbons. The coach which they will use was built at Geelong and was on the Western District run, out Hamilton way, for years. Nearly 150 of the drivers of the old mail coaches survive in Victoria. A horse coach ran as recently as ten years ago in the Apollo Bay district, and its driver, named Kennedy, by an ironical stroke of fate, was killed in a motor truck accident soon after he gave up his coach and horses. One of the guests of honor at the annual meeting of Cobb and Co.'s Coachdrivers Association on Monday will be the Chief Commissioner of Railways (Mr Clapp). When he was invited as a 'Pioneer of Road Transport' the compliment was sincerely meant. It was conveyed more for his father's sake than his own. The late F. B. Clapp (the appellation of Mr was reserved in those stirring days for clergymen and officials) was another of the Yankees who was in the coaching business here in the early days, and, although Clapp and Co. did not rise to the wealth and fame of Cobb and Co., they did set many important contracts." (Cobb and Co.'s Coachmen Live To Grand Old Age, 20 May 1937)

1937 See also Preston, R.

Pritchard, Jack
1894 "With Cobb & Co. in far inland Australia ... an invitation to visit him on his sheep-station in the far Australian interior ... *But what shall we do if this river you speak of is actually in a state of flood?* asked the pale young man. *Oh, it'll be lowering by the time you get there*, replies the agent; *and Jack Pritchard'll put you through all right most careful driver on the road, Jack, you know.* We groan at

this, and retire to the hotel over the way for refreshments and a brief sleep." (With Cobb & Co. in far inland Australia, 28 Jul 1894, p.4)

Purcell, Johnny
1922 "On the 10th January, at Deniliquin, John beloved husband of Hughena C Purcell and loving father of M.J.A., B.K.W. and J., aged 78 years. Late of Cobb and Co." (Family Notices, 16 Jan 1922, p.1)

1923 See also Robinson, James (Robbie)

Pywell, Edward
1893 "A STREET RUNAWAY. A pair of horses attached to Cobb and Co.'s Barwon Heads coach, caused a sensation in Malop and Moorabool streets yesterday afternoon about a quarter to 2 o'clock. The horses, under the charge of Edward Pywell, aged 20 years, a resident of Portarlington, left the stables in Malop-street for the purpose of meeting passengers coming by the steamer Excelsior and picking up those desirous of proceeding to Barwon Heads, via Ocean Grove. Adopting the practice of most of the coach drivers—a rather questionable one—Pywell had the reins of the horses separate, and when nearing the Victoria Hotel one rein fell out of his hand. Having thus lost control of one horse Pywell made an effort to regain possession of the fallen rein by clambering along the coach pole to which the horses were attached. By this time the animals had discovered that they were free, and the pair raced along Malop-street, sharply turned the corner by the Victoria Hotel, and tore down Moorabool-street at a furious gallop. The coachdriver vainly endeavored to steer the horses by the one line of rein he held in his hand, whilst he unsuccessfully tried to pick up the trailing rein, and the terrible rate the horses were travelling at prevented him returning to his seat in the front of the coach. When approaching the wharf the horses swerved to the west side of Moorabool street, and in their mad gallop brought the coach into violent contact with the telephone post close to the office of Messrs Huddart, Parker and Co. The crash was a very forcible one, as whilst the horses cleared away with the pole, fore carriage and front wheels of the vehicle, the main body of the coach was sent flying high in the air, and it fell in front of the office of the shipping company seven yards away, and Pywell was thrown with great violence into the mud on the centre of the road, where he lay motionless.

At the time the accident occurred there were about a dozen cabs backed up against the west side of the approach to the wharf, and when the runaway coach horses were leading towards the rank there was a general rush of cabmen to get their horses and cabs clear. All managed to do so with the exception of a young man named James Leverett, aged 24 years, who was driving a waggonette for Mrs Geo. Upjohn. The coach horses dashed into the side of Loverett's conveyance with fearful force, overturned the cab and threw Leverett on to the roadway ... who was severely injured about the thighs, and had to be removed to the hospital. Pywell was found unconscious and bleeding from a wound over the right eye, abrasions on the face, and cuts about the right arm. In that state the unlucky coach driver was taken in a lorry to the hospital. Late last night Pywell was in

1860 Bourke St. E. Melbourne—Courtesy State Library Victoria

a semi-conscious state, but it was not believed that he had sustained any injuries likely to prove fatal, whilst Loverett was slowly recovering from the shock. The coach and waggonette were badly injured, and one of the coach horses received some slight injuries about the legs and chest. Owing to the accident the Portarlington coach, which is usually driven by Pywell, was somewhat late in leaving Geelong, another driver having to be obtained." (A Street Runaway, 9 Sep 1893, p.3)

Reade, Bill ... 1917 See Bruce, Harry

Reardon, George
"The old drivers to at last lay down their reins were: George Reardon who drove Cobb & Co's last coach on the Mitchell-St. George run in 1918." (Communications Across the Generations, Read 1971, p.188)

1947 See also Richards, J. Frederick (Fred)

Redfern, Jim
1927 "There were other famous drivers in those early days besides Miles, such as 'Cabbage Tree Ned,' 'Bendigo Ike,' 'Jim Redfern' (who is still to the fore, and loves to talk over olden days), Frank Rutherford, and many a good whip besides, but, alas! They have nearly all taken their last trip on this earth, when the voices were silent that rang so merrily in song or story on the track, and the fingers cold that once so skilfully held reins and whip." (Pioneering days in western Victoria : a narrative of early station life, 1927, p.91)

Reynolds, H.
1874 "H. Reynolds deposed : I am a driver in the employment of Cobb and Co., and drive the Melbourne coach on the middle stage, between the Bunyip and the Moe." On the same page another article stated "SEIZURE OF AN ILLICIT STILL. Acting upon information received that an illicit still was in existence on Mr J. Frawley's selection at Pearson's Morass, about nine miles from Sale ... found there a man named Dunn, a servant of Mr Frawley's. A search was at once instituted, and within a short distance of the hut occupied by Dunn, was found under the ground the funnel of a still; a copper worm was discovered in another place, and tied to a fence, and sunk in a water hole, a large boiler capable of holding about 36 or 38 gallons of wort. In the hut were found three hogsheads of wort ready for the still, some empty hogsheads, two bags of sugar, a small quantity of hops, and other materials, all of which were seized, and Constable Martley left in charge until they can be removed into Sale to-day. Great difficulty was experienced in getting the large boiler out of the waterhole, the work occupying fully half an hour, and the Superinteoundent and the constables being for that time up to their middles in water. Dunn was arrested and lodged in the lockup, and will be broughlt before the bench this morning." (Sale Police Court, 2 Jun 1874, p.3)

Rich, Levi ... 1933 See Grover, Robert H. (Wharparilla Bob); 1951 Winkler, Eddie

Richard, Ernie
"The old drivers to at last lay down their reins were: Ernie Richard, who died in June 1968, was the last of Cobb's drivers. He was the youngest driver starting at 14 and drove the coach on the St. George-Bollon run in 1888-1919 at the age of 17 years. He handled mail, both coach and motor lorry for more than 40 years continually." (Communications Across the Generations, Read 1971, p.188)

Richards, A. E. (Ted) ... 1947 See O'Donnell, Dick

Richards, Billy ... 1917 See Richardson, W.; 1947 Richards, J. Frederick (Fred)

Richards, Ernest
1966 "I was very pleased to read Pamela Ruskin's article The Legend of Cobb & Co. (Walkabout, September). However, not all the old drivers are dead, as one of the Gallaghers and Ernest Richards are still living. Richards, the youngest of the drivers, still flourishes at Mitchell. He started driving in 1916 at the age of 16 ... W. R. F. Bolton, Toowoomba, Qld." (Cobb's Drivers, 1 Dec 1966, p.5)

Richards, James (Brummy/Brumby)
1934 "Mr. James Richards ... drove between Cootamundra and Temora for Cobb and Co. during the gold rush to Temora in 1883 ... He also drove the coach from Gundagai in which the bushrangers Moonlight and Rogan were taken to Cootamundra gaol after being beaten in a fight at Wantabadgery. He afterwards drove coaches in the coastal districts." (Cobb and Co. Driver, 11 Apr 1934, p.17)

1934 "BRUMMY RICHARDS DEAD James ('Brummy') Richards, who was one of Cobb and Co's best drivers half a century back, died recently near Sydney. At the start of the Temora gold rush in 1881 he usually drove a three-decked ten-in-hand, and cut but the 34 miles in less than three hours in fine weather. 'Brummy' was born in Birmingham (Eng.) 79 years back." (Brummy Richards Dead, 21 May 1934, p.3)

Richards, James (Old Brummy)
1924 "Brummy's father was a wonderful driver, and, as his son was the king of drivers in later days ... 'Old Brummy'— that was his father's sobriquet—came to Australia, from Birmingham— and he brought the nickname of 'Brummy' with him—where he was a well-known stage-coach driver. He drove in the southern district for many years." (In the Days of Cobb and Co., 23 Dec 1924, p.2)

1924 "THE BOX SEAT. Great Coach Driver. In the romantic early days of N.S.W., when the great coaches of Cobb and Company thundered along the rough bush roads outback, there was no more picturesque figure than driver 'Brummy.' There were great drivers in those hectic times, brave and daring men, who took more risks in one day than the average man takes in his whole life. But 'Brummy,' the old stagers will tell you, was the master ... He tells graphic stories of the numerous occasions when bushrangers, reckless men, who laughed at death, stuck him up ; of the mad rushes to the goldfields, when law and order were almost unknown ; of the great drivers of Cobb and Company ; and of the grim struggles of the pioneers ... As a child he was never happier than when helping harnessing the horses, and riding on the boot of the coaches ... He stayed with Malone until Cobb and Company came into being in 1860. On the Goulburn road 'Brummy's' life (he was 23) was one round of adventure ... 'Brummy' laughingly tells of the time he capsized a coachload of Chinese into a small river between Goulburn and Braidwood. The Chinese were bound for the Araluen digging ... It was a time of great drought, the country was parched, there was no grass, and stock was dying everywhere. The stream was the only one that had not been dried up for miles around, 'Brummy,' by some means or other missed the causeway, and the coach, Celestials, and driver, were treated to a sudden bath ... none the worse for the experience, resumed its journey. 'Brummy' was met at his destination by James Malone, who at that time was a manager for Cobb and Company, and he wanted to know why coach, horses and Chinese, were so wet. Without a blush, 'Brummy,' told him that the drought had broken. He had run into a thunderstorm about ten mile out of the township ... Immediately the word went round that the rain was coming, the town celebrated in the true spirit. It was a wonderful day for the hotelkeepers. There was no rain for months afterwards ... He was sixty years on the box seat. Truly a wonderful record." (The Box Seat, 16 Dec 1924, p.2)

Richards, J. Frederick (Fred) ... 1917 See Richardson, W.; 1917 Anderson, Jim; 1925 Eddie, Nathan; 1940 McMillan, Alexander

1947 "IN THE COBB & CO. DAYS Many Familiar Names. The following interesting history of the old Cobb and Co. days and one of the oldest drivers of the firm, since deceased, will be read with much interest by the present age, and perhaps many of those still living of the time referred to, who may have recollections of the oldest Cobb driver in this district—Mr. J. F. Richards. Mrs. Fred Richards came to Charleville in 1891, and married Frederick Richards in 1898, who was one of Cobb and Co's Royal Mail coach drivers. She travelled with her husband the length and breadth of Queensland, her husband driving coaches on the Charleville to Tambo run, then Winton to Kynuna ... Richmond to Cloncurry, Yuleba to Surat, and St. George. In 1915 he took over as coaching manager at St. George. After 30 years with Cobb and Co. he relinquished his services, and he and his eldest son took over Cobb's coach lines from Mitchell to St. George, and Mitchell to Bollon, and died at Mitchell on September 17, 1937. Mrs. Richards recalls many of Cobb's old-time coach drivers—Jack Burgess, Dave Teys, Jim Davidson, Tom Naylor, Alf Jensen, Alf Lewis, Jack Matheson, Dick O'Donnell, Jack Ferguson, John Gallagher, Billy White, Bill Lumley, Ted Palmer, George Reardon, and Joe and Billy Richards. Mrs. Richards now only knows of two of the remaining spokes left in the old wheels of Cobb and Co., they being Joe Hertzberg and Ted Richards, who are both in the north of Queensland." (In the Cobb Co Days, 21 Nov 1947, p.21)

1937 "FREDERICK RICHARDS The death is announced of Mr. Frederick Richards, of Mitchell, at the age of 67. He commenced with Cobb & Co. in 1894, and for 20 years drove that company's mail coaches in various centres throughout Queensland. In 1914 he was appointed traffic manager for Cobb & Co. at St. George, and held that position until 1919, when he commenced business on his own account as mail contractor on the Mitchell-St. George run. A few years ago, he retired from active association with the Maranoa Motor Services, Mitchell which hold several mail contracts which are being carried on by his two sons. The deceased is survived by his widow and two sons." (Obituary, 30 Sep 1937, p.2)

1948 See also Herchberg/Hertsberg, Joseph (Joe)

Richards, Joe & Richards, Ted ... 1947 See Richards, J. Frederick (Fred)

Richards, Mick ... 1917 See Manning, Ned

Richards, Ned ... 1917 See Richardson, Alf

Richardson, Alf ... 1917 See Richardson, W.; 1917 Manning, Ned

Richardson, Bill (Billy)
1936 "A Downs newspaper man (the late Duncan M. Cameron), in commenting on a journey he took 62 years ago by coach from Warwick to Stanthorpe and back, wrote of Cobb and Co.:—*With a secure knowledge of their own capabilities, like Jehu of old, those Warwick-Stanthorpe coach drivers drove furiously, with a trifle of recklessness as a side line. A sure cure for a torpid liver was that 40 mile ride in the coach in the seventies. The champion whip of the road was appropriately nicknamed 'Hell-fire Jack.' Remember riding on the box seat with him from Warwick to Stanthorpe in 1873, but returning preferred the body of the coach. The manner in which that driver would tool that vehicle between two trees, knocking the bark off both of them with the boxes of the wheels, was amazing.*

An outstanding feature, in connection with those coaching days was the blowing of a bugle by the driver when coming down Blades' Hill, on to Deuchar's Creek bridge. Cobb and Co's first driver on this section was Nick Hart (of 'Thunderbolt,' the bushranger, fame), then came Tom Elmes, an erstwhile Gympie coach driver, and noted whistler, who gave his passengers a whistling concert on many occasions all the way from Warwick to Stanthorpe and back. Other of Cobb and Co's drivers were Harry Lumley, Johnny Miles, Tom Rummery, and Bill Richardson. In the days I am referring to Cobb and Co's coaches provided the excitement, of the day, when, in a cloud of dust, to the accompaniment of clanking traces and cracking whip, they clattered along Albion-street to the post office and thence on to the Commercial Hotel." (Echoes of the Past, 22 Feb 1936, p.8)

1925 See also Atkins, W.

Richardson Brothers ... 1950 See Hickson, Harry

Richardson, Jim
1890 "STANTHORPE. Monday, November 17. Richardson, an old driver from Cobb and Co., has been instructed with the establishment of a coach service between here and Rivertree. He has arrived with the horses and coach, and the service will commence forthwith." (Stanthorpe, 18 Nov 1890, p.3)

1922 "Another time Jim Richardson, of Rivertree, had on the box a very eminent legal personage, and on arrival the boys crowded round to hear what Jim had to say about him. *Never saw such a man*, said Jim. *Kept shootin' out his hands at places and wantin' to know the names of them. Well, I kept on finding names for them till I got tired, and then I said, You so-and-so and such-and-such old blank (and many more blanks), if you don't stop asking (words omitted) questions I'll throw you off the majenta coach. You said all that to him, gasped one* of the crowd. *Of course, I did, every word of it. And what did he say, Jim? Oh, he didn't say nothing,* replied Jim, *I said it under me breath.*" (When Cobb & Co was King, 16 Apr 1922, p.15)

Richardson, Tom
"OLD COBB DRIVER A Blackall man in Brisbane for the last Exhibition once drove for Cobb and Co. He is Tom Richardson, 75 … Born in Victoria he went to Blackall in 1902 to drive for Cobb and Co. from Blackall to Barcaldine. *The seven horse coaches used to do the 70-odd-mile trip in about nine hours with three changes of horses*, he said. By car the trip now took about 2 hours." (Old Cobb Driver, 22 Sep 1949, p.4)

Richardson, W.
1917 "Queensland … drivers … CROYDON TO GEORGETOWN, by Kelly's, the Gilbert River telegraph station, and on past Forest Home, the Cumberland, and Durham, which was a little rough in places and boggy in others. On this line were Jim Macpherson, Bill White (a driver with Cobb and Co. for over 30 years, and still driving on the Winton-Longreach route), and Little Bob, who ran the first horse mail from Cairns to Herberton … GEORGETOWN TO HERBERTON, a rough track requiring the best of horses, tackle, and drivers. On this route were drivers Alf Jensen, Ned Richards, Alf Richardson, Jack Balsall, and Terence Carr … HERBERTON TO PORT DOUGLAS, by the present Atherton and Mareeba (Old Granite Creek), and on to Northedge and Mount Molloy, and across the range to Port Douglas; J. Green and Rod McCrae were the old-time drivers here … HUGHENDEN TO CHARTERS TOWERS: This was run a few years only, Jim Hutchinson being the sole driver, and the time three days each way. As the railway was constructed this route was shortened … HUGHENDEN TO CLONCURRY, along the left bank of the Flinders, by Marathon, Richmond, to Nelia Ponds, and on to Eddington, Leila Vale, and across the Williams to Cloncurry, a journey of 240 miles. Bitterly cold in winter, and in summer a sweltering, hot, dusty ride. On this run were drivers Ned Manning, Big Jim Nowlan, a nephew of an old New South Wales coach contractor, Tom Burke, Mick Richards, and Alf Richardson … HUGHENDEN TO MUTTABURRA, up the Landsborough, was run for 16 years with but one driver, J. Thompson … NORMANTON TO CROYDON, one of the vilest tracks in Queensland. When the floods were out, sheets of water miles wide had to be negotiated, especially when nearing Normanton, while in summer travellers thought they were visited by all the plagues of Egypt, together with a few which originated in the Gulf country. The drivers here were Jack Leonard, and Jack Warner, and in the 'rush' days of the [18]80's and early 90's it was a busy line … RICHMOND TO MACKINLAY, on one of the heads of the Cloncurry, and about 40 miles east of the present Mount Hampden, Cloncurry to Normanton, up the Cloncurry River to its Junction with the Flinders, past Donors Hill, and then on, by Paddy's Lagoon, to Normanton, a weird journey always, of about 260 miles. The drivers on this route included Jack Underwood, Harry Bourke, and Harry Bruce … WINTON AND BOULIA, 249 miles, via the 20-Mile Hotel, Western Hotel, Elderslie, Woodstock, Llanheidol, across the Hamilton at Warenda, and on to Boulia on the Bourke, was one of the loneliest rides in the Western country. The drivers on this route were: Tom Gardner, Alex. McMullen, Frank Ward, and Steve Wall … WINTON TO HUGHENDEN, by Oondooroo, Corfield and Stamford, drivers: W. Markwell, A. Thompson, and Bill Cox … WINTON TO KYNUNA, by Ayrshire Downs and Dagworth up the Diamantina, was run by Jim Foster, Fred Richards (now of St. George), and Bill (his brother), Dick O'Donnell and W. Richardson … WINTON TO HUGHENDEN, by Oondooroo, Corfield and Stamford, drivers: W. Markwell, A. Thompson, and Bill Cox" (Coaching in Australia, 1917, p.45)

Ridley, (Christian name unknown)
1869 "Mr Ridley, the driver of Cobb and Co.'s coach from Ballarat to Castlemaine, telegraphed on Saturday to say that in consequence of the flood the journey could not be accomplished. However, he afterwards undertook the task, and proved himself a first-rate whip by driving through a long tract of flooded country with its bridges many of them swept away, and others scarcely holding together. Some of the passengers booked declined to take their seats, when the coach started, but amongst those who arrived were four females. The Rev. Father Moore was in the Ballarat district on Saturday, and while driving towards a bridge it was intended to pass over, the structure was swept away by the torrent of water rushing in the channel below. Until a few days of fine weather has allowed the flood to subside it is impossible to form even an approximate idea of the large amount of damage done." (Items of News, 18 Oct 1869, p.2)

Rivers, Ridgway
1869 "Rivers Ridgway, charged on the information of George Quigley with intercepting the free passage of the prosecutor and the spring-cart under his care on the Kadina-road, on October 5, pleaded not guilty. Mr. Daly for the prosecutor ; Mr. Brook for the defendant. George Quigley, of Lower Light, publican, said on October 5 he was driving home from Adelaide on the main road to Kadina in a spring-cart. There were two others with him. The defendant, who was in charge of one of Cobb & Co.'s coaches, then drove up on his wrong side and ran into prosecutor's vehicle, breaking the harness, injuring one of the wheels, and cutting prosecutor's leg. The defendant seemed to be driving on the wrong side of the road purposely. By Mr. Brook—The defendant monopolized about 17 yards of the road, which was a chain wide. Thought defendant intended to run into him. Cobb & Co.'s coach used to stop at his public-house, but that had been discontinued within the last six months. Did not remember ever having said he would get Ridgway off the road. Michael Kean and Isabella Redpath said they were with Quigley on the day in question. Defendant drove into them and injured their vehicle. George Tiller stated that he was passing at the time and saw Ridgway drive his coach into Quigley's cart. The information was dismissed. His Worship considering that Quigley might have driven nearer the fence in order to avoid a collision." (Police Courts, 23 Oct 1869, p.3)

Robards, John
1911 "MR. JOHN ROBARDS … emigrated to New South Wales when four years old. His youthful days were spent at Melrose, near Orange, where he was employed by the late Mr. John Tom Lane, one time Police Magistrate at Orange. His avocation was principally among stock. Later on he was driver of Cobb and Co's coaches between Orange and Wellington, and Orange and Molong. On one occasion while taking his team from Orange to Molong he was 'stuck up' somewhere in the

vicinity of Erambie, by a bushranger, one Jimmy Fitzgerald." (Mr. John Robards, 8 Jul 1911, p.3)

Robertson, Jack ... 1953 See Rutherford, James (Jas./Jimmy)

Robertson, J. F ... 1919 See Aisbett, E. J.

Robertson, Jno ... 1925 See Eddie, Nathan

Robertson, John
1899 "The news of the death of Mr. John Robertson, who was formerly connected with the well-known coaching firm of Cobb and Co. (Wagner and Robertson), will be learned with regret by his numerous friends in this district. The deceased gentleman was for some years the local representative of the firm in the old days, when their coaches used to start from their offices at the Shamrock hotel for various centres of population in different parts of the colony which did not then enjoy the advantages of railway communication. Upright in all his dealings, unobtrusive in demeanor, and of a generous disposition, the deceased won the respect and esteem of all who were brought in contact with him. He was a keen sportsman, and during his residence here he was a prominent member of the Bendigo Jockey Club. He died at 'Halewood,' Toorak, on Saturday morning, at the age of 65 years, after a long and painful illness." Meanwhile "In June, 1893, the amount of rain which fell was 5in. 33 points. Yesterday was moderately fine, but the wind was cold. The readings at Mr. J. B. Edwards's, jeweller, on Saturday were :—Thermomter, 9 a.m., 43^0; 12 noon, 44^0; 3 p.m., 47^0; 6 p.m., 47^0; maximun, 47^0; minimun, 41^0." (Obituary, 26 Jul 1899, p.3)

Robinson, Ben
1937 "VETERAN MAILMAN. JERILDERIE, Tuesday. After having carried the mails along the one route between Jerilderie and Finley for 45 years, Mr. Ben Robinson this week terminated his contract. Originally a driver for Cobb and Co., Mr. Robinson in the eighties and early nineties drove a coach between Avoca and St. Arnaud (Vic). In 1892 he came to Riverina and commenced on the Jerilderie-Tocumwal road, via Finley. This contract was then held by his father, the late Mr. James Robinson, of Deniliquin, well known in coaching circles in the Riverina's early days. In later years Mr. Ben Robinson conducted the mail service on his own behalf. With the advent of the railway, the coach service was discontinued between Finley and Tocumwal, but still runs between Jerilderie and Finley." (Veteran Mailman, 7 Apr 1937, p.11)

Robinson, James (Robbie)
1923 "OLD COACHING DAYS. HISTORY OF COBB AND CO. HOW JAMES RUTHERFORD MADE HIS NAME FAMOUS. From 'Deniliquin Independent.' Mr. James Robinson, who was employed by the firm of Rutherford and Company, at Kyneton, when he was 20 years of age (he is now 84), has handed us a copy of the 'Sunday Times' containing stores of the old coaching days of Cobb and Co. 'Robbie,' as he is familiarly called, continued with the firm until the partnership was dissolved, when Messrs. Robinson and Wagner, two members of the old firm, became partners, and established the coaching business in many parts of this State.

Perhaps the principal centres were between Echuca and Deniliquin, and Deniliquin and Hay. The late 'Johnny' Pureell and 'Tom' Kidd were two of the principal drivers on the former line, 'Charlie' Lee (who is still hale and hearty and living on his farm at Booroorban), on the Hay-Deniliquin line. About this time 'Robbie' was sent by Mr. Robertson to Hay as a spare driver and continued in the service until he started out on his own account. Mr. Maurice Parker was the general manager of the firm, with his headquarters at Hay, and Mr. O'Dwyer had charge of the Deniliquin office. It is mentioned in the article that the '22 light greys were groomed like racers,' and the same remark is applicable to the horses driven in those days. All were corn fed and as there were frequent changes along the routes, rain never deterred the delivery of mails up to time. The mail contract for the Hay line alone was up to £2000 per annum, and this price continued for many years until 'Mick' Charters started in opposition and secured the contract. Although a few coaches still carry passengers and mails, the motor car has superseded them, but in very wet weather the old coach or buggy has to be resorted to. The following is the article referred to:—The name 'Cobb and Co.' is about all there ever was to associate Winslow and Freeman Cobb with the great system of passenger transport that served Australia so well in the pre-railway days of the country. The actual founder and conductor of the coaching business, that is still serving the people in the developing areas of far out, was the late James Rutherford, whoso name is inseparably connected with the progress of the Western district of New South Wales ... Headquarters of the business were established at Bathurst, where the new firm erected coach-building factories, establishing others at Goulburn, Hay, Bourke, Charleville, and Castlemaine. For over forty years, under, the management of Rutherford, Cobb and Co. carried passengers and mails over the routes of Australia, and conveyed the gold from diggings to the banks in the town centres.

'CABBAGE-TREE NED.' One of the biggest coaches on the roads of Australia in the 'good old days' was the Leviathan. It could carry 70 passengers, and ran a 20-mile stage between Castlemaine and Kyneton. The team for this was 22 horses, light greys, groomed like racers ... The next biggest team was 12 white horses used on the run from Melbourne to Ballarat ... One of the famous drivers of the early days of the company was 'Cabbage-tree Ned'—Ned Devine ... He was given the sobriquet on account of his specialising in cabbage-tree hats, which he always wore on the road ...

JACK FAGAN'S EXPERIENCE. The work of the management of the service was arduous, but the chances of the journeys were the burden of the men on the box seats of the coaches. Their experiences were thrilling on occasions. Perhaps one of the most exciting trips was that of Jack Fagan ... the gold stolen by the bushrangers in the Eugowra Creek hold up ... One of the old time drivers of this State was Jim Conroy, who should not have had to work for a crust. His father squatted on a block of land in Melbourne—put a fence round the paddock in which his humpy stood, and decided to settle there. News of good things on otter in Sydney attracted him, and he sold the humpy and paddock for £12. Just about where old man Conroy's humpy was is the palatial store of Buckley and Nunn, in Melbourne. Jim had some experience with the 'rangers, but escaped actual bullet contact. On the occasion of a hold-up he suggested to the gang that it was unwise to take so big a chance for so little profit. *I'll bet there isn't a fiver's worth in the mail bags*, he said. *I wouldn't have stayed here all night in the cold if I hadn't thought to get something*, replied the robber. *You'll get something all right*, said the driver. They did. They were arrested and got five years.

SILENT MEMBER. An identity of the roads was Silent Bob Bates. He gave all his attention to the horse ... One of the pupils of Silent Bob was W. H. Hampson, a driver who had little trouble with the bushrangers of the period. He was a dead shot with a revolver, and probably on that account was held in high esteem by those gentlemen. George Adams (Tattersall), well known later as a commercial traveller on the North Coast route, was a pupil of Hampson's, and one of the best of the many excellent whips in the State. He advanced from driver to road manager, and left the coaches for the more profitable business of the bagman.

HIRAM BARNES AND HALL GANG. Hiram Barnes, mentioned previously, took the first Cobb's coaches to Queensland in 1866. In Victoria he had been in charge of a seven-horse team running from Diggers' Rest to Castlemaine. In this State he was on the Forbes-Orange run and was fired at several times by bushrangers and twice wounded. One of the closest calls he had was when Hall and Gilbert erected a barricade three miles out of Forbes and held up the mail in charge of Tom Hunter. Barnes was expected on this journey and it was intended that he should be dealt with. Twenty-five passengers in the coach were tied up and laid by the roadside till all had been searched and robbed. A woman was the exception. She was not bound, and accepting her statement that she had no money or valuables, the 'rangers did not search her. Subsequently she boasted that she had £300 in her hair. This got to the knowledge of the bushrangers, and women in subsequent hold-ups were carefully examined for hidden wealth. Dan Mayne, for many years an identity of Bathurst—proprietor of 'The Sentinel' (for which A. G. Taylor and Jack Hunt did some of the best of their writing), was one of the drivers of Cobb and Co. Jack Barry, who died a year or two ago at Orange, was another of the well-known whips of the time. Peter Torquay was on the box when Frank Gardiner stuck up the coach on the road to Lambing Flat.

One of the veterans of the service recently dead in the Western country, was Jim Breen. He was a staunch admirer of Rutherford, and was always to be found on the box seat when the gov'nor was breaking-in a young 'un. Rutherford was a very fine driver, and specially good with the young 'uns. When Jimmy became too old to help with his advice and vigorous criticism Rutherford gave him a stocked and equipped farm, and placed him on the pension list of the business. When Rutherford was quite a new chum on one occasion he put up at the Springs Creek Hotel and turned his horses into the paddock attached to the premises. When he went into the bar he was asked who he was, and where he was going. For some obscure reason he was locked in a room, the door of which he forced, and from which he returned to the bar. He was then rushed, stripped, and locked up in the stable and the hotelkeeper and two troopers bound him with ropes and a bullock chain, and left him till noon of next day. He brought an action against his assailants, and was awarded £500 damages. With this money he made his start. " (Old Coaching Days, 15 Jun 1923, p.3)

1923 "Old Coaching Days. MR. JAMES ROBINSON'S REMINISCENCES ... Coach drivers in their way were celebrities, and these were many nerve wracking and stirring incidents in which they figured while driving their smart teams of horses over the mountains and plains, day and night, in fair or foul weather. Rain, hail or shine, it was all the same to those intrepid drivers. Cobb and Co. had a reputation in regard to punctual delivery of mails and passengers, and the men who piloted the teams zealously sought to uphold it. As time went on the trail of the iron horse pushed the coaches further away from the big centres ... *Cobb and Co. had grand horses in those days*, Mr. Robinson remarked. *They were looked after like race horses, given the best of food money could buy, and bedded down at night. The harness was always kept scrupulously clean, and so were the coaches. Most of the horses came from Queensland. The drivers looked after them well when on the road, and were very proud of their turnouts* ... Over 40 years ago Mr. Robinson went to Hay for Cobb and Co., and drove special coaches with commercial travellers and their samples between Hay, Booligal, Hillston and other centres, and he was then put on the Urana-Jerilderie service as driver for twelve months. Next he was transferred to Boree 'change' (on the Deniliquin-Hay road), where he remained for five years. His predecessor there was 'Jim' Mason, and his successor 'Johnny' Purcell, two well known Deniliquin identities who have both gone west." (Old Coaching Days, 19 Oct 1923, p.3)

Robinson, Johnnie
1934 "Great Steeplechase Rider ... OLD timers (but old they must be), may recall the steeplechase rider, Johnnie Robinson. He was the acknowledged leader in this branch of racing for many years, and his list of victories totalled a large number. He was contemporary with the romantic poet horse worshipper, Adam Lindsay Gordon, of whom I could only speak but of the mouth of others, as I cannot recall this lovable and tragic minstrel of Australian song. In middle life Johnnie Robinson became a famous reinsman in Cobb & Co.'s coaching service, often driving with masterly skill a team of five gallant steppers to the Bay in the huge coach, 'The Leviathan,' on fete days and special occasions. What a coach of vermilion and gold, with its immense 'C' springs that was! ... Johnnie Robinson was a man of naturally gentle manners, beloved by women and boy passengers and respected by men." (Sporting Memories, 18 Jan 1934, p.19)

Robinson, Thomas
1905 "A well-known resident of Toogong in the person of Mr. Thomas Robinson died on Monday last at Orange ... Deceased was well known throughout the western districts ... The deceased, who was 72 years of age, was for 50 years a resident in Australia. When he first arrived in N.S.W. he entered the service of Mr. Henry Osborne, of Marshall Mount, Wollongong, on the South Coast, and afterwards entered the employ of a Mr. Chalmers, of the same town. Leaving the latter gentleman's employ he accepted an engagement with Messrs. Cobb & Co. as a coach driver, which position he faithfully filled for 25 years. He, however, severed his connection with Cobb and Co., and commenced working for Irvine Bros., of Toogong." (Obituary, 21 Apr 1905, p.2)

Robson, J. M ... 1919 See Aisbett, E. J.

Rochester, William George (Bill)

1936 "Obituary. MR. WILLIAM GEORGE ROCHESTER. One by one the members of the grand old band of heroic drivers for the pioneer, but now extinct, firm of Cobb and Co. pull up their horses and alone cross the dark waters of the River of Lethe … It was a man's job, a job only for the stout hearted and true, men with indomitable pluck and determination. The royal mail had to be delivered and these veteran jehus of the past did it as close to schedule time as conditions would allow. In Phantom Land to-day, there will be a great reunion, for Bill Rochester has gone to join those who went before. He 'let go the ribbons' on Wednesday morning at 10.30, quite conscious almost till the last bugle sounded … As we said before, he drifted into the arena of horses, and over 60 years ago he joined Cobb and Co … he settled for many years in the West of New South Wales, being principally located near Dubbo, but his operations took him as far west as Wilcannia and Bourke and even to the Queensland border … The affinity that exists amongst old servants of Cobb and Co. was again demonstrated at the funeral, which was attended by four colleagues of deceased in former days, in the persons of Messrs John Mitchell (Taree), Richard Oldfield and Wally Morris (Gloucester) and Fred Walden (Nabiac)." (Obituary, 7 Mar 1936, p.6)

1935 Mr. W. G. Rochester stated "In the seventies (1870s) … Fred Walden (Nabiac), his father (Bill Walden) and Jimmy Hampton were the drivers from Wellington to Dubbo, and later to Warren. That was in the days before the iron horse took charge of the road. In those days the Macquarie used to break its banks very often, between Gin Gin and Warren, at which time much of this country would be under water. Then it was that Matt Gaffney on account of his intimate knowledge of the country, was requisitioned to plot the coaches through. In the eighties [1880s], when I was driving there, on two or three occasions, the townspeople used to ride four abreast in front of the leading horses to pilot me out to the Red Hill. At Sandy Creek, some four miles out, a whaleboat, 8ft. long, was kept for the ferrying of passengers and mails across the swollen stream, to and from the coaches on either side. The passengers had to be carried, in those days to the boat. John Mitchell, of Manning-st. Taree (he was not married then) was also one of the drivers. I used to do the carrying. I well remember on one occasion the boys and girls who were attending school in Sydney were returning home for the vacation, and with them a very popular lady, the wife of a very popular boniface of the district. She weighed 17 stone. As mentioned above, I was doing the carrying." (Cobb and Co., 24 May 1935, p.9)

1935 See also Conroy, James (Jim)

Rodgers, (Christian name unknown) … 1930-1940s See Allan, (Christian name unknown)

Roe, Billy
1907 "North Country. LEONORA TO LAWLERS. Soon after daybreak the other morning Cobb's coach, under the skilful guidance of Billy Roe, rumbled out of Tower-street, and once more negotiated the old, rutted track that leads to Lawlers. The town of Leonora, temporarily disturbed by the prancing of the horses, the packing of luggage, by the hoisting aboard of some lady fares who said 'lawk' in an agitated tone of voice, and the concluding 'let her went' of Tom, the energetic coaching agent who saw the conveyance off, relapsed again into slumber. In a moment the thoroughfare was emptied save for a weary dead-beat roosting patiently on the stool of the last pub, waiting for the opening of the bar door. Streaking along ahead was a bloomer-clad cycliste of charming contour—she was out for a morning constitutional and meant to beat the coach into Diorite.

The Four-Mile pub tumbled out with its pyjamas on as we drove up, ready to rake in any surplus revenue that might be floating by. Bung scratched his head in a bewildered fashion and an old lady, who appeared shortly after, fished among some over-night debris for the corkscrew to open a bottle of beer .or two. Finally they rooted the corks out with a nail as an alternative to knocking the heads, off. *Bottles are too valuable to go smashing 'em up like that*, remarked Pyjamas, jamming down a tight-fitting end that scorned to be yanked forth by a mere nail. Our gruel consumed, all hands climbed aboard again and onward went Cobb and Co. in the wake of a fair scorcher, now a mere dust-ball in perspective. Regarding the Four-Mile pub, it may be incidentally remarked that new owners are in possession, and that 'Cutty,' the bright and cheerful genius who engineered its destinies for years, has moved further along to 'Nobby' Hannah's familiar beer depot at Doyle's. 'Cutty's successors are generally considered to be handling the ancient habitation successfully.

The fourteen or fifteen miles, to Diorite were over a parched and dreary stretch of red dust with skeleton trees right and left ; mere desolation, waste, and misery. The two individuals clad in dog-poisoners moving about the roadway were Government surveyors mapping out a track for the problematical railway from Lawlers to Leonora … Lawlers, no mines to exploit and nothing on route that its existence would help to develop, and, secondly, the State's finances are dead against its construction … At Diorite the coach breakfasted at Mrs. Burrows' Currajong Hotel, which takes its name from a huge currajong overlapping the rear of the building. It is the only domicile alive in the crumbling township of Diorite …

At more distant Mt. Clifford, where Mulgu Taylor used to hunt for alluvial in his pre-political days, owners of the local battery are doing much to push on prospecting in the neighbourhood. Unfortunately water for milling purposes is so scarce that crushing operations occur at intervals, and often long ones …

Bidding adieu to Diorite and the scorcher cycliste who, having beaten the coach, was sailing off in triumph to Leonora, Billy steered a steady course to Doyle's. On this stage we encountered 'Red-Flannel,' 'Crooked' Mick, Long Paddy, and other teamster celebrities

'Cutty' lay smoking on a stretcher in front of the pub and dreamily watched the passengers alighting. *Well, I suppose I'll have to get up*, he observed desperately as the crowd filed into the bar. *Warrel y'ave ?* He enquired swinging in behind the jump and making an effort to get at the bottom of an empty long-sleever with an alleged bar-towel … Everybody had beer … someone rang a horse-bell and we all trended into the dining room …

Eleven miles further brought us to Pink Well, the stronghold of my friend Dick, Cobb's enterprising groom, and the ardent admirer of the belle of Poison Creek. Discontinuing his pursuit

of a predatory goanner which had just emerged from the humble domicile where Cobb's henchman dreams away the summer days, he brought fresh horses to the Conch. Although it suits the satirical to poke a bit of fun at him. Dick is a good old soul and about the hardest worker in Cobb's service. May his efforts to be landlord of the Poison Creek pub be crown
ed with success.

Without more ado, Lawlers ! The town was if anything quieter than is its wont. Still, business is very solid at Lawlers. The commercials say so and they ought to know. The most active man in the community seemed to be Warden Clifton, who was making ready for a long trip per motor bike up to Lake Way and over through the mines at Kathleen Valley ...

In the immediate vicinity of Lawlers appearances indicate that mining is on a more prosperous footing than it has been for some time ... To manager Allen of the East Murchison United, or Northern Gold Mines belongs pride of place, however, in the matter ot cheap costs. Bringing his ore a distance of seven miles and covering everything—mining, milling, cynaniduig, and treatment of slimes, as well as capital expenditure—with 15/ a ton is a feat in mining which, considering all the circumstances, has no parallel in the State. It isn't possible to run a mine on closer or more economical lines and keep up efficiency.

Drifting from mining on to the strike, the beer strike at Vivien. This movement was inaugurated recently to force the beer philanthropist running the only pub down to sixpenny rates. For some days the strikers heroically hung off in the mulga, but the great Australian thirst at last prevailed. They claimed to have won a victory by establishing small beers at sixpence a time, same as at Lawlers, but it was a poor old strike, anyhow. When last seen the leading spirits of the attempted revolution were socking away pints as they had never socked them away before. The beer-martyrdom of Bowyangs is a thing short-lived and full of humor.

Lawiers sports are out with a two days race programme of £160 to eventuate on November 19 and 20. Included in this is a £30 cup. It is expected that most of the horses taking part in the Sandstone meeting and not a few from Leonora end will put in an appearance on the Lawlers course which is in excellent condition. One thing about the Lawlers club it has a straight-going committee and secretary who are going to see that the public get clean racing. The meeting has every prospect of being a profitable one." (Leonora to Lawlers, 27 Oct 1907, p.11)

Rogers, Bob ... 1932 See Lowe, Bill; Appendix 1.6

Rogers, F. J.
1856 "An inquest was held before Dr Wilmot, the city coroner, on Tuesday, touching the death of a Chinese man named Ah Moon, aged about 39 years. From the deposition of Dr Clancy it appeared that he had been called to attend deceased about nine o'clock on Saturday night. He found him lying in Messrs Cobb's office, quite dead ... no external marks of violence ... Dr Fletcher had made a post mortem examination of the body, and found the brain congested with its membranes, and extensive adhesions between the membranes of the dura matter and pia matter ; also, an induration and thickening of a portion of the dura matter immediately over the posterior lobe of the left cerebral hemisphere, the posterior and middle lobes being also very considerably congested. He had no doubt as to the immediate cause of death being apoplexy ... F. J. Rogers, the driver of the coach stated, that about three o'clock on Saturday afternoon, he took deceased from the conveyance that had brought him down from Castlemaine to the middle of the Black Forest ... he had no suspicion of anything being the matter with deceased, as, when he last saw him, he was sitting up in the carriage like any other passenger" ... while stated in the same article "SUSPICION OF STEALING A BOX OR FRUIT ... Constable Nicholson deposed that he met the prisoner about half-past eleven o'clock on Monday night, near the Rob Roy public house, in Flindors street, carrying a box of fruit on his head. Upon being questioned, he first of all said that he had brought it from Sydney, and afterwards from the Yarra steamer. At the station house he said he had bought it from a man. James Fox, a watchman on the Wharf, swore that the case belonged to a lot of others which were under his charge. The Bench sentenced the prisoner to one month's' imprisonment with hard labor ... LECTURE ON BREATHING.—We observe that this evening, at the United Presbyterian Church, Dr. Eades will deliver a lecture on 'Breathing,' illustrated by numerous diagrams. Dr. Eades' repute as a pleasing and instructive lecturer, will secure him a large audience. The lecture is to commence at half-past seven." (Local Intelligence, 23 Jul 1856, p.3)

Rogers, Frank
"My mother traced our family history and I was given the names of two original Cobb & Co drivers who are related to me. The first one is Lewis Rogers who died in 1867 and the second is his brother Frank Rogers. Lewis died of pneumonia and is buried in the Presbyterian section of Orange Cemetery." (Lynn Forrest, relation, 2023)

1867 "Saturday, the 26th January, will long be remember here as one of the most disagreeable day's we have had—clouds of Adelaide dust being driven this far by the hot wind that was blowing. Since then the weather has been on the whole very pleasant, being cool mornings and evenings.

Messrs Cobb & Co. have taken the old bus off this line and replaced it with a handsome new, or nearly new, conveyance— one in every way suited to the traffic, and peculiarly adapted for the rough places on the road—so now we have a good bus, an experienced driver (Mr Frank Rogers), who has already won the esteem and confidence of those whose business or pleasure has caused them to travel with him by his courteous and obliging conduct, and a guard, who having an eye to the health of the Meadows community, by preventing their sleeping too late, awakes them before 6 o'clock by a few flourishes of his bugle, and thus invites them to follow his very good example of early rising." (Meadows, 9 Feb 1867, p.3)

Rogers, Jimmy ... 1938 See Anderson, Thomas (Tom)

Rogers, Lewis ... See Rogers, Frank

Rogers, S. F ... 1919 See Aisbett, E. J.

Rogers, Will & Rook, Ned ... 1921 See Griffen, Chas.

Ross, Alec ... 1929 See Corbett, Alec.

Rotten, Henry ... 1935 See Whitney, William Franklin (Frank)

Rowland, Thomas
1873 "The Dubbo Mail Robbery. On Friday morning Cobb and Co.'s coach from We'ling with the Sydney and intermediate mails did not arrive at Dubbo at its proper time, and the cause was soon learnt by telegram. The driver, Thomas Rowland, who is a new hand on the road, left Wellington at the usual hour; and had a break down near Payne's Inn at Ponto. While Mr. Payne and the blacksmith there were repairing the injuries to the coach the driver deliberately opened the Dubbo bag and abstracted some of the letters. While in the act Mr. Payee came upon him, and Rowland said, *John, can't we square it. There's £20, and I'll give you half*. Mr. Payne then spoke to him about the enormity of the offence he had committed, and the driver getting frightened, bolted into the bush. Information was at once conveyed to the police at Wellington; and, in the course of the day. Rowland was arrested by constables Beaton and M'Alister. He has been brought up at Wellington and committed.—Dispatch." (The Dubbo Mail Robbery, 23 Aug 1873, p.3)

Rowley, Anthony
1936 "OBITUARY. COBB AND CO. DRIVER ... Anthony Rowley, who was one of the oldest survivors of the coaching days of the Western district. He was 71 years of age. Mr. Rowley spent practically all his life with horses. As a boy he was apprenticed at training stables at Coleraine and Casterton, and afterwards joined the services of Cobb and Co. (Western Stage Co.), and drove on the Penola mail service coach. Geelong was then the headquarters of Cobb and Co.'s extensive Western district coaching service. After several years on the Western district run Mr. Rowley was transferred to Geelong and placed in charge of the Ocean Grove" (Obituary, 5 Feb 1936, p.8)

Rumley, Tom
1875 Coach breakdown "News arrived here on Friday that Cobb and Co.'s mail coach that left Tenterfield for Warwick on Thursday morning had a spring broken when about four miles from Wilson's Downfall, on the Great Northern Road, but owing to the cool activity of Tom Rumley, the coachman, the restive horses were restrained, and no further casualty occurred."(Tenterfield, 30 Jun 1875, p.2)

1877 "Tenterfield ... two very serious accidents which happened in our locality within the past week. The first occurred on Sunday evening last, to Mr. T. Rumley, the driver of Cobb & Co.'s coach from Stanthorpe to Tenterfield. It appears that he left Tenterfield at the usual hour on Sunday morning ... two or three miles from Boonoo Boonoo the coach broke down, owing to the horses swerving off the road, and running it against a tree, which necessitated the driver to return to town for the spare coach. On the afternoon of the same day he resumed his journey, and when crossing the stony creek on the plain, his horses bolted, and he was thrown heavily to the ground. A report of the occurrence being brought to town, several gentlemen proceeded to the spot, and found ... Mr. Rumley lying on the roadside, in a state of insensibility. He was conveyed to Brown's Hotel, when it was found that he had sustained a compound fracture of his right leg, in addition to other serious injuries. He is now happily improving in health, and it is to be hoped that he will soon recover from the shock to his system." (Tenterfield, 5 Jan 1877, p.6)

Rummery, (Christian name unknown)
1876 "The Storm in the Tin Country. THE tin mining district seems to have felt the fullest force of the late heavy storms. The Stanthorpe Miner says—Never since the opening of the tin mines has this district been visited by a storm of such terrific force ... Mr Rummery, Cobb, and Co's coachdriver, informs us that the state of the country the whole way is something terrific, from fallen timber, ruined bridges, and mutilated roads. The roads in the vicinity of Sugarloaf, Herding Yard, and the Downfall, are in many places completely blocked and dreadfully destroyed by the flood. Several houses, fences, and other property in the localities above mentioned were, more or less, damaged by wind and flood, though happily no injury to the inhabitants appears to have occurred." (The Storm in the Tin Country, 25 Jul 1876, p.3)

Rummery, Thomas (Tom)
1880 "Tenterfield ... A Child Bitten by a Snake.—We learn that on Sunday morning last a child of four years of age, the son of Mr. George Ware, who resides at Yellow Creek, near Tabulam, was bitten on the calf of the leg by a black snake. Fortunately the child's mother was close at hand when the occurrence took place, and appears to have acted with great promptitude; she immediately scarified the wound and sucked it well; she then administered ammonia and brandy, and adopted other means, which we are glad to learn succeeded in saving her child's life ...

COACH ACCIDENT.—We are sorry to learn that an accident of a serious nature happened yesterday morning to Cobb and Co.'s coach on the Warwick line, but which we are glad also to say was not attended by any loss of life. As is well known this coach leaves here at a very early hour on Wednesday morning (4.30), and it being unusually foggy the driver, Mr. Thomas Rummery, in endeavouring to avoid a deep hole of which he was aware some three miles from town, and near Mr. J. H. Sommerlad's farm, ran against a tree with great force, smashing the coach into smithereens. Fortunately the driver and a gentleman passenger escaped with only a severe shaking, although we learn Rummery's position was most critical, for he stuck manfully to his horses, and was dragged a considerable distance. The passenger rode one of the horses back into town, and a spare coach was driven out by Mr. W. Laird, and again proceeded." (Tenterfield, 11 Jun 1880, p.3)

1934 "Quartpot to Stannum, and still later to Stanthorpe. Of the means of transport between Warwick and Tenterfield in the early tin-mining days, Cobb and Co.'s coaches were the more advanced. A coach ran daily (Sundays excepted) from Warwick to Stanthorpe and back. Leaving 'Sam' Evenden's Commercial Hotel at 5 a.m., breakfast was partaken of at the Gap Inn, kept in the days of the writer's earliest, recollections by 'Bill' Gilham; then on through Maryland to Stanthorpe. On the return journey Warwick was reached between 8 and 9 p.m. That was 60 years ago, when it was possible to travel from Warwick to Stanthorpe and back in the one day. To do so to-day there is but one means—per motor car. The coach drivers in those distant

Tom getting 8 pounds 6 shillings and 11 pence. The pair then rode to Warwick, and stayed at John Collins' Horse and Jockey Inn, where Tom did some work. When Tom woke one morning, Charles Bratt had disappeared along with Tom's cheque. Tom and a constable rode to Goomburra Station where Bratt had been contracted to work. (Empire, 6 May 1858 p. 2) They confronted Bratt and he was arrested, convicted and later sentenced to 12 months with hard labour. (Maitland Mercury and Hunter River General Advertiser, 13 May 1858, p.3). Tom was just 18, already showing his determination not to be wronged, less than 12 months after immigrating …

On 15 October 1863 Tom married Hannah Burgess in Warwick. Her parents were Hannah Jackson who died in 1874, and William Burgess, a bricklayer who built some of Warwick's early buildings, including the remains of the flour mill storehouse that stands at number 1 Mill Street off Wantley Street in Warwick … In 1868, Tom's address was listed in Meyer's Directory as Allora and his occupation as bushman … The Electoral Roll for Warwick lists him living in Warwick in 1870 …

From 1864 through to 1871, Tom and Hannah had six daughters. Only three of them lived to adulthood, two dying before 1868 and the last, Alice Mary born in 1871 survived for four years. Their surviving daughters were Hannah Sophia born 6 Jan 1867 married James Hayes Rigby in 1886; Henrietta born 17 Nov 1868 married Joseph William Irwin in 1889; Emily Ann born 11 July 1870, married Donald McInnes in 1893, all in Warwick … Tom was a Cobb and Co. stage coach driver in the 1870s … Tom died, on 11 February 1917 in Brisbane General Hospital." (Information provided by Pamela Fisher, great-great-granddaughter of Henry's brother Tom Rummery, 2022)

1936 See also Richardson, Bill

Russert, Jacob (Jake)
1917 "Jacob Russart was another of Cobb and Co.'s drivers. Once, he recalls, when driving over the Blue Mountains they arrived at Wascoes and found the place full of people. 'Twas polling time, but the day had been tiring and the arrivals wanted a sleep. Tom Harrison, the Telegraph master, was on for a bit of fun, and started pelting Jacob with pillows. This angered Jacob and he picked up Tom, who was in his nightie, carried him to the bar tub where the girls were washing the glasses, and before all soused him in." (Coaching in Australia, 1917, p.27)

1925 See also Eddie, Nathan; 1935 Whitney, William Franklin (Frank); 1935 Conroy, James (Jim)

Rutherford, Frank … 1927 See Redfern, Jim

Rutherford, James (Jas./Jimmy)
1953 "When Cobb and Co. Came To Cunnamulla. Lower Warrego Pioneers. By J. J. O'Carroll. The men who opened the Lower Warrego were a brave lot … Rutherford's and Cobb and Co.'s names in after years were linked with the early days of Cunnamulla and what was later Wyandra, and also on the Diamantina and Farrar's Creek … He [Rutherford] came from New Hampshire, U.S.A., and was a real 'Yankee' in the sense that he came from the part of U.S.A. whose inhabitants were termed as such. Rutherford did not like the term. He came to Victoria as a youngster with Hiram Cobb as a driver. With them were Whitney, J. M. Peck, Wagner and Jack Robertson. With Australians Jesse Brown and Hiram Barnes (father of the late W. H. Barnes and George Barnes whom we knew as members of our State Assembly) they were the first Cobb and Co. coach drivers in Victoria …

Later Hiram Cobb returned to U.S.A. and he sold the coaches to a syndicate comprising the above men except Brown and Barnes who declined the offer to join it … To secure a business head these men got Walter Hall who had been Cobb's booking agent in one of the principal mining towns. This combination went on from success to success, and amassing more money than their business required, they embarked in pastoral pursuits.

The first property they acquired in N.S. Wales was Buckinguy, on the Macquarie. They later came over the border, and Rutherford decided that the site of the town of Cunnamulla would be their headquarters, and the block was called by that name. After, settling down it was found that many travellers were coming along, and Cobbs established a store there, which was the beginning of the flourishing town we now know. Later, the headquarters of the run were moved further south and the holding was consider ably added to. The new location was called Burrenbilla and was held by Cobb and Co. until Rutherford's death in 1912. Not long after Cunnamulla was established Cobbs sent a young man from Buckinguy who was to leave his mark on the pastoral history of the Lower Warrego. He was Arthur Leeds. Rutherford and Whitney took over the running of the pastoral interests of Cobb and Co., and both being keen judges of horse flesh and knowing that Cobb and Co.'s success in the coaching business was due to the superior class of horseflesh they used, they naturally decided that nothing but the best would do them for their herds and flocks on the properties.

Not content, with the holding known as Burrenbilla, Rutherford put his firm's interests further out and his scouts moved up the Warrego and acquired the blocks Claverton, Northam, Yarramanbar and Wyandra, which afterwards, with other blocks, were consolidated and called Claverton. In later years the pastoral interests of Cobb and Co. were taken over by Rutherford and Whitney, but at a later date Whitney again drew out and took Claverton, which he carried on in his own name, while Rutherford retained Burrenbilla and Buckinguy and carried on as Cobb and Co. Then Whitney acquired Coombing Park from Thomas Icely with one of the best merino and Shorthorn studs in N. S. Wales. Then Arthur Leeds went to Claverton (he was related to Whitney), and anyone who knows Queensland sheep and cattle knows how he kept improving the Claverton stock that to-day are among the best in the State. This quality has been maintained by his son, Arthur, who so ably followed him and who now, in addition to managing the Claverton studs, supervises the Coombing Park stud." (When Cobb and Co. Came To Cunnamulla, 10 Sep 1953, p.15)

1924 "The name of James Rutherford was a synonym for all that was honorable, just, and equitable … he told me much of his early history. He said: *I came to Melbourne in 1852, and after an unsuccessful attempt at gold digging at Nyer's Flat (now Bendigo), returned to Melbourne very hard up, and took a contract to clear a paddock … When the contract was finished I took a trip, by boat, to Brisbane, which was then only a struggling village—the chief centre being Ipswich. I then travelled back overland to Melbourne in a tilted cart … An American, named Freeman Cobb, had started running coaches to the diggings, but owing to lack of good management was not successful. Eventually I formed a company to buy him out. The partnership was as follows :—James Rutherford, one share; John Wagner, one share; A. W. Robertson, one share; B. and C. Robertson and Pollock, one share, Walter R. Hall and W. F. Whitney, one share. The purchase money was £23,000—£5000 in cash and the balance in promissory note, and I was appointed manager at £25 a week. Within six months all liabilities were paid off, and we never looked back.* That was the beginning of the great firm of Cobb and Co., which James Rutherford conducted in Victoria, New South Wales, and Queensland, for 50 years, with what success is well known. (An American-Australian, 29 Nov 1924, p.10)

1917 "Start made by Cobb and Co … New South Wales … It was decided that the two-day trip from Bathurst to Forbes should be run in one day, and Rutherford, having first arranged the stages, took the first trip on July 3rd, 1861, with four good horses, and completed the journey in the day. He had a full load of some twenty odd passengers to Bathurst the following day, including the U.S.A. Consul, MacNamara (Sydney), and Miss Guggenheim, a well-known American actress and her troupe" (Coaching in Australia, 1917, p.23)

1923 See also Robinson, James (Robbie); 1925 Eddie, Nathan; 1935 Conroy, James (Jim)

Ryan, Phil (Possible Cobb and Co driver) … 1916 See Hood, Ross

ca. 1910 Cobb & Co. coach at Yuleba, driver Alf Jensen, manager Arthur Senyard near lead horse—Courtesy Queensland Museum Collection

1895 Cobb and Co. coach photographed outside the hotel in Atherton, Queensland—Courtesy State Library of Queensland

Chapter Nine

Drivers

S – V

The Roll Call of Cobb & Co.

Cobb has mustered up its drivers,
There are seven left in all,
At Lennons there is a party,
There the roll they are going to call.

There will be some stirring stories
Each driver tells his tale,
Of course there's bound to be this one
"Never late with the mail." …

Ah; those were the days, I remember,
Trotting along on the plain.
The rattle of coaches was music,
I wish I could hear it again. …

As I write tonight, I am thinking,
Of those men I used to know,
Many gone where they cannot answer,
The Roll Call of Cobb & Co.

H. J. Bennett, Rocky Creek, Yarraman, Qld
(The Roll Call of Cobb & Co, Excerpts, 30 Jun 1955, p.5)

ca. 1895 Cobb & Co. coach at Horse Shoe Bend Hotel, Hughenden-Muttaburra Route,
Tommy Thompson and possibly Billy Smith—Courtesy Queensland Museum Collection

Supporting evidence:

Sampson, (Christian name unknown) ... 1875 See Turner, Bob (Big Bob)

Sawyer, Con ... 1939 See Buller, Jimmy

Scobie, Martin (New Zealand) ... 1875 See Turner, Bob (Big Bob)

Scott, (Christian name unknown) ... 1920 See Gales, A.

Scott, Alex ... 1917 See Wright, Bob

Search, Cecil E.
1934 "Pioneer Looks Back. 45 Years with Cobb & Co ... The young man was Mr. Cecil E. Search, who has retired from active service, at the age of 77, after 45 years with the old coaching firm. Thus is severed another link with the 'golden' days and the coaching days, as Mr. Search is said to be the oldest member of the famous firm whose coach routes formed a network over the whole of ... Australia, and played such an important part in the opening up and development of the country." (Coaching Days, 9 Mar 1934, p.4)

Shaw, F.
1885 "ROCKHAMPTON ... Since the severity of the drought has been disastrously felt by the selectors in this district they have ceased to display any interest in the proceedings of the Central Queensland Farmers and Selectors' Association ... the president (Mr. Hobler) has been spreading the knowledge he has gained after a lengthy residence in the colony in a way that I think few others would have thought of. A few months ago he told members at a meeting that many a life could be saved in the bush by the thirsty traveller killing his horse, heating its flesh over a fire, and sucking the juice from it ... BEENLEIGH ... The Governor and Lady Musgrave will be present, the Governor having kindly consented to open the show. The Ministry and leaders of the Opposition are to be invited. Mr. F. Shaw, of Cobb and Co., will drive the Governor and Lady Musgrave in a four-in-hand from the rail way station to the show ground, the local Mounted Infantry acting as a guard of honour ... MARYBOROUGH ... One of the most promising bowlers among our local cricketers, Jack Mungomery, lost a finger of his right hand the other day by amputation, consequent upon an accident met with his work as a blacksmith" (Country News, 19 Sep 1885, p.476)

Sheppard, (Christian name unknown)
1858 "The Geelong Advertiser says:—The upsetting of Cobb's coach, on Monday afternoon was of a more serious nature than has been made to appear. The coach left Geelong at twelve o'clock, being occupied by no less than 34 passengers including the driver, upwards of 20 of whom were on the roof. It arrived about two o'clock, at the Clyde Hotel, and after changing horses, and renewing the journey, one of the leaders, a rather young horse, became restive and unmanageable, apparently startled by a bullock dray blocking the way. This led to some restiveness amongst the other horses, when the wheels of the coach became locked, which led to its capsize. Three or four persons have received material injury—one a female, seriously. The driver, Mr Sheppard, did not escape unhurt, and considerable damage was done to the carriage." (Ballaarat Gaol Accommodation, 6 Mar 1858, p.5)

Sheraton, Lou ... 1950 See Hickson, Harry

Simmons, Frederick Langton (Fred)
1875 "Coach Accident. An accident happened to Cobb's Whittlesea coach this morning, whilst journeying from that place to town. It appears that the coach was being driven by one of the company's steadiest drivers, a man named Simmons. Just opposite to Croxton Park the horses shied at a laborer who was working at the corner of the road, and the conveyance was swerved by the affrighted animals towards the water-shed. The sudden jerk had the effect of bending the king-bolt, which eventually broke by the continued strain upon it, causing the fore carriage to sever its connection with the other part of the coach. The driver was thrown to the ground ... The accident which is the first that has occurred on this line is safely attributable to the stupidity of the man who persisted in working on the crown of the road notwithstanding he must have heard the approach of the coach ... Frederick Langton Simmons, aged 32 years, the driver or the coach, was admitted to the Hospital." (Coach Accident, 30 Aug 1875, p.3)

1886 "COLONIAIL COACHING AND THEIR JEHU'S ETC. By C.B ... *I'm a P.O.F.* said an old friend once, when discussing the subject of Friendly Societies; *and perhaps you never heard of that Order before ; what do you think is the full title ?* Thinking for a while, and knowing the jocular bent of my friend, I innocently said, *I suppose it is a Lodge of Particular Old Fools.* The solution convulsed the company. *That's one for you*, said my friend. I was wrong, though, for the initials meant *Personal Odd Fellow*. Well, readers, you will probably say I am one of that Order, when I tell you, that for pleasant travelling on pleasure bent, I prefer the old English stage, or the leather-spring Cobb's coach to the iron horse; and I do not object to a rough bush road, or a few miles of 'Corduroy,' when a steady, good tempered Jehu sits on his throne. A little jolting or shaking is an excellent antidote for a sluggish liver, which latter is the plague of many a pent-up citizen.

But I have not always had a good-tempered Jehu 'to rattle my bones over the stones.' In the good old times, before the iron horse invaded Tasmania, there was an orthodox English stage coach, running from Launceston to Hobart, a distance of about 120 miles. The road presented a charming variety of scenery, mountain, dale, and level plain, with objects of interest to tourists all along. On my first trip there, I experienced the discomfort of having one of the most sullen, disagreeable, old buffers of a Jehu, that ever handled 'the ribbons' I ever met, either in England or the colonies. 'Old Davie,' for that was his name, was a cure : unsociable, reserved, and churlish to a degree. Fortunately, the Guard was the very reverse : cheerful, obliging, chatty, ever ready to interest strange passengers in the districts he passed through by explanation, or answering enquiries; relating historical yarns of places and people en route ; making a long journey apparently short and delightful. It was an exciting journey up and down the mountain zig-zag convict-made roads, and caused the hearts of the timorous to beat pit-a-pat, as down, down, down, the four-in-hand dashed on, often of their own accord, for the surly 'Old Davie' was often seen actually nodding on the throne of Jehu, and the Guard's attention had to be called to his somnambulistic state ...

My next experience was in South Australia with a five-horse Cobb's, from Adelaide to Mount Barker, driven by a Jehu, pleasant and affable. A most exciting, pleasurable, and exhiliarating trip. The first halt before ascending the Mount is at the Vine Inn, Glen Ormond, where the attention of passengers is directed to a large black dog at the hotel door. *Throw him a penny and he will buy a biscuit*, said one; and sure enough, in the most business-like manner, the dog picked up the coin and trotted off inside, and brought out the biscuit. This is repeated as every coach stops, and I was informed that the landlord sometimes netted from £20 to £25 a year by the dog's sagacity. Leaving the Vine, the mountain is approached, first through gullies, till we reach the Mountain Hut, then the ascent begins in earnest. A complete zig-zag, backwards and forwards ; the scenery and excitement being a near approach to the celebrated Blue Mountain Zig-Zag of N.S.W. The 'Eagle's Nest,' and the Eagle Hotel just above ; the villages, and the German township of Hahndorff, are all interesting, and the Jehu a favorite, steady, and trustworthy man.

Coming back to Victoria, Gippsland (before the advent of railways) afforded the tourist some good and pleasurable 'rough riding,' over roads of corduroy and tea-tree and sand ; not without interest and objects of note. The trip by steamer, from Melbourne to Port Albert, in calm weather is charming, from Port Albert to Sale, Cobb's coach, driven by the celebrated 'Tom Plows,' a Jehu well known and universally respected, was the only means of conveyance. Kangaroo and Wallaby were numerous, and afforded amusement to passengers as the coach drove by, and the crack of Tom's whip made them scamper. At one of the road-side hotels, when the coach changed horses, a most singular object of curiosity and interest is pointed out. In the bar of the hotel on a shelf near the ceiling where spare tumblers and bottles were stowed away, a swallow had built its nest in one of the drinking glasses, and for three years had reared its brood. The bird was then flitting about the bar, and the barman reached the tumbler down to show visitors, and as soon as the glass was returned to its place, the bird would perch on the rim.

Crossing the swamp near Sale, over a kind of pontoon bridge, and partly through the water, was another excitement, especially in flood-time, when a boat was often required. 'Tom Plows' was one of those men with whom it is a pleasure to travel, and no matter how high the floods, or however, bad the roads, if 'Tom' was on the box the passengers confidence was established, and safety assured. Another coach road I often travel, is that to the Yan Yean, Morang, Whittle sea, and Plenty district; and, to me, few roads out of Melbourne have a greater charm or a more varied scenery for so short a journey of 25 miles. The conveyance is a leather spring Cobb's, capable of carrying over 30 passengers ; its Jehu is 'Fred. Simmons,' one of the most cheerful, obliging, and good tempered fellows that ever mounted the box, or handled the ribbons. Steady and safe with his team, he is a favorite with all, jocular and pleasant. Washington Irving's characteristics of a coachman describes 'Fred's' case to a T:— He enjoys great consequence and consideration along the road; has frequent chats with the village house wives, who look up to him as a man of great trust and dependence, and he seems to have a good understanding with every bright-eyed country lass.

When off the box he is generally surrounded by an admiring throng. They all look up to him as an oracle. The patronage of the road is given to 'Fred's' coach in an unmistakeable manner, notwithstanding that the fare is higher than that of the Royal mail. His obliging manner has earned it. Passengers often hail his coach, and after looking all over, and peering inside, vexedly call out 'no room!' but 'Fred's' gentle and well-known reminder 'four on a seat inside,' generally provides the accommodation ; but often the coach has been converted into a nursery, not only of babies, but of infants in their teens, and the packing has been as close as that of sardines in an oil tin, or herrings in a cask. Yet, with all this crushing, packing, sweating, and nurring, I never heard a shadow of a murmur or complaint addressed to this popular Jehu of the Whittlesea coach. 'Fred's' jokes are often dry, droll, and amusing to his passengers. Two Chinamen lately seated themselves at the back of the coach, and on turning the corner of Bourke-street, the wind carried away the head-gear of one, who set up a terrific cry, *Hi ! hi ! coachee stop !* Of course the steeds were reined in and John dismounted to have a chase after his runaway Golgotha, exposing his pig tail to the crowd in the street and passengers, much to their amusement ...

On another occasion, on leaving Whittlesea, a not over bright young German was seated on the front seat. During the journey one of the horses got his tail hitched in some way, and the young foreigner was asked to dismount to set it right ; but instead of going to the part indicated he went to the horses head, looking bewildered. *Its his tail, his tail ; don't you know where horses tails grow ; behind, not in front*, cried Fred. The dry manner of delivering the sentence, caused a hearty chuckle, and that young German will remember looking for a horses tail. Fred. is good company at all times, and never allows himself to be drawn into discussions likely to lead to bickering dissensions, but converses with tact and judgment to his many and varied constituents. Other coach roads including Wood end to Daylesford, Avenel to Nagambie, on the Goulburn, etc., have interesting tales to tell if the stones could speak ; but I have run the full length of my tether for this issue, so conclude." (Colonial Coaching and their Jehu's etc, 16 Apr 1886, p.3)

Simmons, Jack ... 1921 See Griffen, Chas.

Sinclair, Dave ... 1917 See Wright, Bob

Skillern, C ... 1919 See Aisbett, E. J.

Slatyer, John
1936 "ABOUT PEOPLE. We extend our sympathy to Mrs. Les. Burrows and Mrs. Les. King, of Bowral, in the death of their father, Mr. John Slatyer, at Goulburn, on Tuesday. He had lived in the Goulburn district for the past sixty years and was at one time a coach driver for Messrs. Cobb and Co. He was greatly interested in musical matters and in addition to being a skilled cornetist was at one time band master of the well-known Goulburn Light Horse Band. Mr. Slatyer was a foundation member of the Goulburn Liedertafel, one of the leading musical societies of the State. He is survived by a widow, one son and three daughters." (About People, 11 Aug 1936, p.3)

Slocum, Hiram
1904 "District News. (FROM OUR CORRESPONDENT.)

GRAYTOWN. On Saturday evening last there passed away one of our oldest residents, Mr. Hiram Slocum, the proprietor of the Bendigo Hotel ... The deceased was 75 years of age, having been born in New York in 1829. He came to this colony in 1853 and for some time he was well known as one of Cobb and Co's drivers. He was a first-class whip and told many stories of his experiences of the diggings days when the roads were bad and the bushrangers were very pressing in their attentions. He came to Spring Creek, soon after the rush and for a long time kept an hotel at Compton's Creek about a mile from the main township. He afterwards purchased the hotel in which he has just died. Mr. Slocum's wife predeceased him about 25 years, and he leaves behind him a grown up family of five sons and four daughters to mourn their sad loss. The funeral took place on Monday, 31st Oct., and was largely attended, the remains being interred in the Graytown Cemetery in the presence of a most representative gathering from the surrounding districts. The funeral service was conducted by the Rev. B. Williams of Heathcote, and the funeral arrangements were carried out in a most satisfactory manner by Mr. H. Baud, Nagambi. (District News, 3 Nov 1904, p.2)

Small, Jimmy ... 1935 See Conroy, James (Jim); Appendix 1.6

Smiles, Frank
1936 "ONE ON THE DEAN! Mr. Frank Smiles, a veteran Cobb and Co. coach driver, tells a star story about Dean Stretch, for many years, known far and wide in this State: The Dean once had a large parish in outback N.S.W. A lover of horses and a good 'whip'. He was presented by a squatter with a fine buggy and four cream ponies. He was driving one day over the plains, wearing a slouch hat and an open shirt, when a swaggie hailed him and asked him for a lift—incidentally a rare thing for swaggies of the old school to do. The cleric was delighted to have company, and someone to open the gates for him. Some approving comments passed on the spanking team of ponies, then the swaggie asked: *When's the rest of the show coming on mister?* The Dean demanded, *What show?* The swaggie looked puzzled, and asked *Ain't you the advance agent for the circus?*" (One on the Dean!, 7 Aug 1936, p.3)

Smiley, Frank
1884 "Mr W. S. Moore, farrier, of Sardinia street, met with a very nasty accident yesterday whilst being driven with a number of other holiday makers to Spring Creek by Frank Smiley, an experienced whip in Cobb and Co.'s employ. The ordinary track was being followed by the driver, but an overhanging tree branch on the left hand side of the road unfortunately struck Mr Moore on the head and inflicted a painful scalp wound. The sufferer at once returned to Geelong, and was attended to by Dr. Newman, who does not anticipate any serious result." (Town Talk, 27 Dec 1884, p.2)

1940 "Pioneers of road transport in Victoria ... The gathering of these veterans of the road at the motor show led to the formation of the Cobb and Co.'s Old Coach Drivers' Association, of which Mr. Frank Smiley, aged 83, is president. He began driving for Cobb and Co. in May, 1877 (63 years ago) on a run from Wickliffe to Warrnambool, and took the last coach from Colac to Camperdown just before the railway was opened in July, 1883." (Link with the Past, 22 May 1940, p. 6)

1954 "THE WORK OF HARRY SMILEY. I recently had the pleasure of meeting Frank Smiley, himself an old-time driver in Victoria and a son of one of the original Americans employed as a driver at the formation of the Cobb and Co. firm in the southern sister State. A fine jovial youngster of 75 years is the same Frank, who was instrumental in forming a Coach Drivers' Reunion Club in Melbourne some time ago, and recently came over here to try and do the same in this State." (Australianites— Cobb and Co. Drivers, 6 May 1932, p.9)

1930 See also Alder, Amos 1937 Atkinson, Frank; 1930-1940s Allan, (Christian name unknown)

Smiley, S. P. (Senior)
1918 "I got on coachdriving for Cobb and Co ... I was driving the night coach from Hamilton to Portland. Tom Ward, Malcolm McCallum, and old Smiley were on the Ballarat line." (The Early Days of Warrnambool, 13 July 1918, p.4)

1937 See also Preston, R.

Smiley, W.
1932 "Old George drove for Cobb & Co. There were coaches running from Dandenong to Cranbourne and the Bass; then to Berwick, and so on. These latter ran after the Main road was made, as before that time horsemen carried the mail, the driving of a trap being an impossibility. Tom Murray, Tom McMahon, and other drivers of recent date, drove coaches, but they do not properly come within the range of the early-day drivers. In 1858 Messrs. Cobb & Co. built stables and offices at the corner of the Main and Pultney streets, and the large underground tank still remains as a memento of the old coaching days. When Mr. Peter Evans bought the building, which he converted into a bootmaking shop, it was often remarked upon why such a small establishment required such a large tank but those who enquired were not aware that that large tank was not more than sufficiently large to water the big string of horses required for the coaches. The coach from Dandenong to Bass ran three times weekly. Its original driver was George Wright ('Old George.'). He was followed by J. Moorhouse, after whom came W. Smiley, and the last driver of that line was Charlie Wilson." (Reminiscences Early Days of Dandenong, 16 Jun 1932, p.7)

Smith, James
1925 "COBB'S COACH DRIVER. There went to Melbourne from Ballarat on Tuesday by invitation from the Motor Exhibition committee, Mr. James Smith, one of the oldest surviving of the famous Cobb's coach drivers in the Western district. Mr. Smith joined Cobb's service in 1875, at Hamilton, and for many years drove the famous coaches between there and Portland, Warrnambool and Ballarat. He stated that there was one man in Melbourne who was boasting that he was the oldest living coach driver, but, added Mr Smith, *That boy was at school when I drove the old Cobb's coach. I'll show him!* Mr. Robert McGregor was one of those who farewelled the veteran on his way to the metropolis to 'show him!' Mr. Smith was enthusiastic over his opportunity to visit Melbourne and compare the motors of to-day with the coach ... He is old, as he confesses, but he is as 'tough as a leather spring.'" (Cobb's Coach Driver, 8 May 1925, p.8)

Smith, Ted
1876 "ACTION AGAINST COBB AND CO. In the District Court on Wednesday, an action was brought up by a man named Fogarty against the firm of Cobb and Co., for injuries sustained by him through being knocked down by coach horses on the Orange and Forbes road … the coach was driven by Ted Smith ; it was going at the rate of about nine miles an hour at the time." (Action Against Cobb and Co, 2 Sep 1876, p.7)

Smith, Walter Oliver
1899 "I am sorry to say I have quite a Chapter of accidents and casualties this week … Messrs. Cobb and Co.'s coach left Barcaldine on Wednesday morning about 3.30 with nine passengers on board. While bowling along about three miles from town, at the rate of six miles an hour, the horses suddenly swerved at a dead dog lying in the track, and became hopelessly entangled, the vehicle turning over, throwing the passengers in various directions. Fortunately the pole broke right off, and the seven horses made a dash for the bush. A man sitting on top of the coach was thrown some distance, but received nothing worse than a shaking … Mr. Walter Smith, the driver, was thrown violently to the ground, and lay unconscious for a few minutes." (The Barcoo, 23 Jan 1889, p.6)

1935 "LIGHTS OF COBB AND CO. LAST OF THE OLD DRIVERS PASSING. (Special for the 'News.') By the death of Walter Oliver Smith at Mount Morgan, there passed away one of the few surviving drivers of the coaches of Cobb and Co., when they operated in Central Queensland. Mr Smith was one of the most capable and trusted drivers employed by the famous coaching company in the Central-West, before the coming of the railway. One of his special duties was to convey the Judge and Crown Prosecutor when on the Central Circuit. His most frequent passengers on these trips was the late Judge Blake, who was mostly accompanied by the late Mr. Justice Real as Crown Prosecutor. The old coach driver had, many amusing stories to tell of these trips.

SCARED OF DINGOES AND SNAKES. The Judge had a horror of snakes and dingoes. Oftimes the part had to camp for the night in the bush. The coachman and Crown Prosecutor would proceed to make themselves comfortable under canvas, but His Honour preferred to sit all night in the coach. Needless to say he did not get much sleep, and in his waking moments, which were frequent, he would disturb the others by calling out to the Crown Prosecutor: *Paddy, wake up man and come here. The dingoes will have you before morning* … The Judge always carried a bottle of brandy on the western trip, which he zealously guarded for use solely in case of snakebite. If there was no-call to use it, and there never was, he would give it to the married coach driver handling the ribbons on the last stage of the circuit.

BUCKET BATH. Judge Blake was very particular about his daily bath, a somewhat difficult matter to arrange in the West in those days. More often than not it would be contrived on the bank of a lagoon or creek, His Honour standing on a log whilst the Crown Prosecutor and coachman, working in relays, doused him with buckets of water. His toilet completed he would arrive in town in time for the Court to sit" (Lights of Cobb And Co., 24 Jan 1935, p.6)

1917 See also Wright, Bob

Smythman, (Christian name unknown)
1880 "THE COACH ACCIDENT.—This has been a very quiet week, and except the accident to Cobb's coach not much to report. After the driver was thrown off the horses started down the Wellington Lane and only stopped at the end—breaking the pole and damaging themselves and the coach. They became entangled and that brought them to a stand still. A fresh coach was sent off as soon as possible, and Mr. Smythyman came to Wellington. Dr. Rygate set his collarbone, and he is getting right again, but was much shaken." (Wellington, 15 May 1880, p.39)

Snell, Charlie
1925 Snakes anecdote "Generally once a year, when the winter has been a wet one at the head of the Darling River and the snow commences to melt at the head of the Murray, there is trouble for the mail contractor running along these rivers. We had 500 miles of such tracks to contend with. The rivers overflow their banks, always by way of creeks or billabongs, and these are nearly always feeders of sometimes big lakes, being miles around, so that when the creek or billabong becomes too deep to cross, it means many miles extra going round it. Sometimes great risks are taken by drivers in crossing these places sooner than go around.

Each day the water gets a little deeper, and the horses get used to it, until you will see the leaders have to swim a few yards before getting their feet again. I've seen the horses swim and plunge twenty yards sometimes before they get their footing again, and the coach half floating and bumping. It used to be very risky work, and only horses used to it could get through. All mails, etc., and passengers had to be put above water line on top of the coach. I remember one incident in particular which occurred when crossing one at these creeks just below Salt Creek on the border of South Australia and New South Wales. This part of the Murray, I should think, would compare favorably with any other part of the world for snakes. They are there in thousands in the long buffalo sort of grass that covers the Murray flats there. On this particular morning we stopped at one of these flooded creeks. Only the driver (Charlie Snell) and myself were aboard, and when the former surveyed the rise in water since he had previously, crossed, he remarked: *It's a bit risky today, but I think we can get across. Anyway, it will be the last time for a month or so. We'll have to go around the lake in future.* Just while we were making everything fast on the coach top, about a dozen snakes came out of the grass on to the road just in front and about the horses. Snell, a bit of a wag, looked at them, and said: *No mail for you today, gentlemen*, and turning to me, added: *I get a visit from this crowd every day. You will see some of them will escort us across the water.* And sure enough they did.

As the horses walked into the water half a dozen of the snakes also, wriggled in, and swam across ahead of us, some turning back and others going right across. I remember that on this morning the horses swam and plunged quite thirty yards, hauling the five-passenger coach after them in the middle of the stream. One of our old drivers, Andy Blake, was a wonderful man at getting along through these annual flooded, conditions. My old friend. Mr. Fred Crews—now a retired, speculator living in Perth, but 50 years ago Adelaide's most dapper and probably best coach driver—used to be the mail contractor on this Murray mail for years" (Coaching in the Commonwealth, 7 June 1925, p.11)

Snell, E ... 1919 See Aisbett, E. J.

Snuffkins, (Christian name unknown)
1933 "THE COACHIE STRIKES A SNAG. As a rule the Cobb & Co. drivers were a civil and obliging lot of men, but Snuffkins proved the inevitable exception. He lorded it over the grooms and passenger-public to such an extent and threatened the world a hiding with his impatient 'maulies' so frequently, that, a number of the squatter boys along the stage subscribed a nice little purse of pounds and got into touch with Abe Hicken, the pugilistic champion in Melbourne, requesting him to send up a lively-fisted party to put the coachie in his place, promising him the purse in return for the favor extended. Up came the lad from Melbourne who, upon requesting the box-sent in the politest manner was told by the bully-driver that he'd *go where he was put.* At the first change of horses the Townie entered the pub adjacent for a drink, when in came the driver breasting the bar and elbowing him aside in the ribs. *You're a bit fussy, aren't you?* said the traveller inoffensively. *Fussy be damned: I'm the boss of this road, and I don't take any back chat from the like o' you. Come outside if you don't like it. Right you are,* said the other, following him into the stable-yard, attended by about a score of bar-loungers eager to see the fun. *I don't suppose I need bother taking my coat off,* said the man from Melbourne *You might just as well,* said the coachdriver, *you'll need your waistcoat and shirt off before I'm done with you.* Two rounds settled it, condition and science won in a walk, and the flash[?] driver had to be assisted up to his seat when the stage was resumed a few minutes later with his late adversary riding proudly on the box-seat beside him as he proceeded upon his way to receive his reward." (The Coachie Strikes a Snag, 11 May 1933, p.2)

Stackpole, T ... 1919 See Aisbett, E. J.

Stephen, J ... 1933 See Leviston, W.

Stephens, Edward
1940 "A Long Life and A Merry One. Some secrets on the art of growing old gracefully—and happily—may be learned by 'youngsters' in their 80s from Mr Edward Stephens, of Stawell, a veteran of Victoria, who will reach his century on May 7. Mr Stephens has set several records. He probably will be the first male citizen born in Victoria to reach the century mark. He has already celebrated his platinum wedding, having been happily married for 73 years. And he does not attribute his old age to a quiet and uneventful life. According to his nephew, Mr Frank Campbell, of Caulfield. Edward Stephens began work as a horse wrangler to his father at the age of 12. A year later he was driving a transport team between Melbourne and Ballarat. He saw the Eureka Stockade at 16 and at 18 was a temporary driver for Cobb and Co. He drove with Freeman Cobb on the first coach to enter Ballarat and he often spoke with Captain Moonlight, the bushranger. At 100 he has a fine head of hair, does not need glasses, walks without a stick, plays the flute, eats heartily and smokes strong tobacco. He was still ploughing and drilling with an eight-horse team at 80, and riding his hack at 95. Following the horses does not always bring grey hairs before their time!" (A Long Life and A Merry One, 18 Jan 1940, p.9)

(Surname unknown), Steve
1858 "We are off through Main Road dust ... on the box is one lucky individual, who is privileged as a familiar for to call the coachman 'Steve,' and sit beside him. *Horresco referens!* I subsequently attained to the seat, but was again for a while deposed, as the Ballan landlady's pretty daughter usurped my place, and 'Steve,' like a sensible good-looking fellow as he was, maliciously swore there was 'only room for two,'—three of us comfortably enjoying the seat all the way to 'Melbourne direct', after the pretty girl aforesaid was transferred to the up coach we met near Pentland Hills." (A Spell Off, 6 Nov 1858, p.2)

Stevenson, George ... 1925 See Atkins, W.

Sting, Rawley
1917 "ST. GEORGE TO SURAT ... as the five horses, with never a protest, swung the coach out by the new hotel and rumbled through the silent Terrace to the Post Office, where bags and packages under the superintendence of Postmaster Roebush, were rolled down the steps of the post office and packed in boot and rear for delivery along the road to Surat, 80 miles distant, Yeulba, and Brisbane. A call at Cobb and Co.'s booking office and store, where more packages were obtained ... The team of five fine white horses were well handled by Driver Rawley Sting ... Bogorrah change house is an iron hut set near the river side, 17 miles from St. George where a pleasant and very welcome breakfast is provided." (Coaching in Australia, 1917, pp.65-67)

Stirling, J. L ... 1921 See Griffen, Chas.

Stokes, (Christian name unknown)
1918 "Driver Stokes writes to Mr. Vines from Wiltshire, England, that he is with a training battalion getting ready to return to France. He is learning French and says things are 'no bong' (soldiers' French for not good). Driver Stokes is well-known to the travelling public, having driven for Cobb and Co. in the Geelong district for over ten years." (News of Geelong and District Soldiers, 31 Jan 1918, p.6)

Stratton, (Christian name unknown)
1930 "History of Rosedale ... Apparently the flood legends of later years were based upon personal experience, the river's most threatening demonstration being in 1866, when 16 feet of water flowed over the causeway. This was the occasion of the tragic happening to Cobb and Co.'s coach, when driver Stratton and his four horses were swept away and drowned in the swirling waters. Lesser episodes were the floods of 1889 and 1899, when the depth of water on the flats was seven feet. Although in these onslaughts of Mother Latrobe the overflow made approach to the town unpleasant and risky the river never invaded its streets, which were constructed above flood levels." (History of Rosedale, 22 Mar 1930, p.10)

Strickland, Joe ... 1928 See Frost, James (Old Jim Frost); 1929 Corbett, Alec.

Sullivan, (Christian name unknown)
1884 "QUEENSLAND. Fatal Coach Accident. Brisbane, Friday. Sullivan, a coach driver at Charters Towers, fell from the box and broke his neck." (Queensland—Fatal Coach Accident,

29 Jan 1884, p.3)

1930-1940s See also Allan, (Christian name unknown)

Summers, Frank ... 1875 See Turner, Bob (Big Bob)

Sutcliffe, Bill ... 1917 See Wright, Bob

Swanton/Swanston, James
1888 "THE END OF COBB AND CO. IN SANDHURST. The noted coaching firm of Cobb and Co., so far as Sandhurst is concerned, is dead killed by the railway. Few names are so well known in Australia, and as long as the memory of coaching days lives the name will live with it. When the fame of the Victorian goldfields had spread over the world and population began to flow in from all countries, an enterprising American firm of carriers, Adam's New York Express Carrying Co., sent an agent, in the person of Mr. Freeman Cobb, for the purpose of opening up a similar express business in the colony. A line of coaches was speedily established between Melbourne and Sandhurst in 1854. The Sandhurst office was in the Mall about where the shop of Mr. Osborne, watchmaker, stands, next the Shamrock hotel. Three remarkably skilful drivers—J. Pack, J. R. Lambert and J. Swanston—were engaged. They were important men in those days, for owing to the dangers of the road, life and limb depended on their skilful handling of the reins. Reminiscences of these early travels are amongst the pleasant and exciting memories of all old Bendigonians. The swimming of the coach in seas of mud and the bumping over the corduroy road, when hats and heads, it is said, used to go through the roof of the vehicle, can be amply testified to.

In 1855 Cobb sold out to T. Davis, who carried on for a couple of years and then sold to the *Victorian Stage Company*, which was composed of the drivers and several others. This company desired that Mr. Crowley, of the Albion Hotel, Sandhurst, should look after the financial affairs of the company in Melbourne, but he did not see his way to do so, but he was their agent in Sandhurst. At the same time Mr. Crowley lent one member of the company, Mr. A. L. Blake, £500 to purchase his share in it, and so lucrative was the carrying trade that in two months time Mr. Crowley had his money back. About 1864, the office of the company in Sandhurst was shifted to the Williamson-street side of the Shamrock Hotel, and it there remained until it finally closed the other day.

Messrs. Watson and Hewitt bought out the *Victorian Stage Co.*, but after a year or so they sold out to Messrs. Robertson, Wagner, and Co., who maintained the business until its close. This firm attended to the public wants with a faithfulness worthy of all praise, and by their energy and enterprise the high repute of Cobb and Co., was firmly established in this and the surrounding districts. They extended the coaching to Inglewood, Heathcote, and Swan Hill. An extraordinary thing in connection with the Cobb and Co. firm, of this and, we believe, of other districts, was its reliability. Ten miles an hour was the travelling rate, and time was kept to the minute, so to speak, no matter what the difficulties or dangers to be overcome. Particular attention was paid to employing only first class men as drivers, and it is most creditable to the Sandhurst branch that very few accidents ever happened, the only serious one we believe, being that at the steep and dangerous gully of the Buckeye, when the coach was capsized and the driver killed. The opening of the Heathcote railway is the last straw that brought this famous company to an end on Sandhurst, that being the only route on which a coach was running from this centre." (The End of Cobb and Co. n Sandhurst, 8 Sep 1888, p.5)

1922 "Of the new firms which now entered into the coaching business, Swanton and Blake are said to have been members of the original 12 partnership of Cobb and Company, and to have themselves driven some of the first of Cobb's coaches" (Cobb and Co, 20 Jun 1922, p.13)

1942 "John Murray Peck, Freeman Cobb, James Swanton and John Lamber, all from the United States, as partners, originated Cobb and Co ... Peck and Swanton, who were outstanding whips (the former once drove a team of 14 coupled in pairs with 40-passenger 'Jack' coach to Melbourne Cup) managed the lines, and often drove themselves. Lamber looked after the Melbourne stables and the providoring, and Cobb, who was a little lame man, ran the office and the finance." (Memoirs of a Stockman, 1942, p.16)

Sweeney, Joseph Francis
1891 "RELICS OF THE FIFTIES. Talking about countrymen, I must not forget to mention the death of Joseph Francis Sweeney, an old time coachdriver, well known throughout the colony as one of Cobb and Co.'s reliable whips in the early days." (Melbourne Notes, 20 Mar 1891, p.2)

Taverner, John ... 1908 See Byrne, F. A.

Taylor, Charles
1940 "MR. CHARLES TAYLOR. One of the few remaining links with the coaching days of Cobb & Co. was broken with the death at the Dubbo District Hospital yesterday morning of Mr. Charles Taylor. Born at Kyneton (Vic.), 75 years ago, he was one of the drivers in that State and the Riverina for Cobb & Co., and had many interesting stories to tell of the stirring coaching days that preceded the growth of the railways. He had resided in New South Wales for many years, having been married at Hay, and he was a familiar figure about Dubbo." (Mr. Charles Taylor, 31 Oct 1940, p.3)

Taylor, J. P ... 1919 See Aisbett, E. J.

Templeton/Templenton, (Christian name unknown) (Later Mrs. Burnside) ... 1930-1940s See Allan, (Christian name unknown)

Templeton, Andy ... 1938 See Templeton, Herb.

Templeton, Ernie (Ern)
1908 "The information to hand states that the accident occurred on the approach to Cobb and Co.'s stables at Tyers ... One brake broke on an incline near Ingleson's farm ... The five horses now got beyond the control of the driver, and tore wildly down the hill, near the bottom of which all the occupants of the coach, seven in all, were tossed out. The coach was capsized. The names of the occupants were Ernie Templeton (driver) ... The driver, Templeton, who has the reputation of being one of the most reliable whips in Victoria, reached Moe at 10.15 p.m., driving the much-damaged coach" (Ladies injured in coach

accident, 5 May 1908, p.3)

1950 "MR E. TEMPLETON. At about 4.30 p.m. last Saturday, Mr Ern. Templeton, of Moore Street, quietly passed away in his sleep. He was 76 years of age and had not enjoyed good health for a long time, although confined to his bed for seven weeks only. During that time, he recovered from an attack of dropsy, but his heart was very weak. The late Mr Templeton was a son of the late Mr and Mrs Andrew Templeton, his father probably being the first driver of coaches between Moe and Walhalla, and with his brothers (Herb, and Will.). He later followed in his father's footsteps. He was a driver for Cobb and Co. until coaching was discontinued. In 1938, when the Back-to-Moe celebrations were held, 'Ern' drove through the town a 'six-in-hand.' His part in the 'back-to' procession was a decided whiff of the past, and as such was appreciated by all old-timers.

For some years, Mr Ern. Templeton was an employee of the Narracan Shire Council and was stationed at Erica where his wife (formerly Miss Elsie Murie) had resided, her people also being pioneers of that district. When they came to Moe, they took up residence in the home always occupied by the Templeton family, in Moore Street. Mr Templeton joined the staff of Williams and Rayner's garage, and drove the mail car from Moe to Fumina for many years. He became just as attached to the car—a Buick that 'did' more than 140,000 miles—as he had been to horses. Deceased had a quiet disposition, but a keen sense of humor. He was always obliging and helpful on his routes, and was highly respected by all with whom he came in contact. He leaves a widow, a daughter (Doris, Mrs A. Budge, of Lower Plenty) and a son ('Bill', of Sydney), and his only surviving sister (Mrs F. E. Knight) resides at Moe West. To all goes the sincerest sympathy of many friends. At deceased's home on Monday afternoon, a service was conducted by Rev. P. Ackland, prior to the long funeral cortege leaving for the Moe cemetery, where Rev. Ackland again officiated. The coffin-bearers were Messrs W. Templeton (son), A. Budge (son-in-law), A. Knight and A. Templeton (nephews). Among the chief mourners as deceased's only surviving brother 'Bob,' who is 72 years of age, and resides in Woodside, South Gippsland. The large and representative assemblage of district residents and the many beautiful floral tributes bore testimony to the esteem in which deceased was held. Mr F. Halden had charge of the funeral arrangements." (Obituary, 31 Mar 1950, p. 7)

1938 See also Templeton, Herb.

Templeton, Herb.
1938 "Cobb & Co's. Coach. The next event of importance was the arrival (from the direction of Walhalla) of Cobb & Co.'s coach, drawn by four horses and driven by Mr. Ern. Templeton, himself an old coach-driver, and a son of the late veteran driver, Mr. Andy Templeton, who drove the first coach into Walhalla. He had as passengers … Messrs. Geo. Nicholson (Melbourne) and Herb. Templeton (Oakleigh), both old coachdrivers" (Cobb & Co's. Coach, 22 Apr 1938, p.3)

Tery, Pat … See Appendix 1.6

Teys, Alex … 1917 See Wright, Bob; 1948 Herchberg/Hertsberg, Joseph (Joe)

Teys, Dave … 1917 See Anderson, Jim; 1938 Anderson, Thomas (Tom); 1947 Richards, J. Frederick (Fred)

Thomas, (Christian name unknown)
1939 "Mrs. Catherine Ann Lenihan, who died on Tuesday, 26th December, had lived in Roma nearly 60 years. Born at Condamine township in 1870, she was the third daughter of the late Mr. Thomas and Mrs. Merritt. Her father was a coachdriver for Cobb & Co., and drove coaches as far west as Charleville. After residing with her parents in Roma for some years, she married the late Mr. William Lenihan, who predeceased her about 14 years. Of a quiet disposition and kindly nature, Mrs. Lenihan made a host of friends. She leaves a family of three sons, Messrs. Thomas P. (Roma), William J. (Brisbane), and Charles M. (Roma)." (Obituary, 30 Dec 1939, p.2)

Thompson, A … 1917 See Richardson, W.; 1917 Wright, Bob

Thompson, Alf & Thompson, Bill … 1921 See Griffen, Chas.

Thompson, Fred. A.
1954 "A COBB & CO. DRIVER SPEAKS OF MUNGINDI … driving a Cobb and Co. coach to Mungindi from 1904 onwards. Mr. Thompson drove on several routes, including Mungindi-Thallon, Thallon-St George, Cunnamulla-Thargomindah and Mitchel-St George" (A Cobb & Co. Driver Speaks Of Mungindi, 20 Apr 1954, p.7)

"The old drivers to at last lay down their reins were: Fred Thompson who drove the last Cobb & Co. Coach in Australia on the Yuleba-Surat run in 1924." (Communications Across the Generations, Read 1971, p.188)

Thompson, Jack
1951 "A well known resident of Hughenden, Mrs. Margaret Thompson, passed away there recently at the age of 83. The late Mrs. Thompson came to Australia from Ireland as a young woman and she had lived over half a century in Hughenden. Her husband, the late Mr. Jack Thompson, was a coach driver for Cobb and Co. for many years, on the Hughenden-Muttaburra and Prairie-Muttaburra runs. Mrs. Thompson is survived by two sons, Henry (Townsville) and George (Hughenden)." (Obituary, 30 Nov 1951, p.3)

Thompson, Joe
1917 "Among other drivers were Peter Torquay, on the Lambing Flat road, when Gardner stuck up the coach; Jim Nairn, driver of the coach out from Bathurst; Dan Mayne; Joe Thompson; and Jack Barry on the Mudgee road, a great one for pulling one's leg." (Coaching in Australia, 1917, p.27)

1925 See also Eddie, Nathan

Thompson, Johnny
1895 "One early Sunday morning before sunrise saw me speeding northward, the only passenger on Cobb's four-horse coach, with Johnny Thompson, the genial driver, as my guide, philosopher, and friend until Hughenden was reached. The morning was beautifully fine, the weather cool and invigorating, and the horses in good heart, and the time sped pleasantly on." (Rockhampton and the West, 30 Mar 1895, p.603)

1953 "Sixty-four years ago Mrs. Sellers' first husband (the late Mr. J. Thompson) was a Cobb and Co. driver on the Aramac-Mutaburra-Barcaldine run … Back about 1890, she and her husband lived on a coach stopping station about 11 miles from Barcaldine on land that Cobb and Co. rented from Corina Station. Teams were changed at this stopping place, which had stables and a grass paddock for the specially bred coach horses. *I was often called out of bed at 3 o'clock in the morning to make tea for passengers—but those were good days*, said Mrs. Sellers yesterday … The company had two types of coaches at Barcaldine, one drawn by five greys and the other, a larger type, drawn by a team of seven greys and bays. *A team of seven—two sets and two and three lead horses—took some driving*, she said. Mrs. Sellers often rode into Barcaldine and out to Corina Station again in Cobb and Co. coaches and says that the coaches were well sprung and gave the passengers a wonderful ride—almost like riding in one of today's modern buses … When railway tracks were laid to Aramac Mr. and Mrs. Thompson went to live and work on Mt. Cornish station not far from Muttaburra. Years later they came to Warwick where Mr. Thompson died … And now, with the Cobb's means of transport improved out of existence by trains, motors and aeroplanes, yet another element of romance has faded away" (Coach Brought Back Memories, 31 Oct 1953, p.2)

1917 See also Richardson, W.

Thoms, Wm.
1877 "LATE EPITOME OF NEWS … Tuesday's 'Tamworth News' says:—Cobb and Co.'s up-coach met with an accident, on Sunday morning, about a mile and a half South of Goonoo Goonoo, which, although not resulting in any serious casualty, caused considerable fright and suffering. The coach left Murrurundi with 14 passengers, the driver, Wm. Thoms, very properly refusing to take two more—importunate to get on—one of whom was an invalid. The night dark and foggy—the fog so thick, in fact, that Mr. Ross, of Inverell, who occupied a box-seat, could not see the leaders' heads. That gentle man bestows unqualified praise on the care and forethought of the driver, who, on foot, led the horse for some miles before, and was so conducting them when the accident occurred. As the coach was thus proceeding along a sideling on the track, which was very slippery in consequence of the rain, it gradually slided downwards, and a sudden jerk at the bottom caused it to capsize. All the passengers received a disagreeable shock … M'Donald was much bruised and shaken. Mrs. Harper of Armidale, and Mrs. Ross, wife of the gentleman before mentioned, were nearly smothered before they were extricated from a heap of passengers, portmanteaus, and bags." (Late Epitome of News, 18 May 1877, p.5)

Thomson, H.
1950 "A link with the early west was severed at Hughenden this week when the death occurred of Mr. H. Thomson, at the age of 91. Mr. Thomson, in his early days, was a driver for Cobb and Co. on the Muttaburra-Hughenden run and on occasions relieved on the Winton and Richmond runs. It is claimed that he was the sole survivor of that great band of pioneers who drove the famous coaches and still lived in the west. Of recent years he resided with his son, Mr. Geo. Thomson, of Byers street, Hughenden. He is also survived by his widow." (Obituary, 24 May 1950, p.2)

Thornton, Matt (Mat.) … 1921 See Griffen, Chas.; 1934 Hole, Mat.; 1934 Alexander, Jack

Todd, (Christian name unknown) (Father of John) … 1948 See Todd, John Henry

Todd, Jimmy
1925 "Jimmy Nicholas … Another man who went through the coaching with me for the past 32 years is little Jimmy Todd, who is not very big but is all man. He is still with me, forgetting coaching and learning sheep. Jim Richards ('Brummy') was generally classed as being one of the best, if not actually the best, drivers in Australia 45 years ago, but the poor old chap has outlived his usefulness, as I saw him a few years ago in Sydney driving a one-horse buggy for a commercial traveller. Right through my coaching experience I have noticed each town or district had its pet driver. Commencing at Goulburn, where the rail from Sydney had reached when I joined Cobb and Co., that town had its pet in 'Brummy.' Jim Richards was favorite further up the line. About Young Cootamundra and Wagga, Jimmy Foy [Loy] was the selected one. Albury had its George Carter; Deniliquin had Tom Ploughs ; Hay had Bill Keast, and Wilcannia Dick Daley, while Broken Hill and that part (held by myself) always did me the honor of wiring to me to come along and drive any Royalty Governors, etc., that may have come to the Hill." (Coaching in the Commonwealth, 24 May 1925, p.11)

Todd, John Henry
1948 "LINK WITH COBB & CO. LAST OF LOCAL DRIVERS DEAD. With the death last Saturday, at the age of 69, of John Henry Todd, another link with the old coaching days was broken. Mr. Todd is said to have been the last of the Cobb and Co. coachmen in this district. He had been living in Hay for about 30 years … From the time he was 17 or 18, Mr. Todd was groom and coachman to Cobb and Co.; his father also had been one of their drivers. When the company passed into other hands—though it still traded as 'Cobb and Co.'—Mr. Todd kept the job on. He drove on several runs; for some years he was on the Hillston-Carrathool run, and also travelled between Hay and Booligal, Hay and Balranald; Deniliquin and Ivanhoe were also on his runs at different periods. His favourite team was four greys … He often spoke of the old coaching days, recalling the wide variety of people whom he had met; he made many friends in his work" (Link with Cobb & Co., 30 Jul 1948, p.2)

Toohey, Denis (Denny)
1923 "This brings to my mind another institution of those early days, to wit, H.M. Mail, per favour of Cobb and Co's. coaches, under the capable whip of Mr. Denis Toohey. It used to be a source of admiration to me as a boy to watch the departure of the mail coach for Orange, with a shout and flourish of Denny's long whip; off and away, tearing through the mud, at an eight to ten mile an hour gait. Often times teams bringing merchandise would be inextricably 'stuck fast' in some bog on the road for a week or two, awaiting the hold up of the rainfall, to get out again." (Pioneering in the Parkes District, 19 Apr 1923, p.25)

Toohey, Pat … 1917 See Anderson, Jim

Toohey, Peter ... 1935 See Conroy, James (Jim)

Torbury, Peter ... 1932 See Breen, Jim (Jimmy)

Torquay, Peter ... 1917 See Thompson, Joe; 1923 Robinson, James (Robbie)

Toy, James (Jim) ... 1934 See Carter, John (Jack); 1935 Conroy, James (Jim)

Toy, Percy ... 1912 See Miller, Ted

Tranter, J. J.
1951 "COBB AND CO. COACH IN SHOW PAGEANT ... Phases of Clarence history and development will be re-enacted and displayed at the night session of the C.P. and A. Society's annual show on Thursday. Among the exhibits will be a Cobb and Co. mail coach, which was at one time on the Grafton-Glen Innes run. This will be a unit in the road transport feature which includes packhorses, buckboards and other vehicles through to the early models of popular cars and trucks to the latest streamlined, powerfull versions. The old coach will be driven by Mr. J. J. Tranter, sen., of Woolgoolga. He was one of the regular drivers when the mail coaches were the chief means of connection between important country centres." (Cobb and Co. Coach in Show Pageant, 10 Apr 1951, p.2)

Treloar, Tom ... 1921 See Griffen, Chas.

Tuite, William Henry
1935 "The death occurred suddenly, at Eulo, on Monday last, of Mr. William Henry Tuite, at the age of 57 years. He was born at Merriwa, N.S. Wales, and had for many years past been a resident of the Eulo and Cunnamulla districts. He will be well remembered by many old western residents, having been for over a quarter of a century a driver of Cobb and Co.'s mail coaches. About 18 years ago he resigned from Cobb and Co. and took over the management of the Gladstone Hotel, Eulo, where he had resided with his wife and family up till the time of his death. He leaves a widow and family of five sons and two daughters to mourn their loss. A son is Ald. W. Tuite, of Murrurundi." (Obituary, 2 Aug 1935, p.5)

1917 See also Wright, Bob

Tully, Frank
1934 "In referring to the death in Melbourne of Mr. Frank Tully, the 'Mallee Harvester.' Murrayville. states:—Mr. Tully who was 61 years of age was born in Hamilton and drove Cobb and Co's coaches from Hamilton to Portland and Port Fairy. He subsequently engaged in station work in the Hamilton and Skipton districts. He came to Cow Plains Station, Cowangie, before the railway was put through, the nearest station on the Victorian side, being Ouyen, and on the South Australian side, Pinnaroo. When Murrayville was opened for settlement, Mr. Tully and family moved to this town, and for years before the railway came through he drove the coach from Murrayville to Pinnaroo. Mr. Tully's house, which the family still occupy, was the first house in Murrayville, and his son Murray of Red Cliffs, was the first child born in Murrayville. Subsequently he was employed by the Shire of Walpeup for many years ... He leaves his widow and seven children to mourn his loss, and one daughter died in infancy. The members of his family are: Messrs. Austin, Samuel, and Frank Tully, and Mrs. Johnson, all of Murrayville; Murray Tully of Red Cliffs; Mrs. C. Crane and Frank Tully, both of Ngallo; and Rosalie, who died in infancy. Two brothers of the deceased, Messrs. W. and M. Tully, live at Hamilton; another brother, Mr. A. Tully, lives at Warrnambool; and his sister, Mrs. E. Bond, lives at Koroit." (Obituary, 30 Mar 1934, p.2)

Turner, Bob (Big Bob)
1875 and republished in The Lorgnette in 1889 "VELVET AND NAGS. By Robert P. Whitworth. (By permission of the Author) ... During a good many years of life in Australia, it has been my fortune to travel much, both by sea and land. I have experienced the dirt and discomfort of the steerage of a coasting schooner, the ease and elegance of the saloon of an ocean steamer. Railway and road, bush and river, horseback and on foot, in dray and in buggy, by coach and by boat ... Each method of travelling has its delights, each its annoyances, its comforts, and its discomforts. None has more of each, or less of each, according to circumstances and temperament, than has that throne, of Jehu, that place of proud pre-eminence, the seat of Phillip 'Cobb's Box' ... These, and for years after, were the palmy days of Cobb's coaches, these were the days that made the name of the line a house hold word throughout the length and breadth of many lands, these were the days that immortalised 'Cobb,' the good rough and tumble old times when it was a favor to get a place at all in Cobb's coaches, and the highest honor mortal man could aspire to, was to obtain a seat on 'Cobb's Box'.

One by one they have left, these hardy pioneers of the road, these men who recked not of danger, who smiled in the face of difficulties, who calmly looked at impossibilities and—overcame them. Furious driving, I grant you, a reckless disregard, sometimes, of their own, and their passengers necks. Probably. But what else would have done, let me ask ? There was no time then to stand, shilly-shallying on the edge of a swamp, no use hesitating at taking a header down a steep gully with a broken boulder or a thick slimy, bottom. It was a shake of the reins, a crack of the stinging whipcord, a heigh ! ho ! houp la ! a mad plunge, a creaking of springs, a straining of harness, a flying of mud and gravel, and a get out at full gallop on the other side, for, you know, Her Majesty's mails must not be delayed, and Her Majesty's lieges, of those days, bronzed diggers for the most part, would not brook many stoppages.

One by one, I say, have these pioneers of the road quitted ... As I have said, I have travelled, many a mile with Cobb, always, when I could, on Cobb's Box. What special charm there is in a box seat, I can hardly tell. It is certainly not the most comfortable position in the coach, exposed as it is to the broiling heat and choking dust of summer, and the piercing wind, rain, and sleet of winter ... for him who shares the throne of the monarch of the road. He becomes part and parcel of the coach, he has a vested interest in the team. He shares in the admiring greeting accorded, as of right, to his companion by passers by, he claims half the smile of buxom landladies and pretty barmaids, he feels himself personally interested in the off wheeler's capped hock, and the grey leader's blind eye, and he even cries, 'Wo, steady, old girl,' when, the kicking mare is being hitched to, at the third stage. He interchanges tobacco and drinks with the great man, he sits on the same seat, his legs are covered with the same rug ... This is Cobb's box, what more would you— could you have ?

All in the morning early, ere yet the magpie hath ceased his rich metallic matin song, ere yet the dee drops are off the grass, ere yet the possum, with querulous whimper, hath sought his lair, ere yet the sun hath risen from his vast bath far away to the eastward, comes a rap at the door of the room in the shanty where you have slept so soundly, you hear the shuffling and scuffling incidental to so many people rising in a hurry, and at an unwonted hour, and in five minutes, half dressed, and ready for the cup of coffee waiting you at the bar, you emerge, yawning, not quite awake, cross, cold, and miserable. Your coffee scalds your throat as you gulp it down, your travelling companions growl and grumble in odd corners, a half clad groom, with bits of hay sticking in his unkempt hair, treads on your toes as he lumbers past, without so much as, 'with your leave,' or 'by your leave.'

The grey morning seems damp, and the air raw and uncomfortable But, by-and-by, the driver comes in, great coated and muffled, but fresh and rosy. *Now then, all aboard.* You mount the box, there is a shaking of reins, a rattle of harness, a little playing up from the chestnut mare, who stands on her hind legs and looks round, as who would say, *now then you sleepy heads, I'm awake, if you are not*, a smack of the whip, a plunge into the collar, and away you go. What a change. By the time you have crossed the creek, and topped the first rise out of the valley, the sun is shooting his golden arrows at you through the thick bush to the right, the atmosphere is growing warmer, the sweet smelling incense to the God of day is wafted from wattle flower, wand May bloom, and tender leaved peppermint on the breath of the fitful morning breeze. You drink in fresh life with every inhalation, see fresh beauty at every glance, the purple and yellow heath glows with a brighter hue, the glossy leaved veronica bushes shine with a richer lustre ... Now for a breather 'Heigh, houp la,' a shake of the reins, a crack of the silken whipcord, and the gallant team breaks into a spanking rack, half trot half canter. How they snort and whisk their tails ... How every buckle and every bit, and every clinking chain tinkles like a silver bell, harmonising merrily with the deep dull diapason of the wheels grinding over the hard road. Ah me ! this is indeed the poetry of motion ...

But there is a dark side to the picture, as I well know. And yet, even that has its joys. The rain, the pitiless sleet, cutting your face like a thousand sharp edged knives. Deep dangerous rivers to ford, steep hills to climb, cold, wet, discomfort. The perils of bad and uncertain roads in the thick darkness, when the glare of the lamps, and the steam from the sweating horses make you feel as if you were perched on the back of a triple eyed dragon, breathing fire and smoke, plunging headlong through briar and brake, slough and quagmire. Yes, even at the worst, it has its pleasures. The excitement, perhaps, of knowing that one trip, one false pull of the rein, one break of the straining harness, and over you go down the precipice that yawns so blackly, and withal, so conveniently, within a foot or so of your near side wheels, and, certainly, the greater pleasure, when it is all over, of knowing that after all, you have come out with your neck unbroken.

Whether with Ned Devine, 'Cabbage tree Ned,' as they call him, up and down the bare hills and steep pinches of eastern Otago ... Frank Summers through the wild gorges and over the terrific sandstone precipices of the Blue Mountain road to Bathurst jolting over the unmade track, and crashing through the timber with Crawford, when he took the first four wheeler from Melbourne to the Ovens in 1853, tearing along the rolling downs with Hoyt and Clapp to Belfast and the West ; axle deep in the tenacious black mud of the Singleton road with big Bob Turner, tearing recklessly on the six horse night coach, through the Black Forest to Bendigo with Sampson and Jackson, plunging, crashing, creaking, straining, with Bill Bowes through the wild gorges, deep swamps, and terrible 'glue pots' of Gippsland, lumbering across the dreary wastes and barren hills of the Liverpool Plains with merry eyed Johnny Patrick, bowling along joyously through the gloomy passes, and over the rapid rivers of the Hokitika road with Martin Scobie and Old Shep., or dashing, full split, and regardless of consequences, over hill and dale, gully and flat, mudhole and 'corduroy' between Geelong and Ballarat with Lame Bradley, 'tis all one.

Those were mad days my masters, days of fun and merriment and wild carouse, days of quick getting, and reckless spending, days when gold was plentiful, and when money flowed like water, such days as we shall never see again. Better so, perhaps, for in that wild Devil's dance, that mad whirl of revel, and riot, and fierce carouse, how many noble souls went down, how many, worthy of a better fate, sucked into the greedy vortex of the maelstrom of dissipation, sank, shattered, ruined body and soul, sank never to rise again ..." (Velvet and Rags, 5 Oct 1889, p.3)

Turner, Syd
1909 "Charleville ... There is a good number, of Northern faces here, and passing through the district, I noticed McPherson the son of the wild Scotchman, going south with a mob of Territory cattle, and another Territory man named Sid Turner, who came in with Ross McClean [?]. Sid Turner is now going to handle the ribbons, for he is going to drive for Cobb and Co. here." (Southern Pastoral Notes, 24 Aug 1909, p.6)

Underwood, Jack ... 1917 See Richardson, W.

Vane, Jimmy (Cabbage Tree Head) ... See Appendix 1.6

Vines, A. N. (brother T. Vines)
1917 "NEWS OF GEELONG AND DISTRICT SOLDIERS Pte. Horace Sibbison has written to Mr. Trounce, of North Geelong, from France, stating he is well. He met two old friends, Alex. Eason and Harry Britter, with whom he played cricket in Geelong. They were principals in a match between the soldiers. Lieut. J. A. Freeman, son of Mr. and Mrs. B. J. Freeman, Waverley, Western Beach, writing by last mail from London on December 2nd, where he has been on furlough, states he is well. He visited Edinburgh, and has quite recovered from the wound he received in his arm. By now he is back in the firing line. Gunner Alec Vines, writing under date of 22/11/17 from Belgium, says:—*I have had most exciting experiences lately, and have come out of everything safe and sound; with shells bursting all round, it is marvellous I have escaped. We are having a quiet time, though still in action and short-handed. Amongst the signallers here I met Don Hall, an old Geelong Grammarian. I had a hot bath the other day, the first for a*

fortnight. Driver Cantwell and I visited a Belgian refugee's shop the other day, and were able to buy an English newspaper, two days old, for 2½d.; we had dinner in a Belgian cottage; the meal consisted of black bread, vegetable soup and fried potatoes. I have been slightly affected with gas, but feel as good as ever again. We are at present living in a ruined Belgian house. which is Paradise compared with where we have been, and we are all doing a bit of cooking—steamed pudding, made from army biscuits and raisin, jellies and Quaker oats form part of our bill of fare. This part is perfectly drained, different to Ypres where, if we got off the duckboard, the mud was up to our knees.

Driver Stokes writes to Mr. Vines from Wiltshire. England. that he is with a training battalion getting ready to return to France. He is learning French. and says things are 'no bong' (soldiers' French for not good). Driver Stokes is well-known to the travelling public, having driven for Cobb and Co. in the Geelong district for over ten years. Private H. H. Hitchins, writing to his mother by yesterday's mail, said he had been on leave in Paris, and enjoyed himself immensely. He is back in the firing line in Flanders. Pte. Will Page, son of Mr. and Mrs. H. Page, of Fenwick-street, a former student in the architectural class at the Gordon College, has written an interesting letter to the principal. He is in France, and still finds time to keep up his architectural training, he writes enthusiastically of the charming architecture he has seen. He mentions meeting Erskine Collins, the news of whose death has since been received.

Signaller Les. Singleton, eldest son of Mr. and Mrs. Peter Singleton, East Geelong, sends word from France that he is still well. At the time of writing he was expecting a second trip to England soon after Christmas. Mr. and Mrs. T. W. Freeman, of Newtown, have received word from their sons, Neil and Alan. Both are well. The former, who holds the rank of major, had a narrow escape from a serious accident. When riding along a snow-covered road in France, his horse slipped, and he was thrown heavily, but escaped with a few bruises. Pte. Stanley Howard, of Brown Hill, Ballarat, who enlisted in Adelaide, paid a visit to his Geelong relatives. He was shot in the stomach three times in action, but is rapidly recovering, and expects to be discharged in a few days.

Sergt, Vivian Lowe, son of Mr. Alex. Lowe, of Little Malop-street, is now at the Divisional Signalling School, Salisbury. He is now sergeant on the staff. He met Stan. and Harold David son. Captain Stan. Davidson, son of Mr. Frank Davidson, who is connected with the First Army Corps Company of Engineers, has sent Christmas greetings, 'Lest We Forget,' to Geelong friends.

Writing to the principal of the Gordon College, Pte. Ian McDonald says he has been five weeks in France. The work is strenuous and exciting in the sector where he is situated, and he would welcome a rest. He says he possesses 'sufficient knowledge of French to buy eggs, butter and similar luxuries.' He sent a number of interesting post cards. Staff Sergt.-Major and Mrs. Hirst, of Kia Ora, 8 Bailey-street, Geelong, have received letters and cards from their son, Sergt. S. Hirst, from France: and also cards from their son-in-law, Pte. F. W. Bartlett from Holland, saying e expected to go to France shortly. They are both well, and wish to be remembered to all friends. Mr. and Mrs. I. Dorman have received letters from their son, Sapper A. H. Dorman. He is well and billeted in Britling-Sea, Essex. News of other Geelong and District Soldier will appear to-morrow." (News of Geelong and District Soldiers, 16 Apr 1917, p.3)

1938 "The first act of the old drivers on reaching Geelong was to visit the cemetery and place a wreath on the grave of the late Mr. A. N. Vines, himself an old driver, and for many years manager of Cobb and Co's Geelong section. It was the late Mr. A. N. Vines who formulated the plan for the stage coach trips during the centenary celebrations, but it was left to his brother, Mr. T. Vines, to carry out the ideas." (Old Coach Drivers, 15 Oct 1938, p.8)

1937 See also Preston, R.

Vines, Joshua (father of T. Vines)
1906 "Joshua Vines, a member of the old coaching firm of Vines and M'Phee, who ran many coaches in the Ballarat, Wimmera and Western districts under the style of Cobb and Co., in the early days, died at Ballarat on Saturday, aged 72." (Obituary, 5 Oct 1906, p.3)

1938 "Geelong Centenary GEELONG, Monday.—Amid cheers from the large crowd assembled, the Cobb and Co. mail coach, with the veteran driver Tom Vines in charge of the five in hand, left the city this afternoon on the first of the Geelong centenary celebrations journeys around the district. The design of the coach was originally approved by the late Mr. Joshua Vines, father of Mr. T. Vines, and was constructed at Cobb and Co.'s works in Geelong 65 years ago. It was used on the Hamilton-Penola service, of which Mr. T. Vines was manager." (Tour in Old Mail Coach, 11 Oct 1938, p.12)

1953 See also Kidman/Kiddman, Charles (Charlie)

Vines, Thos. (Tom)
1919 "The Cobb & Co.'s Old Coach Drivers' Association ... old coach drivers employed by Messrs. Cobb & Co., kindred coaching firms in Australia and New Zealand, and others ... Driver, district employed: Geelong" (Annual report / Cobb & Co.'s Old Coach Drivers' Association, 1919, pp.6-8)

1930-1940s See also Allan, (Christian name unknown); 1937 Preston, R.

Vinge, G ... 1919 See Aisbett, E. J.

A GARDEN AT KALGOORLIE.

Hugh K. Lyptus write "Breakfast over, my bag in the boot of one of Cobb & Co's five horse coaches, I was fortunate enough to scramble on to a box seat, and we were off to Kalgoorlie, which has been fitly named the centre of the Golden Zone. As you go out of the maia street there is a spectacle to be wondered at and even to grow poetical over. In an apparently inhospitable flat an industrious gardeuer has produced as fine a picture as it would be possible for anyone to see. Probably some two acres have bseu cultivated, and almost every kind of vegetable in common use shows to extraordinary advantage. A healthier garden it would be impossible to get, and the result of this man's effort is only an example of what can be done with the exercise of 'sufficient intelligence aud industry." (A Garden at Kalgoorlie, 25 Sep 1896, p.31)

1920 Crossing the flooded Paroo River at Eulo by punt, Billy McDonald driver; Punt worked by hand winches with the coach horses swimming beside the punt (Information from Cobb and Co. driver Ernie Richards ca. 1955)—Courtesy Queensland Museum

Chapter Ten

Drivers

W - Z

The Olden Days of Cobb & Co.

As wistfully we close our eyes,

We seem to see beyond the gates,

And on the box seats, visualize

The welcome from our old time mates,

They're beautiful, those spectre teams,

And as we near life's sunsets glow,

'Tis good to live again in dreams,

The olden days of Cobb & Co.

Wm. Jas. Wye, 1942
(Annual report / Cobb & Co.'s Old Coach Drivers' Association, 1919, p.18)

1906 Cobb & Co. coach, Richmond, A. E. (Ted) Richards driver—Courtesy Queensland Museum Collection

Supporting evidence:

Wagner, John ... 1953 See Rutherford, James (Jas./Jimmy)

Walach, Wm.
1895 "THE DRIVER KILLED.—OTHERS INJURED. Melbourne, January 24.—Cobb's coach on the road from Bruthneen to Omeo was going down Mt. Ash when the brake was found to be useless. The horses became unmanageable. The coach struck the railing of a bridge at the bottom of the hill and capsized. The driver, Wm. Walach, was killed. Wm. Graeber, of Omeo, is still unconscious, and two ladies escaped with little injury." (Victoria, 25 Jan 1895, p.3)

Walden, Fred ... 1936 See Rochester, William George (Bill)

Walden, James
1940 "PASSING OF MR. JAMES WALDEN Mr. James Walden died at the Hospital this morning at the age of 73 years. He was born at Richmond, Victoria, and was well known in this district. He was one of the coach drivers for Cobb & Co. The funeral will take place tomorrow leaving Mrs. A. W. Gurney's residence, 697 Beryl Street at 11 a.m. for the Church of England Cemetery. Fred J. Potter & Son have charge of the funeral arrangements." (Passing of Mr. James Walden, 12 Nov 1940, p.2)

Walden, William (Bill)
1927 "A LINK WITH COBB AND CO… age of 82 … Old-Time Driver Dead. Crossed over on Saturday last, one of the last Cobb and Co. coach drivers, in Mr. William Walden, at the age of 82. For many years, Bill Walden drove the mail coaches on various stages between Orange and Bourke, and he was most interesting to listen to … was as fine a specimen of colonial manhood as one could meet in a day's march. A good judge of a horse, and a man capable of taking his own part in a rough-up." (A link with Cobb and Co, 27 May 1927, p.5)

1932 See also Donovan, Pat; 1935 Rochester, William George (Bill)

Waldren, Bill ... 1932 See Lowe, Bill; Appendix 1.6

Wall, Stan
1925 "COBB AND CO.'S DRIVERS. TO THE EDITOR. Sir,—'Cobb s Coaches,' by T. J. Lonsdale is interesting reading but many 'good whips ' he left out. In my time Tom Gallagher (who subsequently became manager), Stan Wall, Ted Donohue, W. Atkins, Billy Richardson (now a car driver in Southport) and George Stevenson—all these men drove on the principal routes from … Charleville; and a week before Christmas of 1904 I left Charleville for Adavale with the record heaviest loaded coach, so I was informed, and the ribbons were in the safe keeping of Stan Wall. He was only a little fellow but he could drive, and but for careful handling going over the Gray Range we must have toppled over. Yet those were the days and it did one good to see any of these men driving, and generally on time too." (Cobb and Co.'s Drivers, 29 Jan 1925, p.12)

Wall, Stephen Edward (Steve)
1925 "Few men were more widely known and generally respected in this district than Mr Stephen Edward Wall … it became, known on Tuesday morning that he was the victim of a horse accident … He has been associated with horses during the whole of his life. In his younger days keeping a livery stable. Later on the more adventurous life of coach driving appealed to Mr Wall and he took service with Cobb and Co., on the Wilcannia line. He also drove on the Bourke to Thargomindah, Bourke to Barringun, Cunnamulla to Thargomindah lines, and also on that between Charleville and Adavale." (Winton Notes, 6 Feb 1925, p.7)

"On these lines he gained a wide experience and was generally looked upon as one of the best whips on the road. Even now, old coach travellers relate anecdotes of their experiences on the roads with Steve Wall. In 1907 he was transferred to Winton, and drove between Winton and Mackunda, on which line he continued for some years. Some 13 years ago he severed his connection with the old firm, and has since been associated with his sons in mail contracts and droving. Recently, he decided to seek fresh fields and was planning to go South. It was with this in view that he sold his horses and had arranged to give delivery on the day of the accident. He is survived by his two sons. Rowley and William, who, like their father were both good horsemen, but with the advent of the automobile, transferred their attention. His oldest daughter, Hazel, is married to Mr. Fred Vernon, a leading shearer and motorist. Two younger daughters, Stephena and Doreen, twins, were born in Winton, in the old home which the family have occupied for years. They too have inherited the family love of horses, and were the constant companions of their father in riding exercise. At the time the accident happened Mr. Wall was accompanied by his dog, an old favorite" (Death of Mr. S. E. Wall, 7 Mar 1925, p.3)

1917 See also Richardson, W.; 1940 McMillan, Alexander; 1950 Hickson, Harry

Wallace, F. W.
1953 "DROVE COACHES FOR COBB & CO. A man whose colourful career included a period as a coach driver for Cobb and Co. in Victoria and N.S.W., celebrated his 90th birthday at Perth on Saturday … Born in Sussex … As a young man he moved to Queensland, where he worked as a boundary and stock rider." (Drove Coaches for Cobb & Co., 3 Mar 1953, p.7)

Wallace, Jim (Senr.)
1917 "Some 12 miles through open pear country we pass through a cypress pine scrub, a sandy ridge perfectly alive with rabbits and with occasionally a flock of emus with their young, their ungainly indecisive lollop being very amusing to the passengers. We are still on Bullamon run, the property of the Australian Pastoral Co., Ltd., and Jim Wallace, senr., our driver, informs us, a centre in the early days of the most unscrupulous cattle duffers in the State. We mount a low sandy ridge about 24 miles from Thallon, and have a fine outlook over the north country to Nindi Gully, an old time camping place on the Moonie, and a regular change from the 70's. It is now a centre for grazing farms and stations, and has a store, hotel kept by Mrs. M. A. Haines, and a post office and telegraph office." (Coaching in Australia, 1917, p.57)

Wallace, P ... 1930-1940s See Allan, (Christian name unknown)

Wallace, Peter
1947 "Cobb's drivers went over old times. FACTS Adelaide Correspondent. In Adelaide's Alexandra Gardens last Sunday, South Australia's surviving Cobb's Coach drivers held a reunion. Most of them were over 80 and they talked of 50 and 60 years ago. All of them agreed that the modern horse was not in the class of the nags which used to draw Cobb's coaches 'all over the colonies.' Arthur Harman, hale and hearty at 81, said that in the coaching days horses could go 60 miles a day. Now 25 miles was their limit. He claimed to be the only man who had ever driven camels in a coach, and their oldest living driver. Then came stories of the coach of 60 passengers with 12 bay horses that went from the Black Bull Hotel, Geelong, 45 miles to Melbourne to see Lillywhite's first English cricketers play in 1876. When Peter Wallace produced pictures of coaches climbing round steep mountain cuttings in the Walhalla district, his mates cried: *Tell us again, Peter, how you cut the icicles off your horses' ears with your whip.*" (Cobb's drivers went over old times, 2 Feb 1947, p.4)

1919 See also Aisbett, E. J.

Wallett, (Christian name unknown)
1878 "YOUNG. MONDÂY. The horses attached to Cobb and Co.'s coach bolted yesterday from the post-office, with sixteen passengers in the coach. The driver was arranging the luggage when the horses started. A passenger who had been entrusted with the reins jumped off. Wallett, driver, succeeded in recovering the reins, and brought the horses round a telegraph post without injury to coach or horses. A gentleman named Burke, from Wagga, jumped off and dislocated his ancle. All who retained their seats escaped unhurt." (Young, 31 Dec 1878, p.6)

1879 "YOUNG. MONDAY. A serious coach accident happened this afternoon, by which Messrs. Aitken, of Murrumburrah, and Trenery, of Goulburn, are seriously injured. Shortly after Cobb and Co.'s coach left town the horses became restive, and Mr. Aitken being alarmed, jumped off the coach and broke his arm. Mr. Trenery followed suit, and it is at present impossible to state the extent of his injury. The other passengers, who remained in the coach, were uninjured. No blame is attached to Wallett, the driver." Another article stated "NEW YEAR'S DAY. The catering for the delectation of the public to-morrow seems of a very diversified and extended character ... A grand excursion to Sandringham and Sana Souci has been arranged to start at 10 o'clock from tho foot of Erskine-street, and there will be the usual trips to Manly Beach and Watson's Bay, and sports in Ivanhoo Park. The Young Men's Christian Association have organized an excursion to Vaucluse, and numbers of people will no doubt, proceed to Athol Gardens, where there will be fireworks, dancing, athletics, and a concert. The Highland Society of New South Wales has arranged a specially attractive programme of sports ... At Clontarf, one of the prettiest parts of the harbour, there is to be a grand national gathering ... while the sporting fraternity can have their penchants gratified by attending Tattersall's Annual Race Meeting at Randwick ... If any persons cannot obtain satisfaction from a perusal of this list, they had better have recourse to the railway time-tables, and see if they cannot determine upon a trip to the Blue Mountains, or to some picturesque spot to be reached by rail. In the evening there will be opportunities for attending the pantomimes, or for proceeding to the School of Arts, where the Cheevers, Kennedy, and Bent Minstrels are still offering their carefully compiled programme." (Young, 15 Apr 1879, p.5)

Walsh, Bob
1925 "COBB'S COACH ORIGINAL DRIVER. 'Bob' Walsh, who was the driver of Cobb and Co.'s famous coach in the pageant of travel and transport at the Jubilee Show on Wednesday, is a man with a great knowledge of the distant parts of Queensland. His appearance on the box seat must have recalled many memories to those who travelled the Far North in the early days, for he was the original driver of this old vehicle. Yesterday Mr. Walsh said that he had handled the ribbons on the run from Port Douglas to Normanton, via Burke-town, Georgetown, and Croydon, while he had also been for several years on the run from Cloncurry to Normanton." (Cobb's Coach Original Driver, 14 Aug 1925, p.13)

Walsh, William
1895 "A Sensational Coach Accident. THE DRIVER KILLED. A Bruthen (Vic.) telegram of Wednesday, says:—The Omeo-road was the scene of a fatal accident this morning. While Cobb's coach was on the journey to Omeo, at the Mountain Ash Range the brake became useless, and in the descent to Double Bridges the horses became uncontrollable, bolting down the incline at a great pace. The coach struck the railings of a culvert and capsized. William Walsh, the driver, was so seriously injured that he died in a few hours ... Walsh ... was an old and trusted driver for the company ... Walsh, the driver, has been in the employ of Cobb and Co, for 35 years, and was a thoroughly steady and reliable man." (Sensational Coach Accident, 26 Jan 1895, p.4)

Walters, Les
"Les Walters drove the McKinlay-Kinuna track. John Carter was a teacher in Nelia (Nelia is in the Julia Creek area - McKinlay Shire) in the mid-1950s when he knew Les, who at the time was in his late 70s or early 80s. John remembers Les was a WW1 veteran, he had bad arthritis in both hands and loved a bet. He used to bet a casket ticket with someone on the 'trains travelling past and whether the number of carriages would be odds or evens'. John didn't recall Les mentioning any family. He died at Charters Towers." (Contribution John Carter, 2023)

Ward, (Christian name unknown)
1874 "An accident of a very serious character occurred yesterday to one of Cobb and Co.'s coaches ... There were some fourteen passengers inside and two on the box with the driver, named Ward ... Bacchus Marsh district ... one of the breaks ... broke ... The driver then put on the other break, which failed to hold the coach ... The driver, Ward ... would no doubt have steered through in safety, had it not been for ... two wagons, laden with straw ... with a terrific crash she capsized ... being smashed into a thousand pieces—the passenger, of course, all more or less hurt ... the animals escaped almost scatheless." (Serious Coach Accident, 27 May 1874, p.3)

Ward, Frank ... 1940 See McMillan, Alexander

Ward, Joe ... 1908 See Byrne, F. A.

Ward, T ... 1919 See Aisbett, E. J.

Warnemindi, Martin ... 1941 See Chatfield, Harry

Warner, Jack
1939 "Into the mists of the past have gone the days of Cobb and Co.'s coaches, with their daring drivers who could 'spin' many a thrilling story of the days when 'the world was wide.' Another man who can relate incidents connected with the machine days is Jack Wieneke, who I had the pleasure of meeting for the first time at the last Rockhampton Rodeo. Jack knew many of Cobb's drivers on the Western roads from Mungundi through to St. George, then on to Surat and Yeulba, or from St. George to Cunnamulla. Talk to this hardy old veteran like I did, and he will relate stories about Jack Warner, Ted Manning, Tom Anderson, Jimmy Davidson, Billy Mitchell, George Douglas, and others who handed the 'ribbons' for Cobb and Co. in those far-away days.

On one occasion a coach was rattling along the road from St George, and the only passenger was a woman. After passing Surat the woman showed symptoms of becoming a mother, and the driver was in a very awkward predicament, at least so he thought. However, he lashed up the horses and managed to reach Yeulba just before the child was born.

On many occasions prisoners were taken by coach to the Yeulba railway station, and as the vehicle travelled along the bush roads the constable accompanying such men—often desperate characters—had to keep his eyes open to prevent a dash for freedom. On one occasion when a Cobb's coach was on its run in the West a prisoner suddenly jumped from the vehicle and took no notice of the constable's stern command to stop. A corpse rode in the coach the remainder of the journey. Another time when one of Cobb's coaches was travelling at night between Yeulba and St. George, a thief, waiting at the side of the road, climbed on to the back of the vehicle, without being noticed by the driver, then unfastened the mail bags and allowed them to drop to the ground. He secured a valuable haul and got clean away." (Dick Craig's Fight, 28 Apr 1939, p.5)

1917 See also Richardson, W.; 1938 Anderson, Thomas (Tom); 1941 Chatfield, Harry

Warner, William John
1946 "COBB & CO. DRIVER DIES IN BRISBANE. CAIRNS. September 2.—A link with the early coaching days of Cobb and Co. was severed by the death in Brisbane yesterday of William John Warner, for many years a driver between Mareeba and Georgetown. The deceased was born at Toowoomba and was 66 years of age. He had been living in Brisbane for some years, and for some time was associated with the firm of Pink Brothers, grocers." (Cobb & Co. Driver Dies in Brisbane, 3 Sep 1946, p.1)

Waterworth, James
1926 "TWO NONAGENARIANS CAMPBELLTOWN, Saturday. Mr. James Waterworth, Campbelltown's oldest resident, died this morning in his 93th year. He was a coach-driver of Cobb and Co. in the early days. At his late residence is his old coach. Yesterday, the funeral took place of the late Mr. James Bocking, who was only three weeks younger" (Two Nonagenarians, 28 Mar 1926, p.5)

Watson, Harry
1928 "*I was stuck up by Jack Morgan*, said Harry Watson, *that was in 1869, when I was driving the mail between Albury and Wagga.*" (Those were the days, 8 May 1928, p.6)

1930 "MET NED KELLY AT DANCE. MELBOURNE ... A veteran stage-coach driver, Mr Harry Watson ... 87 years ... one of the older brigade of Cobb and Co.'s drivers, the late Mr Watson could relate many thrilling experiences of early coaching days in Victoria. One of the events that stood out in his memory was the time he drove eight greys in a circus coach through Melbourne. He knew Ned Kelly, and was present at dances attended by the bushranger ... In the early days, when it required men of strong will and stronger physique to win out against the hardships that coach drivers had to face" (Veteran Coach Driver Dies, 3 Sep 1930, p.2)

Watson, W. H. ... 1937 See Preston, R.

Watt, C. H. ... 1919 See Aisbett, E. J.; 1937 Preston, R.

Watterson, Jonathon
1897 "COUNTRY NEWS. BALLARAT. Jonathan Watterson, aged 24 years a coach driver in the employ of Cobb and Co committed suicide on Wednesday by cutting his throat with a razor. Deceased, it appears, has been in bad health for some weeks past, suffering from a nervous disease, and recently he spoke of consulting a doctor. While engaged, however, in performing his toilet he decided on terminating his existence" (Country News. Ballarat, 22 Apr 1897, p.6)

Watts, William
1948 "DEATH OF COBB AND CO. DRIVER Mr. William Watts ... was one of the famous band of Cobb and Co. drivers of the early days ... His early life was spent in the Wagga and Hay districts, and later he was engaged for several years as a driver of Cobb & Co's. coaches in the Hay-Balranald district ... Mr. Schiller pays tribute to the deceased as a man of high character, very industrious and thoroughly dependable." (Death of Cobb and Co. Driver, 8 Jan 1948, p.1)

Weaver, Harry ... 1917 See Anderson, Jim

Weldron, Jim ... See Appendix 1.6

Wells, George
1944 "Death of Mr. George Wells DROVE COACH FOR COBB & CO ... in his 83rd year. The late Mr. Wells was born in Gippsland, Victoria, and in his youth was apprenticed to a coach builder. The driving of coaches appealed more to him so he left this to go driving for Cobb & Co. in the Ballarat district, over roads upon which the Kelly gang operated. He was unmolested by this gang on condition he did not carry police escorts. This information was conveyed to him by Kate Kelly, with whom he claimed to have danced on many occasions. Mr. Wells left the Ballarat district almost 56 years ago to come north to Wilcannia ... employed as a coach driver on their extensive mail lines. This employment took him to Bourke, but he returned with a complete new outfit to open up the Wilcannia-Cobar passenger

and mail service for his employers. In his reminiscences of the days of the coach, Mr. Wells often related how when the river had flooded the Tally-walka Creeks, the coach had to be floated across the expanse of water to reach Wilcannia. During one of these hazardous crossings Mr. Wells almost lost his life.

Mr. Wells retired from coach driving to take over the Meadows Hotel which he held, together with the Meadow Glen property attached, for a period of 30 years. Both he and his wife, who predeceased him by three years, were well known for their hospitality and kindness of heart, and many who passed that way only once, remembered for years the figure of the dapper and courteous host, who was never known to refuse help to anyone down on his luck … His passing removes from our midst a definite type—the courteous and hospitable bushman of the old school. Two sons. Messrs. Donald and Douglas Wells; and six daughters, Mesdames F. Booth, Geo. Booth. E. Booth. B. Pretty, C. Fox and M. Broun mourn his passing. A son, the late Mr. Clarrie Wells, died at Wilcannia last November. He leaves also 40 grandchildren and two greatgrandchildren." (Death of Mr. George Wells, 27 Oct 1944, p.1)

Wells, Richard
1944 "DROVE FOR COBB & CO. The Late Mr. Richard Wells … 84 years … In the early days of Glen Innes he was a driver on the Cobb and Co. coaches." (Drove for Cobb & Co., 3 Aug 1944, p.6)

Welsh, William
1880 "THE COACH ACCIDENT AT KERANG. (FROM OUR TRAVELLING REPORTER.) On Tuesday morning about eleven o clock, as already notified by telegram, a very serious accident happened to Cobb and Co.'s mail coach while it was starting for Swan Hill from Cullen's Hotel, Kerang … The passengers numbered four, consisting of two males and two females; one of the former, Sergeant Faussett, of Swan Hill, who was returning home after the escape of the prisoner Gale from the Kerang lockup, was sitting on the box with the driver—William Welsh, a very careful employe of Cobb and Co. The start is made from the hotel yard, immediately on issuing from which a sharp turn has to be made to the left, and then, after 30 or 40 yards, another sharp turn to the right takes place, which brings the coach ,on to the approach to the bridge over the Loddon and between the fences enclosing the same. Everything being ready, the signal was given for the start, on which the leader, there being three horses, swung sharp round and broke the polo short, off across the fore legs of one of the polers, the consequence of which was that the whole team bolted, and in making the last turn on to the bridge capsized the coach. Welsh stuck to the reins, holding even when he was on the ground, and on the passengers being picked up the sergeant was found to have sustained a compound fracture of the right leg, near the ankle, almost severing it. He was removed to the hotel, where Dr. Austin attended him. Dr. M'Intyre, of Swan Hill, afterwards arrived, when the leg was set, but the hopes of saving it are faint. The driver sustained a sprained ankle, bruised elbow, and cut finger. The ladies escaped with cut faces and bruised heads. The other male passenger escaped unhurt, and he and the ladies proceeded on their journey by another coach." (The Coach Accident at Kerang, 8 May 1880, p.1)

Westrien, W.
1919 "The Cobb & Co.'s Old Coach Drivers' Association … old coach drivers employed by Messrs. Cobb & Co., kindred coaching firms in Australia and New Zealand, and others … Driver, district employed: Ocean Grove and Barwon Heads" (Annual report / Cobb & Co.'s Old Coach Drivers' Association, 1919, pp.6-8)

Whatmore, Bobby
1931 "Brewarrina … In the wet season the trip meant any old time at all; and if, perchance, the driver had the bad luck to get his coach bogged, as happened occasionally, he would strap his mail bags to the horses' backs, and lead the way to the nearest accommodation, the passengers following on foot, some of them inconsiderate enough to make uncomplimentary remarks as to the state of the roads and means of transport. Possibly the most popular 'whip' was old Bobby Whatmore, who among other things, had the remains of a decent tenor voice. Even when things have been at bedrock, Bobby has whiled away the tedium for hours. One of his favourite songs was 'Ben Bolt'—resurrected in 'Trilby'." (Brewarrina in the Early 80's, 6 Nov 1931, p.8)

Whisson, James … 1921 See Griffen, Chas.

White, (Christian name unknown)
1868 "STICKING-UP OF COBB & CO.'S MAIL COACH, NEAR GYMPIE. We had hoped the sharp reception which the bush-thieves met from Mr. White, at Currie, the utter absence of all aid in the way of bush telegrams, and the presence of an efficient police force in the immediate neighbourhood, would have prevented the recurrence of this species of scoundrelism on the highway to our Gold-fields, but we are disappointed. With all its risk there are creatures still to be found, it appears, who prefer taking the money of honest men to honestly working to obtain money of their own.

The particulars of the sticking-up, as they have reached us, are as follows:—The coach, with the mails and three passengers, Mr. Power, Mrs. Farley, and Mrs. Thatcher, left Gympie on Thursday morning at a quarter past six o'clock. About half-an-hour after, and when about three miles from Gympie, the coach was descending a hill, and had nearly reached the bottom, when three men, with their faces covered, two of them armed with double-barrelled guns, the other with a single-barreled gun, started from behind some trees, and commanded the driver to stop. The driver not being able to bring up the vehicle so soon as the men liked, they called out again, and threatened immediately to fire if they were not instantly obeyed. The driver called out, he was pulling up as quick as he could, and brought the horses to a stand at the foot of the hill—a steep ascent before him making it vain to attempt to escape by forcing the horses on.

As soon as this coach was stopped, Mr. Power was ordered out, and told to go and hold the horses, when one of the men came up to him and ordered him to shell out his cash, when he drew out of his waistcoat pocket a five pound note, which did not satisfy the fellow ; so he put his own fingers into the pocket and drew out two ten-pound notes … The mail was not a very heavy one, luckily. A mail to Brisbane, with the English mail, had been made up the night previously and sent overland … They seemed very unexcited and methodical in their work, and to Mrs. Farley, who was rather alarmed at their proceedings, they said, Don't be afraid, we never touch ladies' by which we judge that this is not the first piece of villany of the kind they have been at ... The coach not arriving with its accustomed punctuality, the troopers suspected something wrong, and were on their way to ascertain the cause of the detention." (Sticking up of Cobb & Co.'s Mail Coach near Gympie, 5 Sep 1868, p.2)

White, Bill (Billy/Old Bill)
1971 "The old drivers to at last lay down their reins were: Ted Palmer and Billy White on the Charleville-Augathella-Tambo run 1921." (Communications Across the Generations, Read 1971, p.188)

1917 See also McPherson, Jim; 1953 Markwell, W. S.; 1925 Eddie, Nathan; 1950 Hickson, Harry

Whiteman, (Christian name unknown) ... 1873 See Powell, (Christian name unknown)

Whitney, William Franklin (Frank)
1925 "NEW SOUTH WALES INVADED. The first association of this redoubtable combination with N.S.W dates back to 1862 ... they arrived in Bathurst with an imposing procession of 103 horses (80 in harness), ten coaches and two feed waggons, after an uneventful trip from Victoria. On the driving box of the first four coaches to enter Bathurst were James Rutherford (destined to become one of the greatest benefactors and residents of that 'city of the plains'), Frank Whitney, Hal. Hamilton and Charlie Bissell." (Cobb and Company's Coaches, 10 Apr 1925, pp.1,5&28)

1933 "Interesting Old Records. In a recent 'Bulletin' a par. was reprinted from the issue of August 1, 1891. It is interesting to residents of the district, and is as follows:—All the old stage-coach drivers have not become railway gatekeepers or minor tram officials. Walter Hall, of Pott's Point and Mt. Morgan ; Jas. Rutherford of Lithgow, Bathurst, and half a dozen other choice spots ; Frank Whitney, of Coombing Park, Carcoar, the beautiful home of Icelys in days gone by, where Sir Charles Fitzroy, Colonel Mundy and other 'bloods' spent many a roystering evening ; jacob Russart, the wealthy host of the Royal Hotel at Blayney and the local 'Dick Whittington ; 'King' William Orbel host of a golden hotel at Dubbo ; John Fagan J.P. and squatter, of Cowra (he drove the coach on the morning that Gardiner and his gang stuck up the escort at Eugowra Rocks) ; the late Henry Rotten, of Bathurst (M.L.A.), and half a score other prominent citizens handled the ribbons over the Blue Mountains before the iron horse found its way westwards." (Cobb and Co. Drivers, 27 Jul 1933, p.6)

1925 See also Eddie, Nathan; 1953 Rutherford, James (Jas./Jimmy)

Wicks, A ... 1917 See Wright, Bob

Wicks, Billy
1937 "A WOMAN'S DESPAIR AT COBB'S MAIL CHANGE, QUEENSLAND. (By J. H. O'Brehoun.) Reading in the 'Richmond River Herald' of June 22 the story told of the pitiful plight of a Mrs. Hall in outback Queensland, with her little orphan children, coupled with an article which appeared in the Sun newspaper last week, re our old coaching days, recent accounts too of births which have taken place in strange places and under almost incredible circumstances of isolation, in crowds, on the Sydney ferry; in a Sydney taxi cab; and in a fig tree in the '64 flood on the Macleay (if true) reminds me of an excitable incident, strange but true, which occurred on an outback coach road many years ago, when all of us male passengers were hurriedly bundled out and had to mount on the upper deck, and then while the old roadster of the Never Never continued on its way now at an increased emergency speed: Billy Wicks applying his long greenhide, the old craft rocking and swaying alarmingly on its great leathern springs, a babe was born below the deck of that romantic old timer, out there in the wilds miles from nowhere ...

A few makebelieve men of the hold-up breed; but, let-me-see-now, it must be just 56 years since the last of the dinkum bushrangers, the Kelly gang, were wiped out in their last stand in Glenrowan pub. No doubt some readers will recall the cowardly action of the Police in setting a light to the hotel while crowded with innocent people, men, women and little children ... You may recall too how a young Irish priest, who had by chance come along, had rushed into the burning building and had succeeded in dragging out two of the dead outlaws. Thirty years ago I knew that Reverend gentleman very well indeed, the R.C. Bishop of Perth, W.A., now the late Bishop Giboney. R.I. P.

Of course like all things else there are policemen and policemen, just as there were bushrangers and bushrangers. The members of Ned Kelly's gang were gentlemen compared with some of the lowdown scum of creation who plundered the old coaches, lone travellers, and gold escorts. Morgan was a cold-blooded murderer, but the three that hunted in a pack in Victoria ; took the kitty as ruthless villains. History tells they were never captured. Those three sons of Hades of whom I'm thinking, didn't believe in wasting ammunition on their victims if they could avoid it. They were too fiendishly cruel for that kind of death. Instead, they used to tie their victims up to trees and leave them there to die by degrees, and they were fond of boasting to their next unfortunates of the whole jugful of pleasure they always got out of the thoughts of the many lingering deaths for which they were responsible.

This one example of their playful ways I'll let stand for their whole programme : Three diggers, who had done well, were on their way from Mount Egerton to Ballan on horseback. One of the mates, a young Irish chap named Moran, had decided to return to the old folks at home with the gold he had won, but fate, oft cruel, willed otherwise. They were stuck up by these three samples of the devil's brew, and robbed of their all, even of their best articles of clothing. Then, after the cruel fiends had broken a leg of each of the three horses in their devilish play, the three half-clad diggers in cold winter were marched far into the bush, tied up to trees in sight of water, where they were left to die from thirst, hunger and cold; and would have too had fate not relented and again took command in the scheme of things. A new chum, who had got bushed while searching for a straying horse, had by this grim gesture of fate, been guided to the hold-up victims. They had been then there for three days, young

Moran being in a state of collapse from fever and exposure, having been shot in the thigh in a short gun-battle with the outlaws ... The old jade, fate, though had yet another joke to reveal; for as the new chum hastened down the gully for water to relieve the suffering of the tied-up men, he was surprised and overjoyed to find his horse just coming into drink. The victims of the hold up directed their deliverer how to go for assistance, who now mounted made all haste. Young Moran recovered, and smelt more gunpowder smoke when a leaden ball again bit deep into his flesh, in the Eureka Stockade, December 3, 1854. During that short battle in the historic '54, a female child was born in a miner's tent while soldiers' bullets passed right through the walls. That Eureka baby girl died five years ago in Sydney ... Moran, however, made the big comeback, and for years afterward kept an hotel in Bendigo, an Irish wife and an Irish jaunting car ...

Much from time to time has been written in romantic trend around the old rock-aby coach, gone from the roads of Australia fair, with never a word of the mail-change grooms, without which the coach or its passengers never could have gone through. Many of these changing stops were isolations and merely sapling yards on open range, especially where the road ran in stages across wide and unfenced cattle country. Over sheep runs, however, the mail-change grooms were more favourably placed, mostly accommodated with a paddock, even though a few miles square, in which to run the changing horses. On the other hand, however, where the changing stations were in open country, it is obvious, that the first essential in a groom's qualifications was bushcraft, necessary in order to keep in condition and to have rounded up in readiness the change for the oncoming coach in the days of old; and what wonderful unshod grass-feds were they of the Royal Mail, linking of hands across the bushlands, as it were ...

Charleville, then the dead end of Queensland's South western railway. We were heading to cut the coach road leading from that sheep town to little outback Adavale, situated on Black Water Creek. It was to Adavale the wire came, telling Scotty Layton the good news that he, a down and out shearer waiting for a shed, had won the Tattersall sweep of £30,000 (thirty thousand), on the Melbourne Cup of 1892. What luck! (A Woman's Despair at Cobb's Mail Change, Queensland, 30 Jun 1937, p.8)

Wiggins, G. T.
1920 "G. T. Wiggins of Ringwood was one of Cobb's drivers. He was the first to drive a coach, with eight passengers, from Melbourne to Woods Point, via the Yarra track, in 25 hours." (A Southern Arcadia, 6 Feb 1920, p.3)

Wild, Charley ... 1917 See Bruce, Harry

Wiley, William
1888 "Ivanhoe correspondent writes—A pleasant little ceremony took place here on the evening of the 24th instant, at Elliott's Hotel, when about twenty gentlemen sat down to a dinner given in honor of Mr William Wiley, on the eve of his departure from Ivanhoe. After the usual toasts had been honored, a massive gold albert was presented to Mr Wiley as a token of esteem from the people of Ivanhoe. Mr Wiley has been coach driving for Cobb and Co., on this line, for some five or six years, and recently he received notice from the firm, that his services were no longer required. This is considered harsh treatment, as all who know him speak highly of him as being a careful and obliging driver, and his departure from the line is much regretted." (No Title, 28 Sep 1888, p.2)

Wilkinson, (Christian name unknown) ... 1910 See Bates, Robert (Silent Bob)

Wilkinson, Jim (Big Jim)
1926 "Frank Smiley ... His father was one of the mates of Big Jim Wilkinson on the run from Ballarat to Skipton" (Days of Cobb & Co., 27 Mar 1926, p.13)

Willcock, Thomas ... 1917 See Breen, James

Williams, (Christian name unknown)
1954 "Mrs. Elizabeth Jane Williams's husband was a one time driver of Cobb and Co. coaches, running from Hay to Booligal and Deniliquin." (Link With Cobb & Co., 15 Jul 1954, p.7)

Williams, Hugh ... 1920 See Gales, A.

Willocks, Mick & Willocks, Tom ... 1929 See Corbett, Alec.

Wilson, Charlie ... 1932 See Smiley, W.

Winkler, E ... 1919 See Aisbett, E. J.

Winkler, Eddie
1951 "BESIDES playing a vivid and vital part in the development of Australia, Cobb and Co. provided a striking display at the first Melbourne Cup. An unofficial Melbourne Cup had been run the year before, but the first Tuesday in November, 1861, saw fleets of special coaches running a crowd of 4000 people to Flemington ... It was announced that an Australian, Ned Devine, also known as Cabbage Tree Ned, would take a new monster coach—The Leviathan—to the course, carrying 82 passengers ... It was a huge vehicle, requiring 22 horses to haul it. Driving it would be a tough job, even with postillions on the lead and centre horses. The arrangement of this team was interesting. There were two in the wheel, and five sets of four-abreast. Nothing like it had ever been seen anywhere in the world, men said ... cheers arose from the Flat and Leger when the huge Leviathan and its 22 horses came swinging on to the course and sped along the track. Then followed eight-in-hands driven by ... Levi Rich ... Ike Haig followed with another, and then came two more, with Big Sampson and Eddie Winkler at the reins." (The Days of Cobb and Co., 21 Jul 1951, p.13)

Winterbottom, G. T.
1896 "READ THIS CASE. Mr. G. T. Winterbottom, Exchange Hotel, Gawler, S.A., who writes on April 18th, 1893:—Over thirty years since I was coach driving in Victoria for Cobb and Co., and consequently was exposed to all changes of weather. Then it was that the germs of the complaint from which I afterwards suffered were infused into my system. Some years after giving up coaching I was seized with and suffered most terribly from rheumatic fever ; no matter what remedy I tried or what doctors I consulted there was absolutely no relief of any duration to be obtained. Some six months since I commenced a course of Clements Tonic, and now it is very seldom that I have

any pains, and never fever. I am well known here, and numbers of my relatives and friends are aware of the above facts.—I am, Sir, yours truly, G. T. Winterbottom, Exchange Hotel, Gawler, S.A." (Read this Case, 29 Aug 1896, p.13)

Wollen, Dan
1873 "Coach Accident at Weimbilla Creek.—We are authorised by the driver (Mr. Dan Wollen) of Cobb's Coach, to give the following true account of this accident, the report in some of the papers being somewhat exaggerated :—On arriving at Weimbilla Creek, where there is not a bridge, but some logs placed in the bed of the stream to afford a footing, the horses, in attempting to cross, began to swim, as the logs had been carried away by the current. The driver immediately stopped the coach, and with Mr. Daveney's help unhitched the horses, which had not been carried off the bridge, for the best of all reasons—there was no bridge, as we said before. At the request of the driver, Mr. Daveney went across and brought back a horse and released the two other passengers who had remained in the coach. The driver and Mr. Daveney then wheeled the coach to dry land, Mr. D. pushing and steering by the pole, which had not been detached, and consequently required no diving after, the driver. putting his shoulder to the wheel. The horses were then reattached and the party returned in safety to Roach's Mail Station. We are really sorry to have to spoil so fine a romance as that which has been published and to deprive the hero of his laurels, but we, have been requested as we have said, to give the true account of the matter, furnished by the driver of the coach. Of course Mr. Daveney deserves thanks" (Notes and News, 13 Dec 1873, p.2)

Woods, Bill ... 1917 See Anderson, Jim

Woods, George ... See Appendix 1.6

Woodworth, George
1922 "The shipment referred to included the first of the famous 'Jack' or 40 passenger and six-horse coaches brought to Australia, which did so much to enhance and spread the fame of Cobb and Co. They were all thorough-brace swung, and turned out to be the most suitable and popular for the purposes of the goldfields traffic on the main roads. Mr. George Woodworth, who died only last year, was the last survivor of Cobb and Co.'s original drivers, and one of the 13 partners of the Victorian Stage Co., and the first to drive a 'Jack' into Bendigo. He often related that when he first took the ribbons on a 'Jack' it happened he had a light load. She rolled so 'like a ship at sea' that for the whole of his stage from Castlemaine to Bendigo the sensation of top heaviness was so strong that he felt all the time she was going to lurch over his wheelers. But, the old man added with pride, never a Jack was known to leave her braces or lose her centre of gravity." (Old Coaching Days, 10 Jun 1922, p.7)

1937 See also Peck, John Murray

Wools-Cobb, Arthur Henry
1951 "Late Mr. Wools-Cobb was Cobb & Co. Coach Driver. MR. ARTHUR HENRY WOOLS-COBB, a wellknown Dandenong identity … was formerly a famous Cobb & Co.'s. coach driver. His late father, Mr. Alfred Wools-Cobb, came out from England to take over Cobb & Co.'s coach company from its American owner, and up until the time the coaches were superseded by trains, his son, Mr. A. H. Wools-Cobb, drove one of these in the Orbost area." (Late Mr. Wools-Cobb was Cobb & Co. Coach Driver, 23 May 1951, p.1)

Woolworth, George
1925 "George Woolworth, the last survivor of the original American drivers of Cobb and Co., died in Victoria, a nonagenarian, in 1921." (Cobb and Company's Coaches, 10 Apr 1925, pp.1,5&28) while in "An account of the pioneering work of Cobb and Co., and the later expansion and newly formed partnerships which extended throughout Australia. Reference is made to … early drivers, George Woolworth and Frank Smiley" (Memoirs of John Murray Peck)

Workman, Jos.
1920 "Eugowra Gold Robbery. OLD COACHMAN'S EXPERIENCE. The departure of Mr. Jos. Workman from Bathurst to Sydney recently recalls the dramatic robbery of the Eugowra gold escort in 1862 (says the Molong Express). Mr. Workman, who is 76 years old, lived on the Lachlan for 60 years, and drove Cobb and Co.'s coaches in the Cowra, Orange, Forbes and Condobolin districts. He was in the vicinity when Ben Hall and his gang made their profitable raid on the gold escort. The escort was travelling from the Lachlan to Eugowra, when the bushrangers appeared on the scene, and opened fire on the party. Two troopers were wounded, and finally the police were overpowered. The bushrangers escaped with several thousands of ounces of gold, which, so far as the State is concerned, was never recovered. A romance connected with the hiding place of the gold stolen from the escort has recently aroused much interest. The appearance of a number of strangers' activities in the vicinity of the Weddin Mountains has given rise to a report that the strangers' activities had some-thing to do with the 'plant' of the gold. It is reported that the strangers possessed knowledge of the spot where the gold was buried, unearthed it, and carried it away as quietly as they came. There are, however, no means or confirming this report." (Eugowra Gold Robbery, 2 Jul 1920, p.3)

Workman, Ted
1881 "FORBES. August 23. DEAD ON THE ROAD. The coroner (Mr. J. F. Armstrong) told an inquest at J. Flint's Horse and Jockey Hotel on Monday touching the death of a person named James S. Arnott. It appeared that deceased came up from Condobolin on Cobb's coach on Saturday night. On leaving Carrawobity, Arnott, who was under the influence of drink, was lying asleep in the coach, and the driver (Ted Workman) missed him shortly afterwards, but took no special notice of the occurrence … Byrne … found deceased lying dead close to the road … The verdict of the jury was, that James S. Arnott died from dislocation of the neck caused through accidentally falling from the coach." (Forbes, 27 Aug 1881, p.38)

1950 "WIFE OF COBB & CO. DRIVER … The passing of grand old Temora lady Mrs. Mary Jane Workman at the age of 96, depleted still further the rapidly thinning ranks of those who even yet remembered, the days when bushrangers rode the land … After moving around to different parts she married and settled down in Forbes, Condobolin, Grenfell area, where her husband was a driver of Cobb & Co.'s coaches. In this capacity he came to Temora where he became the driver of the coach from Temora to Wyalong. Mrs. Workman made her home here, where she resided for the last 58 years. Her husband predeceased her 36 years ago, and of the family of ten children (five boys and five girls), three sons and one daughter survive, also fifteen grandchildren and one great-great granchild. The surviving sons and daughter are Joe (Temora), Jack (Echuca), Sid (Dubbo), and Mrs. C. A. Wallace (Temora). While at Condobolin great sorrow came into her life when two of her daughters were drowned in the Lachlan River. The youngest girl, aged 10, fell into the river and her elder sister, aged 14, went to her assistance and both were drowned." (Wife of Cobb & Co. Driver, 8 Sep 1950, p.9)

Wright, Bob
1905 "COACH ACCIDENT. Messrs. Cobb and Co.'s coach, due at Charleville on Thursday last, had the misfortune at the 37-mile to meet with an accident through the breaking of the reins. Driver Wright had a miraculous escape, he being powerless after the reins broke. The horses travelled on until they met an over-limb tree. The violent contact with the tree caused the horses to gallop wildly, so much so that one horse got killed on the spot and others injured. Mr. Wright recovered, but is much indisposed." (Coach Accident, 8 Feb 1905, p.2)

1917 "On the formation of the Company in Queensland in 1881, a forward move was made, and, under the governing director, Mr. Rutherford, and roads manager, Tom Gallagher, Queensland was soon grid-ironed by Cobb and Co ... There are no harder worked men than Cobb and Co's drivers in the outside districts of Queensland, as they often have to drive with half-broken horses over half-made tracks, cutting in and out of the bush with nerve and wrists of iron ... Charleville to Augathella, Tambo, and Blackall line, drivers: Maurice O'Brien, Jim Brown, Alex. Teys, Bob Wright, Alf Lewis ... Charleville to Adavale, via the Ward and Langlo, had as drivers, J. Coyne, E. Donohue, Andy Atkins (now holder of a grazing farm near Charleville), Dave Sinclair, and A. Wicks (now at Charleville) ... Charleville to Cunnamulla, down the Warrego, the drivers were: Christie French, A. Thompson, and Bob Nicholson (who after acting as road inspector at Hughenden, took up a grazing farm, and, it is said, after a time sold out for £15,000 and is living retired near Sydney) ... Cunnamulla, via Dynevor Downs to Thargomindah, drivers: E. Athorne, Joe Clarke, Charley Martin, Alex. Scott and W. Tuite, now manager of the line ... Aramac and Muttaburra, Thomson River, drivers: Walter Smith, and Bill Cooper ... Winton to Cork Station, down the Diamantina, was only a run for a while. Muttaburra to Longreach, drivers: Ned Palmer (now inspector in the Central district), Nick Egan, and Bill Hitzman ... Comet to Springsure, driver, Charley Hewson ... Withersfield to Aramac, drivers: Tom Nolan, and Bill Langdon ... Muttaburra and Winton, driver: Jack Long ... In the Central district, Batholomew had a coach running from Westwood in the early 70's to Clermont. This line was purchased by Cobb and Co. in 1877-8. Blackall to Withersfield, then the head of the Central railway line, drivers: Jim Patterson and Bill Sutcliffe." (Coaching in Australia, 1917, p.43)

Wright, George (Old George) ... 1932 See Smiley, W.

Wright, George Freeman
1934 "Death ... 47 Severn-street, Box Hill, loving husband of the late Eliza Ann, and loved father of Violet, George, Lucy, Francis and Alfred, aged 85 years (late coach driver Cobb and Co.)" (Family Notices, 28 Nov 1934, p.1)

Yabsley, Jimmy ... 1932 See Clark, Billy

Yankee Bill
1955 "The early Queensland drivers included H. Barnes, Jerry Murphy, Jim Hunter, Yankee Bill, Jimmy Murphy, Tom Elms, Nick Hunter, Bob McRae, Tom Amies and Tom Kidd." (Cobb & Co. in Queensland, 7 Jul 1955, p.4)

Yeomans, Edward (Ted)
1890 "Accident to a Coach ... A nasty accident happened to Messrs. Cobb and Co.'s coach, which runs between Forbes and Orange, on Sunday night, at Heifer, Station Hill, about 54 miles from Orange. The horses bolted, and the bolt broke, and the coach was overturned. The horses attached to the pole and front wheels galloped away, leaving the main body of the coach in the road with five passengers on board, none of whom were seriously hurt, though all were bruised and shaken. The driver, Edward Yeomans, was thrown into a waterhole, where he lay for some time unconscious. The news was brought to town and another coach, with a doctor and several townsmen, was at once sent to the scene of the accident. They returned to town about 10 p.m., bringing the passengers and mails to Orange." (Australian Star, 20 May 1890, p.5)

1894 "A STICKING-UP CASE. Sydney, June 21. A wire from Condobolin states that on Thursday morning last, when Messrs. Cobb & Co.'s mail coach was on its way from Forbes to Condobolin, and when at Riley's public-house, 20 miles down the river, the driver, Yeomans, was attacked by three men, one of whom attempted to pull him off his seat. Yeomans clubbed his whip to defend himself, when one of the assailants drew a revolver and threatened to shoot him. Two male passengers, who were in the hotel, then rushed out and jumped into the coach. The driver got his horses going, but the attacking party galloped across the leading horses and turned them short round, endeavoring to upset the coach. This attempt failed, and the coach reached Condobolin safely. Yeomans gives as his reason for not reporting the affair that he knew one of the men who attacked him, and was afraid of the consequences. The driver's story is to a certain extent substantiated by the two passengers." (A Sticking-up Case, 23 Jun 1894, p.21)

York, Ollie
"The old drivers to at last lay down their reins were: Massey Hood and Ollie York on the Cunnamulla-Thargomindah run 1922." (Communications Across the Generations, Read 1971, p.188)

COBB AND CO'S LAST COACH.
"Approval has been given by the Prime Minister (Mr. Bruce) to the request made by the Federal Capital League that the Commonwealth should purchase the last coach used in Australia by Cobb and. Co. It is stated that Cobb and Co. had a firm offer for the purchase of the coach from a private individual for £150. They have agreed to sell it to the Commonwealth for £100." (Cobb and Co's Last Coach, 30 December 1924, p. 2)

The Best Driver

1925 "Who was the best driver that Cobb and Co. ever had?" one old chap asked, and then they fell into argument, and after hours of friendly wrangling it was unanimously decided that all of the drivers were the best. As I listened I remembered a piece of poetry that was written over 30 years ago and was found amongst the effects of the late 'Billy' Mitchell, one of Cobb's oldest drivers, its title was *The Whips of Cobb and Co*. It read as follows":-

I've been coaching down in New South, riding in the Royal mail,
On the box in Vic and Tassy, on the boot in snow and hail;
Riding in my sober senses, riding with my lamps alight,
Watching 'Jehu' with the ribbons, seeing if he held them right;
Marked his pull and all his quiver; marked the way he held the whip;
Marked him try to do a straddle; marked his liking for a nip;
Marked his every blooming action; marked his blooming cuddies, too;
Marked his coach from rack to pole point; as a critic ought to do.

And I've got him in the optic, I've got him in me mind,
As I've seen him whip the kiddies to the call of 'whip behind.'
And I feel him mount a boulder, fail to straddle when he ought,
Graze a stump and blame the wheeler, curse him when his whip got caught;
Comb my whiskers with the branches, never thinks to 'pologise;
Dumps me into ruts and gullies, shakes my innards in Gilgais.
And I mark him down as wanting, and his pace as extra slow—
Why he isn't even in it with the Queensland Cobb and Co.

So my mind goes harking backwards to the days of long ago,
Back to old familiar faces in the ranks of Cobb and Co.
And I see a whiskered chivvy—you can guess the 'chiv,' I mean--
It was known as Billy Mitchell; is he still above the green?
Many miles I've ridden with him; many yarns to me he's told;
Many drinks we've had together—'ginger beer'—in days of old;
Many times I've blown his bugle when we reached the sandy lane;
Many times I've held the ribbons when we crossed the Myall Plain.

Harry Bruce and big Jack Warner, both were demons in the dark;
They could drive their blooming carriage where a dingo couldn't bark.
They would never comb your whiskers with the branches overhead;
And they'd 'break her' into gullies like a hearse that bore the dead.
The Andersons and Davy Teyl, and Jim and Micky Carr,
Could steer a team through forest box or stunted coolabah;
And Douglas, with his ready wit and ever-cheerful smile,
Would drive a team of five abreast, or five in single file.

Then my fancy turns to Rogers, good old Jimmy of that ilk;
When he wasn't driving coaches he was mostly sporting silk.
Ride or drive, the same old Jimmy never fence was yet too high;
And you never heard him grumble if the roads were wet or dry.
And Jimmy D—, you know the rest, he's on the Yeulba track,
A man to cheer a gloomy soul, or bring a wanderer back;
A fair and square 'bontoshia,' an' a man I'm proud to know,
Is this more than brilliant unit in the ranks of Cobb and Co.

Last I saw of old Ted Manning, up in Longreach drawing beers—
Chucked the whip and leather ribbons—dealing in the cup that cheers.
Where, I wonder, are the others, Is their balance high or low?
Do they still convey the mail bags for Cobb and Co.?
For I miss 'em in my travels—little Dick, and Tom, and Fred;
Some, I know, have left the coaches; some to other lands have fled;
Now and then I meet a rambler, and Tom had to let them go,
For the drought had played the devil with the whips of Cobb and Co.

Yes, I miss them, good old drivers, with cheerful 'get away';
It was good in sit beside 'em even on the wettest day.
It was good to hear their laughter, listen to the tales they told;
May their years be long and happy 'ere they rest beneath the mould.
Seems as if the gods had chosen men like them to swing the whip
On the sun-scorched tracks of Queensland, where the only joy's a nip.
Never mind, ye western Jehus, in the end to Heaven you'll go
With your rein hand for a token that you wrought for Cobb and Co.

"So far as I can ascertain these verses have never been published previously, nor is the name of the author known.
The verses were typewritten, and thumb worn-evidently they had been handled a good deal."
(Cobb's Coaches, 17 Jan 1925, p.17)

1905 Jack Thompson—Hughenden-Muttaburra route
E. Spike photographer, Courtesy State Library of Queensland

Mrs Mary Jinks
She drove for Cobb and Co, Weekly Times, 22 Aug 1951, p.32, Courtesy State Library Victoria

Name unknown
Gunn Lantern Slide Maker, Courtesy The Sovereign Hill Museums Association Limited, Ballarat, Victoria

Bathurst coach driver, name unknown
Courtesy Ray Green, Bathurst

Frank Duffell
Truth, 9 November 1947, p. 39

John Murray Peck
1941 Annual report and balance sheet/Cobb & Co.'s Old Coach Drivers' Association, p.7, Courtesy State Library Victoria

T. Coyle
The Daily Telegraph, 6 September 1924, p. 13

Freeman Cobb
Gunn Lantern Slide Maker, Courtesy The Sovereign Hill Museums Association Limited, Ballarat, Victoria

Charleville coach drivers, names unknown
Courtesy Ray Green, Bathurst

Harry Lumley
Coaching in Australia, 1917, p.39

Jos. Green
Coaching in Australia, 1917, p.39

Harry Hickson
Morning Bulletin, 23 Mar 1950, p.6

1893 Edward Devine
Courtesy State Library Victoria

Buster White (Fictional hero by Will Lawson)
Gunn Lantern Slide Maker, Courtesy The Sovereign Hill Museums Association Limited, Ballarat, Victoria

William DuRieu
The Journal (Adelaide, SA : 1912 -1923), 15 Sep 1913, p.4

Lou Sheraton
Morning Bulletin (Rockhampton, Qld) 23 Mar 1950, p.6

1872 William Richardson
Courtesy John Oxley Library, State Library of Queensland

John Miles
Coaching in Australia, 1917, p.39

James Lowe
Gold Digging Days, 2 Aug 1937, p.2

Walter Hall
Courtesy State Library Queensland

James Rutherford, aged 26 years
Coaching in Australia, 1917, p.15

James Rutherford
Courtesy of State Library Queensland

Richard Palmer
Gunn Lantern Slide Maker, Courtesy The Sovereign Hill Museums Association Limited, Ballarat, Victoria

John Wagner
Courtesy State Library Victoria

Driver Photographs & Artifacts

Alder, A.
1927 Cobb & Co.'s drivers answer the 1927 roll call in Melbourne (Smith's Weekly, 28 May 1927, p.15)

Alder, Jas. (Jimmy)
1927 Cobb & Co.'s drivers answer the 1927 roll call in Melbourne (Smith's Weekly, 28 May 1927, p.15)

Andrews, C.
1927 Cobb & Co.'s drivers answer the 1927 roll call in Melbourne (Smith's Weekly, 28 May 1927, p.15)

Atkins, Andy
Coach at Langlo Hotel (Queensland Museum Collections)

Bell, J.
1927 Cobb & Co.'s drivers answer the 1927 roll call in Melbourne (Smith's Weekly, 28 May 1927, p.15)

Bradley, T.
1927 Cobb & Co.'s drivers answer the 1927 roll call in Melbourne (Smith's Weekly, 28 May 1927, p.15)

Britton, W. H. J.
1927 Cobb & Co.'s drivers answer the 1927 roll call in Melbourne (Smith's Weekly, 28 May 1927, p.15)

Bromley, G.
1927 Cobb & Co.'s drivers answer the 1927 roll call in Melbourne (Smith's Weekly, 28 May 1927, p.15)

Buckley, J.
1927 Cobb & Co.'s drivers answer the 1927 roll call in Melbourne (Smith's Weekly, 28 May 1927, p.15)

Carlisle, D. H.
1927 Cobb & Co.'s drivers answer the 1927 roll call in Melbourne (Smith's Weekly, 28 May 1927, p.15)

Classen, H. J.
1927 Cobb & Co.'s drivers answer the 1927 roll call in Melbourne (Smith's Weekly, 28 May 1927, p.15)

Cobb, Freeman
[Gunn Lantern Slide Maker] (The Sovereign Hill Museums Association Limited, Ballarat, Victoria)

Corbet, J.
1927 Cobb & Co.'s drivers answer the 1927 roll call in Melbourne image (Smith's Weekly, 28 May 1927, p.15)

Coyle, Thomas (Tom)
1924 Mr. T. Coyle (The Daily Telegraph, 6 Sep 1924, p.13)

Cozens, R. B.
1927 Cobb & Co.'s drivers answer the 1927 roll call in Melbourne (Smith's Weekly, 28 May 1927, p.15)

Crawford, W. C.
1927 Cobb & Co.'s drivers answer the 1927 roll call in Melbourne (Smith's Weekly, 28 May 1927, p.15)

Cuthbert, J. H.
1927 Cobb & Co.'s drivers answer the 1927 roll call in Melbourne (Smith's Weekly, 28 May 1927, p.15)

Davis, G. M.
1927 Cobb & Co.'s drivers answer the 1927 roll call in Melbourne. (Smith's Weekly, 28 May 1927, p.15)

Devine, Edward (Cabbage-tree Ned)
1893 Edward Devine (State Library Victoria)
1902 Ned Devine; Cabbage Tree Ned [Henry Goldman] (State of Library Victoria)

Dowling, Nicholas
1927 Cobb & Co.'s drivers answer the 1927 roll call in Melbourne (Smith's Weekly, 28 May 1927, p.15)

Drayton, J.
1927 Cobb & Co.'s drivers answer the 1927 roll call in Melbourne (Smith's Weekly, 28 May 1927, p.15)

Duffell, Jack
1947 Mr. Frank Duffell (Truth, 9 Nov 1947, p.391)

Durieu/DuRieu, William (Billy)
1913 The Journal (Adelaide, SA : 1912 -1923), 15 Sep 1913, p.4
1913 Mr. William Du Rieu (Observer, 20 Sep 1913, p.40)

Edgcombe, F.
1927 Cobb & Co.'s drivers answer the 1927 roll call in Melbourne (Smith's Weekly, 28 May 1927, p.15)

Fogarty, F. E.
1927 Cobb & Co.'s drivers answer the 1927 roll call in Melbourne (Smith's Weekly, 28 May 1927, p.15)

Gallagher, A. D. (Ned)
1915 Coach in Procession. A. D. (Ned) Gallagher driver (Courtesy Queensland Museum Collection)

Green, Jos.
1917 Mr. Jos. Green (Coaching in Australia, 1917, p.39)

Hall, Walter
1874 Walter Russell Hall [drawn by Helena Forde, Sydney] (State Library of New South Wales)
Pre-1911 Portrait of Walter Hall [T. R. Dibdin] (Mitchell Library, State Library of New South Wales)
Walter Hall (State Library Queensland)

Halvorsen, Herman
Herman Halvorsen, mail coach to Ayr. (State Library Qld, Image number: bur00051, Burdekin Shire Council Library Services)

Harman, Arthur John
Badges: The badges belonged to Arthur John Harman (1866-1962), a coach driver for Cobb & Co. (Cobb & Co's Old Coach Driver's Association [realia], Record ID 9917655723607636. State Library Victoria)

Hewitt, Cyrus
1860 Two men seated in a buggy, Cyrus Hewitt on left, beard, wearing top hat; J. M. Peck on right, moustache, also wearing top hat (State Library Victoria)

Hickson, Harry
1950 Harry Hickson (Morning Bulletin, 23 Mar 1950, p.8)

Hirschberg, Joe
ca. 1915 Joe Hirschberg's coach, Croydon to Forsayth (State Library of Queensland)

ca. 1920 Joe Hirschberg on Duchess to Camooweal Route (Queensland Museum Collections)

Holman, S. C.
1927 Cobb & Co.'s drivers answer the 1927 roll call in Melbourne (Smith's Weekly, 28 May 1927, p.15)

Houston, Dick
1925 On Dick Houston's old run to the New England (The Stirring Days of Cobb and Co., 10 Apr 1925, p.28)

Jackson, Peleg Whitford
1880 Peleg Whitford Jackson (State Library of South Australia)

Jarvis, C.
1955 Cobb & Co coach No. 48 at Lennons Hotel, part of the celebrations for the Cobb & Co Stamp Run (Queensland Museum Collections)

Jinks, Mary
She drove for Cobb and Co, Weekly Times, 22 Aug 1951, p.32 (State Library Victoria)

Jensen, Alf
ca. 1910 Cobb & Co coach at Yuleba, driver Alf Jensen, manager Arthur Senyard near lead horse (Queensland Museum Collection)

Johnston, J.
1927 Cobb & Co.'s drivers answer the 1927 roll call in Melbourne (Smith's Weekly, 28 May 1927, p.15)

Jonson, Andes
1897 Andes Johnson, Cobb & Co. (Cobb's Coach to Orbost, 20 Nov 1897, p.20)

Lamb, Frank
1927 This photograph of Cobb and Co.'s coach which ran between Taroom and Miles was taken some years ago. Mr. Frank Lamb was the driver (No title, The Brisbane Courier, 11 Mar 1927, p.16)

Lambell, W. E.
1927 Cobb & Co.'s drivers answer the 1927 roll call in Melbourne (Smith's Weekly, 28 May 1927, p.15)

Lawton, Tom (Tommy)
1955 The original Cobb and Co. coach, with former driver, Tom Lawton, seen., in centre, drew special applause from thousands who lined the route of the procession (Beautiful effects in floats, 8 Sep 1955, p.7)
1955 Cobb & Co coach No.100 outside Brisbane GPO, Queen Street, driver Tom Lawton (Queensland Museum Collection)

Lowe, James (Jim)
1937 James Lowe (Gold Digging Days, 2 Aug 1937, p.2)

Lumley, Harry
1917 Harry Lumley (Coaching in Australia, 1917, p.39)

Lyall, James A. (Jas)
ca. 1892 Cobb & Co. Coach with driver James A. Lyall, Hamilton c. 1892. The coach is driven by James A. Lyall with 5 horses drawing an impressive carriage crowded with of passengers, inside the coach and on the roof. Some of the passengers are holding placards. The carriage is on the street outside the Bank of Victoria. The company's General Booking Office was next to the Victoria Hotel, Thompson-street, Hamilton. Inscribed in pencil on verso : 'Hamilton / Coach driven by / Jas. A Lyall / c. 1892'. (Royal Historic Society of Victoria)"
1925 Coach driven by Jas. A. Lyall at Hamilton in 1892." (The Old Coaching Days, 3 Jan 1925, p.34)

Maloney, William (Bill/Billy Snr)
1935 A mail coach of the eighties leaving Hill End goldfields for Bathurst. The driver is William Maloney, who still resides at Bathurst, N.S.W. (The Lights of Cobb & Co, 17 Jul 1935, pp.22-23)

Mathieson, Jack
1910 Coach leaving Surat, driver may be Jack Mathieson (Queensland Museum Collection)

McCrae, Roderick
Roderick McCrae—Police Camp Barron River, Port Douglas-Herberton Road (Brisbane John Oxley Library, State Library of Queensland)

McDonald, Wm. (Bill/Billy)
1920 Crossing the flooded Paroo River at Eulo by punt, Billy McDonald driver (Queensland Museum Collections)

McMillan, Ted (Possible Cobb and Co driver)
Ted McMilliam—Front row: G. Wells Snr., H. Dodds, Ted McMillan [noted early coach driver]. Back row: Thomas Graham [grandson of T. Boyd], unidentified, G. Wells Jnr., Joseph Villicott. (Brisbane John Oxley Library, State Library of Queensland)

Miles, John
Coaching in Australia, 1917, p.39

Mills, S.
1927 Image: Cobb & Co.'s drivers answer the 1927 roll call in Melbourne. (Smith's Weekly, 28 May 1927, p.15)

Norton, John Alfonsus
1895 Mail Coach (Ballarat area), John Alfonsus Norton driver (Queensland Museum Collection)

O'Hea, C.
1927 Cobb & Co.'s drivers answer the 1927 roll call in Melbourne image (Smith's Weekly, 28 May 1927, p.15)

Palmer, E. A.
1920 E. A. Palmer coach. E.A. Palmer was a former driver and road inspector for Cobb & Co. who bought all the company's Charleville equipment and plant in 1921. (Queensland Museum Collections)

Palmer, Richard
[Gunn, Lantern Slide Maker] (The Sovereign Hill Museums Association Limited, Ballarat, Victoria)

Peck, John Murray
1860 Two men seated in a buggy, Cyrus Hewitt on left, beard, wearing top hat; J. M. Peck on right, moustache, also wearing top hat (State Library Victoria)
1941 Annual report and balance sheet/Cobb & Co.'s Old Coach Drivers' Association, p.7 (State Library Victoria)

Richards, A. E. (Ted)
Glass plate negative, Cobb and Co's Royal Mail coach, Richmond, North Queensland in 1906. The driver is Mr A. E. (Ted) Richards who drove the coach on the Richmond to

Cloncurry run (National Archives of Australia)

Richards, J. Frederick (Fred)
1910 Heavy load of mail, Julia Creek, driver Fred Richards [J. Backward N.Q.R. photographer] (Queensland Museum Collections)
1911 Bogged coach, Mary Ann Creek, Fred Richards driver (Queensland Museum Collections)
1912 Cobb & Co coach No. 118, between Yuleba to Surat, driver Fred Richards (Queensland Museum Collections)

Richardson, C.
1955 Cobb & Co coach No. 48 at Lennons Hotel, part of the celebrations for the Cobb & Co Stamp Run (Queensland Museum Collections)

Richardson, William
1872 IWilliam was a driver of Cobb & Co Coaches between Warwick and Tenterfield. Later a driver of a 15 seater coach belonging to Richardson's Stanthorpe Texas Royal Mail with passengers (State Library of Queensland)

Robertson, Alexander William
Alexander William Robertson (Glen Eira Historical Society)

Rogers, S.
1927 Cobb & Co.'s drivers answer the 1927 roll call in Melbourne (Smith's Weekly, 28 May 1927, p.15)

Rutherford, James
1872 James Rutherford[T. F. Chuck] (State Library Victoria)
James Rutherford, National Advocate (Bathurst), 19 Nov 1913, p.3 Coaching in Australia, 1917, p.15

Scott, Fred
1924 'The Good Old Coaching Days', The Australasian (Melbourne, Vic. : 1864 - 1946), 18 October, p. 65. , Nov 2023, http://nla.gov.au/nla.news-article140763086

Sheehan, M. J.
1927 Cobb & Co.'s drivers answer the 1927 roll call in Melbourne (Smith's Weekly, 28 May 1927, p.15)

Sheraton, Lou
Morning Bulletin (Rockhampton, Qld) 23 Mar 1950, p.6

Smiley, Frank
1924 'The Good Old Coaching Days', The Australasian (Melbourne, Vic. : 1864 - 1946), 18 October, p. 65. , Nov 2023, http://nla.gov.au/nla.news-article140763086

Smiley, S. P.
1924 'The Good Old Coaching Days', The Australasian (Melbourne, Vic. : 1864 - 1946), 18 October, p. 65. , Nov 2023, http://nla.gov.au/nla.news-article140763086

Smith, Ernie Parr (Possible Cobb and Co. driver)
Coach at Langlo Hotel (Queensland Museum Collections)

Smith, Billy
ca. 1895 Cobb & Co coach at Horse Shoe Bend Hotel, Hughenden-Muttaburra Route, Tommy Thompson and possibly Billy Smith (Queensland Museum Collections)

Taylor, B. F.
1927 Cobb & Co.'s drivers answer the 1927 roll call in Melbourne image (Smith's Weekly, 28 May 1927, p.15)

Taylor, R. F.
1927 Cobb & Co.'s drivers answer the 1927 roll call in Melbourne image (Smith's Weekly, 28 May 1927, p.15)

Thompson, Jack
1905 Hughenden-Muttaburra route [E. Spike photographer] (Brisbane John Oxley Library, State Library of Queensland)

Thompson/Thomson, Fred (Tommy)
ca. 1895 Cobb & Co coach at Horse Shoe Bend Hotel, Hughenden-Muttaburra Route. Driver is Tommy Thompson (Queensland Museum Collections)
ca. 1920 Cobb & Co coach No. 141, Surat to Yuleba Route, driver Fred Thompson (Queensland Museum Collections)
1920 Ballon River Ferry, driver Tommy Thompson (Queensland Museum Collections)
1920 Bainbilla horse change on Yuleba Surat route, Horrobin family property and horse change,Fred Thomson driver (Queensland Museum Collections)
1925 Cobb & Co's last coach run Surat to Yuleb, Fred Thompson driver (Queensland Museum Collections)
1925 Cobb & Co coach from Yuleba to Surat at Beranga Station, driver Fred Thomson, Alice Coleman (nee Wilson) photographer (Queensland Museum Collections)

Wagner, John
1890 John Wagner (1827-1901), a proprietor Of Cobb & Co. [Catani, U.] (State Library Victoria)

Walker, Alex
1872 Alex Walker [identity not confirmed as Cobb and Co.'s Alex Walker] [Chuck, Thomas Foster] (State Library Victoria)

Watson, H.
1927 Cobb & Co.'s drivers answer the 1927 roll call in Melbourne image (Smith's Weekly, 28 May 1927, p.15)

Watt, C. H.
1927 Cobb & Co.'s drivers answer the 1927 roll call in Melbourne (Smith's Weekly, 28 May 1927, p.15)

White, Buster
Buster White [Gunn Lantern Slide Maker] (The Sovereign Hill Museums Association Limited, Ballarat, Victoria)

Whitney, Frank
1900-1915 Mr Frank Whitney amongst workshop, Mandurama, New South Wales [E. A. Lumme] (National Library of Australia)
1900-1915 Mr Whitney holding horse, Coombing Park, New South Wales [Evan Antoni Johann Lumme 1865-1935] (National Library of Australia)

Williams, C.
1927 Image: "Cobb & Co.'s drivers answer the 1927 roll call in Melbourne" (Smith's Weekly, 28 May 1927, p.15)

Winkler, E.
1927 Cobb & Co.'s drivers answer the 1927 roll call in Melbourne (Smith's Weekly, 28 May 1927, p.15)

Right top: Cobb & Co. Drivers answer the 1927 Roll Call in Melbourne—Courtesy State Library of Queensland

Right: The Old Cobb's drivers taken at Gelong [Geelong] (Every-Day Snapshot Co., photographer)—Courtesy State Library Victoria

COBB & CO.'S DRIVERS ANSWER THE 1927 ROLL CALL IN MELBOURNE.

Front Row: G. Wright, R. B. Cozens, W. E. Lambell, S. Holman, H. Watson, N. Dowling, J. Bell, T. Bradley, C. Andrews. Second Row: G. Bromley, C. Williams, W. H. J. Britton, J. Corbett, J. Buckley, A. Alder, F. Edgcombe, J. Alder, H. J. Classen. Third Row: S. Rogers, J. Johnston, D. H. Carlisle, W. C. Crawford, M. J. Sheehan, C. H. Watt, J. H. Cuthbert, R. F. Taylor. Back Row: F. Smiley, J. Drayton, C. O'Hea, E. Winkler, S. Mills, F. E. Fogarty, G. M. Davis, J. P. Taylor.

Remembering Cobb and Co.

1947 Cobb & Co. Coach No. 100 prior to restoration, Charlie Sullivan driver, Charleville Centenary 1947 (George Balsillie photographer)—Courtesy Queensland Museum Collection

2022 Coach No. 100—Courtesy John Elliott, writer/photographer, & Toowoomba Cobb+Co. Museum

Cobb+Co Museum, Toowoomba

The Bolton Family were the pioneers of the Cobb+Co. Museum currently located in Toowoomba. Mr. William Robert Fossey Bolton (Bill), who is no longer with us, received a Scholarship and was schooled at The Toowoomba Grammar School. He was an accountant and practiced in the Public Service, being highly complemented whilst in this employment. Mr Bolton had a strong interest in literature, transport, horses and ultimately Cobb and Co.

In the 1950's, Mr Bolton felt *"Australian children know all about Wells Fargo and the American Express Company,* he says, *but little about the even more romantic and exciting story of Cobb & Co., and of the men who opened up half a continent by their energy, resourcefulness and courage."* (Walkabout, 1 Sep 1966, p.32) so Mr Bolton instigated the idea of a 'horse drawn' private museum, located under his transport depot. The museum included a piece of granite from Scotland.

After a fire in the 1980s, when the coaches were saved because of the quick thinking of Mr John Osbourne, the museum was relocated and developed into the current Cobb+Co Museum, which is a "part of the Queensland Museum and is home to the National Carriage Collection." (Queensland Museum Network, 2022)

Because of Mr. William Bolton's love of Cobb & Co, he interview a number of drivers or their descendants. The following letter is one such letter that has survived the ravages of time—now held for posterity.

1980 Cobb & Co. depot fire, removing Coach 100 from burning Cobb & Co. depot, John Osborne on the right, Chris Goodall on left—Courtesy Queensland Museum Collection

Eugowra Escort Robbery

Images: Letter from William K. Fagan to Mr Bill Bolton

"7-111-1967 Dear Mr. Bolton. I received your letter some days ago with interest, it will be a great pleasure to call and see you some day. With regard to the matter of Cobb & Co being involved at the Eugowra Escort Robbery on the 15th June 1862. I can assure you that Cobb & Co was involved to the extent of being the owners of 'the Coach'. My Grand-Father John Fagan was the Driver for Cobb & Co. at that time, this of course was known to Reg Fagan my Father who often spoke about it to me. Of course I was not born when my Grand-Father died 15 Sept 1912. I visited the 'Site' of the Robbery with the late Reg Fagan who explained it all to me as he had it explained to him by John Fagan his father & driver of the coach. He said it was a Cobb & Co Coach which the company had brought from Melbourne. I may add that John Fagan had been a driver for Cobb & Co in Victoria before they came to this area & of course this was how he got his connection with them in this district. I hope this will be of interest to you. King regards, sincerely William K. Fagan"
(Source: Mr. David Bolton, son of Mr Bill Bolton)

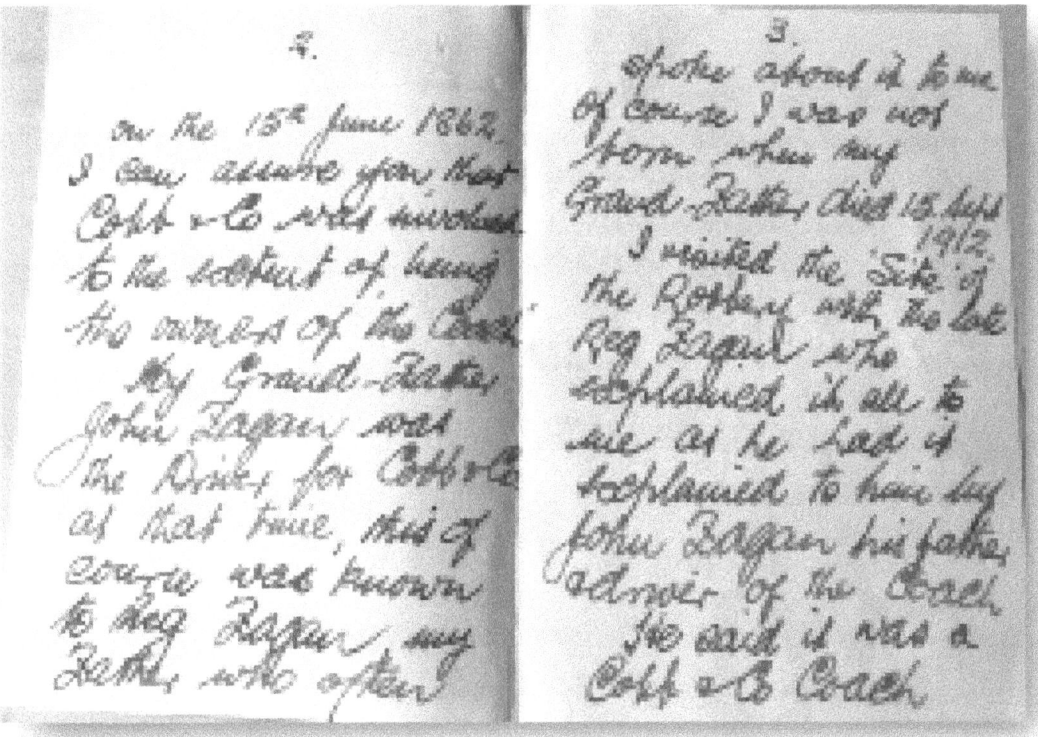

Letter from William K. Fagan to Mr. Bill Bolton—Courtesy of Mr. David Bolton

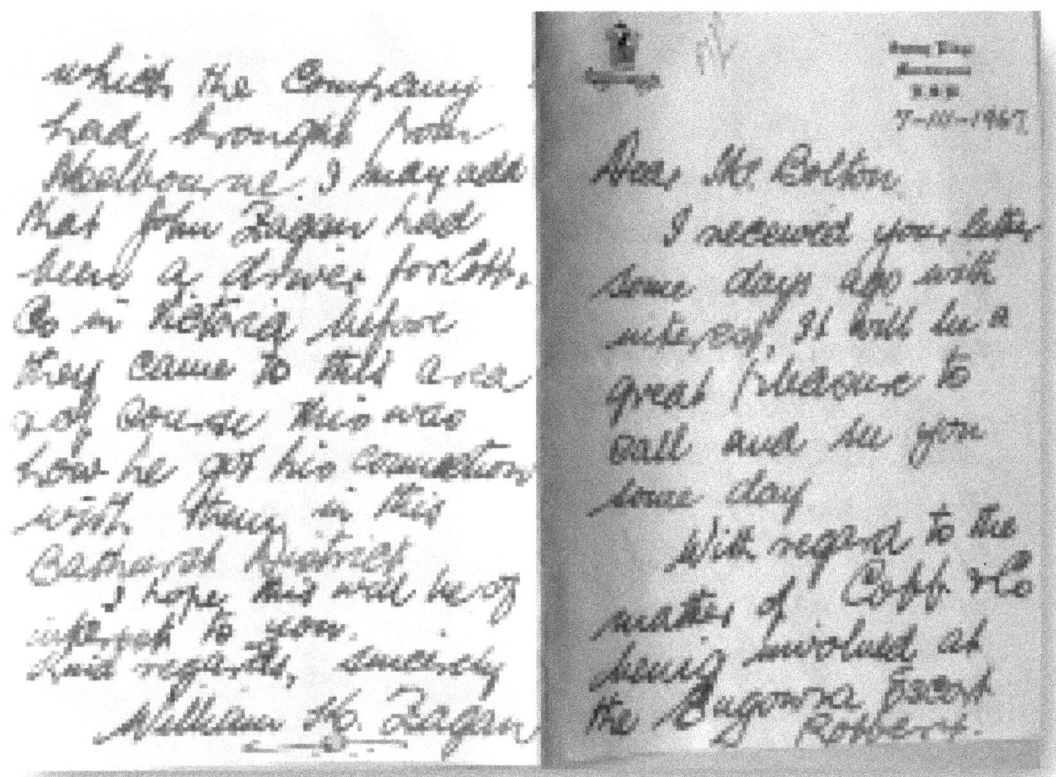

Cobb and Co.

Many spokes in the wheel ... until the wheels turned no more ...

"They were good days—the days of Cobb and Co … along the roads there still remain old and ruined 'Travellers' Rests' and 'Squatters' Arms' to remind us of the days that are gone ; at the rear of these old ruins, with their broken, rusty, and crooked lamp-posts and sign-boards, now hanging dejected and useless, are big tottering wrecks that once were barns and stables ; old slab structures that once accommodated coach-horses and sheltered commercials' buggies; but they have out-lived their usefulness. In some there are the remains of old coaches, and at evening when the light is soft, when the hot sun has sunk behind the hills in the west, little children climb upon the box seat, and clamber inside and play at Cobb and Co. ; methinks, if the spirits of the past revisit the earth, there are ghostly drivers on the box seat driving spectral coach-horses. And the old 'Travellers' Rests' and 'Welcome Homes' and 'Macquarie Arms' are aglow with light and laughter, as the spirits of the long-ago arrive or depart—by Cobb and Co's Royal Mail; but there remains a fragrant memory, to many a perennial source of pleasure—or sorrow?"

For joys, wax dim and woes deaden,
We forget the sorrowful biers
And the garlands glad that have fled in
The merciful march of years.

GORDON, Valé!
(Cobb and Co., 10 Jan 1903, p.1)

"In the winter of 1853, four young Americans who were in the employ of one or the other of the two leading U.S.A. Express (or Carrying) Companies Wells, Fargo and Co (Ben Holliday)., and the Adams Express Co. came out to Victoria:- **Freeman Cobb**, of Brewster, Massachusetts; **John Murray Peck**, of Lebanon, New Hampshire; **James Swanton**, of Omar, in New York State; and **John B. Lamber**, of Leavenworth, out in the far west of those days, Kansas."
(a [?] Drive, 31 July 1937, p.4)

"**George Francis Train**, in his book 'My Life of Many States and Foreign Lands', 1902, says: I told Freeman Cobb, who was then with Adams and Co., that I wanted him to start a line of coaches between Melbourne and the gold-mines, a distance of about sixty miles. I advanced the money for the enterprise, and a line was established, the first in Australia ... These were the first coaches seen in that continent."
(My Life of Many States and Foreign Lands, 1902, pp133-134)

"**Freeman Cobb** came to Melbourne at the end of 1852, or beginning of 1853, with **George Mowton**, to form a branch of Adam and Co, famed in the United States as express carriers."
(Miscellaneous, 5 Oct 1878, p.6)

'The name 'Cobb and Co.' is about all there ever was to associate **Winslow and Freeman Cobb** with the great system of passenger transport in Australia." (Stories of the Cobb & Co Coaching Days, 19 Dec 1920, p18)

"**Winslow Cobb and his brother** (the founders of the coaching business of Cobb and Co)."
(Personal, 29 Apr 1917, p.12)

James Rutherford, Hiram Cobb, J. M. Peck, Wagner and Jack Robertson. With Australians Jesse Brown ... and Hiram Barnes ... they were the first Cobb and Co. coach drivers in Victoria.
(When Cobb and Co. Came To Cunnamulla, 10 Sep 1953, p.15)

1953 They commenced carrying from Liardet's (Port Melbourne) to the City of Melbourne for a start but 'no road' across the swamp between Emerald Hill, now South Melbourne, and the river was such a quagmire that their waggons sank to the hubs ... They advised their principals in the United States against the carrying business, but told them that there was a good opening for a real up-to-date line of coaches to the diggings ... The United States companies turned down the coaching proposition. (a [?] Drive, 31 July 1937, p.4)

The four 'Boys,' as they called themselves, raised all the capital they could, and on January 30, 1854, started, as Cobb and Co., their first coach from the Criterion Hotel, Collins street, Melbourne, for the Forest Creek diggings, now Castlemaine, under the title of, as advertised in 'The Argus' of the day, *The American Telegraph Line of Coaches*. Within 12 months Lamber retired and Arthur Blake went into the partnership. The new firm—Melbourne and Forest Creek, extended the lines to Bendigo, and opened branches to Maryborough and other centres, and later to Swan Hill. Soon other Americans and Canadians ('Yankees' and 'Canuks') followed, some joining Cobb and Co. as drivers. (a [?] Drive, 31 July 1937, p.4)

1857 Freeman and Peck but not Swanton returned to the United States

1857 Thomas Davies bought Cobb and Co., added Ballarat line ... It is said the purchase money was 16,000 pounds (Cobb & Co., 27 Mar 1933, p.4) ... on 13 May 1857 Thomas Davies, Esq [Cobb and Co.] offered 25 mares and geldings each with a wharf-dray and harness for public auction ... business sold to Alexander Walker, who for want of finance had to sell—Tenders for Lines of Coaches, known as Cobb and Co.'s Telegraph and Estafette Lines, 16 Oct 1857 (Advertising, 16 Oct 1857, p.7)—he sold to George Watson and Cyrus Hewitt, who had a livery stable in Melbourne

At various times, other sources state the owners of Cobb and Co. were:

- Mr. Alfred Wools-Cobb, came out from England to take over Cobb & Co.'s coach company from its American owner
- About 1857 Hewitt and Watson sold out to the big firm, the shareholders of which were James Rutherford (U.S.A.), John Wagner (Canadian), A W. Robertson (Canadian), B. and C. Robertson (Canadian) and Pollock, Walter R. Hall (Yorkshireman), and W. F. Whitney
- Hiram Cobb returned to USA and sold to Rutherford, J. M. Peck, Wagner and Jack Robertson—Walter Hall added as business head
- Rutherford said "I formed a company to buy him [Freeman Cobb] out. The partnership was as follows :— James Rutherford, one share; John Wagner, one share; A. W. Robertson, one share; B. and C. Robertson and Pollock, one share, Walter R. Hall and W. F. Whitney, one share." 1924
- 1862 Rutherford joined with Alexander William Robertson, Walter Hall, W. F. Whitcombe and James Wagner
- Mr Thomas Coyle—late in the '60 the firm consisted of Frank Whitney, Walter Hall, James Rutherford, and a wealthy Melbourne racing man named Power—after about ten years of management I was taken in as a partner, with a fifth share in the whole concern
- 1876 George Watson : "I am a partner in the firm of Robertson, Wagner and Co., coach proprietors."

1857 Watson and Hewitt only held the lines and branches to the earlier diggings for a very brief spell, bought out Foster and Vinge on the Sydney road toward the end of 1857, and sold the Ballarat line and branches to Frank B. Clapp and Co (a [?] Drive, 31 July 1937, p.4)

Peck subsequently returned to Australia with a cargo of the famous American 'Jack' coaches and the harness to equip them … The Big 'Jacks' 40 passengers (a [?] Drive, 31 July 1937, p.4) In 1858 a new company was formed to take over Peck's shipment … The new company consisted of 13 partners, Peck, his old original partner, James Swanton, Anthony Blake, George Woodworth, and nine others, nearly all Yanks or Canuks, and formerly drivers or overseers of the old firm, and registered as the Victorian Stage Co., (Swanton, Blake & Co) but, of course, still running under the old Cobb and Co. name. (a [?] Drive, 31 July 1937, p.4)

1860 Watson and Hewitt bought Victorian Stage Company

7 Jun 1861 "Cobb's Coaches —We understand that Messrs. Watson and Hewitt, who have for so long been the proprietors of Cobb's Telegraph Line of Coaches, have disposed of all their interest in the line to Messrs. Robertson, Britton, and Co." (The Comet, 7 Jun 1861, p.3) … then its registration changed to Robertson, Wagner and Co (A. W. Robertson, John Wagner, James Rutherford, Walter Russell Hall, W. Franklin, Walter Bradley [known generally as 'Old Brad' to distinguish him from 'Hoppy Brad,' the famous driver] and R Brunig) but ran under the old magical name of Cobb and Co … Then in 1862 James Rutherford, Walter Hall, Whitney, Bradley and John Robertson (A.W.'s brother) went to Bathurst and established the N.S.W. headquarters … and in 1865 Hiram Barnes went over to Brisbane with 16 coaches

1871 The company divided … Robertson and Wagner took over Victoria and some N.S.W. assets

1871 The company divided … Rutherford, Whitney, Hall and Bradley took some of N.S.W and Queensland … Bradley left mid-seventies, 1880 Hall retired and in 1893 Whitney died

14 August 1924 The last Cobb and Co. coach was taken off the road Surat to Yeulba [on the Yeulba-St. George run] (The Last Coach, 5 Sep 1924, p.16)

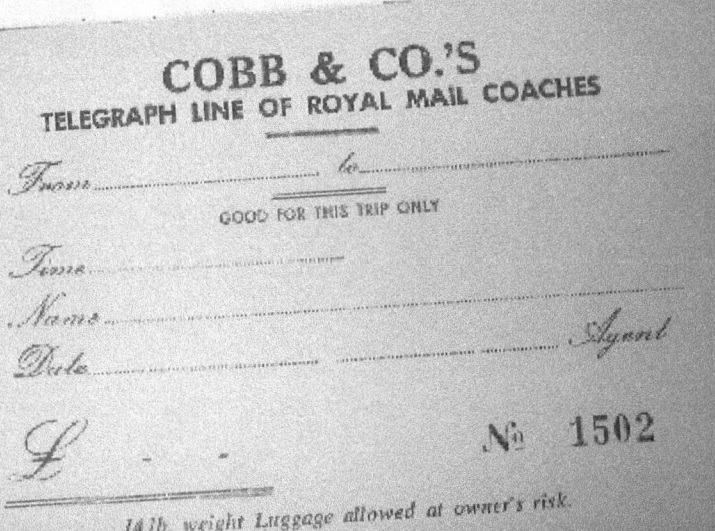

Original Cobb and Co. coach ticket book
—Courtesy Ray Green, Bathurst

1906 Cobb and Co. Alice River, Barcaldine - Courtesy Bathurst District Historical Society

1955 Cobb & Co. coach No.100 outside Brisbane GPO, Queen Street, driver Tom Lawton
—Courtesy Queensland Museum Collection

Waiting for the train, Healesville tunnel (John Henry Harvey, 1855-1938, photographer)—Courtesy State Library Victoria

1909 Haines & Grut Motor Buggy Co, Motor Buggy, Melbourne, Victoria
—Courtesy Museums Victoria

Appendices
Appendix 1.1

1853 George Mowton arrival in Australia, age 35 years, 1 April 1853, Ship Fanny from USA—Inwards Overseas Passenger Lists, p.1, Apr-May 1853, Public Record Office Victoria

Appendix 1.2

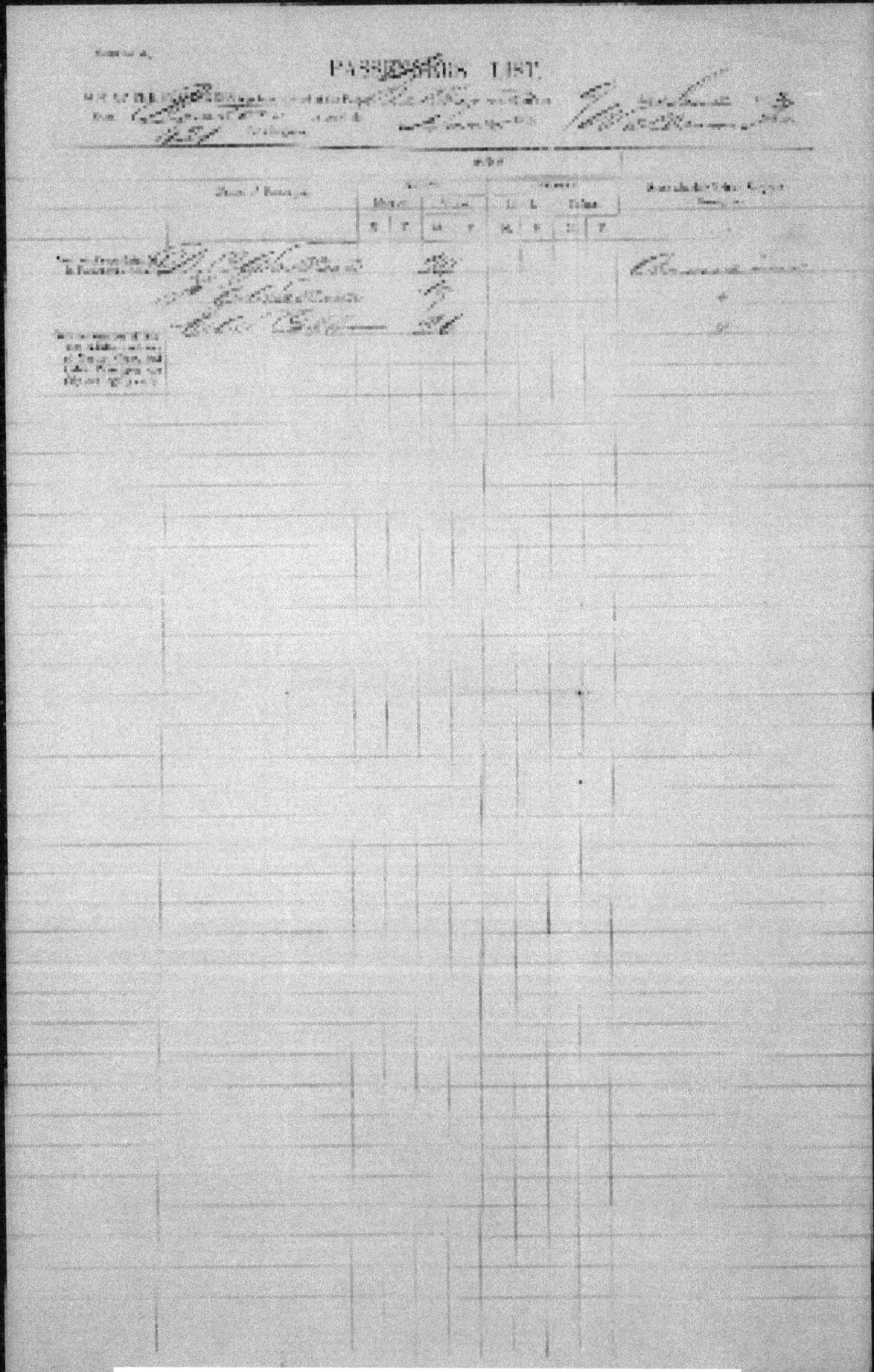

1853 E. W. Cobb arrival in Melbourne, Australia, age 26 years, 9 June 1853, Ship Homer from Boston—Inwards Overseas Passenger Lists, p.65, Jun-Jul 1853, Public Record Office Victoria

Appendix 1.3

1856 Freeman Cobb (aged 30) & J. Lamber (aged 36) departure from Australia to Liverpool, Ship Royal Charter, 24 May 1856—1856 Outward Passengers to Interstate, U.K. and Foreign Ports, p.98, Public Record Office Victoria

Appendix 1.4

1856 Freeman Cobb (aged 30) & J. Lamber (aged 36) departure from Australia to Liverpool, Ship Royal Charter, 24 May 1856—1856 Outward Passengers to Interstate, U.K. and Foreign Ports, p.98, Public Record Office Victoria

Appendix 1.5

1856 E. W. Cobb (aged 30) departure from Melbourne to Sydney, Ship Golden Age, 5 May 1856—1856 Outward Passengers to Interstate, U.K. and Foreign Ports, p.101, Public Record Office Victoria

Appendix 1.6

RELATION TO THE FEMALE RAPIDS, BILL MOBEY, JACK SPEARS,
Charlie Hooper, Hugh Hamilton, Bill Williams, Tom Roberts,
George Roberts, Jim Kidd, Dick Sams, Sam Williams, Dave Roan,
Tom Sharpe, Joe Bordman, Miss Bella Lowe, (sister of W.J.Lowe)
was machinist.

Old identities whom I have driven: Judge Wilkinson,
Judge Bowler, Duke of Manchester, Western and Sharpe.

Jose Jenkins was driving on the Mudgee line one morning
just as the sun was rising. A large kangaroo hopped up and stood
on the side of the road. Joe had a new chum on the box seat
at the side of him. Joe said "No mail to-day,"and cracked his
whip and the 'roo marched off. The new chum said "Is that not
wonderful, but I would like to have his fur coat."

Another incident that happened with a driver named
Frank Morris. He was coming down Cockatoo Hill one day. Something startled the horses. He also had a new chum on the near
side of the box seat, where there was also a brake handle so that
any passenger could assist the driver if it was needed. Frank
said to him: "Put your foot on the brake, please". The new
chum didn't know what he wanted. Frank said again "Put your
foot on the brake will you?" Still he didn't understand. Then
Frank roared "Put your foot on the brake you b.... or your soul
will be in blazes in less than five minutes." They struck a
tree and capsized the coach. Frank was the only one who got
seriously hurt. He had his shoulder broken and five of his ribs
broken, also a severe cut over his left eye.

The horses got away with the front carriage, and went
about seven miles into Sofala and ran against a telegraph post
in front of old Jack Smith's blacksmith shop. The horses were
played out. The bars cut their legs badly

Ted Latham was a manager for Cobb & Company. I think
he had been a driver also. He had a bald head, no more hair
than on the palm of my hand. He wore a wig. One day in a hotel
an argument rose as to strength. There was a big fellow there;
Latham bet him five pounds that he could not lift him off his

[handwritten margin note]: at 7 GREAT SHOCK WHEN HE ATTEMPTED TO LIFT HIM, THE WIG CAME

---

100 OR MORE HORSES WITH THIS REMEDY,AND I CANT HAD ONE DIE
and that was brought about by different people advising the
owner of the horse to give it this, that and the other thing.
the horse was actually poisoned by the different stuff that
he got.

I have seen horses on the streets and gone up and
said, your horse is sick.

There were three members of the firm of Cobb & Company.
I remember Mr. James Rutherford, Senr. I was with him for
most of my lifetime as a general hand or a coach driver.

Mr. Rutherford was the principal of Cobb & Company.
The other members of the firm were Messrs. Whitney and Hall.
I knew Mr. Whitney and also Mr. Hall very well, but was
actually under Mr. James Rutherford all the time I was in the
firm, and he appeared to me to be the head man of Cobb's firm.
I do not think there was ever anything done without Mr. Rutherford was first consulted. This was probably on account of him
being a good manager and knowing better than Mr. Hall or Mr.
Whitney how to act.

Names of old drivers that had driven for Cobb & Company:
Billy Orbel, Jimmy Vane, (better known as Cabbage Tree Head),
Jose Jenkins, Charlie Bisse , Deny Doll, Bob Mugridge, Jimmy
Fitzpatrick, James Lowe, Pat Tery, Harry Page, Frank Bissel,
Harry Holland, Jimmy Frost, Jimmy Little, Jimmy Small, Pat.
Houligan, Pat Donanon, Pat. Farrell, Ross Hood, Jim Moran, Jim
Hunter, Martin Murphy, Tom Kennedy, Peter Lewis, Jim Drew,
Bob Rogers, Harry King, George Woods, Harry Nolan, Adam Nolen,
George Norris, Bill Waldren, Pat. Meagher, Billy Peters, Frank
Morris, Tom Morris, Jack Forman, Jack Lloyd (who after became
manager of Hornby Station for Cobb & Co.) Jim Weldron (also
became manager on the roads) and Albert Hamilton.

There are many more drivers whom I just can't remember.

I fancy they are all dead except two - Jimmie Doran
of Goulburn and Ross Hood of Wellington.

MEMBERS OF THE FACTORY: Davey Brown was Foreman.

Account from Bill Lowe (Cobb and Co. driver from the age of 15)—Courtesy Rutherford Family

Reference List

Special thanks to The National Library Australia and the contributions of the following: State Library New South Wales and Library Council of New South Wales, State Library of Queensland and Queensland Government, State Library Victoria, W & F Pascoe Pty. Ltd, Vincent Fairfax Family Foundation, State Library of Western Australia, State Library South Australia, Orange & District Historical Society collection, Sovereign Hill Museums and Queensland Museum.

'MEMOIRS OF JOHN MURRAY PECK', PECK, Harry Huntington - Victoria in the 1850s. The origins and early history of Cobb and Co., and memoirs of John Murray Peck, one of its founders. Unpublished. https://trove.nla.gov.au/work/227766194?keyword=Cobb%20%26%20Co%20Victoria (Memoirs of John Murray Peck)

1854 'ADVERTISING', The Argus (Melbourne, Vic. : 1848 - 1957), 24 November, p. 6. , viewed 16 Oct 2022, http://nla.gov.au/nla.news-article4800754. (Advertising, 24 Nov 1854, p.6)

1854 'ADVERTISING', The Argus (Melbourne, Vic. : 1848 - 1957), 25 November, p. 6. , viewed 16 Oct 2022, http://nla.gov.au/nla.news-article4800795. (Advertising, 25 Nov 1854, p.6)

1854 'ADVERTISING', The Argus (Melbourne, Vic. : 1848 - 1957), 31 January, p. 3. , viewed 22 Jul 2022, http://nla.gov.au/nla.news-article4802637. (Advertising, 31 Jan 1854, p.3)

1854 'GLEANINGS FROM THE VICTORIA GOLD FIELDS.', The Sydney Morning Herald (NSW : 1842 - 1954), 4 May, p. 5. , viewed 22 Jul 2022, http://nla.gov.au/nla.news-article30940256. (Gleanings from the Victoria Gold Fields, 4 May 1854, p.5)

1855 'ADVERTISING', The Argus (Melbourne, Vic. : 1848 - 1957), 20 November, p. 3. , viewed 16 Oct 2022, http://nla.gov.au/nla.news-article4823798. (Advertising, 20 Nov 1855, p.3)

1855 'BEECHWORTH.', The Age (Melbourne, Vic. : 1854 - 1954), 22 December, p. 6. , viewed 22 Jul 2022, http://nla.gov.au/nla.news-article154859656. (Beechworth, 22 Dec 1855, p.6)

1855 'ORIGINAL CORRESPONDENCE.', Bendigo Advertiser (Vic. : 1855 - 1918), 25 October, p. 3. , viewed 22 Jul 2022, http://nla.gov.au/ nla.news-article88047797. (Original Correspondence, 25 Oct 1855, p.3)

1856 'CASTLEMAINE TOWN COUNCIL.', Mount Alexander Mail (Vic. : 1854 - 1917), 12 November, p. 3. , viewed 05 Aug 2022, http://nla.gov.au/nla.news-article202632854. (Castlemaine Town Council, 12 Nov 1856, p.3)

1856 'LOCAL INTELLIGENCE.', The Age (Melbourne, Vic. : 1854 - 1954), 23 July, p. 3. , viewed 05 Aug 2022, http://nla.gov.au/ nla.news-article154863725. (Local Intelligence, 23 Jul 1856, p.3)

1856 'NIGHT-TRAVELLING ON THE BENDIGO ROAD.', Bendigo Advertiser (Vic. : 1855 - 1918), 30 May, p. 2. , viewed 22 Jul 2022, http:// nla.gov.au/nla.news-article88050345. (Night-Travelling On The Bendigo Road, 30 May 1856, p.2)

1857 'ADVERTISING', The Argus (Melbourne, Vic. : 1848 - 1957), 16 October, p. 7. , viewed 16 Oct 2022, http://nla.gov.au/nla.news-article7140490. (Advertising, 16 Oct 1857, p.7)

1857 'ADVERTISING', The Argus (Melbourne, Vic. : 1848 - 1957), 7 May, p. 3. , viewed 17 Oct 2022, http://nla.gov.au/nla.news-article7131220 (Advertising, 7 May 1855, p.3)

1857 'SIR H. BARKLY IN CASTLEMAINE.', Bendigo Advertiser (Vic. : 1855 - 1918), 23 September, p. 2. , viewed 05 Aug 2022, http://nla.gov.au/nla.news-article88001919. (Sir H. Barkly, 23 Sep 1857)

1858 'A SPELL OFF.', The Star (Ballarat, Vic. : 1855 - 1864), 6 November, p. 2. , viewed 05 Aug 2022, http://nla.gov.au/nla.news-article66051013. (A Spell Off, 6 Nov 1858, p.2)

1858 'BALLAARAT GAOL ACCOMMODATION.', The Age (Melbourne, Vic. : 1854 - 1954), 6 March, p. 5. , viewed 05 Aug 2022, http://nla.gov.au/nla.news-article154858249. (Ballaarat Gaol Accommodation, 6 Mar 1858, p.5)

1858 'CASTLEMAINE.', Bendigo Advertiser (Vic. : 1855 - 1918), 13 January, p. 2. , viewed 28 Jul 2022, http://nla.gov.au/nla.news-article87978110. (Castlemaine, 13 Jan 1858, p.2)

1858 'FEARFUL FIRE AT BEECHWORTH.', Mount Alexander Mail (Vic. : 1854 - 1917), 6 January, p. 2. , viewed 13 Oct 2022, http://nla.gov.au/nla.news-article197087382. (Fearful Fire at Beechworth, 6 Jan 1858, p.2)

1858 'UNCERTAINTY OF MINING LAW.', Mount Alexander Mail (Vic. : 1854 - 1917), 29 October, p. 3. , viewed 05 Aug 2022, http://nla.gov.au/nla.news-article199051761. (Uncertainty of Mining Law, 29 Oct 1858, p.3)

1860 'CENTRAL POLICE COURT.', Geelong Advertiser (Vic. : 1859 - 1929), 23 August, p. 3. , viewed 07 Sep 2022, http://nla. gov.au/nla.news-article148885462. (Central Police Court, 23 Aug 1860, p.3)

1860 'CURRENT TOPICS.', Geelong Advertiser (Vic. : 1859 - 1929), 11 June, p. 2. , viewed 07 Sep 2022, http://nla.gov.au/nla. news-article148791637. (Current Topics, 11 Jun 1860, p.2)

1861 'KING COBB.', The Star (Ballarat, Vic. : 1855 - 1864), 15 February, p. 4. , viewed 29 Jul 2022, http://nla.gov.au/nla.news-article66337398. (King Cobb, 15 Feb 1861, p.4)

1864 'FORBES.', The Sydney Morning Herald (NSW : 1842 - 1954), 17 May, p. 4. , viewed 29 Apr 2023, http://nla.gov.au/nla.news-article13086133 (Forbes, 17 May 1864, p.4)

1864 'MUNICIPAL POLICE COURT.', Bendigo Advertiser (Vic. : 1855 - 1918), 7 July, p. 2. , viewed 03 Oct 2022, http://nla.gov. au/nla.news-article88002307. (Municipal Police Court, 7 Jul 1864, p.2)

1864 'NO TITLE', The Age (Melbourne, Vic. : 1854 - 1954), 7 July, p. 4. , viewed 30 Apr 2023, http://nla.gov.au/nla.news-article155016295 (No title, 7 Jul 1864, p.4)

1867 'FOUNDATION OF THE COLONY.', The South Australian Advertiser (Adelaide, SA : 1858 - 1889), 31 December, p. 2. , viewed 14 Oct 2022, http://nla.gov.au/nla.news-article28803452. (Foundations of the Colony, 31 Dec 1867, p.2)

1867 'ROMA', Dalby Herald and Western Queensland Advertiser (Qld. : 1866 - 1879), 5 October, p. 3. , viewed 23 May 2021,http://nla.gov.au/nla.news-article215449847 (Roma, 5 Oct 1867,p.3)

1868 'MONDAY, 1ST JUNE.', The Sydney Morning Herald (NSW : 1842 - 1954), 5 June, p. 3. , viewed 16 Dec 2022, http://nla.gov.au/nla.news-article13167374. (Monday 1st June, 5 Jun 1868, p.3)

1868 'STICKING UP OF COBB & CO.'S MAIL COACH, NEAR GYMPIE.', Maryborough Chronicle, Wide Bay and Burnett Advertiser (Qld. : 1860 - 1947), 5 September, p. 2. , viewed 27 Jul 2022, http://nla.gov.au/nla.news-article148015785. (Sticking up of Cobb & Co.'s Mail Coach, near Gympie, 5 Sep 1868, p.2)

1869 'CURRENT TOPICS.', Geelong Advertiser (Vic. : 1859 - 1929), 29 September, p. 2. , viewed 24 Apr 2023, http://nla.gov.au/nla.news-article150434446 (Current Topics, 29 Sep 1869, p.2)

1869 'ITEMS OF NEWS.', Mount Alexander Mail (Vic. : 1854 - 1917), 18 October, p. 2. , viewed 14 Oct 2022, http://nla.gov.au/ nla.news-article197309125. (Items of News, 18 Oct 1869, p.2)

1869 'SHIPPING.', The Brisbane Courier (Qld. : 1864 - 1933), 21 August, p. 4. , viewed 13 Oct 2022, http://nla.gov.au/nla.news-article1293875. (Shipping,21 Aug 1869, p.4)

1869 'UNDER THE VERANDAH.', Leader (Melbourne, Vic. : 1862 - 1918, 1935), 27 March, p. 17. , viewed 13 Oct 2022, http:// nla.gov.au/nla.news-article196482306. (Under the Verandah, 27 Mar 1869, p.17)

1870 'ATTEMPTED STICKING UP OF THE DUNOLLY MAIL.',

Geelong Advertiser (Vic. : 1859 - 1929), 22 February, p. 3. , viewed 07 Sep 2022, http://nla.gov.au/nla.news-article150437338. (Attempted Sticking Up Of The Dunolly Mail, 22 Feb 1870, p.3)

1870 'LICENSES UNDER THE LAND ACT.', Bendigo Advertiser (Vic. : 1855 - 1918), 16 December, p. 3. , viewed 15 Sep 2022, http://nla.gov.au/nla.news-article87916306. (Licenses Under The Land Act, 16 Dec 1870, p.3)

1870 'THURSDAY, OCTOBER 27, 1870.', The Argus (Melbourne, Vic. : 1848 - 1957), 27 October, p. 5. , viewed 23 Aug 2022, http://nla.gov.au/nla.news-article5836894. (Thursday, October 27, 1870, 27 Oct 1870, p.5)

1870 'WEDNESDAY, JULY 13.', Queensland Times, Ipswich Herald and General Advertiser (Qld. : 1861 - 1908), 14 July, p. 3. , viewed 29 Apr 2023, http://nla.gov.au/nla.news-article130842140 ('Wednesday, July 13', 14 Jul 1870, p.3)

1871 'GENERAL NEWS.', Southern Argus (Port Elliot, SA : 1866 - 1954), 25 February, p. 2. , viewed 06 Oct 2022, http://nla.gov. au/nla.news-article96872064. (General News, 25 Feb 1871, p.2)

1872 'COACH ACCIDENT.', Weekly Times (Melbourne, Vic. : 1869 - 1954), 6 April, p. 7. , viewed 09 Aug 2022, http://nla.gov. au/nla.news-article219362732. (Coach Accident, 6 Apr 1872, p.7)

1873 'BATHURST.', Evening News (Sydney, NSW : 1869 - 1931), 30 September, p. 2. , viewed 26 Apr 2023, http://nla.gov.au/nla.news-article107169098 (Bathurst, 30 Sep 1873, p.2)

1873 'CONDAMINE.', The Queenslander (Brisbane, Qld. : 1866 - 1939), 19 April, p. 10. , viewed 12 Oct 2022, http://nla.gov.au/nla.news-article27275612. (Condamine, 19 Apr 1873, p.10)

1873 'COUNTRY NEWS FROM COUNTRY PAPERS.', The Sydney Mail and New South Wales Advertiser (NSW : 1871 - 1912), 13 December, p. 765. , viewed 07 Oct 2022, http://nla.gov.au/nla.news-article162662309. (Country News from Country Papers, 13 Dec 1873, p.765)

1873 'DISASTROUS FLOOD AT INVERELL.', The Brisbane Courier (Qld. : 1864 - 1933), 7 January, p. 3. , viewed 06 Oct 2022, http://nla.gov.au/nla.news-article1305964. (Disastrous flood at Inverell, 7 Jan 1873, p.3)

1873 'EPITOME OF NEWS.', The Armidale Express and New England General Advertiser (NSW : 1856 - 1861; 1863 - 1889; 1891 - 1954), 5 April, p. 2. , viewed 09 Oct 2022, http://nla.gov.au/nla.news-article189987058. (Epitome of News, 5 Apr 1873, p.2)

1873 'FATAL COACH ACCIDENT ON THE WESTERN ROAD', The Maitland Mercury and Hunter River General Advertiser (NSW : 1843 - 1893), 14 June, p. 2. , viewed 27 Dec 2022, http://nla.gov.au/nla.news-article18774573 (Fatal Coach Accident On The Western Road, 14 Jun 1873, p.2)

1873 'NOTES AND NEWS.', Dalby Herald and Western Queensland Advertiser (Qld. : 1866 - 1879), 13 December, p. 2. , viewed 24 Apr 2023, http://nla.gov.au/nla.news-article215603426 (Notes and News, 13 Dec 1873, p.2)

1873 'SERIOUS ACCIDENT TO A MAIL DRIVER.', The Goulburn Herald and Chronicle (NSW : 1864 - 1881), 19 November, p. 4. , viewed 28 Sep 2022, http://nla.gov.au/nla.news-article101099690. (Serious Accident to a Mail Driver, 19 Nov 1873, p.4)

1873 'STANTHORPE.', The Telegraph (Brisbane, Qld. : 1872 - 1947), 23 June, p. 3. , viewed 20 Oct 2022, http://nla.gov.au/nla.news-article169485870. Stanthorpe, 23 Jun 1873, p.3)

1874 'ALEXANDRA TIMES.', Alexandra Times (Vic. : 1868 - 1877), 17 January, p. 2. , viewed 14 Oct 2022, http://nla.gov.au/nla.news-arti-cle58214571. (Alexandra Times, 17 Jan 1874, p.2)

1874 'DUBBO.', Empire (Sydney, NSW : 1850 - 1875), 3 June, p. 2. , viewed 27 Dec 2022, http://nla.gov.au/nla.news-article60988543. (Dubbo, 3 Jun 1874, p.2)

1874 'SALE POLICE COURT.', Gippsland Times (Vic. : 1861 - 1954), 2 June, p. 3. (Morning.), viewed 02 Nov 2022, http://nla.gov.au/nla.news-article61907610. (Sale Police Court, 2 Jun 1874, p.3)

1874 'SERIOUS COACH ACCIDENT.' (1874, May 27). The Herald (Melbourne, Vic. : 1861 - 1954), p. 3. Retrieved September 29, 2022, from http://nla.gov.au/nla.news-article244335789. (Serious Coach Accident, 27 May 1874, p.3)

1875 'ACCIDENT TO COBB AND CO.'S COACH.', The Daily Northern Argus (Rockhampton, Qld. : 1875 - 1896), 16 September, p. 2. , viewed 06 May 2023, http://nla.gov.au/nla.news-article213422363 (Accident to Cobb and Co.'s Coach, 16 Sep 1875, p.2)

1875 'COACH ACCIDENT.', The Herald (Melbourne, Vic. : 1861 - 1954), 30 August, p. 3. , viewed 15 Sep 2022, http://nla.gov.au/nla.news-article244175931. (Coach Accident, 30 Aug 1875, p.3)

1875 'COBB'S BOX.', Wagga Wagga Advertiser and Riverine Reporter (NSW : 1868 - 1875), 6 February, p. 4. , viewed 05 Aug 2022, http://nla.gov.au/nla.news-article104117694. (Cobb's Box, 6 Feb 1875, p.4)

1875 'ST. GEORGE.', The Queenslander (Brisbane, Qld. : 1866 - 1939), 14 August, p. 3. , viewed 08 Oct 2022, http://nla.gov.au/nla.news-article18337410. (St. George, 14 Aug 1875, p.3)

1875 'TENTERFIELD', Glen Innes Examiner and General Advertiser (NSW : 1874 - 1908), 30 June, p. 2. , viewed 1 Oct 2020, http://nla.gov.au/nla.news-article217833322 Page identifier http://nla.gov.au/nla.news-page23896014. (Tenterfield, 30 Jun 1875, p.2)

1875 'TENTERFIELD', Glen Innes Examiner and General Advertiser (NSW : 1874 - 1908), 25 August, p. 3. , viewed 1 Oct 2020, http://nla.gov.au/nla.news-article217834526 Page identifier http://nla.gov.au/nla.news-page23896046. (Tenterfield, 25 Aug 1875, pp.2-3)

1876 'A COACH-DRIVER IN TROUBLE.', The Herald (Melbourne, Vic. : 1861 - 1954), 21 January, p. 3. , viewed 07 Aug 2022, http://nla.gov.au/nla.news-article244279268. (A Coach-Driver in Trouble, 21 Jan 1876, p.3)

1876 'ACTION AGAINST COBB AND CO.', The Grenfell Record and Lachlan District Advertiser (NSW : 1876 - 1951), 2 September, p. 7. , viewed 15 Sep 2022, http://nla.gov.au/nla.news-article130883150. (Action Against Cobb And Co, 2 Sep 1876, p.7)

1876 'ADELAIDE.', The Telegraph (Brisbane, Qld. : 1872 - 1947), 22 April, p. 2. , viewed 02 Oct 2022, http://nla.gov.au/nla.news-article169494471. (Adelaide, 22 Apr 1876, p.2)

1876 'CHARLEVILLE TO DALBY PER COBB AND CO.'S COACH.', Western Star and Roma Advertiser (Qld. : 1875 - 1948), 22 January, p. 3. , viewed 01 Nov 2022, http://nla.gov.au/nla.news-article97420439. (Charleville to Dalby per Cobb and Co's Coach, 22 Jan 1876, p.3)

1877 'LATE EPITOME OF NEWS.', The Armidale Express and New England General Advertiser (NSW : 1856 - 1861; 1863 - 1889; 1891 - 1954), 18 May, p. 5. , viewed 25 Oct 2022, http://nla.gov.au/nla.news-article188960107. (Late Epitome of News, 18 May 1877, p.5)

1877 'TENTERFIELD.', The Armidale Express and New England General Advertiser (NSW : 1856 - 1861; 1863 - 1889; 1891 - 1954), 5 January, p. 6. , viewed 01 Oct 2022, http://nla.gov.au/nla.news-article188959464. (Tenterfield, 5 Jan 1877, p.6)

1877 'UNDAUNTED v. MIDLORN.', The Maitland Mercury and Hunter Riv-er General Advertiser (NSW : 1843 - 1893), 6 March, p. 7. , viewed 09 May 2023, http://nla.gov.au/nla.news-article18816269

1878 'LOUTTIT BAY.', Geelong Advertiser (Vic. : 1859 - 1929), 31 January, p. 3. , viewed 07 Sep 2022, http://nla.gov.au/nla.news-article149821413. (Loutit Bay, 31 Jan 1878, p.3)

1878 'Maryborough.', The Brisbane Courier (Qld. : 1864 - 1933), 28 December, p. 6. , viewed 01 Oct 2022, http://nla.gov.au/nla.news-article1377612. (Maryborough, 28 Dec 1878, p.6)

1878 'MISCELLANEOUS.', Warwick Examiner and Times (Qld. : 1867 - 1919), 5 October, p. 6. , viewed 14 Oct 2022, http://nla.gov.au/nla.news-article82121690. (Miscellaneous, 5 Oct 1878, p.6)

1878 'PRESENTATIONS.', South Australian Chronicle and Weekly Mail (Adelaide, SA : 1868 - 1881), 14 September, p. 9. , viewed 08 Oct 2022, http://nla.gov.au/nla.news-article92263944. (Presentations, 14 Sep 1878, p.9)

1878 'SERIOUS COACH ACCIDENT.', Evening News (Sydney, NSW : 1869 - 1931), 11 May, p. 5. , viewed 07 Aug 2022, http://nla.gov.au/ nla.news-article107933123. (Serious Coach Accident, 11 May 1878, p.5)

1878 'TELEGRAPHIC INTELLIGENCE.', The Ballarat Courier (Vic. : 1869 - 1885; 1914 - 1918), 18 January, p. 2. , viewed 07 Aug 2022, http://nla.gov.au/nla.news-article211537403. (Telegraphic Intelligence, 18 Jan 1878, p.2)

1878 'TO NEWSA BY COBB & CO'S COACH.', Gympie Times and Mary River Mining Gazette (Qld. : 1868 - 1919), 12 January, p. 3. , viewed 15 Sep 2022, http://nla.gov.au/nla.news-article168608657. (To Newsa by Cobb & Co's Coach, 12 Jan 1878, p.3)

1878 'YOUNG.', The Sydney Morning Herald (NSW : 1842 - 1954), 31 December, p. 6. , viewed 24 Apr 2023, http://nla.gov.au/nla.news-article28391437 (Young, 31 Dec 1878, p.6)

1879 'ACCIDENT TO COBB AND CO.'S COACH, AT ST. GEORGE.', Western Star and Roma Advertiser (Qld. : 1875 - 1948), 15 November, p. 3., viewed 27 Jul 2022, http://nla.gov.au/nla.news-article97449832. (Accident to Cobb and Co.'s Coach, at St. George, 15 Nov 1879)

1879 'COLONIAL AND INTERCOLONIAL MESSAGES.', Australian Town and Country Journal (Sydney, NSW : 1870 - 1919), 12 July, p. 9. , viewed 29 Sep 2022, http://nla.gov.au/nla.news-article70970995. (Colonial and Intercolonial Messages, 12 Jul 1879, p.9)

1879 'CURRENT NEWS.', The Queenslander (Brisbane, Qld. : 1866 - 1939), 19 July, p. 69. , viewed 14 Oct 2022, http://nla.gov.au/nla.news-article20327400. (Current News, 19 Jul 1879, p.69)

1879 'LATE TELEGRAMS.', Cootamundra Herald (NSW : 1877 - 1954), 14 June, p. 4. , viewed 06 Oct 2022, http://nla.gov.au/ nla.news-article143908144. (Late Telegrams, 14 Jun 1879, p.4)

1879 'STICKING UP THE GYMPIE COACH.', Western Star and Roma Advertiser (Qld. : 1875 - 1948), 8 September, p. 4. , viewed 29 Sep 2022, http://nla.gov.au/nla.news-article97449471. (Sticking up the Gympie Coach, 8 Sep 1879, p.4)

1879 'YOUNG.', The Sydney Morning Herald (NSW : 1842 - 1954), 15 April, p. 5. , viewed 29 Dec 2022, http://nla.gov.au/nla.news-article13432919. (Young, 15 Apr 1879, p.5)

1880 'A BUSH TRIP.', Australian Town and Country Journal (Sydney, NSW : 1870 - 1919), 3 January, p. 18. , viewed 11 Oct 2022, http://nla.gov.au/nla.news-article70939913. (A Bush Trip, 3 Jan 1880, p.18)

1880 'ACTION FOR DAMAGES.', Western Star and Roma Advertiser (Qld. : 1875 - 1948), 26 June, p. 3. , viewed 06 May 2023, http://nla.gov.au/nla.news-article97451001 (Action for Damages, 26 Jun 1880, p.3)

1880 'TENTERFIELD.', The Armidale Express and New England General Advertiser (NSW : 1856 - 1861; 1863 - 1889; 1891 - 1954), 11 June, p. 3. , viewed 04 Oct 2022, http://nla.gov.au/nla.news-article192877276. (Tenterfield, 11 Jun 1880, p.3)

1880 'WALGETT.', The Sydney Morning Herald (NSW : 1842 - 1954), 8 January, p. 5. , viewed 01 Nov 2022, http://nla.gov.au/nla.news-article13447871. (Walgett, 8 Jan 1880, p.5)

1880 'WELLINGTON.', Australian Town and Country Journal (Sydney, NSW : 1870 - 1919), 15 May, p. 39. , viewed 30 Apr 2023, http://nla.gov.au/nla.news-article70943784 (Wellington, 15 May 1880, p.39)

1881 'FORBES.', Australian Town and Country Journal (Sydney, NSW : 1870 - 1919), 27 August, p. 38. , viewed 05 Aug 2022, http://nla.gov.au/nla.news-article70959409. (Forbes, 27 Aug 1881, p.38)

1882 'COACH ACCIDENT.', The Manaro Mercury, and Cooma and Bombala Advertiser (NSW : 1862 - 1931), 8 November, p. 3. , viewed 13 Jul 2022, http://nla.gov.au/nla.news-article115705764. Coach Accident, 8 Nov 1882, p.3)

1883 'ACCIDENT TO COBB AND CO.'S COACH.', The Ballarat Courier (Vic. : 1869 - 1885; 1914 - 1918), 18 April, p. 3. , viewed 06 May 2023, http://nla.gov.au/nla.news-article254661420 (Accident to Cobb And Co.'s Coach, 18 Apr 1883, p.3)

1883 'COUNTRY NEWS.', The Queenslander (Brisbane, Qld. : 1866 - 1939), 17 March, p. 407. , viewed 11 Oct 2022, http://nla.gov.au/ nla.news-article19790009. (Country News, 17 Mar 1883, p.407)

1883 'NO TITLE', The Albury Banner and Wodonga Express (NSW : 1860 - 1938), 14 September, p. 13. , viewed 14 Oct 2022, http:// nla.gov.au/nla.news-article254376869. (No Title, 14 Sep 1883, p.13)

1883 'THE BOX-SEAT DISPUTED.', Evening News (Sydney, NSW : 1869 - 1931), 1 August, p. 6. , viewed 01 May 2023, http://nla.gov.au/nla.news-article111027400 (The Box-seat Disputed, 1 Aug 1883, p.6)

1884 'A TRIP TO MARYSVILLE.', Australasian Sketcher (Adelaide,SA : 1874 - 1885), 9 April, p. 7. (ADELAIDE EDITION), viewed 06 Aug 2022, http://nla.gov.au/nla.news-article246609576. (A Trip to Marysvale, 9 Apr 1884, p.7)

1884 'DREADFUL COACH ACCIDENT.', Kerang Times and Swan Hill Ga-zette (Vic. : 1877 - 1889), 22 April, p. 4. , viewed 17 Oct 2022, http://nla.gov.au/nla.news-article65586506. (Dreadful Coach Accident, 22 Apr 1884, p.4)

1884 'QUEENSLAND.', Tasmanian News (Hobart, Tas. : 1883 - 1911), 29 January, p. 3. , viewed 13 Jul 2022, http://nla.gov.au/nla.news-article162306586. (Queensland—Fatal Coach Accident, 29 Jan 1884, p.3)

1884 'SERIOUS COACH ACCIDENT.', Mount Alexander Mail (Vic. : 1854 - 1917), 15 April, p. 2. , viewed 15 Sep 2022, http:// nla.gov.au/nla.news-article198275458. (Serious Coach Accident, 15 Apr 1884, p.2)

1884 'SERIOUS COACH ACCIDENT.', Western Star and Roma Advertiser (Qld. : 1875 - 1948), 30 April, p. 4. , viewed 01 Oct 2022, http://nla.gov.au/nla.news-article97522774. (Serious Coach Accident, 30 April 1884, p.4)

1884 'TALLAROOK', Seymour Express and Goulburn Valley, Avenel, Gray-town, Nagambie, Tallarook and Yea Advertiser (Vic. : 1882 - 1891; 1914 - 1918), 18 January, p. 2. , viewed 26 Apr 2023, http://nla.gov.au/nla.news-article165089134 (Tallarook, 18 Jan 1884, p.2)

1884 'TOWN TALK.', Geelong Advertiser (Vic. : 1859 - 1929), 27 December, p. 2. , viewed 12 Oct 2022, http://nla.gov.au/nla.news-article150164917. (Town Talk, 27 Dec 1884, p.2)

1885 'A WINTER TOUR IN QUEENSLAND.', Western Star and Roma Advertiser (Qld. : 1875 - 1948), 15 August, p. 4. , viewed 11 Oct 2022, http://nla.gov.au/nla.news-article102732354. (A Winter Tour in Queens-land, 15 Aug 1885, p.4)

1885 'COLONIAL AND INTERCOLONIAL.', The Western Champion (Blackall/Barcaldine, Qld. : 1879 - 1891), 12 March, p. 2., viewed 03 Oct 2022, http://nla.gov.au/nla.news-article79727760. (Colonial and Inter-colonial, 12 Mar 1885, p.2)

1885 'COUNTRY NEWS.', The Queenslander (Brisbane, Qld. : 1866 - 1939), 19 September, p. 476. , viewed 29 Sep 2022, http://nla. gov.au/nla.news-article19800581. (Country News, 19 Sep 1885, p.476)

1885 'QUEENSLAND.', The Age (Melbourne, Vic. : 1854 - 1954), 13 March, p. 6. , viewed 29 Apr 2023, http://nla.gov.au/nla.news-article196954495 (Queensland, 13 Mar 1885, p.6)

1886 'COLONIAL COACHING AND THEIR JEHU'S ETC.', Mercury and Weekly Courier (Vic. : 1878 - 1903), 16 April, p. 3, viewed 10 Aug 2022, http://nla.gov.au/nla.news-article58433514. (Colonial Coaching and their Jehu's etc, 16 Apr 1886, p.3)

1886 'FROM BRISBANE TO ADAVALE.', The Queenslander (Brisbane, Qld. : 1866 - 1939), 8 May, p. 733. , viewed 13 Apr 2023, http://nla.gov.au/nla.news-article19805135 (From Brisbane to Adavale, 8 May 1886, p.733)

1886 'TAMBO.', The Capricornian (Rockhampton, Qld. : 1875 - 1929), 2 October, p. 25. , viewed 02 Nov 2022, http://nla.gov.au/nla.news-article66318508. (Tambo, 2 Oct 1886, p.25)

1887 'ACCIDENT TO ONE OF COBB'S COACHES.', Traralgon Record (Traralgon, Vic. : 1886 - 1932), 23 December, p. 2. (morning.), viewed 15 Sep 2022, http://nla.gov.au/nla.news-article64423732. (Accident To One Of Cobb's Coaches, 23 Dec 1887, p.2)

1887 'BALL'S HEAD.', The Sydney Morning Herald (NSW : 1842 - 1954), 26 October, p. 7. , viewed 05 Aug 2022, http://nla.gov.au/nla.news-article13669003. (Ball's Head, 26 October 1887, p.7)

1887 'THE ADELAIDE FOOTBALL PLAYERS AND VISITORS.', Geelong Advertiser (Vic. : 1859 - 1929), 9 June, p. 3. , viewed 07 Sep 2022, http://nla.gov.au/nla.news-article150399215. (The Adelaide Football Players And Visitors, 9 Jun 1887, p.3)

1887 'WALGETT.', The Maitland Mercury and Hunter River General Advertiser (NSW : 1843 - 1893), 29 January, p. 13. (Second Sheet to The Maitland Mercury), viewed 14 Oct 2022, http://nla.gov.au/nla.news-article18901317. (Walgett, 29 Jan 1887, p.13)

1888 'A MAIL COACH ON FIRE.', The Brisbane Courier (Qld. : 1864 - 1933), 7 August, p. 5. , viewed 18 Apr 2023, http://nla.gov.au/nla.news-article3482213 (A Mail Coach on Fire, 7 Aug 1888, p.5)

1888 'COBB'S COACH.', The Capricornian (Rockhampton, Qld. : 1875 - 1929), 22 December, p. 1. (CAPRICORNIAN ILLUSTRATED CHRISTMAS SUPPLEMENT 1888.), viewed 31 Oct 2022, http://nla.gov.au/nla.news-article65793654 (Cobb's Coach, 22 Dec 1888, p.1)

1888 'NO TITLE', The Riverine Grazier (Hay, NSW : 1873 - 1954), 28 September, p. 2. , viewed 09 Oct 2022, http://nla.gov.au/nla.news-article140548068. (No Title, 28 Sep 1888, p.2)

1888 'QUEENSLAND.', The Australian Star (Sydney, NSW : 1887 - 1909), 13 March, p. 6. (SECOND EDITION), viewed 13 Jul 2022, http://nla.gov.au/nla.news-article229935861. (Queensland—Coach Accident, 13 Mar 1888, p.6)

1889 'CABBAGE-TREE HAT MAKING.', Windsor and Richmond Gazette (NSW : 1888 - 1965), 21 December, p. 6. , viewed 08 Oct 2022, http://nla.gov.au/nla.news-article72561053. (Cabbage-tree Hat Making, 21 Dec 1889, p.6)

1889 'COUNTRY NEWS.', The Argus (Melbourne, Vic. : 1848 - 1957), 25 May, p. 11. , viewed 07 Aug 2022, http://nla.gov.au/nla.news-article6249668. (Country News, 25 May 1889, p.11)

1889 'TAMBO TIT BITS.', The Western Champion (Blackall/Barcaldine, Qld. : 1879 - 1891), 10 December, p. 2. , viewed 02 Nov 2022, http://nla.gov.au/nla.news-article79706627. (Tambo Tit-Bits, 10 Dec 1889, p.2)

1889 'THE BARCOO.', Morning Bulletin (Rockhampton, Qld. : 1878 - 1954), 23 January, p. 6. , viewed 06 Oct 2022, http://nla.gov.au/nla.news-article52275050. (The Barcoo, 23 Jan 1889, p.6)

1890 'STANTHORPE.', Queensland Times, Ipswich Herald and General Advertiser (Qld. : 1861 - 1908), 18 November, p. 3. (Daily.), viewed 20 Oct 2022, http://nla.gov.au/nla.news-article125072410. Stanthorpe, 18 Nov 1890, p.3)

1890 AUSTRALIAN STAR (Sydney, NSW : 1887 - 1909), 20 May, p. 5. , viewed 17 Oct 2022, http://nla.gov.au/nla.news-article230615427. (Australian Star, 20 May 1890, p.5)

1891 'FATAL COACH ACCIDENT NEAR GRENFELL.', The Sydney Morning Herald (NSW : 1842 - 1954), 21 October, p. 6. , viewed 06 Nov 2022, http://nla.gov.au/nla.news-article13847143 (Fatal Coach Accident Near Grenfell, 21 Oct 1891, p.6)

1891 'GRENFELL COACH ACCIDENT.', The Burrangong Argus (NSW : 1865 - 1913), 11 November, p. 2. , viewed 24 Apr 2023, http://nla.gov.au/nla.news-article2476788351891 (Grenfell Coach Accident, 11 Nov 1891, p.2)

1891 'MELBOURNE NOTES.', The Elmore Standard (Vic. : 1882 - 1920, 20 March, p. 2. , viewed 11 Oct 2022, http://nla.gov.au/ nla.news-article253384950. (Melbourne Notes, 20 Mar 1891, p.2)

1892 'COACH ACCIDENT.', Barrier Miner (Broken Hill, NSW : 1888 - 1954), 19 April, p. 2. , viewed 07 Aug 2022, http://nla.gov.au/nla.news-article44082509. (Coach Accident, 19 Apr 1892, p.2)

1892 'YOUNG BLOOD.', National Advocate (Bathurst, NSW : 1889 - 1954), 28 March, p. 2. , viewed 17 Oct 2022, http://nla.gov.au/ nla.news-article156661575. (Young Blood, 28 Mar 1892, p.2)

1893 'A COACH ACCIDENT.', Singleton Argus (NSW : 1880 - 1954), 1 April, p. 4. , viewed 06 May 2023, http://nla.gov.au/nla.news-article82454121 (A Coach Accident, 1 Apr 1893, p.4)

1893 'A STREET RUNAWAY.', Geelong Advertiser (Vic. : 1859 - 1929), 9 September, p. 3. , viewed 30 Apr 2023, http://nla.gov.au/nla.news-article150747819 (A Street Runaway, 9 Sep 1893, p.3)Bottom of Form

1893 'COACH ACCIDENT.', The Albury Banner and Wodonga Express (NSW : 1860 - 1938), 7 April, p. 28. , viewed 27 Jul 2022, http://nla.gov.au/nla.news-article254585979. (Coach Accident, 7 Apr 1893, p.28)

1893 'COACH HORSES.', Western Star and Roma Advertiser (Qld. : 1875 - 1948), 26 July, p. 3. , viewed 27 Jul 2022, http://nla.gov.au/ nla.news-article97466252. (Coach Horses, 26 Jul 1893, p.3)

1893 'LOCAL AND DISTRICT NEWS.', The Lilydale Express (Vic. : 1886 - 1897; 1914 - 1955), 13 October, p. 2. , viewed 11 Oct 2022, http://nla.gov.au/nla.news-article252180879. (Local and District News, 13 Oct 1893, p.2)

1893 'LOCAL AND GENERAL.', Geraldton Advertiser (WA : 1893 - 1905), 5 June, p. 3. , viewed 06 Oct 2022, http://nla.gov.au/ nla.news-article252750130. (Local and General, 5 Jun 1893, p.3)

1893 'OUR MEMBERS.', Victorian Express (Geraldton, WA : 1878 - 1894), 9 June, p. 2. , viewed 17 Oct 2022, http://nla.gov.au/ nla.news-article211602025. (Our Members, 9 Jun 1893, p.2)

1894 'A ROMANCE OF EARLY COLONIAL LIFE.', Geelong Advertiser (Vic. : 1859 - 1929), 29 January, p. 4. , viewed 07 Sep 2022, http://nla.gov.au/nla.news-article150360454. (A Romance Of Early Colonial Life, 29 Jan 1894, p.4)

1894 'A STICKING-UP CASE.', South Australian Chronicle (Adelaide, SA : 1889 - 1895), 23 June, p. 21. , viewed 17 Oct 2022, http://nla.gov.au/nla.news-article92860771. (A Sticking-up Case, 23 Jun 1894, p.21)

1894 'WITH COBB & CO. IN FAR INLAND AUSTRALIA.', Warwick Argus (Qld. : 1879 - 1901), 28 July, p. 4. , viewed 01 Oct 2022, http://nla.gov.au/nla.news-article76646670. ('With Cobb & Co. in far inland Australia, 28 Jul 1894, p.4)

1895 'A SENSATIONAL COACH ACCIDENT.', Wagga Wagga Advertiser (NSW : 1875 - 1910), 26 January, p. 4. , viewed 09 Aug 2022, http:// nla.gov.au/nla.news-article101803928. (Sensational Coach Accident 26 Jan 1895, p.4)

1895 'COLONIAL GOVERNORS.', Coolgardie Miner (WA : 1894 - 1911), 1 June, p. 2. , viewed 06 Oct 2022, http://nla.gov.au/ nla.news-article216660137. (Colonial Governors, 1 Jun 1895, p.2)

1895 'NEWS OF THE WEEK.', Coolgardie Pioneer (WA : 1895 - 1901), 5 June, p. 14. , viewed 14 Oct 2022, http://nla.gov.au/nla.news- arti-cle251478636. (News of the Week, 5 Jun 1895, p.14)

1895 'QUEENSLAND.' The Brisbane Courier (Qld. : 1864 - 1933)

3 June 1895: 5. Web. 4 Aug 2022 <http://nla.gov.au/nla.news-article3603402>. (Queensland, 3 Jun 1895, p.5)

1895 'ROCKHAMPTON AND THE WEST.', The Queenslander (Brisbane, Qld. : 1866 - 1939), 30 March, p. 603. , viewed 06 Oct 2022, http://nla.gov.au/nla.news-article21630443. (Rockhampton and the West, 30 Mar 1895,p.603)

1895 'VICTORIA.', The Australian Advertiser (Albany, WA : 1888 - 1897), 25 January, p. 3. , viewed 22 Jul 2022, http://nla.gov.au/ nla.news-article260521771. (Victoria, 25 Jan 1895, p.3)

1895 COBB & CO'S OLD COACH DRIVER'S ASSOCIATION [realia], Record ID 9917655723607636, State Library Victoria.1895 'Cobb and Co.', Warwick Argus (Qld. : 1879 - 1901), 30 March, p. 4. , viewed 15 Sep 2022, http://nla.gov.au/nla.news-article76649248.

1896 'A VETERAN COACH DRIVER.', Wagga Wagga Advertiser (NSW : 1875 - 1910), 9 May, p. 2. , viewed 07 Aug 2022, http://nla.gov. au/nla.news-article101776515. (A Veteran Coach Driver, 9 May 1896, p.2)

1896 'DEATH OF A MUDGEE WHIP.', National Advocate (Bathurst, NSW : 1889 - 1954), 17 September, p. 2. , viewed 06 Oct 2022, http://nla.gov.au/nla.news-article156707202. (Death of a Mudgee Whip, 17 Sept 1896, p.2)

1896 'READ THIS CASE.', The W.A. Record (Perth, WA : 1888 - 1922), 29 August, p. 13. , viewed 08 Oct 2022, http://nla.gov.au/ nla.news-article211621463. (Read this case, 29 Aug 1896, p.13)

1896 'ST. GEORGE.', Maryborough Chronicle, Wide Bay and Burnett Advertiser (Qld. : 1860 - 1947), 25 February, p. 2. , viewed 29 Dec 2022, http://nla.gov.au/nla.news-article146987795. (St. George, 25 Feb 1896, p.2) Bottom of Form

1897 'COUNTRY NEWS. BALLARAT.', The Argus (Melbourne, Vic. : 1848 - 1957), 22 April, p. 6. , viewed 29 Dec 2022, http://nla.gov.au/nla.news-article9174852. (Country News. Ballarat, 22 Apr 1897, p.6)

1897 'GRENFELL POLICE COURT', The Grenfell Record and Lachlan District Advertiser (NSW : 1876 - 1951), 10 July, p. 2. , viewed 18 Apr 2023, http://nla.gov.au/nla.news-article117235239 (Grenfell Police Court, 10 Jul 1897, p. 2)

1897 'LOCAL AND GENERAL NEWS.', The Ballan Times and Egerton, Gordon, Blakeville and Myrniong Standard (Vic. : 1895 - 1899), 30 September, p. 2. , viewed 29 Sep 2022, http://nla.gov.au/nla.news-article265318802. (Local and General News, 30 Sept 1897, p.2)

1897 'MISCELLANEOUS NEWS.', The Advertiser (Adelaide, SA : 1889 - 1931), 10 March, p. 6. , viewed 09 Oct 2022, http://nla.gov.au/nla.news-article34575978. (Miscellaneous News, 10 Mar 1897, p.6)

1897 COBB'S COACH TO ORBOST Weekly Times (Melbourne, Vic. : 1869 - 1954), 20 November, p. 20. (SPECIAL SUPPLEMENT TO THE WEEKLY TIMES), viewed 15 Sep 2022, http://nla.gov.au/nla.news-page23410402. (Cobb's Coach to Orbost, 20 Nov 1897, p.20)

1898 'A COACHING IDENTITY', The Australasian (Melbourne, Vic. : 1864 - 1946), 3 September, p. 27. , viewed 31 Dec 2022, http://nla.gov.au/nla.news-article138604281. (Coaching Identity, 3 Sep 1898, p.27)

1898 'LOCAL AND GENERAL.', Norseman Times (WA : 1898 - 1920), 16 March, p. 2. , viewed 24 Apr 2023, http://nla.gov.au/nla.news-article149940909 (Local and General, 16 March 1898, p.2)

1899 'ACCIDENT TO COBB'S COACH.', Coolgardie Miner (WA : 1894 - 1911), 15 March, p. 5. , viewed 15 Sep 2022, http:// nla.gov.au/nla.news-article217336986. (Accident to Cobb's Coach, 15 Mar 1899, p.5)

1899 'COACH ACCIDENT.', The Maitland Weekly Mercury (NSW : 1894 - 1931), 19 August, p. 10. , viewed 13 Jul 2022, http://nla.gov.au/nla.news-article127546920. (Coach Accident, 19 Aug 1899, p.10)

1899 'COACH ACCIDENT.', The Telegraph (Brisbane, Qld. : 1872 - 1947), 2 June, p. 5. , viewed 27 Jul 2022, http://nla.gov.au/nla.news-arti-cle175301584. (Coach Accident, 2 Jun 1899, p.5)

1899 'NEWS AND NOTES.', The West Australian (Perth, WA : 1879 - 1954), 29 June, p. 5. , viewed 06 Oct 2022, http://nla.gov. au/nla.news-article3229789. (News and Notes, 29 Jun 1899, p.5)

1899 'OBITUARY.', Bendigo Advertiser (Vic. : 1855 - 1918), 26 June, p. 3. , viewed 21 Oct 2022, http://nla.gov.au/nla.news-article89822862. (Obituary, 26 Jul 1899, p.3)

1900 'IN THE DAYS WHEN THE WORLD WAS WIDE', Lawson, Henry. The Roaring Days p.33, Angus and Robertson, Sydney.

1901 'GEORGETOWN CHIPS.', Morning Post (Cairns, Qld. : 1897 - 1907), 21 June, p. 3. , viewed 03 Oct 2022, http://nla.gov.au/nla.news-article42946725. (Georgetown Chips, 21 Jun 1901, p.3)

1902 'ALONG THE LINE', The Northern Miner (Charters Towers, Qld. : 1874 - 1954), 7 March, p. 6. , viewed 09 Oct 2022, http:// nla.gov.au/nla.news-article79030312. (Along the line, 7 Mar 1902, p.6)

1902 'MY LIFE IN MANY STATES AND IN FOREIGN LANDS.', Train, George Francis. Pp. Xxi. 340. D. Appleton: New York. SR 910.4 T768 Available from: The National Library of Australia. (My Life in Many States and in Foreign Lands, 1902, pp.133-134)

1903 'CABBAGE TREE NED.', The Bendigo Independent (Vic. : 1891 - 1918), 12 December, p. 6. , viewed 27 Jul 2022, httP:// NLA.GOV.AU/NLA.NEWS-ARTICLE223407312. (CABBAGE TREE NED, 12 DEC 1903, P.6)

1903 'COBB AND CO.', Windsor and Richmond Gazette (NSW : 1888 - 1965), 10 January, p. 1. , viewed 22 Oct 2022, http://nla.gov.au/nla.news-article86217886 (Cobb and Co., 10 Jan 1903, p.1)

1903 'CORRESPONDENCE.', The Shoalhaven News and South Coast Districts Advertiser (NSW : 1891 - 1937), 11 April, p. 3. , viewed 29 Apr 2023, http://nla.gov.au/nla.news-article135736400 (Correspondence, 11 Apr 1903, p.3)

1903 'ILFRACOMBE.', The Capricornian (Rockhampton, Qld. : 1875 - 1929), 10 January, p. 31. , viewed 17 Oct 2022, http://nla.gov.au/nla.news-article71945394. (Ilfracombe, 10 Jan 1903, p.31)

1903 'OBITUARY.' The Sydney Mail and New South Wales Advertiser (NSW : 1871 - 1912) 20 May 1903: 1228. Web. 21 Oct 2022 <http://nla.gov.au/nla.news-article165189164>. (Obituary, 20 May 1903, p.1228)

1903 'OBITUARY.', The Malcolm Chronicle and Leonora Advertiser (WA : 1897 - 1905), 27 November, p. 2. , viewed 21 Oct 2022, http://nla.gov.au/nla.news-article228046673 (Obituary, 27 Nov 1903, p.2)

1904 'THUNDERBOLT' (FRED WARD).', The Armidale Chronicle (NSW : 1894 - 1929), 27 August, p. 8. , viewed 13 Apr 2023, http://nla.gov.au/nla.news-article1896653821904 (Thunderbolt [Fred Ward], 27 Aug 1904 , p.8)

1905 'COACH ACCIDENT.', Darling Downs Gazette (Qld. : 1881 - 1922), 8 February, p. 2. , viewed 27 Jul 2022, http://nla.gov.au/nla.news-article180417336. (Coach Accident, 8 Feb 1905, p.2)

1905 'INTERESTING COURT CASE', Morning Post (Cairns, Qld. : 1897 - 1907), 8 December, p. 3. , viewed 09 Aug 2022, http:// nla.gov.au/nla.news-article44419413. (Interesting Court Case, 8 Dec 1905, p.3)

1905 'OBITUARY.', Canowindra Star and Eugowra News (NSW : 1903 - 1907; 1910 - 1911; 1914 - 1922), 21 April, p. 2. , viewed 21 Oct 2022, http://nla.gov.au/nla.news-article144472695. (Obituary, 21 Apr 1905, p.2)

1906 'FROM DAY TO DAY.', The Riverine Grazier (Hay, NSW : 1873 - 1954), 4 September, p. 4. , viewed 04 Aug 2022, http://nla.gov.au/nla.news-article141268054. (From Day to Day, 4 Sept 1906, p.4)

1906 'OBITUARY.', Goulburn Herald (NSW : 1881 - 1907), 22 August, p. 2. , viewed 21 Oct 2022, http://nla.gov.au/nla.news-article100555369. (Obituary, 22 Aug 1906, p.2)

1906 'OBITUARY', The Horsham Times (Vic. : 1882 - 1954), 5 October, p. 3. , viewed 21 Oct 2022, http://nla.gov.au/nla.news-article72935898. (Obituary, 5 Oct 1906, p.3)

1907 'DOUBLE BEREAVEMENT.', The Daily Telegraph (Sydney, NSW : 1883 - 1930), 19 December, p. 8. , viewed 18 Apr 2023, http://nla.gov.au/nla.news-article238262402 (Double Bereavement, 19 Dec 1907, p.8)

1907 'LEONORA TO LAWLERS.', The Sun (Kalgoorlie, WA : 1898 - 1929), 27 October, p. 11. , viewed 27 Jul 2022, http://nla. gov.au/nla.news-article211342998. (Leonora to Lawlers, 27 Oct 1907, p.11)

1907 'OBITUARY.', The North Eastern Ensign (Benalla, Vic. : 1872 - 1938), 19 April, p. 3. (MORNING.), viewed 22 Oct 2022, http://nla. gov.au/nla.news-article70758413. (Obituary, 19 Apr 1907, p.3)

1908 'CIVIL SITTINGS.', The Western Champion and General Advertiser for the Central-Western Districts (Barcaldine, Qld. : 1892 - 1922), 26 September, p. 9. , viewed 02 Nov 2022, http://nla.gov.au/nla.news-article76582340. (Civil Sittings, 26 Sep 1908, p.9)

1908 'DEATH OF AN OLD TIME COACH DRIVER.', Kilmore Free Press (Kilmore, Vic. : 1870 - 1954), 23 July, p. 2. (MORNING.), viewed 08 Aug 2022, http://nla.gov.au/nla.news-article58090989. (Death of an Old Time Coach Driver, 23 Jul 1908, p.2)

1908 'LADIES INJURED IN COACH ACCIDENT.', The Mercury (Hobart, Tas. : 1860 - 1954), 5 May, p. 3. , viewed 29 Sep 2022, http://nla.gov.au/nla.news-article12664990. (Ladies injured in coach accident, 5 May 1908, p.3)

1909 'A GLIMPSE OF THE BUFFALO', Benalla Standard (Vic. : 1901 - 1931), 30 April, p. 4. , viewed 07 Oct 2022, http://nla.gov. au/nla.news-article155347576. (A Glimpse of the Buffalo, 30 Apr 1909, p.4)

1909 'COUNTRY NEWS.', The Ballarat Star (Vic. : 1865 - 1924), 30 August, p. 6. , viewed 27 Jul 2022, http://nla.gov.au/nla.news-article218789786. (Country News, 30 Aug 1909, p.6)

1909 'OBITUARY.', Leader (Orange, NSW : 1899 - 1945), 8 May, p. 2. , viewed 06 Oct 2022, http://nla.gov.au/nla.news-article252386448. (Obituary, 8 May 1909, p.2)

1909 'SERIOUS COACH ACCIDENT.', East Murchison News (WA : 1901 - 1911), 30 July, p. 2. , viewed 07 Sep 2022, http://nla.gov.au/nla. news-article253582433. (Serious Coach Accident, 30 Jul 1909, p.2)

1910 'A PIONEER JEHU GONE.', Glen Innes Examiner (NSW : 1908 - 1954), 17 May, p. 2. , viewed 10 Aug 2022, http://nla.gov. au/nla.news-article180124436. (A Pioneer Jehu Gone, 17 May 1910, p.2)

1910 'PERSONAL & SOCIAL', The Burrowa News (NSW : 1874 - 1951), 10 June, p. 2. , viewed 09 Oct 2022, http://nla.gov.au/nla. news- arti-cle101578748. (Personal & Social, 10 Jun 1910, p.2)

1911 'BUSHRANGER TRICKED.', The Elmore Standard (Vic. : 1882 - 1920, 18 March, p. 4. , viewed 08 Oct 2022, http://nla. gov.au/nla.news-article262617038. (Bushranger Tricked, 18 Mar 1911, p.4)

1911 'COACH ACCIDENT', The Brisbane Courier (Qld. : 1864 - 1933), 23 November, p. 5. , viewed 02 Nov 2022, http://nla.gov. au/nla.news-article19754059. (Coach Accident, 23 Nov 1911, p.5)

1911 'COACH OVERTURNED.', Northern Star (Lismore, NSW : 1876 - 1954), 2 January, p. 2. , viewed 27 Jul 2022, http://nla. gov.au/nla.news-article72265855. (Coach Overturned, 2 Jan 1911, p.2)

1911 'MR. JOHN ROBARDS.', Leader (Orange, NSW : 1899 - 1945), 8 July, p. 3. , viewed 05 Aug 2022, http://nla.gov.au/nla. news-article252605175. (Mr. John Robards, 8 Jul 1911, p.3)

1912 'BLACKALL NOTES.', The Northern Miner (Charters Towers, Qld. : 1874 - 1954), 5 August, p. 6. , viewed 01 May 2023, http://nla. gov.au/nla.news-article79101152 (Blackall Notes, 5 Aug 1912, p.6)

1912 'COACH IN BUSH FIRE.', Huon Times (Franklin, Tas. : 1910 - 1933), 21 February, p. 4. , viewed 29 Dec 2022, http://nla.gov.au/nla. news-article135664913. (Coach in Bush Fire., 21 Feb 1912, p.4)

1912 'LOCAL BREVITIES', Mudgee Guardian and North-Western Representative (NSW : 1890 - 1954), 28 March, p. 21. , viewed 03 Oct 2022, http://nla.gov.au/nla.news-article157642144. (Local Brevities, 28 Mar 1912, p.21)

1912 'MESSRS. COBB AND CO.', Morning Bulletin (Rockhampton, Qld. : 1878 - 1954), 29 April, p. 6. , viewed 09 Aug 2022, http://nla. gov.au/nla.news-article53266882. (Messrs. Cobb and Co., 29 Ap 1912)

1912 'MULGALAND MEMS.', The Sun (Kalgoorlie, WA : 1898 - 1929), 29 September, p. 7. , viewed 11 Oct 2022, http://nla.gov. au/nla.news-article211336351. (Mulgaland Mems, 29 Sep 1912, p.7)

1912 'OBITUARY.', The Bendigo Independent (Vic. : 1891 - 1918), 27 May, p. 6. , viewed 22 Oct 2022, http://nla.gov.au/nla.news-article227962668. (Obituary, 27 May 1912, p.6)

1913 'COBB'S AND A LEGAL PUZZLE', Geelong Advertiser (Vic. : 1859 - 1929), 2 April, p. 4. , viewed 05 Oct 2022, http://nla. gov.au/nla.news-article150677518. (Cobb's And A Legal Puzzle, 2 Apr 1913, p.4)

1913 'CROSSING SMASH AT MARSHALLTOWN.', Geelong Advertiser (Vic. : 1859 - 1929), 11 January, p. 3. , viewed 05 Oct 2022, http://nla.gov.au/nla.news-article150789889. (Crossing Smash At Mar-shalltown, 11 Jan 1913, p.3)

1913 'FIFTY YEARS ON A MAIL COACH.', The Richmond River Express and Casino Kyogle Advertiser (NSW : 1904 - 1929), 13 May, p. 3., viewed 29 Jul 2022, http://nla.gov.au/nla.news-article123880336. (Fifty Years on a Mail Coach, 13 May 1913, p.3)

1914 'BACCHUS MARSH.', The Bacchus Marsh Express (Vic. : 1866 - 1943), 19 September, p. 3. , viewed 11 Oct 2022, http://nla. gov.au/nla.news-article74267462. (Bacchus Marsh, 19 Sep 1914, p.3)

1914 'DEATH OF AN OLD TIME COACH DRIVER.', The Corowa Free Press (NSW : 1875 - 1954), 21 July, p. 4. , viewed 27 Jul 2022, http://nla.gov.au/nla.news-article235103935. (Death of an Old Time Coach Driver, 21 Jul 1914, p.4)

1914 'OBITUARY.', Chronicle (Adelaide, SA : 1895 - 1954), 25 July, p. 45. , viewed 06 May 2023, http://nla.gov.au/nla.news-article88842688 (Obituary, 25 Jul 1914, p.45)

1914 'OBITUARY.', Kerang New Times (Vic. : 1901 - 1918), 1 December, p. 3. , viewed 21 Oct 2022, http://nla.gov.au/nla.news-article87739819. (Obituary, 1 Dec 1914, p.3)

1916 'COACHING IN FLOOD TIME.', Wellington Times (NSW : 1899 - 1954), 24 August, p. 5. , viewed 01 May 2023, http://nla.gov. au/nla.news-article137410698 (Coaching in flood time, 24 Aug, p.5)

1916 'COACHING IN FLOOD TIME.', Wellington Times (NSW : 1899 - 1954), 21 September, p. 3. , viewed 01 May 2023, http://nla. gov.au/nla.news-article137414344 (Coaching in flood time, 21 Sep 1916, p.3)

1916 'DEATH OF MR. JAMES CONROY.', Goulburn Evening Penny Post (NSW : 1881 - 1940), 17 June, p. 2. (EVENING), viewed 07 Oct 2022, http://nla.gov.au/nla.news-article98900896. (Death of Mr. James Conroy, 17 Jun 1916, p.2)

1917 'COACHING IN AUSTRALIA : a history of the coaching firm of Cobb & Co. with guide to the present coaching routes in Queensland.', Lees, William. Brisbane: Carter-Watson Co., Record Number 996938114702061, 21113295690002061 Available at: http://onesearch.slq.qld.gov.au/primo-ex-plore/search?query=any,contains,Lees,%20W%20Coaching%20in%20Austral-ia%20:%20a%20history%20of%20the%20coaching%20firm%20of%20Cobb%20%26%20Co,&tab=all&s-earch_scope=SLQ_PCI_EBSCO&vid=SLQ&lang=en_US&offset=0&fromRedirectFilter=true&pcAvailability=true [Accessed 1 Oct. 2020]. Print. State Library South Bank Collection. (Coaching in Australia : a history of the coaching firm of Cobb & Co. with guide to the present coaching routes in Queensland, 1917) * Note reference to the book Coaching in Australia in 1917 in 'The Genesis of Cobb & Co', The Western Champion and General Advertiser for the Central-Western Districts (Barcaldine, Qld. :

1892 - 1922), 15 September, p. 11. , viewed 18 Mar 2021, http://nla.gov.au/nla.news-article77790761 and in 'Cobb and Co.', 1917, The Queenslander (Brisbane, Qld. : 1866 - 1939), 1 September, p. 3. , viewed 20 Apr 2021, http://nla.gov.au/nla.news-page2539743.

1917 'DEATH OF OLD ORANGE COACH DRIVER.', Leader (Orange, NSW : 1899 - 1945), 5 September, p. 1. , viewed 03 Oct 2022, http://nla.gov.au/nla.news-article117831171. (Death of Old Orange Coach Driver, 5 Sept 1917, p.1)

1917 'DEATH OF OLD ORANGE COACH DRIVER.', Leader (Orange, NSW : 1899 - 1945), 5 September, p. 1. , viewed 07 Aug 2022, http:// nla.gov.au/nla.news-article117831171. (Death of Old Orange Coach Driver, 5 Sep 1917, p.1)

1917 'NEWS OF GEELONG AND DISTRICT SOLDIERS.', Geelong Advertiser (Vic. : 1859 - 1929), 16 April, p. 3. , viewed 09 Oct 2022, http://nla.gov.au/nla.news-article132673457. (News of Geelong and District Soldiers, 16 Apr 1917)

1917 'PERSONAL', Sunday Times (Sydney, NSW : 1895 - 1930), 29 April, p. 12. , viewed 14 Oct 2022, http://nla.gov.au/nla.news-article122793428. (Personal, 14 Oct 1917, p.12)

1918 'DAYS OF COBB & GO.', The Forbes Advocate (NSW : 1911 - 1954), 4 October, p. 7. , viewed 11 Oct 2022, http://nla.gov. au/nla.news-article100309216. (Days of Cobb & Go., 4 Oct 1918, p.7)

1918 'MAIL DRIVER 54 YEARS.', Wellington Times (NSW : 1899 - 1954), 26 September, p. 2. , viewed 03 Oct 2022, http://nla.gov.au/nla.news-article143234079. (Mail Driver 54 Years, 26 Sept 1918, p.2)

1918 'NEWS OF GEELONG AND DISTRICT SOLDIERS.', Geelong Advertiser (Vic. : 1859 - 1929), 31 January, p. 6. , viewed 09 Oct 2022, http://nla.gov.au/nla.news-article119708751. (News of Geelong and District Soldiers, 31 Jan 1918, p.6)

1919 'LANDSBOROUGH.' The Ballarat Star (Vic. : 1865 - 1924) 22 January 1919: 6. Web. 21 Oct 2022 <http://nla.gov.au/nla.news-article213867409>. (Landsborough, 22 Jan 1919, p.6)

1919 'NEWS AND NOTES.', The Richmond River Herald and Northern Districts Advertiser (NSW : 1886 - 1942), 25 April, p. 1. , viewed 18 Apr 2023, http://nla.gov.au/nla.news-article132524250 (News and Notes, 25 April 1919, p.1)

1919 ANNUAL REPORT / COBB & CO.'S OLD COACH DRIVERS' ASSOCIATION. (Anon) Footscray, Vic: The Association. pp.6&7, State Library Victoria. Record ID: 999827033607636. https://viewer.slv.vic.gov.au/?entity=IE2421340&file=FL17322317&mode=browse, viewed 6/9/2022.

1920 'A SOUTHERN ARCADIA.', The Lilydale Express (Vic. : 1886 - 1897; 1914 - 1955), 6 February, p. 3. , viewed 09 Oct 2022, http://nla.gov.au/nla.news-article258378361. (A Southern Arcadia, 6 Feb 1920, p.3)

1920 'ALONE IN AGONY.', Young Witness (NSW : 1915 - 1923), 14 May, p. 3. (LATEST EDITION), viewed 07 Aug 2022, http://nla.gov.au/nla.news-article122441477. (Alone in Agony, 14 May 1920, p.3)

1920 'ON THE ROADS WITH COBB & CO.', Smith's Weekly (Sydney, NSW : 1919 - 1950), 4 September, p. 9. , viewed 03 Oct 2022, http://nla.gov.au/nla.news-article234221223. (On the Roads with Cobb & Co., 4 Sep 1920, p.9)

1920 'STORIES OF THE COBB & CO. COACHING DAYS.', Sunday Times (Sydney, NSW : 1895 - 1930), 19 December, p. 18., viewed 14 Oct 2022, http://nla.gov.au/nla.news-article120522761. (Stories of the Cobb & Co. Coaching Days, 19 Dec 1920, p.18)

1921 'ECHO OF COBB AND CO.', Young Witness (NSW : 1915 - 1923), 10 September, p. 4. (LATEST EDITION), viewed 21 Oct 2022, http://nla.gov.au/nla.news-article113612679. (Echo of Cobb and Co, 10 Sep 1921, p.4)

1921 'IN THE DAYS OF COBB & CO.' Sydney Mail (NSW : 1912 - 1938) 20 April 1921: 8. Web. 22 Oct 2022 <http://nla.gov.au/nla.news-article159037714>. (In the Days of Cobb & Co., 20 Apr 1921, p.8)

1921 'JOTTINGS.', Southern Argus (Port Elliot, SA : 1866 - 1954), 15 September, p. 3. , viewed 14 Oct 2022, http://nla.gov.au/nla.news-article96990982. (Jottings, 15 Sep 1921, p.3)

1922 'COBB AND CO.', Morning Bulletin (Rockhampton, Qld. : 1878 - 1954), 20 June, p. 13. , viewed 06 Aug 2021, http://nla.gov.au/nla.news- article54018319. State Library of Queensland. (Cobb and Co., 20 Jun 1922, p.13)

1922 'FAMILY NOTICES', The Age (Melbourne, Vic. : 1854 - 1954), 16 Jan-uary, p. 1. , viewed 20 Oct 2022, http://nla.gov.au/nla.news-arti-cle205751294 . (Family Notices, 16 Jan 1922, p.1)

1922 'OLD COACHING DAYS.', The Argus (Melbourne, Vic. : 1848 - 1957), 10 June, p. 7. , viewed 06 Aug 2021, http://nla.gov.au/nla.newsar-ticle4629678. (Old Coaching Days, 10 Jun, 1922, p.7)

1922 'WHEN COBB & CO WAS KING', The Sun (Sydney, NSW : 1910 - 1954), 16 April, p. 15. , viewed 03 Oct 2022, http:// nla.gov.au/nla.news-article223948547. (When Cobb & Co was King, 16 Apr 1922, p.15)

1923 'FAR WESTERN[?] VICTORIA.', The Argus (Melbourne, Vic. : 1848 - 1957), 10 November, p. 8. , viewed 07 Oct 2022, http://nla.gov. au/nla.news-article1989223. (Far Western[?] Victoria, 10 Nov 1923, p.8)

1923 'OLD COACHING DAYS.', Macleay Argus (Kempsey, NSW : 1885 - 1907; 1909 - 1910; 1912 - 1913; 1915 - 1916; 1918 - 1954), 15 June, p. 3. , viewed 03 Oct 2022, http://nla.gov.au/nla.news-article234211341. (Old Coaching Days, 15 Jun 1923, p.3)

1923 'OLD COACHING DAYS.', The Corowa Free Press (NSW : 1875 - 1954), 19 October, p. 3. , viewed 12 Oct 2022, http://nla.gov.au/ nla.news-article235914489. (Old Coaching Days, 19 Oct 1923, p.3)

1923 'OLD COACHING DAYS.', The Independent (Deniliquin, NSW : 1901 - 1946), 23 February, p. 5. , viewed 03 Oct 2022, http://nla.gov.au/nla.news-article101552764. (Old Coaching Days, 23 Feb 1923, p.5)

1923 'OLD COACHING DAYS.', The Riverine Grazier (Hay, NSW : 1873 - 1954), 27 February, p. 2. , viewed 13 Oct 2022, http:// nla.gov.au/nla.news-article140118107. (Old Coaching Days, 27 Feb 1923, p.2)

1923 'PIONEERING IN THE PARKES DISTRICT', Western Champion (Parkes, NSW : 1898 - 1934), 19 April, p. 25. , viewed 11 Oct 2022, http://nla.gov.au/nla.news-article113490898. (Pioneering in the Parkes District, 19 Apr 1923, p.25)

1924 'A COBB & CO. VETERAN.', The Macleay Chronicle (Kempsey, NSW : 1899 - 1952), 7 May, p. 3. , viewed 06 May 2023, http://nla.gov.au/nla.news-article174388858 (A Cobb & Co. Veteran, 7 May 1924, p.3)

1924 'AN AMERICAN-AUSTRALIAN', The Daily Telegraph (Sydney, NSW : 1883 - 1930), 29 November, p. 10. , viewed 02 Nov 2022, http://nla.gov.au/nla.news-article245465278. (An American-Australian, 29 Nov 1924, p.10)

1924 'COBB & CO.', The Bathurst Times (NSW : 1909 - 1925), 13 December, p. 2. (SPECIAL HARVEST SUPPLEMENT), viewed 28 Jul 2022, http://nla.gov.au/nla.news-article112113656. (Cobb and Co., 13 Dec 1924, p.2)

1924 'IN THE DAYS OF COBB AND CO.', The Richmond River Herald and Northern Districts Advertiser (NSW : 1886 - 1942), 23 December, p. 2. , viewed 15 Sep 2022, http://nla.gov.au/nla.news-article125957206. (In the Days of Cobb and Co., 23 Dec 1924, p.2)

1924 'PASSING OF COBB & CO.', The Daily Telegraph (Sydney, NSW : 1883 - 1930), 6 September, p. 13. , viewed 04 Oct 2022, http://nla.gov.au/nla.news-article245220526. (Passing of Cobb & Co., 6 Sep 1924, p.13)

1924 'THE BOX SEAT.', The Gundagai Times and Tumut, Adelong and Murrumbidgee District Advertiser (NSW : 1868 - 1931), 16

December, p. 2. , viewed 07 Aug 2022, http://nla.gov.au/nla.news-article121769918. (The Box Seat, 16 Dec 1924, p.2)

1925 'A WAGGA DISTRICT NATIVE.', The Murrumbidgee Irrigator (Leeton, NSW : 1915 - 1954), 21 April, p. 3. , viewed 27 Jul 2022, http://nla.gov.au/nla.news-article155872150. (A Wagga District Native, 21 Apr 1925, p.3)

1925 'COACHING IN THE COMMONWEALTH', Sunday Times (Perth, WA : 1902 - 1954), 17 May, p. 9. , viewed 28 Apr 2023, http://nla.gov.au/nla.news-article58258535 (Coaching in the Common-wealth, 17 May 1925)

1925 'COACHING IN THE COMMONWEALTH', Sunday Times (Perth, WA : 1902 - 1954), 24 May, p. 11. , viewed 28 Apr 2023, http://nla.gov.au/nla.news-article58218298 (Coaching in the Common-wealth, 24 May 1925, p.11)

1925 'COACHING IN THE COMMONWEALTH', Sunday Times (Perth, WA : 1902 - 1954), 31 May, p. 9. , viewed 26 Apr 2023, http://nla.gov.au/nla.news-article58218716 (Coaching in the Common-wealth, 31 May 1925, p.9)

1925 'COACHING IN THE COMMONWEALTH', Sunday Times (Perth, WA : 1902 - 1954), 7 June, p. 11. , viewed 29 Apr 2023, http://nla.gov.au/nla.news-article58219105 (Coaching in the Common-wealth, 7 June 1925, p.11)

1925 'COBB AND CO.'S DRIVERS.', The Brisbane Courier (Qld. : 1864 - 1933), 29 January, p. 12. , viewed 06 Oct 2022, http:// nla.gov.au/nla.news-article20904832. (Cobb and Co.'s Drivers, 29 Jan 1925, p.12)

1925 'COBB AND COMPANY'S COACHES.', Country Life Stock and Station Journal (Sydney, NSW : 1924 - 1925), 10 April, p. 5. , viewed 26 Sep 2022, http://nla.gov.au/nla.news-article128647626. (Cobb and Company's Coaches, 10 Apr 1925, p.5)

1925 'COBB'S COACH DRIVER.', The Horsham Times (Vic. : 1882 - 1954), 8 May, p. 8. , viewed 22 Jul 2022, http://nla.gov.au/nla.news-arti-cle73035337 .(Cobb's Coach Driver, 8 May 1925, p.8)

1925 'COBB'S COACH' The Daily Mail (Brisbane, Qld. : 1903; 1916 - 1926) 14 August 1925: 13. Web. 22 Jul 2022 <http://nla. gov.au/ nla.news-article217592076>. (Cobb's Coach Original Driver, 14 Aug 1925, p.13)

1925 'COBB'S COACHES.', The Brisbane Courier (Qld. : 1864 - 1933), 17 January, p. 17. , viewed 04 Oct 2022, http://nla.gov.au/ nla.news-article20898443. (Cobb's Coaches, 17 Jan 1925, p.17)

1925 'DEAD, AT 93.', The Gundagai Independent and Pastoral, Agricultural and Mining Advocate (NSW : 1898 - 1928), 10 December, p. 5. , viewed 10 Aug 2022, http://nla.gov.au/nla.news-article121746102. (Dead at 93, 10 Dec 1925, p.5)

1925 'DEATH OF MR. S. E. WALL.', Western Herald (Bourke, NSW : 1887 - 1970), 7 March, p. 3. , viewed 14 Oct 2022, http://nla.gov.au/nla.news-article142055997. (Death of Mr. S. E. Wall, 7 Mar 1925, p.3)

1925 'HIGHWAY ROBBERY.', Queensland Times (Ipswich, Qld. : 1909 - 1954), 21 March, p. 14. (DAILY.), viewed 27 Jul 2022, http://nla.gov.au/nla.news-article121936707. (Highway Robbery, 21 Mar 1925, p.14)

1925 'LINK WITH COBB & CO.', The Tumut Advocate and Farmers and Settlers' Adviser (NSW : 1903 - 1925), 27 January, p. 6. , viewed 29 Dec 2022, http://nla.gov.au/nla.news-article112275820. (Link with Cobb & Co., 27 Jan 1925, p.6)

1925 'LINK WITH THE PAST', The Cessnock Eagle and South Maitland Re-corder (NSW : 1913 - 1954), 30 January, p. 2. , viewed 09 Aug 2022, http://nla.gov.au/nla.news-article99364395. (Link with the Past, 30 Jan 1925, p.2)

1925 'LOCAL AND GENERAL', Cootamundra Herald (NSW : 1877 - 1954), 26 January, p. 2. , viewed 29 Apr 2023, http://nla.gov.au/nla.news-article144456346 (Local and General, 26 Jan 1925, p.2)

1925 'OBITUARY.', Healesville and Yarra Glen Guardian (Vic. : 1900 - 1942), 20 June, p. 2. , viewed 21 Oct 2022, http://nla.gov.au/nla.news-article60210142. (Obituary, 20 Jun 1925, p.2)

1925 'OBITUARY.', The Daily Telegraph (Sydney, NSW : 1883 - 1930), 1 September, p. 2. , viewed 21 Oct 2022, http://nla.gov.au/nla.news-article245250983. (Obituary, 1 Sep 1925, p.2)

1925 'PASSING OF COBB & CO', Windsor and Richmond Gazette (NSW : 1888 - 1965), 16 January, p. 3. , viewed 06 May 2023, http://nla.gov.au/nla.news-article85899167 (Passing Of Cobb & Co, 16 Jan 1925, p.3)

1925 'WINTON NOTES.', Townsville Daily Bulletin (Qld. : 1907 - 1954), 6 February, p. 7. , viewed 04 Aug 2022, http://nla.gov. au/nla.news-article61576457. (Winton Notes, 6 Feb 1925, p.7)

1926 'COLLINS'S HOTEL.', Townsville Daily Bulletin (Qld. : 1907 - 1954), 19 June, p. 6. , viewed 18 Apr 2023, http://nla.gov.au/nla.news-article60939188 (Collins's Hotel, 19 Jun 1926, p.6)

1926 'DAYS OF COBB & CO.', Smith's Weekly (Sydney, NSW : 1919 - 1950), 27 March, p. 13. , viewed 03 Oct 2022, http://nla. gov.au/nla.news-article234436562. (Days of Cobb & Co., 27 Mar 1926, p.13)

1926 'GOSSIP', Smith's Weekly (Sydney, NSW : 1919 - 1950), 20 November, p. 15. , viewed 18 Apr 2023, http://nla.gov.au/nla.news-article234435847 (Gossip, 20 Nov 1926, p.15)

1926 'MR. JIM FROST.', The Gundagai Times and Tumut, Adelong and Murrumbidgee District Advertiser (NSW : 1868 - 1931), 6 July, p. 2. , viewed 22 Aug 2022, http://nla.gov.au/nla.news-article123465742. (Mr. Jim Frost, 6 Jul 1926, p.2)

1926 'OBITUARY.', The Gundagai Independent and Pastoral, Agricultural and Mining Advocate (NSW : 1898 - 1928), 6 May, p. 2. , viewed 29 Dec 2022, http://nla.gov.au/nla.news-article121745279. (Obituary, 6 May 1926, p.2)

1926 'OBITUARY', The Hillston Spectator and Lachlan River Advertiser (NSW : 1898 - 1952), 14 January, p. 6. , viewed 21 Oct 2022, http://nla.gov.au/nla.news-article131323499. (Obituary, 14 Jan 1926, p.6)

1926 'OLD COACH DRIVER.', Western Age (Dubbo, NSW : 1914 - 1932), 2 July, p. 3. , viewed 09 Aug 2022, http://nla.gov.au/ nla.news-article137074449. (Old Coach Driver, 2 Jul 1926, p.3)

1926 'OLD COBB & CO. DRIVER.', Warialda Standard and Northern Districts' Advertiser (NSW : 1900 - 1954), 9 August, p. 4. , viewed 27 Jul 2022, http://nla.gov.au/nla.news-article214788954. (Old Cobb & Co. Driver, 9 Aug 1926)

1926 'PASSING OF THE COACH.', Observer (Adelaide, SA : 1905 - 1931), 10 July, p. 60. , viewed 18 Oct 2022, http://nla.gov. au/nla.news-article166326490. (Passing of the Coach, 10 Jul 1926, p.60)

1926 'PERSONOGRAPHS', Truth (Brisbane, Qld. : 1900 - 1954), 13 June, p. 10. , viewed 06 Oct 2022, http://nla.gov.au/nla.news-article199290351. (Personographs, 13 Jun 1926, p.10)

1926 'TWO NONAGENARIANS', The Sun (Sydney, NSW : 1910 - 1954), 28 March, p. 5. , viewed 29 Dec 2022, http://nla.gov.au/nla.news-article224059621. (Two Nonagenarians, 28 Mar 1926, p.5)

1927 'A LINK WITH COBB AND CO', Leader (Orange, NSW : 1899 - 1945), 27 May, p. 5. , viewed 29 Jul 2022, http://nla.gov. au/nla.news-article254405499. (A link with Cobb and Co, 27 May 1927, p.5)

1927 'A PIONEER MAILMAN.', The Land (Sydney, NSW : 1911 - 1954), 25 November, p. 6. , viewed 17 Oct 2022, http://nla.gov. au/nla.news-article102988737. (A Pioneer Mailman, 25 Nov 1927, p.6)

1927 'COACH ACCIDENT.', Glen Innes Examiner (NSW : 1908 - 1954), 5 November, p. 4. , viewed 01 Jan 2023, http://nla.gov.au/nla.news-article180163269. (Coach Accident, 5 Nov 1927, p.4)

1927 'COBB AND CO.', Glen Innes Examiner (NSW : 1908 - 1954), 9 June, p. 10. , viewed 09 Aug 2022, http://nla.gov.au/nla. news-article184223738. (Cobb and Co, 9 Jun 1927, p.10)

1927 'LINK WITH COBB & CO.', Windsor and Richmond Gazette (NSW : 1888 - 1965), 10 June, p. 1. , viewed 06 May 2023, http://nla.gov.au/nla.news-article85955647 (Link With Cobb & Co., 10 Jun 1927, p.1)

1927 'MEMORIES OF MYPONGA.', The Register (Adelaide, SA : 1901 - 1929), 28 October, p. 13. , viewed 07 Oct 2022, http:// nla.gov.au/nla.news-article56514302. (Memories of Myponga, 28 Oct 1927, p.13)

1927 'NO TITLE', The Brisbane Courier (Qld. : 1864 - 1933), 11 March, p. 16. , viewed 18 Apr 2023, http://nla.gov.au/nla.news-article21104111 (No title, The Brisbane Courier, 11 Mar 1927, p.16)

1927 'OBITUARY.', The Brisbane Courier (Qld. : 1864 - 1933), 14 September, p. 17. , viewed 21 Oct 2022, http://nla.gov.au/nla.news-article21173877. (Obituary, 14 Sep 1927, p.17)

1927 'OFF THE FOOTPLATE.', Recorder (Port Pirie, SA : 1919 - 1954), 22 September, p. 1. , viewed 23 Aug 2022, http://nla.gov. au/nla.news-article96053697. (Off the footplate, 22 Sep 1927, p.1)

1927 'PRESS ERROR', The Blue Mountain Echo (NSW : 1909 - 1928), 1 July, p. 6. , viewed 11 Oct 2022, http://nla.gov.au/nla. news-article108961043. (Press Error, 1 Jul 1927, p.6) (Pugh's Queensland almanac, directory and law calendar. 1862-1866, Call Number FER F14499, p.84)

1927 'SMITH'S WEEKLY' (Sydney, NSW : 1919 - 1950), 28 May, p. 15. , viewed 08 Oct 2022, http://nla.gov.au/nla.news-page25332659. (Smith's Weekly, 28 May 1927, p.15)

1927? PIONEERING DAYS IN WESTERN VICTORIA : A NARRATIVE OF EARLY STATION LIFE / by J.C. Hamilton Creator Hamilton, J. C. (James Charles), 1836-1927, Call Number N 919.45 HAM Created/Published Melbourne : Exchange Press, [1912?]. https://nla.gov.au/nla. obj-40129670/view?partId=nla.obj-40138483#page/n88/mode/1up

1928 'A TRIUMPH IN ORGANISATION.', Leader (Orange, NSW : 1899 - 1945), 28 December, p. 6. , viewed 18 Apr 2023, http://nla.gov.au/nla.news-article254509087 (A Triumph in Organisation, 28 Dec 1928, p.6)

1928 'LOOKING BACKWARDS', Freeman's Journal (Sydney, NSW : 1850 - 1932), 11 October, p. 16. , viewed 07 Oct 2022, http://nla.gov.au/nla.news-article118054418. (Looking Backwards, 11 Oct 1928, p.16)

1928 'OLD WESTERN PIONEER.', Molong Express and Western District Advertiser (NSW : 1887 - 1954), 11 August, p. 16. , viewed 05 Aug 2022, http://nla.gov.au/nla.news-article139470930. (Old Western Pioneer, 11 Aug 1928, p.16)

1929 'COBB AND CO. KING PASSES', The Picton Post (NSW : 1907 - 1954), 4 September, p. 1. , viewed 03 Oct 2022, http:// nla.gov.au/nla.news-article112204114. (Cobb and Co. King Passes, 4 Sep 1929, p.1)

1929 'COBB AND CO.'S COACHING DAYS: GOLOURFUL PAGE OF HISTORY CLOSED.', Sunday Mail (Brisbane, Qld. : 1926 - 1954), 30 June, p. 23. , viewed 16 Dec 2021, http://nla.gov.au/nla.news-article97696763 (Cobb and Co.'s Coaching Days: Colourful Page of History Closed, 30 Jun 1929, p.23)

1929 'CRACK-O'-THE-WHIP.', The Gundagai Times and Tumut, Adelong and Murrumbidgee District Advertiser (NSW : 1868 - 1931), 5 July, p. 2. , viewed 11 Oct 2022, http://nla.gov.au/nla.news-article122750230. (Crack-o'-the-Whip, 5 Jul 1929, p.2)

1929 'DEATH OF MR. C0RBETT.', Leader (Orange, NSW : 1899 - 1945), 4 March, p. 5. , viewed 05 Aug 2022, http:// nla.gov.au/ nla.news-article254520287. (Death of Mr. Corbett, 4 Mar 1929, p.5)

1929 'MAIL DRIVER'S DEATH', The West Wyalong Advocate (NSW : 1928 - 1954), 6 August, p. 3. , viewed 07 Aug 2022, http://nla.gov.au/nla.news-article188326214. (Mail Driver's Death, 6 Aug 1929, p.3)

1929 'MR. RICHARD HALCROFT.', Molong Express and Western District Advertiser (NSW : 1887 - 1954), 3 August, p. 8. , viewed 03 Oct 2022, http://nla.gov.au/nla.news-article139474593. (Mr. Richard Halcroft, 3 Aug 1929, p.8)

1929 'OBITUARY.', The Brisbane Courier (Qld. : 1864 - 1933), 3 August, p. 14. , viewed 21 Oct 2022, http://nla.gov.au/nla.news-article21433986. (Obituary, 3 Aug 1929, p.14)

1929 'OBITUARY', The Burrowa News (NSW : 1874 - 1951), 9 August, p. 6. , viewed 07 Oct 2022, http://nla.gov.au/nla.news-article102379029. (Obituary, 9 Aug 1929, p.6)

1929 'PENSIONER FOUND DEAD.', Western Mail (Perth, WA : 1885 - 1954), 12 December, p. 27. , viewed 22 Jul 2022, http:// nla.gov.au/nla.news-article37681806. (Pensioner found dead, 12 Dec 1929, p.27)

1929 'TEDDY MORGAN', Glen Innes Examiner (NSW : 1908 - 1954), 6 Au-gust, p. 4. , viewed 26 Apr 2023, http://nla.gov.au/nla.news-article180832073. ('Teddy' Morgan, 6 Aug 1929, p.4)

1929 'TEDDY MORGAN', The Scone Advocate (NSW : 1887 - 1954), 9 Au-gust, p. 4. , viewed 31 Dec 2022, http://nla.gov.au/nla.news-article157995579. (Teddy Morgan, 9 Aug 1929, p.4)

1929 'VETERAN COACHMAN.', The Manning River Times and Advocate for the Northern Coast Districts of New South Wales (Taree, NSW : 1898 - 1954), 21 August, p. 3. , viewed 29 Apr 2023, http://nla.gov.au/nla.news-article173805198 (Veteran Coachman, 21 Aug 1929, p.3)

1929 'WHIPS OF COBB & CO.', The Australian Worker (Sydney, NSW : 1913 - 1950), 20 February, p. 5. , viewed 31 Oct 2022, http://nla.gov.au/nla.news-article145971259. (Whips of Cobb & Co., 20 Feb 1929, p.5)

1930 'BARNEY MCTIERNAN.', The Bombala Times (NSW : 1912 - 1938), 14 November, p. 5. , viewed 29 Apr 2023, http://nla.gov.au/nla.news-article14129959 (Barney McTiernan, 14 Nov 1930, p.5)

1930 'COBB'S COACHES RECALLED', Gilgandra Weekly and Castlereagh (NSW : 1929 - 1942), 27 November, p. 7. , viewed 25 Apr 2023, http://nla.gov.au/nla.news-article113687044 (Cobb's Coaches Re-called, 27 Nov 1930, p.7)

1930 'DROVE FOR COBB & CO.', Windsor and Richmond Gazette (NSW : 1888 - 1965), 8 August, p. 3. , viewed 27 Jul 2022, http://nla.gov.au/nla.news-article85884124. (Drove For Cobb & Co, 8 Aug 1930, p.3)

1930 'GOSSIP FROM EVERYWHERE', Smith's Weekly (Sydney, NSW : 1919 - 1950), 16 August, p. 13. , viewed 01 May 2023, http://nla.gov.au/nla.news-article234425615 (Gossip from Everywhere, 16 Aug 1930, p.13)

1930 'HISTORY OF ROSEDALE', Weekly Times (Melbourne, Vic. : 1869 - 1954), 22 March, p. 10. , viewed 14 Oct 2022, http:// nla.gov.au/nla.news-article223899508. (History of Rosedale, 22 Mar 1930, p.10)

1930 'MEMORIES OF COBB & CO.', The Age (Melbourne, Vic. : 1854 - 1954), 6 May, p. 11. , viewed 31 Oct 2022, http:// nla.gov.au/nla.news-article203084695 (Memories of Cobb & Co, 6 May 1930, p.11)

1930 'MR. P. J. BYRNE.', Moree Gwydir Examiner and General Advertiser (NSW : 1901 - 1940), 4 August, p. 3. , viewed 11 Oct 2022, http://nla.gov.au/nla.news-article111701786. (Mr. P. J. Byrne, 4 Aug 1930, p.3)

1930 'OBERON NEWS', Lithgow Mercury (NSW : 1898 - 1954), 26 September, p. 6. (TOWN EDITION), viewed 09 Oct 2022, http:// nla.gov.au/nla.news-article219577490. (Oberon News, 26 Sep 1930, p.6)

1930 'OBITUARY.', The Brisbane Courier (Qld. : 1864 - 1933), 2 June, p. 18. , viewed 06 Oct 2022, http://nla.gov.au/nla.news-article21559214. (Obituary, 2 Jun 1930, p.18)

1930 'OBITUARY', The Burrowa News (NSW : 1874 - 1951), 29

August, p. 4. , viewed 21 Oct 2022, http://nla.gov.au/nla.news-article102367739. (Obituary, 29 Aug 1930, p.4)

1930 'OLD COACH DRIVER'S Scorn.', The Evening News (Rockhampton, Qld. : 1924 - 1941), 6 August, p. 5. , viewed 07 Aug 2022, http://nla.gov.au/nla.news-article201509234. (Old Coach Drivers Scorn, 6 Aug 1930, p.5)

1930 'VETERAN COACH DRIVER DIES', The Riverine Herald (Echuca, Vic. : Moama, NSW : 1869 - 1954; 1998 - 2002), 3 September, p.2. , viewed 06 Aug 2022, http://nla.gov.au/nla.news-article116320268. (Veteran Coach Driver Dies, 3 Sep 1930, p.2)

1930-1940S 'CABBAGE TREE NED : COBB & CO'S COACH DRIVER'. A newspaper article and photograph on a cardboard backing, plus the covering letter from donor E. J. Mickle. Royal Historical Society of Victoria (RHSV), viewed 27/12/20022, https://ehive.com/collections/6420/objects/752143/cabbage-tree-ned-cobb-cos-coach-driver

1931 'ADMINISTRATION OF JUSTICE BILL.', The Riverine Grazier (Hay, NSW : 1873 - 1954), 9 June, p. 2. , viewed 23 Aug 2022, http://nla.gov.au/nla.news-article140664748. (Administration of Justice Bill, 9 Jun 1931, p.2)

1931 'AN OLD COACH DRIVER', The Southern Mail (Bowral, NSW : 1889 - 1954), 27 February, p. 4. , viewed 29 Jul 2022, http://nla. gov.au/nla.news-article128539649. (An Old Coach Driver, 27 Feb 1931, p.4)

1931 'AUSTRALIANITIES', Northern Star (Lismore, NSW : 1876 - 1954), 27 October, p. 10. , viewed 17 Oct 2022, http://nla.gov.au/nla.news-article94255559. (Australianities, 27 Oct 1931, p.10)

1931 'BREWARRINA IN THE EARLY 80's', Narromine News and Trangie Advocate (NSW : 1898 - 1955), 6 November, p. 8. , viewed 12 Oct 2022, http://nla.gov.au/nla.news-article98917914. (Brewarrina In The Early 80's, 6 Nov 1931, p.8)

1931 'DAYS OF COBB & CO.', The Gloucester Advocate (NSW : 1905 - 1954), 30 January, p. 4. , viewed 14 Oct 2022, http://nla. gov.au/nla.news-article159587892. (Days of Cobb & Co., 30 Jan 1931, p.4)

1931 'DAYS OF COBB & CO.', The Wingham Chronicle and Manning River Observer (NSW : 1898 - 1954), 16 January, p. 8. , viewed 06 May 2023, http://nla.gov.au/nla.news-article166286916 (Days of Cobb & Co., 16 Jan, p.8)

1931 'EARLY DAYS.', Narromine News and Trangie Advocate (NSW : 1898 - 1955), 24 July, p. 7. , viewed 29 Jul 2022, http://nla.gov. au/nla.news-article98921371. (Early Days, 24 Jul 1931, p.7)

1931 'MR. TOM ROBERTS', Glen Innes Examiner (NSW : 1908 - 1954), 19 September, p. 2. , viewed 17 Oct 2022, http://nla.gov. au/nla.news-article185891367. (Mr. Tom Roberts, 19 Sep 1931, p.2)

1931 'OCTOGENARIAN'S SAD END.', Portland Guardian (Vic. : 1876 - 1953), 18 May, p. 4. (EVENING), viewed 01 Jan 2023, http://nla.gov.au/nla.news-article64295134. (Octogenarian's Sad End, 18 May 1931, p.4)

1932 'AUSTRALIANITIES.', Macleay Argus (Kempsey, NSW : 1885 - 1907; 1909 - 1910; 1912 - 1913; 1915 - 1916; 1918 - 1954), 6 May, p. 9. , viewed 13 Jul 2022, http://nla.gov.au/nla.news-article234242364. (Australianites—Cobb and Co. Drivers, 6 May 1932, p.9)

1932 'AUSTRALIANITIES', Glen Innes Examiner (NSW : 1908 - 1954), 3 September, p. 2. , viewed 07 Oct 2022, http://nla.gov.au/nla.news-article184608041. (Australianities, 3 Sep 1932, p.2)

1932 'COBB & CO. DAYS', Lithgow Mercury (NSW : 1898 - 1954), 22 March, p. 2. (TOWN EDITION), viewed 29 Sep 2022,http://nla.gov.au/nla.news-article219677463. (Cobb & Co. Days, 22 Mar 1932, p.2)

1932 'COBB & CO. DRIVER DISAPPOINTED', Western Age (Dubbo, NSW : 1914 - 1932), 23 March, p. 3. , viewed 09 Sep 2022, http://nla.gov.au/nla.news-article137151666. (Cobb & Co. Driver Dis-appointed, 23 Mar 1932, p.3)

1932 'COBB & CO.', Narromine News and Trangie Advocate (NSW : 1898 - 1955), 19 February, p. 5. , viewed 29 Apr 2023, http://nla.gov.au/nla.news-article98916700 (Cobb & Co, 19 Feb 1932, p.5)

1932 'COBB AND CO, DRIVER DISAPPOINTED', Leader (Orange, NSW : 1899 - 1945), 18 March, p. 2. , viewed 13 Jul 2022, http://nla. gov.au/nla.news-article255171130. (Cobb and Co, Driver Disappointed, 18 Mar 1932, p.2)

1932 'COBB AND CO. COACHMAN', The Gundagai Independent (NSW : 1928 - 1954), 21 November, p. 4. , viewed 17 Oct 2022, http://nla.gov.au/nla.news-article224984605. (Cobb and Co. Coachman, 21 Nov 1932, p.4)

1932 'COLAC.', The Age (Melbourne, Vic. : 1854 - 1954), 31 October, p. 11. , viewed 01 Nov 2022, http://nla.gov.au/nla.news-article205496194. (Colac, 31 Oct 1932, p.11)

1932 'DRIVERS OF THE PLAINS', The Daily Telegraph (Sydney, NSW : 1931 - 1954), 1 April, p. 9. , viewed 03 Oct 2022, http:// nla.gov.au/nla.news-article246332977. (Drivers of the Plains, 1 Apr 1932, p.9)

1932 'DROVE FOR COBB'S', Goulburn Evening Penny Post (NSW : 1881 - 1940), 15 February, p. 2. (DAILY and EVENING), viewed 29 Apr 2023, http://nla.gov.au/nla.news-article99555313 (Drove for Cobb's, 15 Feb 1932, p.2)

1932 'EARLY CAMPERDOWN HISTORY.', Camperdown Chronicle (Vic. : 1875 - 1954), 9 June, p. 5. , viewed 07 Oct 2022, http://nla.gov.au/nla.news-article23363799. (Early Camperdown History, 9 Jun 1932, p.5)

1932 'IN THE DAYS OF COBB & CO.', The Port Macquarie News and Has-tings River Advocate (NSW : 1882 - 1950), 8 October, p. 6. , viewed 13 Oct 2022, http://nla.gov.au/nla.news-article105959477

1932 'MR. GEORGE GILBERT.', The Central Queensland Herald (Rockhampton, Qld. : 1930 - 1956), 10 November, p. 23. , viewed 01 Jan 2023, http://nla.gov.au/nla.news-article70308292. ('Mr. George Gilbert, 10 Nov 1932, p.23)

1932 'OBITUARY.', Dungog Chronicle : Durham and Gloucester Advertiser (NSW : 1894 - 1954), 16 December, p. 5. , viewed 21 Oct 2022, http://nla.gov.au/nla.news-article141133621. (Obituary, 16 Dec, 1932, p.5)

1932 'OLD COACHING DAYS', Cairns Post (Qld. : 1909 - 1954), 18 October, p. 4. , viewed 28 Jul 2022, http://nla.gov.au/nla.news-article41175091. (Old Coaching Days, 18 Oct 1932, p.4)

1932 'REMINISCENCES EARLY DAYS OF DANDENONG.', The Dandenong Journal (Vic. : 1927 - 1954), 16 June, p. 7. , viewed 07 Oct 2022, http://nla.gov.au/nla.news-article201112973. (Reminiscences Early Days of Dandenong, 16 Jun 1932, p.7)

1932 'TALES OF THE BUSH.', Narromine News and Trangie Advocate (NSW : 1898 - 1955), 20 May, p. 6. , viewed 06 Oct 2022, http://nla.gov.au/nla.news-article98921578. (Tales of the Bush, 20 May 1932, p.6)

1932 'WHIPS OF COBB AND CO.', Sydney Mail (NSW : 1912 1938), 24 February, p. 15. , viewed 12 Oct 2022, http://nla.gov.au/nla.news-article160082745. (Whips of Cobb and Co., 24 Feb 1932, p.15)

1933 'COBB & CO.', Bowen Independent (Qld. : 1911 - 1954), 27 March, p. 4. , viewed 17 Oct 2022, http://nla.gov.au/nla.news-article196464732

1933 'COBB AND CO. DRIVERS', Cowra Free Press (NSW : 1911 - 1937), 27 July, p. 6. , viewed 09 Oct 2022, http://nla.gov.au/nla.news-article262351504. (Cobb and Co. Drivers, 27 Jul 1933, p.6)

1933 'FAME AND FORTUNE', The Central Queensland Herald (Rockhampton, Qld. : 1930 - 1956), 23 March, p. 55. , viewed 23 Aug 2022, http://nla.gov.au/nla.news-article70333125. (Fame and Fortune, 23 Mar 1933, p.55)

1933 'FAMILY NOTICES', The Age (Melbourne, Vic. : 1854 - 1954), 25 August, p. 1. , viewed 21 Oct 2022, http://nla.gov.au/nla.news-arti-cle204371480. (Family Notices, 25 Aug 1933, p.1)

1933 'OLD COBB AND CO. DRIVER', Glen Innes Examiner (NSW : 1908 - 1954), 23 February, p. 3. , viewed 13 Jul 2022, http://nla.gov.au/nla.news-article183566236. (OLD COBB AND CO. DRIVER, 23 Feb 1933, p.3)

1933 'OLD LINK BROKEN', The Armidale Express and New England General Advertiser (NSW : 1856 - 1861; 1863 - 1889; 1891 - 1954), 9 January, p. 4. , viewed 18 Apr 2023, http://nla.gov.au/nla.news-article193022428 (Old Link Broken, 9 Jan 1933, p.4)

1933 'OLD-TIME COACH DRIVER', Sunraysia Daily (Mildura, Vic. : 1920 - 1937), 7 March, p. 5. , viewed 03 Oct 2022, http://nla.gov.au/nla.news-article265684418. (Old-time Coach Driver, 7 Mar 1933, p.5)

1933 'PERSONAL NEWS', The Albury Banner and Wodonga Express (NSW : 1860 - 1938), 23 June, p. 46. , viewed 06 May 2023, http://nla.gov.au/nla.news-article102258893 (Personal News, 23 Jun 1933, p.46)

1933 'THE AGE' (Melbourne, Vic. : 1854 - 1954), 21 June, p. 11. , viewed 21 Jun 2022, http://nla.gov.au/nla.news-page19051453. (Former Cobb and Co. Drivers, 21 Jun 1933, p.11)

1933 "OBITUARY." The Grenfell Record and Lachlan District Advertiser (NSW : 1876 - 1951) 19 June 1933: 2. Web. 21 Oct 2022 <http://nla.gov.au/nla.news-article112822425>. (Obituary, 19 Jun 1933, p.2)

1934 'A PIONEER COACH DROVER', Kilmore Free Press (Kilmore, Vic. : 1870 - 1954), 13 September, p. 2. (MORNING), viewed 29 Dec 2022, http://nla.gov.au/nla.news-article58079118. (A Pioneer Coach Drover, 13 Sep 1934, p.2)

1934 'BRUMMY" RICHARDS DEAD', The North Western Courier (Narrabri, NSW : 1913 - 1955), 21 May, p. 3. , viewed 17 Oct 2022, http://nla.gov.au/nla.news-article133265580. (Brummy Richards Dead, 21 May 1934, p.3)

1934 'COACHING AND THE COACHING DAYS.', The Riverine Grazier (Hay, NSW : 1873 - 1954), 13 February, p. 4. , viewed 04 Aug 2022, http://nla.gov.au/nla.news-article136892195. (Coaching and the coaching days, 13 Feb, 1934)

1934 'COACHING DAYS.', The Charleville Times (Brisbane, Qld. : 1896 - 1954), 9 March, p. 4. , viewed 06 Oct 2022, http://nla.gov.au/nla.news-article76674018. (Coaching Days, 9 Mar 1934, p.4)

1934 'COBB AND CO. DRIVER NOW A SQUATTER.', Manilla Express (NSW : 1899 - 1954), 16 March, p. 4. , viewed 03 Oct 2022, http://nla.gov.au/nla.news-article192359572. (Cobb and Co. Driver Now a Squatter, 16 Mar 1934, p.4)

1934 'COBB AND CO. DRIVER.', The Sydney Morning Herald (NSW : 1842 - 1954), 11 April, p. 17. , viewed 03 Oct 2022, http://nla.gov.au/nla.news-article17072343. (Cobb and Co. Driver, 11 Apr 1934, p.17)

1934 'COBB COACH VETERAN', The Herald (Melbourne, Vic. : 1861 - 1954), 26 May, p. 1. , viewed 27 Jul 2022, http://nla.gov.au/nla.news-article243251752. (Cobb Coach Veteran, 26 May 1934, p.1)

1934 'ECHOES OF THE PAST', Warwick Daily News (Qld. : 1919 -1954), 25 August, p. 3. , viewed 04 Oct 2022, http://nla.gov.au/nla.news-article177327839. (Echoes of the Past, 25 Aug 1934, p.3)

1934 'FAMILY NOTICES', The Age (Melbourne, Vic. : 1854 - 1954), 28 November, p. 1. , viewed 29 Sep 2022, http://nla.gov.au/nla.news-article205069423. (Family Notices, 28 Nov 1934, p.1)

1934 'HARRY PECKMAN', The Dubbo Liberal and Macquarie Advocate (NSW : 1894 - 1954), 11 January, p. 2. , viewed 14 Oct 2022, http://nla.gov.au/nla.news-article131582430. (Harry Peckman, 11 Jan 1934, p.2)

1934 'MR. ARTHUR MICHAEL O'MALLEY', The Northern Champion (Taree, NSW : 1913 - 1954), 22 August, p. 2. , viewed 03 Oct 2022, http://nla.gov.au/nla.news-article162137946. (Mr. Arthur Michael O'Malley, 22 Aug 1934, p.2)

1934 'OBITUARY', Ouyen Mail (Vic. : 1915 - 1918, 1931 - 1941), 30 March, p. 2. , viewed 21 Oct 2022, http://nla.gov.au/nla.news-article255666742. (Obituary, 30 Mar 1934, p.2)

1934 'OUT AMONG THE PEOPLE', The Advertiser (Adelaide, SA : 1931 - 1954), 25 October, p. 17. , viewed 06Oct 2022, http://nla.gov.au/nla.news-article74118771. (Out among the People, 25 Oct 1934, p.17)

1934 'SPORTING MEMORIES OF S.A.', Chronicle (Adelaide, SA : 1895 - 1954), 18 January, p. 19. , viewed 14 Oct 2022, http://nla.gov.au/nla.news-article92359480. (Sporting Memories, 18 Jan 1934, p.19)

1935 'DEATH OF COBB AND CO'S DRIVER.', Leader (Orange, NSW : 1899 - 1945), 22 February, p. 2. , viewed 03 Oct 2022, http://nla.gov.au/nla.news-article255413659. (Death of Cobb and Co's Driver, 22 Feb 1935, p.2)

1935 'LIGHTS OF COBB AND CO.', The Evening News (Rockhampton, Qld. : 1924 - 1941), 24 January, p. 6. , viewed 25 Apr 2023, http://nla.gov.au/nla.news-article198329483 (Lights of Cobb And Co., 24 Jan 1935, p.6)

1935 'OBITUARY', The Scone Advocate (NSW : 1887 - 1954), 2 August, p. 5. , viewed 21 Oct 2022, http://nla.gov.au/nla.news-article158987807. (Obituary, 2 Aug 1935, p.5)

1935 'OBITUARY', Wagga Wagga Express (NSW : 1930 - 1939), 8 June, p. 2. , viewed 21 Oct 2022, http://nla.gov.au/nla.news-article207542707. (Obituary, 8 Jun 1935, p.2)

1935 'OLD COACHING DAYS', Cowra Free Press (NSW : 1911 - 1937), 11 November, p. 8. , viewed 13 Oct 2022, http://nla.gov.au/nla.news-article261785688. (Old Coaching Days, 11 Nov 1935, p.8)

1935 'OUT IN THE BUSH', The Maitland Daily Mercury (NSW : 1894 - 1939), 17 September, p. 12. , viewed 03 Oct 2022, http://nla.gov.au/nla.news-article127104907. (Out in the Bush, 17 Sep 1935, p.12)

1935 'VETERAN COACH AND COACHMAN', The Argus (Melbourne, Vic. : 1848 - 1957), 8 June, p. 24. , viewed 14 Oct 2022, http://nla.gov.au/nla.news-article12246865. (Veteran Coach and Coachman, 8 Jun 1935, p.24)

1935 'WELLINGTON DISTRICT NEWS.', Wellington Times (NSW : 1899 - 1954), 29 August, p. 4. , viewed 18 Apr 2023, http://nla.gov.au/nla.news-article142898980 (Wellington District News, 29 Aug 1935, p.4)

1936 'ABOUT PEOPLE', The Southern Mail (Bowral, NSW : 1889 - 1954), 11 August, p. 3. , viewed 17 Oct 2022, http://nla.gov.au/nla.news-article118718721. (About People, 11 Aug 1936, p.3)

1936 'COBB & CO. DRIVER', Wagga Wagga Express (NSW : 1930 - 1939), 18 July, p. 4. , viewed 17 Oct 2022, http://nla.gov.au/nla.news-article207545993. (Cobb & Co. Driver, 18 Jul 1936, p.4)

1936 'COBB AND CO. DRIVER.', Daily Examiner (Grafton, NSW : 1915 - 1954), 3 July, p. 10. , viewed 13 Jul 2022, http://nla.gov.au/nla.news-article194278164. (COBB AND CO. DRIVER, 3 Jul 1936, p.10)

1936 'DAYLESFORD.', The Age (Melbourne, Vic. : 1854 - 1954), 4 April, p. 7. , viewed 14 Oct 2022, http://nla.gov.au/nla.news-article205263876. (Daylesford, 4 Apr 1936, p.7)

1936 'ECHOES OF THE PAST', Warwick Daily News (Qld. : 1919 -1954), 22 February, p. 8. , viewed 01 Oct 2022, http://nla.gov.au/nla.news-article177296432. (Echoes of the Past, 22 Feb 1936, p.8)

1936 'ECHOES OF THE PAST', Warwick Daily News (Qld. : 1919 -1954), 29 February, p. 8. , viewed 20 Oct 2022, http://nla.gov.au/nla.news-article177297043. (Echoes of the Past, 29 Feb 1936, p.8)

1936 'MAINLY ABOUT PEOPLE', Wellington Times (NSW : 1899 - 1954), 12 November, p. 12. , viewed 18 Apr 2023, http://nla.gov.au/nla.news-article142909640 (Mainly About People, 12 Nov 1936, p.12)

1936 'NEW BOOKS', The Corowa Free Press (NSW : 1875 - 1954), 17 July, p. 1. , viewed 01 Jan 2023, http://nla.gov.au/nla.news-article236860579. (New Books, 17 Jul 1936, p.1)

1936 'OBITUARY.', The Age (Melbourne, Vic. : 1854 - 1954), 5 February, p. 8. , viewed 05 Oct 2022, http://nla.gov.au/nla.news-article205238180. (Obituary, 5 Feb 1936, p.8)

1936 'OBITUARY.', The Manning River Times and Advocate for the Northern Coast Districts of New South Wales (Taree, NSW : 1898-1954), 7 March, p. 6. , viewed 05 Aug 2022, http://nla.gov.au/nla.news-article171465674. (Obituary, 7 Mar 1936, p.6)

1936 'OLD COACH DAYS', Warwick Daily News (Qld. : 1919 -1954), 22 July, p. 2. , viewed 15 Jul 2022, http://nla.gov.au/nla. news-article177381956:(Old Coach Days, 22 Jul 1936, p.2)

1936 'ONE ON THE DEAN!', The Young Chronicle (NSW : 1902 - 1910; 1913 - 1915; 1924 - 1934; 1936 - 1940), 7 August, p. 3. , viewed 29 Dec 2022, http://nla.gov.au/nla.news-article233923430. (One On The Dean!, 7 Aug 1936, p.3)

1937 ' A WOMAN'S DESPAIR AT COBB'S MAIL CHANGE, QUEENSLAND.', The Macleay Chronicle (Kempsey, NSW : 1899 - 1952), 30 June, p. 8. , viewed 24 Apr 2023, http://nla.gov.au/nla.news-article173113247 (A Woman's Despair At Cobb's Mail Change, Queensland, 30 Jun 1937, p.8)

1937 'A [?] DRIVE', The Australasian (Melbourne, Vic. : 1864 - 1946), 31 July, p. 7. , viewed 12 Oct 2022, http://nla.gov.au/nla.news- article141807670. (a [?] Drive, 31 July 1937, p.4)

1937 'ANCIENT COACH', Mudgee Guardian and North-Western Representative (NSW : 1890 - 1954), 16 September, p. 15., viewed 07 Aug 2022, http://nla.gov.au/nla.news-article162238211. (Ancient Coach, 16 Sept 1937, p.15)

1937 'COBB AND CO. DRIVER DIES', The Herald (Melbourne, Vic. : 1861 - 1954), 24 June, p. 10. , viewed 13 Jul 2022, http://nla.gov.au/nla.news-article244629833. (Cobb And Co. Driver Dies, 24 Jun 1937, p.10)

1937 'COBB AND CO.'S COACHMEN LIVE TO GRAND OLD AGE', The Herald (Melbourne, Vic. : 1861 - 1954), 20 May, p. 10. , viewed 13 Jul 2022, http://nla.gov.au/nla.news-article244632128. (Cobb and Co.'s Coachmen Live To Grand Old Age, 20 May 1937)

1937 'DUBBO MOURNS', The Dubbo Liberal and Macquarie Advocate (NSW : 1894 - 1954), 30 March, p. 1. , viewed 08 Oct 2022, http://nla.gov.au/nla.news-article131589978. (Dubbo Mourns, 30 Mar 1937, p.1)

1937 'GOLD DIGGING DAYS', Daily Advertiser (Wagga Wagga, NSW : 1911 - 1954), 2 August, p. 2. , viewed 11 Oct 2022, http://nla.gov.au/nla.news-article143598736. (Gold Digging Days, 2 Aug 1937, p.2)

1937 'GOLD-MINING DAYS', The Grenfell Record and Lachlan District Advertiser (NSW : 1876 - 1951), 21 June, p. 1. , viewed 29 Sep 2022, http://nla.gov.au/nla.news-article111752829. (Gold-Mining Days, 21 Jun 1937, p.1)

1937 'OBITUARY', Balonne Beacon (St. George, Qld. : 1909 - 1954), 30 September, p. 2. , viewed 21 Oct 2022, http://nla.gov.au/nla.news-article213762997. (Obituary, 30 Sep 1937, p.2)

1937 'OBITUARY', Goulburn Valley Stock and Property Journal (Vic. : 1916 - 1942), 26 May, p. 6, viewed 21 Oct 2022, http://nla.gov.au/nla.news-article219773888. (Obituary, 26 May 1937, p.6)

1937 'OBITUARY', Narandera Argus and Riverina Advertiser (NSW : 1893 - 1953), 14 September, p. 2. , viewed 21 Oct 2022, http://nla.gov.au/nla.news-article100799195. (Obituary, 14 Sep 1937, p.2)

1937 'Old Coaching Days.', The Age (Melbourne, Vic. : 1854 - 1954), 25 May, p. 19. , viewed 01 Jan 2023, http://nla.gov.au/nla.news-article203877795. (Old Coaching Days, 25 May 1937, p.19)

1937 'OLD COACHING DAYS.', The Age (Melbourne, Vic. : 1854 - 1954), 8 February, p. 14. , viewed 07 Aug 2022, http://nla.gov.au/nla.news-article206194870. (Old Coaching Days, 8 Feb, 1937, p.14)

1937 'OVERLAND MAIL CENTENARY', The Argus (Melbourne, Vic. : 1848 - 1957), 25 May, p. 7. , viewed 30 Apr 2023, http://nla.gov.au/nla.news-article11066749 (Overland Mail Centenary, 25 May 1937, p.7)

1937 'VETERAN MAILMAN.', The Sydney Morning Herald (NSW : 1842 - 1954), 7 April, p. 11. , viewed 29 Dec 2022, http://nla.gov.au/nla.news-article17357890. (Veteran Mailman, 7 Apr 1937, p.11)

1937 'WEE WAA AND DISTRICT NEWS', The North Western Courier (Narrabri, NSW : 1913 - 1955), 2 September, p. 2. , viewed 14 Oct 2022, http://nla.gov.au/nla.news-article133296281. (Wee Waa and District News, 2 Sep 1937, p.2)

1938 'COBB & CO. COACH AGAIN ON RUN TO BALLARAT', The Advertiser (Adelaide, SA : 1931 - 1954), 11 March, p. 10. , viewed 27 Jul 2022, http://nla.gov.au/nla.news-article74213879. (Cobb & Co. Coach Again On Run To Ballarat, 11 Mar 1938, p.10)

1938 'COBB & CO.', The North-Western Watchman (Coonabarabran, NSW : 1936 - 1949), 27 January, p. 10. , viewed 06 May 2023, http://nla.gov.au/nla.news-article263575625 (Cobb & Co., 27 Jan 1938, p.10)

1938 'COBB & CO'S. COACH.', The Narracan Shire Advocate and Yallourn Brown Coal Mine, Walhalla and Thorpdale Lines Echo (Moe, Vic. : 1923 - 1943), 22 April, p. 3. , viewed 27 Jul 2022, http://nla.gov.au/nla.news-article264534943. (Cobb & Co's. Coach, 22 Apr 1938, p.3)

1938 'COBB AND CO.', Daily Advertiser (Wagga Wagga, NSW : 1911 - 1954), 13 January, p. 8. , viewed 27 Jul 2022, http://nla. gov.au/nla.news-article143729851. (Cobb and Co., 13 Jan 1938, p.8)

1938 'FORTY YEARS AGO', Kalgoorlie Miner (WA : 1895 - 1954), 19 December, p. 4. , viewed 30 Apr 2023, http://nla.gov.au/nla.news-article87490791 (Forty Years Ago, 19 Dec 1898, p.4)

1938 'OLD COACH DRIVERS At Geelong', The Argus (Melbourne, Vic. : 1848 - 1957), 15 October, p. 8. , viewed 09 Oct 2022, http://nla.gov.au/nla.news-article12511491. (Old Coach Drivers, 15 Oct 1938, p.8)

1938 'ON THE TRACK.', Townsville Daily Bulletin (Qld. : 1907 - 1954), 31 August, p. 11. , viewed 09 Aug 2022, http://nla.gov. au/nla.news-article62166056. (On the track, 31 Aug 1938, p.11)

1938 'PERSONAL ITEMS', The Albury Banner and Wodonga Express (NSW : 1860 - 1938), 27 May, p. 5. , viewed 06 May 2023, http://nla.gov.au/nla.news-article102335108 (Personal Items, 27 May 1938, p.5)

1938 'QUEANBEYAN REMINISCENCES', Queanbeyan Age (NSW : 1927 - 1954), 20 September, p. 1. , viewed 01 Jan 2023, http://nla.gov.au/nla.news-article265335826. (Queanbeyan Reminiscences, 20 Sep 1938, p.1)

1938 'TOUR IN OLD MAIL COACH', The Argus (Melbourne, Vic. : 1848 - 1957), 11 October, p. 12. , viewed 09 Oct 2022, http://nla.gov.au/nla.news-article12505832. (Tour in Old Mail Coach, 11 Oct 1938, p.12)

1938 'VETERAN OF THE ROAD', Goulburn Valley Stock and Property Journal (Vic. : 1916 - 1942), 12 October, p. 18. , viewed 06 May 2023, http://nla.gov.au/nla.news-article219768833 (Veteran of the Road, 12 Oct 1938, p.18)

1939 'DICK CRAIG'S FIGHT.', Townsville Daily Bulletin (Qld. : 1907 - 1954), 28 April, p. 5. , viewed 06 Oct 2022, http://nla. gov.au/nla.news-article61462416. (Dick Craig's Fight, 28 Apr 1939, p.5)

1939 'OBITUARY.', Cairns Post (Qld. : 1909 - 1954), 14 January, p. 14. , viewed 02 Oct 2022, http://nla.gov.au/nla.news-article42150397. (Obituary, 14 Jan 1939, p.14)

1939 'OBITUARY', Western Star and Roma Advertiser (Qld. : 1875 - 1948), 30 December, p. 2. , viewed 21 Oct 2022, http://nla.gov.au/nla.news-article98085757. (Obituary,, 30 Dec 1939, p.2)

1939 'PIONEER DRIVER.', The Wingham Chronicle and Manning River Ob-server (NSW : 1898 - 1954), 10 February, p. 2. , viewed 13 Jul 2022, http://nla.gov.au/nla.news-article167880451. (Pioneer

Driver, 10 Feb 1939, p.2)

1939 'REMINISCENCES', Kilmore Free Press (Kilmore, Vic. : 1870 - 1954), 2 March, p. 1. , viewed 03 Oct 2022, http://nla.gov.au/nla.news-article58111351. (Reminiscences, 2 Mar 1939, p.1)

1939 'THE BULLETIN', Call Number NX 252, Created/Published Sydney, N.S.W.: John Haynes and J.F. Archibald, 1880-1984, Issue Vol. 60 No. 3095 (7 Jun 1939). https://nla.gov.au/nla.obj-578436455/view?sectionId=nla.obj-583239899&searchTerm=coach+driver&p artId=nla.obj-578459847#page/n19/mode/1up/search/

1939 THE BULLETIN, Call Number NX 252, Created/Published Sydney, N.S.W.: John Haynes and J.F. Archibald, 1880-1984, Issue Vol. 60 No. 3095 (7 Jun 1939). https://nla.gov.au/nla.obj-578436455/view?sectionId=nla.obj-583239899&searchTerm=coach+drive r&p artId=nla.obj-578459847#page/n19/mode/1up/search/coach+driver

1940 'A LONG LIFE AND A MERRY ONE', The Argus (Melbourne, Vic. : 1848 - 1957), 18 January, p. 9. , viewed 24 Apr 2023, http://nla.gov.au/nla.news-article11272199 (A Long Life and A Merry One, 18 Jan 1940, p.9)

1940 'COBB AND CO DRIVER PASSES', South Coast Bulletin (Southport, Qld. : 1929 - 1954), 18 October, p. 4. , viewed 06 May 2023, http://nla.gov.au/nla.news-article188881120 (Cobb and Co Driver Passes, 18 Oct 1940, p.4)

1940 'DRIVER FOR COBB & CO.', Border Watch (Mount Gambier, SA : 1861 - 1954), 22 August, p. 5. , viewed 07 Aug 2022, http:// nla.gov.au/nla.news-article7810133. (Driver For Cobb & Co., 22 Aug 1940, p.5)

1940 'EX-COBB AND CO. DRIVER DIES', The Daily Telegraph (Sydney, NSW : 1931 - 1954), 27 April, p. 5. , viewed 15 Sep 2022, http://nla.gov.au/nla.news-article247490161. (Ex-Cobb And Co. Driver Dies, 27 Apr 1940, p.5)

1940 'LATE MR. A. MCMILLAN WAS COBB & CO. DRIVER', The Telegraph (Brisbane, Qld. : 1872 - 1947), 12 October, p. 2. (LATE CITY CABLE NEWS), viewed 01 Oct 2022, http://nla.gov.au/nla.news-article186272304. (Late Mr. A. McMillan Was Cobb & Co. Driver, 12 Oct 1940, p.2)

1940 'LINK WITH COBB AND CO.', Barrier Miner (Broken Hill, NSW : 1888 - 1954), 2 March, p. 3. , viewed 09 Aug 2022, http://nla.gov.au/nla.news-article48342767. (Link With Cobb and Co., 2 Mar 1940, p.3)

1940 'LINK WITH THE PAST', The Age (Melbourne, Vic. : 1854 - 1954), 22 May, p. 6. , viewed 21 Jun 2022, http://nla.gov.au/ nla.news-article206765222. (Link with the past, 22 May 1940, p. 6)

1940 'LITHGOW PIONEER', Lithgow Mercury (NSW : 1898 - 1954), 26 April, p. 2. (TOWN EDITION), viewed 31 Dec 2022, http://nla.gov.au/nla.news-article220785230. (Lithgow Pioneer, 26 Apr 1940, p.2)

1940 'MR. CHARLES TAYLOR', The Dubbo Liberal and Macquarie Advocate (NSW : 1894 - 1954), 31 October, p. 3. , viewed 08 Oct 2022, http://nla.gov.au/nla.news-article132630067. (Mr. Charles Taylor, 31 Oct 1940, p.3)

1940 'OBITUARY', The Argus (Melbourne, Vic. : 1848 - 1957), 20 August, p. 2. , viewed 21 Oct 2022, http://nla.gov.au/nla.news-article11300252. (Obituary, 20 Aug 1940, p.2)

1940 'PASSING OF MR. JAMES WALDEN', Barrier Miner (Broken Hill, NSW : 1888 - 1954), 12 November, p. 2. , viewed 29 Dec 2022, http://nla.gov.au/nla.news-article48364855. (Passing of Mr. James Walden, 12 Nov 1940, p.2)

1940 MEN OF COBB & CO. / by E.J. Aisbett, Creator Aisbett, E. J, Holding Library Call Number Np 388.3 AIS, Holding Library National Library of Australia, Created/Published Melbourne : Cobb & Co's Old Coach Drivers' Association, 1940, Images 28, p.15, https://nla.gov.au/nla.obj-3106019092/view?partId=nla.obj-3106019811#page/n16/mode/1up)

1941 'RURAL REMINISCENCES', Queensland Country Life (Qld. : 1900 - 1954), 6 February, p. 4. , viewed 29 Apr 2023, http://nla.gov.au/nla.news-article97069230 (Rural Reminiscences, 6 Feb 1941, p.4)

1941 ANNUAL REPORT AND BALANCE SHEET / COBB & CO.'S OLD COACH DRIVERS' ASSOCIATION. (1941). Mont Albert, Vic: The Association. Annual report and balance sheet / Cobb & Co.›s Old Coach Drivers› Association. (slv.vic.gov.au). Record ID: 999827043607636. (Annual re-port and balance sheet / Cobb & Co.'s Old Coach Drivers' Association, 1941)

1942 'COBB AND CO. COACH DRIVER'S DEATH', Glen Innes Examiner (NSW : 1908 - 1954), 12 November, p. 7. , viewed 22 Jul 2022, http://nla.gov.au/nla.news-article182096122

1942 'DEATH OF COBB & CO. COACHMAN', Border Watch (Mount Gambier, SA : 1861 - 1954), 18 June, p. 1. , viewed 21 Oct 2022, http://nla.gov.au/nla.news-article80048407. (Death of Cobb & Co. Coachman, 18 Jun 1942, p.1)

1942 'MEMOIRS OF A STOCKMAN', Peck, Harry Huntington, printed by Stockland Press, 16-20 Queensberry Street, North Melbourne (Memoirs of a Stockman, 1942, p.16)

1943 'MEMORIES AND MUSINGS', Advocate (Melbourne, Vic. : 1868 - 1954), 29 April, p. 10. , viewed 03 Oct 2022, http://nla.gov.au/ nla.news-article172206271. (Memories and Musings, 29 Apr 1943, p.10)

1943 'PASSING OF A PIONEER COACH MAN.', Healesville Guardian (Lilydale, Vic. : 1942 - 1954), 24 April, p. 3. , viewed 23 Aug 2022, http://nla.gov.au/nla.news-article61122352. (Passing of pioneer coach man, 24 Apr 1943, p.3)

1944 'DEATH OF MR. GEORGE WELLS', Western Grazier (Wilcannia, NSW : 1896 - 1951), 27 October, p. 1. , viewed 07 Aug 2022, http://nla.gov.au/nla.news-article139554470 . (Death of Mr. George Wells, 27 Oct 1944, p.1)

1944 'DROVE FOR COBB & CO.', Glen Innes Examiner (NSW : 1908 - 1954), 3 August, p. 6. , viewed 03 Oct 2022, http://nla. gov.au/nla.news-article185424342. (Drove for Cobb & Co., 3 Aug 1944, p.6)

1944 'OBITUARY', Chronicle (Adelaide, SA : 1895 - 1954), 1 June, p. 2. , viewed 06 May 2023, http://nla.gov.au/nla.news-article92712683 (Obituary, 1 Jun 1944, p.2)

1944 'OBITUARY', Chronicle (Adelaide, SA : 1895 - 1954), 1 June, p. 2. , viewed 06 May 2023, http://nla.gov.au/nla.news-article92712683

1944 'ON THE TRACK', Townsville Daily Bulletin (Qld. : 1907 - 1954), 13 November, p. 3. , viewed 06 Oct 2022, http://nla.gov. au/nla.news-article61931781. (On the Track, 13 Nov 1944, p.3)

1945 'MR. F. WRAY', Catholic Weekly (Sydney, NSW : 1942 - 1954), 26 April, p. 17. , viewed 29 Apr 2023, http://nla.gov.au/nla.news-article146484319 (Mr. F. Wray, 26 Apr 1945, p.17)

1946 'COBB & CO. DRIVER DIES IN BRISBANE.', Townsville Daily Bulletin (Qld. : 1907 - 1954), 3 September, p. 1. , viewed 07 Aug 2022, http://nla.gov.au/nla.news-article62992089. (Cobb and Co. Driver Dies in Brisbane, 3 Sep 1946, p.1)

1946 'VETERAN COACH DRIVER DIES', The Age (Melbourne, Vic. : 1854 - 1954), 27 June, p. 3. , viewed 09 Aug 2022, http:// nla.gov.au/nla.news-article206105734. (Veteran Coach Driver Dies, 27 Jun 1946, p.3)

1947 'COBB & CO VETERAN', Truth (Brisbane, Qld. : 1900 - 1954), 9 November, p. 39. , viewed 01 Oct 2022, http://nla.gov.au/nla. news-article203234615. (Cobb & Co Veteran, 9 Nov 1947, p.39)

1947 'COBB & CO. COACHES FOR AUST. PICTURE', Maryborough Chron-icle (Qld. : 1947 - 1954), 6 June, p. 5. , viewed 12 Oct 2022, http://nla.gov.au/nla.news-article146897581. (Cobb & Co. Coaches for Aust. Picture, 6 Jun 1947, p.5)

1947 'COBB COACH-DRIVER TO COMMERCIAL PILOT', The Murrumbidgee Irrigator (Leeton, NSW : 1915 - 1954), 16 May, p. 4. , viewed 22 Jul 2022, http://nla.gov.au/nla.news-article156168311.

(Cobb Coach-Driver to Commercial Pilot, 16 May 1947, p.4)

1947 'COBB'S DRIVERS WENT OVER OLD TIMES', The Sun (Sydney, NSW : 1910 - 1954), 2 February, p. 4. (FACT and OPINION), viewed 05 Oct 2022, http://nla.gov.au/nla.news-article229997195. (Cobb's drivers went over old times, 2 Feb 1947, p.4)

1947 'DROVE COBB AND Co.'s. COACH!', Queensland Times (Ipswich, Qld. : 1909 - 1954), 11 November, p. 1. (DAILY), viewed 03 Oct 2022, http://nla.gov.au/nla.news-article118386977. (Drove Cobb and Co.'s Coach!, 11 Nov 1947, p.1)

1947 'FOLLOWING IN FATHER'S DUST', The Central Queensland Herald (Rockhampton, Qld. : 1930 - 1956), 11 December, p. 9. , viewed 29 Dec 2022, http://nla.gov.au/nla.news-article75578110. (Following in Father's Dust, 11 Dec 1947, p.9)

1947 'IN THE COBB CO. DAYS', The Charleville Times (Brisbane, Qld. : 1896 - 1954), 21 November, p. 21. , viewed 03 Oct 2022, http://nla.gov.au/nla.news-article76546721. (In the Cobb Co Days, 21 Nov 1947, p.21)

1948 '50-60 YEARS AGO', Balonne Beacon (St. George, Qld. : 1909 - 1954), 3 June, p. 3. , viewed 04 Aug 2022, http://nla.gov.au/ nla.news-article213766484. (50-60 years ago, 3 Jun 1948, p.3)

1948 'DEATH OF COBB AND CO. DRIVER', The West Wyalong Advocate (NSW : 1928 - 1954), 8 January, p. 1. , viewed 07 Aug 2022, http://nla.gov.au/nla.news-article185957017. (Death of Cobb and Co. Driver, 8 Jan 1948, p.1)

1948 'DROVE OVER HIS OLD COBB AND CO. COACH ROUTE', Lachlander and Condobolin and Western Districts Recorder (NSW : 1899 - 1952), 26 July, p. 4. , viewed 09 Aug 2022, http://nla.gov.au/nla.news-article214410680. (Drove Over His Old Cobb and Co. Coach Route, 26 Jul 1948, p.4)

1948 'FAMILY NOTICES', The Argus (Melbourne, Vic. : 1848 - 1957), 3 Au-gust, p. 2. , viewed 23 Aug 2022, http://nla.gov.au/nla.news- arti-cle22688572. (Family Notices, 3 Aug 1948, p.2)

1948 'LINK WITH COBB & CO.', The Riverine Grazier (Hay, NSW : 1873 - 1954), 30 July, p. 2. , viewed 29 Jul 2022, http://nla. gov.au/nla.news-article137226379. (Link with Cobb & Co., 30 Jul 1948, p.2)

1948 'MR GEORGE GUILD PALMER PASSES', The Riverine Herald (Echuca, Vic. : Moama, NSW : 1869 - 1954; 1998 - 2002), 12 November, p. 2. , viewed 22 Jul 2022, http://nla.gov.au/nla.news-article116546787. (Mr George Guild Palmer Passes, 12 Nov 1948, p.2)

1948 'OBITUARY', Townsville Daily Bulletin (Qld. : 1907 - 1954), 14 May, p. 2. , viewed 21 Oct 2022, http://nla.gov.au/nla.news-article63050886. (Obituary, 14 May 1948, p.2)

1949 'FOUND HIS HAPPINESS IN HILLS', The Herald (Melbourne, Vic. : 1861 - 1954), 8 November, p. 7. , viewed 23 Aug 2022, http:// nla.gov.au/nla.news-article244146055. (Found His Happiness In Hills, 8 Nov 1949, p.7)

1949 'OLD COBB DRIVER', Balonne Beacon (St. George, Qld. : 1909 - 1954), 22 September, p. 4. , viewed 27 Jul 2022, http:// nla.gov.au/nla.news-article215369106. (Old Cobb Driver, 22 Sep 1949, p.4)

1949 'VETERANS RECALL PIONEERING DAYS', The Age (Melbourne, Vic. : 1854 - 1954), 20 May, p. 2. , viewed 29 Apr 2023, http://nla.gov.au/nla.news-article206070991 (Veterans Recall Pioneering Days, 20 May 1949, p.2)

1950 'COACHING REUNION', The Herald (Melbourne, Vic. : 1861 - 1954), 28 October, p. 11. , viewed 13 Jul 2022, http://nla.gov.au/nla.news-article244347941.(Coaching Reunion, 28 Oct 1950)

1950 'JEHUS OF YESTERYEAR TO BE GUESTS', The Age (Melbourne, Vic. : 1854 - 1954), 26 April, p. 2. ("The Age" International Motor Show Supplement), viewed 17 Oct 2022, http://nla.gov.au/nla.news-article187640498. (Jehus of Yesteryear to be Guests, 26 Apr 1950, p.2)

1950 'OBITUARY', Townsville Daily Bulletin (Qld. : 1907 - 1954), 24 May, p. 2. , viewed 21 Oct 2022, http://nla.gov.au/nla.news-article63461998. (Obituary, 24 May 1950, p.2)

1950 'REMINISCENCES OF COACHING DAYS', Morning Bulletin (Rockhampton, Qld. : 1878 - 1954), 23 March, p. 9. , viewed 28 Jul 2022, http://nla.gov.au/nla.news-article56937460. Coaching Days, 23 Mar 1950, p.9)

1950 'WIFE OF COBB & CO. DRIVER', The Forbes Advocate (NSW : 1911 - 1954), 8 September, p. 9. , viewed 03 Oct 2022, http://nla.gov.au/nla.news-article219098248. (Wife of Cobb & Co. Driv-er, 8 Sep 1950, p.9)

1951 'COBB AND CO. COACH IN SHOW PAGEANT.', Daily Examiner (Grafton, NSW : 1915 - 1954), 10 April, p. 2. , viewed 31 Dec 2022, http://nla.gov.au/nla.news-article195308646. (Cobb and Co. Coach in Show Pageant, 10 Apr 1951, p.2)

1951 'COBB AND CO. DAYS', The Charleville Times (Brisbane, Qld. : 1896 - 1954), 26 July, p. 10. , viewed 03 Oct 2022, http:// nla.gov.au/nla.news-article79312787. (Cobb and Co. Days, 26 Jul 1951, p.10)

1951 'IN THE DAYS OF COBB & CO.', Narromine News and Trangie Advocate (NSW : 1898 - 1955), 19 January, p. 2. , viewed 09 Aug 2022, http://nla.gov.au/nla.news-article100191539. (In the Days of Cobb & Co., 19 Jan 1951, p.2)

1951 'LATE MR. WOOLS-COBB WAS COBB & CO. COACH DRIVER', The Dandenong Journal (Vic. : 1927 - 1954), 23 May, p. 1. , viewed 27 Jul 2022, http://nla.gov.au/nla.news-article222352453. (Late Mr. Wools-Cobb Was Cobb & Co. Coach Driver, 23 May 1951, p.1)

1951 'OBITUARY.', Victor Harbour Times (SA : 1932 - 1986), 10 August, p. 3. , viewed 21 Oct 2022, http://nla.gov.au/nla.news-article168552800. (Obituary, 10 Aug 1951, p.3)

1951 'OBITUARY', Cloncurry Advocate (Qld. : 1931 - 1953), 19 October, p. 1. , viewed 21 Oct 2022, http://nla.gov.au/nla.news-article170140942. (Obituary, 19 Oct 1951, p.1)

1951 'OBITUARY', The Evening Advocate (Innisfail, Qld. : 1941 - 1954), 5 September, p. 6. , viewed 21 Oct 2022, http://nla.gov.au/nla.news-article212299012. (Obituary, 5 Sep 1951, p.6)

1951 'OBITUARY', The Northern Miner (Charters Towers, Qld. : 1874 - 1954), 11 August, p. 3. , viewed 21 Oct 2022, http://nla.gov.au/nla.news-article81601300. (Obituary, 11 Aug 1951, p.3)

1951 'OBITUARY', Townsville Daily Bulletin (Qld. : 1907 - 1954), 30 November, p. 3. , viewed 21 Oct 2022, http://nla.gov.au/nla.

1951 'SHE DROVE FOR COBB AND CO.', Weekly Times (Melbourne, Vic. : 1869 - 1954), 22 August, p. 32. , viewed 05 Oct 2022, http:// nla.gov.au/nla.news-article224486334. (She drove for Cobb and Co, 22 Aug 1951, p.32)

1952 'COBB DRIVER DIES', The Express, Melton (Vic. 1943 - 1954), 18 October, p. 2. , viewed 27 Jul 2022, http://nla.gov.au/nla.news-article254844377. (Cobb Driver Dies, 18 Oct 1952, p.2)

1952 'OLD COACH-DRIVERS NEVER DIE', The World's News (Sydney, NSW : 1901 - 1955), 12 July, p. 7. , viewed 31 Oct 2022, http://nla.gov.au/nla.news-article139913795

1953 '£5 BY COBB & CO. TO BALLAARAt', The Argus (Melbourne, Vic. : 1848 - 1957), 16 April, p. 30. , viewed 13 Apr 2023, http://nla.gov.au/nla.news-article23239006 (£5 by Cobb & Co. to Ballaarat, 16 April 1853, p. 30)

1953 'COACH BROUGHT BACK MEMORIES', Warwick Daily News (Qld. : 1919 -1954), 31 October, p. 2. , viewed 04 Oct 2022, http:// nla.gov.au/nla.news-article191100763. (Coach Brought Back Memories, 31 Oct 1953, p.2)

1953 'COACH RUNS IN EARLY DAYS', Kalgoorlie Miner (WA : 1895 - 1954), 17 June, p. 8. , viewed 09 Oct 2022, http://nla.gov.au/nla. news-article256922770. (Coach Runs in Early Days 17 Jun 1953, p.8)

1953 'COBB AND CO. DRIVER DIES', The Daily News (Perth, WA : 1882 - 1955), 2 May, p. 2. (SPORTS), viewed 09 Aug 2022, http://nla.gov.au/nla.news-article266134474. (Cobb and Co. Driver Dies, 2 May 1953, p.2)

1953 'DEATH OF A COBB DRIVER', Brisbane Telegraph (Qld. : 1948 - 1954), 5 February, p. 5. (SECOND EDITION), viewed 03 Oct 2022, http://nla.gov.au/nla.news-article217190223. (Death of a Cobb Driver, 5 Feb 1953, p.5)

1953 'DEATH OF MR. S. C. COLEMAN', Western Herald (Bourke, NSW : 1887 - 1970), 16 January, p. 6. , viewed 25 Apr 2023, http://nla.gov.au/nla.news-article103924864 (Death of Mr. S.C. Cole-man, 16 Jan 1953, p.6)

1953 'DROVE COACHES FOR COBB & CO.', Examiner (Launceston, Tas. : 1900 - 1954), 3 March, p. 7. , viewed 01 Oct 2022, http://nla.gov.au/nla.news-article61079564. (Drove Coaches for Cobb & Co., 3 Mar 1953, p.7)

1953 'DROVE FOR COBB & CO.', Sunday Times (Perth, WA : 1902 - 1954), 17 May, p. 27. , viewed 01 Nov 2022, http://nla.gov.au/nla.news-article59553881. (Drove for Cobb & Co, 17 May 1953, p.27)

1953 'LONGREACH-WINTON FOR COBB & CO.', Queensland Country Life (Qld. : 1900 - 1954), 11 June, p. 14. , viewed 03 Oct 2022, http://nla.gov.au/nla.news-article97021083. (Longreach-Winton for Cobb and Co., 11 Jun 1953, p.14)

1953 'WAS A COBB AND CO. COACH DRIVER', Narandera Argus and Riverina Advertiser (NSW : 1893 - 1953), 28 September, p. 2. , viewed 22 Jul 2022, http://nla.gov.au/nla.news-article101629694. (Was a Cobb and Co. Coach Driver, 28 Sep 1953, p.2)

1953 "WHEN COBB AND CO. CAME TO CUNNAMULLA" Queensland Country Life (Qld. : 1900 - 1954) 10 September 1953: 15. Web. 14 Oct 2022 <http://nla.gov.au/nla.news-article100664189>. (When Cobb and Co. Came To Cunnamulla, 10 Sep 1953, p.15)

1954 'A COBB & CO. DRIVER SPEAKS OF MUNGINDI.', North West Champion (Moree, NSW : 1915 - 1954), 20 April, p. 7, viewed 01 Oct 2022, http://nla.gov.au/nla.news-article179270863. ('A Cobb & Co. Driver Speaks Of Mungindi, 20 Apr 1954, p.7)

1954 'GOLD, MEN AND HORSES!', The Age (Melbourne, Vic. : 1854 - 1954), 16 January, p. 14. , viewed 16 Oct 2022, http:// nla.gov.au/nla.news-article206084410. (Gold, Men and Horses, 16 Jan 1954, p.14)

1954 'LINK WITH COBB & CO.', The Age (Melbourne, Vic. : 1854 - 1954), 15 July, p. 7. , viewed 08 Oct 2022, http://nla.gov.au/nla.news-article205695292. (Link With Cobb & Co., 15 Jul 1954, p.7)

1954 'OBITUARY.', The Gloucester Advocate (NSW : 1905 - 1954), 21 September, p. 2. , viewed 02 Nov 2022, http://nla.gov.au/nla.news-article160381158. (Obituary, 21 Sep 1954, p.2)

1955 'BEAUTIFUL EFFECTS IN FLOATS', The Central Queensland Herald (Rockhampton, Qld. : 1930 - 1956), 8 September, p. 7. , viewed 01 Nov 2022, http://nla.gov.au/nla.news-article79254064. (Beautiful effects in floats, 8 Sep 1955, p.7)

1955 'COBB & CO. IN QUEENSLAND', Balonne Beacon (St. George, Qld. : 1909 - 1954), 7 July, p. 4. , viewed 01 Oct 2022, http://nla.gov.au/nla.news-article215346078. (Cobb & Co. in Queens-land, 7 Jul 1955, p.4)

1955 'OBITUARY', Balonne Beacon (St. George, Qld. : 1909 - 1954), 10 November, p. 2. , viewed 03 Oct 2022, http://nla.gov.au/nla.news-article215352467. ('Obituary', 10 Nov 1955, p.2)

1966 'WALKABOUT', Call Number Nq 919.4 WAL, Created/Published Melbourne : Australian National Travel Association, 1934-1978, Issue Vol. 32 No. 9 (1 September 1966), p.32

1966 COBB'S DRIVERS, Walkabout, Call Number Nq 919.4 WAL, Created/Published Melbourne : Australian National Travel Association, 1934-1978, Issue Vol. 32 No. 12 (1 December 1966) p.5. (Cobb's Drivers, 1 Dec 1966, p.5)

1971 'COMMUNICATIONS ACROSS THE GENERATIONS : AN AUSTRALIAN POST OFFICE HISTORY OF QUEENSLAND.', Rea, Malcolm. M. (Read at a meeting of the Society on 22 July 1971). Journal of the Royal Historical Society of Queensland 9 (2) 168-226 [online] pp.168–226., viewed 08 Feb 2021, Available at: https://espace.library.uq.edu.au. The University of Queensland. (Communications Across the Generations, 1971)

2022 INDEPENDENT AUSTRALIA, 'All or nothing', viewed 12 may 2023, https://independentaustralia.net/politics/politics-display/all-or-nothing-including-a-first-nations-voice-to-parliament,16618#:~:text=Quoting%20former%20Prime%20Minister%20Tony,for%20change%20in%20the%20Constitution. (Independent Australia, 2 Aug 2022, p.1)

Index

A

'Aaron Sherritt shot dead' 68
Abbot 16
Accidents 6, 20, 27, 28, 29, 30, 34, 35, 37, 38, 44, 45, 53, 59, 61, 62, 66, 67, 72, 73, 76, 81, 90, 92, 94, 105, 106, 107, 112, 113, 139, 144, 147, 148, 149, 159, 161, 164, 165, 201
Adams 9, 16, 26, 41, 42, 59, 63, 67, 73, 126, 135, 182
Adams and Co. 9, 182
Aisbett 16, 18, 19, 20, 21, 24, 27, 34, 36, 40, 42, 48, 49, 53, 60, 61, 63, 66, 72, 75, 82, 84, 85, 88, 92, 93, 95, 102, 103, 105, 107, 108, 112, 115, 122, 123, 124, 129, 134, 136, 138, 145, 148, 149, 154, 159, 160, 163, 198
Aitken 16, 60, 159
Alder 16, 17, 18, 22, 34, 43, 59, 62, 68, 82, 92, 93, 103, 124, 126, 146
Alexander 18, 29, 58, 61, 66, 67, 72, 81, 82, 90, 102, 105, 106, 122, 133, 151, 158, 159, 183, 192, 196, 197, 202, 203
Alford 18
Allan 18, 20, 29, 49, 51, 59, 63, 65, 73, 76, 90, 92, 106, 107, 108, 112, 124, 137, 146, 149, 154, 158
American Telegraph Line of Coaches 9
Amies 18, 21, 60, 80, 85, 90, 114, 165
Anderson 18, 19, 43, 49, 52, 60, 88, 89, 100, 102, 108, 114, 123, 133, 138, 150, 152, 160, 164
Andrews 19, 22
Athorn 19, 76
Athorne 19, 165
Atkins 19, 24, 52, 95, 133, 148, 158, 165
Atkinson 16, 19, 20, 49, 60, 66, 115, 124, 146
Australian cricketer 85
Avery 20, 74

B

Babies 43, 95, 160, 163
Bail up & stuck up! 27, 40, 44, 48, 64, 68, 74, 105, 109, 122, 124, 134, 136, 150, 160, 162
Bain 20, 64
Balsall 20, 134
Bamberger 20
Bannear 20, 67
Barnes 18, 20, 21, 26, 35, 40, 41, 59, 127, 136, 140, 165, 182, 184
Barnett 21
Barrie 21, 109
Barrir 21, 95
Barry 21, 59, 108, 130, 136, 150
Bates 21, 22, 26, 59, 65, 73, 74, 89, 101, 103, 115, 122, 123, 135, 163
Bell 17, 22, 41
Bennett 22, 34, 67, 124, 143
Bernie 22, 23, 126
Birrell 23
Bissel 23
Bissell 23, 58, 162
Bissu 23, 95
Black Forest 58, 75, 127, 138, 153
Blackwell 24
Blake 24, 29, 58, 88, 147, 149, 183, 184
Bloomfield 24
Blue 23, 24, 67, 81, 127, 140, 145, 153, 159, 162, 201
Bolton 6, 24, 43, 126, 132, 177, 178
Bourke 24, 30, 39, 43, 44, 64, 65, 66, 83, 84, 93, 94, 103, 115, 116, 118, 119, 130, 134, 135, 137, 145, 158, 160, 195
Bourne 24
Bowes 24, 153
Bradley 24, 25, 74, 75, 106, 114, 122, 130, 153, 184
Brady 25, 59, 84, 126
Brayshaw 26, 93
Breen 16, 21, 22, 26, 42, 49, 59, 61, 74, 90, 103, 115, 136, 152, 163
Brenyer 26, 93
'Bridget Coleman's murder' 74
Bristow 26, 30
Britten 27
Brown 27, 30, 34, 116, 125, 139, 140, 154, 165, 182, 193
Bruce 27, 80, 93, 122, 131, 134, 163, 167
Brumfield 27, 28, 43
Brummy 28, 66, 123, 132, 133, 151
Brush of straw 67
Buchanan 28
Buckland 28
Bugle/mailhorn 41, 42, 71, 93, 95, 106, 108, 133, 136, 138, 167
Buller 28, 126, 144
Bullock 29, 107
Burgess 29, 124, 133, 140
Burke 29, 102, 134, 159
Burnside 18, 29, 149
Burrowes 29
Burrows 21, 29, 137, 145
Burstall 29, 43
Bushrangers 10, 34, 44, 124
'Bushranger tricked' 16
Butler 29, 108
Byrne 27, 29, 30, 31, 68, 73, 85, 118, 149, 159, 164
Byrnes 29, 31

C

Cabbage Tree Ned 26, 49, 135
Cairns 34, 125, 134, 196, 197, 200, 201
Camels 116, 159
Cameron 34, 133
Cann 34
Carbis 34, 67, 68, 72
Carlisle 17, 34
Carr 34, 134, 167
Carter 34, 36, 40, 42, 67, 74, 93, 95, 127, 151, 152, 159, 192
Cartrini 34, 35
Cawker 35, 96
Chamberlain 35, 85
Chatfield 18, 19, 35, 65, 76, 100, 105, 112, 125, 160
Chick 36, 52, 108
Chinese Diggers 17, 48, 68, 81, 132, 138
Chisholm 36
Clapp 36, 106, 130, 153, 184
Clark 36, 37, 43, 63, 89, 123, 128, 165
'Classes of passengers' 95
Clifford 37, 137
Clint 37
Clowry 37
Cobb+Co Museum, Toowoomba 177
Cobb, Freeman 9, 10, 12, 29, 37, 41, 42, 58, 74, 126, 135, 141, 148, 149, 168, 182, 183, 187
Cobb, Hiram 38
Cobb, Winslow 9, 12, 135, 182
'Cockeydejong Swamps - phantom lights' 91
Cole 38, 39, 79, 102
Coleman 39, 40, 74
Colke 40
Colman 40, 67
Comerford 40
Conroy 16, 20, 21, 22, 26, 29, 34, 40, 42, 49, 52, 60, 61, 62, 63, 66, 74, 80, 84, 88, 90, 93, 101, 102, 103, 107, 109, 115, 135, 137, 140, 141, 146, 152
Cook 17, 42, 125
Cooke 42, 67
Coomber 42
Coombes 42
Cooper 6, 42, 59, 60, 64, 102, 165
Corbett 24, 28, 29, 37, 42, 43, 52, 61, 64, 66, 94, 104, 105, 119, 122, 128, 138, 148, 163
Corduroy roads 25, 79, 127, 145, 149, 153
Cork 43, 165
Cornelius 17, 43
Cousens 19, 43
Cousins 43, 76
Cox 43, 134
Coyle 43, 44, 95, 168, 183
Coyne 44, 165
Cozens 44, 68
'Cranley Shooting' 74
Crewes 44, 67
Crimmins 44
Crogan 44, 45
Crossen 45
Crow 45, 78
Cummings 45, 93
Cunningham 45, 124
Currie 45, 77, 161
Cuthbertson 45

D

Dailey 48, 84
Dallas 48, 130
Dallis 48
Daly 49, 52, 91, 134
Danes 18, 49

Davidson 19, 49, 59, 108, 133, 154, 160
Davis 49, 129, 149
De Graves 49, 130
Devine 20, 26, 40, 49, 59, 66, 68, 106, 135, 153, 163, 168
Dickson 27, 50
Dilworth 50
Discom 50, 67
Discombe 50
Doherty 27, 50, 51
Doil 51
'Dolly Varden shield' 10
Donnelly 51
Donohue 19, 52, 83, 158, 165
Donovan 43, 52, 119, 158
Doran 52
Dougharty 52
Douglas 44, 49, 52, 53, 93, 125, 134, 159, 160, 161, 167
Douglass 52
Dowdle 53
Dowling 53
Doyle 29, 53, 60, 95, 137
Drew 53, 67
Drood 53, 93
Droughts 9, 18, 25, 35, 37, 51, 59, 77, 82, 105, 112, 116, 132, 133, 144, 167
Dryer 53, 67
Duffell 53, 76, 168
Duncan 53, 79, 133
Dunleavy 53
Dunn 31, 48, 53, 132
Dunstall 53
Durack 53, 54, 73
Durieu 54
DuRieu 54, 169

E

Eales 58
Eastley 58
Eddie 16, 21, 22, 23, 25, 26, 49, 52, 58, 59, 61, 65, 72, 73, 74, 91, 95, 103, 108, 114, 115, 123, 124, 132, 133, 134, 140, 141, 150, 162, 163
Edgcombe 59
Edwards 18, 20, 59, 60, 66, 113, 135
Egan 53, 60, 78, 165
Ellis 16, 60
Elmes 60, 133
Elms 18, 60, 165
Empson 60

Enright 19, 60
'Eugowra Escort Robbery' 178
Eureka Stockade 148, 163
Evans 17, 60, 146
Everett 42, 60
Eyre 60, 61

F

Fagan 26, 41, 58, 61, 63, 73, 135, 162, 178
Farrar 61, 140
Farrell 61
Fawcett 61, 81
Fegan 61
Ferguson 61, 133
Fergusson 61
'Ferrying passengers' 137
Field 43, 52, 61
Fillery 61
Finemore 61
Fire 5, 9, 18, 19, 20, 25, 35, 40, 59, 60, 64, 77, 81, 83, 84, 87, 93, 100, 106, 109, 112, 119, 124, 125, 130, 134, 139, 145, 148, 162
Fires 9, 40
First Nations Peoples 40, 41, 49, 54, 74, 84, 102, 125
Fitzpatrick 61, 80
Flannery 61
Floods 5, 6, 9, 18, 19, 20, 25, 28, 31, 35, 40, 42, 59, 60, 64, 77, 81, 83, 84, 87, 93, 100, 106, 109, 112, 117, 119, 124, 125, 129, 130, 134, 139, 145, 147, 148, 161, 162
Fogarty 61, 62, 130, 147
Forbes 17, 20, 24, 26, 31, 41, 42, 43, 52, 53, 62, 63, 64, 72, 129, 136, 141, 147, 164, 165, 195, 203
Forcett 61, 106
Foreman 62, 95
Forsyth 62
Fossett 62, 89
Foster 27, 62, 134, 184
Fowler 17, 62, 90, 130
Fox 37, 62, 63, 66, 123, 138, 161
Fraser 63, 89, 101
Frayer 63
Free 63, 101, 130, 191, 193, 195, 199, 200, 201
Freerer 18, 63
French 63, 148, 154, 165

Frisco 63
Frost 43, 63, 64, 94, 129, 148

G

Gales 20, 64, 88, 91, 144, 163
Gallagher 19, 35, 59, 65, 133, 158
'Game of Horse Loo' 52
Gardener 65
Gardiner 26, 44, 58, 61, 64, 65, 74, 75, 83, 109, 136, 162
Gate-opener job 81
Geaghan 65, 66, 123
Getson 65
Ghosts 89, 91, 118
Gilbert 26, 48, 65, 134, 136
Giles 18, 65, 102
Gill 21, 65
Gillespie 65, 66
Gilliam 66, 84
Gilligan 43, 64, 66
Girdham 66
Girdlestone 66, 67
Glasson 20, 66
Goode 18, 66
Goodfellow 66
Gordon 34, 59, 66, 67, 105, 123, 136, 154, 198
Graham 20, 66
Grant 66, 67, 75
Green 4, 67, 122, 124, 128, 134, 168, 184
Greer 67
Griffen 16, 20, 24, 34, 40, 42, 44, 50, 53, 66, 67, 72, 90, 93, 104, 112, 119, 129, 138, 145, 148, 150, 151, 152, 161

H

Haig 72, 163
Haines 61, 72, 130, 158
Halcroft 72
Hall 18, 26, 34, 44, 48, 49, 61, 63, 64, 65, 67, 72, 75, 83, 92, 93, 116, 127, 136, 140, 141, 154, 162, 164, 169, 183, 184
Halliday 72, 94
Hamilton 30, 35, 37, 40, 58, 60, 68, 72, 73, 77, 94, 96, 107, 130, 134, 146, 152, 154, 162, 201
Hampson 16, 26, 41, 59, 73, 74, 135
Hampton 65, 74, 75, 137
'Handling the ribbons' 10, 41, 95, 100, 104, 147
Hanning 75

Harding 75
Harman 75, 159
Harmon 18, 76
Harris 37, 48, 68, 75, 83, 92, 125
Hart 48, 68, 75, 76, 133, 139
Hauman 18, 76
Hayden 76
'Headless rider' 89
Heap 76
Heathwood 76
Heelan 76
Hemers 76
Herchberg 19, 43, 53, 76, 103, 124, 133, 150
Hertsberg 19, 43, 53, 76, 103, 124, 133, 150
Hertzberg 35, 76, 133
Hewson 76, 165
Hickson 60, 76, 77, 78, 94, 105, 133, 144, 158, 162, 168
Highfields 45, 78
Hildebrand 78
Hill 4, 9, 24, 27, 29, 30, 42, 44, 49, 50, 62, 65, 67, 73, 80, 85, 88, 89, 90, 91, 95, 101, 103, 115, 118, 122, 124, 126, 133, 134, 137, 149, 151, 154, 161, 165, 168, 169, 183, 190, 192, 195, 197, 201
Hiller 80, 93
Hillman 80
Hirschberg 80
Hitzman 80, 165
Hobbs 80, 130
Hodgson 80, 104
Hogan 80, 123, 130
Holbery 80
Holden 18, 80
Hole 61, 80, 81, 90, 93, 122, 151
Holland 20, 82, 154
Holliday 82, 182
Hollister 82
Holloway 82
Holman 17, 68, 82, 129
Hood 52, 82, 83, 94, 95, 119, 141, 165
Hopkins 84, 107
Hotels 43, 66, 77, 81, 82, 83, 95, 145
Houligan 84
Houston 84
Hoyle 30, 85
Hoyt 85, 153
Hunter 18, 63, 85, 95, 124, 136, 140, 165, 196, 203

Hussey 85, 130
Hutchinson 85, 134

I

Ike 35, 67, 68, 72, 85, 106, 129, 132, 163

J

Jackson 40, 75, 88, 93, 106, 119, 140, 153
Jarvis 64, 88, 122
'Jehu and his Team' 57
Jenkins 88, 100, 105
Jennings 88
Jensen 19, 88, 133, 134
Jinkins 88, 95
Jinks 88, 89, 168
Johnson 1, 4, 22, 31, 89, 152
Jones 37, 54, 62, 66, 72, 88, 89, 90, 101, 104, 109, 119, 128, 129
Jonson 89
Jordan 89

K

Kangaroo 73, 115
Kavenagh 89
Keast 68, 81, 89, 90, 151
Keightly 90
Kellier 90
Kelly 16, 18, 28, 68, 80, 90, 100, 106, 124, 134, 160, 162
Kelton 18, 90
Kennedy 90, 94, 130, 159
'Kentucky Waters' 74
Keough 67, 90
Kidd 18, 90, 135, 165
Kiddman 49, 90, 91, 103, 154
Kidman 49, 58, 90, 91, 103, 115, 116, 117, 118, 119, 154
Kilpatrick 64, 91
King 17, 24, 35, 63, 66, 76, 91, 92, 94, 96, 104, 115, 116, 118, 123, 127, 129, 133, 145, 162, 178
Kingsland 91, 92
Kirk 91, 92, 119

L

Lairy 92, 96
Laity 17, 18, 60, 92
Lakewood 92, 93
Lambell 92
Lambert 9, 73, 74, 92, 149
Land 42, 45, 92, 101, 106, 136, 191, 202
Langdon 92, 165
Langley 92
Latewood 64, 92, 93
Lawrence 67, 93, 101, 125
Leary 26, 43, 45, 53, 80, 92, 93, 103, 122
Lee 81, 82, 93, 103, 119, 135
Leftwitch 93
Lennon 93, 122
Leonard 82, 93, 134
Le Sueur 93
'Letter wager' 105
Levi 40, 68, 74, 75, 88, 93, 105, 115, 132, 163
Leviathan coach 40, 41, 80, 84, 106, 135, 136, 163
Leviston 93, 148
Lewis 23, 78, 89, 94, 95, 133, 138, 165
Little 10, 24, 35, 43, 58, 64, 94, 104, 106, 134, 154
Lizards 36, 65
Lloyd 23, 94
Long 5, 15, 18, 34, 67, 74, 94, 127, 137, 148, 165
Loveday 94
Lovelock 94
Lowe 21, 23, 53, 82, 88, 90, 91, 94, 95, 102, 104, 119, 138, 154, 158, 169
Lumley 19, 59, 93, 95, 108, 129, 133, 139, 168
Lunley 92, 96
Luscott 96
Lyall 35, 96

M

Macadamised roads 82
MacDonald 100
Macgilcuddy 19, 100
Mack 88, 100, 122
Mackenzie 100, 104
Macnamara 100
Macrac 35, 100, 105
Madden 22, 100, 101
Maddicks 101
Madrill 101
Maher 101
Mallon 101
Malone 21, 42, 89, 101, 132
Maloney 42, 95, 101, 102
Mannin 102
Manning 19, 29, 41, 102, 119, 133, 134, 137, 160, 167, 195, 200, 201, 203
Markus 102
Markwell 102, 105, 134, 162
Martin 35, 79, 90, 95, 102, 103, 114, 126, 144, 153, 160, 165
Mason 27, 103, 136
Matheson 103, 133
Mathieson 103
Matthews 17, 91, 103
May 9, 12, 16, 17, 19, 20, 21, 24, 27, 29, 34, 37, 38, 39, 45, 48, 49, 53, 54, 60, 61, 68, 74, 76, 77, 78, 80, 82, 89, 91, 94, 96, 101, 103, 104, 116, 117, 118, 129, 130, 132, 137, 140, 146, 148, 150, 151, 153, 158, 159, 160, 161, 164, 165, 167, 183, 187, 189, 190, 191, 192, 193, 194, 195, 196, 197, 198, 199, 200, 201, 202, 203
Mayne 26, 59, 63, 103, 136, 150
McAnally 103
McCleary 103
McCormack 59, 76, 103, 122
McCrae 103, 134
McCullough 41, 42, 103
McDonald 80, 93, 103, 154
McFarland 67, 104
McFarlane 67, 72, 104
McGlinchy 104
McGroda 95, 104
McGroder 43, 104
McIntyre 72, 104
McKenzie 16, 91, 104, 115
McLean 105
McMahon 105, 146
McMillan 78, 102, 105, 133, 158, 159
McMullen 77, 105, 134
McNickle 105
McPhee 60, 105
McPherson 24, 105, 153, 162
McRae 105, 165
McTiernan 105
Meagher 105
Medical condition - Dropsy 61, 150
Merritt 43, 105, 150
Mesbitt 24, 36, 61, 72, 88, 106
Mickle 18, 106, 192
Miles 106, 107, 132, 133, 139, 169
Millard 18, 107
Miller 29, 33, 36, 42, 49, 79, 107, 108, 116, 126, 152
Milne 18, 108, 116
Mitchell 19, 29, 43, 49, 59, 60, 71, 93, 95, 103, 108, 115, 122, 125, 132, 133, 137, 160, 166, 167
Montgomery 108
Moore 31, 67, 73, 101, 109, 122, 134, 146, 150
Moorhouse 109, 146
Moran 21, 61, 109, 123, 127, 162, 163
Morecroft 109
Morgan 62, 68, 100, 101, 109, 112, 125, 147, 160, 162
Morris 27, 67, 112, 137
Mosch 35, 112
Mother 160
Mowton 9, 182, 185
Moyse 67, 112
Mugridge 112
Mulholland 18, 112
Murphy 18, 19, 24, 95, 112, 113, 114, 165
Murray 9, 16, 24, 27, 31, 34, 41, 58, 73, 74, 76, 81, 87, 114, 116, 118, 126, 127, 128, 146, 147, 148, 149, 152, 164, 168, 182, 198

N

Nairn 22, 59, 114, 150
Nankervis 115
Nash 21, 115
Nathan 16, 21, 22, 23, 25, 26, 42, 49, 52, 58, 59, 61, 65, 73, 74, 91, 95, 103, 108, 115, 123, 124, 133, 134, 140, 141, 150, 162
Naylor 102, 115, 133
Nesbitt 115, 130
Netterfield 40, 93, 115
Newman 115, 146
Nicholas 49, 52, 53, 75, 76, 80, 89, 91, 108, 115, 116, 117, 118, 119, 151
Nicholls 58, 91, 115
Nicholson 43, 119, 138, 150, 165
Nolan 83, 119, 122, 165
Norris 27, 119
Northway 67, 119
Nowel 94, 119

O

Oakley 18, 122
Obrien 122
O'Brien 35, 102, 107, 122, 165
O'Connor 44, 122
O'Dea 122
O'Dell 22, 122
O'Donnell 64, 122, 132, 133, 134
Oldfield 27, 122, 137
O'Leary 43, 122
O'Malley 43, 122
Orbel 122, 162
Orbell 123
O'Sullivan 123
Ottey 123, 130

P

Pack 123, 149
Page 17, 21, 123, 154, 202
Paine 23, 28, 63, 65, 66, 123
Palmer 22, 25, 37, 59, 76, 108, 123, 124, 125, 133, 162, 165, 169
Parker 17, 118, 124, 131, 135
Parrington 124
Partington 18, 20, 66, 124
Paterson 105, 128
Patrick 30, 31, 90, 114, 123, 124, 128, 129, 153
Patterson 36, 90, 125, 165
Pay 77
Payne 17, 23, 83, 107, 126, 138, 139
Pearse 126
Peck 9, 24, 29, 34, 58, 64, 74, 75, 126, 127, 140, 149, 164, 168, 182, 183, 184, 198
Peckman 127
Pedrara 127
Peters 128
Peterson 128
Petrasson 128
Phillips 123, 124, 128
Pickering 128
Piesley 43, 128
Pillett 128
Pittman 36, 37, 128
Ploughs 89, 128, 151
Plows 128, 145
Plush 128, 129
Pollard 129
Post Office 20, 79, 148
Potter 101, 129, 158
Powell 118, 129, 162
Power 44, 113, 114, 129, 161, 183
Prater 67, 129
Preston 21, 25, 48, 49, 61, 62, 63, 66, 68, 72, 80, 82, 85, 90, 115, 123, 129, 130, 146, 154, 160
Pritchard 130
Purcell 59, 130, 136
Pywell 131

R

Rabbits 158
Reade 27, 131
Reardon 132, 133
'Red as a lobster' 78
Redfern 44, 85, 132, 140
Reynolds 132
Rich 68, 74, 132, 163
Richard 72, 105, 122, 123, 132, 137, 161, 169
Richards 19, 29, 59, 61, 76, 88, 94, 103, 105, 115, 122, 124, 125, 132, 133, 134, 150, 151
Richardson 19, 20, 24, 27, 34, 43, 60, 62, 65, 67, 76, 78, 85, 88, 93, 95, 102, 103, 105, 107, 122, 132, 133, 134, 139, 140, 150, 151, 153, 158, 160, 169
Ridley 134
Rivers 74, 118, 134
Robards 134
Robertson 28, 30, 35, 42, 59, 66, 75, 84, 89, 108, 115, 116, 134, 135, 140, 141, 149, 182, 183, 184, 197
Robinson 16, 21, 22, 26, 42, 49, 61, 74, 80, 83, 85, 90, 93, 103, 107, 131, 135, 136, 141, 152
Robson 136
Rochester 75, 108, 112, 122, 136, 137, 158
Rodgers 18, 137
Roe 137
Rogers 60, 67, 94, 138, 167
Ross 43, 59, 82, 83, 119, 138, 141, 151, 153
Rotten 138, 162
Rowland 138, 139
Rowley 139, 158
Rumley 139
Rummery 133, 139, 140
Russert 59, 140
Rutherford 9, 26, 27, 38, 40, 41, 43, 44, 58, 63, 73, 75, 94, 116, 127, 132, 134, 135, 136, 140, 141, 158, 162, 165, 169, 182, 183, 184
Ryan 31, 83, 141

S

Sampson 18, 67, 68, 72, 75, 144, 153, 163
Sawyer 28, 144
Saying - 'Hell for leather' 122
Saying - 'Let her go for Buck's the rider' 84
Saying - 'Three, sheets in the wind' 31
Saying - 'To rattle my bones over the stones' 144
Scobie 144, 153
Scott 20, 35, 64, 125, 144, 165
Search 19, 93, 144
Shaw 20, 27, 105, 144
Sheppard 144
Sheraton 76, 77, 78, 144, 169
Simmons 67, 128, 144, 145
Sinclair 145, 165
'Singer Sewing Machines' 63
'Singing in the coaches' 81
Skillern 145
Slatyer 145
Slocum 145, 146
Small 146
Smiles 146
Smiley 17, 18, 20, 35, 61, 66, 68, 105, 106, 109, 114, 129, 130, 146, 163, 164, 165
Smith 27, 31, 34, 39, 67, 83, 104, 114, 127, 146, 147, 165, 195, 196, 201
Smythman 147
Snakes 25, 28, 35, 36, 51, 76, 139
Snell 24, 147, 148
Snuffkins 148
Stackpole 148
Stephen 18, 72, 82, 93, 148, 158
Stephens 148
Stevenson 19, 106, 148, 158
Sting 148
Stirling 67, 148
Stokes 148, 154
Stratton 148
Strickland 43, 64, 148
'Stuck in mud' 83
Suicide 128, 160
Sullivan 18, 60, 123, 148
Summers 89, 149, 153
Sutcliffe 149, 165
Swanton 9, 24, 38, 74, 92, 123, 126, 127, 149, 182, 183, 184
Sweeney 149

T

Taverner 30, 149
Taylor 93, 101, 125, 136, 137, 149
Templeton 18, 119, 149, 150
Terms
    billabong 16, 147
    cow catcher 65
    fag 112
    hotel loafers 31
    metalled roads 68
    nags 159
    neddies 95
    ostler 25
    ruffian 16, 100, 104
    smithereens 139
    swagman 64
    tin Lizzie 117
    wireless 40, 64, 81
Tery 150
Teys 19, 34, 76, 133, 150, 165
'The Hairy Man' 101
Thomas 19, 25, 26, 27, 29, 30, 34, 43, 50, 59, 60, 65, 80, 92, 96, 102, 103, 109, 126, 136, 138, 139, 140, 150, 160, 163, 183
Thompson 21, 59, 83, 103, 114, 128, 134, 150, 151, 152, 165, 168
Thoms 151
Thomson 59, 78, 83, 151, 165
Thornton 18, 67, 81, 151
Todd 151
Toohey 18, 19, 64, 151, 152
Torbury 26, 152
Torquay 136, 150, 152
Toy 34, 108, 152
Tranter 152
Treloar 67, 152
Tuite 152, 165
Tully 152
Turner 24, 25, 36, 49, 61, 83, 85, 88, 124, 144, 149, 152, 153
'Two on the box seat' 148

U

Underwood 134, 153

V

'Valuables
    hidden in carcase of mutton' 95
    hidden in curtains' 124
    hidden in hair' 136
Vane 19, 153
Verses
    'Here's a song of Cobb and Co.' 33
    'I've been coaching down in New South, riding in the Royal mail' 167
    'Long Jim of Cobb & Co.' 15
    'So my mind goes harking backwards to the days of long ago' 71
    'The Lights of Cobb & Co.' 47, 121
    'The Olden Days of Cobb & Co.' 157
    'There was talk of flood, or the fear that sprang' 87
    'The roaring camps of Gulgong and many a Diggers' Rest' 73
    'The Roaring Days' 99
    'The Roll Call of Cobb & Co.' 5, 67, 143
Vines 18, 60, 65, 91, 130, 148, 153, 154
Vinge 154, 184

W

Wages 17, 39, 44, 93, 106, 118
Wagner 28, 30, 75, 89, 108, 115, 116, 134, 135, 140, 141, 149, 158, 169, 182, 183, 184
Walach 158
Walden 52, 94, 137, 158
Waldren 158
Wall 19, 77, 105, 134, 158
Wallace 18, 75, 79, 103, 158, 159, 165
Wallett 159
Walsh 50, 159
Walters 159
Ward 27, 30, 42, 48, 105, 109, 123, 125, 134, 146, 159, 160, 165
Warnemindi 35, 160
Warner 19, 27, 35, 49, 52, 93, 102, 108, 134, 160, 167
Waterworth 160
Watson 68, 75, 130, 149, 159, 160, 183, 184, 192
Watt 73, 130, 160
Watterson 160
Watts 160
Weaver 19, 160
Weldron 160
Wells 116, 126, 160, 161, 177, 182
Welsh 161
Westrien 161
Whatmore 161
Whisson 67, 161
White 4, 24, 53, 59, 65, 66, 78, 80, 88, 95, 102, 115, 118, 123, 124, 133, 134, 161, 162, 169
Whiteman 129, 162
Whitney 23, 44, 58, 59, 61, 72, 73, 116, 123, 138, 140, 141, 162, 183, 184
Wicks 162, 165
Wiggins 163
Wild 27, 163
Wiley 163
Wilkinson 21, 116, 163
Willcock 26, 163
Williams 48, 64, 67, 75, 134, 146, 150, 163
Willocks 43, 163
Willow tree - First in Bathurst 66
Wilson 83, 113, 139, 146, 163
Winkler 72, 132, 163
Winterbottom 163, 164
Wollen 164
Woods 19, 85, 95, 163, 164
Woodworth 74, 127, 164, 184
Wools-Cobb 164, 183
Woolworth 164
Workman 164
'Wreck of the Loch Ard' 68
Wright 19, 27, 37, 42, 44, 52, 60, 63, 73, 74, 76, 80, 90, 92, 94, 103, 119, 122, 123, 126, 129, 144, 145, 146, 147, 149, 150, 152, 162, 165

Y

Yabsley 36, 37, 165
Yeomans 43, 85, 165
York 9, 35, 82, 94, 126, 146, 149, 165, 182, 199

www.ingramcontent.com/pod-product-compliance
Lightning Source LLC
Chambersburg PA
CBHW041710290426
44109CB00028B/2835